A NEW HISTORY OF
CHRISTIANITY

VIVIAN GREEN

CONTINUUM · NEW YORK

1996

The Continuum Publishing Company
370 Lexington Avenue, New York, NY 10017

First published in Great Britain by
Sutton Publishing Limited
Phoenix Mill, Thrupp, Stroud,
Gloucestershire, GL5 2BU

Library of Congress Cataloging-in-Publication Data

Green, Vivian Hubert Howard.
  A new history of Christianity/by Vivian H.H. Green.
    p.   cm.
  Includes bibliographical references and index.
  ISBN 0-8264-0863-X
  1. Church history.   I. Title.
BR145.2.G74   1996
270–dc20   96-25163
                                                            CIP

Typeset in 10/13pt New Baskerville.
Typesetting and origination by
Sutton Publishing Limited.
Printed in Great Britain by
WBC Ltd, Bridgend.

Contents

Foreword

by

The Rt Revd Lord Runcie

It is disconcerting to read a four-hundred page history of Christianity, only to find that I have already taken my place in the story by page 328. However, this is a tribute to the thorough way in which Vivian Green has set the events of very recent church history in the context of two thousand years. Readers will be able to trace the way in which the turbulent history of the twentieth-century world-wide Church has been shaped by events in places and centuries remote from the centres of power and activity in the modern Church. This book is the best sort of history: the facts are there, with a chronology to guide one through the thicket of events, but there is more than that – for history is not a mere recital of facts. It is always viewed through the eyes of one particular human being, and so the story can never properly or satisfactorily be told without the declaration of opinions. Vivian Green has not been afraid to express his views on events both remote in time and contemporary; with his lifetime's experience of the historian's craft, he is an expert guide through Christian history.

The outstanding quality of Green's writing is honesty. The Church is presented here warts and all – because the Body of Christ, as it is incarnated in human society, is often a body full of sores and disease. No adequate theology of the Church could pretend otherwise. So here we are shown the faults of Christian faith in the past, especially its intolerance towards other forms of truth. Perhaps the most dreadful blemish is its record in relation to Judaism, which has had such terrible consequences in the twentieth century. The most important lesson which history can teach is humility. Perhaps from the story of two millennia of a religious tradition, we can learn that the Christian faith is very young; it represents a small sliver of human experience of the divine. I believe this is a heartening truth. It enables us to combine a good deal of penitence with pride in the promises of faith. When in the twentieth century we find perplexity about doctrine and change – amply chronicled in these pages – we are seeing the pains of youth, not the decay of age. A faith which finds its focus in Cross and Resurrection rather than 'unchanging certainties' seems to me more likely to create the spiritual energies we shall need for the next century.

Preface

To survey two thousand years of Christian history in a single volume may seem an over-ambitious and even arrogant task. The nature of the subject-matter is such that there must be inevitably a high degree of selectivity and many areas in which such a book may only hope to skim the surface of available knowledge. Some, for instance, may feel that the English Church, proportionate to its membership, receives more than its fair share of attention. Others will surely query some of my historical judgements, but in a field strewn with denominational mines and partisanship I have tried to be objective. There must surely be some justification both for seeking to explain why Christianity is what it is today, and for trying to put the modern church into its historical perspective. I have tried to show how the development of the most influential society in world history has evolved both in its positive and negative aspects, by what appears in some sense as a series of variations on the theme of the cross and the sword.

My indebtedness to past and present historians of the church will be abundantly obvious to any reader; but I should be less than generous if I did not particularly stress my debt to those modern English historians whose works I have liberally pillaged to my own profit, notably Owen Chadwick, the doyen of modern Church historians, and John McManners together with his fellow contributors to *The Oxford Illustrated History of Christianity*. I have to thank Mrs Sarah Sjogren for typing the original manuscript and my friend William Scoular for reading the script and making invaluable critical comments.

Vivian Green

Chronology of Events

361–3	Julian last non-Christian emperor
370	Basil, Bishop of Caesarea, promotes monastic life
374–97	Ambrose, Bishop of Milan
381	Council of Constantinople condemns Arianism
386	Jerome settles in a monastery at Bethlehem; responsible for the Latin Bible (Vulgate)
395	Augustine appointed Bishop of Hippo (*d.* 430)
401–7	Pope Innocent I asserts primacy of Rome
410	Goths sack Rome; Roman troops withdraw from Britain
c. 410	Monasteries established at Marseilles (John Cassian) and Lérins
416	Teaching of British cleric Pelagius condemned by church council at Carthage
c. 425	Augustine completes *The City of God*
430–61	Pope Leo I
431	Council of Ephesus condemns Nestorianism and reaffirms Nicene Creed. Bishop Palladius sent to Ireland; but Patrick (*d. c.* 460) main agent in conversion of the Irish
451	Council of Chalcedon affirms orthodox view of union of divine and human natures in one person in Christ; rejected by the Mono-physites
476	Ending of the Roman Empire in the west
496	Conversion of Clovis, King of the Franks
c. 525	St Benedict founds monastery at Monte Cassino
527–65	Emperor Justinian I: restores rule over N. Africa (Vandals) and Italy (Ostrogoths)
532–8	Building of the cathedral of Santa Sophia at Constantinople
c. 543	Death of Benedict of Nursia at Monte Cassino
563	Columba goes to Iona
571–94	Gregory of Tours, author of the *History of the Franks*
589	Visigoths converted to Catholic Christianity
590	Columbanus leaves Ireland and introduces Celtic monastic usage into Gaul and N. Italy
590–604	Pope Gregory the Great
596–7	Augustine despatched to convert the Anglo-Saxons
597	Death of Columba at Iona
615	Columbanus founds monasteries at Luxeuil and Bobbio
627	Conversion of Northumbria
632	Conversion of East Anglia. Death of Mohammed
636	Byzantines defeated by the Arabs at Yarmuk, losing Syria
638–56	Arabs conquer Palestine, Iraq, Syria and Egypt
649	Lateran Synod condemns Monothelitism
651	Aidan, 'apostle' of Northumbria, dies
664	Synod of Whitby accepts Roman dating of Easter
669–90	Theodore, Archbishop of Canterbury
680	Council of Constantinople condemns Monophysitism and Monothelitism
711–16	Arabs conquer Spain
716	Boniface's first missionary journey to Frisia
726–843	Iconoclastic controversy in Byzantium
731	Bede completes *Ecclesiastical History*
732	Arabs defeated by Franks near Poitiers

751	Pepin anointed Frankish king by the Pope
754	Pepin's donation to the papacy establishes Papal State. Boniface killed
771–814	Charlemagne, King of the Franks; promotes Carolingian Renaissance
790	Alcuin, Northumbrian scholar, head of Charlemagne's Palace School (*d.* 804)
793	Vikings sack monastery of Lindisfarne
800	Charlemagne crowned Holy Roman Emperor
814–21	Monastic reform under the lead of Benedict of Aniane
830–65	Anskar of Bremen evangelizes Denmark and Sweden
c. 850	Pseudo-Isidorian Decretals forged
863	Cyril and Methodius convert Moravia; Bible and service books translated into Slavonic
863–7	'Photian Schism' – breach between Patriarch Photius of Constantinople and Pope Nicholas I
871–901	Alfred Anglo-Saxon king
910	Abbey of Cluny founded in Burgundy, becomes a centre of monastic reform
959–88	Dunstan, Archbishop of Canterbury, promotes reform of the Anglo-Saxon Church
961	Foundation of monastery at Athos
962	Otto I crowned emperor at Rome
963	Pope John XII deposed
963–84	Ethelwold, monastic reformer, Bishop of Winchester
966	Conversion of Poland
987–8	Vladimir, Prince of Kiev, baptized by Byzantine missionaries
993–1002	Emperor Otto III, crowned at Rome in 996, works in collaboration with Pope Sylvester II (Gerbert of Rheims)
995	Conversion of Norway
997–1038	Hungary Christianized under King Stephen
1009	Destruction of the Church of the Holy Sepulchre at Jerusalem
1012	Romuald founds monastery of Camaldoli in Tuscany
1038	Order of Vallombrosa founded
1046	Synod of Sutri; Emperor Henry III deposes three popes
1049–54	Pope Leo IX inaugurates Church reforms
1054	Fracture of relations between Rome and Constantinople
1070–89	Lanfranc Archbishop of Canterbury
1071	Seljuk Turks defeat Byzantines at Manzikert
1073–85	Pope Gregory VII (Hildebrand) seeks to reform Church and rid it of lay control, giving rise to the Investiture Controversy
1075	*Dictatus Papae* issued
1077	Emperor Henry IV does penance at Canossa
1084	Carthusian Order established by Bruno at the Grande Chartreuse
1093–1109	Anselm Archbishop of Canterbury
c. 1093–1133	Building of Durham Cathedral
1095	Pope Urban II preaches crusade against Muslims at Synod of Clermont
1098	Cistercian Order founded
1099	First Crusade takes Jerusalem
1115	Foundation of Clairvaux under St Bernard
c. 1116	Peter Abailard (*d.* 1142) teaching at Paris
1118	Order of Templars founded

1120	Praemonstratensian Order founded by Norbert of Xanten
1122	Concordat of Worms settles Investiture Contest
1137–44	Abbot Suger builds abbey of St Denis
1140	Synod of Sens condemns Abailard's teaching
1146	St Bernard preaches the Second Crusade
1153	Death of St Bernard
1154–59	Hadrian IV, the only English Pope
1160–1226	Building of first Gothic cathedral at Laon
1162–70	Thomas Becket Archbishop of Canterbury
1170	Becket murdered at Canterbury (canonized 1174)
1176	Foundation of Waldensians by Peter Waldo
1179	Hildegarde of Bingen, mystic, dies
1187	Saladin defeats the Christians at Hattin and recaptures Jerusalem
1189–92	Third Crusade
1190	Order of Hospitallers founded
1194	Rebuilding of Chartres Cathedral (after a fire)
1198–1216	Pope Innocent III
1202	Decretal *Venerabilem* asserts supremacy of Pope
1204	Crusaders capture Constantinople and institute the Latin empire
1209–29	Crusade against Albigensians (Cathars)
1215	Fourth Lateran Council
1216	Dominicans recognized by Pope Honorius III
1221	St Dominic dies (canonized 1234)
1223	Pope Honorius III confirmed the Franciscan rule
1226	St Francis of Assisi dies (canonized 1228)
1232	Roman Inquisition set up
1264	Feast of Corpus Christi instituted by Pope Urban IV
1274	Thomas Aquinas, scholastic writer, dies
1280	Albertus Magnus, scholastic writer, dies
1291	Mamelukes conquer Acre; end of Christian rule in Near East
1293	First Christian missionaries in China
1302	Pope Boniface VIII issues *Unam Sanctam*, asserting universal jurisdiction of Pope
1308	Duns Scotus, scholastic writer, dies
1309–72	Avignonese Captivity; the popes at Avignon
1312	Destruction of Templars
1314–21	Dánte Alighieri writes *The Divine Comedy*
1323	Franciscan doctrine of Christ's poverty condemned as heretical
1327	Meister Eckhart, mystic, dies
1327–47	William of Ockham, scholastic writer, propagates nominalist philosophy
1343	Bull *Unigenitus Dei* proclaims jubilee year to be celebrated every 50th year (in 1389 every 33rd year: in 1470 every 25th year)
1377	Pope Gregory XI returns to Rome from Avignon
1378–1415	The Great Schism: a divided papacy
1384	John Wycliffe dies; Lollardy in England
1387–1400	Geoffrey Chaucer writing *The Canterbury Tales*
1415	John Huss burned; Council of Constance called to reunite and reform the Church
c. 1418	*Imitatio Christi*, ascribed to Thomas à Kempis

1431–49	Council of Basle
1438–9	Council of Ferrara–Florence; reunion of Roman and Byzantine Churches but rejected by Byzantines
1453	Turks capture Constantinople; Santa Sophia converted into a mosque
1460	Pope Pius II condemns appeals to a general council (in *Execrabilis*)
1479	Spanish Inquisition established
1483	Martin Luther born
1484	Bull *Summis desiderantes* condemns witchcraft
1492	Ferdinand and Isabella conquer emirate of Granada; Spain united under Catholic rule; Jews and Moors expelled
1493–4	Pope Alexander VI partitions newly discovered lands between Spain and Portugal
1495–1517	Cardinal Ximenes reforms Spanish Church
1506	Rebuilding of St Peter's, Rome, starts
1508–12	Michelangelo paints Sistine Chapel
1516	Erasmus's New Testament published
1517	Luther posts 95 theses against indulgences at Wittenberg
1519	Luther debates with Eck, denying papal supremacy. Cortés invades Aztec empire
1521	Luther excommunicated by the Pope; outlawed by Diet of Worms
1521–2	Luther at Wartburg Castle
1522	Leo X bestows title Fidei Defensor on Henry VIII
1523	Franciscans arrive in Mexico. Zwingli leads reform movement in Zurich
1524	Luther completes translation of Bible into German
1524–6	Peasants' Revolt in Germany led by Anabaptist Thomas Müntzer
1525	Tyndale makes translation of New English Testament. Matteo da Bascio founds Capuchin Order
1527	Reformation in Sweden and Denmark
1529	Diet of Speyer; German states take name of Protestant German Protestant princes form Schmalkaldic League Luther debates with Zwingli at Marburg
1530	Diet of Augsburg; Augsburg Confession states Lutheran faith
1531	Henry VIII recognized as supreme head of English Church Zwingli killed at the battle of Kappel
1533	Thomas Cranmer appointed Archbishop of Canterbury
1534	Loyola founds Society of Jesus. Act of Supremacy: severance of English Church from Rome
1534–5	Anabaptist rule in Munster
1535	Thomas More executed
1536	Calvin's *Institutes of the Christian Religion* published. Dissolution of monasteries starts in England
1537	Pope Paul III asserts that American Indians entitled to liberty and property
1540	Pope Paul III approves Jesuit Order
1541	Calvin chief pastor in Geneva (until 1564). John Knox begins reformation in Scotland
1542–52	Francis Xavier's missions in India and Japan
1545	Council of Trent first convoked; dispersed 1547; reassembled 1551–2, 1562–3
1546	Luther dies

1682	The Quaker William Penn establishes the State of Pennsylvania. Gallican Articles promulgated in France
1685	Louis XIV revokes Edict of Nantes
1689	John Locke's *Letters Concerning Toleration*. English Toleration Act (excluding Roman Catholics and Unitarians)
1692	Christian worship permitted in China. Affair of 'Salem' witches in Massachusetts
1701	Society for the Propagation of the Gospel founded
1702	Papal legate sent to China to deal with the problem of Jesuit compromises
1713	Bull *Unigenitus* condemns Jansenism
1721	Tsar Peter I suspends the Moscow patriarchate and replaces it with a synod
1723	Zinzendorf founds Moravian colony in Saxony
1724	Voltaire's *Lettres Philosophiques* published
1726	Start of the Great Awakening in America
1727–58	Jonathan Edwards preaching in America
1727–68	Reimarus teaching in Hamburg; beginnings of Higher Criticism of the Bible
1728	Church of Utrecht (Old Catholics) separates from Rome
1731	Protestants expelled by Archbishop of Salzburg
1732	Moravian missions abroad started
1738	John Wesley's 'Conversion' experience
1740	Pope Benedict XIV. George Whitefield preaching in America
1742	Handel's *Messiah* first performed in Dublin
1751–65	Diderot's *Encyclopaedia* published
1759	Jesuits expelled from Portugal and subsequently from France (1762), Sapin and Naples (1767)
1762	Rousseau's *Social Contract* published
1767	Jesuit *reductio* of Paraguay terminated
1770	George Whitefield dies
1773	Pope dissolves Jesuits
1781	Emperor Joseph II's Patent of Toleration
1786	Synod of Pistoia favours Jansenism
1787	Constitution of United States separates Church and State
1789	French Estates-General decrees sale of Church property
1790	Civil Constitution of the Clergy in France
1791	John Wesley dies
1792	Baptist Missionary Society founded
1793	'DeChristianization' in France; festival of the Goddess of Reason in Notre Dame
1795	London Missionary Society founded
1799	Church Missionary Society founded
1801	Concordat between Napoleon and the Pope
1804	British and Foreign Bible Society founded
1807	Britain bans slave trade. First Protestant missionary in China
1808	Roman Catholic see of Baltimore made Metropolitan see in the USA
1810–11	Primitive Methodist Church founded
1810–24	Foundation of South American republics
1813	East India Company allows entry of missionaries
1814	The Society of Jesus reconstituted by the Pope. Consecration of first Anglican bishop in Asia for the see of Calcutta
1815	Bible Christians founded

1817	Union of Lutheran and Calvinist Churches in Prussia. Robert Moffatt begins missionary work in South Africa
1820–51	Dr J. Phillips, London missionary superintendent at the Cape
1821	Greek revolt against Turks
1826–30	Suppression of religious orders in many South American republics
1829	Roman Catholic Emancipation Act in the UK
1831	G.W. Hegel, philosopher, dies
1832	Autonomy of the Serbian Orthodox Church
1833	John Keble's Assize Sermon at Oxford inaugurates the Oxford Movement. Emancipation of slaves in British Empire
1834	Friederich Schleiermacher, German theologian, dies
1835	D.F. Strauss's radical *Life of Jesus* published
1836	First Roman Catholic and Anglican bishops appointed in Australia. Great Trek in South Africa
1840	David Livingstone begins missionary work in Africa
1842	G.A. Selwyn first Anglican bishop in New Zealand. Treaty of Nanking permits entry of Christian missionaries into China
1843	Disruption of the Scottish Church
1844	Adventists in USA expect the Second Coming (form Church of Seventh Day Adventists in 1861)
1845	J.H. Newman received into Roman Catholic Church
1846–78	Pope Pius IX
1847	Sonderbund (religious war) in Switzerland. Brigham Young moves Mormons to Salt Lake City
1848	Pope Pius IX flees Rome. Karl Marx and Engels publish Communist manifesto. Oneida Christian Communist community established in USA
1850	Roman Catholic hierarchy in UK reconstituted
1851–1930	Adolf Harnack, German Protestant theologian
1852	Holy Synod established in Greece
1854	Pius IX promulgates the Immaculate Conception of the Blessed Virgin Mary as an article of faith
1857	Indian Mutiny. Foundation of Universities Mission to Central Africa (UMCA)
1858	Treaty of Tienstin allows work of Christian missions in China and legalizes opium trade
1859	Darwin's *Origin of Species* published
1860	*Essays and Reviews* published. F.C. Baur, German theologian, founder of the Tübingen School, dies
1861	Bishop Mackenzie, first head of UMCA, dies
1863	Attempt to depose Bishop Colenso of Natal. J.E. Renan's *La Vie de Jesus* published
1864	*Syllabus of Errors* published
1865	James Hudson Taylor founds China Inland Mission. Samuel Crowther, first Black Anglican bishop in Nigeria
1867	First Lambeth Conference of bishops
1868	Archbishop Lavigerie of Algiers founds the White Fathers
1870	First Vatican Council: papal infallibility decreed
1871	Murder of J.C. Patteson, missionary bishop of Melanesia. Re-establishment of the Old Catholic Church
1872	L.A. Feuerbach, radical German thinker, dies

1872–9	*Kulturkampf* in Prussia
1873	David Livingstone dies
1878–92	Missionary rivalry in Buganda
1878–1903	Pope Leo XIII
1884	Tembu National Church set up
1886	Roman Catholic hierarchy established in India
1889	Albrecht Ritschl, German Protestant theologian, dies
1890	Archbishop Lavigerie initiates '*ralliement*' in France
1891	Leo XIII publishes encyclical *Rerum Novarum* on social order
1894–1906	Dreyfus case in France
1896	Leo XIII condemns Anglican orders in encyclical *Apostolicae Curae*
1900	Boxer Rebellion in China; attacks on Christians
1903–14	Pope Pius X (canonized 1954)
1905–7	Separation of Church and State in France
1907	Pius X condemns modernism in encyclical *Pascendi*
1908	Union of Presbyterians, Congregationalists and Dutch Reformed Church in South India
1910	Missionary conference at Edinburgh. Revolution in Mexico: oppression of the Church
1913	J. Chilembwe, nationalist prophet, in Nyasaland. Albert Schweitzer goes as medical missionary to Africa
1914	Assemblies of God, an affiliation of Pentecostal Churches in USA
1914–22	Pope Benedict XV
1915	Ku Klux Klan in USA reorganized
1916	Charles de Foucauld murdered in N. Africa
1917–18	Bolshevik Revolution in Russia; reinstatement of Moscow patriarchate, followed by separation of Church and State and persecution of Christians
1919	World Christian Fundamentalist Association founded in USA. Karl Barth's *Commentary on Romans* published. Church Assembly established in UK
1920	Jeanne d'Arc canonized
1921	Church of Simon Kimbangu (Church of Jesus Christ) founded in Congo
1921–51	Rudolf Bultman, founder of form criticism, professor at Marburg
1922–39	Pope Pius XI
1925	J.O. Oshitelu, founder of the Church of the Lord (Aladura)
1927	Faith and Order Movement inaugurated at Lausanne
1927–8	Failure of Prayer Book revision in England
1929	William Temple Archbishop of York (of Canterbury 1942–4). Lateran Treaty. Mother Teresa begins work in Calcutta
1932	United Methodist Church: union of Wesleyan and Primitive Methodists. Reinhold Neibuhr's *Moral Man and Immoral Society* published
1933	Concordat between the Pope and Hitler. Paul Tillich, theologian, leaves Germany for USA
1934	Synod of Barmen, foundation of German Confessional Church
1935	Karl Barth leaves Germany for Basle. Pastor Niemöller imprisoned
1937	Pius XI denounces Nazi teaching in the encyclical *Mit Brennender Sorge*
1938	F. Buchman, founder of the Oxford Group, inaugurates Moral Rearmament
1939–58	Pope Pius XII
1940	Taizé Community founded by Roger Schutz
1943	Stalin allows re-establishment of Russian patriarchate. Bonhoeffer executed.

1944–61	Geoffrey Fisher Archbishop of Canterbury
1946	Abolition of the Eastern rite (Uniat) in Russia
1947	Foundation of the Church of South India (Anglicans, Methodists and South India United Church)
1948	World Council of Churches set up at Amsterdam
1948–9	Communists in China expel Western missionaries
1949	Billy Graham commences evangelistic work
1950	Papal encyclical *Humani generis* queries biblical criticism. Pius XII proclaims the Bodily Assumption of the Blessed Virgin Mary to be an article of faith
1951	Beginning of the Three Self-Help Patriotic Movement in China
1958–63	Pope John XXIII
1958–64	Khruschev initiates further attacks on the Orthodox Church
1960	Archbishop Fisher received by the Pope at Rome
1961	Orthodox Churches join World Council of Churches
1961–74	Michael Ramsey Archbishop of Canterbury
1962–5	Second Vatican Council
1963–78	Pope Paul VI
1964	Western missionaries expelled from Sudan
1966	Archbishop Ramsey visits the Pope. Pentecostal and charismatic movements increasingly influential. Cultural Revolution in China; all Christian churches closed
1967	Western missionaries expelled from Guinea
1968	Papal encyclical *Humanae Vitae* condemns birth control. Martin Luther King murdered. Conference of Latin American bishops at Medellin, Columbia, attended by Paul VI, first Pope to visit South America
1970	World Alliance of Reformed Churches (Congregational and Presbyterian). Church of North India and Pakistan formed. General Synod replaces Church Assembly in UK
1972	Collapse of proposals for Anglican–Methodist reunion
1974–80	Donald Coggan Archbishop of Canterbury
1978	Pope John Paul I. John Paul II elected Pope
1979	Churches in China opened for public worship. Pope John Paul II criticizes liberation theology (at Puebla, Mexico). Mother Teresa awarded Nobel Peace Prize
1980	Archbishop Romero of San Salvador murdered
1980–1991	Robert Runcie Archbishop of Canterbury
1981	Attempted assassination of the Pope
1982	Pope visits Britain
1986	Desmond Tutu appointed Archbishop of Cape Town
1988	Barbara Harris appointed first woman bishop in USA (Massachusetts). Millennium of Russian Christianity
1989	Archbishop Lefebvre excommunicated
1989–90	Collapse of Communist regimes followed by liberation of the churches in Communist states
1991	George Carey appointed Archbishop of Canterbury
1993	Church of England approves ordination of women

Introduction

Among early historians, the Northumbrian monk, Bede of Jarrow, whose *Ecclesiastical History* was completed in 731, was a scholar endowed with an unusual aptitude for basing his material on an accurate and impartial assessment of the evidence at his disposal. 'In accordance with the principle of true history [*quod vera lex historiae*]', he wrote in the preface, 'I have simply sought to commit to writing what I have collected from common reports, for the instruction of posterity.' However, despite his skill at recognizing the need to evaluate his sources, Bede's final purpose remained religiously didactic:

> Should history tell of good men and their good estate, the listener is spurred on to imitate the good; should it record the evil ends of wicked men, so effectively the devout and earnest believer is kindled to eschew what is harmful and perverse.

For Bede, man's history lay inevitably within the providence of God.

Otto of Freising, the twelfth-century Cistercian monk and bishop, and author of a history of the world which he entitled *Chronicon of the Two Cities* (the earthly and the heavenly), placed the course of history even more firmly within a divine framework. He subdivided his history into eight books, the first seven of which described the history of the world from the creation of Adam to AD 1146, the year in which he was writing. The eighth book told of the anticipated culmination of history with the coming of the Antichrist, followed by the Last Judgement, which was to be the providential conclusion to human history. According to Otto, history was not a series of isolated events but

> there were from the beginning of the world four principal kingdoms which stood out above all the rest, and that they are to endure unto the world's end, succeeding one another in accordance with the law of the universe, can be gathered from the vision of Daniel.

For many centuries the writing of Christian history was powerfully affected, and in some degree distorted, by the confessional bias of those who essayed to write it. In a European world that for so long accepted the claims of the Christian Church as a divine society and which held what might be described as a fundamentalist view of the universe, it was hardly surprising that so many scholars, and indeed some even now in the twentieth century, came to regard history as the providential dispensation of God, divinely ordained and guided. Just as the Marxist historian would try to compress his material into a particular ideological pattern, so historians of Christianity have been tempted to portray the history of their faith as pointing to a moral and telling a divine tale, underlining and throwing into relief God's supposed plan for mankind, posing moral judgements which betrayed a similar ideological stance.

It was only slowly that this scenario, poised against a providential cosmic backcloth, gave way to a more distinctively secular approach. The fifteenth-century Renaissance scholar Flavio Biondo, the first writer to describe the age in which he was living as the *medio evo*, the middle ages, was also one of the first historians to divide history into periods of secular repression and progress. Yet the belief that history bore the hallmarks of a divine plan was slow to disappear. The eighteenth-century politician Edmund Burke observed that history was fundamentally the divine 'march of the Providence of God'. Burke's statement was intrinsically theological as well as political, hinting at a theory for the theologian to test and handle and one which properly lay outside the historian's scope. For while faith is a historical fact, the beliefs which give rise to it may well lie outside the normal process of history and be inaccessible to the historian's judgement. It is plainly not the modern historian's task to invoke history, let alone to seek to adapt it, to demonstrate or to disprove a religious and supernatural view of the universe. The historian, using the best evidence at his disposal, has to make a judgement on the course of events within the framework of the known world.

Man's understanding of the nature of God has changed and evolved throughout history, and what this book seeks to do is to demonstrate the Church's capacity to absorb, develop and readjust, proving its continuous ability to adapt itself to political and social, as well as intellectual change. The harsh, holy deity of the Old Testament was transformed in the New, as having the features of a loving Creator. Later, God and the court of heaven itself were interpreted in the light of a hierarchical society presided over by kings who sometimes believed themselves as an embodiment of divine power, as had the Roman emperors of an earlier age. At the hands of some theologians the medieval doctrine of the atonement itself became a reflection of the feudal relationship which bound the vassals to their lord, knit by a series of complex obligations.

Similarly, the representation of Christ, of whom no contemporary visual image was created, changed in response not merely to the imagination of the individual artist but also to dictation from the social and theological ethos of the time at which that particular painting or sculpture was being made. So the face of Christ depicted on the walls of the Roman catacombs, beardless and beautiful with short hair and fine curls, could remind worshippers of bygone heroes like Alexander the Great and other divine beings venerated in the ancient world. With the legitimation of Christianity the image of Christ not surprisingly acquired the attributes proper to an emperor, seated on a jewel-encrusted throne, his head, like that of the emperor, surrounded by a halo, dignified, middle-aged, bearded like a philosopher, a teacher and a lawgiver. In the medieval world two artistic types seemed to jostle with each other: that of the Byzantine Christ – magisterial, aloof, impassive, blackbearded; and that to which the Gothic world seemed increasingly attracted – younger, spiritual, handsome, humane yet transcendent, as in the statue of the 'beau dieu' in Amiens Cathedral, an ideal hero for an aristocratic society. If Renaissance artists like Leonardo da Vinci and Michelangelo were drawn to idealize Christ as a divine and handsome hero, there were others, more affected by the bleakness of so much of common life, who displayed Christ as the Man of Sorrows, bearing the sins and sufferings of a fallen world. Every generation seemed to draw the Christ it needed, so that his face came to represent the aspirations and fears of a changing world.

This book traces the development of the Church as a power structure, often exercising its authority and imposing its teaching in ways not dissimilar to those employed by secular rulers. 'When I came to the throne of St Augustine', Archbishop Runcie recalled in his *Authority in Crisis*, 'I was reminded of the men of power who had sat there before me by the pikes from the Archbishop's private army. And I was reminded by them of the temptation to gain the Church's ends by the world's means.' But this book is also a study in religious history since there is a spiritual message at the heart of Christianity, determined by a belief in cosmic truths, doctrines of redemption and salvation, of judgement and eternity, expressed in earthly symbols, great cathedrals and small parish churches, through painting, sculpture, literature and music.

In large measure the book is concerned with the means by which the worldly and spiritual elements of Christianity have been constantly interwoven, bringing about what may be metaphorically described as the clash between the cross and the sword. After the legalization of Christianity by the Emperor Constantine, the Church was often tempted to embrace the sword in the name of the cross. Towards the end of the twentieth century changing circumstances have removed the sword from the Church's grasp, leaving the Church to preach the cross without the sword, standing, as it were, 'naked to mine enemies', as Cardinal Wolsey put it in Shakespeare's *Henry VIII*.

Although the book is entitled *A New History*, it is not intentionally innovative, nor radical nor revolutionary in its approach. It has been written with an attempt to minimize, if not to escape, bias, and to tell the remarkable story of how Christianity has evolved from a fringe society, spurned by the world around it, to become the single most important influence on western civilization.

CHAPTER ONE

Christian Beginnings

'It is my custom, Sire,' Pliny, the governor of Roman Bithynia in Asia Minor, informed the emperor Trajan in *c*. AD 112, 'to refer to you in matters about which I am not sure. . . . I have never been present at any trial of Christians; therefore I do not know what should be the customary penalties or investigations. . . . The contagion of this superstition has spread not only in the cities, but in the villages and the countryside, yet it seems capable of being checked and set right.' The emperor replied circumspectly, telling Pliny that the Christians were not to be deliberately sought out: 'if they are informed against, and the charge is proved, then they are to be punished, but with this reservation – that if anyone denies he is a Christian, and actually proves this to be so by worshipping our gods, he shall be pardoned.'

Forty-three years later, in 155, Polycarp, the aged bishop of Smyrna, was summoned before the proconsul and charged with being a Christian. 'Swear', the magistrate urged him in an effort to make him affirm his loyalty and so bring about his release, 'Curse Christ.' 'Eighty and six years', Polycarp replied, 'have I served him, and he has done me no wrong; how then can I blaspheme my king who has saved me?' 'I have wild beasts', the proconsul threatened; 'if you don't repent, I will have you thrown to them.' Polycarp responded, 'Send for them.' In despair at the bishop's obduracy the magistrate told him, 'If you don't despise the wild beasts I will order that you be burned alive.' 'You threaten the fire', Polycarp told him, 'that burns for an hour and in a little while will be quenched; but you are unaware of the fire of the judgement to come, and the fire of the eternal punishment which is kept for the ungodly.' Under pressure from the clamour of the mob, the proconsul gave orders for Polycarp to be burned to death. Twenty-two years further on, many Christians, some of them migrants from Asia, died in the arena in Lyons in France fighting the wild beasts in the public games.

These two episodes do not merely demonstrate that the imperial authorities favoured a comparatively moderate policy towards the early Christians, violent spasmodically as the mob could be, but they show how Christianity had spread early from the eastern to the western Mediterranean, how strong were the convictions of its leaders, and how it was slowly beginning to attract the attention of the world outside the small Christian communities.

In the first century of the Christian era pagan writers hardly ever alluded to the Christians. Tacitus spoke of their founder 'Christus, executed at the hands of the procurator Pontius Pilate in the reign of Tiberius'. Suetonius described the Christians as 'a set of men adhering to a novel and mischievous superstition'. But both Tacitus and Suetonius were writing many decades after the events they were recording. For a full century after Christ's execution the Christian sect must have struck the normal Roman, if he was aware of it at all, as a socially and politically unimportant, if conceivably perverse, community of men and women.

THE ORIGINS OF THE CHRISTIAN CHURCH

Christianity lacked an objective account of its origins. There was no contemporary biography of Christ. St Paul's Epistles and the Acts of the Apostles may have been written within twenty or thirty years of Christ's death. St Mark's seems to have been the first gospel. St Luke's was probably written in the 70s, and St Matthew's followed, probably composed after the fall of Jerusalem to the Romans in 70. St John's Gospel is generally thought to have been the last of the gospels to be composed but some scholars have recently claimed priority for it. All these authors were interested parties, doubtless believing that what they were writing was historically true, but their object was not to write history but to transmit a religious message, 'the good news' of salvation in Jesus Christ which they had personally experienced. As historical accounts the gospels were not trustworthy; the nativity stories recorded by Luke and Matthew were historically implausible. They relied on oral tradition, conceivably on earlier writings which have been lost and on their own vivid personal experience. Some at least of those upon whom they relied for information must have known Jesus personally. Yet nevertheless the origins of the Christian Church remain comparatively obscure.

Why Christianity appeared when it did or, even more pertinently, why Christians thought God should have chosen that particular time in history for his incarnation in a man, Jesus Christ, constituted then and later an unanswerable puzzle. There seemed nothing in the contemporary historical situation which made so momentous and miraculous an intervention in human history probable, necessary or even desirable, let alone possible. That Christianity spread with comparative rapidity may have been as much a social as a religious phenomenon, its teaching providing its followers with personal answers in a society in which there was evidently some measure of disillusionment.

The Roman world in which Jesus Christ spent some thirty years of his existence was a polyglot and a polytheistic society. Diverse in race, character and language, it was relatively free from internal strife and moderately efficiently governed. The genius of Rome may have been less creative than that of Greece, but it had assimilated and incorporated many diverse peoples into a single *imperium*, so that to be a Roman citizen, as St Paul was himself to proclaim, was a meaningful dignity. In spite of continuous trouble on Rome's extensive frontiers and occasional political crises, the empire as yet possessed a solidity and a stability relatively unknown in the Mediterranean world for some centuries.

Religious belief in the empire was as diverse as its peoples. The emperor was himself the embodiment of the state religion, its high priest or *pontifex maximus*. After his death, he was often but not necessarily accorded the honours of a god, and in his lifetime worship given to him in the form of incense was a pledge of loyalty. Unlimited as was his earthly power, the emperor was still the servant of the celestial deities, Greek and Roman, who guided the destiny of the world. It was to seek their patronage and to propitiate their anger that sacrifices were made and public games held. For the majority of Romans, what we may describe as a state religion cannot, however, have instilled a deep sense of the numinous, or of the guardianship of the nether world. What counted for the average man or woman more than the distant if capricious deities was the everyday influence of the local spirits of the grove or spring, of the household god whose shrine was decked with flowers and gifts. Materialistic as the Roman world may sometimes appear to be, its peoples were aware that there existed supernatural cosmic forces of infinite power and caprice which governed the world of nature and of men. Men's anxiety and apprehension at the Christians' denial of the gods was understandable, and understandable too was to be the future appeal of the Christian faith.

The classic religions rooted in antiquity had been supplemented by the so-called mystery religions, cults imported from the East, involving the veneration of the Great Mother, of Isis and of Osiris, and of Mithras. In their elaborate ceremonial, initiation rites and esoteric teaching these cults satisfied the emotional needs of their worshippers in ways which the worship of the Roman and Greek gods did not. In their emphasis on rebirth, the ritual of blood sacrifice and eventual resurrection they bore a superficial resemblance to Christianity, even though the connection was a tenuous one. That they first appeared in the volatile religious world of the Near East may help to explain why this was the crucible in which Christianity itself originated.

For if there was nothing in the greater part of the Roman world to explain the rise of a religious leader and teacher such as Jesus Christ was thought to be, in the turbulent land of Palestine the soil was already well fertilized for a religious groundswell. Christianity's roots were to be found in the Judaic rather than the Roman or Hellenic world. The first Christians were thought, understandably, to be yet another Jewish sect; indeed, without the legacy of Judaism Christianity would itself be incomprehensible. Since the fall of the Kingdoms of Judea and Israel the Jews had been governed by a series of alien rulers whom they deeply resented. Alien rule, whether of the Romans or the Herodian princes, evoked fierce nationalistic and religious feeling.

If there was a party among the Jews ready to collaborate with the Roman occupiers, represented more specifically by the strongly conservative Sadducees from among whom the High Priest was sometimes selected, there were also more radical groups who entertained messianic hopes. They harboured expectations of the appearance of a divine messenger or leader 'the teacher of righteousness' who would 'restore the kingdom to Israel', whether by expelling the occupying power by force or by some more mysterious cosmological event which would bring the world to an end and so inaugurate the kingdom of God. One of these radical groups, the Essenes, who lived in the desert near the Dead Sea and whose teaching, preserved in scrolls, was recovered between 1947 and 1956 from caves not far from Qumran, possibly a centre of their activities, were puritanical and ascetic in their life-style. While the dating and interpretation of the scrolls which provide the earliest texts of parts of the Old Testament books have caused bitter controversy, they at least indicate the seething religious atmosphere in which Jesus was to appear as a radical teacher. Like the Samaritans the Essenes refused to recognize the Temple (which Herod had recently rebuilt) as a religious centre because they regarded it as a symbol of corruption and political compromise. John the Baptist with his call for repentance may very likely have had connections with such a group, and in his turn his teaching may have influenced Jesus Christ himself. Indeed the 'teacher of righteousness' in his teaching and even in his death seemed to prefigure Jesus. Whatever their internal divisions, the Jews remained a race apart, refraining from inter-marriage and sustaining their identity by cultic and cultural isolation. The sacred writings formed the bastion of their religious faith which they sought to preserve by special ordinances, insisting, for instance, on circumcision and certain food taboos. Hostile to the worship of images they were strongly monotheistic. Their god, Yahwe, was the providential guardian of the people, utterly holy, requiring of his followers that they should seek to follow the moral commandments which he had revealed to his prophets. Judaism did not merely represent racial solidarity but a coherent belief in a future destiny. Jewish expectations, more especially as they were diffused among the more nationalistic and radical members of society, notably the Zealots, explain why Jesus's teaching initially attracted a following, and in some respects may point to the genesis of that teaching itself.

What cannot be wholly explained is the man Jesus himself. Indeed, he may be inexplicable. The gospel writers give only a fragmentary account of Jesus's career, placing it in a setting of Old Testament prophecy. They were not biographers, and they may have superimposed early Christian teaching on surviving oral traditions. They give a glimpse of the historical Jesus and some intimations of the divine Christ, but it was to be only through the life and teaching of the early Church that such experiences were articulated into doctrines which in their turn were to supply the Church with what it would claim to be its divine foundation.

They tell us that Jesus was born of a labouring family to a woman called Mary by a virgin birth, a historically and biologically improbable event, if later theologically explicable. Yet it was only in the two last years of his short life that Jesus achieved prominence as a teacher and healer. Both by his teaching, in which originally he may have been influenced by John the Baptist, said to be his cousin, and by his charismatic character he won followers, and among some people the expectation grew that he was the promised Messiah, whose coming had been predicted in the sacred writings. The New Testament suggests that Jesus had a vivid consciousness of God as the heavenly father and that he represented, indeed incarnated, a new way of life which he was to demonstrate through his loving concern for his fellows. There was nothing in his teaching, which was basically pacifistic and profoundly moral, to suggest that he would actually lead the people in a revolt against Roman rule but his following may have given the appearance to the Jewish authorities of a subversive semi-revolutionary organization. After a comparatively short ministry he was arrested at the instigation of the Jewish religious authorities, with the apparent complicity of the Roman procurator Pontius Pilate, who scented a political threat, so that what started as a charge of blasphcmy was to appear ultimately as sedition. After a summary trial he was executed by crucifixion, probably in March 36, when he was in early middle age.

Jesus's death was the beginning rather than the end of the matter. For the disciples became convinced through their own experience that after his entombment Jesus miraculously reappeared, retaining his spiritual identity without losing his earthly provenance before eventually returning to God the Father of whom he had been the revealed expression. To what extent before his death his followers believed that Jesus was the son of God is far from clear nor were Jesus's own allusions to his identity completely free from ambiguity though on at least one occasion he claimed a messianic role. Such events can only be accepted by the eye of faith, for they were self-evidently incapable of a satisfactory historical or rational explanation. Upon such slender foundations a great edifice was to be raised.

For the early Christians Christ's resurrection, which seemed preposterous to pagan writers, offered humanity the hope of redemption from the sin which marred their existence and the possibility of victory over death. There is no real evidence that Jesus intended to set up a continuing Church, or establish a new religion outside Judaism; Jesus seems to have seen himself essentially as a prophet who came to inaugurate the imminent consummation of God's kingdom on earth. It was only when this proved to be a false expectation that his followers, at first equally expectant of the second coming, changed his role to that of the divine son of God. Although the small community of Jewish Christians had their hopes splintered by Jesus's death, they were inspired by the belief that he had triumphed over death, and they were welded together by a common faith and a common life which were to find expression in a society, a *koinonia*, an infant Church. Moreover, though Jesus had 'ascended' to his Father, Christians came to believe that, as the Acts of the Apostles was to record of the feast of Pentecost, the Holy Spirit of God was itself still operative in the world, inspiring and guiding this Church. If the historian can do no more than record what the early Christians sincerely believed to be true, he is bound to recognize that whether or not they were simply the victims of an illusion or a legend manufactured by St Paul and the emerging Christian Church, a profound change of mood affected the infant Christian community after Christ's death. Henceforth a core of committed Christians acted as if God had entrusted to them a divinely appointed task, which they were to mediate not merely to their fellow Jews but the Gentile world as well.

The first Christians, Jews by race, emerged naturally enough as a Jewish sect, but they early discarded some Jewish customs and beliefs and offended orthodox Jews by their assertion that in Jesus Jewish messianic hopes were fulfilled. More liberal-minded Jews, especially those living in the Hellenistic world, had long taught that the Jews were entrusted by God with a mission to all people. It would not be long before the early Christians decided that they had a message for the Gentiles as well as the Jews, though how far this was Christ's own teaching remained to some extent unclear. The issue as to how far the early Christians should retain Jewish customs soon caused a vigorous debate. The first leader of the Church in Jerusalem, Jesus's half-brother James, believed that even if the Gentiles accepted the Christian faith they ought to keep strictly to the formularies of the Mosaic code which Jesus had come to fulfil; but he was opposed by his brother apostle, Peter, who declared that while the Christians were bound to keep the prescriptions of the Mosaic law relating to food, they were not thereby obliged to be circumcised or to observe the ancient Jewish religious festivals. The Church soon began to emerge from its Jewish shell with a broader vision of its message to the world than that with which it had started life.

This development became the more decisive through the conversion of St Paul, an orthodox Jew who had been engaged in the persecution of the early Christians, to the Christian faith. He was literally the second founder of Christianity, for he carried the Christian message of which he was both interpreter and in some sense a creator enthusiastically into the Gentile world, to the towns of Asia Minor and Greece, Lystra, Iconium, Thessalonica, Philippi, Beroea, Corinth, and Athens; eventually after appealing, as he was entitled to do as a Roman citizen, he was sent for trial in Rome where, with Peter, he died in the Neronian persecution. Paul, a courageous leader of strong convictions, gathered around himself a group of like-minded men and women, Apollos, Epaphras, Epaphroditus, Junius, Timothy and Barnabas. His preaching attracted crowds and nearly always met with interest, occasionally with hostility and sometimes, as at Athens, with scepticism, but the seed sown rarely failed to bear fruit. He kept in touch with the infant Christian churches by letters, written between 49 and 62, in which he interpreted the Christian message, at times laying a gloss on early teaching about Jesus, and exhorting his correspondents to keep the faith. At his departure for Rome he left behind him Christian communities scattered across the eastern Mediterranean world whose zeal he had fostered and whose backslidings he rebuked.

Christianity's spread can only be mapped imprecisely. The sea routes across the Mediterranean, free from piracy, provided the opportunity for travellers, merchants and others to carry the Christian message to the Mediterranean ports and their hinterland. Christian Jews and Greek-speaking migrants were the principal agents by whom that message was transmitted. Rome, which had a sizeable Jewish colony, had had a Christian community even before St Paul arrived. Over a century later Irenaeus of Lyons, writing *c.* 180, spoke of Christians in Spain, Germany, and Britain, and Tertullian, probably writing rhetorically, spoke of places in Britain 'inaccessible to the Romans, subdued to Christ'. Christianity, as one would expect, probably spread more rapidly in the eastern than in the western Mediterranean. The Phrygian bishop Abercius, in the second half of the second century, found Christian congregations beyond the River Euphrates and in the province of Adiabene. The king of Edessa, Abgar VII, was said to be a Christian sympathizer whose predecessor, Abgar V, was rumoured actually to have corresponded with Jesus, as a legendary if unlikely letter in Syriac preserved in the archives supposedly demonstrated. Later legends told of St Thomas's apostolate in the Parthian kingdom of King Gundopher who ruled at Taxila in the Punjab. Seemingly more probable was the journey of a Christian traveller Panaenus who went from Alexandria to India at the end of the second century and found there a Christian colony which was said to have been established by St Bartholomew. Some such stories may be of the stuff of legend, but they hid nuggets of truth.

THE EARLY CHRISTIAN COMMUNITY

Within a century and a half Christianity was widely if thinly spread throughout the Roman world and had even crept beyond its borders. Since the Church kept a low profile in a predominantly pagan environment, it seems unlikely that there can have been much outright evangelistic missionary work, but it must have spread by informal contacts: family relationships, friendships and house meetings. Even sporadic persecution, leading to the dispersal of Christian groups may have acted as a means of dissemination. Christians were not segregated from pagan society but in most respects a part of it.

Yet Christianity was a unique social phenomenon, for Christians differed from their pagan neighbours in their beliefs and way of life. Their beliefs were crystallized in simple confessions of faith in which catechumens or candidates for baptism were instructed. There was for hundreds of years no official creed nor a recognized rota of sacred writings and no agreed or uniform text. The early Christians had the benefit of the Jewish Septuagint in which they read or misread prophecies relating to the revelation of Jesus as the Messiah. The gospels and epistles were soon incorporated in the sacred writings, though it was not until 382 that Pope Damascus authorized a complete text of the canonical books of the Old and New Testaments.

Bishop Polycarp had spoken of New Testament books being read at the church of Smyrna in 107–8. Papias of Hierapolis, writing about 130, commenting on traditions relating to the authorship of St Matthew's Gospel, declared that greater importance should be attached to oral traditions handed down from the apostles than to written books. Funerary paintings in the Roman catacombs show Christians at the Last Judgement holding books in their hands. The possession of a written text was in fact to prove immensely important, providing the youthful Christian Church with some advantage over the pagans who were more dependent on oral myths.

Although Christian belief was still in a transitional state, its fundamentals were already sufficiently clear to separate it off from pagan faiths and mystery religions, even if in some of its ceremonies and notions there was superficial resemblance. Its insistent monotheism and its condemnation of the worship of all other gods removed it from the pagan pantheon. The Christian conviction that salvation came through Jesus Christ and that through his resurrection men and women might enjoy the expectation of eternal life was a conception which seemed ludicrous to the intellectual pagan. It was hardly surprising that without the discipline of an officially recognized creed or the authority of sacred scripture the history of the early Church should have been dogged by an explosion of ideas and beliefs that threatened the integrity of what was ultimately recognized as orthodoxy.

That such ideas did not take over the early Christian Church was probably due to the way in which the Church of the early Christian community soon acquired an effective organization. It is unclear how exactly or how uniformly a Church order of deacons, priests or presbyters and bishops came into being, but the growth of a Christian ministry was a natural sequel to the Church's needs. There had to be someone to carry out baptisms, to preside over the Eucharist and to supervise the community's charitable activities.

Nor is it plain that there was at first any real differentiation between a bishop and a presbyter, though a bishop was soon to emerge as the chief representative of the Christian community. In the late second century Hegesippus declared that the chief Christian churches looked back to the apostles as their founders and Irenaeus of Lyons supposed that it was to the bishops as successors of the apostles that the preservation and dis-semination of the Christian faith was transmitted. 'Therefore,' he wrote, 'obedience is due to those presbyters who . . . are in the succession after the Apostles, and who with their episcopal succession have received according to the will of the Lord the charisma of truth.'

The bishop soon became the leading figure in the Christian congregation, elected by a mixed suffrage, by other bishops, by Church elders and laity and through, as it was believed, the guidance of the Holy Spirit. Ruling in the place of God, the bishop was endowed with great responsibilities, settling disputes within his flock, administering the Church's funds, presiding over its worship and caring for the poor, widows and virgins. He laid hands on newly baptized Christians and had authority to impose penance for sin and, if needs be, to exclude sinners from the Church.

Bishops met with other bishops in greater or smaller synods whereby they could consult together and correlate their views on doctrine and discipline, so giving the Church a degree of uniformity in its teaching and maintaining some sort of contact between the small Christian communities scattered over the Roman Empire. Since early Christianity was in the main an urban phenomenon, the bishops of the major Roman cities, Rome, Antioch, Alexandria, became important and influential in the life of the Church. Because Rome was for long the centre of secular administration, the Church there was soon to acquire a prestige which led other churches to appeal to its bishop for guidance in matters of dispute. In 190 Bishop Victor of Rome threatened the churches of Asia Minor with excommunication for failing to adopt the Roman date for the celebration of Easter. Bishop Stephen, for the first time asserting that his primatial position was based on the Petrine text, engaged in vigorous controversy with Bishop Cyprian of Carthage over questions relating to baptism. Bishops were often described as Latin *papa* or Greek *pappas*, but it was not until the sixth century that the bishop of Rome was described as *papa*.

It was the life-style of the early Christians which most distinguished them from their pagan contemporaries. Ideally, belief in Jesus Christ had a life-changing dimension. Christians were admitted into the Church by the rite of baptism which was the outward sign of their spiritual regeneration. After baptism they attended the Eucharist and the common meal. 'On an appointed day,' the pagan governor Pliny told the emperor, 'they are accustomed to meet before daybreak and to recite a hymn antiphonally to Christ, as to a god, and to bind themselves by an oath, not for the commission of any crime but to abstain from theft, robbery, adultery and breach of faith, and not to deny a deposit when it was claimed. After the conclusion of this ceremony it was their custom to depart and meet again to take food, but it was ordinary and harmless food.' The Eucharist was performed in a room in an ordinary house or in a small building set apart for the purpose; but such gatherings, the nature of which underlines how comparatively small were these early Christian congregations, took place in secret, probably for fear of disturbance either by the curious or the hostile. Such secretiveness led to unjustified charges of Thyestean (i.e. cannibalistic) feasts.

At their baptism the Christians had renounced sin and if they lapsed they were liable to do penance. Tertullian described how 'Christian sinners spend the day sorrowing and the night in vigils and tears, lying on the ground among clinging ashes, tossing in rough sackcloth and dirt, fasting and praying'. A penitent adulterer was 'led into the midst of the brethren and prostrated, all in sackcloth and ashes . . . a compound of disgrace and horror, before the widows, the elders suing for everyone's tears, licking their footprints, clasping their knees'.

It was perhaps in their attitude to sexuality that the Christian differed most distinctively from the non-Christian. Sex, some Christian writers stated, had come into the world as a result of the fall of Adam and Eve and was intrinsically sinful. In practice pagans accepted the exposure of children and abortion, and the re-marriage of widows, nor did concubinage, as St Augustine's own experience was later to demonstrate, carry any stigma. Active homosexuality (though not in general male prostitution) was socially accepted. The Christian writer Tatian said, with some hyperbole, that the Romans considered 'pederasty to be particularly privileged and try to round up herds of boys like herds of grazing mares'. In fact many pagan Romans deplored sexual indulgence and were as sedate in their private lives as the Victorians. Like the Jews Christians condemned the exposure of children and incestuous marriage, disapproved of fornication and adultery, supposed abortion to be 'murder of the creation of God' and homosexuality a sin which was bound to provoke God's anger. While they could hardly escape the conclusion that marriage was natural and God-given, many writers insisted that it was only for procreation. Many thought that it was second best, 'a respectable form of adultery' as Athenagoras put it. The rigorists Tatian and Tertullian went further, calling it a 'defilement and fornication'. Augustine unconvincingly revealed his anti-feminism when he wrote 'if it was company and good conversation that Adam needed, it would have been much better to have two men together as friends, not a man and a woman'. It was hardly surprising that the Church came to disapprove of second marriages and came more and more to deprecate the marriage of the clergy (though St Peter had, for instance, been a married man).

The Church came early to place great stress on chastity and the virtues of virginity. Jesus, it was pointed out, was never married and his mother Mary was a virgin. 'Christ and Mary', Jerome wrote, 'were both virgins, and thus consecrated the pattern of virginity for both sexes.' 'Virginity', the rigorist Novatian wrote in 250, 'makes itself equal to the angels; it exalts the angels, because it must struggle against the flesh to master a nature which the angels do not possess.' In the book of Revelation St John had described the 144,000 virgins in heaven, men who were singing on their harps and had never had intercourse with women. Some Christians, the philosopher Origen commented, 'practise total chastity, others marry only once because they think that the person who marries, or marries a second time, is damned'; but Origen had himself castrated so that he should not be tempted while he taught his female pupils, a somewhat extreme step which, as the Council of Nicaea was to state, disqualified a man from being a priest.

In his commentary on St Matthew, Origen was, however, to disclaim such conduct as an unjustified way of safeguarding chastity.

If the Christian conception of family life differed from that of the pagans, there was a more positive side to Christian society which may have assisted in the process of converting others to the Christian position. For the Christian *koinonia* was evidently a caring fellowship, an extension of the family itself. The early Christians did not seek to revolutionize society nor to condemn slavery, holding indeed that slaves had to submit to their masters, but they taught that the masters must treat their slaves with 'patience, equity and philanthropy'. Above all they stressed brotherhood, concern and compassion, not merely for fellow Christians but for all men and women. In the mid-fourth century the pagan emperor Julian, deploring the anti-social attitude of his fellow pagans, asserted that 'the Jews do not allow any of their own people to become beggars and the Christians support not only their own but also our poor'. The Christians upheld an ideal of charity and love, humility and purity which was in many respects alien to contemporary society. The Church was concerned to look after the widows, the virgins and the poor, and to care for those who were sick or in prison. Moreover, the Christians disapproved of and did not participate in, except as press-ganged victims, the immensely popular and brutally perverted gladiatorial shows when, as Byron was later to write, men and beasts were 'butchered to make a Roman holiday'. It was Christian opinion that was eventually to curb and ultimately to stop the appalling blood-lust of the Roman amphitheatre. They condemned necromancy and idolatry, abstained from luxurious costume and unnecessary finery, and in their care for each other they must have created a pattern which drew others into their ranks.

If the churches appeared to be extensions of a kinship group they were also nuclear societies. In every congregation there was a hard core of committed men and women who guided and organized the fellowship; but the membership must have varied in its degree of commitment. The churches always carried passengers, though the number was greatly to increase after the acceptance of Christianity by the established order in the state. The strongly committed have always constituted a comparatively small percentage of the whole. Some accepted church membership for family or even business connections and, after Christianity became a tolerated religion, for reasons of fashion and convention. St Paul's letters showed how, even in the days of the infant Church, Christians were liable to lapse morally and spiritually from the high ethical and spiritual standards which they had embraced. Even before Christianity became the established faith, elections to bishoprics were occasionally tarnished by bitter rivalry. In the angry controversy which centred on the so-called heretical views of Paul of Samosata, bishop of Antioch in the 270s, his critics charged him with too great a familiarity with women (whom he had apparently recruited for his church choir) and with living too luxuriously. There must too have been a floating membership which did not persist, more especially when persecution loomed. Once this occurred the conflict of loyalties and self-interest created major problems in every church. As Christianity became more socially respectable, so the standards set by some Christians became more reminiscent of the world which they had specifically rejected. In practice the difference between Christian and pagan may have been less than the search for Christian perfectionism might suggest.

For the Christians' separateness from non-Christian society must not be overstressed. They did not live in a ghetto and, though regarded with suspicion by some, they had friends and relatives among their pagan neighbours. They inherited the thought patterns of the contemporary world, more especially of Judaic civilization and were beset by superstitious belief. They believed that they were surrounded by spiritual beings, whether demons sent by the Devil or Satan to tempt them or by guardian angels who watched over every baptized person. They received guidance through dreams and visions, which were thought to provide glimpses of another world. They had an ever-present fear of the literally interpreted fires of hell reserved for sinners and non-believers. 'Here', as the martyr Papylus of Pergamum stated, 'the fire burns briefly, but there it burns for ever, and by it, God will judge the world. It will drown the sea, the mountains and the woods. By it God will judge each human soul.' Yet in spite of what must have seemed to their pagan neighbours their idiosyncratic beliefs, for the most part Christians moved peacefully and without hindrance in a predominantly non-Christian world for the first three hundred years of Christian history.

Who were these early Christians? The Church's adherents were more likely to be found in the towns than in the countryside. In AD 251 whereas in Rome the Church had 154 ministers caring for 1,500 widows and poor people, a North African council of 256 showed that of eighty bishops only four were located in rural areas. It is doubtful whether Christianity made more than a limited appeal to slaves and the desperate poor, and more probable that the majority of its followers were drawn from the humbler free classes. 'We see them,' Celsus, the second-century critic of the Christians wrote, 'wooldressers, cobblers, and fullers, the more uneducated and common individuals, not daring to say a word in the presence of their masters who are older and wiser. But, when they get hold of the children in private, and silly women with them, they are wonderfully eloquent.' The Christian writer Athenagoras, writing c. 177, was in part agreement. 'With us you will find unlettered people, tradesmen and old women, who though they are unable to express in words the advantages of our teaching demonstrate by acts the value of their principles.' Inscriptions record a Christian butcher in Phrygia, a Christian woodcarver in Bithynia and a Christian member of a boat owners' guild in Ostia. There were Christian town councillors, lawyers and even soldiers who seemed, though there were exceptions, able if needs be to participate in token sacrifices. A Christian athlete, who had won prizes in the pagan games, was an elder in the town of Eumenaia.

From the start Christianity evidently made a great appeal to women, perhaps in part because it refrained from treating them as sexual objects and cared for virgins and widows. St Paul tells of Phoebe who helped the Christians at Corinth and of Lydia, the seller of purple, a luxury good. A catalogue of goods confiscated from the church of Cirta in North Africa taken during the persecution of AD 303 lists 38 women's veils, 82 ladies' tunics and 47 pairs of women's slippers but only 16 men's tunics. The Church made a particular point of caring for widows, many of whom because of the early age of marriage, were still comparatively young; later legacies from rich widows in part enabled the Christian community to carry out the social work involved in looking after the sick, the destitute and the orphaned. The Church provided women with a vocation, and in the figure of the Blessed Virgin Mary, the object of growing devotion, an example to follow.

Sooner or later Christianity would infiltrate the upper classes of society. Surprisingly early St Paul alluded to Christians in 'Caesar's household', presumably imperial slaves, and his own converts included Erastus, a steward or *aedile* at Corinth, and both at Ephesus and Cyprus he made contact with important people, notably the Roman governor of Cyprus, Sergius Paulus. The Roman historian Dio Cassius, writing some hundred years or more later, asserted that in 95 the emperor Domitian had his cousin Flavius Clemens and his wife Domitilla and the consul Acilius Glabrio arrested and charged with atheism, since they had 'slipped into Jewish customs' which would imply that they had been converted to Christianity. Clemens and Glabrio were sentenced to death; Domitilla was sent into exile. The mistress of Marcus Aurelius' successor, the emperor Commodus, at the end of the second century was said to have been a secret Christian sympathizer who intervened on behalf of Christians sentenced to the mines. But such influence in high places must as yet have been comparatively rare. Christianity grew only slowly and remained a minority movement.

PROBLEMS OF BELIEF IN THE EARLY CHURCH

The Church's growth was attended by internal problems which threatened its unity and led to bitter controversy; though the animus to which doctrinal controversies gave rise could then and later be seen also as a testimony to the vitality and dynamism of the Christian community.

In Phrygia, a former priest of Cybele, Montanus, who preached that he was a medium for the Holy Spirit or Paraclete, taught the imminent second coming of Christ, and the need for Christians to live lives of strict austerity, marked by strict continence and fasting, to prepare for it. He was assisted by two females, Prisca and Maximilla, one of whom was said to have glimpsed Christ in a vision garbed as a woman. This charismatic millennial movement soon won a following in Asia Minor, its beliefs strengthened by the earthquakes and famines which had recently struck the region, among its sympathizers the eminent theologian Tertullian. But the Asian bishops condemned Montanus's teachings. He was excommunicated, appealing in vain to the bishop of Rome. But Montanism did not quickly die, for it penetrated to many parts of the Mediterranean.

Although the intellectual Tertullian became a Montanist, Montanism was not primarily an intellectual movement but the rise of Gnosticism, if in some respects only peripherally Christian, showed that Christianity had moved from the market place to the academe.

Although Gnosticism was severely criticized by Christian writers it had a serious purpose and was trying to deal, if ineffectively, with a real problem: how to place the Christian faith within the context of philosophy and to present it as a rational alternative to superstitious pagan belief. In practice Gnostic teaching, less the product of Judaism than of Syrian and Egyptian Hellenism, with an admixture of necromancy, ended by more or less explaining Christianity away. Gnostics held that *gnosis* or knowledge was itself a particular and saving grace of the Holy Spirit. 'It is', the Gnostic writer Valentinus wrote in his *Letter to Rheginus*, 'not only baptism that frees us from the power of fate but *gnosis* – the knowledge of what we were, why we have come into being, what we are and at what point we have been placed in the cosmos, whither we are hastening, from what we have been redeemed, and what is birth and rebirth.' Most of the Gnostic writers, Valentinus, Basilides, Menander to mention only a few, supposed there to be a series of emanations from the divine being, God, some mystical and allegorical, of which Christ was likely to be the ultimate expression. The Incarnation, the Passion, and the Resurrection were in Gnostic writings only symbols rather than actuality. There was a strong element of dualism, of mind separated from matter, hence of the mental as opposed to the physical in Gnostic teaching, for they taught that the spirit had to be liberated from its earthly body.

Dualism was to have its classic spokesman in the late third century in an influential Iranian teacher. Mani, born *c.* 216, grew up in a Jewish-Christian community of Baptists in southern Iraq. Like St Paul upon whom he appears to have modelled himself, he experienced an evangelical vision of 'the boundless heights and unfathomable depths' of ultimate reality and he travelled as far as India. Returning to Iran he first won the favour of the ruling king, Sapor I, but then in 276 aroused the hostility of his successor, Bahram I, who had him flayed alive. Mani taught that the eternal principles governing the universe were light and darkness between which there was unending conflict. Satan had stolen the particles of light which had been confined to the human brain. The religious prophets, among them Jesus, the true spirit of light in the guise of a man, though never born of a woman or actually suffering crucifixion, and of whom Mani was himself the last emanation, aimed to save mankind by releasing the particles of light imprisoned in the human body. It would be impossible to save the existing world, which was ultimately doomed to extinction, but by recognizing Mani's gospel of light, his followers could bring about the release of the light particles imprisoned in their own bodies and so progress to a higher, spiritualized existence in the future world. Since the essence of evil is unregulated desire, Mani stressed the need for austerity in living, especially for his elect; he preached abstinence from sex and a selective vegetarianism – he believed even vegetables shed tears when they are eaten and palm trees shouted out when they are pruned; melons alone as fleshless vegetables were well favoured.

Although Mani described himself as an 'apostle through the will of Jesus Christ' his movement was only peripherally Christian, but in some respects it appealed very much to the more rigorist Christians, and he established a church which had a hierarchy of deputies, bishops and elders. Originating on the outskirts of the Roman Empire Mani's teaching penetrated into the Greek-speaking countries of the eastern Mediterranean, winning disciples, among them in his early years the African father St Augustine with a following in Iran and India. For Mani's religion was linguistically more mobile than Christianity, its founder Syriac-speaking and its faith, as Mani said, was 'for all languages'. The dualistic components of Manichaeism, the basic antagonism between light and darkness, the spirit and the flesh, were an enduring ingredient in Christian thinking, notably among the heretical Bogomiles and Cathars in the middle ages.

The Christian faith was as yet in many respects theologically under constant siege both from its more eccentric interpreters whether Montanists, Gnostics, or Manicheans, as well as from its pagan critics. Some of the latter wrote forcefully. In 165 Lucian of Samosata wrote of his disillusionment as he discovered that his Christian comrades seemed both credulous and fanatical. In a penetrating survey another pagan, Celsus, dismissed the Christians as superstitious, silly and disloyal. The Christian God, Celsus urged, was like an angry old man, and the Christian revelation unpersuasive. 'If Jesus really wished to display his divine power, he would have appeared to the actual men who had reviled him.' The Christians were like 'frogs holding a symposium round a swamp or worms in a conventicle in a corner of the mud, debating which of them were the most sinful and saying "God reveals all things to us beforehand and gives us warning He forsakes the whole universe and the course of the heavenly spheres to dwell with us alone"'. To Celsus the existence of many gods seemed to accord more with the natural order of the universe than belief in monotheism.

Both the need to provide instruction in the Church's teaching and to define its true beliefs led to a series of apologetic writings designed to refute the Church's critics. In his book *Against the Heresies* Irenaeus, an Asiatic who became bishop of Lyons, denouncing the Gnostics, demonstrated pungently that the Christian God, who was the same God as Yahwe the God of the Jews, had revealed himself through Jesus Christ in accordance with scriptural teaching. Justin, a Christian convert who taught at Rome, in his *Apologia* and *Dialogue with Trypho* while declaring that Christian teaching was intrinsically superior to Greek philosophy, admitted that there were elements in Stoic and Platonic philosophy compatible with the teaching of the Christian faith. Both Abraham and Socrates he deemed were 'Christians before Christ'. Incidentally, there seemed to be evidence of some accommodation between the thought patterns of the Judaic and the Hellenic world, so that Christianity might even be interpreted as the consummation of Greek philosophy as well as the fulfilment of Old Testament prophecy. In a rich display of learning Clement of Alexandria, another convert from paganism, showed that educated men and women could follow an apostolic style of life without necessarily discarding their cultural roots.

In the course of nearly three centuries, a Christian apologetic, intellectually vigorous, diverse in its opinions, had come into being; Irenaeus of Lyons, Tertullian, Origen, an original and even radically oriented mind, Cyprian the bishop of Carthage, the learned and atrabilious Roman presbyter Hippolytus, were only a few among the figures who were arguing that Christianity was intellectually respectable. If they wrote and taught mainly for the clergy, what they wrote showed that some at least among the Christians, more especially the bishops, were highly educated men.

REPRESSION AND PERSECUTION

Although Christianity was, unlike Judaism, a *religio illicita*, an unlicensed religion, for the greater part of three centuries Christians were left undisturbed. Comparatively few in number, as Christ and St Paul had seemed to advise, they were punctilious in stressing their loyalty to the emperor, even if they were unwilling to pay ritual sacrifice to him. Subservient to the established order, obedient by nature, at first believing that the end of the world was imminent, they could not in general be regarded as a real threat to the safety of the state.

The first violent persecution certainly took place at Rome in 64 at the emperor's orders when the Christians were made a scapegoat for the terrible fire which swept the city on 19 July which some attributed to the emperor Nero himself, eager to clear a site for a new palace. 'Consequently,' Tacitus wrote, 'to get rid of the report Nero fastened the guilt and inflicted the most exquisite tortures on a class hated for their abominations, called Christians by the populace. . . . Accordingly an arrest was first made of all who confessed; then, upon their information, an immense multitude was convicted not so much for the crime of arson, as of hatred of the human race. Covered with the skins of beasts, they were torn by dogs and perished, or were nailed to crosses, or were doomed to the flames.' Although the Christian leaders, Peter and Paul, probably perished in the holocaust it seems extremely doubtful that there were, as Tacitus had suggested, 'an immense multitude' of Christians in the city. It was because the Christians were a small and unpopular community that it was easy to seize upon them. Unless there was, as seems possible, a small-scale outbreak under the emperor Domitian nearly two hundred years were to pass before a persecution was initiated by imperial legislation.

The Christians' earliest enemies were less the pagans than the Jews. Paul's travels showed how they stirred up riots and instigated violence against the Christians. The head of the Christian community, James, who was obliged to retreat from Jerusalem to the Greek city of Pella, was murdered in 62. Ironically enough the Christian cause was well served by growing Roman hostility towards the Jews. In the late 60s the tactless policy of a Roman procurator, Gessius Florus, had provoked a Jewish uprising against Roman rule. Subsequently the Romans laid siege to Jerusalem which was courageously and even sacrificially defended, more especially by the puritanical sect of the Essenes, while the small Christian community evacuated the city. Jewish obduracy so infuriated the normally humane Emperor Hadrian that he made circumcision, which he seems to have identified with castration, a penal offence. In fury the Jews under Bar Kochba, who was described as the new Messiah, led a desperate uprising against the Romans which ended inevitably in the defeat and dispersion of the Jews. Even the name of Jerusalem was obliterated; henceforth it was to be called Aelia Capitolina. Rome rather than Jerusalem would become the principal Christian city.

The Jews were no longer, and perhaps had not been for some time, any real danger to the Christians but the intellectual and religious skirmish had long-term effects. The Jews remained hostile, particularly at festival times, as that of Purim, burning Christian crosses, attacking Christian beliefs such as that of the Resurrection which they termed sorcery, and actively supporting persecution. The Christians were, however, to repay the Jews in their own coin, and in the long term, with the rise of anti-Semitism, were horridly to get the better of the battle.

Where there was persecution it tended to be sporadic, local in its range, representing the pressure of public opinion rather than government policy. The small Christian communities sometimes aroused the distrust of their pagan neighbours, if only because of their secretive and masonic character. What was more to the point were the rumours that the Christians' denial of the gods and their failure to propitiate them by making sacrifices could account for the misfortunes which befell the whole community in the shape of famine, earthquakes, plagues and other disasters. 'If the Tiber reaches the walls, if the Nile does not rise to the fields,' Tertullian commented, 'if the sky doesn't move or the earth does, if there is famine, if there is plague, the cry is at once "Christians to the lions!" What, all of them to one lion?'

In some instances mob violence was actually aroused for reasons of personal interest. From time to time there were those who had their eyes on

Christian property and, as Melito of Sardis said, denounced the Christians to the magistrate in the hope of later acquiring it. In one such outbreak which occurred at Smyrna in Asia Minor between 155 and 158 twelve Christians were sentenced to be the prey of apparently reluctant lions and the aged Bishop Polycarp was burned alive. About the same time the Christian writer Justin Martyr, denounced by a fellow philosopher, was scourged and beheaded at Rome. One of the worst of the early persecutions took place in 177 at Lyons. The local nobles, resentful of the expense of providing gladiators for the public games, learned that it was possible at no cost to themselves to substitute condemned criminals. The Christians, some of whom were immigrants from Asia Minor, were conscripted for the games at the great festival on 1 August and paid the penalty. The victims were tortured, beaten, put on the rack, had their bodies clawed by an iron scraper while melted lead was poured on their private parts. 'Those standing round', the Church historian Eusebius wrote later, 'were struck with amazement, at seeing them lacerated with scourges, to their very blood and arteries, so that now the flesh congealed in the very inmost parts of the body, and the bowels themselves were exposed to view. Then they were laid upon conch shells from the sea, and on sharp heads and points of spears on the ground, and after passing through every kind of punishment and torment, were at last thrown as food to wild beasts.' But such horrific events were comparatively rare in the first three centuries of the Church's history. Once the crisis had passed at Lyons the Christian community appeared to resume its ordinary tolerated existence. The Church's properties were not even confiscated, and the presbyter Irenaeus was elected as bishop in succession to Pothinus who had perished in the massacre.

The emperors followed in effect a policy of coexistence, made easier by the comparatively small numbers of Christians and their passivity. The emperor Trajan had told his governor, Pliny, that Christians were not to be purposely sought out. Trajan's successor, Hadrian, in a letter to the proconsul of Asia, Minucius Fundanus, in 124–5, advised that a Christian who was accused of definite crimes should be tried by due process of law, and if the charge failed the Christian was entitled to bring a counter-charge against his accuser.

Yet the Christians lived inevitably in a climate of social and religious insecurity. While their religion remained only a *religio illicita* they could be required to sacrifice to the gods. If they failed to offer incense on a pagan altar, so recognizing the existence of the tutelary deities, they were liable to punishment. The more zealous Christians refused to cooperate and voluntarily paid the penalty but there must have been others who were ready to compromise as the long and often bitter debate about whether the sin of apostasy could be forgiven or what was an adequate penance for it clearly demonstrated. For every Christian who suffered death there must have been hundreds who survived either by quiet concealment or by their readiness to pay the nominal lip service to the gods that the magistrates required.

There was a short but sharp bout of persecution under the emperor Maximus between 235 and 238 in which Hippolytus who had recently claimed to be Bishop of Rome and his successor Bishop Pontian were arrested and despatched to the island of Sardinia, 'the island of death'. This was a precursor to a major change of imperial policy which occurred when in late 249 the emperor Decius issued an edict commanding all his subjects, excepting the Jews, to sacrifice to the gods.

What then caused the imperial government to embark for the first time on a policy of universal persecution is unclear. While it was claimed that the growth in Christian numbers alarmed the emperor there is no real evidence to suggest that there had been a major increase in the Christian population. There may have been, as his successor Valerian's edict in 258 seems to indicate, some degree of Christian infiltration into the official classes which caused some alarm at the imperial court. Valerian's rescript referred to senators, Roman knights, respectable women (*matronae*) and imperial slaves who were Christian sympathizers. Dionysius, the bishop of Alexandria, added that the emperor's court was 'full of the faithful'. Decius' predecessor, the emperor Philip, was rumoured to have favoured the Christians; 'he was more kindly to us Christians' Bishop Dionysius of Alexandria commented. Indeed, even before the outbreak of the persecution, there were riots in Alexandria against the Christians who were somehow identified with the unpopular fiscal reforms which Philip had introduced. Decius may have wished to distance himself from his predecessor and underline his legitimacy as a 'divine' emperor. More probably, given the current economic stagnation and the troubles on the frontiers, he may have wished to assure himself of divine favours 'so that the immortal gods may pass on to future generations what our ancestors have built up'. If Decius wished to be the 'restorer of the Roman past' his anti-Christian policy becomes explicable.

The persecution, though violent, was short-lived. All the emperor's subjects were required to show honour to the gods. Suspected Christians had to attest their acceptance of paganism and undertake an act of sacrifice, receiving in return a certificate sealed in the presence of a local commissioner. 'I have always continued to sacrifice,' so a surviving certificate belonging to one Aurelia Charis from the village of Theadelphia in Egypt reads, 'and show piety to the gods and now, in your presence, I have poured a libation and sacrificed and eaten some of the sacrificial meat. I request you to certify this for me below.' Those who agreed to carry out these sacrifices, the *libellatici*, had their names enrolled. How many genuine Christians did so to save their lives and to wait until the storm had passed it is impossible to say. 'Some', Eusebius wrote later, 'advanced with greater readiness to the altars, and boldly asserted that they had never before been Christians. . . . Some fled, others were taken . . . some after a few days' imprisonment abjured before they entered the tribunal. Others, however, who were firm and blessed pillars of the band . . . became admirable witnesses of his kingdom,' among them the Bishop of Rome, Sixtus II, who with his deacons was beheaded, and Bishop Fabian who suffered a similar fate. Not that the magistrates wished to create martyrs. What they wanted was a compliant people, and they could neither understand nor sympathize with the obdurate stand of the committed Christian. Decius' death on the northern frontier brought the persecution to an end, but it was only a temporary respite, for his successor the emperor Valerian, together with his son Gallienus as co-emperor, followed a similar policy, issuing edicts ordering that bishops and elders should be punished and forbidding Christians to hold meetings or enter the 'cemeteries' under pain of death. Valerian's legislation was even more all-embracing in its implications, for it aimed to destroy the Christian infrastructure. Perhaps, like Decius, Valerian wished to win the pleasure of the gods by following so stringent a policy, but if so the gods did not respond, for a year or so later the emperor was captured and killed by the Iranians and his son, Gallienus, who is said to have had a Christian wife, Salonina, reversed his father's policy and ordered that Christian churches, properties and cemeteries should be restored.

This short but severe spate of persecution had brought to the fore two issues which had always been a sequel to apostasy and martyrdom, both of which had some bearing on the development of the early Church. What was to be the fate of those who had complied with the imperial orders, though they had not in effect given up their faith, when the persecution came to an end? Then and later the Church was divided between the precisians, who believed either that full readmission to the Church was not possible or only possible after the severest of penances, and who were to form the North African Donatist Church; and those who held that after a lapse of time and penance, backsliders should be received again into the Christian congregation. At the time of the Decian persecutions a group led by Novatian argued for the strict position, but the moderates, led by the bishop of Carthage, Cyprian, who was himself to die a martyr's death in 258, urged that readmission was possible, the penance depending on how serious the lapse from the faith had been. After a bitter dispute the policy of moderation was ultimately to prevail. Had it not done so the Church might have dwindled to a small and relatively unimportant sect.

'The blood of the martyrs', Tertullian had observed long before the outbreak of the Decian persecution, was the 'seed' of the Church. The martyrs were its athletes and warriors. They were to be revered as a cloud of witnesses interceding for the faithful in heaven. At death they had experienced a 'second baptism'. 'There are two things', Melito of Sardis wrote in the 170s, 'which give remission of sins: baptism and suffering for the sake of Christ.' They constituted, as Gregory of Tours put it some centuries later, 'the snowwhite number of the elect', linked, as another bishop of the later fourth century, Vitricius of Rouen said, 'by a bond to the whole stretch of eternity'. The martyr's death, like that of Christ, was sacrificial. Ignatius of Antioch spoke of the martyr's blood as the wine and the body crushed by wild beasts as the 'pure bread' of Christ.

In their deaths they pointed heavenwards. 'Today,' said one such after hearing his sentence, 'we are in heaven.' Perpetua, awaiting martyrdom at Carthage, described the dreams of triumph with which Christ consoled her. When she went into the arena, she walked proudly, even helping the embarrassed young gladiator to kill her, 'having guided his wavering hand to her throat'. When the slave girl Blandina was martyred at Lyons, hanging upside down on a pillar, 'she seemed to hang there in the form of a cross and by her concerted prayers she aroused great eagerness in those who were struggling too, for they saw in their struggle and with their physical sight, him who was crucified on their behalf in the person of their sister Blandina.' If in heaven a virgin was accounted as worth sixty times more than the ordinary Christian, a martyr would be worth a hundredfold.

It was not only a literature which grew up about the martyrs, doubtless often embellished by pious legend, but the martyrs' tombs in the cemeteries on the outskirts of the towns became places where the faithful gathered on the purported anniversaries of their death. Readings took place, exaggerated or fictional as they might be, relating the martyrs' heroic deeds 'both as a memorial for those who have already completed and a training and preparation for those who follow suit'. There were feasts, *laetitiae*, of which purists such as St Augustine disapproved.

Their burial places became holy shrines and their relics were sought after – pieces of skin, ashes or dust from the place of their execution. Such shrines became in some sense not only a reminder of but an actual extension of eternity, for there the Christian was surrounded by a heavenly crowd of witnesses. Moreover, as intimates of God they were placed in a position to intercede for the faithful. As Gregory of Nyssa declared, 'They address to the martyr their prayers of intercession as though he were present.'

Some forty years of peace followed the ending of Valerian's policy of persecution. 'Who could describe', the historian Eusebius exclaimed rhetorically, 'those vast collections of men that flocked to the religion of Christ, and those multitudes crowding in from every city, and the illustrious concourse in the houses of worship?' Comparative toleration at least promoted confidence, and led to some growth in numbers of the Christian community. When in 272 Paul of Samosata, Bishop of Antioch, fell foul of his fellow bishops for emphasizing unduly the human nature of Christ, the bishops excommunicated him and appealed to the pagan emperor Aurelian to ensure that the bishop vacated his church. The emperor, a strong devotee of the sun god, *sol invictus*, who described himself not without some justification as the *restitutor imperii*, ordered the appellants to accept the verdict of the bishop of Rome and the Italian bishops.

What brought about a renewal of persecution, of which an attack on a

Manichaean congregation seemed the precursor, remains somewhat obscure. Even more than Aurelian Diocletian, emperor since 284, deserved the title of restorer of the empire. At his accession the empire was in crisis, often split by civil strife, decimated by plague, damaged by inflation and consequent debasement of the coinage with the barbarian tribes lapping over the borders. To seek to arrest this decline Diocletian embarked on a massive programme of reform and reconstruction. He introduced a series of fiscal measures seeking to control prices and wages and secured the empire's frontiers against the barbarians and the Iranians. In the first two decades of his reign there were few signs that he had his eye on the Christian churches; his wife the empress Prisca and her daughter Valeria were said to be Christian sympathizers.

Then everything changed. Diocletian who surrounded himself with oriental pageantry had an autocratic view of his position which may have made him look back longingly to the past when the gods showered favours on the emperor. Although there were some signs that paganism was in decline, inscriptions to the pagan gods seeming to diminish in the second half of the third century, it was in many respects still strong. Cities still placed themselves under the protection of the gods, arranging festivals and games in their honour. Oracles were still invoked, shrines bedecked. Diocletian was said himself to have consulted the oracle of Apollo at Didyma, near Miletus, which countenanced an attack upon the 'just on earth'. The influence of the philosophers at his court at Nicomedia worked in the same direction. In the confused and nervous atmosphere of the times Christianity seemed to be a greater threat than it actually was, challenging the tutelary deities and so bringing misfortune on the empire.

Whether the emperor feared the infiltration of Christians into court circles we do not know, but he was certainly intent on weeding out court officials and army officers who were suspected of being Christian. Yet in practice the Christians were still very much in the minority, their churches inconspicuous, their influence by and large limited. On 23 February 303 Diocletian, in company with his colleague Maximus, issued a decree ordering the destruction of churches, the banning of all services, the burning of the scriptures and the loss of all privileges by the Christians. They were deprived of the legal protection they had previously enjoyed as citizens. Further edicts ordered the imprisonment of the clergy and commanded all Christians throughout the empire to offer pagan sacrifices.

On Diocletian's part it was a great gamble but it did not pay off. It is true that more Christians died in this persecution than in any previous one, greatly expanding the calendar of saints, but the vast majority of Christians did not suffer martyrdom. They went underground or submitted; even the Bishop of Rome, Marcellinus, apparently handed over the copies of the scriptures and offered incense, so in practice disqualifying himself for his high office. The severity of the persecution varied greatly from region to region. It was worst in those parts of the empire, notably North Africa, ruled by the anti-Christian Emperor Maximin who ordered all the goods in the markets to be sprinkled with blood or libations from pagan sacrifices. Christians were everywhere harried and their leaders imprisoned or, as was the case with some bishops including Bishop Marcellus I, compelled to act as keepers for the imperial camels and grooms for the imperial horses. While, as in other persecutions, city mobs took advantage of the situation to loot Christian property there were places where the Christian communities, harmless, law-abiding and socially respectable, were likely to be respected by their pagan neighbours who were willing to connive at their escape. Of a martyr at Edessa it was said that 'some of the Jews and pagans took part in shrouding and burying his body with the Christian brethren'.

It was in effect too late in the day for the 'Great Persecution' to succeed. Wearied by his task Diocletian himself abdicated the imperial diadem in 305 'to grow cabbages' at Salona. The empire passed under the control of two emperors of the east and west and their respective Caesars. Although persecution continued in the eastern half of the empire, it soon began to slacken in the west. Gaul and Britain were controlled by Constantine Chlorus, a believer in the sun god, whose wife Helena was or became a Christian. When Constantine died at York in 306, his son Constantine, who certainly continued to pay lip service to the pagan gods, relaxed Diocletian's religious policy. In 311 he and his eastern colleague Galerius issued an edict ending the persecution and licensing Christianity and Church worship. Two years later Constantine came into conflict with his rival Maxentius and in the hard-fought battle of the Milvian Bridge he emerged the decisive victor.

The battle proved to be a religious as well as a political victory, for Constantine attributed the outcome to the God of the Christians. His future biographer, Eusebius, Bishop of Caesarea, declared that the emperor had become sufficiently acquainted with the Christian faith to put his trust in God, and received a sign, a cross of light shining through the rays of the sun through which could be seen the words 'In this sign, conquer.' *In hoc signo, vince.* In the night he was said to have been granted a vision of Christ himself bearing the cross in his hand, a vision which led him to adopt as his standard the cross in a horizontal transom, carrying the monogram of Christ, *chi-rho.*

The incident has led to a crop of speculation. If Constantine thought he saw a vision, was it simply a peculiar concatenation of clouds in the sky through which the sun was filtering? Was he even invoking the Christian God? Could it have been the sun god to whom his father had been devoted? When, in 315 the Roman Senate erected an arch to commemorate Constantine's victory, the inscription stated simply that he owed his victory to the 'inspiration of the godhead' and the relief shows his army protected by the sun god, *Sol Invictus.* If he knew something already of the Christian faith, who were his instructors? Possibly his mother, the empress Helena. Possibly Hosius, Bishop of Cordova, an ecclesiastic much in his confidence.

Such speculations cannot be resolved. Constantine had halted the persecution of Christians and ordered the restoration of their property. Whether Constantine had calculated the effect of his change of policy or was acting according to his new-found faith, it was soon clear that he had become a professed Christian. In 313, with the consent of his eastern colleague Licinius, he issued the edict of Milan which proclaimed a policy of toleration for all faiths. In a letter which he sent the following year to Ablabius, the governor of Roman Africa, the emperor declared that it had been he to whom 'God has entrusted by his divine will the rule over the whole world in order I should watch over it. . . . I shall not be really or fully secure and able to trust in God's Almighty goodness which freely dispenses happiness and salvation until all men offer worship in harmony and brotherliness to the all-Holy God in the prescribed forms of the Christian religion.'

The 'conversion' of the emperor Constantine was undoubtedly one of the most momentous events in history. After three hundred years the Christian Church had come of age. A minority movement had triumphed and was soon to become the religion of the majority, so initiating a tremendous social and religious revolution. On the eve of the critical battle of the Milvian Bridge Constantine was said to have been vouchsafed a vision of the cross. In the sign of the cross he had triumphed, but if the cross had triumphed it had been because of the sword. In establishing Christianity, as he was soon to do, as the supreme religion of the Mediterranean and western Roman world, a Christianity which was itself soon to adopt an intolerant stance towards its rivals and critics, the Roman emperor had endowed the Church with the powers of the sword. In the centuries that followed the cross and the sword were to be involved in a constant and sometimes violent battle of will.

CHAPTER TWO

The Church Triumphant

The setting was the emperor's palace at Nicaea, a city 30 miles south of the then capital of the eastern empire, Nicomedia. Eleven years after the edict of Milan granting toleration to the Christians, in 325, some three hundred bishops, mainly from the eastern empire, gathered in the hall of the imperial palace. The emperor Constantine, 'resplendent as one of God's angels in heaven', took his seat on a small golden throne and informed the bishops that he hoped that the triumph which he had won over his enemies would be followed by a victory over divisions in the Church and by the restoration of its unity.

If the Church was split by controversy over doctrine, the Church and the empire, hitherto separate, were to become fused into a single entity, the empire ideally a microcosmic expression of the heavenly kingdom governed by God's living representative, the emperor, to whom had been entrusted authority over all peoples. He was indeed already as *pontifex maximus* its pagan high priest, and he continued to hold the title which was only discarded by the emperor Gratian in 382. At one bound the Church had acquired a new God-given head who was henceforth to summon and preside over its oecumenical councils. Christianity had triumphed over paganism, but in so doing became in many respects its political and social, and even religious, heir. In Europe Christianity was henceforth to be the dominant faith maintaining its authority by the message of the cross and the discipline of the sword; and it was difficult to differentiate between the two.

THE DEFEAT OF PAGANISM

Naturally the triumph of Christianity did not mean the sudden extinction of paganism which was an unconscionably long time dying, for it was long to survive as a cultural undergrowth especially in the countryside. Momentarily in 361 when Constantine II's nephew Julian became emperor on the sudden death of his uncle, it seemed that paganism might regain power and the process of Christianization might be stayed. Brought up as a Christian, Julian decided to revive the ancient cults and to eliminate Christianity. So he ordered the pagan temples which had fallen into disuse or which had been destroyed to be rebuilt; the sacrifices were revived and pagan games encouraged. Although the emperor Julian who prided himself on his enlightenment followed a policy of tolerance, even allowing the bishops whom his predecessor for religious reasons had exiled to return to their dioceses, among them the stormy bishop of Alexandria, Athanasius, inevitably the Christians lost out. The influence which they had exercised at the imperial court for the last half century waned as pagan philosophers such as Maximus of Ephesus replaced the bishops as the emperor's protégés. Since Christianity was no longer favoured by the emperor it ceased to be fashionable and those who had become Christian for social reasons returned to the old gods. Yet the paganism which Julian had embraced was unlikely to be deeply popular. He wanted to reform the pagan priesthood so that it would approximate more closely to the Christian clergy. He strongly stressed the moral aspect of pagan teaching.

Austere and even puritanical Julian, often shedding the appurtenances of majesty and shabby in appearance, was unlikely to attract the favour of the populace. In fact his time was short, for he was killed in 363 while leading his army against the Iranians.

Although there was to be one further but abortive attempt to make a pagan an emperor when the schoolmaster Eugenius was raised to the purple in 392, Julian's death meant that henceforth the highest authority in the empire would be Christian and that the Christian faith would not only be maintained by social pressures but supported by the forces of law and the arm of the sword. Whereas during Julian's restoration the pagan mobs had burned Christian churches, it was henceforth the Christians who set out to destroy the relics of paganism. Sixty people, for instance, lost their lives at Sufes in Byzacena (in North Africa) when a Christian mob destroyed a statue of Hercules; at Carthage another mob set about shaving off Hercules' newly gilded beard.

Although paganism would never again endanger the Christian faith, it continued as a philosophical movement, Platonist in its teaching, to have a following among intellectuals. In the late fourth century certain aristocratic coteries were drawn to the humanistic writings of pagan philosophers such as Plotinus and Porphery. The pagan humanists, who had not lost their intellectual tartness, ridiculed such Christian beliefs as the Virgin Birth and the Resurrection. Porphery stated that the scriptures were unreliable, finding the contents self-contradictory and untrustworthy, for the gospel writers were simply clumsy deceivers. Even Jesus was unworthy of veneration, for much of his teaching was trivial in its nature, obscure in its meaning and socially reprehensible. If Jesus had really been what he claimed to be, he should have used his powers to convince Pilate, Herod and the High Priest as well as the apostles, so saving the world without the consequent torments and bloodshed which seemed the legacy of the Church.

In practice, the process of acculturation was bringing about a steady absorption or soaking up of pagan concepts by Christian thought. Where pagan culture could be Christianized the Church evidently held that there could be no objection to the retention of pagan customs. The celebration of Christmas as the natal day of Christ, first apparently mentioned in a Church calendar of 336, was a seeming Christian answer to the pagan festival of *Natalis Solis Invicti* which carried with it the flavour of the merrymaking of the Roman Saturnalia. Christ became unconsciously identified as the 'New Sun' of the world, piercing the world's drear darkness with the returning light. Later still the festival of the Resurrection, about the exact date of which there continued to be a long debate, would be called by the name of the Anglo-Saxon goddess Eostre. But where festivals seemed only a reminder of the pagan past and could not be conveniently given a Christian interpretation, the Church was likely to be less tolerant, disapproving, for instance, of the celebration of the Kalends of January, probably because of its proximity to the Christmas festival. The syncretistic nature of Christianity, which became even more apparent after it became an authorized and accepted faith may, however, partly help to explain why it was so successful in winning converts, since for many of its simple-minded adherents, then and later, the distinction between the new Christian faith and their old pagan beliefs must have appeared blurred.

While membership of the Christian Church grew slowly in the third century, it was imperial favour, expressed by legislation in favour of the Church, which assured the final triumph of Christianity in the fourth century. 'No oppressor's sword has been drawn against us,' Vitricius, the bishop of Rouen, said at the close of the century, 'we have free access to God's altars; no savage enemy lies in wait for us . . . no torturer has attacked us . . . no blood is shed now, no persecutor pursues us.' It had become socially respectable to be a Christian, and was soon to become a necessary qualification for public office, power and influence.

The exercise of patronage, which formed an important feature of late imperial society, furthered the growth of the Christian community, for Christians, who had acquired a standing in society, were likely to favour their fellow worshippers. Religion had become a powerful social bond. From being a persecuted body the Church had graduated to a privileged society. Fresh legislation allowed Christians to make wills in the Church's favour and relieved Christians from the necessity of taking part in pagan sacrifices and games, which some towns continued to celebrate. Although the gladiatorial shows were actually abolished by Constantine I in 326, the edict was for long largely ineffective. Even Augustine attested to the fascination which brutality could exercise: 'without knowing what was happening', the spectator 'drank in madness . . . drunk with the lust of blood'. In 327 Constantius II prohibited soldiers and officials from taking part in the games; but it was not until 681 that imperial legislation seems to have been genuinely effective. Meanwhile measures were introduced to check Jewish hostility towards Christians, to forbid the pagan practice of the exposure of new-born infants and to ensure some degree of Sunday observance, but such legislation was only partially effective.

The clergy were probably the principal beneficiaries of this pro-Christian legislation. They were given exemption from certain taxes, such as the poll tax levied on all between the ages of fourteen and sixty-five, and they managed to secure other special rights in law. Bishops too were accorded some special privileges, such as exemption from the scourging or torture which judges could impose on witnesses who were thought to be hostile. The bishops themselves began to enjoy a measure of coercive jurisdiction in civil suits. After 412 their own courts were given a legal status; with this step the clergy appeared not merely as a separate but as a privileged class, a status they were long to enjoy in European society.

The early Christian emperors had not at first followed a coercive anti-pagan policy, fearful of alienating their pagan subjects and hoping that paganism would simply die out from lack of support. It was not until the closing years of the fourth century that the emperor Gratian refused the office of *pontifex maximus*, that of pagan high priest, and withdrew the subsidies which were still being paid to the pagan priests and Vestal Virgins of Rome. His successor, Theodosius, clamped down much more heavily, prohibiting pagan sacrifices and depriving pagan temples of their property. A Christian who became a pagan was henceforth liable to certain disabilities but pagans were encouraged to convert to Christianity. Indeed, departure from the Christian faith became close to an act of treason, so that both paganism and heresy were now to feel the heavy hand of the law.

CHURCH-BUILDING

It is difficult to estimate with any degree of precision how rapidly the pagans adopted Christian belief, but there can be little doubt that Christian communities were expanding at a fast rate before the close of the fourth century. The physical appearance of the Roman towns was changing as an era of church-building signified the victory of the Christian faith. In the building of churches the emperor himself was to give a lead. In Constantinople he erected two large churches, one of which he dedicated to the Holy Apostles where he intended to be buried and the other to the 'Holy Peace'. His example was followed throughout the empire. In Rome Constantine built the Basilica Constantiana, later San Giovanni in Laterano or St John Lateran, and the basilica of St Peter and St Paul. In the basilica of St Peter and St Paul a mosaic showed Constantine presenting a model of the church to Christ and St Peter 'since', as the inscription below it read, 'under thy guidance, the world has risen triumphant to the skies, the victor Constantine has raised this hall to thee'.

Church-building, often in the classical style of architecture, continued at a rapid rate in the fifth century, a visual reminder of the victorious Faith and the truths it claimed to embody. Under the patronage of popes such as Damasus and Leo I the churches did not merely express the Christian character of the city, a *theopolis* was what Leo I called Rome, but formed an appropriate scenario for the exercise of papal power, and the glorification of the office of Rome's bishop. The Roman people, as Leo told them, were a 'holy people, an elect nation, a priestly and royal city, because, through the see of St Peter established here, the head of the world; ruling more widely now through divine religion than it ever did by worldly dominion'.

The church became the physical centre of religion in a way which was in many respects novel. In earlier centuries the Christians treated their house churches primarily as places to repair for worship and as a physical entity the church appeared to be no more sacred than any other domestic building. Holiness was expressed not in the church but primarily through the life of the community. Now the church was to become itself a holy place, its decor and design in some sense a reflection of heaven. 'This is none other than the house of God and this is the gate of heaven.' Developments in the ceremonial of the liturgy and the adoption of the rich vestments by the priest, who had in earlier times not worn any special clothing, helped to give the church the attributes of a holy place. In the transformation of the role of the church the cults of the saints, more especially of the martyrs, already held in such veneration by the faithful, and of their relics, were thus to play a conspicuous part.

MARTYRS, SAINTS AND PILGRIMAGES

All Christians were aware that the world in which they lived was a temporary abode, for they were all, as St Augustine reminded them in moving language, pilgrims after eternity, as members of this 'Church which is now travelling on its journey to which is joined that heavenly Church where we have the angels as our fellow citizens.' All worship was designed to remind the worshippers of that other supernatural world. The Eucharist itself bridged the gulf between the here and now and eternity. It was against this backcloth that the commemoration of the dead, more especially of the martyrs and saints, became the more comprehensible. The martyr's tomb had long been regarded as a sacred place, the anniversary of his death commemorated by a gathering of the Christian community. The martyrs' favour in God's sight had enabled them to become intercessors with God on behalf of those who sought his help. 'Just', said St Ambrose, 'as the sick cannot themselves invoke the assistance of a doctor, but have to request his attendance through others, so when the flesh is weak, and the soul is sick with sin, we cannot direct our feeble steps to the throne of the Great Physician. Hence the angels, who have been given us as guardians, must be entreated for us; the martyrs must be entreated, whose patronage we claim by the pledge of their bodily remains.' 'By the patronage of the martyrs,' Prudentius, invoking St Laurence, declared, 'I may obtain healing.'

What was novel about the situation after the legitimization of Christianity was the capacity to give the veneration of saints its full scope, hitherto denied by the state's refusal to countenance the full freedom of the Church. Buried originally in cemeteries outside the city walls, the bodies of the martyrs could now be brought into newly built basilicas. There was even what sometimes seemed to be an unseemly search for the bodies of potential saints. 'They collected the bones and skulls of criminals who had been put to death for numerous crimes . . . and made them out to be gods,' wrote Eunapius of Sardis. The buildings of churches to house their remains changed the townscape, often transforming what had been the city's previous centre with its forum and temples into a galaxy of religious buildings. In some sense it was the bishops who annexed the cult by bringing the saints and their relics into the churches, for if there was a danger that the saints might be 'privatized', the bishops were to appropriate the cults to their own advantage while making them available to the whole Christian community.

St Ambrose, Bishop of Milan, discovered the bodies of two martyrs, Gervasius and Protasius, buried at the church of SS Felix and Nobor, allegedly constructed on the site of an ancient Christian cemetery. He had them translated with great ceremonial into the new basilica which he had built just outside the city walls and placed under the altar in the sarcophagus he had prepared for himself, 'Thanks be to Thee, Lord Jesus, that at this time when Thy Church needs greater protection than ever Thou has raised up for us the Spirits of the Holy Martyrs. Such are the defenders that I desire. . . . On account of thee I fear no ill will, their patronage is as safe as it is powerful.' It was to prove a very convenient find since Ambrose was then at loggerheads with the Arian empress Justina who sought to oust him from his bishopric. So at one and the same time the bishop asserted his own power and dignity and made the saint available for the community. If the bishop was the church's earthly patron, the saint was the heavenly patron. 'Where once long rest', said Bishop Alexander, 'had robbed them from our gaze, they blaze with light on a fitting pedestal, and their gathered crown now blooms with joy . . . from all around the Christian people, young and old, flow in to see them, happy to tread the holy threshold, singing their praises and hailing with outstretched hands the Christian faith.' 'The philosophers and the orators have fallen into oblivion,' Theodoret of Cyrrhus wrote, 'the masses do not seem to know the names of the emperors and their generals; but everyone knows the names of the martyrs better than those of their most intimate friends.'

The saints were not only available to intercede in heaven but by reason of their holiness their bodies were likely to possess a dynamic which could perform miracles. Healings and exorcisms took place at the shrine, demonstrating God's power and care for mankind. When the presumed body of the first martyr St Stephen was discovered outside the village of Carpharganala in North Africa in 415 'the earth trembled and a smell of sweet perfume came from the place such as no man had ever known of, so much that we thought that we were standing in the sweet garden of Paradise. And at that very hour, from the smell of that perfume, seventy-three persons were healed.' The saints were present in a special manner at their tombs where they exhibited their miraculous properties. 'The Spirit of God', it was said of the tomb of St Zeno at Verona, was present in the place. As *membra Christi* the saints brought with them the touch of heaven and like guardian angels acted as protectors of those who invoked them.

If the body of a martyr or saint conferred holiness, it was soon apparent that a particle of his body could be equally efficacious. 'In the divided body,' Theodoret of Cyrrhus wrote, 'the grace survives undivided and the fragments, however small, have the same efficacy as the whole body.' 'For when a martyr suffers,' Bishop Maximus of Turin said, 'he suffers not only for himself, but for his fellow-citizens. . . . So all the martyrs be most devoutly honoured, yet specially those whose relics we possess here. For the former assist us with their prayer but the latter also with their suffering.' The relics of St Stephen were distributed to many churches, Jerusalem, Hippo and Minorca. It became essential for every church to have its own relics, and without a relic it could not be consecrated, as the canon law of the Catholic Church still states. There were those who criticized the cult of relics as a pagan practice but they were fighting a losing battle.

Relics were an earthly extension of the holy martyrs, embodying intrinsic powers capable of performing miracles. 'It is well known,' Cyril of Jerusalem stated, 'that such external objects as handkerchiefs and aprons have cured the sick after touching the martyr's body.' These *brandea*, as they were called, might include pieces of the tomb, oil from lamps in the shrine and dust around them. On a visit to the shrine of St Julian at Brioude, the Frankish bishop Gregory of Tours abstracted a piece from the tomb which he then had placed in his church at Tours where it proved to have miraculous properties. In his account of St Peter's tomb at Rome, Gregory of Tours described how the pilgrim 'should he wish to bring back a relic from the tomb, he carefully weighs a piece of cloth which he then hangs inside the tomb. Then he prays confidently and, if his faith is sufficient, the cloth, once removed from the tomb, will be found to be so full of divine grace that it will be much heavier than before. Then he will know that his prayers have been granted.'

Earthly visitors sought daily for heavenly treasure. Constantine's mother the empress Helena, was said to have discovered a piece of the True Cross. Two monks claimed to have found the body of St John the Baptist in the ruins of Herod's palace at Jerusalem. Little historical credence can be given to these legends but the stories illustrate what people of that age believed and the integrity of their faith. The cult of the saints reinforced Christian belief in the afterlife and underlined the Church's identity with its traditional past. Yet while the martyrs were honoured the Church taught, as St Augustine stressed, that they were to be venerated but not worshipped. 'Victory', as Bishop Vitricius of Rouen put it, 'is certain when we fight along such allies with Christ for our general.'

The growing popularity of pilgrimages had similar roots. A pilgrimage acted as a spur to devotion, and brought heaven in touch with earth. 'No other sentiment', Paulinus of Nola wrote at the end of the fourth century, 'draws men to Jerusalem than the desire to see and touch the places where Christ was physically present.' Etheria, an intrepid Spanish nun, who visited Egypt, Palestine, Asia Minor and Constantinople at the end of the fourth century wrote a detailed account of the places she had been to, identifying them with the events of the Old Testament (e.g. Moses' brook; the place where the Golden Calf was made) and the New Testament. An incipient tourist trade was already in train as pilgrims brought back souvenirs of their trips. Moreover, a distinctive but probably inaccurate Christian topography had been invented.

THEOLOGICAL CONTROVERSIES

While the Christians came together to venerate the saints and martyrs, and to look forward to that other world where they too might hope to reign with the saints, their leaders, bishops, clergy and monks were involved in deep and bitter conflict over the doctrinal detail of what they believed. Nor was this a ferment which was confined to the clergy, for it involved the lay authorities which were to take sides with this or that party.

Although such controversy gave rise to violence and acrimony, it was a tribute to the vitality of a Church so freed from the threat of persecution that it could devote itself to trying to define more clearly the fundamental problems of belief. Such theological debate, natural in so far as that there was as yet no finalized consensus of doctrine, had occurred frequently in the Church before Constantine, but when Christianity was legitimized the situation changed, firstly because debate could take place in an open forum and secondly, and more importantly, because the emperor as the visible representative of God became himself personally involved. What had been principally a matter for the Church became an issue which concerned the authorities of the state as well.

At first sight it might seem extraordinary that any one outside an élite group of bishops and clergy should be so obsessed with the interpretations of such esoteric issues as the exact relationship of Christ the Son to God the Father or the fusion or singularity of the divine and human natures in the person of Christ; but such questions, presumably because of clerical propaganda, even aroused the passions of the populace. 'If you ask a man for change, he will give you a piece of philosophy concerning the Begotten and the Unbegotten; if you inquire the price of a loaf he will reply – "The Father is greater and the Son inferior" or if you ask whether the bath is ready, the answer you receive is that the Son was made out of nothing.' The Arian heresy was even propagated by popular music.

The Arian heresy had been long in festering. Christians did not doubt that Christ was truly the Son of God, for in him God had become incarnate. This was the essence of orthodox Christian belief. But what did this mean precisely? Did it mean that as God's son Christ was created in time after his father and so lacked the qualities which his father had possessed eternally and was as a result necessarily inferior or subordinate to him? An Alexandrian presbyter, Arius, concluded that this logically must be so. God, he argued, is alone the father. He must have existed originally for himself alone, but he had created or begotten the son, the word, the logos out of nothing by his will. But the logos was to be a creature and could not be fully equal to his creator or even be God in substance since he was limited by his own nature. Christ must therefore be inferior to God, but was no less essential to man's redemption.

Arius' critics argued that he was minimizing the meaning of the Incarnation which required that Jesus Christ should be in every way God incarnate. Yet they had to agree that since he was in possession of a full human nature in some sense Christ had to be differentiated from God the Father. The problem had appeared to have been resolved at the Council of Nicaea, which the emperor Constantine eager to restore the unity of the Church had called in 325, and which had asserted that Jesus Christ was of the 'same substance', *homousios* was the technical expression used, as God; though fully human Christ was also fully God without any diminution.

But this was far from being the end of the controversy, for the Arians who did not give up easily remained strong and influential, especially among the eastern bishops who had acquired a strong leader in the patriarch of Constantinople, Eusebius, who won the support of the emperor Constantine's son, Constantius. The anti-Arians, stronger in the western Church, had a stalwart champion in Athanasius, the bishop of Alexandria, who was sent into exile at Trier in 336. More than once restored to his episcopal see, Athanasius wrote a series of pungent treatises, of which the *De Incarnatione* defined the orthodox position.

The Arian party was itself soon fractured into a more extreme and more moderate group. It was left to the emperor Theodosius to call a general council at Constantinople in 381 which confirmed the findings of Nicaea, now redrafted, and rejected Arianism. 'Let the heretics have no place for celebrating their mysteries, no opportunity for exhibiting their demented obstinacy.'

What would have happened without the intervention of the emperor it is difficult to say, for the history of the Arian controversy had shown once again the significance of Church–state relations in determining even matters of faith. This is not of course to say that the emperor was himself unaffected by the advice proffered to him by his bishops, and by what may be called the pressure of informed public opinion. Yet the sword which he wielded could be the last resort, as the case of the Spanish heretic, Priscillian the bishop of Avila, demonstrated in 385. Priscillian who apparently held semi-Manichaean views was put to death ostensibly on a charge of sorcery. In fact it was the first instance, but very far from being the last, of capital punishment being meted out by the state as a punishment for heresy.

No sooner was Arianism officially condemned than a new debate broke out in the Church as to the relationship of the divine and human natures in Christ, which was more especially a matter of controversy between the theologians of the rival schools of Antioch and Alexandria. Nestorius who had been appointed patriarch of Constantinople had argued that there were two separate persons in Christ, the divine and the human. He taught that the Virgin Mary was not the mother of God but only of Christ, not *theotokos* but *Christotokos*. His critics accused him of tearing Christ into two, minimizing his divinity as well as lowering the status of the Virgin Mary. Once more Christ's incarnation was in danger of being minimalized. His chief critic was Cyril of Alexandria who insisted on the dynamic unity of the two natures in Christ. At a Church council at Rome, Pope Celestine, to whom both sides had appealed, condemned Nestorius' teaching and ordered him to be deprived of his see, a decision reaffirmed by the general council of the Church which the emperor had called at Ephesus in June 431. The issue would not, however, lie down, and was revived by a Constantinopolitan monk Eutyches who taught that Christ really had only one nature, the divine having absorbed the human nature. The issue was eventually to be resolved by yet another general council of the Church which the emperor Marcian called at Chalcedon in October 451 which stated that Christ was one person with two natures united 'unconfusedly, indivisibly, and inseparably'. The Chalcedonian definition was accepted henceforth as final by a majority of the Christian Church.

In the process there had occurred the first significant fragmentation of the Church. The Monophysites, as the followers of Nestorius came to be called, continued to have a strong following, more especially on the borders of the Byzantine Empire. Their religious sympathies were to make them the readier to accept Muslim conquest in the seventh century. They penetrated Iran and established Christian communities in Arabia even establishing a patriarchal see, presided over by the Catholicos or Patriarch of the East, at Seleucia-Ctesiphon on the Tigris which was moved to Baghdad in 775. By and large they were treated tolerantly by the caliphs of Baghdad but were later to suffer as a result of the invasions of Timur or Tamurlane at the end of the fourteenth century, leading many Nestorians to take refuge in Kurdistan where their descendants survive as the so-called Assyrian Christians. They had a long if disturbed history in India, and penetrated China. The Sigan-Fu stone, a monument in north-west China, described their arrival at the then capital of the Tang dynasty in the eighth century. In more recent times some attempts to reunite them with Rome have been only partially successful. In the Coptic Churches of Egypt and Ethiopia, and in the Assyrian Church of Kurdistan, they continue to survive in spite of an unfavourable political climate.

Although there were then small Christian communities which had crept outside the umbrella of the Roman Church and even of the Roman Empire within a century and half of the legitimization of Christianity, in the greater part of eastern and western Europe orthodox teaching, as defined by the

Council of Chalcedon in 451, provided the framework of belief within which the Christian worked and prayed.

THE GROWING PRESTIGE OF THE ROMAN SEE

The place which the Church had acquired in society brought about its institutionalization as an organized body and in particular a growth in the status and influence of the Church of Rome. Everywhere the bishop's position became increasingly prestigious. He was generally exempt from many forms of taxation, often lived in some splendour, lavishing his money on the building of churches as well as works of charity. The bishoprics, very varied in their resources as in their areas of jurisdiction, were grouped into provinces presided over by a head bishop or metropolitan. The chief city of the province became the metropolitan's administrative centre, so that the ecclesiastical organization became to an increasing extent a spiritual counterpart to secular government.

Constantinople, Antioch, Alexandria, Carthage and Rome were the most important churches but the fourth century saw a striking development in the prestige and influence exerted by the Pope or bishop of Rome. From early times the martyrdom of the apostles Peter and Paul there had given to Rome a particular spiritual distinction. At the end of the second century St Irenaeus had stated that Peter and Paul had jointly governed the Church there, presumably as presbyter bishops, for whether the monarchical episcopate had come into existence at so early a date must be doubted. St Ignatius described the Church of Rome 'as having the presidency of the district of the Romans'. As early as the second century the Pope occasionally intervened in the affairs of churches outside his immediate jurisdiction. It was only, however, very sporadically that the Church of Rome was as yet resorted to as a final court of appeal for the universal Church.

The triumph of Christianity made at first comparatively little difference to the powers exercised by the Pope as bishop of Rome though a later legend, lacking any historical basis, asserted that the emperor Constantine had bestowed on Pope Sylvester I, who had allegedly cured him of leprosy and baptized him, the primacy of the Church and the temporal dominions of the western empire, a claim which medieval Popes were often to invoke to strengthen their own positions. But the way in which the Popes supported orthodox teaching in the theological controversies of the fourth century, albeit the controversies brought the Popes into occasional conflict with the emperor, did much to enhance their standing in the western Church. So the Council of Sardica in 343, attended ultimately only by bishops from the west as their eastern colleagues withdrew to Philadelphia, not only restored the orthodox champion Athanasius to the see of Alexandria from which the pro-Arian emperor Constantius had expelled him but asserted that the bishop of Rome was the final court of appeal for bishops who had been deposed. Such pretensions did not always succeed. Reaping imperial displeasure Pope Liberius was sent into bleak exile in Thrace and pathetically agreed to accept a semi-Arian interpretation of the creed.

Roman claims received a major fillip under his successor, Damasus I, of whom the pagan Prefect Praetextatus jokingly observed 'Make me the bishop of Rome, and I will straightway become a Christian.' Liberius's death had been followed by a disputed and scandalous election which itself showed, if in the worst sort of way, the growing importance of the Roman see. In the course of the prelude to the election Damasus had hired a gang of toughs who stoned the Julian basilica where the rival candidate, Ursinus, had his headquarters so that in the ensuing battle 137 people died. Damasus was an able man of some intellectual ability, for he wrote turgid verses and was a patron of St Jerome who was for three years his secretary, and apparently at his suggestion revised the Latin text of the Bible to produce the single Vulgate edition. He refurbished the shrines of the martyrs buried in the catacombs of suburban Rome and propagated the cult of their relics. All-in-all he was an ambitious and arrogant prelate who kept a splendid court, described by his critics as the 'ear-tickler of the ladies' and accused, probably falsely, of adultery. At the same time he proved to be a vigorous opponent of heresy, more especially of Arianism and a determined proponent of Roman claims to primacy based on Christ's promises to Peter to whom he was the rightful heir. Damasus's pontificate showed what a long way the Roman see had come since Diocletian's persecution of the Church, and how the Pope was acquiring power and prestige.

His successors continued to follow his policy, though neither the emperor nor all the bishops took kindly to papal claims to universal jurisdiction. Pope Siricius had issued decretal letters, the first of which was sent to Himerius, the bishop of Tarragona in Spain, which was held to have the force of law. Even more substantial claims were made by Innocent I who insisted that the Roman practice both in liturgy and discipline ought to be the norm for all other churches. Bishops, he said, after condemning the heresy of Pelagius, must submit all matters of faith to the Pope. In 429 Pope Celestine I despatched Germanus, Bishop of Auxerre, to head a mission to extirpate the Pelagian heresy in Britain, and two years later sent Palladius as the first bishop to preach the gospel to the Irish.

The Petrine authority, giving the Pope supreme and universal power in the Church, was stressed firmly by Leo I as the 'primate of all the bishops'. Angered by the pretensions of the Gallic bishop, Hilary of Arles, Pope Leo ordered Hilary to stay in his diocese and secured from the emperor Valentinian III a decree reaffirming the Pope's ecclesiastical jurisdiction over the western Church. Pope Leo's prestige and courage were such that in 452 he was able to induce the leader of the Huns, Attila, who was then ravaging Italy, to withdraw. The eastern Church continued to have reservations over such extensive papal claims. Although the Council of Chalcedon had in 451 recognized the 'voice of St Peter' in the *Tome* of

Leo I, the council gave to Constantinople the same patriarchal status as that of Rome only admitting the primacy of the latter.

Thus within a century and a half of Constantine's conversion the Church had gone some way to recognize the primacy of Peter and to accept the Pope as the final court of appeal in matters of doctrine and discipline.

THE CHAMPIONS OF ORTHODOXY:
ST AMBROSE, ST JEROME, ST AUGUSTINE

In maintaining the standards of Christian orthodoxy and morality the Church had some eloquent and able advocates, most notably St Ambrose, St Jerome and St Augustine who were greatly to influence Christian teaching. Ambrose, the son of the Praetorian prefect of Gaul, born at Trier in 339, followed a legal career but was appointed governor of the province of Aemilia Liguria, of which Milan was the chief city. When Milan's Arian bishop Auxentius died in 374 Ambrose, though as yet an unbaptized layman, was made, if at first very unwillingly, the bishop. He soon acquired a reputation as a preacher and theologian, fiercely opposing both paganism and Arianism which, he said, 'collected poisons from every heresy'. 'The Arians', he said, 'were worse than Jews and pagans, more blasphemous than Anti-Christ, more insolent in belief than the Devil himself.' If Ambrose was first and foremost a major champion of orthodoxy, he was equally concerned to maintain Christian standards in public life. When the powerful emperor Theodosius perpetrated a brutal massacre at Thessalonica in reprisal for the death of the governor, Ambrose forced him to do public penance. He was a strong supporter of the monastic movement and played an important part in the conversion of St Augustine in 386.

His younger contemporary St Jerome came from Dalmatia and was well educated, especially in rhetoric, and widely travelled before at Trier he decided to become a monk. As a result of some dispute he left Aquileia for Palestine where in a dream God condemned him for being a Ciceronian rather than a Christian. He took the warning seriously, gave up the classics and learnt Hebrew and spent five years in the desert of Chalcis in Syria as a hermit. He came back to Antioch where he continued with his writing and thence went to Rome where Pope Damasus entrusted him with the massive task of producing a standard Latin text of the Bible. At the end of three years during which he became the guide of a group of dedicated Christian ladies, Paula and others who were living a semi-monastic life as widows, he returned to Palestine, settling at Bethlehem where he lived as a monk and Paula established a nunnery.

Jerome was cantankerous and egocentric but the most prodigious scholar of his time, his sardonic wit and flawed nature redeemed by his passionate devotion to his faith. Apart from the Vulgate his achievement was immense, as a fervent supporter of ascetic monasticism, as an advocate of a sound exegesis of scripture, and as a champion of the Roman primacy. In spite of his closeness to Pope Damasus he was a strong advocate of a rigorist morality challenged, as he saw it, by contemporary materialism.

It was an indication of the heightened vitality of the Christian Church that it should have produced in a century three such extraordinary men as Ambrose, Jerome and Augustine. The first thirty years of Augustine's life had proved a veritable spiritual pilgrimage. Born of a pagan father and a Christian mother, Monica, at Tagaste in North Africa, he had studied at the university of Carthage, becoming passionately interested in philosophy and embracing Manichaeism. He lived for fifteen years with a mistress by whom he had a son, Adeodatus. Then to his mother's disappointment he migrated to Rome where he started a school of rhetoric, only to be so offended by his pupils' behaviour that he moved to Milan where he fell under the influence of Ambrose.

It was in Milan in the summer of 386 that an African visitor, Ponticanus, finding a copy of St Paul on Augustine's table, told Augustine and his friend Alypius of the doings of St Antony and the Egyptian monks. As Augustine wrote in his *Confessions*:

> While he was speaking, O Lord, You were turning me around to look at myself. . . . I saw it all and stood aghast, but there was no place where I could escape from myself. . . . There was a small garden attached to the house where we lodged . . . I now find myself driven by the torment in my breast to take refuge in this garden, where no one could interrupt that fierce struggle, in which I was my own contestant, until it came to its conclusion. . . . I tore my hair and hammered my forehead with my fists. I locked my fingers and hugged my knees. . . . In this way I wrangled with myself, in my own heart, about my own self. I probed the hidden depths of my soul and wrung its pitiful secrets from it, and when I mustered them all before the eyes of my heart, a great storm broke within me, bringing with it a great deluge of tears. . . . I was asking myself all those questions . . . when all at once I heard the sing-song voice of a child in a nearby house "Take it and read, take it and read" . . . I stemmed my flood of tears and stood up, telling myself that this could only be a divine command to open my book of Scripture and read the first passage on which my eyes should fall. So I hurried back to the place where Alypius was sitting, for when I stood up to move away I had put down the book containing St Paul's Epistles. I seized it and opened it, and in silence I read the first passage on which my eyes fell: "not in revelling and drunkenness, not in lust and wantonness, not in quarrels and rivalries. Rather, arm yourselves with the Lord Jesus Christ, spend no more thoughts on nature and nature's appetites." I had no wish to read more, as I came to the end of the sentence, it was as though the light of confidence flooded into my heart and all the darkness of doubt was dispelled.

In 388 Augustine returned to his home town at Tagaste where with some friends he set up a monastic community, but shortly afterwards, visiting the town of Hippo Regius, he was pressed by the people to be ordained. Four years later, in 395, he became assistant to the aged Bishop Valerius and after his death sole bishop until he died in 430 as the barbarian Vandals besieged the town.

Augustine was *par excellence* the champion of Catholic orthodoxy, his understanding of heresy drawn from his own experience. He demolished the Manichaean faith by stressing that God was the sole creator and that evil consisted ultimately in the deprivation of some good which should perfectly exist; human imperfection was the sequel to man's original sin and misuse of free will. He was a strong opponent of the Donatists, a schismatic group which held that those clergy who had lapsed under persecution were invalidated from conferring the sacraments and could not be received back into the Church. The schism had originated in 311 when the Donatists had refused to accept Caecilian as bishop of Carthage because he had been consecrated by Felix, Bishop of Aptunga, a *traditor* (so-called because he had surrendered the scriptures to be banned by the pagan magistrates). They claimed that the Church should consist of the worthy, barring the impure and forging for themselves an identity as a chosen people. They acquired a substantial following in North Africa where the more extreme readily resorted to violence to attain their ends. Augustine, repudiating their views, insisted that the unworthiness of the minister did not affect the validity of the sacrament whose minister was Christ, a view incidentally strongly expressed by the novelist Graham Greene in his portrait of the whisky priest in *The Power and the Glory*; he was ready to sponsor the use of force to suppress the heresy.

The third target of Augustine's attack were the views put forward by the British cleric Pelagius who had asserted that man was responsible for his own good and evil deeds, and could save himself by his own free will without the necessary assistance of divine grace. He claimed that man had been created good by God, and through the remission of sins at his baptism would by his will be able to attain perfection (though few would in practice be able to do so). It is 'the easiest thing in the world to change our will by an act of will'. Augustine strongly refuted these views in a series of polemical treatises and Pelagius and Celestius were condemned and excommunicated by the Pope.

Augustine was probably the most influential of all the great fathers of the Church. The Church was 'Our Mother, prolific with offspring: of her we are born, by her milk we are nourished, by her spirit we are made alive.' All history was only comprehensible, he insisted, in the light of God's providence. 'The centuries of past history would have rolled by like empty jars if Christ had not been foretold by news of him.' 'God is the unchanging conductor as well as the unchanged creator of all things . . . he is ordering all events according to his providence, until the beauty of the completed course of time . . . shall have played itself out, like the great melody of some ineffable composer.' He had a deep understanding of Christian theology and showed a masterly insight in interpreting it. As a result of his own conversion and in reaction to Pelagianism he developed a strong view of the overpowering grace of God. Through Adam's fall man inherited a mortal disease which could only be averted by the grace of God. Out of mankind irretrievably lost to sin God elects some to receive unremitted salvation. To resist Pelagianism Augustine had fashioned the doctrine that in Adam all men and women had sinned, a notion of collective punishment of the innocent which his Pelagian critic Julian of Eclanum described as cruel and unjust.

Augustinianism was not merely to condition much of the thinking of the early medieval Church but it strongly influenced the teaching of the early Protestant reformers Martin Luther and John Calvin, and proved a powerful ingredient in the thought-pattern of both the Protestant and Catholic Reformations.

THE EMERGENCE OF MONASTICISM

It was hardly surprising that all three of these fathers of the Church had strong associations with monasticism, for in many respects it was monasticism which formed the main antidote to the materialism of contemporary Christianity. It was the most positive and influential expression of Christianity after its triumph over paganism. Although monasticism is often described as a protest against the prevailing laxity of the Church it was more a positive than a negative movement, fixed on spiritual objectives which had antecedents dating back to the third century. The monk and the nun took the Christian vocation, as he or she saw it, literally by trying to live lives of absolute abnegation. 'Tossed,' as Paulinus of Nola put it, 'we must strip ourselves of encumbering possessions on the planks of Christ's cross.' The monks, Orosius wrote, were 'Christians who, having renounced the multifarious activities concerned with worldly things, confine themselves to the work of faith'.

The precursor of the monastic movement was the hermit, Antony, a legendary figure whose very existence has been doubted by some historians. Hearing the reading in church in which Jesus said 'If you will be perfect, go, sell all that thou hast and give to the poor, and come, follow me', he withdrew into the desert where he struggled with temptation in the form of demons. The monk, perhaps because of the austerity of his life and the spiritual introspection of his lonely days, became often the victim of hallucinatory visions. So the Devil appeared to Antony as a 'little black boy, his appearance matching his mind, with flashing eyes and fiery breath, and horns on his head, half man, half ass'. The Devil tried to arouse Antony's carnal desires, but Antony withstood him.

Antony's reputation for holiness drew disciples to him, and he organized them into a community of hermits living a rule of life before he retired once more into a solitary existence in the desert. His life by St Athanasius, a classic of Christian hagiography, was for long one of the most influential of religious books.

The first monks were solitaries – the word *monachos* means solitary – living in caves or huts in the desert, remote from centres of population, supporting themselves by cultivating vegetable patches and by the alms of the faithful. They seemed self-indulgent in their abasement of the flesh which they equated with temptation and sin. St Thalelaeus lived for ten years in a tub suspended between two poles. St Symeon Stylites who began his monastic life by living for forty days in a cave with his right leg fastened to an iron chain 'though the iron chain did not hinder the flight of his soul' eventually settled for life at the top of a pillar 40 cubits high. He attracted many admiring disciples. 'They came', the Syrian bishop Theodoret reported of those who came to watch and stayed to pray, 'in many thousands, enslaved to the darkness of impiety, [to be] enlightened, by the station upon the pillar. They renounced with their shouts their traditional errors, they broke up their venerated idols in the presence of that great light (Symeon); and they foreswore the ecstatic rites of Aphrodite, the demon whose service they had long accepted . . . they renounced also the diet of the wild ass or the camel.' Near Nisibis there lived a group of Boskoi or grazing monks. 'When meal time came they took sickles and sallied forth to cut grass, and on this they made their repast as if they were cattle.' Others, the so-called Dendrites, lived in trees. Another strange group, the Messalians or Euchites, lived on alms and engaged in charismatic dancing. They taught that as a result of Adam's fall everyone had a demon substantially united to his soul which could only be exorcized by unceasing prayer. Their extremism was to be condemned by the Church council of Ephesus in 431. To mortify the flesh some attached weights to their necks and loins. Macarius who had killed a gnat, feeling that he had deliberately missed a chance for self-mortification by so doing, lived for six months in the marshes of the River Nile near Scete, allowing the gnats to do their worst. For seven years he lived on the barest food so that the bones of his face 'stood out naked beyond the want of man'.

Such deprivations combined with fasting helped to produce the conditions in which the monk was convinced that he was fighting with the Devil and experiencing visions. It was universally agreed that some form of self-denial, some embrace of the ascetic life, was an essential ingredient in the monastic vocation. 'As their fervour cooled,' John Cassian wrote in the early fifth century, referring to Christians after the triumph of Christianity, 'many combined their confession of Christ with wealth; but those who kept the fervour of the apostles . . . withdrew from their cities and from the society of those who thought this laxness of living permissible for themselves and for the Church to spots on the edges of towns, or more remote places, and there practised privately and in their own groups the things which they remembered the apostles had instituted for the whole Body of the Church.'

The monk deliberately separated himself from the world. In popular veneration the monks appeared to be the successors of the martyrs, for while the martyr gave up his life for Christ's sake, for the same reason the monk surrendered all earthly riches and temptations, entering a social group whose life was rooted in prayer and meditation, involving a rejection of the intrinsic features of normal social existence – property, sex, comfort, the pleasures of food and drink, and entertainment. He surrendered his will, and took vows of poverty, chastity and obedience. By curbing his own will and mortifying the flesh he achieved liberation from the mortal bonds of the society he had rejected and so won a victory over temptation and the Devil. John Cassian gave an instance of the monk's exemplary obedience when he described the monk John who was ordered to water a dry stick 'twice daily', though fully aware that it would never sprout, but he continued to bring water, walking 2 miles to do so. 'The good of obedience . . . holds the primacy among the other virtues.' With the cessation of persecution martyrdom was no longer likely, but the monk, like the martyr, was engaged in a continuous warfare with the world, the flesh, and the Devil, seeking the same reward as the martyr through his unqualified commitment to Christ.

What began as a solitary, individualistic movement soon became communal or cenobitic. Drawn by curiosity or veneration, uplifted by their sacrificial lives, the hermits gathered groups of disciples who sought to copy their life-style. The Egyptian Pachomius, a convert from paganism, became a hermit but about 320 at Tabbenisi on the right bank of the Nile established a monastic community which grew in an astonishing way, soon numbering, so it was said, some three thousand monks. A rule of life became a matter of necessity where such large numbers were involved. By the time of Pachomius's death in 346 there were nine monasteries for men and two for women. Another Egyptian, Shenoute, energetic and masterful, who became abbot of Atribis, followed Pachomius's example by founding large monastic communities, one of some 2,200 and another of 1,800 nuns, which he controlled by enforcing a written profession of obedience and by an austere discipline which involved flogging and severe punishment for faults.

From Egypt monasticism was to spread over the eastern Mediterranean world, to Syria, Palestine and Greece. Hermitages and monasteries sprang up all over the Holy Land. At Edessa in Syria St Ephrem set up a monastic school. St Basil, who had studied at Athens, visited the monasteries of Egypt, Palestine and Syria before establishing his own monastery which followed a more humane rule of life than that prescribed in the Egyptian communities. While there was no departure from ascetic demands made on the monk, Basil provided for manual labour in fields and workshops, and encouraged the setting up of hospitals and orphanages. Basil's influence over future monastic development in Byzantium and later Russia remained pre-eminent.

The monastic tide flowed from the eastern to the western Mediterranean. The fourth-century bishop of Tours, St Martin, established a group of hermits at Ligugé near Poitiers and Marmoutier on the River Loire; Martin's life written by Sulpicius Severus, like Athanasius's life of St Antony, became a classical account of the monastic vocation. John Cassian, a Scythian who had visited Egyptian monasteries and settled as a monk at

Bethlehem, moved in 415 to Marseilles where he founded two monasteries and wrote the *Institutes* which laid down the rules for the monastic life. About the same time St Honoratus, later archbishop of Arles, who with his brother Venantius had gone on a pilgrimage to the holy places of Syria and Egypt, founded a monastery on the island of Lérins close to Cannes.

Lérins was to be a monastic nursery for many churchmen and scholars. The Gallic bishops who were educated there took the monastic ideal into their dioceses, injecting monastic values with greater or lesser success into the larger community, clerical or lay. In his sermons Caesarius, Bishop of Arles, advised his listeners to follow the monastic example, more especially by constant reading of the scriptures, or if they were illiterate by getting someone to read it to them. He advised the adoption of the monastic hours and warned against the temptation of gossip, drink and dirty jokes. 'We must', he averred, 'know that it is not enough for us to have received the name of Christian if we do not do the deeds of a Christian.' From Lérins the monastic impulse passed to Spain and Celtic Ireland which became the scene of an exceptional monastic society in the late fifth and early sixth centuries.

These many monasteries did not at first follow a single rule of life, though plainly there was some degree of basic uniformity. Each house was in general separately governed by its own abbot. In the western world this situation was to change with the appearance of the Rule of St Benedict, though it took some time before it was universally accepted. Benedict himself, apparently disgusted by the laxity of Roman society, had retreated to live as a hermit in a cave at Subiaco in southern Italy where he attracted followers who were to form a monastic community. Subsequently he moved to Monte Cassino where he remained as abbot until his death in the middle of the sixth century and where he composed the rule which bears his name.

In practice, modern research has shown that St Benedict's rule was based largely on an earlier composition known as the Rule of the Master, while Benedict, like St Antony, remains for some a legendary figure of doubtful historicity. If Benedict did not personally draw up the rule, the rule was itself a masterly creation remarkable for its practicality and common sense. Its essential characteristic, by comparison with the rules of Pachomius, St Basil (though he did not draw up any actual set of rules) and John Cassian, was its intrinsic moderation. It laid comparatively less emphasis on austerity, penance and mortification of the flesh and more on harmony of living within the community. It did, of course, assume that the monk would live a life of total self-abnegation and obedience, obedience to the spiritual precepts of the gospel, obedience to the rule, obedience to the abbot who was placed as Christ's deputy in the community. The monk had to live his life according to a liturgical pattern built around the lengthy night-office and the remaining monastic hours, Matins (or Lauds), Prime, Terce, Sext, Nones, Vespers and Compline.

Yet the Rule of St Benedict was replete with humanity, stressing the quality of mercy towards the weak and the sick, providing, as St Benedict phrased it a 'school of the Lord's service, in which we hope we have laid down nothing harsh or burdensome'. The rule combined a life of prayer and meditation with manual labour in the fields and workshop.

The Rule of St Benedict only gradually ousted the individual rules of other monastic founders, but in time it was to prove universal in its appeal and application in western Europe. By the sixth century, given the vigorous growth of monasticism in Celtic Ireland, monasticism was thus not merely a major ingredient in Christian life but in its generation of spirituality one of the most formative and fecund aspects of the Christian Church. It constituted too a social, economic and political ingredient in the community, wielding a growing influence over both clergy and laity, separate from the world and yet very much a part of it. The monks were the champions of orthodoxy and the scourge of heresy. In the cultural decline which accompanied the collapse of the Roman Empire in the west the monasteries conserved the learning of the past, their libraries forming reservoirs of scholarship which were to irrigate the barren waters of the neo-Roman world.

In the two centuries which elapsed after Constantine's acceptance of the Christian faith the triumph of Christianity had changed the face of Europe. Towns took on a new appearance as Christian basilicas replaced the ancient forums and temples and Christian cemeteries and shrines, once located on the city's confines, came psychologically as well as physically within the city walls. More significantly, there occurred a process of Christianization of contemporary culture as Christian values displaced pagan concepts or at least absorbed them.

Yet simultaneously with the steady process of Christianization political, social and economic changes were taking place which at least in the west were to put the Church at risk. In the east the Roman Empire was to continue for another thousand years until it fell to the Ottoman Turks in 1453, leaving Russia as its legatee. There the accord between Church and State was to continue and a distinctive form of spirituality was to develop.

For men and women in the fifth century the Roman Empire, identified by many of them with *Christianitas* itself, had seemed eternal, though St Augustine made it plain in his magisterial *The City of God* that the best-governed of earthly states was inferior in absolute terms to the heavenly city. Yet within little over forty years after Augustine's death, in 476, the last puppet emperor of the west, the ironically named Romulus Augustulus, left his shadowy throne. Henceforth the Christian Church in the west had to resolve the problem of how best to cope with barbarian princes, often neo-pagan in attitude and, if nominally Christian, likely to be Arian rather than Catholic in sympathy. If the Christian Church of the fourth and fifth centuries had had to seek to Christianize the once pagan Roman society and state, in the next two centuries it now had to do the same to barbarian peoples, Ostrogoths, Visigoths, Vandals, Franks, Anglo-Saxons, who occupied and governed the lands of the former Roman Empire in the west.

CHAPTER THREE

The Matrix of Medieval Christianity

At the edge of the western world, there was a rocky islet, Skellig Michael, 7 miles from the south-west coast of Ireland, its precipitous cliffs 600 feet in height washed by the stormy Atlantic waves. There, often shrouded by winter fog, and constantly swept by fierce gales, a small body of monks lived in six stone bee-hive cells which still survive. The monks existed on vegetables and herbs grown on small artificial terraces, supplemented by gannets' eggs.

While the Irish monks on Skellig Michael were living out their austere lives, another Irish monk, Columba, migrated from Ireland to found a monastery on the island of Iona off the Scottish coast. Later he was to preach the gospel to the pagan Picts of western Scotland. His biographer Adamnan narrated how he and his fellow monks came to Loch Ness where they were told that a savage water-beast terrorized the natives. Subsequently the monster attacked one of Columba's companions 'with gaping mouth and with great roaring rushing towards the man swimming in the middle of the stream'. But Columba:

> raised his holy hand and drew the saving sign of the cross in the empty air; and then, invoking the name of God, he commanded the savage beast and said: 'You will go no further. Do not touch the man; turn backward speedily.' The beast did as the saint commanded and the pagan barbarians who were there at the time, impelled by the magnitude of this miracle they themselves had seen, magnified the God of the Christians.

These are compelling and dramatic scenes: the monks isolated on their remote and craggy island devoted to prayer and scratching the soil; the Irish monk Columba carrying the gospel to a barbarian people. And all this was seemingly more than a thousand miles away from what had occurred in the imperial city of Constantinople in 537 when the Emperor Justinian, accompanied by his wife Theodora, consecrated the greatest church in Christendom to the Holy Wisdom, Santa Sophia.

The original church of the Holy Wisdom had been built by the emperor Constantine but it had been destroyed by fire in the bloody Nika riots of 532 in which the factions of the Greens and Blues, named after the rival charioteers, joined forces to attack the government at the conclusion of the chariot races in the Hippodrome. To celebrate his victory over the rioters and to atone for the bloodshed which was said to have cost some thirty thousand lives, Justinian ordered the church to be rebuilt. On it he was to spend some 23 million gold solidi. In its vast space, its marvellous dome, its glittering polished marble, green, red, yellow and blue, reflecting the light from the high windows, and its brilliant mosaics it was the most magnificent church in the world. No building expressed better the junction of heaven and earth where God and man met, presided over jointly by the emperor and the patriarch. Nor could there be a greater contrast between the small stone oratory on Skellig Michael and the roughly constructed church of Iona than this stunning building.

Yet the shaggy Celtic monks and the Byzantine emperor represented twin aspects of Christian history in those centuries sometimes if incorrectly called the Dark Ages, Christianity triumphant in the majesty and beauty of Santa Sophia and Christianity still burgeoning and striving in the austerities of Celtic monasteries and stimulating the missionary labours of St Columba.

THE CHRISTIANIZATION OF THE BARBARIAN PEOPLES

The triumphant Christian Church was confronted in the west by a new crisis created by the twin problems of how to christianize and catholicize the barbarian peoples who had infiltrated, settled and conquered the western empire; and how, simultaneously, to contend with a new threat, the menace of militant Islam. While the eastern empire remained a unified dominion which under the emperor Justinian even attempted, if with but temporary success, to regain its lost territory in the western Mediterranean, the Roman Empire in the west had for the most part disintegrated as the barbarian peoples settled in its lands and took over its governance: Ostrogoths in Italy, Visigoths in southern France and Spain, Vandals in North Africa, Franks in Gaul, Angles, Jutes and Saxons in Britain, Lombards in northern Italy, followed later by fresh waves of warlike peoples, Avars, Magyars, Vikings, not to speak of the Arabs who were to conquer and occupy vast areas of the empire both in the east and the west.

The rise of Islam was to shatter further the integrity of the Christian world, especially in the Mediterranean. The Arabs, unified by the genius of a religious leader Mohammed, became a superbly effective militant force, and conquered the Byzantine provinces of Syria, Egypt and Iraq. They defeated the Byzantine army at Yarmuk and overcame the Sassanid princes of Iran. Arab armies advanced along the North African coast. By 711 they had crossed the Straits of Gibraltar and had invaded Spain, shortly afterwards sending armed probes into southern France before a marauding army intent on sacking the abbey of St Martin at Tours received a setback at the hands of the Frankish prince Charles Martel in 731. Some fourteen years earlier, in 717, they had laid siege to Constantinople.

Islam was long to represent a threat to Christian Europe, even conceivably to imperil its very existence. Yet Islam and Christianity enjoyed a common heritage. The Muslim holy book, the Qur'ān incorporated Christian teaching, recognizing Moses and Jesus among the prophets though it rejected the divinity and resurrection of Christ. Islamic teachers claimed that their faith originated with Abraham. 'Abraham was neither a Jew nor a Christian saint but he of the pure faith who submitted to God', in other words a true *muslim*. The Qur'ān asserted that God granted a son Isaac to Abraham's wife, Sarah, from whom the Jews were descended. Sarah banished Abraham's son by the slave girl Hagar, Ishmael, to the desert but Abraham rescued Ishmael and his mother and took them to a barren valley, Mecca, where Gabriel gave them a spring of water. Abraham and Ishmael established the sanctuary of the Ka'ba at Mecca within which were the graves of Hagar and Ishmael from whom the Arab peoples were descended. Mohammed was the last and greatest of the prophets who had restored to the Arabs the true religion of their ancestor Abraham.

Because of their common heritage as 'peoples of the Book who had partaken of God's revelation' the Muslims did not compel either the Jews or the Christians to change their faith but they treated them as second-class citizens, granting them protection and freedom of person, property and worship in return for payments of tribute and tax. Islam was thus able to incorporate Christian communities into its domains with comparative ease whereas Christian Europe, basically intolerant of any faith but its own, lamentably failed to assimilate the Muslims. The Muslims in their turn were to be very largely immune to Christian missions, and the only resort to which Christians could turn to defeat Islam was the sword, as the sorry story of the crusades was later to demonstrate.

If Islam was to continue to menace the frontiers of Christendom, the Church seemed to be assailed everywhere by the forces of evil, by paganism and even where the barbarians had accepted Christian baptism by the heresy of Arianism. Beneath the surface of a nominally Christianized society there continued to lurk the superstitions of the past, beliefs in sorcery and charms, either the heritage of a world only superficially Christian or of a society still intrinsically pagan. The classical culture of the ancient world lay in tatters, its manuscripts preserved but rarely read in the gloomy fastness of monastic libraries. The culture of the literate élite, bishops and monks, had become distinctively Christian, but it sailed on in a sea of darkness. A fortress mentality had enveloped the Christian Church. No wonder that the churches of the age, early Romanesque in type, had such thick walls, their windows mere narrow apertures, their towers squat, the interiors heavy with must and incense, their walls and pillars often decorated with grotesque sculptures depicting in vivid, crude colours the Last Judgement and the horrors of hell. Rape, pillage and sudden death, a commonplace even in royal courts, reflected the vengeance of a wrathful God on man's sin. No wonder that the greatest of the popes of the time, Gregory the Great, pondered his commentary on the book of Job. It was only through the sacrifice of Christ on the cross that men and women had any chance of redemption, but few would be chosen.

In a world where there were forces at work which seemed to threaten the very existence of the Christian Church, the Church eventually managed to win through by a long and hard haul. It could not conquer but it might hope to contain Islam whose potential for further expansion was beginning to be limited. It managed to convert the pagan peoples on the periphery of the former Roman Empire and to counter heresy. To achieve this in part it was obliged to accept a series of compromises which led to the further assimilation of non-Christian elements into the fabric of its teaching.

The Church's task was made easier by the survival of Roman Christianized culture in the western European countries – Anglo-Saxon Britain was an exception – and by the comparative ease with which the barbarian peoples accepted the Christian faith, if only because it seemed to them a symbol of a superior culture which they were eager to embrace. But although the barbarian princes accepted Christianity, the majority preferred the Arian or heretical type. As a result the Catholic Christians regarded the Goths, originally converted by Ulfilas in the fourth century, as enemies of the true Church.

It was the Goths who under their king Alaric in 410 captured and sacked Rome, causing consternation in the Catholic world, for while Rome was no longer the imperial capital it housed the martyrs and saints. 'What will remain standing if Rome falls?', St Jerome asked rhetorically while Augustine realistically began to write his classic *City of God* to contrast the vanity of earthly states with the eternal city of God.

Although the Roman Empire in the west came to an end with the enforced abdication of Romulus Augustulus in 476, the barbarian settlers were in a minority living within the continuing influence of *romanitas*. Neither Germanic pagans such as the Franks nor Arian Christians such as the Goths and the Vandals could displace even if they had wished to do so the massive loyalty of the majority of the population to the ceremonies and beliefs of the Catholic Church. The Catholics sometimes experienced sporadic bouts of persecution at the hands of the Arian Goths. The Visigothic king Euric banished Catholic bishops and kept sees vacant. The Ostrogothic king Theodoric had Boethius, the author of the classic *Consolation of Religion*, executed. But for the most part pagan warriors, Arian kings and Catholic bishops coexisted. The kings increasingly valued the bishops as educated administrators. The Ostrogothic king Theodoric had had a Catholic mother Ereleava and for the greater part of his reign was tolerant of his Catholic subjects. In 589 the Spanish Visigothic king Leovigild renounced the Arian faith and was reconciled to Rome.

When the eastern emperor Justinian began a policy of reconquest of lands lost to the barbarians in North Africa and Italy, the Catholic Church was to be the main beneficiary of his success. The Arian Vandal kingdom in North Africa was brought to an end and the Catholics reacquired among much else the basilica of St Cyprian at Carthage. The Byzantines regained a foothold in the toe of Italy, enabling at least the partial elimination of Ostrogothic Arianism; though northern Italy was occupied by a new group of Germanic invaders, the Lombards, who had been converted to the Arian faith and were long to be a thorn in the side of the Roman Pope.

The Franks who occupied northern and central France, conquering the Burgundians in 534, were pagans but under the lead of their warrior king Clovis were converted to Catholic Christianity. Clovis was married to a Burgundian princess, Clotilde, herself a Catholic. Clovis vowed to be baptized if he was victorious over the Alemanni. Whether Clovis was baptized then in 496 or more likely in 508 as a sequel to his victory over the Visigoths at Vouillé seems unclear. Gregory of Tours tells us that in the latter campaign the Frankish warriors received signs of heavenly support as they passed by the shrines of St Martin at Tours and St Hilary at Poitiers.

The Catholic Church had then in large measure regained its influence in the west before the end of the sixth century, a move which in part at least was a sequel to the pontificate of an able Pope, Gregory the Great. Its bishops acquired great influence at royal courts and like many monasteries became the recipients of handsome patronage which made the Church a massively wealthy institution, owning estates and the serfs who worked them.

By contrast with the western barbarian states the conversion of the former Roman province of Britannia had virtually to be done all over again. At what point Christianity had first filtered into Roman Britain remains obscure, but by the fourth century the British Church evidently had its own bishops, some of whom travelled to general councils on the Continent, their expenses subsidized by the imperial fisc, while mosaics in Roman villas and silver vessels show that the Church must have had a relatively substantial following. Yet paganism, represented by devotion to the old Roman deities, by adherence to the mystery religions especially by soldiers serving on the frontiers, and by the Britons' continued faith in the Celtic deities, remained deeply entrenched, even on the eve of the departure of the Roman legions. In the early fifth century Roman-British princes governed the country. While they were Christian, they may have been influenced by the teaching of the native British heretic, Pelagius, for the Frankish bishop Germanus of Auxerre travelled twice to Britain apparently to resolve problems which were caused by religious discord there. How far such controversy weakened the power of the ruling Romano-British prince Vortigern is unclear, but it was internal as well as external foes which led him to call to his aid barbarian warriors from the Continent, the pagan Anglo-Saxons. After their arrival the Anglo-Saxons turned against their employer and in a series of campaigns (the outcome of which may have fluctuated more than the surviving sources suggest for there was evidently some sort of Romano-British Christian revival at the end of the fifth century), they conquered and colonized the country, leaving only the western periphery, Wales and Cornwall, in Romano-British Christian possession.

The Anglo-Saxons were a vigorous pagan people who wrought the virtual destruction of the Christian Church in Britain. Britain had never been as thoroughly Romanized or Christianized as the rest of the Continent; and though Christianity almost certainly continued to have a vestigial existence, as an organized body it disappeared, or was pushed to the Celtic peripheries of the British Isles. The British monk Gildas, the only contemporary whose writings survive, spoke dramatically of the blood and slaughter, rape and pillage which was the Christians' fate at the hands of the Anglo-Saxons.

In effect the conversion to Christianity would have to be done again. Neighbouring Ireland had never been Romanized or Christianized but simultaneously with the beginnings of the Anglo-Saxon raids on England, first at the initiative of Bishop Palladius whom Pope Celestine I sent in 431–2 and then under the mysterious but charismatic leadership of a Romano-British Christian, Patrick, whose historic existence has been doubted by some, Celtic Ireland was converted to the Christian faith. Christianity in Ireland, monastic in its organization, proved to be a vigorous plant with a strong penitential and missionary impulse. From the Celtic monastery which Columba, a voluntary exile from his native Ireland, set up at Iona off the west coast of Scotland missionaries were despatched not merely to convert the Picts but under the lead of Aidan to reconvert the Northumbrians and in time to penetrate to other Anglo-Saxon kingdoms.

The reconversion of Britain was a pincer movement, for while the Celts played the major part in missionary enterprise, initially it had been a Roman monk, Augustine, at the behest of Pope Gregory the Great, who landed in Kent in 597 and founded the church at Canterbury. The ingredients in the conversion and eventual baptism of the Kentish king Ethelbert were not unfamiliar: a Christian wife, the Merovingian princess Berta, the daughter of Charibert king of Paris; some awareness among the men of Kent of the glamour of Christian and imperial Rome; admiration for the power of the Christian kings of the Franks, brutal thugs as they may seem to have been; and as always faith in the greater efficacy of the Christian God. The Roman mission only made slow progress outside Kent, hindered by dissent with the Celtic missionaries at work in other parts of the country over the date of Easter, a controversy which was eventually resolved by a Roman victory at the Synod of Whitby called by the Northumbrian king in 664, but the conversion of England, if not without its setbacks, was at least superficially complete by the end of the seventh century.

THE CHARACTER OF THE CHURCH IN THE DARK AGES

Although pockets of paganism continued to exist, more especially in northern and eastern Europe, at least superficially the barbarian threat to Christianity had been met and momentarily neutralized. Where Roman civilization had penetrated deeply as in France and Spain barbarian culture was an overlay, freely assimilated, as the history of Roman law showed, by what was still predominantly a post-Roman society. The infrastructure of the Church had not been greatly affected by the barbarian takeover, its administrative features and its social obligations inherited from the imperial age remaining largely intact. Even in newly converted Britain a system of episcopal government was imposed on tribal society. If bishops were more immediately selected from post-Roman aristocratic society, sooner or later men of barbarian origin would take high office. Even in Britain where for some decades the bishops were largely chosen from migrant clergy native Anglo-Saxons came sooner or later to dominate the episcopate.

The bishop's functions remained primarily pastoral, sacramental and administrative in character. What was new was the marked increase in the bishop's secular role which both the instability of the times and the literacy of the bishop's court served to encourage. Bishops became important as advisers to kings, serving as the lynch pins of royal administration. As the holders of substantial estates they were soon sometimes to be even further involved in secular administration as suppliers of warriors for the king's army. Kings needed the support of their bishops while bishops required the protection and patronage of the kings. Often selected from the ranks of the aristocracy there was always a danger of the bishops adopting the life-style of the lay nobles.

The king's conversion was the one essential ingredient in the success of missionary enterprise leading to the subsequent Christianization of his peoples. Once the king had accepted baptism, his nobles followed suit and the peasants had little alternative except to follow their lord's example. But how much the first generation or so of the converted understood of their newly acquired faith may be doubted. The task of instruction must have been well beyond the capacity of a single bishop and many of the clergy who would have been imperfectly trained, and had sometimes to use interpreters to get their message over. For many converts baptism must therefore have appeared little more than a mechanical or magical act; and their understanding of their new found faith may have been little more than a transposition of what they already believed as pagans now placed within a comparatively crude framework of Christian belief. Popular Christianization, as the history of Christian missions throughout the ages has demonstrated, was a gradual and patchy process. It was ultimately as much an effect of social pressure and infection as of genuine personal commitment, the process doubtless stimulated by the sculptures and paintings, rough but dramatic, which decorated the walls of the churches, and by the magical ceremonial of the Mass itself. By the time of the second and third generation Christians the faith had become a formal expression of the society to which they belonged.

The arguments which the missionaries used to combat pagan beliefs were simplistic but, given the limited literacy of many of the converts, compelling. God created the universe. There is only one God. The pagan gods and goddesses are mere sticks and stones. God sent his son Jesus Christ to offer salvation to all those who believe in his name; and for those who do not there await the vivid pains of hell. Those who believe will receive their due reward, possibly in this life and certainly in the next. The supernatural power of the Christian God was an agency for victory in war, and in general for material prosperity as well as personal happiness. All this was encapsulated in a holy book, the Bible, interpreting the revealed Word of God, which itself formed a semi-magical means of communication to the illiterate.

Through the medium of enactments made at councils of bishops and clergy the Church, supported by the king who embodied such decrees in his own newly articulated code of law, sought to eliminate pagan superstition and customs and to enforce a Christian moral code of behaviour. Social pressures and ecclesiastical penalties led to the partial elimination of sexual irregularities, even if the Church's effort to drive out the 'old Adam' proved often as fruitless then as it has since. The ways in which so-called Christian princes resorted not infrequently to murder and brutality sometimes led Christian bishops to protest, as Boniface did at the immoral life of King Ethelbald of Mercia, but more often than not, needing royal support, they had to acquiesce in the moral delinquency of princes who held, as the clergy themselves taught, that their power came from God.

There is, then, insufficient evidence to show to what extent the mass of the population understood Christian belief or practised Christian morality. As in earlier times when such questions seemed of indifferent importance the Church was ready to compromise and even to embed pagan customs into the Church's infrastructure. Gregory the Great, for instance, told Augustine to convert Anglo-Saxon temples into churches, so substituting the sacrifice of the Mass for the animal and, at one time human, sacrifices offered to the pagan gods. In some respects the infiltration of pagan attitudes into a Christian ethos was more subtle. Christ was made to appear as a warrior leader, an ideal to which a pagan king could aspire, and his apostles became his chieftains. The Germanic epic, the *Heliand*, portrayed Christ as a warring lord. The Anglo-Saxon epic poem *Beowulf*, full as it was of Christian allusions, adopted the Germanic pagan virtues. The beautiful eighth-century Northumbrian ivory casket, known from its nineteenth-century purchaser as the Franks Casket, portrayed on one and the same panel the pagan legend of Wayland the Smith and the story of the Adoration of the Magi. The values of the pagan heroic saga crept, if unevenly, within the umbrella of Christian morality.

The conversion of the barbarian kings to Christianity transformed the concept of kingship itself with benefits, at least superficially, both to king and Church. Kings were taught to embrace the Christian virtues. The laws which they decreed began to be threaded through with Christian concepts. Above all they were encouraged to do justice and to show mercy to their subjects, duties which they owed to God. Kings did indeed sometimes take their obligations seriously, standing in some dread of their bishops and even on occasions doing penance for sin; some Anglo-Saxon kings abdicated their thrones and in the search for holiness became pilgrims to the holy city of Rome.

In return the Church, which had formerly been ready to accept the semi-divine authority of the emperor, as it was still doing in the Byzantine Empire, gave a divine imprimatur to kingship bestowing a semi-sacral character on the king through the rite of coronation, a ceremony based on the anointing of David by Saul. Although some form of sacral ordination by the laying on of hands or blessing may have been a feature of Celtic kingship, the rite of coronation seems to have originated in the eighth century when Pepin was anointed king of the Franks in 751. In England the first royal anointing took place in 787 when Ecgferth, the son of King Offa of Mercia, was 'hallowed as king'.

The central act of the coronation was the anointing of the king's head by the bishop with oil mixed with balsam or aromatic herbs; it was preceded by promises which the king made to fulfil his Christian duty to his people, and it ended with his investiture with various insignia of office of which the crown was the most important. Coronation had the effect of confirming the king's status, specifically conferring grace so that he could carry out his function more effectively. The king-elect became, by an act of symbolic rebirth, the king.

While coronation enhanced the royal power, it gave the Church an integral part in the conferring of such authority, so serving especially at a later date to strengthen the claims of those who were to argue that the spiritual power was superior to the temporal. If coronation promoted the status of the king, it did the same for the Church, signifying the marriage between secular and sacred within the framework of *Christianitas*.

THE PAPACY IN THE DARK AGES

The authority which princes exercised in collaboration with the Church in the so-called Dark Ages was made the greater by the comparative weakness of the Roman papacy. While the Pope remained a prestigious figure, venerated by new generations of Christian converts as the vicar of St Peter and Christ, his significance in world politics was limited. The popes enjoyed a substantial income from their vast estates in Italy, Sicily, Dalmatia, Gaul and North Africa but they lived under the shadow of the authority of the eastern Byzantine emperor who had acquired a foothold in Italy itself through the Byzantine exarchate of Ravenna. Papal elections had to be confirmed by the emperor, a right later delegated to the Byzantine exarch in Italy, before the Pope's coronation. Relations between the popes and the eastern emperor were as a result often strained and embittered by theological controversy. Yet the Pope needed imperial support against an enemy nearer home in the shape of another barbarian invader of Italy, the Lombards, Arian Christians, who actually besieged Rome in 579. As a consequence the Pope was too much in need of imperial support to defy the emperor.

Momentarily indeed the Church had had in Gregory the Great a head who from 590 to 604 proved to be a leader of exceptional skill and determination. In the absence of effective civil government he became the virtual ruler of Rome and indeed of much of Italy, making immense efforts to provide relief for those suffering from plague, famine and strife. He established friendly relations with the Catholic monarchs of Visgothic Spain and Frankish Gaul; and in 596 he despatched one of his own monks, his prior Augustine to evangelize Kent. While he was a determined advocate of the Roman supremacy, rejecting, for instance, the bishop of Constantinople's claim to be called the 'oecumenical' patriarch, he was personally a man of deep, even mystical spirituality, so austere in his life-style that excess of fasting led to ill-health. His book *The Pastoral Care*, later to be translated into Anglo-Saxon by King Alfred, in which he outlined the duties of a bishop, in effect set out what was to be his own life's object, the unceasing care of the flock over which he was placed as Christ's shepherd of souls. Pope Gregory the Great made an enduring impact on the papacy, but his successors were less well placed to build on his foundations. Between the pincers of Byzantine overlordship and the Lombard menace, they for the most part marked time.

MONASTICISM

The mainspring of Christianity between the sixth and eighth centuries continued to be found in the monasteries, more especially in the monasteries of Celtic Ireland where Christian societies preserved ancient learning, and became centres of a rigorous asceticism and of enthusiasm for the propagation of the Christian gospel. In non-Romanized Irish tribal society the Irish monastery became the religious counterpart of the tribe. Many Irish monasteries, like Skellig Michael, were small and located in near-inaccessible places but others, like Clonmacnoise, were large, perhaps numbering thousands of monks, and more centrally situated.

Like the monks of Syria and Palestine, the Irish monks, presided over by abbots, frequently a blood-relation of the founder of the monastery, lived austere and ascetic lives, often subjecting themselves to exotic forms of self-mortification. Imbued with a deep sense of guilt, the need for repentance before forgiveness led to the production of penitentials the use of which was to spread throughout the western Church. These monastic con-glomerations, perhaps carrying over cultural traditions inherited from the druids and an earlier race of Irish holy men, were also homes of con-temporary scholarship with libraries rich in scriptural and patristic learning. In their scriptoria the monks engaged in illuminating manuscripts, often with exquisite and original designs. Their reputation for learning attracted scholars from Anglo-Saxon England and Gaul.

There was another significant element in the Irish monastic life-style – travel. In general the monastic rule required that the monk must not wander abroad except at the express wish of the abbot of his house. But the Irish monk had an 'itch' to travel, less to spread the gospel than to perform an act of penance. It was this which sent Columba (who felt the need to do penance to atone for helping to bring about a blood feud involving his family) to the island of Iona off the Scottish coast where he founded a house which soon attracted a large following.

The preaching of the gospel may have been incidental but it was a necessary part of the monk's role. Columba helped to convert the pagan Picts. An Ionan monk, Aidan, was despatched to assist the Northumbrian king Oswald (who had himself been a political exile at Iona) to take the lead in the re-Christianization of the Anglo-Saxon kingdom of Northumbria, for the process of conversion of Northumbria started by Bishop Paulinus at the invitation of King Edwin had been brought to an abrupt end when Edwin was killed by the pagan king of Mercia at the battle of Hatfield.

The monasteries of Anglo-Saxon England, Augustine's monastery at Canterbury alone excepted, at first Celtic in type, served as beacons of the faith in the newly Christianized kingdoms. Aidan, acting as both bishop and abbot, presided over the Northumbrian Church from his island head-quarters at Lindisfarne (Holy Island), and it was Celtic monks who converted the East Saxons and the Mercians and helped in the conversion of East Anglia. And where they went they brought their own particular features, austerity of life, love of the scriptures and an intense desire to preach the gospel.

It was inevitable that their influence should spill over on to the Continent. Contacts between Anglo-Saxon England and the Frankish Church were already in existence. On his journey to Kent Augustine had been consecrated a bishop by the Frankish bishops. Kentish princesses were to be consigned to Frankish nunneries. The monk Wilfred, stern critic of the Celts as he became, resided for some time at Lyons and was later made a bishop by the Frankish bishops at Compiègne. An Irish monk, Fursey, who had been prominent in the conversion of East Anglia, journeyed to Gaul where he was given a monastic house by the Frankish minister Eorcenwald at Lagny-sur-Marne. Another Frank, who had studied in Ireland, Agilbert, was made a bishop of the West Saxons. Deprived of his bishopric because he had not properly learned Anglo-Saxon, he took a prominent part in the debate at the Synod of Whitby which resolved the disputes between Celt and Roman over the date of Easter, and ended his days as bishop of Paris and was buried in the church of the nunnery at Jouarre.

Columbanus, another Irish noble who became a monk, travelled with twelve companions as a penance to Gaul. There acquiring the favour of the Frankish king Childebert II, he founded two monasteries at Anneguy and Luxeuil but he was not universally popular and had to flee Burgundy, eventually making his way to Bobbio, 40 miles north of Genoa which was to become a great centre of scholarship. Equally influential as one of the major locations of medieval learning was the abbey of St Gall, founded by one of his Irish companions. Monks including Columbanus who preached to the Alemanni at Bregenz on the lake of Constance, helped to spread the Christian faith among the pagan peoples of north-east Gaul and southern Germany. St Amand who died in 695 preached among the Basques, the Slavs, the northern Franks and in the Low Countries, and became known as the Apostle of Belgium. Later, as Irish society itself became more chaotic and was disrupted by internecine warfare and by the Viking raiders who shipped their unfortunate captives, monks among them, to the Arab slave markets of Spain and North Africa, the Irish missionary and monastic impulse showed signs of faltering. Indeed Catholic bishops began to find the undisciplined activities of some of their Irish brethren, the so-called 'choroiepiscopi' or wandering bishops, an increasing irritant.

The Irish penetration of Europe had been supplemented and followed by another wave of Christian migrants, enthusiastic men and women from Anglo-Saxon monasteries. It was through their missionary endeavour, in part promoted by a common sense of kinship with the Germanic peoples of the Continent that Christianity was to penetrate the Low Countries and southern Germany and to pave the way for the reform of the sluggish Frankish Church.

THE ANGLO-SAXON CHURCH

The ebullience of the Anglo-Saxon Church at the end of the seventh and in the early eighth centuries was astonishing. The Church had been injected with a new lease of energy after the dispute over the date of Easter had been resolved in favour of the Romans, even though immediately a chaotic situation had developed, partly due to the onset of plague which decimated the higher clergy, among the dead the archbishop of Canterbury. But the new archbishop, Theodore of Tarsus, an aged and learned Greek, turned out rather surprisingly to be a skilled administrator and an inspired leader. In Anglo-Saxon missionary enterprise, which appeared to be the product of the union of Celtic charisma and Anglo-Saxon organization the lead was taken by Wilfred, successively bishop of York and Hexham. Originally a product of the Celtic monastery of Lindisfarne, his stays at Rome and Lyons had made him a firm upholder of the monastic rule of St Benedict and a strong advocate of Roman claims which resulted in the victory of the Roman party at the Synod of Whitby in 664. As importantly Wilfred was the first to take the gospel to the pagan Frisians though their eventual conversion to the Christian faith was secured by one of his pupils from Ripon, Willibrord, whom Pope Sergius made archbishop of Utrecht. He owed his success in part to the support which he received from the Frankish king who saw in the expansion of the Christian faith a useful device for defending the boundaries of his state along the Rhine against the Frisians, the Bavarians and the Saxons. In the missionary activity of the seventh and eighth centuries, as in later times, the cross and the sword were inextricably intermingled.

Willibrord had wished his successor as archbishop in the Low Countries to be another Anglo-Saxon, a Devonian, Winifrith better known as Boniface. But Boniface extended his missionary activity to Hesse and Bavaria. Backed by the Pope Gregory II who consecrated him a bishop in 722 Boniface was given a commission to convert the heathen, supported, as Willibrord had been, by the Frankish princes. He carried out a swift and successful evangelization of Hesse, Thuringia and Bavaria. His methods were straightforward and even dramatic. He demonstrated the power of the Christian God by felling the sacred oak at Geismar.

The newly converted lands were soon criss-crossed by monasteries and nunneries, often staffed by Anglo-Saxon monks and nuns, which served as fortresses of the faith. Pope Gregory III empowered Boniface to establish bishoprics in the newly converted territory, enabling him to create a permanent ecclesiastical framework. At no stage in earlier or later history did English Christianity prove to be of such effective influence on the Continent.

The monastery had become the essential Christian unit in the further Christianization of society, winning the favour and benefactions of princes and noblemen, not merely because the latter were impressed by the monks' dedicated lives but because they could act as patrons and owners largely free from episcopal jurisdiction. For the monastic structure seemed better suited to houses located on rural estates founded by kings and nobles than to urban monasteries under episcopal control. A fresh development was that of the double monastery where men and women lived side by side, their roles complementing each other in what was at least technically an asexual society. Economically self-sufficient through the rich endowments which it collected the monastery served as a social centre for its neighbourhood, providing alms for the poor and sometimes acting as a school. It was the principal, perhaps the only, home of scholarship; its scriptoria produced biblical commentaries, theological tracts, ecclesiastical chronicles, all sometimes brilliantly illuminated. The Anglo-Saxon bishop and versifier Aldhelm was abbot of Malmesbury before he became bishop of Sherborne. Bede, the greatest scholar of his age, spent most of his life as a monk of Jarrow drawing on the rich resources of its library for his commentaries.

There was no lack of vocations to the monastic life. While the standard of life was far from luxurious, the monastery provided a less meagre livelihood for monks and nuns than that enjoyed by many peasants, so often oppressed by poverty and famine. In spite of monastic discipline, monastic existence was reasonably comfortable and secure, made the more bearable by the conviction that the religious stood a better chance of heaven than the secular clergy and the laity. For the laity the monastery was above all the power-house of prayer, its Masses and its daily offices a continuous chain of petition to God.

The very success of monasticism had, however, its own dangers. In later life Bede complained bitterly of the way in which nobles established what passed for monasteries to avoid secular taxation. There were early some signs of increasing laxity in the observance of the monastic rule. In 748 Chrodegang, Bishop of Metz, in an effort to revive monasticism's ancient glories founded the abbey of Gorze as a centre of reformed religious life, and drew up a rule for canons of cathedral churches living in community and devoted to prayer.

It was a symptom of a growing feeling among would-be reformers that the Church in general had become somewhat careless and lax. Pope Gregory the Great had earlier observed that bishoprics in the Frankish Church could only be bought for money. Ecclesiastical dignitaries became a useful source of income for lay nobles. Such was the slack state of the Frankish Church that Boniface pressed upon the Frankish king the urgent need for reform. Under the aegis of the Frankish princes Carloman and Pepin Boniface presided over a series of reforming councils between 742 and 747 which issued a number of reform decrees, though how far they were to be implemented must remain debatable.

THE CAROLINGIAN RENAISSANCE

This cooperation between the Anglo-Saxon churchman and the Carolingian prince was to open a new phase in the history of the Church. The Carolings were the real rulers of France, replacing in fact but not in theory the shadowy Merovingian kings who retained the dignity but not the power. The Popes, drifting between fluctuating friendship and intermittent hostility with the Byzantines and Lombards and often themselves the prey of Roman noble factions, realized that their one hope of freeing themselves from their enemies was to win the support of the powerful Caroling family. In 739–40 Pope Gregory III appealed to its head, Charles Martel, sending him relics and other gifts and requesting him to defend 'the Church of God and his peculiar people'. His successor Pope Zachary buoyed up by strong sentiments of loyalty to the papal see evinced at a Frankish Church council in 747, responded favourably to Pepin's suggestion that he should replace the nominal head of state. Pepin despatched the Merovingian king Childeric III to a monastery and was anointed as king of the Franks by Boniface.

This close relationship between the Roman Pope and the Frankish king was further strengthened when Zachary's successor, Pope Stephen II, threatened by the Lombard king, Aistulf, defied the wintry storms and crossed the St Bernard Pass to meet the king at Ponthion (near Chalons-sur-Marne) on

6 January 754, requesting his help against the insurgent Lombards. To support his argument Stephen referred to the legendary donation of the western empire which his predecessor Pope Sylvester I had supposedly made to Constantine, suggesting that he had something to give the French king in return. Persuaded by the supplications of the priest who was under Christ the head of the Church and aware of the territorial and diplomatic advantages which might accrue to him should he intervene, Pepin agreed to help, guaranteeing the Pope's claim to substantial territory in Italy which included not only Rome but Ravenna, the exarchate in Byzantine hands, and Lombard lands. The Pope anointed Pepin, his wife and sons and nominated him 'patrician of the Romans'. The papal state was in effect in the making.

These important developments were to be extended in the reign of Charles, or Charlemagne as he is better known, who succeeded his father in 768. Charlemagne was an exceptional personality, portrayed by his biographer Einhard in flattering but realistic terms as very strong, tall, a robust hunter, more unusually a swimmer (in the hot springs at Aachen where he built his palace), interested in learning, speaking Latin, Frankish and even a little Greek, though he never acquired the skill of writing. Like most successful princes of his time essentially he was a warrior, following an expansionist policy which brought him control over Aquitaine and the Lombards; he pursued a long and brutal series of campaigns against the Saxons to whom he offered the alternative of baptism or death. His matrimonial life was not without its hazards.

Yet Charlemagne had an unusual conception of his office which raised him above the level of contemporary princes. While he believed that he derived his authority directly from God, he was convinced that such power was combined with responsibility, more especially towards the Church. The movement for the Church's revival, implicit in the work of Boniface and his associates, became the policy of the Frankish king. The clergy were to be the tools by which society was itself to be trained and rejuvenated for the service of God.

Charlemagne's legislation was intended to protect orthodoxy and to eradicate heresy. He approved, for instance, the condemnation of the doctrinal errors promulgated by two Spanish bishops, Felix of Urgel and Elipandus of Toledo, who argued that as Christ was truly human, he could only be God's adopted son.

More positively as the champion of orthodoxy he tried to ensure that there was regularity in the liturgy and Church order. He took care to ascertain that suitable men were nominated to high office in the Church. His capitularies (Frankish royal ordinances) underlined the responsibility of the clergy to live a religious life and to forswear secular pursuits and tried to ensure that monasteries observed the Rule of St Benedict. In 787 in a capitulary to Baugulf, the abbot of Fulda, Charlemagne commanded that there should be opportunities for study in all monasteries and bishops' residences and 'let those who can teach'. Two years later, in 789, he ordered that 'there may be schools for reading-boys; let them learn psalms, notes, chants, the computus and grammar, in every monastery and bishop's house'.

The initiative for the reform of the Church came from the king. Yet he was loyal to the Pope as head of the Church, and, like his father, became involved in the complex politics of Italy. Pope Hadrian I had renewed the appeal to the Frankish king to save him from the Lombards, a request to which Charlemagne acceded, invading Italy, capturing Pavia and dethroning the Lombard king, Desiderius, taking the iron crown of Lombardy for himself. He confirmed the promises which his father had made to Pope Stephen, but he did not relinquish his real power as the Pope's overlord. It was an indication of Charlemagne's position in the Church that the new Pope, Leo III, sent him the keys of St Peter's tomb and the banner of Rome when announcing his election.

Leo III had enemies in Rome who assaulted him, tried to gouge out his eyes and tongue, with the intention of forcing him to a monastery, but he managed to escape from this predicament and made his way to Charlemagne's court at Paderborn. Charlemagne's leading adviser, the scholar Alcuin judiciously advised the king that he was not empowered to pass judgement on the successor of St Peter (who was charged by his enemies with adultery and perjury). He did however promise him protection. In late November 800 Charlemagne arrived in Rome where the Pope took an oath of purgation. The council of notables, Franks and Romans, whom Charlemagne had summoned, then condemned the Pope's accusers to death, but Leo felt either strong or merciful enough to commute the sentence to one of exile. When two days later Charlemagne rose from praying at the tomb of St Peter at the start of the Christmas Mass, the Pope placed an imperial crown on the king' head. The congregation acclaimed Charlemagne emperor and the Pope himself knelt to make an act of homage.

What was the significance of this dramatic scene? It could be seen simply as a reward for all that Charlemagne had done for the Pope, saving his office and even possibly his life. It seems unlikely that, as Einhard suggested, Charlemagne was taken by surprise. While it appears improbable that in making Charlemagne emperor the Pope intended consciously to restore the Roman Empire of the west that had perished with Romulus Augustulus's deposition in 476, yet Charlemagne may have seen himself as a co-emperor, reflecting his suspicion and even dislike of the Greeks. Alcuin had earlier commented that the recent behaviour of the Byzantine empress Irene who had deposed her son, the legitimate emperor, and had him blinded, had illegitimized the Byzantine claim to the imperial title. Given the massive dominions over which Charlemagne ruled, more extensive than any other prince since the ending of the Roman Empire, the title of emperor, which was in fact to be used subsequently by other rulers, among them the Anglo-Saxon and Spanish monarchs, would have seemed an appropriate description of his pre-eminence in the Christian world. Rather than a restoration of the old western empire Charlemagne's *imperium* was personal to himself, a shrewd gesture made by the Pope which would consolidate his understanding with the Frankish king, and which for Charlemagne himself was a fitting culmination of his achievements in peace and war.

In Charlemagne Church and State, cross and sword, became more significantly fused than they had been before. He had responsibility for the welfare of the Church. The Church legitimized his policy, prayed for his success in war (though Alcuin remonstrated with him for enforcing so brutal a policy of conversion on the Saxons), and upheld all that he did with spiritual sanctions, such as the threat of excommunication, against his enemies. For his part the emperor upheld the Church, its privileges and immunities and sought to ensure that it tried to fulfil the divine injunctions which had brought it into being.

In particular he attached great importance to education and scholarship, not merely for the clerical order but for the laity as well. He gathered at his court a group of scholars and churchmen, the Northumbrian Alcuin of York, the Italians Paul the Deacon and Peter of Pisa, the Spaniard Theodulf, Bishop of Orlèans. Charlemagne ordered members of his court as well as the children of the nobility to attend a school where they were to be instructed in the seven liberal arts. The empire became dotted with schools, usually connected to monasteries and cathedrals presided over by distinguished scholars, Alcuin at Tours, Theodulf at Orlèans, Hincmar and Remigius of Auxerre at Rheims, Rabanus Maurus at Fulda and Adalhard and Paschasius Radbertus at Corbie. This revival of learning was limited in scope and lacking in originality; its outlook was conservative and its range was conditioned by its theological objectives.

The revival of learning and religion, restricted as it must have been in the main to the educated élite, did not end abruptly with Charlemagne's death in 814. His son, Louis the Pious, was sympathetic to his father's policy and in 817 approved the systematic organization of the Benedictine rule made at the Synod of Aachen at the behest of Benedict, who had established a reformed monastery at Aniane in Languedoc in 779. The Church was enriched by the scholarship of men such as Agobard, the archbishop of Lyons, an unusually original mind, sceptical of witchcraft and superstition; Hincmar, the archbishop of Reims, a theologian of distinction who engaged in the current controversy over predestination; and his friend, John Scotus Erigena, an Irishman who was sufficiently well acquainted with classical texts to try to reconcile Christian and classical ideas.

Yet by the closing years of the ninth century the sands of the Carolingian renaissance were running out. Such a decline was perhaps due less to a natural fall in religious enthusiasm than to political and social factors. The empire had ceased to be a political unity as its heirs fought each other for their inheritance. Furthermore the break-up of Charlemagne's empire coincided with a new crisis which constituted a threat to Church and state, the appearance of the marauding Vikings.

THE VIKING THREAT

The Vikings were pagan pirates who looted monasteries, churches and shrines less because they were anti-Christian than because such places were thought to house treasure and to be relatively defenceless: the monastery of Lindisfarne was attacked in 793, of Jarrow in 794, of Iona in 795. In Anglo-Saxon England they inflicted immense damage on a Church which was already showing some signs of decay, destroying churches and burning and dispersing their libraries, and so disrupting the organization of the Church that many English dioceses were without bishops and some, Hexham, Dunwich and Leicester, disappeared for centuries. Viking ships threatened Paris in 845. In 882 they sailed up the Rhine to Cologne and Trier. Sooner or later the soldiers became colonists. They spent the winter of 843 at Noirmoutier at the mouth of the River Loire. In 851 they wintered in Thanet in Kent. As a result of internal divisions and military incompetence the major Anglo-Saxon kingdoms, Northumbria, Mercia and East Anglia, fell under Danish rule constituting the Danelaw with York their chief town. Half a century later the French king Charles the Simple bestowed what was to be the duchy of Normandy on the Viking chief Rollo.

Psychologically the Vikings constituted a major threat to the existence of the western Church. For Alcuin their attack on the monastery of Lindisfarne was an expression of God's wrath at human sin. The Vikings seemed a savage and bloodthirsty people, devoted to the war god Woten, who gave them victory. Even if the horrifying ritual of the blood eagle may be a later legend, they behaved cruelly to their victims. King Alfred's decision to translate into English Orosius's tract *Historiarum adversus Paganos* which catalogued the miseries of the pagan past and exhorted the Christian to remain loyal to the faith in spite of adversity reflected the contemporary attitude to these fierce warriors.

Yet the periphery of their aggression was in fact limited, confined to Britain and Ireland and to the coastal regions of France and the Low Countries. Moreover within a comparatively short time they had accepted Christian baptism and conversion, and as soon as they ceased to represent a direct threat the work of renovation could begin. In England Alfred who in spite of adversity had kept his rich kingdom of Wessex more or less intact rebuilt the churches and encouraged learning, like Charlemagne establishing a palace school. With the help of his scholarly advisers, among them Bishop Asser, though whether he was the author of *The Life of Alfred Long* must be doubted, and the Frank, Grimbald, the king personally sponsored the translation of important religious texts: works such as Bede's *Ecclesiastical History* translated into English, and Gregory the Great's *Pastoral Care*, were designed to help improve the standards of clerical life, a copy of which was to be sent to every bishop with an illuminated bookmark, of which the brilliant Alfred jewel in the Ashmolean Museum at Oxford may be a specimen. Alfred's policy of renovation and revival was followed by his successors as West Saxon kings; but the revitalization of English monastic life had to wait until the middle of the tenth century.

THE REVIVAL OF MONASTICISM

While there was an element of continuity with the earlier English monastic tradition, the Anglo-Saxon religious revolution received a strong injection of adrenalin from its contacts with the continental Church. If the reforms of Benedict of Aniane had become a dead letter, two new centres of growth had come into existence, in the Low Countries at the monastic houses of Gorze and St Peter's Blandinium at Ghent, patronized by Arnulf the count of Flanders, and in central France at Cluny near Mâcon in Burgundy where Duke William of Aquitaine founded a monastic house in 910, both movements concerned to return to the pristine rule of St Benedict. Under a succession of able abbots, Berno, Odo, Odilo, Cluny attained such a reputation that many other monasteries in France and Italy including Benedict's monastery of Monte Cassino adopted its reforming programme. Lotharingian and Cluniac reform did not merely stress the importance of cultivating a strict and regimented spiritual life, but emphasized the corporate worship of the community through the medium of the choir offices and the Mass which were celebrated with solemn splendour.

While the English monastic reformation was not specifically Cluniac, its leaders were much influenced by their contacts with the continental Church. Archbishop Dunstan of Canterbury had stayed at the monastery of St Peter's at Ghent; Bishop Ethelwold of Winchester had sent his clerk, Osgar, to the Cluniac house of Fleury-sur-Loire (which had acquired by dubious sleight of hand the body of St Benedict himself from Monte Cassino) from whom Ethelwold learned of the reforms which he was himself to introduce with great effect at his own monasteries of Abingdon and Winchester. Oswald Bishop of Worcester too had studied at Fleury where he had been clothed with the Benedictine habit by its abbot Wulfled. A new version of the monastic rule, the *Regularis Concordia*, providing for the reinforcement of a purer monastic practice, was drawn up by Bishop Ethelwold with the help of visiting monks from Fleury and Ghent.

Although the impact of such religious reforms was limited – monasticism hardly existed north of the River Humber – they had revitalized the Anglo-Saxon Church. The episcopate, largely chosen from monks, proved to be more conscientious. Monasteries and nunneries were reformed and refounded. There was a revival of learning which was accompanied by the production of a spate of splendid illuminated manuscripts and which led to the translation of religious texts into the vernacular. Great churches, few of which survived the Norman Conquest, resplendent with colour and decoration, were built; and monastic craftsmen created beautiful works of art in ivory, gilt and stone. It is impossible to know how deeply this religious revival penetrated into parochial England, but the monks who became bishops tried to raise the standards of the parish priests, emphasizing the celibacy of the clergy and the need to repress drunkenness and concubinage.

There were thus by the early eleventh century positive signs of a religious renaissance in the western Church, mainly monastic in its inception, and patchy in its covering. For its effectiveness it largely depended on the support and patronage of the godly prince. In Britain its culmination was to be the coronation at Bath on Whit Sunday 973 of the West Saxon king Edgar by Archbishop Dunstan as the overlord of all Britain. Eleven years earlier the Pope John XII had crowned the German king, Otto I, as emperor, so inaugurating the Holy Roman Empire which was to last until 1806. In their treatment of the Church the German emperors inherited the mantle of Charlemagne.

THE PAPACY IN DECLINE

If the reformed monastic orders gave the lead, the papacy had by this time undoubtedly sunk to a very low ebb. In theory papal power had actually ballooned after the Pope crowned Charlemagne in 800; forged documents, usually known as the Pseudo-Isidorian Decretals, were circulating in western Europe asserting the superiority of the spiritual to the temporal power. Pope Nicholas I declared that as the Pope was God's representative on earth he had authority over the whole Church. Princes were not entitled to interfere in Church matters but the Pope had a moral right to guide the secular power as well as to have its support and protection.

But this was an unusual flurry of activity as the papal see became more and more the victim of competing Roman families. Popes were made and unmade at the bidding of the papal treasurer Theophylact and his ambitious wife Theodora. Pope Sergius III's affair with the couple's equally determined daughter, the fifteen-year-old Marozia, resulted in the birth of a future Pope John XI. When Marozia fell from power in 932, the popes continued to be nominated by her son Alberic II, prince of Rome, who ruled the city from 932 to 954. The Roman court became the scene of faction fighting and even violence; both Leo V and his rival the anti-Pope Constantine were imprisoned and executed, John X was suffocated by a pillow, Stephen VIII died of his injuries in prison and Benedict VI was strangled by orders of his successor. John XII, the bastard son of Alberic II, was made Pope at the age of eighteen. His private life was reputedly so scandalous that gossips described the Lateran palace as a brothel. Fearful of criticism, John XII sought the help of the German king Otto I, bestowing the imperial crown on him in St Peter's on 2 February 962, so renovating the empire. In return Otto confirmed the donations of Pepin and

Charlemagne, extending still further the domains of the papal state, but the friendship between the Pope and the new emperor was short-lived. Otto summoned the Pope to answer for his misbehaviour and deprived him of his office. John refused to accept the sentence, re-established himself in the city by force of arms, only to die, still in his early twenties, with, so gossip asserted, a married woman in his arms.

In practice the restoration of the Roman Empire in the west had reinforced the political inferiority of the papacy. The emperor by reason of his divinely given authority had responsibility for the Church as well as the empire. At the end of the tenth century a remarkable understanding was reached briefly in the pontificate of Sylvester II, who as the scholar and teacher of dialectic Gerbert of Reims had been the tutor of the future emperor Otto III. Otto III had an almost mystical vision of his theocratic responsibilities; he was depicted in a gospel book from Aachen as an incarnation of Christ in majesty. The extraordinary partnership of Pope and emperor brought about the organization of the recently Christianized Churches of Poland and Hungary to whose king the Pope despatched a royal crown. Pope Sylvester was a scholar of outstanding brilliance, not merely in literature where he collected manuscripts of classical Latin authors but in mathematics and science, a pioneer in the study of the abacus, celestial globes and even the organ; but he was never popular with the Romans. Otto III was dead of malaria by 1002; Sylvester only survived him a year. The millennial year 1000 which some had believed would coincide with the end of the world and the second coming of Christ had passed uneventfully.

Whatever the emperor may have believed to have been his responsibility for the Church's good, whatever the impact that the monastic revival had made, lay nobles, more especially in Germany, were exploiting the Church more and more for their own ends, appropriating its estates, appointing unsuitable candidates, often close relatives, to high ecclesiastical office which sometimes changed hands for money payment. There was a sinister process of secularization at work.

But no lead came from Rome where the papal office after Sylvester's death became again the prey of local nobles, first the Crescentii and then the counts of Tusculum. The prestige of the papacy perhaps reached its nadir in 1032 with the election of the youthful Benedict IX. Like his predecessor a layman at the time of his election, in character violent and dissolute, the opposition to his rule resulted in the election of two anti-Popes. It was to clear up this unholy mess that the German emperor, Henry III, believing that he had a responsibility to God for the good of the Church, marched into Italy and summoned the three would-be Popes to appear before him at a synod at Sutri near Rome. All three popes were ejected from office, and a German bishop appointed in their stead. It was a critical choice, for the time was ripe for the enemies of abuse to take hold of the papacy and so promote the further reform of the Church.

THE BYZANTINE CHURCH

The inauguration of a period of papal reform more or less coincided with a schismatic break with the Greek Church of the east. On 16 July 1054 the Pope's envoy to Constantinople, Humbert of Silva Candida, placed a papal bull on the altar of the cathedral of Santa Sophia excommunicating the Greek patriarch, Michael Cerularius and his supporters. The patriarch replied in kind. The bulls of excommunication were not to be cancelled until at the initiative of Pope Paul VI and the patriarch Athenagoras they were rescinded on 7 December 1965.

In effect the churches of western and eastern Europe had been drifting apart for some centuries. While the break between Rome and Constantinople was not inevitable, political and cultural as well as linguistic and racial differences, exacerbated by theological disputes, made the parting of the ways likely. No less than the western empire the Byzantine empire had been imperilled by external foes; Goths, Slavs, Avars, Iranians, Muslims, Bulgars and Seljuk Turks seized and occupied imperial territory.

The eastern empire was then steadily contracting, even if it retained its inner integrity. At moments of desperation the Greeks regularly turned for help to God and the saints. When Thessalonica was saved from the Avars, the townspeople gave thanks to their patron St Demetrius for delivering them. The Byzantine ethos remained powerfully, even passionately, Christian in character. In the west there was a virtual diarchy as between the barbarian Germanic kings and the Catholic Church, but in Byzantium Church and State were largely fused, as exemplars of the heavenly city of which the emperor and the patriarch were living representatives. In this society the emperor's role was unique. 'Crowned', as Eusebius of Caesarea wrote, 'in the image of the heavenly kingdom, gazing upwards, he steers and guides humans on earth according to the pattern of his prototype [God].' The emperor was a 'religious' person, depicted on the mosaics of Ravenna as Melchisedech, the priest-king of the Old Testament. At the great feasts he carried the offertory into the sanctuary, normally reserved only for priests, and laid them on the altar. The emperor, under Christ, was the Church's defender, appointing the patriarch of Constantinople (constitutionally from a list of three names presented to him by the holy synod but often by the simple exercise of his own will) and depriving him of his office if needs be, calling and presiding over Church councils. Yet fundamental as was the emperor's role in the Church, his autocracy did not necessarily go unchallenged.

The organic Christian unity of the state was reflected in its religious make-up. Constantinople was a city of fine churches and innumerable monasteries, some three hundred of the latter; 'how stately, how fair, how many monasteries', Fulcher of Chartres wrote of his visit, 'how many palaces . . . how many works of art, marvellous to behold. It would be wearisome to tell of the abundance of all good things; of gold and silver; garments of varied appearance and such sacred relics.' The patriarch, secondary in position to the Pope though often disputing papal jurisdiction, was assisted by a holy synod of bishops within the region of the city. The bishops, more often than not, though not as yet invariably as later became the case, were celibate monks but the parish priests were married men, often employed in some form of secular occupation, though debarred by canon law from becoming innkeepers, bankers, brothel owners or civil servants.

The Byzantine Church was essentially monastic in character, catering for women's vocations as for men's. Each monastery had its own rule and was governed by its abbot, without reference to other houses. The hermit or solitary, a more familiar figure in the east than in the west, living an ascetic life of meditation and prayer, was more highly regarded than the monks living in community. The essential function of both monks and nuns was seen as the pursuit of holiness. Byzantine monasteries may have devoted less time to study, scholarship and education than their western counterparts, but they took seriously the obligation of hospitality and sponsored works of charity, establishing hospitals, orphanages and houses for the poor. Yet the greatest stress was placed on abnegation of the world, as was fully demonstrated by the siting of the monasteries of the Meteora clinging to the perpendicular rocks of the Thessalian mountains or by the extraordinary monastic republic of the Holy Mountain of Athos, founded by St Athanasius the Athonite in 961 where access was forbidden to all females, animals as well as men.

The difference in the religious ethos of western and eastern Christianity as well as of language and race (though there were still in the eighth century Syriac or Greek Popes) must have struck the visitor from the west. Such differences were underlined by disputes over the definition of the faith itself and the claims made by Rome to jurisdiction. The definition of faith agreed at the Council of Chalcedon in 451 had not been generally accepted throughout the empire and the support which the anti-Chalcedonians or Monophysites commanded, especially in Egypt and Syria, was a threat to the unity of the empire, more especially after the Muslim explosion, for the Monophysites had some sympathy for Islam's strongly monotheistic creed.

The emperor believed that it was his duty under God to reconcile the conflicting factions, so restoring unity to the seamless robe of Christ's Church and strengthening his rule within his empire. But such a policy cut constantly across the Pope's concern to protect orthodox doctrine. The emperor Justinian tried to resolve the controversy by condemning the writings of three – dead – critics of Cyril of Alexandria, the champion of orthodoxy: Theodore of Mopsuestia, Theodoret of Cyrrhus and Ibas of Edessa. Justinian's wife had by bribery and intimidation secured the election of a Greek, Vigilius, to the papacy in the hope that he would support her husband's policy. The Pope, however, frightened by the hostile reaction of the western Church to imperial policy, vacillated, was arrested on imperial orders, retracted, was brutally attacked at the altar and then fled to Chalcedon where he was persuaded to ratify the findings of the fifth oecumenical council of Constantinople of 553 which had followed Justinian in condemning the three chapters, the writings of the churchmen suspected of favouring Nestorianism, which Justinian had banned in 542–3. It failed in its purpose to reconcile the Monophysites or to bring peace to the church.

The Church remained bitterly divided. In 638 the emperor Heraclius, fresh from his triumph over the Iranians, wanting to win over the Armenians who were Monophysites and whom he had freed recently from Iranian occupation, made a fresh attempt to reconcile the contending parties. Advised by his patriarch Sergius, he published an edict the *Ekthesis* which declared that while there were two natures in Christ there was only one will. Although Pope Honorius in an unguarded moment approved the formula, his successors vigorously condemned it as a new heresy called Monothelitism.

In a further attempt to pacify the Church Heraclius's successor Constans II published yet another document, the *Typos*, which forbade the discussion of either Monothelite or Dyothelite beliefs and required that teaching should be confined to the decrees of the first five general councils of the Church. His decision infuriated the Pope, Martin I, who held a council at Rome of some hundred western bishops which anathematized Constans's edict. The Byzantine exarch in Italy forthwith bundled the Pope, ill with gout and dysentery, on board ship for Constantinople where he was imprisoned, tried for treason, flogged and condemned to death, a sentence which was commuted to banishment to the Crimea where he eventually died of ill-treatment. Yet Monothelitism had little future and was in practice to be condemned at the sixth general council of Constantinople in 681.

A further cause of stumbling which led to hostile repercussions in the west occurred in 726 when the emperor Leo the Isaurian published an edict declaring all images and icons to be idols and ordered their destruction. This edict was likewise designed to win over the Monophysites (who minimized the human side of Christ's nature), possibly to appease the Muslims, who forbade all pictorial representation of God, and represented the influence which the Paulicians, a sect of Armenian origin with dualistic or Manichaean tendencies, had had on the emperor's upbringing. The issue was a theologically significant one since to refuse to portray Christ with a human body seemed to cast doubts on his humanity.

There was an immediate outcry, both in Constantinople where the patriarch Germanus protested and at Rome, to which Germanus had appealed, where Pope Gregory III condemned the iconoclasts. The popes had no wish to break with the emperor or the eastern Church, but they were forced to condemn iconoclasm. It was this rift with Byzantium which obliged the popes to look for succour to the Frankish king. At the close of the eighth century the empress Irene in collaboration with Tarasius, the new patriarch of Constantinople, reversed her predecessors' policy. The seventh general council, held at Nicaea in 787 which was attended by legates of Pope Hadrian I, decreed the restoration of icons and defined the veneration (but not the adoration or worship) to be paid to images.

The decisions of the second council of Nicaea did not wholly mollify the west, partly because the copy of the decrees sent to Charlemagne had been translated incorrectly and were subsequently condemned by the Frankish bishops, nor could Charlemagne's imperial aspirations be warmly greeted in Byzantium. The conflict was not indeed yet dead even in the eastern Church, for the inconoclasts had supporters, especially among the soldiery. Iconoclastic policy was reintroduced by the emperor Leo V the Armenian, with persecution, deposition and imprisonment of his orthodox opponents, of whom the foremost was the monk, Theodore of Studios. The death of the emperor Theophilus in 842 brought peace to the Church, for on the first Sunday in Lent 843 the patriarch Methodius celebrated the festival of the icons, a day ever since commemorated in the eastern Church as the Feast of Orthodoxy.

Yet if peace had been brought to the Byzantine Church, relations between Rome and Constantinople remained contentious. In 858 the emperor appointed a distinguished civil servant, a layman, Photius, as patriarch in place of the patriarch Ignatius who appealed to Pope Nicholas I. The Pope supported Ignatius, excommunicated Photius and expatiated on the inalienable rights of the bishop of Rome. Photius called a synod to protest at Rome's intervention and in 867 declared that the Pope himself was excommunicate and deposed. The squabble was brought temporarily to a close in 869 when a further council at Constantinople deprived Photius of his office. When in 877 the emperor Basil restored Photius, the Pope lay low; for Ignatius the initial cause of the dispute was now dead. Six years later the emperor Leo VI deposed Photius, who retired to end his days in the convent of Armenteia.

The Photian schism had been fermented by a struggle for jurisdiction over the newly Christianized Church of Bulgaria, jurisdiction over which the Roman Church sought to claim unsuccessfully. In compensation for the loss of Bulgaria Rome managed to secure a hold over Moravia where the brothers Cyril and Methodius, despatched by the Byzantine emperor Michael II, had been given permission to use Old Slavonic in the liturgy. Cyril who had been librarian of the church of Santa Sophia invented the Glagolitic alphabet and so became one of the founders of Slavonic literature. Unwisely on Methodius's death in 885 Pope Stephen V forbade the use of the Slavonic liturgy and sought to Germanize the Moravian Church, with the result that some of Methodius's followers took refuge in Bulgaria. By its narrow policy the Roman Church had lost the opportunity to establish a Slav-speaking Church.

The patriarch Photius had raised doubts about the Roman formula of the creed, alleging that to the Nicene creed the western Church had added the words 'And the Son' to the phrase 'the Holy Ghost who proceeds from the

Father'. This interpolation, which must have seemed to the non-theological layman mere hair-splitting, expressed what the theologians called the Double Procession of the Holy Ghost. And this so-called '*filioque* clause' was one of the main points at issue – the other one was the use of unleavened bread in the Eucharist – which led to Cardinal Humbert's delegation to Constantinople in 1054, and the subsequent schism between the eastern and western Churches which fractured the unity of the Church.

This further major fragmentation of Christian unity, for there were already semi-independent Churches on the periphery of the Byzantine Empire, Syrian, Jacobite, Coptic, Ethiopian, coincided with the burgeoning of a major Christian revival in western Europe, introducing a period of immense brilliance and fertility into almost every aspect of the Christian Church. In spite of a crop which had sowed some tares, the previous half a millennium had borne much fruit. Although Islam continued to send a shiver down Christian spines, there were comparatively few pagan enclaves left. The Church was now fully organized into provinces under metropolitans, bishops and parish priests. Monasteries and nunneries, full of vital life, abounded. Cathedral schools trained the Church's future priests in theology and canon law. Another vast spate of church-building was about to start. A tremendously impressive ecclesiastical structure had come into existence, involving every man and woman, holding them in thrall from birth to death, promising them the hope of heaven and threatening them with the fires of hell. The joys of heaven were reserved for only a few; the mass of mankind was inexorably condemned to the pains of hell, so realistically portrayed in contemporary sculpture and painting.

The medieval world was a believing society. Men and women had no difficulty in accepting a God that ruled the universe, a deity with unlimited powers, bestowing benevolence at his will and punishing the wicked. He appeared as a harsh judge rather than a loving saviour. New converts must understandably have thought of him in terms of the deities whom they had rejected at their baptism. But just as at a royal court there were suppliants for mercy, so at the court of heaven there were intermediaries, his Son Jesus Christ, his mother, the Blessed Virgin and the saints who might intercede on behalf of fallen humanity. Men and women were told that Jesus Christ had come to save the world, but apart from the theologians they can have had little understanding of the bitter debates about the relationship of the Father to the Son which soured the Church politics of the age. For most men and women life was an uphill struggle, for they were the constant prey of temptation, engineered by Satan and his myrmidons. The natural order itself manifested the providence of God and the power of the Devil. Even the very sunbeams were alive with supernatural agencies. The world was full of *miracula signa*, of earthquakes, of shooting stars, of famines and portents which revealed the providential purpose of God.

The church, a physical entity, stone or wood, served by a priest, was at the very centre of human existence. For most men and women the bishop, like the lord, was a remote figure, but the local priest, often of the same kith and kin as the villagers he served, was an everyday figure. While the origins of the parochial system are obscure, by the end of the early Middle Ages all over Europe single priests were serving their small flocks in the churches which more often than not the local lord had built. The priests were supported by the tithes, the church-scot and other fees which their parishioners had to pay. While the layfolk may have grumbled at such exactions, yet they did not doubt that the priest was the mediator between the omnipotent and omniscient God and sinful man.

The Church was thus the chief medium of communication between the supernatural and the natural world. Each church was likely to house the relics of a saint who was the subject of veneration. Such remains did not form merely a material expression of enduring holiness but were a highway to the court of heaven. Princes and prelates were alike enthusiastic collectors of relics. The Frankish king Clovis II who outraged the monks of St Denis by taking the saint's arm for his own oratory became with his wife Balthild the special patron of the shrines at St Denis, Auxerre, Soissons, Sens, Orlèans and Tours 'so it might please them better to pray for the mercy of Christ the highest king of all on behalf of the king and for peace'. The Anglo-Saxon king Athelstan was a compulsive collector of relics. The monks of Lindisfarne, their monastery sacked by the Vikings, took the body of St Cuthbert with them as they wandered in search of a safe refuge. The emperor Otto I acquired the body of St Maurice from Burgundy and took it to Magdeburg so that the soldier saint might assist him in his war against the Slavs. The reliquary of St Faith, still in the monastic church of Conques, accompanied the monks on their progress to their estates.

The Church was the house of God where heaven mingled with earth above all in the sacrifice of the Mass. What happened exactly was to be a cause of theological debate but no one doubted that Christ was really present in the Mass. 'Can any of the faithful doubt', Gregory the Great wrote, 'that at the hour of the sacrifice [of the Mass] the heavens open at the priest's calling, that in this mystery of Jesus Christ the choirs of angels are present, the height joined to the depths, earth linked with heaven, the visible united with the invisible?' At least in great churches and abbeys the ceremonial of the liturgy itself tended to become more elaborate, assisted by the ringing of bells, by the swinging of thuribles of incense, by the smoke of candles, the singing of boys' choirs and by the sound of the organ.

A Venetian priest built an organ at Aachen in 826; in the late tenth century Bishop Ethelwold had organs constructed at Abingdon and Winchester. The priest was the remedial officer of early medieval society, affording comfort by caring for the sick and dying, baptizing, marrying and burying his flock, not merely as a magician but as a servant of God seeking however inadequately to dispense what he knew of the love of Christ through whose sacrifice on the cross men and women had been granted, so he taught, the hope of eternal redemption.

CHAPTER FOUR

The Medieval Church: Renovation and Retroaction

Through the summer and autumn of 1215 bishops and their retainers from all over Europe began to converge on Rome for the general council of the Church summoned by Pope Innocent III.

The council passed decrees which touched every aspect of the Church's life, seeking to regulate the lives of clergy and laity alike. Its members articulated, officially for the first time, the doctrine of transubstantiation which declared that the bread and wine of the Eucharist were miraculously changed into the body and blood of Christ at the moment of consecration in the Mass. They ordered all men and women to confess their sins and receive absolution from the priest before they received communion on Easter Day. They insisted that the election of bishops should be free from secular interference, and they laid down the precise duties which the clergy were obliged to perform. Bishops were told to seek out and to punish heretics and if needs be to hand them over to the secular arm for condign punishment. They decided that measures should be taken to curb the growing influence in society of the Jews, decreeing that the Jews, like Christians, should pay tithes to the clergy and that they should not be employed in any official position. Furthermore the Jews were ordered always to wear a distinguishing badge, either a piece of yellow or red cloth or, as in Italy, a hat of particular colour. In its legislation the Lateran Council, so called because it met in the church of St John Lateran, represented a summation of all that had been achieved by the revival which had been taking place in the Church's life in the course of the previous two centuries.

Within a year the council's begetter, Pope Innocent III, was dead. He had been one of the most completely successful of all the vicars of St Peter whose writ ran from the Irish Sea to the eastern Mediterranean and ranged from Scandinavia to furthest Christian Spain. A skilled canonist and a man of spiritual insight, Innocent had a high and all-embracing view of his office, which he had inherited from previous pontiffs and was to pass on to his successors. 'The Creator of the Universe', he had declared in October 1198, 'set up two great luminaries in the firmament of heaven: the greater light to rule the day, the lesser light to rule the night. In the same way for the firmament of the universal Church, which is spoken of as Heaven, he appointed two great dignities: the greater to bear rule over souls (these being, as it were, days), the lesser to bear rule over our bodies (these being, as it were, nights). These dignities are the pontifical authority and the royal power. Furthermore, the moon derives her light from the sun, and is in truth inferior to the sun in both size and quality, in position as in effect. In the same way the royal power derives its dignity from the pontifical authority: and the more closely it cleaves to the sphere of that authority the less is the light with which it is adorned: the further it is removed, the more it increases in splendour.' That such claims in Innocent's reign should have been actually realized in practice, for he had made the German emperor his ward, obliged the French king to put away the wife he had bigamously married and persuaded John of England to become his vassal, would have been inconceivable two hundred years earlier.

THE REGENERATION OF THE CHURCH

The papacy had seemingly reached its nadir in the tenth century, while in many countries kings and nobles rather than bishops and priests virtually controlled the Church, princes, more especially in Germany, treating churches as their own personal property and appointing their kinsmen to high ecclesiastical office.

And yet in spite of this apparent vacuum in spiritual leadership, there were forces in reserve which properly harnessed and directed could create the conditions for the Church's revival. Papal claims were not merely held in reserve but learned clergy were already hunting in monastic and cathedral archives and libraries for precedents which would strengthen the privileges of the Pope and the clerical order even, as did the clerical authors of the so-called Pseudo-Isidorian Decretals, forging documents to support their claims. There were not merely precedents in papal history recorded in papal registers, which could be invoked which showed the Pope's wide powers of jurisdiction and asserted his capacity to interfere in secular affairs, but the Church had a reservoir of law and tradition with which no secular state could compete. Moreover, inherent in the Church's organization were the means by which such ideas could be successfully implemented, if only circumstances would provide the men and the means. The spiritual artillery was already in existence. What was needed was a fuse to set it alight.

The revival of spiritual life in the monasteries in the tenth and early eleventh centuries, stemming from the Burgundian abbey of Cluny where the monks tried to eliminate the lax observances which had crept into monastic existence by keeping more strictly to the Rule of St Benedict, could be described as such a slow fuse. Simultaneously similar movements stirred the sluggish life of the Church in the Low Countries, Lorraine and Anglo-Saxon England. It was the Cluniac monks who set the pace. Many monasteries came to base their rules of life on Cluny and were bonded into a congregation of houses under Cluny's direction. Cluniac monks, patronized by secular lords impressed by their religious enthusiasm, were appointed to bishoprics. Through the influence of reformed monasticism a spiritual adrenalin began to seep through the Church.

What the incipient religious revival so far lacked was the backing of the rich and powerful laity and a lead from Rome itself. When finally the emperor Henry III held a council at Sutri in 1046 which rid Rome of the three would-be Popes and two years later appointed a German rather than a Roman, a distant kinsman of his own, Bruno, Bishop of Toul, already reputed to be a Church reformer, as Pope Leo IX, the cause of Church reform received a real stimulus. Leo IX immediately entered on a programme of reform, denouncing simoniac bishops who had purchased their offices, and, unlike his immediate predecessors, travelling widely, calling synods of the Church at Rome, Siponto, Salerno, Vercelli, Mantua and Bari, Rheims and Mainz where he promulgated reform decrees, seeking to enforce clerical celibacy and condemning secular interference in the election of bishops. He gathered around himself a notable group of like-minded men, such as Humbert of Moyenmoutier and Archdeacon Hildebrand, already fervently impressed by Cluniac ideas, so transforming the moribund papal curia into a powerhouse for reform.

In one respect Leo IX's pontificate was fatal for the future of the Church, for at the end of his papacy the relations between the eastern and western Churches, already under severe strain, reached breaking point, so creating a major fracture in the unity of the Church. Henceforth there were to be two major Churches in Christendom, the Roman and the Eastern or Greek Orthodox. Yet if the eastern Mediterranean was lost to the Roman Church, the Church in western Europe was in the full flush of a reform movement designed to revitalize its spiritual life, to liberate it from the abuses which had characterized its immediate past and to establish afresh the universal jurisdiction of its spiritual head, the Pope. The regional power structures, local liturgies and law codes were henceforth to be made subject to the papal primacy and to the supervision of a universal Church which was to impose a single ritual, the Mass, and a system of ethics and doctrine of which the clergy were the exclusive guardians and from which men and women could only deviate at peril both to their bodies and their souls.

Under Leo's immediate successors the movement gathered pace. Nicholas II, concerned with preventing the unhealthy influence which the Roman barons had exerted over papal elections, decreed that the Pope should henceforth be chosen by the cardinal bishops with the assent of the Roman clergy and people and the confirmation of the emperor. He banned clerics from obtaining churches from the laity and reinforced decrees forbidding clerical marriage and simony. It was a policy followed by his successor Alexander II, who told people that they must no longer attend Masses celebrated by married priests and forbade the laity from taking a positive part in the investiture ceremony by which bishops took office. Legates were despatched to foreign countries to transmit papal decrees and to hold synods at which they could be promulgated. Alexander's wish to bring the Anglo-Saxon Church more effectively within the papal fold led him to despatch St Peter's banner to Duke William of Normandy when he invaded England in 1066. It was an indication of the universal recognition of the Pope's moral authority that his decrees were so widely accepted, for he had no weapons save spiritual ones to ensure that they were enforced.

Under Alexander's successor, Archdeacon Hildebrand, Pope Gregory VII, the reform movement was to proceed apace. A man of powerful intellect, deep spirituality and inflexible will, arrogant as well as dedicated, he was to voice ideas about the nature of papal power, which had been hitherto only implicit and hinted at rather than definitively proclaimed. Now explicitly articulated, they marked a major revolution in the content of papal claims not merely to spiritual but also to temporal overlordship, receiving a classic formulation in the *Dictatus Papae* which was issued in March 1075. 'The Roman Church', the document declared, 'has never erred and never will err till the end of time.' 'The Roman Church was founded by Christ alone.' 'The Pope can be judged by no one.' 'A duly ordained Pope is undoubtedly made a saint by the merits of St Peter.'

While Gregory's claims were to bring him into conflict with secular princes, his final objective remained essentially spiritual for he had a vision of Christian society, kings, bishops, monks and laymen working in collaboration under the guidance of Christ's representative on earth to fulfil God's will. What, he believed, had so far made this impractical had been the sinister intrusion of lay standards into clerical life, and the resistance of the laity to guidance by the Church. Their neglect of scriptural injunctions brought them within the dominion of Satan, and what was worse, the clergy whom they appointed aided and abetted them.

What Gregory tried to do provoked a storm of protest both in France and Germany, leading to a prolonged, bitter and violent struggle with the emperor, involving a historic if somewhat Pyrrhic victory for the Pope as the emperor supplicated in the snow outside the papal castle of Canossa. Yet, in spite of controversy which led to the installation of a rival as anti-Pope and to his own death in exile, by the sheer force of his personality and the use which he made of loyal and able legates Gregory VII managed to exercise a wide-ranging supervision over the Church, from distant Scandinavia to Poland and Hungary and to Spanish Castile where the king, Alfonso VI, agreed to replace the existing Mozarabic liturgy with the Roman service books. The Hildebrandine revolution, as it has been termed, formed the foundation from which the medieval papacy operated.

While the Pope's claim to universal moral supremacy was not novel, it was stated more explicitly by Gregory and his successors than it had ever been before. In theory they pronounced that the Pope's authority was temporal as well as spiritual, and because the spirituality took precedence over the temporality the Pope had a dominical right to interfere in all moral issues. 'He alone can use the imperial insignia; he can depose emperors; he can absolve subjects from their allegiance; all princes should kiss his feet.' The forged Donation of Constantine, the pretended document by which the first Christian emperor had supposedly handed over the western empire to the Pope, became incorporated in canon law, and until it was shown to be a forgery in the fifteenth century was another weapon in the papal arsenal. But Gregory's claim and that of his successors was based less on Constantine's supposed legacy than on the belief that the Pope was the living successor of St Peter to whom Christ had consigned authority over his Church, and so ultimately over all mankind. 'It is your good pleasure that the Christian people, who have been committed to you, should specially obey me because you have given me your authority.'

The claim to temporal lordship provoked bitter controversy which was never properly stilled and which, in spite of the magisterial achievements of Innocent III, had steadily less and less chance of realization. The Pope's critics insisted that such a claim to temporal dominion was unsubstantiated in history, tradition or scripture. The English king, William I, supported by his archbishop Lanfranc, flatly refused to accept it on the grounds that none of Gregory's predecessors had ever made such an outrageous demand before.

Broadly speaking the situation in England reflected the issues that were at stake. Although William I's archbishop, the scholarly Lanfranc, supported Gregorian reform, seeking, for instance, to promote the celibacy of the clergy, he held to the traditional view that Church and State had their own spheres of influence, and that the Pope had no overriding right to interfere in matters of state. William I's successor, William II, a warrior king, his conscience pricked by the onset of serious illness, who had hitherto treated bishoprics as lay fiefs, eventually appointed a pupil of Lanfranc's, Anselm, as his successor.

An austere and aged Italian monk from Lanfranc's abbey of Bec, an original theologian, Anselm was to be at a loss in the king's court. 'You are', Anselm confessed, 'yoking an untamed bull and a weak old sheep to the same plough.' Quarrels over the homage which new bishops had to pay the king and the receipt of the pallium (the badge of office which had to be sent from Rome) and the archbishop's duties as a royal tenant-in-chief, led Anselm to go into exile on the Continent where he learned more explicitly of the papal condemnation of investiture of bishops by laymen, and so to a more forthright championing of papal claims. When Anselm returned to England, he found William II's successor, Henry I, as adamant in his defence of what he regarded as his royal rights.

Eventually the issue was settled by a compromise, which showed that the claims of the more extreme papalists had little chance of acceptance. If the bishops paid homage for their lay fees, the king would not insist on lay investiture, a settlement not very dissimilar to that reached between the

Pope and the emperor at Worms some fifteen years later. In effect such an agreement showed that the papal claims to universal jurisdiction, if now promoted by the articulation of canon law and administered by an increasingly sophisticated bureaucracy, could only operate effectively if *regnum* and *sacerdotium* worked in cooperation.

The crown remained in firm control of the English Church under Henry I and Stephen though the political chaos of Stephen's reign had provided the English Church with the opportunity for winning a greater degree of autonomy, more especially with respect to its right to make its own elections to bishoprics and abbacies.

When, therefore, Henry II initiated a policy which entailed the elimination of the 'evil habits', including the greater freedom enjoyed by the English Church, that had grown up in the reign of Stephen, he decided that the so-called 'liberties' of the Church had to be delimited. To supervise this policy in 1162 he chose as his archbishop Thomas Becket, for seven years his efficient chancellor, a churchman, though only yet in deacon's orders, who had studied canon law on the Continent and had been a member of the previous archbishop, Theobald's, household. Once made archbishop Becket, a highly intelligent man, egotistically pious, intransigent and unsullied in his private life, became the defender of the Church's liberties which Henry wished him to restrain. In particular Henry objected to the power of Church courts which limited royal jurisdiction over criminous clerks, demanding that if such clerks should be found guilty in an ecclesiastical court, they should be handed over for sentence to the royal courts.

In the Constitutions which the king issued at a royal council at Clarendon he sought to define the limitations on the Church's rights in terms of jurisdiction and appeals to the court of Rome. After some prevarication Becket was ultimately defiant, seeking refuge on the Continent only to return after six years following a superficial reconciliation with the king which left nothing resolved. 'If the customs he [Henry] demands', Becket told the Pope, 'were to prevail, the authority of the apostolic see in England would disappear altogether or be reduced almost to nothing.' In anger at his archbishop's continued defiance Henry is said to have declared 'What a set of idle cowards I keep in my kingdom, who allow me to be mocked so shamefully by a low-born clerk.' Some days later five royal knights slew Becket in his own cathedral.

Henry had not really intended this to be the outcome, and outwardly adopted the role of a penitent, agreeing to withdraw the innovations he had made, though as he told Bishop Bartholomew of Exeter later, in fact he had made no real changes, and in practical terms, albeit criminous clerks continued to be brought before Church courts until the Reformation brought an end to their jurisdiction, the Crown's real control over the English Church remained as great as ever. In the process the English Church indeed acquired a martyr, for Becket had been canonized three years after his murder, and his shrine became a focal point of pilgrimage, donations and prayer. Simultaneously the prestige and authority of the papacy, strengthened by its effective bureaucracy, had certainly been consolidated before the twelfth century ended with the pontificate of Innocent III.

At no time then were the Pope's magisterial claims totally accepted, nor were they ever wholly abandoned. 'We', as Innocent III proclaimed, 'are the successor of the Prince of the Apostles, but we are not the vicar of any man or Apostle, but the vicar of Jesus Christ himself.' Thus while papal claims were often strongly and successfully resisted by secular princes the papacy had then established its moral authority. Although the papacy had as yet no armed forces at its disposal, papal decisions in the western Church possessed universal validity. This was in part because the secular powers were ill-matched, when it came to using intellectual arguments, to combat the Church's claims. Kings claimed to possess an independent spiritual power which God had directly given them to care for his Church; they referred back to the Old Testament description of Melchisedech as a priest-king. But they had no real means to challenge doctrinally the Petrine headship of the Church.

From the tenth century onwards the papal claims had the backing of a relatively new instrument, the compilation of a Church or canon law. It was a code which examined and tried to resolve a host of questions, both moral and procedural, which affected both the laity and the clergy. Simultaneously the papal curia became the most sophisticated bureaucratic administrative centre in Europe, communicating papal decisions on innumerable matters, important and trivial, by a network of agencies, legates, metropolitans, archbishops and bishops. To reaffirm and implement papal policy general councils of the Church were occasionally summoned, some seven in all between 1123 and 1311. As more and more appeals, many dealing with the minutiae of Church business in lands distant from Rome, were presented for decision by the Pope or his advisers, there was a massive explosion of business at the papal court. The Church had become a highly efficient and bureaucratic organization, knitting western Europe into an ideological unity. It may never have achieved its temporal ends but it was the most elaborate power structure in western Europe.

Ideally the Church should have been the seamless robe of Christ, the microcosm on earth of the court of heaven. The reformers were genuinely concerned that it should rid itself of its abuses and recover its pristine role which had been submerged by the laxity of the past. If there was a key word in the reformers' vocabulary it was *justitia*, justice, which ought not merely to inspire the clergy to a proper performance of their task but which should ideally condition the right relationships between men and women in lay society. Justice should dictate kings' relationships with their subjects and lords' with their serfs. It should direct merchants in their dealings with their customers by enforcing a just price for their goods and by banning usury, at least to Christians. It should ensure the sanctity of the marriage law, which was revised and more closely defined, and condemn all that was sexually perverse and unnatural. Obviously the practice was always to fall short of the ideal, but the regeneration of the papacy had elevated the concept of justice as a principle for Christian life.

The revival of the papacy released the floodgates of reform. It introduced an era of improved appointments to high offices in the Church, a thinning out of the worldly prelates and an increase in the number of spiritually minded, dedicated churchmen, of whom the saintly Anselm of Canterbury was to be in some sense the doyen. Church councils set about trying to eliminate the practices of simony and nepotism, and to ban clerical marriage. It may be doubted how far these reforms penetrated down to the lower ranks of the clergy but at least they made possible a run of conscientious and caring parish priests. Time would show the flaws.

THE MONASTIC RESURGENCE

Of all the agencies involved in this Christian renaissance monasticism was probably the most important, both as a preparatory force and as a means by which the ideals of the reformed papacy were to be circulated. In recognition the Popes themselves patronized the monastic orders, often rewarding them by giving them exemption from episcopal authority. In the revival of religion, spiritually and intellectually, the monks were to be the Church's chariots of fire, at least initially. Renascent monasticism was to make an indelible mark on contemporary civilization, not only through the vows of poverty, chastity and obedience which the religious took to underline their commitment to Christ but by the services which monks and nuns performed in the community, in almsgiving and hospitality, in charity and teaching and by the influence which they wielded at the courts of the powerful. Monasteries tended to be built in the remote countryside but they were to be the spiritual flagstaff of the medieval world.

Although the reformed Benedictines of Cluny continued to be a vigorous force in the Church's life, by the early eleventh century there were signs that the inspiration of the older monasticism was beginning to falter. Not merely did the learning of the older orders seem too conservative and old fashioned but to some critics the Cluniac monks laid too much stress on the ceremonial minutiae of the religious services and were too concerned with the ornate decoration of their churches.

Even before the papacy had emerged from its undue hibernation, there had been clear signs of a resurgence of monasticism as men gathered together to follow an eremitic life, living lives of self-sacrifice and self-denial, devoted to solitary prayer and labour but, like the Egyptian monks of earlier centuries, coming together in community to worship. There were the Basilians which a Greek, Nilus of Calabria, had set up at Grottaferrata in the Alban Hills outside Rome which for long followed the Greek rite; the

Camaldolensians instituted by a Cluniac monk, Romuald, who was driven by a desire to copy the austere desert fathers of old; and the Vallombrosans which another former Cluniac, John Gualbert, set up near Florence, to live according to the strictest precepts of the Benedictine rule without even recourse to manual labour. A monastic renaissance was soon in full flood. 'Flocks of adherents,' as Guibert, Abbot of Nogent, who died in 1124, put it, 'men and women, people of all ranks, gathered to join them. . . . In manors and towns, cities and castles, and even in the very woods and fields, there suddenly appeared swarms of monks speeding in every direction, and busily engaged, and places in which had been lairs of wild beasts and caves of robbers became known as the sites of holy men and saintly habitations.'

A German, Bruno, who had been master of the cathedral school at Rheims, founded one of the most impressive of the new orders when in 1084 in the mountain valley of the Chartreuse he built a monastery 'on a high and dreadful cliff', as Guibert of Nogent described it, 'under which there is a deep gorge in a precipitous valley. . . . [The monks] all have their own separate cells round the cloister in which they work, sleep and eat. On Sunday they get their food from the cellarer, that is, bread and beans, the latter, their only kind of relish, being cooked by each in his own cell. . . . They have fish and cheese on Sundays and the chief festivals. . . . Gold, silver, ornaments for the church they get from no one, having none in the place but a silver cup. . . . They hardly ever speak in any place, for when it is necessary to ask for anything, they do so by signs. Their dress is a hair shirt and few other clothes. . . . Although they submit to every kind of privation, they accumulate a very rich library. The less their store of worldly goods, the more do they toil laboriously for that meat which does not perish, but endures for ever.' Of all the medieval monastic orders the Carthusians, as they came to be called, were to remain most loyal to the precepts of their founder.

Perhaps because they were established before the monastic resurgence gathered full force and perhaps because of the high demands they made upon their members the Carthusians were less numerous than the Cistercians, though they too were stimulated by a similar desire to live a life of self-denial. The Cistercians may too have had more skilled leaders than the Carthusians, one of whom was an English monk, Stephen Harding, from Sherborne in Dorset who drew up the *Carta Caritatis* which defined the rule. It provided for there to be a close but flexible relationship between the founding abbey and its daughter houses, which were to be visited annually by the abbot and to meet together in a general chapter held at Cîteaux in the autumn. The Cistercians' houses were thus closely knit together. Even more significantly they had a brilliant propagandist in St Bernard of Clairvaux, a genius of fiery and dynamic spirituality who exercised great influence in both Church and state.

By the time of his death in 1153 there were over 360 Cistercian monasteries, 122 of them in Great Britain, 88 in Italy, 56 in Spain and over

100 in German-speaking lands. With their expansion there had come prosperity. Efficient administration of their monastic property, the successful cultivation of their lands, the rich profits of sheep farming made the Cistercians wealthy which led to an inevitable relaxation of standards of austere living.

A life of self-denial and austerity had been the Cistercians' original objective. A community of hermits dwelling together at Molesme in Burgundy, feeling that they were not living as strictly as they aspired to do, migrated to Cîteaux, a spot situated in the diocese of Chalons 'inaccessible by reason of thickets and thorns and inhabited only by wild beasts'. When the Cistercians founded new houses, they chose remote sites covered with brush, scrub and forest but the monks and the lay-brothers were soon to convert them into fine pastures for sheep.

The Cistercians' rule of life was as strict as that of the Chartreuse. Reacting against the over-elaborate Benedictine churches, their own places of worship were plain and unadorned, without silver or jewelled crosses and ornaments and even void of bell-towers. 'They resolved,' as a contemporary described the Cistercian way of life, 'to establish themselves and to observe the rule of St Benedict, rejecting everything that was contrary to it, such as the use of coats, capes, worsted cloth, hoods, pants, combs, counterpanes and bed-clothes, together with a variety of dishes in the refectory.' Their food was simple, consisting of dishes made from vegetables, fish, flour, eggs and cheese, without meat or lard. Although they did not have to keep perpetual silence, no provision was made for recreation or general conversation as in the Benedictine houses. Detached from the life of the world, they enjoyed a degree of freedom which some of the older orders lacked, for they were not entangled in obligations to provide armed knights for military service and they were largely free of control by the local bishops. To help in the work of land clearance and cultivation, they enrolled lay brothers, *conversi*, who took monastic vows but because of their lack of literacy expressed their vocation in manual labour and administration, often living at separate granges on the monastery's wide estates.

The Augustinians or Austin Canons, so-called because their rule of life was supposedly based on advice given by the Church father St Augustine, had originated as a group of different communities, some, like the Praemonstratensians, severe in type, adhering to a rule of rigid abstinence, and others, like those of the abbey of St Ruf near Avignon, more flexible in their demands. The Austin Canons lived more in the world than the more austere orders for, if as Urban II declared, the older orders were following the example of Mary, the Austin Canons took over the role of Martha. 'The rule of the canons regular', at Barnwell Grange in Cambridgeshire was described 'as the Rule of St Augustine, who drew his brethren to dwell together and tempered the rigour of his rule to their infirmity. Like a kind master, he did not drive his disciples with a rod of iron, and invited those who love the beauty of holiness to the door of salvation under a moderate rule.' The Austin Canons were to contribute positively in a quiet way to the regeneration of religious life, especially in towns where they set up schools and hospitals for the sick, lepers and pregnant women.

By the late twelfth and early thirteenth centuries conventional monasticism, if still probably the most powerful single religious force in the Church, appeared to be responding less successfully to the needs of contemporary society. The monks' spiritual enthusiasm became more dilute as the monasteries, partly as a result of the generous benefactions from their patrons who desired their prayers, acquired great estates. What was a vocation tended to become a profession. The scholarship the monks practised stood on old, tried ways and they were often suspicious of the new theology that was investing the Church. In the manner they governed their properties and treated their dependants they differed ultimately little from the secular lords. They still indeed fulfilled their duties of almsgiving, hospitality and caring for the sick, but in other respects their outlook often appeared simply as a religious expression of the oppressive secular society in which they lived.

The founding of the friars was not primarily a reaction to the decline of the older orders, but an expression of the deep reservoir of religion in contemporary clerical and lay society. Francis of Assisi was above all a simple-minded enthusiast who had been caught by the flame of the gospel message and who from the time of his conversion burned with a consuming fire. 'As ye go, preach, saying, The Kingdom of Heaven is at hand. Heal the sick, cleanse the lepers, raise the dead, cast out devils. Freely ye have received, freely give. Provide neither gold nor silver, neither scrip for your journey, neither two coats, neither shoes nor yet staves.' For eighteen years until his death in 1226 Francis tried to put Christ's commands literally into practice. He gave his goods to the poor, laboured with his own hands and lived on alms. The Church at first reacted hesitantly to such simple enthusiasm which contrasted starkly with the opulence of some of its pastors. Only reluctantly the Pope agreed in 1217 to approve a simple rule of life for the friars and later he was to declare that Francis's testament was invalid. Yet the friars were to provide the new life-blood for the Church.

There were many orders of friars, Augustinians, Trinitarians and so forth, but after the Franciscans the Dominicans were to prove the most influential. St Dominic was concerned to convert the critics of the Church, more especially the heretical Cathars in the south of France, by preaching the gospel and by following its precepts in their own lives.

The friars who soon spread into every European country represented a new force in Christian society. Unlike the monks who lived often in houses remote from large cities, the friars preferred to operate in towns, regularly living in their more squalid suburbs. At first, following Francis's example, they embraced poverty absolutely, divesting themselves of their material possessions, living on alms and devoting their lives to preaching the gospel, sometimes in churchyards and the open air rather than in the churches. Their churches, like those of the Cistercians, were plain buildings free of decoration but they were as much preaching houses as places for the celebration of the Mass. 'One comfort I found,' Jacques de Vitry wrote in 1216, 'many people of both sexes – rich people of the world – having left all for Christ, were fleeing from the world, who were called friars minor. . . . These people gave no heed to temporal things but with fervent desire and impetuous energy labour every day to withdraw perishing souls from the vanities of the world and lead them with them. . . . They live after the model of the primitive church. . . . They receive nothing, but live by the work of their hands.'

Both monks and friars contributed positively to the fabric of Christian civilization in the Middle Ages. Although the monks lived supposedly cloistered lives in enclosed monasteries, their habits, the Benedictines in black, the Cistercians in white, made them a familiar sight in town and countryside. They were the servants of the sanctuary who had dedicated their lives to God, giving up all worldly goods, ambitions and desires for a life of stern self-abnegation and self-sacrifice. Their fine churches were powerhouses of prayer working not merely on behalf of their own salvation but for sinful humanity. No wonder when they fell from grace they evoked stern criticism.

But their scope was never confined to religion pure and simple. Many monasteries became fountains of scholarship and learning; some monks were highly respected eminent theologians, others were chroniclers of the history of their houses and their countries. Monks were employed as copyists and in the illumination of manuscripts, a labour which more than anything else occupied the highest proportion of their working hours. They built up extensive libraries; by 1170 Christ Church, Canterbury, had at least six hundred books. Some ran schools, mainly for the instruction of boys in the cloister who were to become monks. They established hospitals and cared for the sick. Monasteries were for long the only places where medicine, albeit of a traditional kind, was studied; the larger foundations had a resident physician. They took care of the poor and indigent. The English *Regularis Concordia* of the late eleventh century laid down that each monastery should provide accommodation for a certain number of poor and as a gesture of their obligation the monks and the abbot were to take their turn in washing the feet of three such pensioners; at Evesham the abbot provided for thirteen poor men daily. Men, women and children fleeing from the scourge of war and famine found a refuge within their walls. They gave hospitality to travellers, sometimes kings and nobles, but also to more ordinary kinsfolk, and to the pilgrims who came to pray before the relics of the saints in their care. To many the monastic ideal, seeming to enshrine the *exemplum Christi*, was a potent ingredient in the revival of religion and if in time the monasteries became rich and lax, the original flame was never entirely extinguished.

The friars added a new category to the monastic ideal, and were to form a leaven in the Church which the Church might well have rejected had not Popes Innocent III and Gregory IX with intuitive genius realized that the friars were likely to be faithful servants of the papacy. Although the stricter friars were to fall out with the Popes over the doctrine of absolute poverty to which they strongly adhered, and which the Pope was eventually to condemn as heretical, the friars were in general to prove loyal supporters of the papacy. They were even more importantly an evangelical force reconciling the laity to the Church through the medium of their popular preaching, and their care for the sick and poor. But they were also to penetrate to royal courts, often acting as confessors to kings, so winning royal patronage. Moreover in the burgeoning intellectual movement of the mid-thirteenth century both the Dominicans who from the start appreciated learning as a tool in the task of evangelization and the Franciscans, who like their founder had at first rejected intellectual work, were to play a very prominent role in the scholastic revolution.

DEVELOPMENTS IN CHRISTIAN THOUGHT

The revival of Christian scholarship was a major ingredient in the Christian renaissance, an indirect sequel both to the restoration of papal power and the Church's interest in and support for higher education so essential for the training of its future teachers. The scholarship of the so-called Carolingian Renaissance had been largely static and that which had been harbingered by the tenth-century reformers in Anglo-Saxon England lacked sophistication or, except in manuscript illumination or in translations into the vernacular, any real originality.

Yet the tools for a regeneration of learning were already at hand, in the monastic libraries which housed patristic texts and even volumes of classical antiquity. Cathedral schools, the earlier homes of higher education, were to be supplemented by universities. Scholarship in the shape of Christian theology and philosophy was no longer to be merely an appendage to faith but an integral part of it, providing a rationale for belief. Whereas in the past learning had depended on authoritative texts which were accepted without question criticism henceforth became a part of higher education, so long, however, as it did not question the basic truths of Christian teaching. 'Dialectic', wrote Lanfranc, the scholarly archbishop of Canterbury whose monastic school at Bec was the most highly reputed in northern Europe, 'is no enemy of the mysteries of God, rather it confirms them.' 'That which we hold by faith,' his successor as archbishop the monk Anselm declared, 'can be proved by formal arguments.'

The more conservative theologians were made uneasy by the stress that was being placed on dialectic, but the application of logic to theology within the framework of orthodox doctrine which itself remained ultimately unquestioned threw up a richly diverse literature which aimed to a greater or lesser degree to close the gap between faith and reason. There were those like Manegold of Lautenbach and Bernard of Clairvaux who believed that the gap was unbridgeable, and that faith was the only valid ground for religious belief, arguing that since God was an ineffable, omnipotent being without limits, he was beyond the powers of investigation by the human mind. 'He involves', as Senatus, the prior of Worcester said scathingly of one modern critic, 'the ineffable secret of the Deity by subtle objections that scarcely a word can be said about God that does not require someone to explain it.'

Yet in the heady intellectual atmosphere of the cathedral schools and the youthful universities of Paris and Oxford scholars made some attempt to rationalize the mysteries of the Christian faith, believing that by so doing they would ultimately strengthen faith rather than weaken it. In the vanguard was its stormy petrel, Abailard, teacher, monk and lover, who endeavoured to place the 'buttresses of reason' upon the 'foundation of authority'. In his *Sic et Non* Abailard set some 385 supposedly opposed texts from the Scriptures and the patristic writings side by side in the hope that their meaning might be reconciled, for 'by doubting we come to questioning, and by questioning we come to the truth'.

The vitality of Christian thought in the thirteenth century was to be further demonstrated by the rediscovery of the lost works of the ancient Greek philosopher Aristotle, which had been preserved in the libraries of Byzantium, Syria, Sicily and Spain. Aristotelian ideas, with their stress on the evolving and organic nature of being, seemed to these early medieval scholars providential precursors to Christian philosophy. Regarded with suspicion by the more conservative thinkers, and actually condemned by a Church council in 1210, Aristotle's works were studied with growing appreciation by thinking men. A few scholars (deeply influenced by the Spanish Arabic Averroes), more particularly Boethius of Dacia and his colleague Siger of Brabant, absorbed so much of Aristotelian materialistic philosophy that they fell into heresy. More moderate Christian writers, however, aware of the dangers implicit in assimilating Aristotelianism lock, stock and barrel, sought to reconcile Aristotle's naturalistic philosophy with the Christian's revealed faith.

This was more especially the task which two exceptionally learned Dominican friars, Albertus Magnus, later bishop of Ratisbon, and his pupil Thomas Aquinas set themselves. In a series of massive compilations, of which the *Summa Theologica* was the crown, Aquinas attempted to reconcile the revealed truths of the Christian faith with Aristotle's theory of being. The marriage was in some sense an unequal one, for Aquinas qualified his findings by stating that faith was still necessary to complete what nature had initiated, as he made plain in a famous phrase, '*Gratia non tollit sed perfecit naturam*'. Yet he had made the novel assertion that the worlds of nature and or faith were complementary rather than antithetical. Aquinas was criticized in his own time, and even more vigorously and penetratingly within half a century after his death by the so-called nominalist school of philosophers represented by Duns Scotus and William of Occam, both Franciscans.

The reform of the papacy and the universal influence that it was exercising, the religious zeal of the monks and friars, the revival of learning which was flooding through the early universities had released a tremendous surge of energy in the Church. It found everywhere a physical as well as a personal expression: in thousands of parish churches, in the great Gothic abbeys and cathedrals, so soaring in height and so full of light, in the brilliance of medieval illumination and bindings of immutable beauty, in painting and sculpture which were themselves given a more naturalistic and humane touch by the new insights into theology, and in the marvellous array of crosses, censers, copes, and the like, all exquisite examples of craftsmanship inspired by faith. It had too an undoubted social expression which suffused lay society in town and countryside. The Church, the wealthiest of institutions in medieval Europe, did not stand for social equality, indeed forcefully upheld the notion of hierarchy and established order, but it believed strongly that there was a just order of persons as of things any disturbance of which had to be attributed to the powers of evil. It sponsored the notion of just governance, denouncing tyranny (and even justifying the removal of the tyrant), and supported the concept of a just market price. In some sense the Church was effectively the only career open to talents at this time, so that the peasant's son who became a priest reached a social status higher than that of his forebears and put even a bishop's mitre or a cardinal's red hat within his grasp.

A resurgent Christianity filtered through all classes, even if it drew its practitioners from a small body of élite men and women. For the life of interior devotion was then, as it must always be, a speciality of the few, though for those who managed to practise it, it resulted in works of classical spirituality. It found expression in the vocations of innumerable hermits and mystics, monks and nuns, of the nun Hildegarde of Bingen, the Dominican Meister Eckhart, the English mystics Richard Rolle, Walter Hilton and Julian of Norwich, all of whom sought to penetrate the veil of darkness screening man from his maker by ascending the ladder or scale of perfection. The 'sharp dart of longing love' smote the deep 'cloud of unknowing'. Perhaps no age had such an abiding sense of God's love and the court of heaven by which man's providential destiny was shaped.

This encomium to medieval Christianity may, however, sit uneasily in the actual context of medieval society, where life was brief and often cruel, famine and disease frequent, poverty and suffering widespread. Then religious belief seemed threaded more by fear than love. Not surprisingly the achievements of the Church nearly always fell short of its ideals and aspirations, the cross fell too often under the shadow of the sword. Papal claims to universal sovereignty at first sight appeared to meet with an astonishing measure of success, but they were to bring their own nemesis.

What more dramatic episodes can there be than the sight of the German emperor Henry IV standing a suppliant in the snow before Pope Gregory VII at the castle of Canossa, or of the English king Henry II baring his naked back to receive a token beating from the monks at Canterbury as a penance for the murder of Thomas Becket? Fundamentally there was much that was hollow and unreal about such triumphs. Papal success was always qualified and became increasingly so. Neither the Norman English kings nor the German emperors in practice really committed themselves to the overlordship which the Pope demanded, and as the laity increased in wealth and influence, so the political claims of the Church became more hypothetical.

THE BUREAUCRATIZATION OF THE PAPACY

Although later medieval Popes, such as Boniface VIII in his bulls *Ausculta Fili* (1301) and *Unam Sanctam* (1302), continued to make theoretically unlimited assertion of their spiritual and even temporal authority, the gap between what was claimed and what was achieved grew steadily wider. Secular sovereigns who believed that God had equally conferred authority on them exercised increasing supervision over the churches in their own lands, virtually nominating bishops, curbing the visits of papal legates to their countries and in other ways exercising an authority under God which was not effectively answerable to God's vicar.

It was not therefore surprising that the Pope himself came more and more to have the attributes and trappings of a secular prince, both as the ruler of the papal state and through his interference in politics, disguised as matters of religious moment. His long conflict with the emperor had been waged not merely by threats of excommunication but by calls to friendly-disposed princes to assist him by force of arms. The Pope's claim to feudal suzerainty over Sicily had led to a violent struggle with the French Angevin princes who had acquired the island. By the mid-thirteenth century a papal army was itself being recruited to defend the papal territory; and warfare became a method for sustaining papal policy.

Boniface VIII was the last of the great medieval Popes who pushed the claims of the *plenitudo potestatis* to the utmost and as a result was involved in a bitter struggle with the French king, Philip IV, and died ignominiously as his captive at Anagni. Two years later a French archbishop, though technically a subject of the English king, Edward I, since he was archbishop of Bordeaux, became Clement V, an event which led to the removal of the papal see from Rome to the papal enclave of Avignon where it remained until 1370. The Avignonese Popes did not lack a high conception of the duties of their office. They tried, for instance, to act as mediators in the bloody wars between France and England. They even sponsored a mission to China; but the prestige of the papacy suffered, more especially as the end of the Avignonese papacy was followed by a division in the Church known as the Great Schism when two and even at one time three Popes claimed to be the true successor of St Peter.

It was less, however, the warlike stance of the papacy or its inner divisions which seemed to bring into question the Pope's office as the vicar of Christ as much as the papacy's very efficiency as an institution. There had been such an implosion of business at the papal curia that as a result the apostolic mission of the Church was sometimes lost to view, buried in the complexities of an increasingly elaborate bureaucratic machine. 'See', St Bernard had written to the Pope as early as 1150, 'where all this damnable business is leading you! You are wasting your time! I will speak to you as Jethro spoke to Moses and say, "What is this thing you are doing to the people? Why did you sit from morning to evening listening to litigants? What fruit is there in these things? They can only create cobwebs."' More and more the central offices of the Church were enmeshed in an intricate tangle of documents, bulls, dispensations, decrees and arbitrations. The Pope was not merely inundated with requests to bestow his patronage on a vast army of supplicants from every country but the papal curia had become a court of first instance which had to adjudicate in an unceasing series of disputes. Business so multiplied that the papal bureaucracy seemed in danger of suffocation and the spirit was subordinated to the letter of the law.

Under the Avignonese Popes the situation worsened as authority became more and more centralized. It had always been recognized that the Pope had the right to confirm appointments to bishoprics but now the Pope as universal ordinary of the Church claimed for himself the final authority, though he kept it in reserve rather than put it into practice, of making appointments to all bishoprics and benefices in the Church, a claim much resented by kings and private patrons.

Simultaneously there was some decline in the Pope's moral authority. His weapons for securing compliance with his edicts, apart from purely spiritual matters where his authority was less likely to be challenged, became increasingly ineffective and even immoral. He could use his power to excommunicate his opponents but over-indulgence in excommunication robbed the instrument of its spiritual terror. He could issue, as Alexander III did on Scotland for expelling a bishop of St Andrews and as Innocent III did on England under King John in 1208, an interdict which virtually banned the faithful from participation in the sacraments and privileges of the Church, but such spiritual weaponry was increasingly treated with disdain.

The ever more frequent use which the Pope made of the system of indulgences, which, properly handled, could have had a positive usefulness, alleviating the harsh system of penance, led to a devaluation of the indulgence as a form of spiritual currency. When, in 1095, Pope Urban II preached the First Crusade, he had undertaken to bestow a plenary indulgence on all who took part, promising that a crusader who died in a state of penitence for his earthly sins would be received into heaven immediately. Innocent III extended the system, offering indulgences to all those who helped the crusade with money or advice. The indulgence became a familiar aspect of Christian life; remission of sins was promised to an increasing number of people in return for payments, or visits to holy places or churches. It was justified on the ground that, as Pope Clement VI argued in a famous bull, Christ had made available by his sacrifice for sin on the cross a treasury of merit on which the Pope as his vicar was able to draw on behalf of the faithful. 'One drop of Christ's blood', so the bull declared, 'would have sufficed for the redemption of the whole human race. Out of the abundant superfluity of Christ's sacrifice there has come a treasure which is not to be hidden in a napkin or buried in a field, but to be used. This treasure has been committed by God to his vicars on earth, to St Peter and his successors, to be used for the full or partial remission of the temporal punishment of the sins of the faithful who have repented and confessed.' The indulgence came later to be applied on behalf of the dead supposedly to release them from the pains of purgatory. In theory the doctrine of indulgences was hedged about with theological qualifications, for to be effective it required confession and contrition, and it could not remove guilt. However, in the popular mind, it was a simplistic method of blotting out past sin.

THE CRUSADES

The indulgence system was a product of the crusade, the holy war designed in the first instance for the recovery of Jerusalem and the holy places from their Muslim occupiers, but later used by kings and Popes to justify armed war against their enemies whether infidels, heretics or even political opponents. The occupation of the holy places had long been a reproach to the Christian Church, felt the more bitterly in the more aggressive thrust of Christianity in the late eleventh century, more especially after the Byzantine Christians lost their Asiatic territory after the battle of Manzikert in 1071. Pope Urban II stirred the imagination of princes and people alike by summoning them at the Council of Clermont in 1095 to take up the cross to liberate the Holy Land from Islam. Princes and nobles were moved by the prospect of a war which not merely gave the promise of loot and adventure but of spiritual reward. The crusading army captured Jerusalem, set up a Christian feudal kingdom and restored papal control over the holy places, for a Latin patriarch was enthroned in Jerusalem. The papacy, well served by the diversion of Norman warriors from potential attack on papal territory in southern Italy, agreed that the crusaders should keep the lands that they had conquered by the force of arms.

Subsequent crusades were motivated by a similar mixture of the sacred and profane. After the Turks captured Edessa in 1144 St Bernard preached a crusade with fervent enthusiasm, but it turned out to be a catastrophic blunder, nor was the Third Crusade led by the emperor, the French and English kings and designed to halt the rapid erosion of the kingdom of Jerusalem, really anymore successful. Indeed, by the end of the twelfth century the Muslims had retaken the Holy Land. Characteristically, Innocent III conceived of a crusade for its recovery but his plans went awry as the Venetians diverted the fleet to an attack on the Christian Greek empire of Constantinople. The crusaders sacked the imperial city and restored the domination of the Roman Church, not indeed in Jerusalem but in the capital of eastern orthodoxy. While the Pope disapproved of the method, yet there was some satisfaction to be found in the renewed control of the Roman Church in the eastern Mediterranean.

This infamous crusade of 1204 was not the last. For the next two hundred years or more Pope after Pope tried to persuade western rulers to sponsor expeditions against Islam. Some armies did set out with the papal blessing, but such success as they achieved was ephemeral.

The crusading ideal was founded on religious assumptions but it became easily perverted to secular ends. The so-called crusading orders showed how ambivalent it could be. The Knights Hospitallers had been founded to care for the sick but they became involved in active warfare. It was not a far cry from the defence of pilgrims to sorties against the enemy. A similar duality was a feature of the Knights Templar, founded in 1118. They too took religious vows but their principal object became the defence of Jerusalem and the Holy Land where the ruins of their castles, serving equally as monasteries and barracks, still survive. Their great wealth aroused the cupidity of princes, among them Philip IV of France who, with the connivance of Clement V, brought their suppression in 1312 after a series of dubious charges including necromancy and homosexuality had been brought against them. A third crusading order, the Teutonic Knights, originating in a tent hospital set up by German pilgrims before Acre in 1189, also combined care of the sick with warfare, for they were to be particularly active in conquering parts of Baltic and Russian lands and so coercing the pagan inhabitants to embrace the Christian faith.

The Church saw the conversion of the heathen and non-believer to the Christian faith as part of its divine task; but persuasion was often supplanted by coercion. In 1088 an archbishop of Toledo was told 'by word and example to convert with God's grace the infidels to the faith'. In 1218 St Francis had taken a mission to the Egyptian sultan, and in the fourteenth century groups of friars penetrated the Mongol empire of China. Yet, by and large, the Church regarded Islam as a creation of Satan and a threat to the integrity of the Christian faith which had to be destroyed, by force if necessary. While Pope Innocent IV certainly declared that the coercive conversion of Muslims could not be justified, he qualified this by stating that force could be legitimately used to ensure that the gospel could be preached in Islamic territory. A later Pope Clement V said that the existence of Muslims in Christian lands was an 'insult to the Creator'. In 1492 the Spanish sovereigns were to conquer the last Islamic kingdom in Spain, the emirate of Granada, with appalling consequences for its Moorish inhabitants. In its exclusivity the Christian Church had no place outside its well-defined frontiers for dissenters, whether Muslims, Jews, heretics or sceptics.

To justify the use of force in general, the Church had developed the concept of a 'just war', which continues to govern the Church's attitude to armed conflicts. Some Christians felt qualms about the Church's participation in warfare. The Church laid down that those who took part in war were liable to lengthy penances and in an attempt to limit the ravages of warfare it tried to forbid fighting at weekends or during the seasons of Lent and Advent, but such efforts had proved impracticable and unavailing. The Church, if sometimes with reluctance, justified final recourse to the sword to save, as it would have argued, the cross, and it was to continue, whether Catholic or Protestant, to do so.

The crusades which were a good illustration of the so-called just war had brought the Roman Church face to face with the Greek Orthodox Church with which it had parted company in 1054. The temporary restoration of the authority of Rome in some parts of the eastern Mediterranean as a result of the establishment of the Latin kingdom of Jerusalem and later the foundation of the Latin empire of Constantinople had come to an end by the middle of the thirteenth century. But the Greek Church itself was confronted with ever greater danger as the Ottoman Turks advanced into the fast-contracting Byzantine Empire. Placed between the infidel in the shape of Islam and the schismatic in the shape of Rome, in his extremity the Byzantine emperor, John VIII Palaelogus (in the hope that western Europe might help him defeat the Turk), sent out feelers for a reunion of the Churches. As a result representatives of the Roman and Greek Orthodox Churches met in council first at Florence and then at Ferrara in 1438–9. Although the Byzantines actually accepted the intransigent terms which the Roman Church presented as the price of reunion, reunion was soon to prove a dead letter, rejected by the non-Byzantine Greek Churches and in spite of its personal implementation by the Byzantine emperor it was highly unpopular with the populace of Constantinople. The union was formally proclaimed in the church of Santa Sophia on 12 December 1452. Less than six months later Constantinople fell to the Ottoman Turks. The Greek Church survived on sufferance as a subject of the Muslim sultan.

MONASTICISM IN THE LATER MIDDLE AGES

If the medieval papacy had through historical circumstances succumbed in part to secular trends, so too the monastic orders had in part lost some of the high idealism which had formed the dynamic of the monastic revival.

There continued to be many houses where prayer, hospitality and study threaded daily life, but there was a certain dour quality about later medieval monasticism. Benedictine houses, its old stately oaks, continued to represent earlier tradition both in the elaborate ceremonial of their daily worship and in their continued pursuit of learning, conservative in character as this tended to be. Many great houses seemed in practice similar in their ethos to large business enterprises; they were administered by capable monastic officials, the obedientiaries; domestic and manual labour was more and more supplied by paid servants; and the abbeys, like all business concerns, were liable at least to liquidity crises. By and large the number of monks was declining, indicating some diminution in the number of monastic vocations, while their standard of living became increasingly bereft of its original austerity. Yet if individual houses from time to time experienced economic crises, many monasteries were immensely wealthy. Their mitred abbots lived in some state, and were treated as princes of the Church.

Of the new orders the Cistercians had paid the penalty of success, for failing at first to indulge in lavish building and expenditure in which other monasteries were involved, they had reinvested their profits more especially from sheep farming in land. With wealth there had come inevitably a relaxation in their adherence to the simplicity of the *Carta Caritatis*. It would be easy, as at all times in the history of the Church, to point a finger at squalid scandals and salacious gossip to which human frailty always gives rise, but late medieval monasticism was afflicted less by corruption than by tedium and formality, perhaps more especially by the psychological disease known to medievals as 'acedia'. Monks entered monasteries less as a result of any deep vocation than to embark upon a profession which would provide a reasonably comfortable and rewarding life. Nuns, often refugees from the marriage market or non-starters in it, found some degree of satisfaction in living in what seemed more often to have been like a relatively comfortable boarding house than an ascetic religious community.

Even the friars experienced a decline from the high standards of earlier days. Less enriched by endowments than the older monasteries they kept to some degree of austerity in their houses which, by comparison with those of the older orders, were only moderate in size. But 'brother' and 'sister' poverty had been thrust out of the door or at least confined to the doorstep, for eventually after a long and bitter conflict between those who sought to keep, as they thought, the letter of St Francis's rule, the Spiritual Franciscans, and their critics who managed to persuade the Pope that if the Pope acted as the trustee for their properties, no objection could be made, Pope John XXII declared absolute poverty to be a heresy and its proponents heretics. The friars brought some contempt upon themselves by the devices they invented to gather money without in effect actually touching the coins; and the life-style of some led to accusations of hypocrisy. There were still flashes of vitality, for there were those like the Observants instituted in Italy in 1368 who sought to remain loyal to the more austere standards of the past. The provincial of the friars of the Strict Observance, Bernardino of Siena, held congregations spellbound by his eloquence, not unlike that of St Paul as Pope Pius II commented, preaching a gospel of moral regeneration. Nonetheless two centuries after St Francis's death both Franciscans and Dominicans seemed pale shadows of their earlier progenitors.

DEVELOPMENTS IN SCHOLASTICISM

The religious orders were still in the forefront of intellectual endeavour sponsoring houses for their own members at the universities. Yet Christian scholarship too had undergone a series of major changes since Aquinas had penned his magisterial volumes, seeking to synthesize all knowledge into a unity. In reaction to Aquinas's philosophy of realism, modernism in the shape of what was called nominalism came more and more to dominate university teaching. Where Aquinas and those who followed him had sought to weld reason and faith in an indissoluble unity, in their different ways Duns Scotus and William of Occam, both Franciscan friars, questioning his findings, concluded that reason could not demonstrate effectively the truths of faith which depend on the revealed will of God, and the dogmatic teaching of the Church which the individual must accept in faith. In highly sophisticated arguments which only a small intellectual élite could properly understand, the nominalists insisted that human knowledge of the divine is demonstratively limited.

The modernists had in fact driven a wedge intellectually speaking into the bulkhead of traditional faith. Nominalist philosophy could act as acid on the theological convictions of earlier ages. Late scholastic philosophy was in so many respects complex and arid, but there were Christian thinkers who wished to return to the simpler formulas which they assumed to be features of apostolic Christianity. Some turned to the *devotio moderna* which in its emphasis on scriptural teaching formed the life-line which was to link late medieval Catholicism to early Protestantism and the Catholic reform movement.

MEDIEVAL HERESY

Although the Church appeared a monolithic structure outside which there was no salvation its teaching had never gone completely unquestioned. Indeed what the Church calls heresy has been an endemic feature of Christianity and may well be regarded as a testimony to the vigour and vitality of the Christian faith rather than as a destructive and hostile force. Yet because of the sanctions which the Church as a monolithic power structure had at its disposal, fear of imprisonment, even torture and death together with the ultimate threat of hell fire, the doubter and the sceptic for the most part lay low. There were intellectual stalwarts who were to criticize its conventional teaching. Such a one was the eleventh-century Frenchman Berengar of Tours who questioned whether it was possible to assert, as the advocates of transubstantiation, including Archbishop Lanfranc, were doing, that any material change took place in the elements of the Mass at the consecration. Berengar was excommunicated and he eventually recanted. In the Church's view the heretic was not only endangering his own soul but because of his intransigence was in peril of infecting the whole community. His crime was worse than that of murder, and if he failed to see the evil of his ways then death was the only acceptable solution.

Heresy had roots in the social context of a Church which seemed to some to have departed from the apostolic teaching of the gospel, which was too permeated by materialism, was too wealthy, worldly and authoritarian. All heretical movements wished to return to what they usually incorrectly assumed to be pristine Christianity, of which the existing Church was the antithesis.

The first major medieval heresy, that of the Cathars or Albigensians, which flourished for some time in the south of France, had most of these ingredients. It had a strong following among the peasantry who resented the wealth of the Church and its oppressive demands. It had strong support too from some of the Provençal nobility, as greedy for Church property as for the message of the gospel, and intent on defending their autonomy against the armies of the orthodox French king. The Cathars formed their own Church, with their own ministers and sacraments, seeming to their enemies to be a satanic parody of the true Church. Dualistic in their theology, they aimed to liberate that which was truly spiritual from its material embodiment by ascetic living and by abstaining from sex and sensuality. They criticized transubstantiation. 'They believe that Christ's body and blood is in no way created by the [priest's] consecration and that it cannot be received by us in communion', but they had their own sacraments. That 'which the chaplains elevate in the Mass', a Cathar heretic caustically told an inquisitor, 'is just some type of turnip.'

Made anxious by their rapid spread the Pope sent missions to persuade the heretics to return to the true faith, threatening them with excommunication and hell fire. But neither the threats nor the missionary efforts of the friars were enough to suppress the heresy and the sword had to be invoked to support the cross. A crusade was proclaimed and brutal deeds were perpetrated on both sides, in the course of which the Cathars showed unrelenting courage, even if it was the courage of despair. By 1227 the end was in sight, though Catharism long continued to have a following which kept the Inquisition busy.

About the same time another group of heretics appeared, the Waldensians, named after a rich merchant of Lyons, Peter Waldo who, struck by Christ's command to his followers to give their goods to the poor (St Matthew 19:21) followed his command literally. He attracted disciples, creating small communities which repudiated the wealthy and luxurious living they associated with the contemporary Church. A Church council held at Verona in 1184 allegedly condemned Waldo's teaching, and in 1209 Innocent III proclaimed a crusade against his followers. In the later Middle Ages Waldensian communes were to sprout in the Dauphinois alps, in Provence, in southern Italy and Germany, the message carried by their wandering preachers. The Waldensians were long to suffer persecution, but they were to survive, even in the twentieth century forming the Chiesa Evangelica of Piedmont with some twenty thousand members.

To combat heresy the Church established the Roman Inquisition. In 1232 Pope Gregory IX appointed an Inquisitor, who was usually to be a Dominican friar, to search out those suspected of heresy, trying in the first place to get them to confess their errors. When the accused man or woman was brought before the Inquisitor and his assistants, they were allowed a defence counsel, but the procedure was stacked against the accused. If he or she were found guilty and remained obdurate they were sent to prison. In 1252 Pope Innocent IV issued a bull *Ad extirpanda* which allowed torture to be used to break the accused's will. Although the medieval Inquisition lacked some of the more horrific aspects of the later Spanish Inquisition, it was a grim instrument for battering the remnants of Catharism and other heretics into submission.

In the later Middle Ages there were two major outbreaks of heresy, Lollardy in England and Hussitism in Bohemia, both of which threatened an erosion of orthodoxy and the power and privileges of the Church. Lollardy's founder, the Yorkshireman John Wycliffe, was an Oxford don who came to criticize the prevailing nominalist scholastic philosophy and in its stead wished to return to a more conservative theology, based in part on the ideas of the patristic writer St Augustine. In philosophical terms it was described as realism. Wycliffe was a backward-looking rather than a forward-looking writer.

From his philosophic standpoint he concluded that the only primary authority for the Christian was the word of scripture, directly inspired by God, and to be literally interpreted. Scripture, he argued, was silent about the claims and powers of the Pope and much else which went on in the contemporary Church. The Church, he said, consisted ultimately of the elect to whom God has vouchsafed his grace.

He began to gather a following, first at Oxford where he attracted a number of young dons through whom Lollard ideas were disseminated in other parts of the country. At Northampton, for instance, so one of its citizens complained in 1382, the 'mayor by assent of the Lollards there sent messengers to Oxford and to other places to hire preachers of Lollardy, to be brought to Northampton to preach there every Sunday during Lent last past at the Cross in the churchyard in the marketplace of Northampton'.

But Wycliffe had also won the patronage and protection of the powerful English nobleman John of Gaunt, Edward III's son. Like other English lay landowners Gaunt was attracted by Wycliffe's theory of lordship or dominion which questioned the holding of property if the holder was not in a state of grace or was not fulfilling the trust for which the land had been originally donated. Such arguments could be utilized to justify the confiscation by the state of the endowments of the Church. For some forty or so years after Wycliffe's death, which took place in 1384, there was a group of knights and gentry who put forward similar views and in 1410 actually presented a petition to parliament for the disendowment of the Church and the distribution of its properties to found universities.

In the main Wycliffe's teaching was promulgated by clergy sympathetic to his evangelistic ideas, the so-called 'poor preachers', garbed in sombre russet cloth, who preached in areas where Lollardy attracted a following, in London and Bristol, at Leicester where William Swynderby who was not a graduate formed a Lollard group (where as early as 1380 two chaplains, Richard Waytestayhe and William Smith, were charged with taking the wooden image of St Katharine as fuel to cook a meal), at Northampton, in East Anglia, at Tenterden in Kent, in the Cotswolds with a lively group at Burford and in the Chilterns, penetrating to the north of England and even Scotland, for an English priest charged with Lollardy was burnt at Perth and it was a Scot, Quentin Folkhyrd, who sent Lollard tracts to Prague in 1410.

Lollardy spread by preaching, by discussion groups and by reading the Bible in English, for an English translation was made by a number of scholars, led possibly but doubtfully by Wycliffe himself. If in its early stages Lollardy had patrons among the gentry and merchants, its principal following was drawn from among artisans and craftsmen, parchment makers, tradesmen, weavers, millers, butchers, thatchers, and other skilled workers, so that its critics described it as the 'lay party'. It had a particular fascination for women, for some Lollards evidently justified their ordination and even their capacity to celebrate the Eucharist.

For all its academic origin and its own recourse to books as a means of instruction, Lollardy was basically an anti-intellectual movement. *Sola scriptura*, only one of many ingredients in Wycliffe's own thought, became the principal criterion in later Lollardy. The Lollards were, as their opponent Reginald Pecock called them, the 'Bible men'.

For the Church as well as the State, Lollardy appeared a subversive movement, destructive of all authority. It attacked the Pope and the hierarchy, the doctrine of transubstantiation, confession, monasticism, the worship of saints and relics, pilgrimages, fasting – the whole gamut of what constituted practical Christianity in medieval England. Its adherents admitted to eating meat on fast days, one of them, Margery Baxter justifying herself by saying that it was more economical to consume the left-overs rather than incur debt by buying fish at the market. Lollards failed to fulfil their obligation to go to church, preferring as did William Tryvet of Gascote near Leicester in 1413 to lie in bed. They neglected confession, did not raise their eyes at the elevation of the host; Eleanor Higges of Burford was even charged that she had put the sacrament in her oven and eaten it.

Whatever its supporters thought of it as an 'alternative' or separate Church, its conception of what constituted the Church, the elect, showed that it had moved away from orthodox thought.

It was inevitable that Lollardy's followers should suffer persecution, more especially after the English parliament passed the act *De Haeretico Comburendo* in 1401, declaring that a heretic adjudged guilty by a Church court could be handed over to the State for burning at the stake. So the records became littered with the purchase of faggots for the ugly and cruel death to which men and women, possibly misguided but certainly sincere, had to submit, their fates carefully described by the Elizabethan hagiographer John Foxe in his *Book of Martyrs.*

It must, however, be added that the bishops often tried to be patient and even lenient, only proceeding to the last extremity when the accused proved wholly obdurate. There must have been others like Reginald Pecock, the bishop of Chichester, who believed that the Lollards should be persuaded of their errors by argument, but Pecock himself fell eventually victim to the establishment and was deprived of his bishopric and imprisoned in 1457 for placing too much trust in reason to the detriment of scripture and the traditional teaching of the Church.

Although Lollardy was to survive in the late fifteenth century as a comparatively weak underground movement, it had nonetheless given coherent expression to a measure of disillusion with some of the fundamental aspects of medieval religion. Nor can its radical character be overlooked. While it has been fashionable to stress the medieval and traditional aspect of Wycliffe's teaching, John Bale was not absolutely incorrect in describing him as the 'morning star' of the Reformation, the *Doctor Evangelicus.* John Wycliffe himself died undisturbed in his Leicestershire rectory of Lutterworth in 1384, but thirty-six years later, in response to the condemnation of his heresy (together with that of John Huss) by the general council of Constance, his body was disinterred and his bones were flung into the waters of the neighbouring River Swift.

The teaching of Jan Huss and his followers in Bohemia was similar to that of Wycliffe whose books Huss had read and even plagiarized, but Huss's anti-papalism became identified with Bohemian nationalism, where after his execution it won the support of the Bohemian nobility and merchants. Although Hussitism was later to become irretrievably split between moderates and extremists, it was to continue as a minority movement in Bohemia, Hungary and Poland. The German reformer, Martin Luther, regarded Huss as one of his precursors.

THE CONCILIAR MOVEMENT

The outbreak of large-scale as opposed to isolated, individual heresy more or less coincided with the ignominy of division within the Church itself, not over any doctrinal issue but because neither Churches nor nations could agree over the headship of the Church itself, for when in 1378 there was a papal election, the first at Rome since Pope Gregory XI returned there from Avignon in 1370, some of the cardinals declared that Pope Urban VI had been elected under pressure from the Roman mob and proceeded to elect Robert of Geneva as Pope Clement VII. For over thirty years the Church had two Popes. Different nations gave their allegiance either to the Urbanist or Roman or the Clementist or Avignonese candidate. Religious orders were equally divided by the absurd spectacle of two competing vicars of Christ, indeed after the council of Pisa in 1409 which had unsuccessfully tried to resolve the schism, of that of three Popes.

Christendom's divisions were healed by the calling of a general council of the Church which the emperor Sigismund summoned in 1415 at the lakeside town of Constance. At last, after much debate, in 1417 the council rid itself of the three rivals and elected a fourth as Pope, Martin V, whom Christendom accepted gratefully as the universal pontiff. The council had ventilated novel ideas on authority in the Church, claiming by the decree *Haec Sancta Synodas* of 6 April 1415 for its general councils an even higher power than that of the Pope himself, which was bestowed directly by Christ.

Such a concept was highly unwelcome to the Pope and was by the bull *Execrabilis* issued by Pius II on 18 January 1460 specifically condemned, but it had sowed further doubts as to the extent of the *plenitudo potestatis* of the Pope which had been exercised with such panache by Gregory VII and Innocent III. Even in the still predominantly Catholic Christian Church where Lollardy and Hussitism might appear to be no more than passing irritants, the Pope's real power, especially in political matters, had contracted. If he was to exercise full jurisdiction he could only do so by negotiating agreements with national sovereigns which in practice left them with substantial authority over the Church in their own countries. Such were the Pragmatic Sanction of Bourges of 1438 and the Concordat of Bologna signed with the French king, the Concordat of Vienna with the emperor, while in the Iberian Peninsula Portugal in 1514 and Spain in 1523 acquired more or less full rights over the colonial Churches in their dominions.

The long crisis of the Great Schism meant that when unity had been restored to the Church the Pope had to restore his own authority in the Papal States and replenish the papal coffers, both objects which he achieved with remarkable success, if at some cost to his moral authority. The papal civil service was to multiply at an alarming rate since in order to raise money in the short term the Popes sold offices for a capital sum and in return supplied the buyer with an annuity. A fine mesh of legal fictions and administrative devices continued to envelop the machinery of curial business. Everything, dispensations, the legitimation of bastards, permission to eat meat in Lent, promises to benefices, all cost money. Even if we dismiss the more scandalous stories told by their enemies and critics of Popes like the Borgia Alexander VI and the warlike Julius II, there had evidently been a fall in the esteem with which the vicar of Christ and the successor of St Peter could be regarded.

There were then indications that after a time of great vigour and creative vitality, mirrored in the reformed Church, in a dynamic monasticism and in intense intellectual activity, in some respects the Church had come to rest on its oars. At least in its higher levels it had come to adopt secular modes of behaviour and policy, making full use of its coercive authority and approving the use of the sword not merely against malefactors and in defence of the states of the Church but against infidels, heretics and other deviants. It had become increasingly intolerant of minorities, whether heretics or sceptics, Jews or homosexuals.

Yet the Protestant Reformation was an accident of history waiting to happen rather than its inevitable outcome. The supposition that the Church at the close of the Middle Ages was in such a state of decay and corruption that a Protestant Reformation was a necessary development was without foundation. If there had been, as we have seen, developments in the Church which sapped its spiritual impetus, a measure of secularization, over-bureaucratization, a dilution of spirituality, there had been simultaneously already many signs of a Christian renaissance, stirrings of reform in the monastic orders, movements of lay devotion, all of which might seem to suggest a future Christian resurgence within the Church.

The majority of men and women did not query the supremacy of the Pope, the role of the clergy, the efficacy of the sacraments or the fundamentals of their faith. Clergy and laity alike accepted the primacy of Rome and continued to make pilgrimages to the holy city. The Pope like the king was prayed for every Sunday in every church. Innumerable bequests, as evidenced in wills, from Christians in all walks of life demonstrated the popular devotion to traditional teaching. Many of the religious practices which the Protestant reformers were so strongly to trounce, shaped by popular devotion, were for long to be adhered to. While there may have been some decline in donations, more especially to the friars and monastic orders, lay people still gave generously to the Church. In the late Middle Ages there was an astonishing abundance of church-building. The Church, whatever its defects, remained in popular opinion the gateway to salvation, the visible expression on earth of the invisible Church triumphant in heaven. It provided the means by which men and women could achieve grace. It was only when a different highway to salvation was to be offered that its dominance was to be in danger. While people may well have wanted to eliminate existing abuses, it is doubtful whether most people wanted a religious revolution that would challenge their fundamental beliefs.

But if the Protestant Reformation could not have been foreseen and could be justifiably described as an accidental outcrop of a situation in which religion was only one ingredient, it was evident that by the closing years of the fifteenth century western Europe, and the Church with which it was still largely co-terminous, was experiencing a social and cultural ferment which presaged an historical metastasis. If there were few indications as yet of any major change in the patterns of agricultural life or industrial production, the face of the Western European world was undergoing something of a face-lift as many of the old landmarks began to shift.

In particular nation states were growing in power, as authority, supported by new and improved armaments, became increasingly concentrated in sovereign states, so diminishing the international character of *Christianitas*. Such states were often engaged in hostilities with each other and with the advancing power of Islam. As one observer noted:

> Battles be reaped well nigh in every coast of the marches, Christian men's lordships decrease and go downward, and the lordships of the heathen men grow upwards and increase. For surely our Christian princes, within these forty years and less, have lost more than the third part of Christendom.

The frontiers of Europe were contracting as the threat from the aggressive Turkish invaders continued to loom large.

Within many a European city a wealthy merchant class had come into existence. Better educated than in the past, it often resented the powers exercised by the Church on whose vast possessions it cast envious eyes. Simultaneously cultural developments had occurred, often patronized by rich merchant families like the Medici of Florence, which provided fresh insights into the nature of man and his destiny, which by so doing fed a feeling of unease, for both literature and art were in some sense being humanized and even desacralized. The growing use of the vernacular impinged on the predominance of Latin, the language of the Church and its liturgy and of the Vulgate Bible. The values of the classical past received a fresh airing, at the hands of more advanced writers to the disadvantage of traditional teaching. While rich patrons continued to subsidize church-building, they were more interested in founding universities and schools than in setting up monasteries. Communications were being slowly transformed by the invention of the printing press, which was to be the main vehicle for Protestant propaganda, perhaps even more important than the spoken word. So the rise of an educated laity challenged increasingly the more or less monopolistic control exercised over intellectual life by the Church.

All these changes created inchoate apprehension in the minds of some contemporaries. There had been constant outbreaks of plague, endemic since the pestilence of 1348–9, which had not merely long-term demographic effects, reducing the population and diminishing the supply of labour, but also raising fundamental theological questions about the nature of such visitations. Were such tragic and inexplicable incidents a demonstration of the wrath of God, of God's judgement on a sinful world and even a corrupt Church? It was hardly an accident that one of the more popular images of the age was that of 'le danse macabre' with its gloomy reminder of mortality. For some there was a renewed interest in the coming of AntiChrist, which would precede the Second Coming of Christ and the Last Judgement. Some conservative observers were disconcerted by what seemed to them to be a growing questioning of the social order, manifest not merely in the radical teaching of heretical movements like Lollardy and Hussitism, but in an apparent lack of respect for the divinely created chain of being. The powers that were ordained of God had to submit to death and rebellion. In England four kings were murdered and one slain in battle and two archbishops put to death. Young men, some complained, criticized their elders 'so rebellious and unbuxom as they all day become. There is another leprosy of young folk that they be much smitten with nowadays and this is vain laughter and idle words and many other vain japes.' It was hardly surprising that the Protestant Reformation was to be in the main the work of the young rather than the old. 'There is no trust nor worldly stability in mundane glory; now it is no more; to-day a lord, to-morrow a lost man, to-day a doughty warrior, to-morrow dead on the field of battle.' Many felt, even if they could not articulate their fears, that the world was changing and did not know how best to respond.

Simultaneously a new world was coming into sight, promising rich material rewards, as exploration began to open up more of Asia, America and Africa, a world of which medieval men and women had never had more than an inkling, revealing mysteriously and in a sense disquieteningly that there were masses of people who had so far lain outside the redemptive message of Christ and who had apparently been beyond the range of Christian revelation.

What was happening constituted a cultural and social, rather than a specifically religious, crisis but the Christian Church, as always in its history, was going to have to adjust to the changing situation, leading in effect to the mutations which were to provide both the Protestant and Catholic Reformations and so crudely to bring Catholic medieval Europe to an end. If these ingredients were to be for some time straws in the wind, the wind was to increase to gale force and the straws became bricks and even brickbats.

CHAPTER FIVE

Popular Religion: Faith and Fable

In *The Canterbury Tales* (Everyman, edited by A. Burrill) Geoffrey Chaucer described the ideal parish priest:

> A good man was ther of religioun
> And was a poore Parson of a town;
> But riche he was of holy thought and werk.
> He was also a lernèd man, a clerk
> That Cristes gospel gladly wolde preach.
> His parishioners devoutly wolde he teach.
> Benigne he was, and wondrous diligent,
> And in adversite ful pacient;
> And such he was i-proved ofte to be.
> To cursen for his tithes ful lothe was he,
> But rather wolde he given out of doute,
> Unto his pore parishioners aboute,
> Of his offrynge, and eek of his substaunce.
> He coude in litel thing have sufficience.
> Wyd was his parish, and houses far asonder,
> But yet he lafte not for reyne or thonder
> In siknesse and in meschief to visite
> The ferthest in his parisshe, smal and great
> Uppon his feet and in his hand a staf.
> This noble ensaumple unto his sheep he gaf,
> That ferst he wroughte, and after that he taughte
> Out of the Gospel he those wordes caughte. . . .
> A bettre priest I trowe ther nowhere non is.
> He wayted after no pompe nor reverence,
> Nor made himself spiced in conscience,
> But Cristes love, and his apostles twelve,
> He taught, and ferst he folwed it himself.

The parish priest rather than the Pope was the central figure in the ordinary Christian's life. Through him men and women learned the rudiments of their faith. It was he who mediated God's ways through the sacraments to man.

Priest and layman lived in an enclosed and authoritarian society,

Christianitas, split between the Catholic Church of the west and the Greek Orthodox Church of the east, yet both equally rooted in a Christian concept of existence. Two groups of non-Christians dwelt within its confines, the Jews and the Muslims, with whom Christians had a limited measure of cultural and social coexistence but little religious empathy. The Jews, forbidden to hold land or engage in most occupations, made themselves serviceable by their financial skill, but though tolerated in the Dark Ages, they became more and more outcasts from Christian society, condemned as members of a race accused of having rejected the Messiah and of having crucified Christ, for which, as the liturgy made plain, they were eternally accursed. A few Christian scholars interested in Hebrew were more kindly disposed, but in general the Jews were regarded with hostility and suspicion, obliged to live in designated areas of towns, forced to wear a special badge and refused the right to own property, and as in England in the thirteenth century actually expelled from some countries. They were subject to occasional brutal pogroms and were accused unjustly of monstrous crimes, including child murder.

The Muslims had rejected Christ as the Messiah, but they were more heretics than unbelievers. In Spain, there was, under some enlightened Christian monarchs, a cross-fertilization of culture and social intercourse which involved Christians, Jews and Muslims. But for the Church Islam constituted a continuing threat to the faith. The crusades, if finally unsuccessful in the near East, eventually brought about the triumph of Christian arms in Spain, culminating with the fall of Granada in 1492, and the subsequent victimization by Church and State of both Jews and Muslims.

Beyond the frontiers of the known world, peopled by legend rather than knowledge, there were strange lands and fabled animals where the Church had not really penetrated. Rumour spoke of a fabulous Christian land, the kingdom of Prester John, but no one had ever been there or knew where it was. By some it was identified with Ethiopia where the Coptic Church survived as an isolated Christian society. Travellers' tales and distant trading caravans had opened a small window on the Far East, but of its religious life the Church knew little, though there still remained a small Christian community of long standing in India. The friars had reawakened the missionary urge, even trying vainly to convert the Muslims, and had penetrated the Mongol empire of China where some converts were made and a church organized. But in general *Christianitas* was a confined and self-contained society.

It was fundamentally Christian in the sense that its history had been, as we have seen, conditioned by the teaching and fortunes of the Church, the regeneration of the papacy, the influence of monks and friars and an essential Christian philosophy taught at schools and universities. How much the majority of men and women understood of what their religion was about it is difficult to know. Society was in effect religiously two-tiered: the professionals, the clergy, and the rest, the laity; though the separation between them must not be overstressed. The clergy in proportion to the population were very numerous, and though not all of them wore a special dress to indicate their calling, they were physically very present in every town and village. They formed a privileged caste, employing their status in defence of their own interests and, as they construed them, of those of the Church, and enjoying numerous privileges – immunity from taxation, military service, the jurisdiction of the criminal courts – their property and persons in some measure sacrosanct. They were the most literate part of the population.

THE ECCLESIASTICAL HIERARCHY

There was a distinctive hierarchy within the Church which was governed by statutes and order as much as lay society; it consisted of popes, archbishops and bishops, cathedral clergy, monks and friars, abbesses and nuns, parish priests, chaplains, and a heterogeneous and numerous clerical proletariat.

The Pope was a distant, almost legendary figure. Between 678 and 752 there had been eleven Syrian and Greek Popes but in the high Middle Ages the Pope was most likely to be an Italian. A solitary Englishman, Nicholas Breakspeare, became Pope as Hadrian IV in 1154; and in the fourteenth century there was a series of French Popes. For Christians Rome as the seat of the apostles was the holy city to which many would go as pilgrims; but medieval Popes did not always reside there. Between 1100 and 1304 the Popes spent 122 years away from Rome and 82 in the city.

Papal elections had often been the scene of bitter conflict. Since Pope Nicholas II had ruled in 1059 the cardinals had the right to elect the Pope, after 1179 by a two-thirds majority. In 1271 Pope Gregory X declared that the cardinals should be shut up 'in conclave' without contact with the outside world to forestall outside interference until the election was made. Many Popes were challenged by rivals who were supported by different princes. There were at least seventeen anti-Popes between 1073 and 1503. Of 88 Popes who held office between 590 and 1058 only 13 reigned for ten or more years, and 2 for more than twenty. Although the choice of the cardinals occasionally fell on an elderly or feeble Pope who could not be expected to live long, and once idiosyncratically simply on a holy man, Celestine V who was soon pressurized into resignation, the Popes were generally men of wide diplomatic skill, trained in canon law and scholastic theology. Some medieval Popes, especially in the later Middle Ages, used their office to enrich their own relatives and to extend their territorial power in Italy.

In their governance of the Church the Popes were assisted by the cardinals who formed a sort of papal cabinet, 'the hinges (*cardines*)', as Pope Eugenius III described them in 1148 'round which the whole Church revolves'. The Pope also used special legates to carry his missives to foreign countries. For administrative convenience the Church was divided into provinces over which a senior bishop or metropolitan presided; the metropolitan had the right to summon and preside over provincial synods and exercise some degree of supervision and discipline over his suffragans.

Below the Pope ecclesiastical society was headed by the bishops, of whom the Pope as bishop of Rome was himself the chief, deriving their ministry from Christ and his apostles. 'Each bishop', as Rudolph Glaber put it, was 'the bridegroom of his own see, showing the likeness of the Saviour'. At the bishop's consecration he received as the symbol of his office the staff conferring on him pastoral oversight of his flock and a ring as a token of the mystical marriage between him and the Church. In the early Middle Ages there had been a bitter struggle as the Church tried to prevent lay authorities from taking part in the investiture ceremony. 'If the hands of a layman', Pope Paschal II commented in 1102, 'deliver the staff which is a sign of the shepherd's office, and the ring which is the seal of faith, what are bishops doing in the Church at all?' All the bishops, including the Pope, enjoyed what was termed *potestas ordinis*, the power implicit in their ordained ministry, but the Pope, by reason of his office as the vicar of St Peter, had a supreme jurisdictional authority. Bishops had to take an oath of obedience to him, and he could deprive them of their office.

There were some nine hundred bishoprics in the western Church, of which three hundred were in Italy and some one hundred and eighty in the eastern Mediterranean. While the bishoprics of Italy and the eastern Mediterranean were small and poorly endowed the great prizes of the Church, such as the English sees of Canterbury, York, Winchester and Durham, and the archbishoprics of Cologne, Mainz, Trier and Rouen enjoyed revenues as great as those of any lay prince.

While the bishop's functions in theory should have been primarily religious, given his higher education and administrative skill he was often involved in the service of the State. This not only led to his being often away from his diocese, but to a dichotomy in his vocation. Bishops were inevitably pulled two ways, by the service they owed their prince and by the service they owed the Church; and not infrequently they found it difficult to find a balance between the two. If the bishop's prince was in conflict with the Pope, as, for instance, happened in England in the reign of King John, or if his prince was pursuing policies which seemed to contravene Christian principles, where was the prior loyalty?

Whatever the bishop's secular duties, he was above all by reason of his office Christ's representative in the diocese. He had the sole right to ordain the clergy, to appoint to benefices within his gift, to visit monasteries within his jurisdiction, to hold synods for his clergy and to grant dispensations, though for these reference had often to be made to Rome. Sometimes he had assistant bishops who acted in his stead in the performance of his sacramental duties as well as those who helped him in the actual administration of his diocese, vicars-general, archdeacons, rural deans. The parish clergy must often have dreaded the visitation of their bishop or of his officials as a burden on their slender resources. The Lateran Council had tried to limit the cost which fell on those who had to entertain them but even so it laid down that an archbishop might bring 50 retainers, a bishop 30, an archdeacon 7 and a rural dean a mere 2. To avoid the expense involved in such visitations many English parishes paid an annual tax known as a procuration to the bishop or archdeacon. There were bishops reputed for the sanctity and austerity of their lives, but for the most part bishops were held in awe rather than affection, seemingly more concerned with dealing with the shortcomings of the faithful, clerical and lay, repressing dissent and persecuting heresy than disseminating the love of Christ.

THE PAROCHIAL CLERGY

Such judgements may seem, as indeed they are, far too general for there were saints as well as sinners among the bishops. It is even more difficult to make generalizations about the function of the parish priest during a period of some four hundred or so years. It was he, often drawn from the same social background as the members of his flock, through whom were mediated the things of God. Often very inadequately trained either in a grammar school or in a bishop's household, and later at a university, council after council complained of his perfunctory knowledge of the scriptures and theology, and even of Latin. Bishops carried out a superficial examination of clerks before ordination or appointment to a living, and in the later Middle Ages occasionally despatched a would-be incumbent to remedy his deficiencies by study at a university.

But complaints about clerical ignorance were a medieval commonplace. 'The ignorance of priests', Archbishop Pecham declared in 1281, 'casteth the people into the ditch of error.' 'Very few priests', Nicolas de Clamanges said in the early fifteenth century, 'indeed are capable of reading even slowly, syllable by syllable, much less of understanding the words and their meaning. What fruit can they produce in others when they themselves find what they read gibberish? How ill they manage to obtain God's grace for others when they themselves offend him and dishonour their ministry by their ignorance and the unworthiness of their lives?' On the other hand the abundance of manuals on the pastoral duties of the clergy suggests that there were at least some priests ready to purchase and read them; and such lists of clerical libraries as survive show that there were some reading men among them.

There can, however, be little doubt that a deep understanding of Christian theology was reserved for a privileged few, not that this can have been a matter of much moment to the parish priest's flock. What they wanted, as Chaucer's portrait makes plain enough, was a pastor who would by his personal example bring home to them the message of the gospel. He

Constantine the Great (274–337), the first Christian emperor of Rome. This marble bust of the emperor was originally located in the apse of Constantine's basilica, and is now at the Palazzo dei Conservatori, Rome. (Mansell Collection)

The Baptistry of St John Lateran, built c. 310 by Constantine the Great. Originally a square building, it was changed c. 350 into a circular building to provide a baptistry. Under Pope Sixtus III (432–40) a porch was added and the circle extended into an octagon. (Hulton Getty)

A mosaic (1132–43) depicting the Three Fathers, Gregory, Basil and John Chrysostom, from the Palatine Chapel, Palermo. (Mansell Collection)

The interior of Santa Sophia, facing east, Istanbul. Built as a Christian cathedral by the emperor Justinian in 532–8, Santa Sophia was converted into a mosque by Turks who captured the city (then Constantinople) in 1453. (A.F. Kersting)

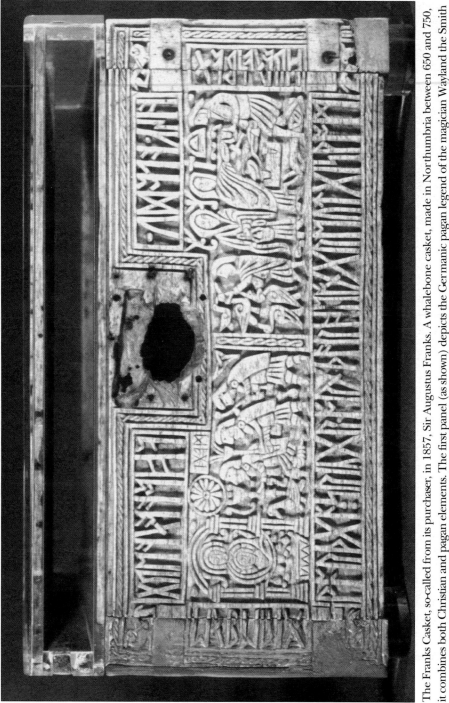

The Franks Casket, so-called from its purchaser, in 1857, Sir Augustus Franks. A whalebone casket, made in Northumbria between 650 and 750, it combines both Christian and pagan elements. The first panel (as shown) depicts the Germanic pagan legend of the magician Wayland the Smith and a representation of the Adoration the Magi. (British Library)

St Boniface baptising converts above and suffering martyrdom in 754 below. He defends himself using the Gospel book as a shield. (Staatsbibliothek Bamberg: Msc. Lit. 1, f. 126v)

Pope Innocent III, fresco in the lower church of Sacro Speco, Subiaco. Pope from 1198 to 1216, Innocent III summoned the Great Council of the Church in 1215, during which decrees were passed which affected profoundly all aspects of Church life for clergy and laity alike. (Alinari/Mansell Collection)

St Francis, detail from fresco by Cimabue in the lower church of San Francesco, Assisi. Canonized in 1228, two years after his death, Francis's simple doctrine of putting into practice that which Christ had preached, was greeted with initial hesitation by the thirteenth-century Church. (Alinari/Mansell Collection)

The Palace of the Popes at Avignon, the home of the papal see from 1309 to 1370. It was begun in 1334 under Pope Benedict XII and extended under his successor Clement VI. (Hulton Getty)

was their man of God to whom they owed religiously a prior allegiance. It was only in the parish church that they could be married or buried.

THE MASS

The parish priest's prior duty was to take the services, Matins, Mass, Vespers. The Mass was the central act of worship which the parishioners were obliged to attend on Sundays and holy days. In the tenth and eleventh centuries the doctrine of the Eucharist was to be fully articulated and eventually crystallized in the doctrine of transubstantiation, becoming a powerful sacramental vehicle which raised the prestige of the priest who was alone able to celebrate it, providing a ritual which unified the Church and the community, and offering to all Christians access to the supernatural world, giving grace on earth as well as hope of eternal salvation.

In the ninth century Paschasius Radbertus of the abbey of Corbie had written that 'from the substance of bread and wine that same body and blood is miraculously consecrated', for if God was able to implant Christ's body in the Virgin Mary, he must equally be capable of enabling it to be present in the bread and wine of the Eucharist. He evoked a rejoinder from one of his younger colleagues, the monk Ratramnus, who argued that if there was a change it was purely figurative or symbolic, a position taken later by Berengar of Tours who insisted that as Christ's body was in heaven it could not be also on the altar. But Archbishop Lanfranc accounted Berengar a heretic and it was Paschasius Radbertus's interpretation which eventually, at the Lateran Council of 1215, became the unassailable doctrine of the Church.

In popular belief the Host was God. The wafer made of wheaten bread, often baked in religious houses with appropriate ritual, became at the moment of its consecration by the priest 'Goddys' flessh', 'Cristes own bodi . . . as hale as he toke it of that blessed maiden', so wrote Robert Mannyng in *Handlyng Synne* (*c.* 1303). The Eucharist became a repository of supernatural power, its efficacy unaffected by the character of the celebrant. 'Just as physical food succeeds in restoring the hungry,' Humbert of Romans wrote, 'thus, this food protects the spiritual life.' 'Just', so Jacques de Vitry wrote, 'as by Adam's tasting all died, so by tasting Christ we all recover life'. 'When the bread', as Hugh of St Cher put it, 'becomes Christ's body nothing at all remains of the bread', but it was not ordinary food simply to be digested and excreted, 'not bodily food', Jacques de Vitry again, 'but food of the soul; not of the flesh but of the heart'.

Christ, theologians agreed, was bodily present after the first consecration of the bread, for by the contemporary doctrine of concomitance flesh and blood were both equally present in the sacramental matter, teaching which was to justify the giving of communion in one kind to the laity, a practice which became normal in the later Middle Ages. The Host encapsulated the story of man's redemption, of the human Christ who was born to the Virgin Mary only to endure at his father's hands a sacrifice to redeem mankind. Naturally the Eucharist was treated as a holy object, even the crumbs of which had to be recovered and protected from mice, vermin and dirt. It was kept in a pyx often made of silver and ivory with a lock, and sometimes fashioned in the form of the Virgin, often hanging over the altar. When the Eucharist was taken to the sick and dying the ceremonial was marked by the carrying of lighted candles, the ringing of bells and the proffering of incense. As the procession passed people fell on their knees, earning an indulgence by so doing. On Maundy Thursday the Host was placed in the Easter Sepulchre to be adored and restored to the pyx on Easter Sunday morning.

In the twelfth century the elevation of the Host became the apex of the service. Bells rang, candles were lighted, censers of incense were swung. The people gazed in rapt adoration, experiencing a spiritual communion. God was 'seen here on earth every day when he was elevated by the hands of the priest, and comes into the company of men'. The laity were actually obliged to take communion only once a year, on Easter Sunday, but some took it thrice, as synodal decisions recommended, but each time only after confession and penance. The unworthy received it at their peril as horrific stories demonstrated. Caesarius of Heisterbach related how an unworthy priest who was celebrating the Mass found that the Host had turned to hot coals in his mouth.

The laity received communion in the one kind under the species of bread, for the chalice was withheld from them, in part for fear that some particle of the sacrament might be lost or spilled, but the move was a further step in the enhancement of the priest's prestige and power. It was, however, common to give each communicant, after the reception of the bread, a draught of unconsecrated wine and water from the chalice to make sure that no crumbs of bread remained in the communicant's mouth. Loaves of bread, brought by the parishioners and blessed by the parish priest, *le pain bènit* or eulogia, were sometimes distributed to the people after the service.

There were stores of miraculous stories concerned to support the physical interpretation of the Eucharist, usually by way of rewarding the good or, more often, of punishing the wicked, and designed to refute or convert the sceptic. The Host was depicted as being actually transformed into bleeding flesh or a child or even the Lamb of God. Edward the Confessor, according to Matthew Paris, saw a child transfixed between the hands of Archbishop Wulfstan as he celebrated the Eucharist. Geoffrey de la Tour described how a Host 'in the mannor of a lytel bright clerenes' flew miraculously into the mouth of a woman reputed for her holiness. An unknown English poet told of a woman whose doubts about transubstantiation made her feel that she should not consume the consecrated element. She placed it on the branch of a pear tree which blossomed unseasonably and a baby was discovered in the place of the Host. In a very early story another woman possessed by similar doubts baked the consecrated bread in an oven, only to discover that it had turned into a bleeding finger. When a pet monkey who had eaten the Host was burned to death the owner found the sacrament intact in its stomach. When in the early sixteenth century the rood and altar at Rickmansworth were set on fire by 'wretched heretics' and the pyx melted 'notwithstanding the blessed body of our Lord Jesus Christ . . . nothing perished'. Many such stories were a response to supposed Jewish hostility. It was narrated that a Jew who had attacked the Host had been converted by seeing a child torn asunder in its place. A Jew offered a Host to his dog which not only rejected the offering but savaged the Jew. Others were designed to convert the doubter or the sceptic. The heretic Gautier of Flos had his faith restored by witnessing a baby in the Host. The legend of the Holy Grail grew up around the quest for the vessel used at the Last Supper often depicted iconographically as the first celebration of the Eucharist.

The devotion to the sacrament received an additional boost with the creation of the feast of Corpus Christi. The feast seems to have originated in the diocese of Liège, representing the influence of the Cistercians and Dominicans but more especially the piety of the sisterhoods of women known as bèguines, one of whom Juliana of Cornillon, working in a leper hospital, had a vision which led her to advocate the institution of a Eucharistic feast. It was only a local usage until Jacques Pantaleon, who had been at one time archdeacon of Campines in the diocese of Liège, was elected Pope as Urban IV and in 1264 by the bull *Transiturus* established Corpus Christi as a universal feast, though it was only celebrated sporadically until John XXII elevated the feast, together with that of the Holy Trinity, to be a feast of universal usage in 1334. The liturgical office for Corpus Christi may well have been written by Thomas Aquinas whom John XXII canonized. Corpus Christi was to be promoted by the granting of special indulgences, by the preaching of special sermons, by the creation of social fraternities or guilds, and by the performance of mystery and miracle plays.

The Mass had become, as it were, the pendulum of the power structure of the medieval Church and the centre of the laity's devotion. Challenges made to the doctrine of transubstantiation, as by the Cathars in the thirteenth century and later by John Wycliffe, constituted heresy. It was the miracle of the Mass which separated Catholics from Protestants and still in the twentieth century makes any ultimate reconciliation or reunion between the Churches impossible. 'Is it', an early Protestant was to ask, 'else but a piece of bread or a little pretty piece round Robin?' On this issue Churches were divided, men and women were to die at the stake.

While all the parishioners were in theory obliged to attend Sunday Mass, in fact attendance seems to have been often irregular, for some at least preferred to 'lygge and swete and take the mery mornynge slepe', as Robert Mannyng put it. 'Upon Sonedayes,' Langland wrote in *Piers Plowman*, 'to cesse . . . godes seruyce to huyre bothe matyns and messe and after mete, in

churches to huyre here evensong every man ouhte.' In practice the daily
services were probably ill-attended, except the Mass on holy days and
sometimes Saturdays which was regarded as honouring the Blessed Virgin
(who alone had faith in the Resurrection on Easter Eve, i.e. Saturday). The
priest was himself expected to celebrate the Mass daily and to recite the
daily office.

THE FUNCTION OF THE PARISH PRIEST

The parish priest was encouraged to preach but it seems only rarely to have
been within his competence. Bishop Grosseteste of Lincoln told his clergy
to preach in English and required the priest whom he had appointed to the
rectory of Cassington first to 'learn all the Sunday homilites'. Popular
preaching by the friars may have spurred on parish priests to copy their
example. In the later Middle Ages there were in some large-town churches
highly reputed preachers who drew large congregations: among them
Geiler von Kaysersberg at Strasbourg; Heynlin von Stein at Basle; Vincent
Ferrer, Giovanni Capistrano and Bernardino of Siena in Italy. William
Lichfield, the fifteenth-century rector of All Hallows the Great, London, left
behind a collection of 3,083 sermons written in English.

The parish priest was required to know and teach the Ten Commandments, the Creed, the Lord's Prayer and the Ave. His services were crucial to
his parishioners at every moment of their existence. If the new-born baby
was to avoid the pains of hell he must be baptized immediately, for 'A soul
of a child that is born and not christened', as Walter Hilton wrote in the
fourteenth century, 'hath no likeness of God; he is nought but an image of
the fiend, and a brand of hell; but as soon as it is christened, it is reformed
to the image of God.' If there was a likelihood that the child might die
before it was brought to church, then anyone could throw water on it 'in
the name of the Father, and of the Son, and of the Holy Ghost', so as to
avert the pains of hell fire. There was a common belief that the vessels and
clothes used in baptism possessed magical properties. Confirmation, which
Robert Mannyng described as the confirmation of what the priest had done
in baptism by the bishop, should have followed baptism, but it was practised
infrequently, in part because of the simple difficulties which a bishop had in
trying to visit his large diocese.

The priest officiated at his flock's marriages, gave them extreme unction
on their death-beds and conducted their burial services. It was to him that
they went at least once a year to confess their sins, for private confession
had more or less replaced public confession. Confession was the gateway by
which a man, whose sinful disposition and sinful acts lay under the wrath
and judgement of God, received remission of his sins. While a few
theologians insisted that if a sinner was to receive absolution he had to be in
a state of absolute contrition, most theologians were satisfied that what was

known as attrition, sorrow that was less than adequate compensation for the sin committed, was enough to earn grace and forgiveness. The priest imposed the appropriate penance and gave absolution. While absolution must have afforded the layman or woman psychological consolation, even though the priest was bound by the seal of secrecy confession had placed him or her at the mercy of the priest. The penitential system was a spiritual discipline which enabled the Church to control its members and reinforced its power over them.

The Church's final sanction for an erring member was excommunication, involving the tolling of the church bell, tossing a lighted candle to the ground to symbolize expulsion from the church, and cursing the sinner in God's name 'sleeping and waking, going, sitting, standing, lying above ground and underground, speaking, riding, eating, drinking, in wood and water, in field and in town'. The excommunicate was to be excluded from the services of the Church and condemned 'with Judas that betrayed our Lord Jesus Christ' to suffer the torments of hell.

The parishioners had to provide their parish priest's everyday needs. Some priests, especially those who for one reason or another held more than one living, had substantial incomes, but the majority were probably not very much better off than most of their flock. Normally the parish priest held some land, varying in area, the glebe which he might well farm, an occupation which must have brought him closer to the peasants whom he served. His principal source of income was the tithe, the scriptural authority for which was deduced from the vow which Jacob made in Genesis, 'Of all that thou shalt give me I will surely give the tenth unto thee.' The payment of tithe in England did not become a legal obligation on all landowners until the early Middle Ages, confirmed in the laws of tenth-century Anglo-Saxon kings. Tithe was levied on every conceivable product, on the greater or 'garb' tithes of corn, the lesser tithes on hay and other kinds of natural production, on garden produce, whether cultivated, such as vegetables, or non-cultivated, such as timber or teasels, on the issue of animals, cows, sheep, goats, pigs, horses, geese, chickens, swans, doves, bees and what they produced, wood, milk, honey, beeswax, and the products of human labour. At Tadcaster, for instance, the church claimed on tithe from the income of all merchants, bakers, carpenters, quarrymen, masons, limeburners, carters and brewers as well as casual labourers.

In theory the tithe should have been distributed in four parts, one for the bishop, one for the maintenance of the fabric of the church, one for the rector of the parish and one for the relief of the poor. In practice the greater part of the tithe, the amount of which varied much from parish to parish, went to the rector and where the rectory had been appropriated, as often happened, to a monastery which appointed a vicar to do the duty, it went to the religious house. The Church was most insistent that tithes should be paid down to the last penny, a requirement which caused conflict between the parish priest and his flock and constant litigation. Doubtless, like many a modern taxpayer, the parishioners tried to conceal as much of their produce as they could, but the Church proved to be a hard taskmaster. Church councils, for instance, deprecated those tithe-payers who deducted their expenses before paying their tithes. Those who failed to pay a tithe made themselves liable to the penalty of excommunication, for by refusing to pay they were guilty of robbing God.

The priest normally had other sources of income the levying of which affected his parishioners. They were expected to donate gifts in money or in kind at the great Church festivals of Christmas, Easter and the festival and dedication of the church, and at the day of the celebration of the anniversary Mass (said on the day of the man or woman's death each year). There were dues at weddings, the churching of women, at confessions and funerals. The clergy received eggs at Easter, cheese at Whitsun, chickens at Christmas and what was left of the *pain bènit* or the loaves blessed at Mass. The priest was also entitled to collect mortuary, the second best animal or vessel (the lord had the best) when a man died, a donation that was based on the theory that the dead man would probably have failed in his lifetime to pay his tithes in full. Since it was also the Church which supervised the making of wills, clerks because of their literacy often acting as testators, lay persons were in general generous in their bequests to the Church.

The parish priest may well have tried to fulfil his vocation to the best of his capacity but Church council after council, generation after generation, reiterated complaints about the behaviour of the clerical proletariat. They were insufficiently learned, unable to expound the scriptures and unready to preach. Their personal lives only too frequently fell short of what the Church required of them. The Hildebrandine reformation had had as one of its main aims the elimination of clerical marriage and the imposition of celibacy. In 1076 Archbishop Lanfranc forbade the ordination of priests unless they were celibate (though he permitted those already married to keep their wives). His successor Anselm forbade the clergy to be married and ordered those who had wives to put them away. In 1127 provision was made for disciplining and even enslaving clerical concubines. While some of the bishops themselves had mistresses, it was a rule impossible of strict enforcement but there seems to have been a gradual improvement in the sexual habits of the higher clergy, which may have helped the lower clergy to comply more fully with the letter of the law. Even so some priests, the *uxorati*, continued to be married while many others had a permanent companion, *concubinari* or *focarii*, hearth mates who probably acted as the priest's housekeeper. 'The cohabitation of clerks with concubines', Pope Alexander IV told Archbishop Gray 'was notorious.' Others simply sinned with their spiritual daughters, and doubtless sometimes with their spiritual sons. It is naturally impossible to quantify the extent to which the rule of celibacy was broken, simply to state that it was natural that it would be.

Church councils reiterated the need for the priest to withstand worldly temptations, gaudy clothes, pointed shoes, fashionable hair styles, taverns and alehouses, dicing and gambling, wenching and sporting with hawks and hounds. In 1220, for instance, the clergy were forbidden to wear pointed shoes or cloaks with sleeves. Two centuries or more later the canonist William Lyndwode stated that the clothes of the clergy should not be either red or green, neither too shabby nor too smart. Their hair should be cut so as to represent their profession, not only showing the top of the head but also the nape and over the ears as to make of the remaining hair a circlet or corona. The priests' everyday clothes and mildly worldly habits may well have helped him to identify more easily with his congregation.

CHURCH LIFE

The church itself was not merely a place of worship but an active centre of communal life. In its architecture as much as in its services it was a lesson in the Christian story. The Church festivals were themselves enriched by drama, more especially at Easter when the internment and resurrection of Christ were symbolically re-enacted. The great cathedrals overtopped the town houses, their towers and spires leaping heavenwards, symbolizing the Church triumphant over the rampant powers of evil. The church, wrote Honorius of Autun at about the same time as Suger, Abbot of St Denis, was building the first of the great Gothic churches, corresponded in all its parts to the ultimate truths of theology. The transparent windows, which keep out the weather and bring in the light, are the doctors who withstand the hurricane of heresy and pour in the illumination of doctrine. The window glass reveals heavenly things, as in a glass darkly. '*Ecclesia materia significat ecclesiam spiritualem.*' The parish church, so much smaller and not infrequently rather dilapidated, was no less to the layman the home of God. The sounds of its bells recalling the layman to its function floated over the village and countryside. All its furnishings had meaning. The bells, which had been consecrated to God's service, could keep thunderstorms at bay; the altar might house the relics of a saint; the font for baptism, the rood with the figures of the Virgin Mary and St John on either side of the crucified Christ. If the church was rich enough there would be stained glass in the windows which spoke of the scripture story or the legends of the saints. The walls of the church were often covered with paintings. Every object in the church helped to familiarize the villager with the basic elements of the Christian faith.

The parish church managed to conflate the sacred with the profane, even though the purists disapproved of the secular activities which took place there. It was a sanctuary where the outlaw from justice could find refuge. It was a place where games and even dancing occasionally occurred as did funeral wakes, parish feasts and scot-ales. Men sometimes slept within its walls and the sick went there to be healed.

THE RELIGION OF THE LAITY

The mass of the peasantry can have had only a comparatively superficial and ambivalent understanding of the Christian faith. Some nobles and rich merchants and educated townspeople would have been better informed. But for the mass of the faithful religion was a curious conflation of superstition and myth, animistic in origin, in some ways a hangover from the pagan past, which was somehow tied in and domesticated by the Christian Church. Everyday life was threaded through with magic and folk-lore, with charms and spells which could affect a man's health, a woman's fertility, the failure or success of the crops. Paper specially blessed by a priest could be nailed to a door to keep away demons or, inscribed with scriptural texts, placed around the necks of patients suffering from diseases of the throat. On St John Baptist Day, coinciding with the midsummer solstice, bonfires were lit in celebration and men and women danced with abandon. The Church's condemnation of dancing was in part rooted not merely in the fear that it led to sexual indulgence but that it was associated with the ancient pagan festivals. In the everyday world where the success or failure of the harvest could mean life or death, these age-old charms and spells had a distinctive role.

Hobgoblins and foul fiends, fairies, pixies and elves, demons and devils stalked the world. Chroniclers wrote gravely about green-skinned men who lived in underground caverns. William of Newburgh described a fairy banquet which, by chance, a rider had come across near Willy Howe, an early barrow in the East Riding of Yorkshire. Men believed in metamorphosis, and in the sinister activities of werewolves and vampires. Two 'werwolves' were burned at Besançon in 1521; and a man was charged with turning himself into a mouse at Rome in 1424. The Church warned people against the dangers of worshipping stones, wells or trees, or of placing too much credence in the interpretation of dreams or the chattering of magpies.

This widespread belief that the world was peopled by supernatural agencies, hostile to men and women, capable of bringing on physical lust and mental illness, of raising tempests, destroying crops and causing other natural calamities was a tribute to the influence exerted by the forces of Satan or the Devil, basic to Christian mythology. Satan was the begetter of sin, the arch-tempter who with his disciples, the fallen angels, was constantly at work. If Christ had triumphed over Satan, yet to test mankind the Devil seemed at liberty, as it were, to freewheel in the world, a professional magician with a sleight of hand with which few saints could compete. He could take the form of an animal, a spider, a bear, a black pig, a toad, a cat, a goat; but as many a sculpture showed, still to be seen adorning the columns of French Romanesque churches, Satan was more often depicted as a monstrous human being with bestial characteristics, 'like', as a monk of Cluny said, 'a small black Ethiopian horribly deformed, with horns coming out of his ears and fire from his mouth as if he was about to eat the very flesh of the sick monk'. Satan could maim cattle, cause earthquakes and plague. A devil, one writer noted, could be seen emerging from the mouth of an epileptic whom a saint had cured. A boy cured of possession had actually seen the Devil shaking his fist in anger at the shrine where he had been healed. He was capable of having sexual relations, and operative in inducing men and women to sexual lust. Guibert of Nogent told of a monk who through the connivance of a Jew 'skilled in medicine who understood magic' sold his soul to the Devil. He asked the Devil what sacrifice he should give him. 'You shall make a libation of your seed,' the Devil told him. 'When you have poured that out to me, then you shall enjoy the rewards of your sacrifice. . . . And so with that horrible libation he declares his renunciation of his faith.' 'The Devil', Martin Luther wrote in 1529, 'makes ceaseless attempts on our lives and discharges his anger by causing accidents and bodily hurt. In several cases he has broken a person's neck or made him lose his reason. At other times he has drowned people and frequently he has pushed them to suicide or other atrocious misfortune.'

It was the omnipresence of the Devil and his agents which in part accounted for the growing belief in witchcraft and sorcery, even if it was not until the sixteenth century that the campaign against witches, resulting in the persecution by the Churches of so many innocent people, Catholic as well as Protestant, was to reach its climax. Witches in league with the Devil were capable of causing all kinds of calamity and misfortune. 'It has lately come to our ears,' Pope Innocent VIII declared in the bull *Summis Desiderantes* of 1484, condemning witchcraft,

> that in some parts of northern Germany . . . many persons of both sexes unmindful of their own salvation . . . have abandoned themselves to devils, *incubi* and *succubi*, and by their incantations, spells, conjurations, and other accursed charms . . . have slain infants yet in the mother's womb, as also the offspring of cattle, have blasted the produce of the earth, the grapes of the vine, the fruits of trees. . . . The witches, furthermore, afflict and torment men and women . . . ever and above this they blasphemously renounce the faith which is theirs by the Sacrament of Baptism, and at the instigation of the enemy of mankind they also shrink not from committing and perpetrating the foulest abominations and the filthiest excesses to the deadly peril of their own souls.

Witchcraft, hitherto a sporadic and intermittent phenomenon in the medieval world of the reality of which some churchmen had earlier been sceptical, now emerged as a universal form of nonconformity of which society had to be purged. As a sequel to the papal bull the Dominican inquisitors, Heinrich Kramer and Jakob Sprenger, whom the Pope had authorized to extirpate what was virtually a new heresy, drew up a classic textbook of demonology, the *Malleus Maleficarum*, the forerunner of many similar publications that were to appear in the sixteenth and seventeenth centuries.

Witches, so it was held, anointed themselves with a deadly unguent, said to be manufactured from the flesh of unbaptized children, more conceivably from ingredients such as aconite and belladonna which could cause hallucinations, which enabled them to fly, stark naked, on their beasts, horse, goats, rams, dogs and the traditional broom sticks to their nocturnal assemblies or sabbaths where they engaged in the obscene worship of their master the Devil whose arse they reverently kissed.

In many respects medieval Christianity was governed by fear – fear of the Devil, fear of the Church – and obsessed by sin and guilt. The ultimate penalty which the Church held out to man for his wrong-doing was the promise of eternal torment in the fires of hell. The brevity of human life and the daily experience of death formed a grim reminder of that other existence on the threshold of which man lived out his daily life. The damned, Richard Alkerton said, preaching in 1406, were to be 'boiled in fire and brimstone without end. Venomous worms . . . shall gnaw all their members unceasingly, and the worm of conscience shall gnaw the soul. . . . This fire that tormenteth you shall never be quenched, and they that tormenteth you shall never be weary neither die.' Alkerton's contemporary John Myrc had a similar picture of the 'pyt of hell' in which the damned would be pitch-forked for evermore with 'sowles bulmyng vp and don, cryng horrybuly and a noyse of fendes crying; "Sle, sle, sle, sle, open the broche, rost hote, cast ynto the cawdren, sethe fast yn puche and cood and brymston, and hot leed!"' The west fronts of many a church, such as those at Conques and Bourges, provided a graphic picture of what most men and women could expect, for many were called but few would be chosen.

THE CULT OF THE BLESSED VIRGIN MARY AND THE SAINTS

How could a man or a woman avert the Devil and all his wiles? The Church taught that the only effective way lay in the acceptance of its teaching and sacraments, in the penitential system, in the payment of its dues, in attendance at the Mass where was re-enacted the sacrifice which Christ had paid to ransom mankind from sin and Satan, and in following Christ's example in daily life. Yet present as Christ was in the Host, he was inevitably a remote and distant figure. Although medieval sculptures came to depict an increasingly humane Christ, he was the Son of God who like the king seemed to a medieval petitioner more a judge – and a wrathful one at that –

than a loving father; his love and mercy were conditional. Where else could the suppliant turn for mercy and reassurance?

'If you fear the Father,' St Bernard declared, 'there is Christ the Mediator. If you fear him, there is the Mother, pure humanity. She will listen to you. The son will listen to her, the Father to him.' 'The Virgin has with Jesus', Guibert of Nogent said, 'the power which a mother in this world has over her son. A mother does not pray; she orders. How, then, would [Jesus] not listen to his Mother?' Mary, solicitous of the needs of men and women, was more sympathetic to human frailty than God could be. There were innumerable stories which told of the miracles of mercy that she had performed. A nun who found that she was pregnant asked the Virgin to help her; so she was able to give birth in her sleep, and the baby was cared for by a priest. Mary's cult gained ever more and more in popularity. Her own conception was believed to be miraculous and her person, as Duns Scotus taught, was immaculate. Her bodily assumption, Peter Damian declared, was even more glorious than that of her son. In the tenth century the *Ave Maria* was added to the Lord's Prayer, and held to be as efficacious. Pope Urban IV ordered that the Hours of the Virgin should be said everyday and her office every Sunday. There were countless relics of Mary in numberless churches – strands of her hair, her milk, her clothing – at, among other places, Constance, Laon, Astorga, Boulogne, Chartres and Verdun.

Mary was the epitome of all that was good in womanhood. The Church, predominantly a male society, was basically anti-feminist in attitude, holding that woman was the temptress by which man fell and that man was in many respects her rightful superior. Woman, as a friar commented, was more carnal than a man 'as is clear from her many carnal abominations'. Eve was the mother of all women, but Mary was her redeemer. 'Eve,' said the fifteenth-century preacher William Lichfield, 'our oldest mother in Paradise, held long talk with the adder, and told him what God had said to her and to her husband, of eating of the apple and by her talking the fiend understood her feebleness and her unstableness, and found thereby a way to bring her to confusion. Our Lady Saint Mary did on another wise. She told the angel no tale but asked him discreetly things that she knew not herself. Follow therefore our Lady in discreet speaking and hearing, and not cackling Eve that both spoke and heard unwisely.' 'Mary', St Bernadino of Siena declared, 'has raised you above shame, sterility, frailty. If some men say it was women who made us fall, I say that it is true but it was woman who raised us up again.'

The saints were, as they had long been, another avenue by which the faithful could petition in the court of heaven. 'The martyrs assist us by their prayers and by their passion. With them we have a familiarity, for they are always with us and abide with us, that is, guard us while living and receive us at death.' In an attempt to regulate the process by which saints were added to the Church calendar Pope Alexander III had reserved the right of canonization to the Pope, requiring evidence of the would-be saint's moral worth, supported by the miracles which he or she had performed before or after death. This measure did not prevent any number of illicit cults springing into being and gathering their own band of devotees.

The saints were not remote figures but familiar members of the local community, invoked as patrons of churches and guilds. St Eligius or Eloi was the patron saint of goldsmiths, St Crispin of shoemakers, St Julian of innkeepers, St Nicholas of grocers, St Christopher of travellers, St Margaret of women in childbirth. Some were invoked for specific disorders: St Blaise by sufferers from infections of the throat, St Geneviève from fever, St Sebastian, St Adrian and St Roch for plague, St Vitus for hydrophobia, epilepsy, demonic possession and victims of the dancing mania. 'One', Erasmus noted in his *Encomium Moriae*, 'is good for toothache [St Apollonia whose teeth had been knocked out by her persecutors], another solaced women in childbirth [the girdle of St Foy at Conques helped the expectant mother], a third, for recovering stolen goods, a fourth, for making a voyage prosperous, and a fifth to protect the flock.' In time of pestilence the monks regularly carried the statue of St Foy, accompanied by the playing of cymbals and the blowing of horns through the valleys of the Auvergne. In Navarre an image of St Peter was taken in procession and submerged in the river in the hope of bringing rain. The saints could be as capricious as their devotees, punishing those who scoffed at them or failed to celebrate their festivals, afflicting the offenders with illness or madness. Alternatively the worshippers might blame the saints for failing to listen to their prayers. There were instances of men beating the saint's image because the saint had not responded.

It was their relics which, as it were, established their credentials. Throughout the Middle Ages there was an extensive and profitable trade in relics as king, churchmen and churches competed for them. Abbot Angilbert enumerating the relics housed in his monastery in 801 listed a piece of wood of the True Cross, a strip of Jesus's vestment, water from the River Jordan, a piece of the stone on which Christ sat, wood from the three tabernacles made at the time of the Transfiguration, hair from St Peter's beard and samples of the Virgin's milk, hair and clothes. After Constantinople fell to the crusaders in 1204 there was an enormous dispersal of relics throughout Europe. When Louis IX of France, himself a saint, built the Sainte Chapelle at Paris he gave it a piece of the crown of thorns, part of the cross, a piece of the holy lance and fragments of the purple cloak of Christ, all of which he had obtained from the Byzantine emperor.

In parallel with the multiplication of relics there was a proliferation of shrines to house them. The eighth-century Council of Nicaea had laid down that all new churches should possess a relic, and other churches which did not have them should seek to obtain them. Housed often in gorgeously decorated reliquaries made of precious metal the relic rather than the saint became the object of the worshippers' adoration. In his *Chronicle*, the monk of St Denis described a procession in the abbey of St Denis which occurred on 25 June 1414:

The monks, preceded by men dressed in tunics, and dalmatics of silk, carrying on their shoulders reliquaries containing the holy bodies of SS Osman, Hilary, Eugenius, Hippolytus, Eustace and the head of St Benedict, sang canticles in honour of these and other saints. At their head was the precentor, wearing a most precious cope, and followed by other ecclesiastics who carried the gold cross, the royal *oriflamme*, the chin of St Mary Magdalene and the finger of St Louis . . . gilt statuettes of St Mary and St Nicholas, and the hand of the apostle Thomas. Finally came the reverend Abbots of St Denis and Pontlevoy with . . . the insignia of the passion of our Lord, that is to say, the Crown of Thorns, the Holy Nail and a [piece] of the Cross of our Lord.

Relics had intrinsic miraculous powers capable of curing sickness. The sick and the diseased visiting the saints' shrines would drink water or wine containing dust from the shrine. The ability to engender miracles was a necessary attribute of sanctity, 'so that the invisible God may clearly be seen in the march of events'. 'If', Abbot Samson wrote, 'He created the laws of matter in accordance with His whim, why should he not alter them whenever he chooses?' 'Merit', Pope Innocent III declared, 'without miracles and miracles without merit are both equally insufficient if a saint is to be venerated by the Church Militant.'

There was intense competition among churches and churchmen for the possession of such relics. The monks of Fleury-sur-Loire had purloined the body of St Benedict from the monastery of Monte Cassino which he had founded in southern Italy for their own church; but later the monks of Monte Cassino insisted that they had rediscovered the real body of the saint. In 1080 it was reported that the remains of St Matthew had been discovered at Salerno while Archbishop Leoteric of Sens claimed to have found a part of Moses' rod in the foundations of his church 'at the news of which the faithful converged on Sens not only from every province of France but even from Italy and overseas'. It was claimed that St Mary Magdalene in expiation of her sins had travelled to France and died at St Maximin, but was buried at Vézelay which became a notable centre of pilgrimage. In due course the monks of St Maximin, jealous of Vézelay's fame and wealth, alleged that a sweet odour had led them to the real body in their own church. The manufacture of relics meant that there were multiple specimens of the same instrument of holiness, enough wood, as Erasmus said sardonically, of the True Cross to build a battleship. When Hugh, the bishop of Lincoln, visited the abbey of Fécamp in Normandy, where the principal relic was a supposed arm of St Mary Magdalene, in his eagerness to secure a particle of the relic, he bit off a piece of the finger.

When the monks remonstrated with him, he replied 'If a little while ago I handled the sacred body of the Lord with my fingers in spite of my unworthiness and partook of it with my lips and my teeth, why should I not treat the bones of saints in the same way?' Similarly when Count Fulk of Anjou visited the church of the Holy Sepulchre at Jerusalem he too bit off a piece of the stone for a reliquary at home. Some kept pieces of such sacred objects in reliquaries which they hung about their necks or in their belts. Hugh of Lincoln had a tooth of St Benedict which had been given him by the monks of Fleury set in his ring. From time to time the Church sought to limit this excessive competition for sacred objects. The Lateran Council of 1215 ordered that relics should only be exposed in a reliquary and tried to do away with the trade in relics. But there was no stopping the cult of the saints. The guardians of the shrines found them prestigious and profitable, though the costs of hospitality sometimes weighed against the profits, and to the people they afforded hope and consolation. Their virtual disappearance from the Protestant world must have been a major traumatic experience.

PILGRIMAGES

The pilgrimage was a natural sequel to the veneration of saints. Although it dated back to the early days of the Church, it reached its climax in the Middle Ages, attracting not merely warriors and nobles, churchmen of all ranks but men and women of all classes, though doubtless few peasants could afford to go further than their local shrine.

Pilgrims have visited the holy places from early times, but the crusades gave an additional fillip to such visits, nor did the pilgrimages terminate when Palestine fell again under Muslim rule. Indeed, the Muslims themselves found Christian pilgrimages a source of profit, drawing handsome revenues from the tolls and tributes they exacted, and from the sale of souvenirs, such, for instance, as mass-produced reproductions of the Church of the Holy Sepulchre or specimens of the 'earth from which God fashioned Adam', recommended more particularly as a preservative against epilepsy. Once in the Holy Land, which most pilgrims reached after a long and distinctly uncomfortable voyage, usually starting at Venice, the pilgrims made a Cook's tour, bathed, if they could, in the River Jordan, visited Emmaus where Jesus had been recognized by his disciples in the breaking of the bread, and Arimathea where Joseph was born and Samuel was buried. They saw the tree from which Judas Iscariot hanged himself, the place where the apostles wrote the creed, the footprint in the stone left by Christ before his Ascension, and the chain with which Goliath was bound after his fight with David. The high point of their trip would have been a visit to the Church of the Holy Sepulchre, and to the Church of the Holy Nativity at Bethlehem.

Rome was the other obvious centre of pilgrimage. After Pope Boniface VIII appointed the year 1300 a jubilee or holy year, Rome was to be thronged with pilgrims, eager to win the promised plenary indulgence for all who visited its great basilican churches. The original jubilee was intended to commemorate a hundred years, but Pope Clement VI in 1343 reduced the interval to fifty years, and Urban VI to thirty-three years, the supposed number of years of Christ's life, a decision which was, however, not accepted by his rival, the Avignonese Pope. It was left to Paul II in 1470 to proclaim that the jubilee was to be celebrated every twenty-five years.

Europe was pockmarked with shrines which attracted a greater or smaller number of pilgrims, for some fell from favour with the passing of time. The shrine of St James the Great at Santiago de Compostella in north-west Spain was one of the most popular. St James's tomb had been revealed in vision to Bishop Teodmiro of Iria in 814 some seven hundred or more years after his death. After the Spanish Christians defeated the Moors at the battle of Clavijo in 834, a victory attributed to the saint's intervention, King Alfonso II built a church which was later transformed into one of the finest of medieval cathedrals. But every country had many shrines: in England, St Thomas at Canterbury, St Winifred at Holywell, St Cuthbert at Durham, the Blessed Virgin Mary at Walsingham and the Holy Rood at Bromholm.

Pilgrims were attracted to shrines in some places because of their association with wonder-working images, such as the crucifix of Lucca or the Virgin of Chartres or the Holy Blood of Hailes or the figure of Christ on the rood at Boxley which allegedly moved its eyes, shed tears and foamed at the mouth. But there were many reasons for going on pilgrimage, to enjoy travel and adventure, to fulfil a sentence imposed as a penitence, to recover health:

The holy blisful martir for to secke
That them hath holpen when they were weeke.*

It was, above all, an act of piety which brought a spiritual reward. Those who went wore a special costume so that they might be identified: a long coarse tunic, a 'sclavein', a cross on their garb, a scrip or loose bag usually made of leather round their waist in which they kept their money and their food, and they carried a staff, all of which may have been blessed by the Church in a special ceremony. Each of these articles was given a symbolic meaning. The staff, for instance, drove away wild animals but was also a symbol of man's defiance of the Devil. To indicate where he had been the pilgrim wore a badge, a palm from the Holy Land (hence the name 'palmer'), cockle-shells from Santiago, most of which were commercialized as small leaden discs. Professional pilgrims, as some modern tourists in their cars, covered the wide brims of their hats with badges. King Louis XI of France,

---

* (Chaucer, ed. A. Burrill.)

an assiduous pilgrim who founded the fine flamboyant pilgrim church of Notre Dame de l'Épine near Chalons, wore a hat 'brimful of images, mostly of lead and pewter, which he kissed when good or bad news arrived', so Claude de Seyssel commented. Even badges were regarded as having spiritual power and curative properties.

The pilgrimage was yet another milestone on the road to salvation. 'A man', commented the Milanese, Santo Brasca, who had gone to Jerusalem in 1480, 'should undertake this voyage solely with the intention of visiting, contemplating and adoring the most Holy Mysteries, with great effusion of tears, in order that Jesus may graciously pardon his sins, and not with the intention of seeing the world or from ambition or to be able to say "I have been there" or "I have seen that" in order to be exalted of his fellows.'

Pilgrims who were expected to go to confession before starting off could, like the crusaders, expect indulgences which offered a remission from sin, though they did not release the sinner from guilt, a distinction which some of the more simple-minded pilgrims may not have taken in. The more Masses they attended, the more holy places they visited, the greater the indulgence for which they could hope. Gerald of Wales reckoned that he had earned 92 years of indulgence as a result of attending some 395 Masses in Rome. The Roman churches, competing for custom, publicly advertised their indulgences. 'It is plain that whoever goes truly penitent to St James and asks for his help with all his heart will certainly have all his sins expunged.'

Whatever degree of secret scepticism may have existed, outwardly religion permeated popular and public life, devised to ward off the Devil and to win God's favour. Litanies and processions of barefoot penitents were held in times of natural disaster. Crucifixes lined the roads and were sometimes placed in the fields to recall to God that the Christian was mindful of his mercy. Merchants and workers formed guilds which always had a religious aspect, with special Masses on the festivals of their patron saints. Laymen and women joined together in religious confraternities, sometimes with their own chapels and found an outlet for their piety in the foundation of hospitals, almshouses and schools. The mystery plays were both a source of edification as well as entertainment. The richer members of the community were able to pave their way to heaven by the endowment of chantries where chantry priests said Masses or obits for their departed souls.

THE LAST THINGS

And at the end of life, what then? Men and women lived on the threshold of another existence which few of them seemed to have questioned. There must surely have been sceptics, like the count of Soissons who, told the story of the Resurrection, laughed 'What a fable! What woolly talk', but most looked forward to life in eternity. Their lot might be the torments of hell but more conceivably the limbo of purgatory where those who died in the grace of God were to expiate their remaining faults before they were able to enjoy the beatific vision in heaven. The concept of purgatory was based on the notion that men must inevitably die without having made complete restitution for the sins they had committed in their lifetime. Although purgatory was a temporary state it could be one of acute suffering and length, the period and degree of which might be reduced by the offering of prayers and Masses on the victim's behalf. Ultimately the faithful followers of Christ might expect to dwell with Christ in glory. Their souls would be with Christ but their bodies would rest in limbo until Christ descended from heaven at the second coming at the general Resurrection. The whole superb scenario, both so fearful and exhilarating, was subsumed in the splendid poetic epic of Dante's *Divine Comedy*. It was this system of salvation which the Protestant Reformation was soon to dislocate and modify and in part destroy. Some might argue that one fable was to be replaced by another.

CHAPTER SIX

The Protestant Reformation

On 16 April 1521 a 38-year-old German Augustinian friar Martin Luther, then a professor at Wittenberg University in Saxony, entered the city of Worms, accompanied by an imperial herald, for he was travelling under safe-conduct from the young emperor Charles V. He had been summoned to attend a meeting of the imperial diet to answer charges of heresy. Although he had been everywhere greeted warmly by the people, Luther knew that he was being called upon to recant, and was in danger of death or imprisonment if he remained adamant. 'We shall enter Worms,' he told his friend Spalatin 'in spite of all the gates of hell and the powers of darkness. . . . Find me somewhere to stay.' Eventually lodgings were found for him and his companions at the hospice of the Knights of St John.

At four in the afternoon he appeared in the meeting hall before a crowded audience. The pale young emperor and some of the dignitaries were seated but most had to stand tightly packed. Did he, Luther was asked, acknowledge that he had written the books stacked on the table in front of him? Would he be ready to recant anything that he had written to which reasonable objections could be made? To some of the onlookers Luther seemed unsure of himself, and he asked for further time to consider his answer to the second of these questions.

When he reappeared in the late afternoon of the second day, apparently more confident, he spoke clearly, defending his writings and even venturing to criticize the Pope. 'Everyone', he said, 'is witness to the fact that the laws promulgated by the Pope and the doctrines made by men ensnare, harass and torture the consciences of believers in the most woeful manner.' What he had written was founded firmly in the scriptures. 'If Christ himself, who knew he could not err, did not scorn to hear testimony against his teaching even from the humblest servant, how much more must I, who am a servant subject to error in all I do, ask that someone bring testimony against my teaching. . . . Bring testimony, convict me of my errors, from the Prophets and the Gospels! Correct me from these, and I will gladly recant and be the first to cast my writings in the fire!' 'Unless I am convinced by testimony from the Holy Scriptures and clear proofs based on reason – because, since it is notorious that they have erred and contradicted themselves, I cannot believe either the Pope or the Council alone – I am bound by my conscience and the Word of God. Therefore I could and will recant nothing, because to act against one's conscience is neither safe nor salutary.

So help me God!' Some accounts give a more incisive ending 'Here I stand and I can do no other. So help me God!'

Luther's response caused a great commotion which the emperor brought speedily to an end by leaving the chamber. Luther, still escorted by the imperial herald, pushed his way through the serried, hostile ranks and shortly afterwards left Worms. Some thirty-four or five years later the emperor Charles, having abdicated his great offices, and living in the quiet of his monastic retreat at Yuste in Spain, expressed his regret that he had honoured the safe-conduct which he had given the reformer. 'I did wrong in not killing Luther at the time . . . as a result this mistake of mine assumed gigantic proportions.'

PRELUDE TO THE PROTESTANT REFORMATION

In fact it was doubtful whether Luther's execution could have arrested the progress of the Protestant Reformation, though it might conceivably have diminished its impact. It was plain that even in the most orthodox circles there was an insistent demand for the reform of abuses, though not for the doctrinal changes which were to be the most characteristic feature of the Protestant Reformation. There were, however, clear signs of religious ferment generated by various developments which were occurring in the late Middle Ages.

Growing criticism of abuses had been promoted by outspoken publications which the printing press made available to an increasingly literate public. In his *Praise of Folly*, for instance, Erasmus had poured scorn on some of the absurdities of current religious practice. Even more influential was his widely read *Enchiridion Militis Christiani* (1504) or Instruction of a Christian Soldier. If Erasmus wrote the *Apocalyntosis* which recounted the supposed reception of the worldly Pope Julius II in heaven, even the papacy was not spared his barbs. Nor was Erasmus the only satirist who poked fun at religion.

The intellectual climate in the late Middle Ages was favourable to change. Contemporary scholasticism, nominalism, which seemingly concentrated much of its attention of debating the minutiae (such as whether it would be possible for God to have become incarnate in a cucumber or an ass) rather than on the fundamentals of faith, was in some intellectual circles increasingly discredited. Well-known scholars of a radical turn of mind, Valla in Italy, Reuchlin in Germany, Colet in England, were, like Erasmus, attracted to the humanist theology made possible by Renaissance scholarship which the rediscovery of the original Hebrew and Greek texts of scripture, hitherto available only in the Latin Vulgate of St Jerome, brought into existence. Concerned to take the dust-covers off the Latin Vulgate Erasmus published in 1516 a fresh edition of the Greek New Testament which if not free from error at least showed up the mistakes and even doctrinal tendentiousness in Jerome's version, while in Spain under the patronage of Cardinal Ximenes a Complutensian Bible was published. Erasmus himself even suggested that everyone should be enabled to read the Bible in his or her own language, so that its message should strike the mind and soul of each reader with the freshness of the true gospel which the Holy Spirit would then teach him to interpret and impart. Humanism fertilized the ground for the Protestant reformers, making possible a more sympathetic response to Protestant criticism of the contemporary Church and to its stress on scriptural theology. 'Luther's dogmatic attacks on the foundations of the medieval Church', so Euan Cameron has commented, 'matured like cuckoo's eggs in the humanist nest.' Yet though it was to be popularized, humanist theology was pabulum for only a small scholarly élite, some of whom, like Sir Thomas More and even Erasmus himself, remained loyal to the Catholic faith.

The Protestant Reformation had had its precursors, John Wycliffe and the Lollards in England, John Huss in Bohemia, both of whom had substituted the authority of scripture for that of the Pope, even if they had not adumbrated the doctrine of justification by faith. While they had largely succumbed to the persecutory pressures of the Church, subliminally they remained a potential threat, for small groups of their adherents in England and central Europe kept their teaching alive and so formed an undergrowth which could in certain conditions be set ablaze. Wycliffe and Huss were to be seen later not unjustly as the prophets of the Protestant Reformation, and their unseen influence on the growth of religious agitation was not inconsiderable.

Moreover, significant changes had been taking place, if on a small scale, in the religious ethos of fifteenth-century Europe. Some measure of monastic reform, with a greater emphasis on austerity of life, had already occurred, more especially in Germany. The semi-monastic association known as the Brethren of the Common Life, sited in the Low Countries, was advocating a return to literal scriptural teaching and to holiness of living. Its best-known member, Thomas à Kempis, wrote a classical devotional book *The Imitation of Christ* stressing private prayer and moral renewal which could be interpreted as diminishing the force of sacramental religion. There was in some quarters, especially among pious laymen and laywomen, a spirit of devotion which encouraged the believer to bypass the formalities of religion and to seek an intimate and personal contact with God the Creator. The Brethren of the Common Life ran schools where they tried to put their ideas into practice, at one of which, at Deventer, Erasmus himself had been a pupil. Religious life in late medieval Europe was neither static nor in decay. In many places there were the green shoots of reform.

The political scene seemed to suggest a further disintegration of the fabric of *Christianitas* as national states grew in power. There was less concern to defend *Christianitas* against common enemies. While the Turks continued to menace the integrity of Christian Europe, besieging Vienna in

1529 and dominating the Mediterranean at least until their defeat at the battle of Lepanto in 1571, the European powers showed little crusading ardour. The French were even ready to ally with the Turk against their common enemy, the emperor. The Venetians and the English were more interested in profitable trade than the pursuit of religion. The Spaniards had unleashed cruel crusades against the Moors to unify Spain, but Spanish Catholicism had become intertwined with national feeling. Paradoxically because the Church in Spain and France, as a result of agreements with the Pope, had fallen much under the dominance of the national monarch, neither in Spain nor in France, unlike in Henry VIII's England or Gustavus Vasa's Sweden, did the rulers feel any need to precipitate a religious reformation in order to win control over the Church.

What ordinary men and women felt about the Church on the eve of the Reformation really eludes us. Although they grumbled, as they had ever done, at the various fees which the Church exacted, and expressed disgust at the luxury of dignitaries and the moral failings of many a parson, by and large they did not query the basic beliefs of their religion or the demands and obligations it imposed. They found spiritual solace in the Church's liturgy and traditional devotions. Their wills are replete with religious sentiment. They neither questioned papal supremacy nor the Church's doctrine, though the support which early Protestant agitation received suggests that there was a measure of disillusion with the faith. Yet in its radical iconoclasm the Reformation was to overturn the very elements in Catholic devotion to which ordinary laymen and women were most attached.

While the Protestant Reformation was to be the work of a resolute minority, it drew for its support on popular feeling which was as much socially as religiously motivated. The enthusiasts on both sides of the great divide were to work on formal church goers, shepherding them into opposite camps, but there was an element of hooliganism of which the religious enthusiasts also availed themselves. The bully-boys, the rent-a-gang mob, engaged in violence to crush the opposition. Men and women who probably knew very little about the cause they were embracing were to interrupt religious processions and services with shouts and secular songs. Images were to be pulled down and desecrated with blood and beer. Men spat, urinated and defecated into holy water stoups and fonts. Letters of indulgence and other religious documents were used as lavatory paper. Satirical plays and carnival processions ridiculed the clergy and Catholic ceremonial. The priest who carried a Bible instead of a Host at the Corpus Christ procession at Basle was loudly cheered. Nor was such violence confined to one side. There were some signs of a generation gap in this ferment, for the reform preachers and their followers were younger than their opponents.

The ingredients which brought the Reformation about were largely adventitious. Its early spread was the result of a congeries of factors, political and social in their nature as well as religious. That the elector of

Saxony, for instance, gave Luther the support which he needed to survive occurred because he esteemed Luther as a highly reputed professor at his cherished newly founded university of Wittenberg. In many a German city it was the merchant classes, the rich bourgeoisie, who seized the opportunity to overthrow an unpopular oligarchical patriciate or to displace a cathedral chapter and seize clerical property. There had been in any case a long-standing distrust of Rome in Germany enhanced by a strong if amorphous nationalistic feeling. The princes found in the acceptance of reformed ideas an opportunity to diminish further the power of the Church and to confiscate ecclesiastical estates. Yet fundamentally the Reformation remained a religious movement, which was filling some sort of spiritual vacuum, providing believers with a rich faith through the open Bible. In its beginnings the course which it was to take was to be in large measure determined by the magnetic force and genius of its early leaders, Martin Luther, Huldreich Zwingli and John Calvin.

MARTIN LUTHER AND THE GERMAN REFORMATION

Martin Luther, the son of a prosperous copper-miner with a peasant ancestry, had an intelligent, incisive mind, if less well ordered than that of Calvin. Educated in the scholastic philosophy of the nominalist school at Erfurt, from which he may have deduced his strong belief in the unfettered will and sovereignty of God and in man's need for a prescriptive faith, there were to be hints of his growing belief in the doctrine of justification by faith in the lectures which he was giving before 1518 at the newly founded university of Wittenberg. 'God cannot accept a man unless the grace of God is justifying him.'

In Luther's view, as in that of St Augustine, and in some sense of St Paul, man's fall from grace had left him and his offspring so utterly depraved that even his good works failed to satisfy God. Man could only be effectually saved by his faith in the redeeming merits of Christ through whose sacrifice on the cross alone there was the power to take away sin. The faith which enables man to attain this is itself a gift from God. 'A sure and constant trust', as his fellow reformer Melanchthon put it, 'in God's good will towards us . . . nothing else than trust in the divine mercy promised in Christ.' The sinner had thus to be justified by the merits of Christ's atoning work which, imputed to men and women, removed their guilt and enabled them to advance towards sanctification.

The doctrine challenged traditional Catholicism. The rigid structure of the penitential system appeared stale and unavailing set side by side with the absolute necessity of accepting in heart and mind Christ's redemptive sacrifice as the only remedy for sin. Confession, penitence, absolution, purgatory, indulgences and intercessions to the saints could no longer provide any remedy. In place of the authority of the Church, Luther had substituted the authority of the Word of God contained in the Bible. In practice he was to discover that it was easier to invoke the authority of scripture than to apply it; while it could not err its texts did not always bear the same weight. To ascertain its basic authenticity it had to be read in the light of its teaching on the promised justification through Christ's redemption. While the reformers readily used the textual skills which recent humanist scholarship had made available, they were not above fitting the text to suit their own doctrinal conjectures. Luther, for instance, appended the word 'alone' to the text from Romans 3:28, 'the just shall live by faith', so giving it additional substance.

Luther's conclusions, enunciated over a long period of time, were not only the result of a lengthy intellectual and spiritual pilgrimage but the outcome of an agonizing voyage of personal self-discovery. His father had hoped that he would adopt a legal career but at the age of twenty-three Martin had had a traumatic experience, in the form of a sudden escape from death in a thunderstorm, which led him to become an Augustinian friar. The life of abnegation which he practised, for this was a reformed order of friars, with an obsessive strictness had not, however, as he had hoped, brought him into a closer relationship with God. It was only by reading the scriptures that he found in a personal surrender to Christ the key which freed him from the feeling of guilt which had caused him such depression and torture of mind.

The episode which made the Saxon professor into an international figure could not have been foreseen. The youthful Albert, Archbishop of Mainz who had acquired oversight of the sees of Magdeburg (in which Wittenberg was itself located) and of Halberstadt found difficulty in paying the fees to Rome for a dispensation to hold these offices in plurality. Consequently he borrowed money at interest from the German bankers, the Fuggers of Augsburg, and to pay for the loan proclaimed an indulgence, the income from which would go in part to pay for the rebuilding of the Church of St Peter's at Rome and the remainder to repay the bankers.

Luther's master, the Elector Frederick banned the indulgence seller, John Tetzel, from setting foot in Saxony, not because he disapproved of indulgences, for he was himself the proud owner of some 17,433 relics in his castle church, but because he disliked Archbishop Albert and resented the loss of cash which the sale of indulgences in his territory would entail. As the sale of indulgences seemed to Luther to devalue the Christian concept of true penitence for sin, he wrote a letter of protest to the archbishop, enclosing ninety-five theses explaining his objections, which subsequently he probably but not certainly affixed on All Saints' Eve, 31 October 1517, to the door of the castle church at Wittenberg.

If Luther at first seemed a reluctant champion of his views, public opinion informed by pamphlet literature began to swing behind him. Contrariwise the papacy, alarmed by the whiff of heresy, called on Luther to answer for his controversial opinions. At the diet of Augsburg in October

1518, confronted by the Thomist scholar Cardinal Cajetan, Luther was again ordered to recant, but he slipped away under cover of darkness, declaring that he would appeal from the Pope to a general council with whom rested final authority in the Church. In the summer of 1519 he was again involved in a public debate, together with his colleague, Carlstadt, in the castle of Pleissenberg at Leipzig where his opponent was the masterful and skilled controversialist John Eck. To Eck's satisfaction, Luther ventured to justify John Huss, so throwing doubt on his earlier appeal to the authority of a general council (by which Huss had himself been condemned). For Luther the Word of God alone was the sole final authority, *sola fide, sola scriptura.*

The die was now cast. Luther who had the pen of a ready writer, with a range of language which moved from obscene polemic to intense spirituality, was soon to provide masses of published material largely written in superb German prose for the youthful printing presses which found a ready market for his work in Germany and beyond. In 1520 he published three major treatises, *To the Christian Nobility of the German Nation,* in which he called on the German princes to undertake the reform of the Church; *The Babylonish Captivity of the Church,* attacking the Church's teaching on the sacraments; and *Of the Liberty of a Christian Man* in which he reiterated the basic importance of justification of faith to the believing Christian.

The papacy was unable longer to tolerate the animadversions of a solitary German monk who questioned its authority and, worried by growing popular support for his views, issued a bull *Exsurge Domine* on 15 June 1520, condemning forty-one propositions in Luther's writings, ordering his books to be publicly burned and commanding Luther to retract within two months or suffer the pains of excommunication. Luther responded by burning the papal bull on a bonfire together with books of canon law and the papal decretals. The excommunication was finalized on 3 January 1521. Such was the background which led to Luther's summons to the Diet of Worms and his confrontation with the emperor.

By his defiant stand at Worms Luther had placed himself outside the bounds of toleration either by the Pope or the emperor, and henceforth could only be restrained by the force of law and of the sword. To ensure his safety the Elector Frederick arranged a collusive kidnapping as he returned from Worms, and his semi-incarceration in the castle of Wartburg where he grew a beard and called himself Squire Georg; but the trauma of his lonely residence and spiritual torment led to nightmares in which he imagined he was persecuted by demons. He plunged himself feverishly into writing pamphlets and tracts and an enduring masterpiece, a translation into German of the New Testament.

Meanwhile the Reformation was catching fire. His teaching was being disseminated with surprising rapidity throughout Germany and beyond. He had willing instruments in the young men, some of them former monks and friars, who had studied under him at Wittenberg and whose preaching carried his message. The printing press formed another essential tool. No less than 4,000 titles were circulating in Germany before 1530, carried from town to town by pedlars and traders, and read aloud in public places, inns, markets and workshops, and even placarded on the walls. The endemic criticisms of a worldly Church, the feeling of German nationhood, the inflammatory preaching of Protestant friars and priests, the aspirations of an urban bourgeoisie, the dissatisfactions of the proletariat had created a populace as ready to ignite as dry tinder.

In Luther's absence Wittenberg under his fiery colleague Carlstadt itself became the scene of violent religious revolution. The Mass was replaced by a revised liturgy which provided for communion in both kinds, both bread and wine, for the layfolk. Town ordinances confiscated funds bequeathed for Masses and transferred them to provide stipends for priests, relief for the poor and dowries for poor girls. Side altars were removed. Begging and brothels were banned. Luther, conservative by instinct, was so alarmed by this radical militancy that he reappeared in Wittenberg in his friar's garb and brought the violence to an end. But what had happened in Wittenberg was to be repeated in many other German towns.

In 1524 Luther still had twenty-two years of active life in front of him, continuing to pour out a series of writings in which he endeavoured, not always with success, to clarify his doctrinal position but nonetheless creating a corpus of theology which laid inescapably the foundations of Protestantism. He lived simply in Wittenberg with his wife, the former nun Catherine von Bora, looking after their children, talking to the students some of whom lodged there and engaging in a very wide correspondence. Latterly he suffered much from ill-health, and from depression accentuated by his disquiet about the way in which the Reformation was developing.

Even before his death some were beginning to query his judgement. Fearful of the danger to public order, he had made intemperate attacks on the peasants who in 1524–5 rose against their landlords in southern Germany, some appealing to the evangelical faith to justify what they were doing. Luther urged the princes to 'brandish their swords, to free, save, help and pity the poor people forced to join the peasants – hit the wicked, stab, smite, and slay all you can'. Nor had the curious case of the German Lutheran prince, Philip of Hesse, whose bigamous marriage Luther and Melanchthon had both sanctioned, finding a convenient precedent in the behaviour of Abraham and the Old Testament prophets, redounded to his reputation.

In practice Luther had been obliged to compromise with the world to ensure the survival and expansion of his evangelical Church, for while Luther had hoped originally that the Church would be governed by its congregation, the brotherhood of all believers became a mirage and the future of Lutheranism was determined more and more by the 'godly' prince. 'These times', Luther had written during the Peasants' War, 'are so extraordinary that a prince can win heaven more easily by bloodshed than by prayer.' Religion and politics became bloodily more and more intermingled. In 1529 a number of princes meeting at the diet of Speyer had issued a protest against the religious policy of the emperor – hence the name Protestant. Two years later they formed an alliance, the Schmalkaldic League, resulting in a prolonged civil war.

Although Lutheranism came to depend upon the German princes, its strongest roots were in the imperial free cities, a large majority of which accepted Protestantism at an early date, and in Swiss towns like Basle and Zurich. The cities housed an educated merchant class, many not merely envious of Church patronage and property but eager to read the pamphlet literature. They could call on a working-class proletariat not merely ready to riot but seeking some compensation for what was often an oppressive existence. It was within the cities that Lutheran church organization took its characteristic shape.

In less than half a century a Lutheran Church, distinct from that of Rome, came into existence with its own organization, order and liturgy. If princes and town councils had the last word, appointing the consistory, the Church's governing body, consisting of laymen and ministers which dealt with disciplinary offences, Lutheranism was basically congregational. Its liturgy remained in some respects conservative, for while Luther had vehemently rejected transubstantiation, he insisted on the real presence in the Eucharist, chalking on the table at Marburg Castle in the course of his debate with Zwingli in 1529 the words 'This is my body'. Luther had written a *Great Catechism* for the clergy and a *Little Catechism* for the laity which became the principal means of instruction for both the parish and home. The Bible constituted the final authority. Luther had completed his translation of the Bible with the German Old Testament in 1524, and some hundred thousand German Bibles were to be printed at Wittenberg alone between 1534 and 1584. Equally important were the German hymns, some fifty or more composed by Luther himself, which were sung at first more at home than in church. The continuing strength of Lutheranism came from its social solidarity. It took a prominent and enlightened part in education, utilized its funds to promote social welfare, to foster poor relief and to care for the sick and needy.

Lutheranism spilled over into non-German lands, Denmark, Sweden and Finland, but its missionary impulse was limited, and its intrinsic unity was not easy to sustain. It had gradually acquired legitimacy. The year after Luther's death, 1547, the capture of the Protestant leader, Elector John Frederick at the battle of Mühlberg, gave the emperor an opportunity to impose a religious settlement, the Interim of Augsburg, which he hoped might pacify both sides. It allowed the Protestants to have a married clergy and to have communion in both kinds, but there was strong opposition, so much so that shortly before he abdicated Charles V agreed, if reluctantly, to a new settlement, the Peace of Augsburg, which declared that every land which had been Lutheran before 1552 should remain so, and that henceforth it was for the ruler of the state to decide whether the official religion should be Catholic or Lutheran. While the Peace of Augsburg assured the future of Lutheranism in Germany (though it made no mention of Calvinism which had a growing following there), it only papered over the cracks, for the Lutherans continued to be sharply divided, between, if the issue can be unduly simplified, the moderates led by Melanchthon with their headquarters at Wittenberg, and the rigorists led by Matthias Flacius Illyricus, a learned but contentious divine from Jena and Magdeburg. Eventually a somewhat spurious unity was imposed through the acceptance in 1577 of a confession of faith known as the Formula of Concord. Yet in spite of such persistent controversy Lutheranism continued to flourish and even to expand, if at a decreasing rate.

Over Lutheranism the spirit of Martin Luther hovered as the Titan among the reformers. Over-vehement, deeply emotional, uneasily fenced in by a feeling of guilt, yet unyieldingly convinced of his faith in Christ's redemptive work he was without doubt the founding father of the Protestant Reformation. He would have wished to strengthen the message of the cross but found that he had unleashed a sword. He wanted to restore a united, apostolic Church but he had seeded a series of societies that were by their very nature fissiparous.

ZWINGLI AND CALVIN

The Swiss reformer Huldreich Zwingli has his own claims to originality, for though he was much influenced by Luther, he made a significant contribution to the development of Protestantism. Whereas Luther had been educated in a predominantly scholastic atmosphere, Zwingli had imbibed humanist ideas, owing much to Erasmus and his teachers at Vienna, and was in many respects more radical in attitude than Luther. Appointed a parish priest of the Grossmünster at Zurich in 1518, for the next fifteen years he propagated reformed views, attacking indulgences and the Pope, clerical celibacy – he had married a widow, Anna Reinhard – and the sacrifice of the Mass, emphasizing the authority of the literal words of scripture as both inspired and infallible. 'The Word of God is certain and cannot fail; it is bright and does not let man err in darkness; it recalls itself, it makes itself plain, and illumines the human world with all salvation.' At Zurich the Lord's Supper was divested of its medieval ceremonial and given a purely commemorative interpretation. The unleavened bread and wine were placed in the centre of the nave rather than on an altar at the east end of the church. The ministers, wearing their everyday garb, facing the congregation, carried the bread on a large wooden trencher for distribution to the people.

While Zwingli was above all a fervent advocate of Protestant teaching, he became deeply involved in Swiss politics, supporting strongly the territorial ambitions of Zurich as against the bishop of Constance and the Catholic cantons around the lake of Lucerne. So the Protestant Reformation became inextricably entangled with the ascendancy of Zurich to defend which Zwingli approved, if unavoidably, the use of force. It was the magistrates who had the final say in religious as in political matters. It was they who ordered that the Anabaptist preachers, whose teaching they believed threatened both the political and social order as well as religious subversion, should be drowned in the lake. Zwingli himself fell in battle in 1531 at Kappel by the lake of Zug in a war against the Catholic cantons that fundamentally had little to do with religion.

In spite of the ambiguous character of the Zwinglian reformation which had spread to Bern and other parts of Switzerland under the guidance of Zwingli's son-in-law Heinrich Büllinger, its exponents exerted influence beyond the borders of Switzerland, more especially over English churchmen in the reign of Edward VI. But Zwinglianism was to be absorbed by the more potent Calvinism. By the Consensus Tigurinus of 1549 Zurich accepted Calvin's teaching on the sacraments; and the Helvetic Confession determined that the belief of the Swiss Protestant churches should be along Calvinistic lines.

John Calvin who owed much to Erasmus and Luther was to have greater influence on the evolution of Protestant Christianity than any other reformer. A Frenchman from Noyon in Picardy he had studied theology and classics at the Collège Montaigu in Paris followed by courses in civil law at Orlèans and Bourges. Possessed of a clear and disciplined mind, he was not devoid of humanist interests as his edition of Seneca's *De Clementia*, published in 1532, showed. At Paris he became associated with a group of scholars and churchmen, influenced by Luther's teaching, who were working for reform, so much so that, finding the academic and ecclesiastical atmosphere in France unsympathetic, and perhaps fearful for his own safety, he moved to Basle, an intellectual and religious frontier-town, forward-looking in Church matters, where he began to write his epochal *The Institutes of the Christian Religion*, published in 1536 and dedicated somewhat ironically to the French king Francis I. It may have been at this time that he underwent a 'converting' experience, for in his later *Commentary on the Psalms* (1557) he wrote, 'At last God tamed my course in a different direction by a hidden bridle of his providence. . . . By a sudden conversion to docility, he turned a mind too stubborn for its years.'

In 1536 Calvin first came to Geneva, a city which had long aspired to win independence from the joint overlordship of its bishop and the duke of Savoy. Helped by the city of Bern which, following the example of Zurich, had accepted the Protestant faith and which wished to occupy the Vaudois, the Genevans accepted a religious as well as a political alignment with Bern, with financial assistance from Basle. The Bernese despatched a French-speaking Protestant, William Farel, who had persuaded the people of Lausanne to expel their Catholic bishop, to preach reform in Geneva. Farel invited Calvin to help him in the work of reforming and reorganizing the

Genevan Church; but there were acute religious and political divisions in Geneva which in 1538 expelled both Calvin and Farel.

Three years later, in 1541, Calvin, who had been acting meanwhile as pastor to the French reformed congregation at Strasbourg which, under the lead of Johann Sturm, had become a prestigious centre of reform, was invited to return. He was to remain in Geneva until his death in 1564, becoming the most influential man in the city and winning an international reputation. Yet Calvin was never to hold any official position save that of pastor, for he was never a citizen, remaining simply an *habitant* or resident alien until 1559 when he was made a *bourgeois*, a category of the second rank carrying certain limited voting rights. His prestige was the more surprising as he lacked the boisterous personality of Martin Luther. He was a reserved, rather charmless man, increasingly irritable as ill-health made its impact, living an austere domestic existence with his wife, Idelette de Bure, widow of an Anabaptist, whose death in 1549 seemed to have greatly grieved him.

In his early years Calvin met with much opposition, led by a party known as the Libertins, and it was only by 1555 that his moral dominance became secure, made so by the influx of Protestant refugees, the majority of whom were artisans including some wealthy men who, because of their financial and social standing, were admitted as *bourgeois*. So the complexion of Geneva's electors changed decisively in favour of Calvin and his supporters.

The Calvinist objective appeared an effective form of religious and moral totalitarianism. The city of Geneva was to be moulded into the 'most perfect school of Christ that ever was in the earth since the days of the Apostles,' as John Knox phrased it, brought into being not merely by persuasive preaching but by social pressures backed ultimately by law and the threat of force.' Yet the government of Geneva was not directly theocratic. The city's moral and religious life was regulated by a series of elected councils on which laymen and ministers both sat. It was the city council which had the last word in the choice of pastors who never possessed civil jurisdiction. Yet in practice the distinction between the civil and religious authorities was blurred, Church and state appearing one society 'distinct in function, but inseparable in being'.

It was the city council which approved the *Ecclesiastical Ordinances*, drawn up by Calvin in 1541, which governed the religious and moral lives of the citizens down to the smallest detail. The Venerable Company of Pastors met together once a week to study the scriptures. It was the duty of the elders, appointed by the councils after consultation with the consistories, to keep a vigilant eye on the morals of the citizens, and to report to the Venerable Company any deviations from the right way. The elders, meeting with the pastors every Thursday, reported cases of potential heresy, irregular attendance at church or any criticism of the ministers. Every unacceptable aspect of life came under their watchful eye: sorcery, fortune-telling, financial extortion, gambling, indecorous conversation, bawdy talk, playing of cards and any sexual irregularity as well as inappropriate dress. An ordinance, for instance, forbade the wearing of slashed breeches, for 'we see that, by the loopholes of the breeches, they wish to bring in all manners of disorders'. The pastors were required to make a yearly visit to the homes of each of their parishioners to ensure that their households were keeping the rules of the Church; but they had no power to impose a civil penalty, a right reserved to the city council. Such inquisitions were not wholly novel, for the medieval Church had had a wide range of powers for dealing with moral offences, but it was the strenuous concentration of effort designed to make Geneva a pattern of the apostolic Church which made that city so significant a powerhouse of religious reformation. The pastors were not indeed only concerned with disciplining defaulters but with the enforcement of justice in trading, and with protecting the sick, children, widows, orphans and the aged. Calvin felt that what was achieved fell far short of his ideal, but although he possessed no direct authority this experiment which he had engineered was to be international in its impact.

By 1555 most of Calvin's critics had left the city. Others were in one way or another suppressed. A manufacturer of toys and playing-cards, the latter banned, who had criticized Calvin, was obliged to walk through Geneva wearing only a shirt, carrying a lighted taper and calling on God to forgive him. Jerome Bolsec, a former Carmelite friar who had taken refuge in Geneva, had in October 1551 attacked Calvin's doctrine of predestination on the grounds that this teaching made God into a tyrant and that by implication Christ died not for all men but only for the elect. He was imprisoned and later banished. The Spanish physician, Michael Servetus, already in trouble with the Inquisition for his anti-Trinitarian views, made an ill-advised and surreptitious visit and at Calvin's instigation he was accused and arrested, and eventually sentenced to death on 27 October 1553. While Calvin, like most of his contemporaries, would have approved of the death penalty for heresy, he was not personally a bloodthirsty or cruel man. What was done in Geneva was executed by order of the city council.

Whatever many Genevans may have felt privately about the regime under which they lived, its very intransigence was to make it a beacon of light for Protestants throughout Europe. Geneva was to be swamped with refugees and visitors from other countries; no less than 4,770 foreign refugees came into the city between 1549 and 1559 of whom 1,536 were artisans. They stimulated trade and manufactures, among them publishing and the watch-making industry, adding greatly to the city's prosperity. They swelled the numbers of the university and the academy. Geneva became a centre for the training of ministers and the publication of Protestant tracts for export abroad. Literature printed at Geneva flooded into Europe, carried by indefatigable colporteurs, so that 'Nothing in Europe was safe from the fiery brand which set everything in flames'.

Calvinism owed its success to Calvin's systematic theology, as expressed in *The Institutes of the Christian Religion* and to the Church structure which enshrined it. His theology was rooted in a magisterial conception of God, as uncreated Creator, omniscient and omnipotent, the embodiment of absolute sovereignty but no arbitrary tyrant, since God would not act contrary to his nature. Of his own volition he made available to man, a sinner who could not achieve salvation by his own efforts, the possibility of redemption by the atoning sacrifice of Christ on the cross. The Church was the earthly medium yet divinely sanctified by which the Christian found salvation. Perfectly the Church was the invisible company of the elect, imperfectly the community of believers on earth, good and bad. 'Wherever', he wrote, 'we see the Word of God preached and purely listened to, and the sacraments [i.e. baptism and the Eucharist] ministered according to the institution of Christ, we cannot doubt that a Church exists.' Confronted by the reality that only some men and women respond to the gospel, Calvin concluded that since the gospel could not be inherently inefficacious, this could only be explained in terms of predestination, a doctrine which he may have owed not merely to St Augustine but to the later medieval scholastics such as Gregory of Rimini and Hugolino of Orvieto. 'We assert that by an eternal and immutable counsel God hath once for all determined both whom he would admit to salvation and whom He would admit to destruction.' For Calvin predestination was less important than it was for future expositors of his teaching (with the consequent and bitter controversy over the belief that Christ died only for the elect), for it was the doctrine of election which helped to provide the members of the evangelical Churches with their inner strength and a sense of their identity. Calvinism which was to provide the backbone for the Protestant movements in France, Scotland and Holland, also exercised a major influence on the Church in Germany and England and through the settlements made by the Puritans in New England became a permanent feature of North American religious life.

THE REFORMATION IN FRANCE

The French Church, more especially in its higher echelons, was ripe for reform. As a result of agreements reached between the Popes and the French kings, the Concordat of Bourges in 1438 and the Concordat of Bologna in 1516, the king had acquired a virtual monopoly over all higher appointments in the French Church, exploiting his power in such a shameless way that it became a form of clientage. High birth, fortune and royal service rather than pastoral zeal became the chief recommendation for appointment to a bishopric; of 129 bishops appointed in the reign of Francis I, 93 came from the noblesse. Bishops tended to dispense their patronage in similar ways, using benefices to reward their clients.

But the reform movement in France was for long a tender plant. Its leading figure Lefèvre d'Etaples had anticipated Luther by stating that justification by faith was a *sine qua non* of the faith, and before he died in

1536 he had published a fourth edition of the French New Testament. Too reserved personally to become a leader, he had acquired a patron in Guillaume Briçonnet, Bishop of Meaux, who won the support of the French king's sister, Marguerite d'Angoulême. The Catholics strongly resisted the onset of reform. The Sorbonne condemned Luther's teaching; Briçonnet recanted and Lefèvre moved to Geneva. The French king had already acquired such power over the Church that unlike his English colleague it seemed more to his interest to deter the reformers than to support them. The state instituted *chambres ardentes* to try cases of heresy. The persecution, stimulated by the posting in 1534 of placards denouncing the Mass in Paris and other chief towns of northern France and even on the door of the king's own château at Amboise, was indiscriminate in its range.

The future of the reform movement in France was to be revolutionized by the link established with Calvin in Geneva. As a Frenchman Calvin was personally particularly interested in promoting the reform movement in his own country. The academy at Geneva became a training-ground for French pastors. French refugees, equipped often with false passports and sometimes travelling in disguise, returned to preach to clandestine congregations. Books and pamphlets were exported from Geneva in great numbers and, in spite of their illegal nature, found ready purchasers, so that the contraband book trade became a lucrative venture. Between 1555 and 1562 the Venerable Company of Preachers provided the French reformed Church with some eighty-eight pastors. By 1561 Admiral Coligny declared that there were some 2,150 reformed congregations in France.

More importantly Calvin supplied the reformed congregations with a Church structure which was able to withstand its many enemies. Its first national synod was held in Paris in 1559, attended by representatives of some twelve Churches and an emissary from Geneva. It drew up a constitution based on the model of Geneva with a very similar ecclesiastical organization and discipline. The ecclesiastical organization of the reformed Church, with its national synod, provincial synods, colloquies, operating as a series of concentric circles, formed a highly efficient administrative structure.

French Protestantism had a diverse following, but was essentially an urban phenomenon and weak in the countryside; its principal supporters were merchants and artisans of the towns where there was a higher rate of literacy and a long tradition of anti-clericalism. Of 160 persons interrogated by the *chambres ardentes* between 1547 and 1550, 55 were clergy (including 30 monks and 25 seculars), 6 were seigneurs, 14 royal officers, 9 lawyers, 16 merchants and 60 artisans and small shopkeepers. Of 561 who attended Huguenot services in November 1560, 36 were city notables, 24 were merchants, 87 were lawyers, physicians and apothecaries, and 387 were artisans and shopkeepers, among them 135 textile workers, but only 27 were described as peasant farmers. Where Protestantism did sprout in the countryside, it was likely to be either a product of long-standing anti-clericalism or of seigniorial influence.

For after the late 1550s Protestantism found some support among the noblesse, some won over by the opportunity to confiscate Church estates which as the Baron de Rochefort commented had been given by them to the Church for purposes which it had ceased to fulfil. A number of aristocratic wives in particular became fervent advocates of the reformed faith. For many of the lesser nobility the attack on the Church became a means of rehabilitating their fortunes affected by the current economic depression.

By the middle of the sixteenth century there was everywhere prescription for a bloody strife. The Protestants indulged in riots of image breaking and the pillage of churches and the Catholics replied in kind. With the treasury heavily in debt, without the capacity to exercise its patronage in such a way as to enable it to identify with either side, the crown seemed powerless to control the situation. The queen dowager, Catherine de'Medici, a woman of little spiritual depth, tried if in vain to process a policy of accommodation in order to pacify both parties. In September 1561 she called a colloquy of theologians to the convent of Poissy near Paris, where a French cardinal on seeing Beza and his fellow Calvinists enter observed 'Here come the Genevan dogs' to which Beza responded 'The Lord's sheepfold needs faithful sheepdogs to drive off the wolves.' In January 1562 Catherine commanded the Huguenots to restore to the Catholics the churches which they had seized and forbade Huguenot public worship in towns, though as a mild concession she allowed it to take place in private houses and places outside the town walls.

The wars of religion lasted some thirty years and though sporadic in their nature they were characterized by savage barbarity. In 1572 on St Bartholomew's Day, Catherine, in the hope of settling the question (and incidentally of releasing her impressionable young son Charles IX from the influence of the Huguenot Admiral Coligny) ordered a general massacre of all the Huguenots in Paris, an example followed in other towns. Religion became a power struggle between competing factions, involving Spanish intervention on the Catholic side.

At last in 1589 Henry of Navarre, Henry IV, became king. Henry was a Huguenot but a moderate who counted the unity and peace of his kingdom as more precious than the minutiae of theological debate. He decided to abjure heresy and simultaneously to seek to satisfy the religious aspirations of his fellow Huguenots. The Edict of Nantes, issued in 1598, gave the Huguenots liberty of conscience throughout France as well as freedom of access to all hospitals, universities and schools. They were to be allowed to worship freely in all cities where they had been able to do so between January 1596 and August 1597 but nowhere within 5 leagues of Paris. Contrariwise the Catholics were given freedom to worship in Huguenot towns. The edict, which provided an uneasy religious peace until Louis XIV ordered its revocation in 1685, was imperfect, setting up a state within a state; but by legislating for the coexistence of Protestant and

Catholic in a single state it marked a major advance in the history of religious toleration.

THE REFORMATION IN SCOTLAND

Like the French Church the late medieval Scottish Church was characterized by many abuses: 'the corruption of morals and profane obscenity of life in churchmen of almost all ranks, together with crass ignorance of literature and all the liberal arts'. As in France religious change became deeply intertwined with political rivalries, notably the support which the French, intermarried with the Stuart royal family, gave to the Catholics, and the English support for reformed ideas, and the encouragement they gave to the Scottish nobles to keep their greedy eyes on the properties of the Church.

After a period of confusion and religious strife the lead in propagating Protestantism along definite Calvinistic lines was to be taken by John Knox. After Knox had been released from the French galleys, which had captured him in 1547 as a result of French intervention in Scottish affairs, he travelled abroad, preaching at the court of Edward VI and working with Calvin in Geneva before he returned to Scotland to find the Protestant cause gathering strength under the 'lords of the congregation'. The Catholics under Queen Mary, the widow of a former French king, had French support, the Protestants the backing of Elizabeth and the English to whom Mary was to surrender in 1567.

Under Knox's stern and fervent lead, Protestantism gained ground. The Scottish parliament abolished the authority of the Pope and declared that the saying or hearing of Mass should be a criminal offence. The nature of reform was crystallized in three statements of which Knox was the principal author, the first of which was the *Scots Confession*, approved by parliament in 1559 and to be superseded by the *Westminster Confession* in 1644; it affirmed justification by faith and declared the true Church to be 'invisible known only to God, who alone knoweth whom he has chosen'. *The Book of Common Order*, which made provision for common worship, was based upon the model of Geneva. *The Book of Discipline*, which bore traces of Calvin's *Ecclesiastical Ordinances*, aimed at a complete 'Reformation of Religion in the whole realm', seeking to ensure the proper appointment of godly ministers and the imposition of discipline on those who contravened the Church's rules for godly living. The Scottish Reformation was rigorously Calvinistic, both in its more attractive spiritual and more repellent human aspects.

THE REFORMATION IN THE LOW COUNTRIES

It was Calvinism which was to provide the essential ingredient in resistance to Spanish rule, in the fight for Dutch independence and in the espousal of

Protestantism in the Low Countries. The Low Countries, consisting of strongly particularist provinces, resentful at the loss of the political privileges under imperial and Spanish rule, and of the money they had to dole out for Spain's wars in which they had no interest, had reacted strongly to the centralized policy of their Spanish masters, more especially to Philip II's sensible if injudicious design to remodel the Church in the Low Countries and the fear that as a consequence the Inquisition would be introduced.

Lutheranism and Anabaptism had early made some headway, religious discontent promoted further by a growing depression in industry and trade. A long and bloody struggle erupted as the Spanish king sought to bring his wayward subjects more directly under his religious and political guidance.

It was in this situation that in the Low Countries, as in Scotland and France, Calvinism became a significant war-head, especially after 1562. Although the religious extremists were for long only a minority in the country, they were to be fuelled not merely by a constant stream of Calvinist propaganda but by an influx of Calvinist preachers and *agents provocateurs* from France and England. By 1572 there were seventeen communities of Dutch Calvinist refugees in England; and some sixty thousand Dutch fled the country under Alva's rigorous rule. A continuous stream of preachers, the *predikants*, some trained in Geneva, others from France, England and Germany, returned home to encourage the brethren to indulge in image breaking and religious pressures of one sort and another. 'The audacity of the Calvinist preachers', a government sympathizer wrote in 1566, 'has grown so great that in their sermons they admonish the people that it is not enough to remove all idolatry from their hearts; they must also remove it from their sight. Little by little, they are trying to impress upon their hearers the need to pillage the churches and abolish all images.' A combination of religious enthusiasm with the pressures which a dominant but militant minority could bring on the less committed, promoted by trade depression, the high cost of bread and unemployment, powered the resistance to Spain.

An efficient system of communication between the Dutch Protestants circulating underground came into existence, 'the churches under the cross' with sympathizers from abroad. The Calvinists took over the former Roman churches and organized their own Church along Calvinist lines with elders and deacons chosen by the congregation and ministers selected by the elders or the town magistrates who kept a tight rein on the Church. The Calvinists remained a minority of the population, for many were deterred from membership of the Church by their fears that if the Catholics again got the upper hand their lives and property would be endangered, while others disliked the strict control over the Church exerted by the elders which required a rigorous examination of the beliefs and morals of each individual member.

Eventually the Low Countries became religiously divided as Flanders remained in Spanish Catholic hands, and even in the United Provinces Calvinism was itself split by the rigorists who accepted Calvinist teaching in its most rigid form and their critics who sought to modify the more intransigent interpretation of predestination, leading in the early seventeenth century to bitter and violent quarrels. Even so, in the lengthy process which brought the Dutch their independence from Spain, Calvinism was a major ingredient, not merely in helping to mould the Dutch Reformed Church in Holland itself but in shaping the religious history of South Africa.

THE ENGLISH REFORMATION

The English Reformation followed a different course for whereas in Scotland, France and the Low Countries it was at least in part a movement of protest against the established government and had some popular support, in England the impetus to the repudiation of Rome stemmed from royal initiative, springing from the desires of a king, Henry VIII, troubled in conscience and so egocentric as to interpret public policy in terms of personal need.

Hence, while there were at least some strong popular elements in the continental reform movements at a comparatively early date, initially the English reform movement was largely determined by competition between influential factions or interest groups, mainly aristocratic in composition, bound together by ideological loyalties, to a greater or lesser degree religious in character, and able by pressure or coercion to secure the compliance of their clients.

Nor was the English Reformation in any sense an inevitable reaction to the deficiencies of the late medieval Church. While there were, as there had always been, numerous complaints about clerical behaviour, non-residence and pluralism (in London between 1521 and 1546, 112 out of 326 clergy were non-resident), anti-clericalism, often fuelled by endemic litigation about the payment of tithes and other fees (such as the case of Richard Hunne who refused to pay his parish priest the mortuary fee for burying his infant son and was subsequently brought to court, charged with heresy and found hanging in his cell) was sporadic and did not represent deep-seated hostility to the clergy. In practice the performance of clerical and episcopal duty in England on the eve of the Reformation was relatively high and better than it was in many other countries. Ecclesiastical courts, if regarded jealously by common lawyers, functioned effectively. Many churches were being restored and built. There was little evidence to suggest that the English people wished to reject the Pope, or to change the doctrine of the Church.

There were perhaps some straws in the wind in the continued existence and even possible resurgence of Lollardy. Some bishops, Longland of

Lincoln in particular, took the threat to orthodoxy from the Lollards sufficiently seriously to renew the persecution of offenders. Yet Lollardy remained the faith of a small minority, confined to certain regions of the country, in the main Bristol, Coventry, Norwich, Essex, Kent, the Chilterns and the Cotswolds. By itself it had no capacity to inaugurate a religious reformation, but its continued existence constituted a life-line between the earlier critics of the Church and those who were being attracted to the new ideas circulating in Germany. It would not be long before dissentient groups were to reprint Lollard works as Protestant propaganda. The early heretic Thomas Bilney seems to have ingested Lollard ideas; the theology of the future Protestant bishop Hugh Latimer was more Lollard than Lutheran in substance. Such Lollard groups as there were might merge with those who were persuaded by the ideas being propagated by Luther which, through the medium of the printing press made an astonishingly early appearance in England. The couriers were likely to be German or Dutch merchants, possibly members of the German Steelyard in London, who fraternized with London traders and a small group of clergy sympathetically inclined to evangelical religion. Church and State were sufficiently alarmed to ban the import of Lutheran books and to make bonfires of heretical literature.

There were small groups of scholars and clergy in London and Cambridge excited by Luther's ideas. Thomas Cranmer, then a young Cambridge don, used to meet with like-minded men at the White Horse tavern in Cambridge; and his later thought, screened as it seemed to be by his political opportunism, was Luther's evangelical doctrine of salvation. Oxford University stamped heavily on colporteurs of Lutheran literature, but it was an Oxford graduate, William Tyndale, who was strongly supported by London merchants when he set about his epochal translation of the Bible into English. In 1524 Tyndale went to Wittenberg and thence to Cologne where part of his translation of St Matthew's Gospel was printed.

Luther's advocacy of the Bible in the vernacular fitted in with the assumptions of humanist scholarship, though Luther was not himself properly speaking a humanist, which had influential proponents in England, among them Erasmus who spent some dreary days teaching Greek at Cambridge between 1511 and 1514, John Colet, the dean of St Paul's, much esteemed as a preacher who stressed the original text of scripture, Sir Thomas More and a number of bishops, among them Richard Foxe who founded an Oxford college, Corpus Christi, more specifically to forward the 'new learning'.

There would, however, have been no real likelihood of Lollardy, Lutheranism or humanism developing into a reform movement in early sixteenth-century England had not Henry VIII for personal reasons precipitated the break with Rome, and had not various interest groups seen that there might be some profit, whether religious or material, in supporting religious change.

It must at the time have seemed comparatively easy to believe that the Pope could be induced to issue Henry with a dispensation from his marriage to Catherine of Aragon in order that he might marry Anne Boleyn and sire an heir to the throne, for Catherine had been wed in the first instance to Henry's elder brother, Arthur, and as the book of Leviticus reminded him, 'if a man shall take his brother's wife it is an impurity'. But Catherine herself vehemently opposed the divorce, claiming that the marriage to Arthur had not been consummated. More to the point she had a powerful patron in her Catholic nephew, the emperor Charles V. Subsequently the king's chief minister Cardinal Wolsey and the Pope, Clement VII (whose principal city Rome had in 1527 been sacked by imperial troops), were at their wits' ends as to what could be done to meet the king's request and indeed unsure as to what even theologically and canonically was the correct course to follow.

Henry grew impatient. Wolsey was disgraced and new stars appeared at the Tudor court, favourable to the divorce and to the promotion of the new religious ideas to which Anne Boleyn was herself personally sympathetic. Thomas Cranmer, a protégé of the Boleyns, who was made archbishop of Canterbury in spite of protests from Catherine of Aragon untied Henry's marriage knots leaving him free to marry Anne. Aware of papal disapproval he began to hedge the Church in England into an increasingly Protestant frame; what he was trying to do was only circumscribed by his prescriptive belief in obedience to the king as God's living representative on earth. In this he was to be assisted by an able and ambitious layman, Thomas Cromwell, a convinced adherent of evangelical Protestantism. With the king's support they made the break with Rome more substantial, using parliament, representative of the nobility and gentry, anti-clerical in attitude, as a vehicle for legislation which cut the ties with Rome, banning the sending of fees and appeals to Rome and declaring that the king, under Christ was the head of the English Church.

Since the monasteries were seen as the chief strongholds of the old religion and were besides the wealthiest property owners in the country, both the king and Cromwell then directed their attack on them, first the smaller houses and then by 1539 the remainder. In striking at the monasteries the king could replenish his exchequer, emptied by the expenses of his ill-conceived wars, and remove a pillar of Romanism. Cromwell, now the king's vice-regent in matters ecclesiastical, sent round a commission to investigate the monasteries. While there can be little doubt that many houses were past their prime, and a few like Dorchester Abbey near Oxford were scandalous in their neglect of the rule, the tale of their offences, supposedly unearthed by the commissioners, reads like the findings of some modern salacious tabloid. In 1536 the smaller monasteries surrendered their estates and three years later the great oaks, the large monasteries, succumbed. The crown acquired a handsome addition to its revenues which it was soon to squander; the upper classes' attachment to the Protestant faith was strengthened by the acquisition of monastic property. To emolliate his critics the king used part of the spoils to found six new bishoprics. But it was a sorry story, for many monasteries were respectable communities conscientiously seeking to carry out their obligations, and the country lost irretrievably a rich cultural and religious heritage.

In religious matters Henry was both an instinctive conservative and a political pragmatist. When Cromwell sought to consolidate the Protestant cause by negotiating an understanding with the German princes, which committed Henry to a marriage with Anne of Cleves whom he found unbearably unattractive, the faithful minister paid for his mistake with his life. The pro-Catholic though not pro-Roman party manipulated a religious reaction as a consequence of which the Ten Articles of 1539, Protestant in flavour, were replaced by the Six Articles of 1542 which moved backward in a Romanist direction, among other things condemning clerical marriage, so that Cranmer, married secretly to a niece of a German reformer, Osiander, had hurriedly to send his wife back to Germany. 'The people', Marillac reported, 'show great joy at the king's declaration touching the Sacrament, being much more inclined to the old religion than the new opinions.' But the power of the pro-Roman party headed by the duke of Norfolk evaporated after the execution for adultery of Norfolk's niece, Catherine Howard, the king's fifth wife. Her successor was pro-Protestant; and the king's son and heir was consigned to the care of a Protestant tutor. Henry who had deteriorated into an obese, tyrannical monster suffering from the agonies of an ulcerated leg, died in 1547, his hand resting in that of his loyal archbishop.

How deep and how religious was the English Reformation when Henry died? There were many good religious men and women who had been appalled by the course of events. Sir Thomas More, scholar and humanist, and John Fisher, the bishop of Rochester, had been beheaded for denying the king's headship of the Church. There were many lesser men and women who suffered a similar fate. James Mallet, the treasurer of Lincoln Cathedral who had the temerity to say that 'Woo worth then that begun the divorce between the kyng and quene Kateryne, for syns we had never a good world', was hanged, drawn and quartered in 1542. At Exeter in 1537 local women attacked the workmen who were pulling down St Nicholas's Priory. More serious than individual protests was the armed rising in the north, the Pilgrimage of Grace. While it had other causes, it was fundamentally support for the old religion and the monasteries which drew hundreds of men to the rebels' banner, impaling the five wounds of Christ, which momentarily posed a very real threat to the government's authority.

Yet in some respects the foundations for a successful Protestant reformation had been laid. The papacy and all its agencies had been expelled. Under the guidance of Archbishop Cranmer the liturgy had been given a Protestant direction and the Bible in English was being placed or

ordered to be placed in every English church while the vestiges of the
Roman past, shrines, images and wayside crosses, were being destroyed.
There were other signs of Protestantism's increasing hold. The number of
wills which were definitely Protestant in language was growing. There was a
decline in bequests to chantry priests and to religious guilds and
fraternities. Requests for commemorative sermons were tending to replace
propitiatory Masses, trentals, obits and the like. Protestant tracts, such as
Simon Fish's *Supplication for Beggars*, had a wide reading public.

Nonetheless the majority of men and women had neither wanted nor
greeted the Reformation. Not even the king knew exactly what sort of
reformation was taking place. The majority of his subjects must have been as
confused as their master. Far from indifferent to the disappearance of the
old rituals and customs, they acquiesced in the new order because, short of
rebellion with all its dire consequences, they had no real alternative.
'*Indignatio principis mors est.*' – 'The prince's wrath means death.' 'These
things', a London priest confessed in 1536, 'will not last, I warrant you: you
shall see the world change shortly.' The religious changes had led to some
decline in the Church's pastoral efficiency marked by a fall in the number
of ordinands which had been increasing in the first few decades of the
century. In London, for instance, 840 men had been ordained in the
episcopate of FitzJames (1506–22), 306 in Tunstal's time (1522–30),
97 under Stokesley (1530–9) and 46 under Bonner (1540–7). The
injunctions obliging every parish church to have an English Bible, to
remove images and to abolish the veneration of saints, as the
churchwarden's accounts show, were only reluctantly and slowly obeyed.

Henry's heir, the young Edward VI, had been brought up under
Protestant tutelage and the appointment as regent of his uncle the duke of
Somerset meant a further Protestantization of the Church in a radical
direction. Cranmer, who had sometimes walked so uneasily in the late king's
court, became Somerset's guide. Right-wing bishops like Stephen Gardiner
of Winchester and Edmund Bonner of London were placed under
detention and replaced by left-wing clerics, among them Ridley who became
bishop of London, the preacher Hugh Latimer who was restored to his see
of Worcester and Hooper, made bishop of Gloucester, who, as Fuller
observed, 'after he came back to England in 1549 seemed to have brought
Switzerland with him'. 'Our king', Hooper had commented, just before
Henry's death 'had destroyed the Pope but not Popery.' This was what the
reformers now proceeded to do. The chantries and similar societies, some
2,347 in all, were dissolved, their properties passing to the crown. Their
disappearance must have been psychologically and spiritually disturbing, for
chantry priests had said Mass for the dead, to diminish, so it was believed,
their years in purgatory. The very shape of eternity was being changed by
government legislation.

Further royal injunctions ordered the destruction of all remaining images
and relics of superstition and forbade processions in church or around the

churchyard. Every church had to have a pulpit from which the preacher was required at least once a quarter to preach a sermon. Forbidden were the blessing of candles at Candlemas, ashes on Ash Wednesday and palms on Palm Sunday. Popular customs like the Plough Monday gatherings, maypoles, hocking (the collection of money after Easter week), and rogation processions were banned. A whole world of visual and auditory imagery, whether superstitious or not, dear to the majority of the English people and closely associated with the communal life of the parish were trampled upon without anything positive being put in their place. Churches were reglazed and coated with white lime.

Evangelical Protestantism was making its impact. Cranmer himself contributed to a *Book of Homilies*, a collection of twelve sermons on key topics which the clergy were to read aloud so as to instruct their people in the faith. Even more important was the first Book of Common Prayer, much of it compiled personally by Cranmer, providing a uniform service book in English prose of which Cranmer was an undoubted master. The book was moderately rather than radically Protestant in tone.

Such changes were not fast enough for the more extreme, more particularly for the Protestant pastors from abroad who had flocked to England at Cranmer's behest. Between 1547 and 1553 some forty or more settled in England, in their missionary fervour and doctrinal views more harshly evangelical than Cranmer himself. The newer teachings were propagated throughout the country by some one hundred or so licensed preachers. Remarkably such changes were put into practice more by persuasion than force, for only two heretics died in Somerset's brief spell of power.

Yet many people were upset and confused by the rapid rate of change. There was a dangerous rising in the south-west of England whose leaders called for the restoration of the Latin Mass, with communion in one kind and a ban on the English Bible, the restoration and adoration of the sacrament, of ashes and palms, and the condemnation of heresy. Cranmer's new prayer book was stigmatized as 'like a Christmas game'. But parish accounts show that churchwardens were, if in a somewhat patchwork fashion, complying with the government's injunctions, purchasing copies of the *Book of Homilies*, the English Bible, the Book of Common Prayer, removing the stone altars and replacing them with the wooden Lord's table. In a sermon which he preached at Paul's Cross Bishop Barlow held aloft an image which had movable joints so that it could turn its head and bless the people to discredit the reverence paid to images; with the bishop's approval 'the boys broke the idols in pieces'. But most gave only a grudging assent to what was done and resented the pace of change.

With the fall and execution of Somerset and the governance of his successor, the duke of Northumberland, the English Reformation veered in an even more aggressively Protestant direction. Northumberland seems to have been a self-seeking cynic who was ready to exploit and despoil the

Church for his own interest but he found allies in the clerical extremists. Cranmer drew up the second Book of Common Prayer in 1552 which embodied a purely memorialist interpretation of the Eucharist. John Knox managed to get inserted in the prayer book the so-called Black Rubric which explained that kneeling at the communion was not intended to indicate any adoration of the holy sacrament. The book, the highwater-mark of Protestantism in the Church of England, became law in 1552, but its life was short for the 'godly imp' Edward VI died in 1553.

Edward's successor, his sister Mary, was welcomed not merely because she was the legitimate heir but because she was identified with the old religion. The Edwardian legislation was repealed. Catholic ritual and ceremonial, Rogationtide processions, Plough Monday gatherings, May games, were restored. The images, chalices, crosses and vestments where they survived were unpacked or new ones, involving the parish in some expense, were ordered; service books were replaced by the missal. The heresy laws had been restored. The irascible Bonner, now back in London, tried to repress nonconformity, arresting some four hundred seemingly disaffected men and women, but of these the majority were ultimately ready to accommodate themselves to the Roman faith, standing as penitents in white sheets 'in a marvellous dump and sadness' at the choir of their parish churches after Mass. The married clergy were obliged to send away their wives, some 88 out of 319 in the county of Essex alone. There was a spate of enforced resignations from benefices, a third in London, which were not easily filled. A few monasteries were restored, among them Westminster and the Carthusian house at Sheen, but the lay proprietors who had made a meal out of monastic land were in no mood to give it back, and on this score Mary and Pole had to mark time. They had plans for revitalizing the Church and ridding it of its abuses, but its finances were in such disorder as a result of despoliation that they were unable to accomplish much of what they wanted to do, nor was time on their side.

Mary's religious policy had led to an immediate flight abroad of better-off Protestants, first of all the foreign ministers, then clerics, university dons and merchants, among them Protestant printers who continued to publish books to help the reformed cause. Five bishops were executed: Ridley and Latimer were burned at Oxford and were followed a few weeks later by Archbishop Cranmer who, after a mood of prevarication and recantation, very probably brought about by psychological pressures, died heroically.

Protestantism was forced underground. 'You're in the confines of Babylon', as John Philpot told his sister, 'where you are in danger to drink of the whore's cup, unless you be vigilant in prayer.' Some sought to pay lip service alone by attending the Mass but not fully participating, refusing to kiss the pyx, or avoiding the elevation by hanging down their heads or so seating themselves that they could not actually see it. But in the last resort they could not avoid the extreme penalty. 'You have the Word,' as Dr Weston, a former rector of Lincoln College, Oxford (who had won

Mary's favour and been rewarded with the deanery of Westminster but with his 'burned breech' fell from grace for being a 'bawdy beast') said, 'and we have the Sword.' 'As a good surgeon', so Bonner justified the burnings, '[who] cutteth away a putrefyed and festred member, for the love he hath to hole body, least it infecte the other members adjoynge to it.' The mass of Mary's martyrs were not well to do or influential, but tradesmen, weavers, clothworkers and labourers with a fair sprinkling of women, drawn by and large from the south-east of the country. The martyrs served the cause of Protestantism well, converting 'what had been to date a largely foreign-inspired minority clique into a national legend'. Martyrdom was to strengthen the Protestant faith just as the early Christians had been encouraged by the deaths of its saints. Books like Jean Crespin's *History of the Martyrs* (1554) and John Foxe's *Book of Martyrs* (1563) provided pabulum for the Protestant cause. Even so, had Mary not died in November 1558, followed shortly by her arch-henchman Pole, it seems perfectly possible that England might have remained a predominantly Catholic country.

The work of rendering Protestant a religiously divided country remained an uphill task, gathering pace only slowly, and it was not until the close of Elizabeth's reign that Protestantism could be described as the religion of the majority of the English people. Elizabeth's religious instincts were conservative, looking back to the doctrinal and ceremonial practices of her father's reign, but she could not disavow Protestantism without, as the daughter of Anne Boleyn, seeming to admit her own illegitimacy, and she needed the support of the Protestant exiles in manipulating the carefully poised balancing act which formed the religious settlement of the early years of her reign. Bishoprics were filled with sound Protestants. Acts of Parliament restored the supremacy of the crown (with Elizabeth as supreme governor rather than supreme head of the Church) and a Protestant liturgy which managed to combine the spirit of the Cranmerian prayer book of 1549 with the letter of the second prayer book of 1552; the communion sentences, for instance, embodied what could be interpreted as both the doctrine of a real presence and a purely commemorative observance.

Such a settlement had something of the makeshift about it, what Patrick Collinson has described as 'an enforced coalition of contrary religious traditions and tendencies, crudely distinguishable as very protestant, not-so-protestant and crypto-papist'. The queen and her archbishop fought a rearguard action against the Protestants who demanded a further godly reformation of the Church. The extremists wanted to eliminate what Bishop Jewell called the 'scenic apparatus of divine service', replacing the surplice by the Geneva gown and removing all traces of what could be interpreted as Roman Catholic practice. Archbishop Parker, doubtless at the queen's command, drew up a series of ecclesiastical articles in an attempt to clip the extremists' wings, detailing clerical dress and stating that a 'comely surplice with sleeves' was the appropriate garb for the performance of divine worship. It was unfortunate that Parker's successor as archbishop, Edmund

Grindal, took a more distinctively Protestant line and arousing the queen's anger by so doing had his post sequestered a year after his appointment, though he remained as archbishop until his death in 1583.

It was in the closing decades of Elizabeth's reign that the English Church's tentative features became more explicit. The danger to the stability of the Church came from two quarters, the surviving Catholics and the extreme Protestants or Puritans. While Catholicism still had deep roots in some parts of the country, noticeably Lancashire and Yorkshire, Hampshire and Sussex, where it had much support among the local gentry, in reality it was becoming something of a paper tiger. A Catholic community, separate from the established Church and serviced by at least 150 priests, the majority in Lancashire, had come into existence before the missionary priests arrived from abroad. For the most part papists were not at first sought out and persecuted if they complied nominally with the letter of the law.

But by the early 1570s the situation was changing, politically rather than ecclesiastically, raising Protestant fears of a possible Catholic revanchism: by the rising of the northern earls against the government in 1569, by the Pope's excommunication of Elizabeth in the following year, by the Ridolfi plot and the massacre of the Huguenots on St Bartholomew's Day in Paris in 1572 which sent a ripple of alarm throughout Protestant Europe.

A further impetus to renew government action against the Catholics was the arrival of the so-called missionary priests, trained at Douai. Often courageous if indiscreet men, they were more concerned to provide pastoral care for the Catholics than to make converts. New laws were enacted as a result of which Catholicism became identified with treason. From 1581 onwards convicted recusants were liable to pay a fine of £20 a month for non-attendance at church; a number of missionary priests died bravely. As a result Catholicism was at least contained. The English Catholics were in some respects divided, for the old Catholic noble and gentrified families were by and large averse to foreign intervention.

Puritanism was rather a different proposition, if only because it was itself so amorphous, ranging from those who wished simply for a further reformation of the Church along Protestant lines to groups who denounced the structure of Church government itself as unscriptural. One such separatist group was the congregation at Norwich led by a quarrelsome cleric, Robert Browne, who migrated to Middleburg in Holland. Extreme Puritanism offered a radical challenge to the constitution and organization of the established Church. 'There is not', as one of them wrote, 'to be found in the New Testament so much as one syllable whereby there may be the least surmised of such thing' as government by bishops. But the majority of those who would have described themselves as Puritans still thought of themselves as members of the national Church, unready to renounce its basic formulas, including the supremacy of the crown and government by bishops but wanting a reduction in religious ceremonial, such as making the sign of the cross, the bestowal of the ring in marriage and the wearing of vestments. They appealed constantly to the authority of scripture and the 'discipline of the primitive Church'.

Archbishop Whitgift tried to bring the more extreme advocates of Puritanism to heel, insisting that Puritan clergy should accept and use the prayer book. He employed the recently constituted Court of High Commission to prosecute the more recalcitrant. Strongly backed by the queen he managed to prevent a threatened Puritan takeover, but he could only limit not eliminate their influence in the English Church. The Puritans had strong backing among many nobles and country gentry and were influential in many towns. They attained, for even Whitgift was intellectually a Calvinist, theological dominance at the universities, if not without some bitter controversy. Both the newly founded Cambridge colleges, Sidney Sussex and Emmanuel, were virtually Puritan seminaries.

By the close of Elizabeth's reign a recognizably Protestant Church was emerging in the 'new Israel', as the Puritans liked to describe England. The victory of Protestantism had been achieved in the first instance by a policy of coercion, propagation and patronage by the governing bodies in Church and State, but other factors were also at work. Catholicism was to become more and more identified with the national enemy, Spain. In the main the essence of the change was to be found in the slow process of indoctrination and evangelization. In the years immediately following Elizabeth's accession the old ceremonies continued to persist in many areas. Even a high proportion of JPs in the north favoured the old religion while many a parish priest continued as before, ignoring episcopal mandates.

Time had, however, worked in the Protestant favour. The Catholic JPs gradually disappeared. The older clergy died out and were replaced by younger men trained in the Protestant tradition, for the elimination of Catholicism at the universities and their strong adherence to Protestant teaching was to be a major factor in the education of future ministers and schoolmasters. There was a flood of Protestant propaganda for those who could read. In a sense the triumph of Protestantism was a matter of new generations. It had everywhere an appeal to women, but in general it was also a movement of youth. 'My father' one young man commented, 'is an old doting fool and will fast upon the Friday; my mother goeth always mumbling on her beads.' 'Ye shall see that every boy in the street shall spit in the priests' faces and hurl stones at them.' Protestantism had a measure of social appeal. 'Did not Christ die as well for a craftsman and poor men as for gentlemen and rich men?' The availability of the vernacular Bible, the Word of the living God, had met a religious need, liberating its readers from the control of the priesthood, the demands of the penitential system and the superstitious and idolatrous ceremonies of the Church, and providing an avenue to salvation.

The Elizabethan Church had been, and in many respects was to remain, diversified in practice and even divided in its beliefs. The Elizabethan bishops, as nominees of the crown, their estates often exploited ruthlessly by the crown and its agents for their own ends, had only a qualified control over their flocks. Yet slowly in a shambling sort of way a national Church had come into being, and with it gradually a more highly educated and conscientious clerical order. It attained too a certain measure of doctrinal coherence. Its doctrinal beliefs were summarized in the Thirty-nine Articles of 1571, and its revised code of law was crystallized in canons approved in 1597 and revised and extended in 1604. The Church took as its authority, as Bishop Jewell observed in the *Apologia*, the scriptures and the practice of the primitive Church, to which Richard Hooker would have added in his masterly *Of the Laws of Ecclesiastical Polity*, the first four books of which were published in 1594, the traditions of the Church and the rational judgement which God had implanted himself in man. The Church which was emerging at the end of Elizabeth's reign had received a strong injection of Protestant doctrine without surrendering all its Catholic inheritance while its moral tone had been largely set, though not necessarily engineered, by Puritan emphasis on the axiomatic authority of the Bible, the observance of Sunday, and sexual purity with a high sense of duty entailing personal responsibility and integrity. Its trials were not over but at least it had achieved some degree of recognizable definition.

THE REFORMATION IN SCANDINAVIA

The course of the Reformation in England was in many respects different in character from religious changes in the greater part of Europe. Its nearest equivalent was what had happened in Sweden under the lead of Gustavus Vasa who had thrown off the Danish yoke of the Catholic king Christian and restored independence to his country. To consolidate his authority Gustavus needed to do two things, to make the monarchy financially stable and to win the support of the Swedish nobility of which he himself had been originally a member. Since the Swedish Church was rich, the Swedish parliament or *riksdag* meeting at Vasteras in June 1527 agreed to dissolve the monasteries and to restore to its original owners all property which had been alienated or donated to ecclesiastical foundations since 1430. In this way both crown and nobility would benefit financially. A further clause permitted the preaching of Lutheranism which had already won adherents in Sweden under the masterful leadership of Olaus Petri who translated the New Testament into Swedish and who with his colleague Laurentius Andreae reformed the service books along Lutheran lines. A later Swedish king, John III, an amateur theologian himself, sought to reconcile the contending Catholic and Protestant factions by drawing up a religious compromise known as the *Red Book* in 1575, but it was harshly criticized and his son and successor, Sigismund, a Roman Catholic, lost his throne as a result of his faith. For the Swedes had been won over indissolubly to

Protestantism, itself harnessed to the interests of the Swedish state. A not dissimilar development had occurred in Denmark where the reformation of the Church and the consolidation of monarchical authority went hand in hand.

THE RADICAL REFORMATION

Although the Reformation depended for its ultimate survival on popular support, it was not initially a popular movement but rather the work of a powerful minority which won powerful backers who for self-interested as much as religious reasons gave the reformers their support: in England, Denmark and Sweden the king, in Germany the princes and town councils, in France some members of the nobility and gentry, in the Low Countries townsfolk and those opposed to Spanish domination. But everywhere by preaching, education and propaganda they gradually won over the populace. There were, however, fragmented minorities, proletarian and powerfully religious in character, sometimes with distinctive social objectives, which demanded a more radical reformation.

The Radical Reformation was rooted in social and economic unrest and in a literal adherence to the word of the scriptures, which seemed to justify rebellion against injustice and oppression. Since the layman no longer required the services of a priest to understand the word of God, all men and women could interpret the scriptures if they were genuinely guided by the Holy Spirit.

In general the radical reformers, generically often described as Anabaptists, were religious exclusivists, believing that they alone were the 'saved' and that they constituted a 'fellowship of holy being' for whom heaven was reserved. They were a separate people called by God to keep themselves unspotted from the world, who lived under the shadow of an eschatological expectancy, believing that the second coming of Christ was imminent. Such was, for instance, the pivot of the teaching of Melchior Hoffmann, the Dutch precursor of Anabaptism who in his pamphlet *The Return of the Lord* (1530) divided history into three ages, the last and final period of which began with Luther. After three and a half years of chaos he prophesied that Christ would come in judgement and inaugurate a new heaven and earth, with Strasbourg as the 'New Jerusalem'.

Within their communities they believed strongly in the brotherhood and sisterhood of all true believers, rejecting the use of force and the rigours of the law, advocating simplicity of living and costume and practising some form of communalism in property. The majority of Catholic and Protestant churches regarded these aberrant and sometimes fiery pietists with a mixture of scorn and fear similar to that with which the Romans had regarded the early Christians. As a likely source of subversion to the established order in Church and State they were invariably to be subject to persecution, their sufferings, as they saw them, a fitting prelude to the millennium.

The earlier episodes in the history of Anabaptism did something to reinforce this judgement. One of the principal leaders in the Peasants' War of 1524, Thomas Müntzer, saturated with the imagery of the Book of Revelation, taught that the elect had to prepare for the second coming of Christ. 'Harvest-time is here, so God himself has hired me for his harvest. I have sharpened my scythe, for my thoughts are most strongly fixed on the truth, and my lips, hands, skin, hair, soul, body, life curse the unbelievers.' His apocalyptic aspirations involved a return to a primal and paradisal state of nature and the holding of all things in common. When the German peasants, enraged by what seemed to be threats from the seigniorial order to their improving economic and social status, took to arms, Müntzer saw his opportunity to put prophecy into practice. The promised miracle did not, however, materialize and the prophet only escaped from the battlefield of Frankenhausen to suffer execution.

The fear which Anabaptism evoked in the established order was reinforced by the dramatic events which took place at Münster in 1534. There a Lutheran preacher Bernt Rothmann acquired a following among the burghers and the city's guilds. Subsequently he identified himself with the Anabaptists who had migrated to Münster. Preaching the imminence of Christ's second coming and advocating the holding of goods in common, Rothmann attracted an influx of the impoverished and depressed from outside the town eager to share in the profits and joys of the 'New Jerusalem'.

Among the immigrants was a fiery Dutch Anabaptist Jan Matthys who replaced Rothmann as leader, urging the righteous to prepare for the millennium by taking up the sword against their enemies. One of Matthys's followers, Jan Benkelsz or Jan of Leyden, was a disturbed young man of messianic aspirations and charismatic personality. He proclaimed that Münster would be the new Jerusalem, and had to prepare for this by being 'purified of all uncleanness', which involved the expulsion of Lutherans and Catholics and the institution of communal ownership. All books except the Bible were banned. In defence of their faith the elect, in Rothmann's words, were to arm themselves 'not only with the humble weapons of the apostles for suffering, but also with the glorious armour of David for vengeance . . . in order, with divine strength and help, to eradicate all ungodliness'.

Jan Benkelsz, handsome and eloquent, was both a megalomaniac and a mystic who, following the biblical command to 'increase and multiply', legalized polygamy. 'My spirit desires your flesh', so the aspiring male put it to the womenfolk. Jan was proclaimed the messianic king of all the world, the successor of David, foretold by the prophets of the Old Testament, until Christ should reclaim his kingdom. Jan's emblem was a globe of the world pierced by two swords and surmounted by a cross with the words inscribed 'One king of righteousness over all'. This fantastic religious authoritarianism, however popular in its appeal, was brought to an end by the blockade and siege of the town by the bishop's forces.

Although there were other outbreaks of militant Anabaptism, in practice the radical reformers, if exclusive and separatist, tended to be pacifistic. The Hutterites, named after Jacob Hutter who was executed in 1536, established a communal settlement, a *Bruderhof* or house of brothers in Moravia where they tried to emulate the conditions of the early Church. They believed in common ownership and the common life, and acquired a reputation for industry and thrift. But the Hutterites became victims of the Thirty Years War in the early seventeenth century and were expelled from Moravia, moving hither and thither, until in 1874–9 they settled, still loyal to their traditional tenets, in South Dakota and Canada. Similar in attitude were the Mennonites, named after Menno Simons, a Dutch Anabaptist who died in 1561, who lived in a congregational society excluded from the world which they had renounced; their traditions are maintained in native austerity by the Amish Mennonites in the USA.

On the Anabaptist fringe were the Socinians, more theologically oriented than some of the other Anabaptist groups, for in their scrutiny of the New Testament they found no real support for the Christian doctrine of the Trinity. Established originally at Rakow in Poland where the townspeople sought to establish yet another 'New Jerusalem', the anti-Trinitarians found a leader in an Italian radical theologian, Fausto Sozzini who worked in Poland from 1580 until his death in 1604. The Catholic Church in Poland eventually drove out the Socinians, but their intellectual influence percolated to England, Holland and Germany; and to the Socinians Unitarianism traces its origin.

THE PROTESTANT ETHOS

The Reformation had not seriously fractured the framework of Christianity within which most men and women lived out their brief lives. There were certainly a few sceptics, such as for instance had been the spy and humanist Giordano Bruno, and some atheists but the basic formulas of the Christian faith had not been significantly challenged. The universe remained a supernatural entity governed by the providential dispensation of God. The verdict which the fathers of Chalcedon had reached on the nature of Christ went uncriticized, except by a small minority of religious extremists. Nor for that matter had the Reformation effected any major changes in the ethics and standards of Christian living.

But if Christian belief emerged fundamentally unscathed, a major religious revolution had occurred. The Church, already divided into its eastern and western halves, was fragmented further by Protestantism, itself fissiparous by nature. It had erected a theological divide in Christendom which could not be effectively bridged. The attempts made to heal the breach, and to find an accommodation between the two Churches, from Melanchthon and Contarini in the sixteenth century to their more modern successors, have been doomed to failure. The authority of the Church mediated by the Pope had been replaced by the authority of the scriptures mediated in the last resort by the individual believer. 'The Bible,' as William Chillingworth observed in 1638, 'the Bible only I say is the religion of Protestants.'

The Reformation had swept away many of the fundamental tenets of the Catholic Church, more especially the high road by which Christians had been taught they could attain salvation. Both the penitential system of grace, confession and absolution and the offering of the Mass, denounced by Protestants as blasphemous, had been rejected. Only two sacraments, baptism and the Eucharist, had been retained, and even so some of the reformers had been careful to urge that both were only signs of God's grace but did not themselves confer grace.

The hieratic structure of the Church had been transformed. The reformers differentiated between the invisible Church which was the community of the faithful, the body of the elect, of those predestined to be saved, and the visible Church, consisting of those who professed faith in Christ. They had a structured ministry, though apart from the Church of England and some Lutheran churches they dispensed with the episcopate, but the minister was no longer a priest who mediated between God and man, but a preacher expounding the Word of God, who by his exhortation, by the instruction he gave through the catechism and by his example was to transmit his faith to his congregation.

Fundamentally the Reformation was a clerical movement, but its success was in part due to the support which it had evoked from laymen and women. The early preachers had deliberately set out to win over the laity, engaging them in debate, urging them on to action against the old faith and enticing their cooperation by 'flattering their susceptibilities'. Since the layman or laywoman could no longer rely on the mediating capacity of the Church to assist him or her towards salvation, he or she had to assume personal responsibility before God for the faith which alone could secure God's forgiveness. The reformed Churches came, however, to exert a formidable programme of discipline, keeping as strict a control over their members' private lives, and exercising, if needs be, the penalties of excommunication and expulsion, as the old Catholic Church, so as to justify John Milton's comment that 'new presbyter is but old priest writ large'.

The churches were themselves transformed. Since the early Protestants utilized the medieval churches which they had taken over from the Catholics, so outwardly there might have appeared comparatively little change. Not many new churches were built, though among them was the French Huguenot temple constructed at Charenton in 1623. But there were major changes in their interiors. The stone altars had been replaced by wooden holy tables. The frescoes were whitewashed. The oak screen dividing the nave from the chancel might remain but the rood loft and the figures of the Blessed Virgin and St John on each side of the crucified Christ were taken down. The images were smashed and replaced by boards with scriptural texts or the Ten Commandments. In many churches organs were dismantled, for the Calvinists held them to be a worldly distraction. The reading desk and the hour glass to time the sermon appeared in many English churches. The pulpit became the most symbolic piece of church furnishing, for the sermon was henceforth to be the main vehicle for conversion to the Word of God.

Gone too were many of the social functions with which the Church had been so intimately associated, the Masses for the dead at the side altars, the family chantries, the meetings of the religious fraternities, the Corpus Christi processions, the pageants at midsummer and other seasons as well as many of the secular activities which had taken place in the church or the churchyard.

The divorce between the sacred and profane which stricter church men had always desired now became permanent. Popular rites and festivals were condemned as, in the words of the Lutheran Caspar Huberinus in 1569, 'unchristian, pagan, idolatrous, frivolous, seductive, ungodly and devilish'. At first the Protestant reformers had been ready to use drama, ballads and popular songs to discredit their Catholic opponents, but by the 1570s and 1580s, and in German towns even earlier, the Protestant churches took strong measures to oust the secular from the sacred. Carnivals were abandoned. The traditional mystery plays came to an end. Minstrelsy, secular music and playgoing were henceforth associated with an unacceptable worldliness. The theatre in particular became the target of Puritan abuse, reaching its consummation in William Prynne's *Histrio-mastix* of 1637. The visual aspects of religion, the images, stained glass, book illustrations, with their symbolism were largely cast aside and the practice of worship became in the main auditory, a matter of hearing rather than of seeing. While worship gained in reverence, it lost in familiarity. Medieval congregations had often chattered and laughed in church but the Protestants were keen to ensure decency and dignity in the Lord's house. Churchwardens and beadles were ordered to suppress irreverent conduct. The Irish Church canons of 1634, for instance, ordered the churchwardens to exclude noisy young children from the service. Yet there seems to have been little notion, as was common in Catholic countries, that churches should be kept open for prayer or private devotion, for it was assumed that this would take place in the home.

There was a renewed emphasis on the need for Sunday to be observed strictly, something which stern moralists had long been demanding, if in vain. For in the world of medieval Catholicism Sunday was often a time for plays, for football, even for bear-baiting and other entertainments, and church ales, which were sometimes held to raise money for church repairs. The Swiss reformers had abolished all holy days except Sunday while in his

True Doctrine of the Sabbath the Puritan Nicholas Bownd recommended that the strict Mosaic regulations for keeping the Sabbath should be transferred to the Christian Sunday. There was much popular resentment at this and other measures designed to limit what the Puritans regarded as desecration of the Lord's day. King James I and his son issued *The Book of Sports* allowing the playing of harmless games on Sunday but parliament in 1625 and 1627 forbade bull-baiting, bear-baiting and play-acting on Sunday, ordered drovers, carriers and waggoners not to drive their carts nor butchers to sell or kill meat on a Sunday, and discouraged men from meeting for sport outside their own parish. For centuries to come strict Sunday observance was to be a grave and often gloomy legacy of Protestantism.

Protestantism stressed the family virtues and the sanctity of marriage. Whether in this respect it differed in substance from Catholic teaching may well be doubted, for both had a paternalistic and patriarchal view of family life. Both Catholic and Protestant deplored what to contemporaries seemed to be a growth in marital infidelity and in the spread of prostitution, but attempts to stem such trends by banning prostitution and by punishing sexual misbehaviour by obliging offenders to undergo some humiliating act of penance clearly failed. The abolition of clerical celibacy led the Protestant to present the ideal of the pastor as a father and a husband. If Protestantism taught that wives should be obedient to their husbands and that children should obey their parents, it emphasized that husbands should be faithful to and love their wives, for women were 'no dish-clouts . . . nor no drudges, but fellow-heirs with them of everlasting life, and so dear to God as the men', as the Protestant writer Thomas Becon stated. Protestantism may, however, have given the family a more distinctively religious role, for it encouraged family prayers and the regular reading of the Bible in the vernacular and religious books like Foxe's *Book of Martyrs*. Luther's hymns were sung less in church than in the family circle.

The Reformation had taken from women a vocation, that of the nun, which many had found rewarding, but women had played a very prominent part in the Reformation, some suffering martyrdom for their faith. Whether the part which women played in the Reformation was because of their 'natural propensity' to religion or because Protestantism provided women with an outlet for sublimated desire and a relief from the tedium of constant child-bearing and housewifely duties must remain unclear. By and large Protestantism seems, if somewhat obscurely, to have enhanced the female role.

This may in part have been connected with what was one of the more significant effects which Protestantism had on society, the appearance of the clerical family. Many priests in the past had had unofficial families, but Protestantism placed a legal stamp on clerical marriage, reckoning it to be one of the distinctive features of a true ministry. This was certainly not the opinion of Queen Elizabeth I: 'Her Majesty', Cecil told Archbishop Parker in 1561, 'continueth very evil affected to the state of matrimony in the clergy', but that very same year we know that at least half the clergy in the archdeaconry of London had wives. In Strasbourg in 1609 only two out of seventy-one reformed ministers were unmarried. There was, moreover, a pattern of clerical intermarriage; the ministers' wives were often themselves daughters of the clergy. Their sons too often followed their fathers in the clerical profession, sometimes founding clerical dynasties. Of ninety-five pastors in the north German state of Oldenburg in the last half of the sixteenth century fifty-five had been the sons of pastors.

The Protestant pastor differed from the Catholic priest. The latter often came from a humble background and was indifferently educated, at least until the Catholic Reformation took effect, but the Protestant clergyman, unless he was a pastor in a dissenting sect, was more often than not the product of the urban middle class, neither noble nor of the peasantry, probably a graduate of a university or educated at a gymnasium or training college, such as that set up by Johann Sturm at Strasbourg in 1538, and trained in theology. Within the mainstream reformed churches there was a distinctive and self-conscious clerical profession, forming often an intellectual élite in secular society, which by its standing, manners and even dress may, in a number of respects, have distanced itself from the people whom it served.

The social and political implications of the Protestant Reformation can not be summarized succinctly. It has been claimed, more especially by Max Weber, that the emphasis which Protestantism placed on the native virtues of thrift, industry, sobriety, respectability, individual responsibility, integrity, and what Luther called *Der Beruf* or vocation, meant that it played a significant part in the creation of a capitalist ethic; but capitalism and the encouragement of mercantile activity have never been a Protestant monopoly. Politically the early reformers had advocated obedience to the powers that be, and argued that obedience to authority was a necessary corrective to human disorder, sin and immorality. But confronted with 'ungodly' rulers they progressed from passive disobedience to the approval of armed revolt. The sword no less than the cross became a godly weapon, justifying, for instance, the armed reaction of the Huguenots in France and the Puritans in seventeenth-century England. The Protestant ethic certainly had its part to play in the history of political protest.

The Reformation, then, constituted a revolution, religious in character but with a social and political significance. It involved the destruction of much of the fabric and teaching of the medieval Church. Yet to evaluate its true significance in the history of the Christian Church it has to be placed side by side with the Catholic Reformation, with which fundamentally it had much in common.

CHAPTER SEVEN

The Catholic Reformation

On a cold December morning in 1545 the clergy were assembling in the church of the Holy Trinity in the city of Trent (modern Trento in Italy, but then part of the Empire), the cardinals donning red copes braided with gold and mitres of white damask. Fra Domenico intoned the *Veni Creator* and the procession moved slowly to the cathedral of St Vigilius, where the bishop of Brescia preached the sermon, telling the assembled company which included representatives of the emperor Charles V that it was their task to defend the faith and sacraments of the Catholic Church, to rid it of greed and ambition, to promote charity among Christians and to oppose the Turks 'the scourge of God'. It was the opening of a Church council which was to last on and off for eighteen years and which was eventually in many respects to change the character of the Roman Catholic Church.

When eighteen years later the council, now swollen to as many as 400 bishops, met for the last time on 4 December 1563, as the fathers eagerly packed their bags to escape the Alpine winter, a major venture had come to an end. Often interrupted, even in some ways disappointing in its conclusions, the Council of Trent, the last great council of the Catholic Church before the Vatican Council of 1870, had crystallized in its achievements the objectives of the Catholic Reformation, defining and refashioning the faith and discipline of the Church.

It was a very far cry from the urbane environs of Trent to the bleak wilderness of the French province of Quebec where two Jesuit fathers who had been pioneers in mission work in Canada since 1615 were captured in 1649 by the Iroquois Indians, tortured and killed. The Iroquois, spurred on by the English, had been fighting the Huron Indians, who were allies of the French and who had responded favourably to the missionary efforts of the Jesuits. 'Even after they had been stripped naked and beaten with sticks on every part of their bodies', so reads the graphic account of the Jesuits' death, in the *Martyrology*:

> Father Brébeuf continued to exhort and encourage the Christians who were around him. One of the Fathers had his hands cut off, and to both were applied under the armpits and besides the loins hatchets heated in the fire as well as necklaces of red-hot lance blades round their necks. Their tormentors then proceeded to girdle them with belts of bark steeped in pitch and resin to which they set fire. At the height of these

torments Father Lallemant raised his hands to heaven, and with sighs invoked God's aid, whilst Father Brébeuf set his face like a rock [as] though insensible to pain. Then, like one recovering consciousness, he preached to his persecutors and to the Christian captives until the savages gagged his mouth, cut off his nose, tore off his lips, and then, in derision of holy baptism, deluged him and his companion martyr with boiling water. Finally, large pieces of flesh were cast out of the bodies of both the priests and roasted by the Indians, who also tore out their hearts before their death by means of an opening above the breast, feasting on them and on their blood, which they drank while it was still warm.

What happened in the Canadian wastes was indirectly a sequel to the proceedings of the Council of Trent, for the council had not merely revitalized the Catholic Church, but in part made possible the reawakening of the missionary spirit which sent Brébeuf and his companion to their heroic fate.

THE SOURCES OF THE CATHOLIC REFORMATION

The Catholic Reformation was not, as is sometimes stated, simply a Roman answer to the Protestant Reformation, but rather it was a parallel movement rooted in a similar religious background. They were both concerned with reforming abuses in the Church which had been so widely echoed in the fifteenth century and which had not been stilled by papal condemnation of the conciliar movement. Catholics as well as future Protestants owed much to the inspiration of what is usually known as the *devotio moderna* which was directed towards the revivification of the spiritual life by meditating on the gospel message. Thomas à Kempis's life of Christ was, for instance, to be one of the favourite books of Ignatius Loyola, the founder of the Jesuits. The Christian renaissance by rehabilitating the works of the early fathers of the Church and of St Augustine in particular provided a common foundation for both Catholic and Protestant reformers.

Before the Protestant reformers began to preach there were many hints, seedlings rather than trees, of what they were to seek to do in late medieval Catholicism. In fifteenth-century Europe there were many examples of reforming bishops, such as Niccolo Albergati in Italy, a Carthusian, who became bishop of Bologna in 1417; Archbishop Antonino of Florence; and Lorenzo Giustiniani, the patriarch of Venice; while in Spain Cardinal Ximenes de Cisneros, statesman and scholar, promoted monastic reform. Reform was even on the lips of the Renaissance Popes, though what they tried to do was of little effect, in part because of the fears of the curial officials for their vested interests.

The most positive indication that within the Catholic Church things were stirring was to be found in the reform and resuscitation of the religious orders, which were to act as a forerunner to a renewal of spiritual energy at the top. The signs of the monastic renewal can be seen in the appearance of what might be described as splinters from some of the older orders, of groups of religious who wanted to revive a more disciplined and spiritual life, together with the foundation of new orders of stricter observance, such as the German congregation of Bursfeld which had ninety abbeys and the reformed Augustinian friars which had eighty-three houses, including those of Erfurt and Wittenberg where Luther was to study. Among these new orders were the Camaldolese, which under the guidance of Paolo Giustiniani aimed at a life of absolute poverty, and the rigorist Capuchins founded by Matteo da Bascio who were concerned to return to the traditional life of self-denial which they associated with the original rule of St Benedict.

Other priests had a more outgoing attitude, wishing to communicate their message to the working clergy to raise their pastoral standards and to sponsor works of charity. The Oratory of Divine Love, set up originally at Genoa in 1497, consisted of a small group of priests, some of good birth and intellect, who decided to express their Christian vocation through lives of prayer, mortification and charity, so holding up an ideal for the priesthood to follow. The Theatines, founded by Gaetano di Thiene (who was bishop of Thiene or Chieti) established confraternities at Vicenza and Verona and a hospital at Venice, so providing an example for the parochial clergy in the hope that this might help to remedy 'the corruption of manners and of souls, which had spread far and wide among the Christian people'. The Somaschi, who had been set up in 1528 by Girolamo Miani, a Venetian noble and soldier, devoted themselves to helping the sick, founding orphanages and rescuing prostitutes. The Barnabites, formed in 1530, were first and foremost missionary priests, attracting congregations by their fervent and at times histrionic preaching. While members of these orders took monastic vows, they were not cloistered monks. They formed a leaven in the Church, reaching out beyond their own houses as far as the outer limits of the papal curia itself, so that patrons and members of these orders began to be appointed to bishoprics whence, as did Gian Matteo Giberti after he was made bishop of Verona, they introduced measures of reform in their own dioceses. This monastic renaissance was, however, limited in its achievements, traditional in type and more or less confined to Italy, but its function was significantly preparatory.

THE SOCIETY OF JESUS

The Society of Jesus used its world-wide influence to surpass all the other new or reformed religious orders, becoming a centrifugal force in Christianity and spreading the Catholic Reformation, which became 'its main prop and chief instrument'. The Jesuits' founder, Ignatius Loyola, a

Basque by birth, the youngest of eleven children of a noble and by profession a soldier, at the age of thirty had been seriously wounded when the French were besieging Pamplona in 1521. In his convalescence at Arevalo he turned to religion, reading devotional books like the life of Christ by Ludolf the Carthusian and seeking a life of prayer and mortification at Manresa near the abbey of Montserrat where he passed nights in solitary vigil, in fasting and in mortification of the flesh, beating himself with barbed chains. He underwent a mystical experience emerging a new man dedicated to the service of Christ. There too he began to write what was to be the textbook of his society, *The Spiritual Exercises*. Momentarily he turned his attention to evangelizing the Muslims but returned from a visit to the holy places to study at Barcelona, Alcala and Salamanca where he was suspected of heresy, eventually making his way to the Collège Montaigu at Paris which in earlier times had housed both Erasmus and Calvin. It was here at Paris after graduation with six friends at Montmartre in 1534 that he took the monastic vows of poverty, chastity and obedience. Once again the youthful Jesuits played with the idea of preaching a mission to Islam and went to Venice to make preparations; but this was to remain a dream while the reality was the papal approval of Loyola's order by the bull *Regimini Militantis Ecclesiae* in 1540 of which, after a show of reluctance, Loyola became the first general.

The Jesuit ideal was an expression of Loyola's spiritual genius. Loyola's *Spiritual Exercises*, in part structured by the military cast of Loyola's mind, formed a handbook by which the reader was led through the disciplined use of his intellect and imagination from the renunciation of sin and self to union with God. *The Spiritual Exercises* formed a drill book for the Christian who aspired to become a disciplined and devoted soldier of Christ. Loyola did not believe in a purely contemplative piety but held that spiritual renewal must eventuate in religious activity.

The Jesuit was of the world but was freed from all worldly ties. Before he was admitted to full membership of the order, he had to undergo a long novitiate, so that by the time of his admission his will was tempered and honed for his missionary vocation. His vow of obedience to the Pope and to the general of his order was primary and unconditional. 'He must let himself be carried and ruled by his superior', Loyola declared in the Jesuit constitution, in a phrase actually borrowed from the rule of St Francis, 'as if he were a dead body (*perinde ac cadaver*), that lets itself be carried anywhere and handled anyhow, or like an old man's staff, which he who holds it in his hand may use to help himself wheresoever and howsoever he may wish.'

What was significant about this new religious society was the extent to which the traditional monastic rules were modified. The Jesuits were no longer obliged to recite the daily monastic hours nor to wear a particular monastic habit. Unconsciously rather than deliberately Loyola had fashioned a society well suited to propagate the ideals of the Catholic Reformation, deepening the sense of vocation of the monastic clergy, refuting and reconverting Protestants and taking the Christian gospel to pagans and infidels. The Jesuits did not neglect the poorer members of society, for they played a prominent part in parish missions, targeting the wealthier and influential members of the community. In their turn acting as patrons the latter founded universities and schools where the Jesuits proved to be skilled and sympathetic schoolmasters, with a modern curriculum and sensible teaching methods. There was, however, to be no questioning of the fundamentals of dogma and belief and they were politically safe. Although they were regarded with considerable suspicion by princes such as Philip II of Spain because of their prior loyalty to the Pope, they soon won increasing influence at royal courts where they were chosen to be confessors.

That they became unpopular can hardly be denied. The adjective jesuitical became a pejorative term. They were to be involved in bitter and prolonged controversy, charged by their critics with moral casuistry. Moreover their early history was marked by acute divisions within the order itself. Yet of all the forces which were operative in the Catholic Reformation the Jesuits were certainly the most important, even by Loyola's death in 1556 attracting a thousand members and making an impact in Asia and America. Their theologians, notably Lainez and Salmeron, were influential figures at the Council of Trent where they championed traditional orthodoxy and stressed the primacy of the Pope.

THE COUNCIL OF TRENT

The Council of Trent was to form the engine room of the Catholic Reformation, for it was the council which refashioned doctrine and discipline and re-established the power and prestige of the Pope. For long the bureaucratic nature and the power of vested interests at the papal curia had frustrated every major attempt at reform. Neither the Pope nor his advisers had forgotten that the general council of Constance had claimed an authority higher than that of the Pope himself, and they were fearful that another general council might lead to a diminution in papal authority, a fear that was fanned by the demands that were being made for a general council in the empire where papalists saw the dreadful hand of Luther at work. The delay in calling a council had been augmented by the political state of western Europe savaged by the scourge of constant war fought between the French king and the German emperor.

The death of the well-meaning but supine Clement VII in 1534, the same year that witnessed the formation of the Society of Jesus, opened the way to the election of a Pope, Paul III, who was to prove a patron of reform. At first glance a churchman of traditional type, a man of aristocratic lineage who had fathered children before he became a priest, he saw the advisability of calling a general council, favouring a group of reforming churchmen, among them the Venetian Gasparo Contarini, whom he brought into the curia, making tentative moves towards the calling of a council. In the first place, apart from introducing much-needed reforms among the Roman clergy, he set up a special committee consisting of reforming theologians, some of them members of the Oratory of Divine Love, to prepare a report which they presented to the Pope in February 1537. It was a strongly worded document which did not mince words in accounting for the sickness of the Church, and it made radical proposals to 'restore the Church of Christ, which was crumbling down, nay had almost fallen in headlong ruin'. It set alarm bells ringing down the corridors of the curia; and endeavours were made by interested parties to suppress its findings.

But Paul III could not renege on his plans for a general council, much as he may have wished to do so. A council had been summoned to meet at Mantua in 1537 but neither it nor a further council called at Vicenza in 1538 materialized. It was only on 6 June 1542 that the Pope at long last convoked a council to meet at Trent where after long delays the first session opened in December 1545.

Even so it was slow in getting down to business and so small in number as to be very unrepresentative. In the winter of 1547 an outbreak of plague led the papal legates to seek to transfer it to Bologna, a move which was strongly resisted by the German and Spanish bishops who saw in the attempt a ploy for strengthening papal control over the proceedings. The full council did not meet again at Trent until 1551–2 but the meetings, rarely attended by as many as fifty bishops, were pretty abortive. It was not until Easter Sunday 1561 that the bishops again foregathered at Trent where the last session took place in December 1563.

The council's proceedings were predisposed to strengthen rather than to weaken papal authority. The Cardinal de Lorraine commented sourly that when the Holy Spirit was needed, it was fetched in a bag from Rome. This was not wholly just. In a monarchical age which was moving in the direction of absolute monarchy the Pope could not acquiesce in any diminution in his powers without loss to the administrative and spiritual efficacy of the papacy. The cardinal legates were in constant communication with Rome, and the conciliar secretariat presided over by Massarelli provided a strong element of continuity which the council needed.

Arguably the council might have been unable to reach such decisions as it did without a final recourse to papal authority. A bitter debate raged in the council as to the nature of episcopal authority. The Italians argued that bishops derived their authority directly from the Pope while their critics, in the main Spaniards, declared that a bishop's powers were directly conferred by God. The implications of this argument were radical, for if, as the Spanish bishops argued, the bishop was responsible to God, surely it was his duty always to reside in his diocese.

Given the complex political situation and the intrinsic difficulties the council reached some major decisions. Although some, notably in Germany, still hoped that the way could be paved for a reunion of the conflicting

Churches, the possibility of a compromise which would satisfy Catholic and Protestant was a forlorn cause. Protestant doctrine had created an abyss which without concessions of fundamental importance on both sides could not be bridged.

But the council did articulate doctrine in such a way as to redefine it, if in ways which made a compromise with Protestantism unlikely. It upheld the Roman teaching on the doctrine of justification and reaffirmed the traditional teaching on the power and effectiveness of the sacraments, which had been fixed as seven in number in 1439. There could be no question about the truth of the doctrine of transubstantiation. 'If anyone says that in the most holy sacrament of the Eucharist there remains the substance of bread and wine together with the Body and Blood of our Lord Jesus Christ, and denies that marvellous and singular conversion of the whole substance of the wine into the Blood, even though the species of the bread and wine remain, which the Catholic Church most appropriately calls transubstantiation, let him be anathema!' Although the council had not formulated any new doctrine it had redefined traditional teaching afresh and reasserted the essentials of faith and salvation in such a way as to provide the corpus of orthodoxy on which all future theological thinking in the Roman Church was to be based.

In more practical terms the council was determined to rid the Church of the abuses which had crippled its efficiency and even stunted its faith. The fathers issued a series of regulations which were designed to ensure that all ranks of the clergy carried out their sacred duties properly. Even the Pope was urged to take good care in choosing the cardinals. The bishops were told to preach regularly, to hold diocesan synods and to conduct visitations. The council sought to cope with the long reiterated complaints about the parish priest. They were to be strictly celibate; and if they were living in concubinage they were to put away their concubines forthwith on pain of deprivation of their living. They were to live in their parishes, to wear appropriate clerical dress and to celebrate Mass reverently.

Perhaps the most important innovation that was made was the requirement that seminaries ('perpetual nurseries of ministers for the worship of God') should be founded in which the priests could be properly trained. If the Catholic priest was to compete with his better-educated counterpart, the Protestant minister, he must be adequately trained both in teaching the gospel and in the refutation of heresy. 'If', the relevant canon stated, 'they are not well educated, young people are all too easily led astray by the pleasures of the world. Thus unless they are formed in piety and religion at the tenderest age, before vicious habits have entirely taken hold of them, it is impossible for them to persevere perfectly in ecclesiastical discipline without the special and powerful protection of almighty God.'

When the council ended, there were still a number of unresolved issues but these the bishops were content to leave to the discretion of the Pope. The lay Catholic princes gave only a grudging approval to the Tridentine decrees, fearful that they portended papal interference in Church affairs which they had for the most part controlled themselves. While the Poles and Portuguese greeted the council's decrees, Philip II of Spain in 1564 only accepted the council's decisions in so far as his 'royal rights' were 'in no ways infringed', a formula which he was later to invoke to the detriment of papal authority. The French kings were even less cooperative, refusing to legalize the decrees and later, in 1615, condemning a declaration which the French bishops made to ensure that the decrees were implemented. The emperor also gave only qualified approval, refusing to allow the publication of any decrees which might impinge on his authority.

Perhaps the greatest obstacle to the full implementation of the Tridentine decrees was the in-built conservatism both in manners and doctrine of the Church. Old habits died hard as well as slowly. Neither nepotism nor pluralism could be fully eliminated, even at the papal curia itself. Aristocratic families in France and Germany continued to have a lien on bishoprics; the Gondis who monopolized the see of Paris between 1569 and 1662, the Rohans who held the see of Strasbourg from 1704 to 1803, the La Rochefoucaulds. The bishops did not hold provincial or diocesan synods as regularly as the council had required. They were slow to found seminaries and reluctant to carry out visitations. Nor was there seemingly any decline in the ostentatious wealth of the higher clergy, many of whom still seemed to be separated socially and even spiritually from the run-of-the-mill parish priests, against whom there continued to be perennial complaints of neglect of duty and poor quality of life. The transformation of the parochial scene was slow. Although a diocesan synod held at Lyons in 1577 laid down that candidates for holy orders had to submit to an examination before ordination, it was not until 1657 that ordinands were required to attend a seminary, nor until after the mid-seventeenth century that four new seminaries were created.

Even so, there was no denying that a great change was taking place. If there was not, as in the Protestant Reformation, a doctrinal break with the past, the Roman Catholic Church of the late sixteenth and seventeenth centuries was no longer the old medieval Church writ large. It had re-emerged, streamlined and refashioned. All this was not simply a result of the work of the council alone but was the outcome of changes that had their roots in the later Middle Ages.

THE REVIVAL OF THE PAPACY

At the centre of the revival of the papacy was the re-enforced authority of the Pope. In the fifteenth century, partly as a result of the conciliar movement and the increase in the power which secular rulers exerted over Church affairs, the Pope's power contracted. The Pope had to come to terms with a situation in which his political influence was to continue to diminish. But he sought to compensate, if unconsciously, by centralizing the affairs of the Church on Rome, and stressing his spiritual authority. All this could not be done without a radical transformation of the holders of the papal office and the curia. The Popes took immediate action to purge their own city of the corruption which had so long characterized it, a move which was much resented by many of its pleasure-loving citizens. The ascetic Dominican who became Pope Pius V in 1566, a somewhat narrow-minded if humble devôt, tried to eliminate immorality and excessive luxury, removing prostitutes from the streets and punishing adulterers by whipping or imprisonment. He curbed the sale of public offices, which made the curia so lukewarm in the pursuit of reform, and imposed measures of discipline on lay and religious alike. His later successor and protégé, the vehement Sixtus V, in five years of rule transformed the city, replanning it and restoring the economy of the Papal States by putting down banditry, encouraging industry and agriculture, draining the marshes and effectively restoring the papal finances (which unfortunately led him in some measure to resort to the sale of offices again). His heavy taxation and repressive discipline made him so unpopular with his subjects that on hearing of his death they immediately removed his statue from the Capitol. By the end of the sixteenth century the Popes had gone some way to restore not simply their authority over the Church but the moral and spiritual leadership which their high office demanded.

By the time of Sixtus V's death in 1590, Rome had been re-established as the religious capital of the Roman Catholic Church. Both the faith had been strengthened and the administrative structure made infinitely more effective. The Pope approved the issue of a *Catechism* (1566) for which the Council of Trent had asked as early as 1546, together with (in 1568) a reformed breviary and (in 1570) a Roman missal; a new if not wholly satisfactory edition of the Vulgate was published in 1593.

The curial administration underwent a significant facelift. The college of cardinals was remodelled, the number of its membership being fixed in 1586 as 70, consisting of 6 bishops, 50 priests and 14 deacons, a number not exceeded until the pontificate of Pope John XXIII. The curial departments of state were reorganized. New congregations had already been created: the Inquisition in 1542 to deal with heresy and error; the Index (1570) for censorship and banning of books and so forth. In 1588 by the bull *Immensa Dei* Sixtus V created fifteen permanent congregations of organized committees, incorporating those which were already in existence but adding four new ones, so creating a modern framework for government, a system that was to remain virtually unchanged until the Second Vatican Council. A Congregation for the Conversion of the Infidels had been set up in 1568 and it was later, in 1622, reorganized as the powerful and influential Congregation de Propaganda Fide, which supervised the ever-expanding missionary work of the Church.

The revitalization of the Church released a surge of evangelistic activity in

Europe, Asia and America for the promotion of which colleges were founded in Rome, run by the Jesuits, to train priests in missionary work abroad: a German College in 1573, a Hungarian College in 1578, and an English College in 1579. There were also special colleges for the Greeks, Catholics who accepted the eastern rite, for Maronites, Armenians and converts from Islam or Judaism. These latter ventures originated with the learned Pope Gregory XIII who also established a printing press for eastern languages and patronized the Vatican library. His name was to be indelibly associated with the reform of the calendar.

The papacy had thus re-emerged as purged and purified, strengthened in authority by delimiting the powers of both cardinals and bishops; Sixtus V insisted that all bishops should make regular visits to Rome, and report on their dioceses. By largely abandoning the pretensions to temporal supremacy made by their medieval predecessors, in favour of a working compromise with the great powers, the Popes had recovered something of the moral prestige which a few decades earlier they seemed to be in danger of losing. There was to be no realistic threat to papal autocracy of any significance until the closing decades of the twentieth century.

THE CATHOLIC REFORMATION AND EDUCATION

What happened at Rome was less significant for the implementation of the Tridentine decrees than what was to occur in local churches, more especially through the foundation of schools, colleges and seminaries which helped to raise the standards of the local clergy. The Council of Trent had envisaged a seminary in every diocese, but for various reasons this was an ideal which could not be fulfilled. In Italy twenty seminaries were founded between 1564 and 1584; in Spain where four had been set up before 1564, another twenty-six were established between 1567 and 1600. In France where the state never acknowledged the Tridentine decrees officially it was not until after the middle of the seventeenth century that seminaries became widespread. Seminaries were set up to train priests to work in the mission fields of Protestantized countries; there were English colleges at Douai, Saint-Omer, Paris, Louvain and Liège, Irish colleges at Paris, Louvain, Salamanca and Rome, and a Scots college at Pont-à-Mousson, later moved to Douai, and at Rome.

The seminaries, which housed young men whose ages ranged from twelve to twenty-four, varied much in quality and in the type of instruction they provided. The curriculum was traditional in type, marked by a revival of interest in the teaching of Thomas Aquinas whom Pope Sixtus V had made a doctor of the Church, and less concerned with the metaphysical subtleties of the late medieval schoolmen. More stress was placed on the study of scripture. Moulded by the natural conservatism of the teaching, the priest was likely to be suspicious of critical thought, especially in religious matters.

Virtually, for the first time, the Church had brought into operation systematic training for clergy, so that, indoctrinated by the faith and discipline of the Tridentine decrees, they could pass on their teaching to the lay people. Such training may also have helped to foster a distinctive clerical profession, creating a self-conscious class which, perhaps even more than in the Middle Ages, was separated from the laity by its uniform (upon the wearing of which bishops were now insistent) and by its cast of mind.

As influential as the establishment of these special seminaries for the training of priests was the part played by the Catholic reformers in founding colleges, schools and academies for the education of the laity. In 1546 Guillaume du Prat, the enlightened bishop of Clermont-en-Auvergne, offered the Jesuit father Le Jay the decayed university of Billom in his diocese which the Jesuits then transformed into a highly successful centre of education. The Jesuits' methods, epitomized in the *Ratio Studiorum*, printed in 1599, were, for their age, remarkably humane. The mind had to be persuaded rather than hammered into subjection. Emulation and competition in the form of rewards and prizes helped the young men to climb the path of higher education. The Jesuits' success and skilful teaching methods were much esteemed by the wealthier laity upon whom they concentrated their attention. It was partly through the education which their sons received that the scions of the affluent bourgeoisie and aristocracy absorbed the spiritual and cultural ideals of the Catholic Reformation. Nor was girls' education neglected. An order of nuns, the Ursulines, originating with Angela Merci who had set up a girls' school at Brescia, spread fast, more especially in France where there were some 255 Ursuline houses by the middle of the seventeenth century. Women played as important a part in the Catholic as they did in the Protestant Reformation, more especially in promoting the cult of the spiritual life.

THE NEW RELIGIOUS ORDERS

While the Jesuits were certainly the leading agents in the dissemination of the Catholic Reformation, other religious orders, both old and new, became vibrant proponents of its ideals. Older, unreformed orders received short shrift from a resurgent papacy. Pius V, zealous for the correction of abuses, suppressed the Umiliati and encouraged the reform of the Franciscans and Cistercians. Teresa of Avila, a practical visionary if ever there was one, established the discalced Carmelites who won the patronage of the Spanish king Philip II. Her contemporary Peter of Alcantara set up a branch, severe in its practice, of the Observant Franciscans. The Brothers of Mercy, founded by John of God, cared for the sick. Jane Frances de Chantal, directed by the holy bishop of Geneva, Francis de Sales, founded a convent at Annecy in 1610 which flowered into the Order of Visitation, whose adherents ran some hundred and fifteen houses in France before Chantal's death in 1641.

Another French representative of the new monasticism was Vincent de Paul, spurred on to charity by his fervent evangelism. The members of the order which he set up to help the sick were reminded that they had to 'love one another as being persons whom Jesus Christ has united and bound through his love'. In 1624 he founded the Congregation of the Mission to carry the faith into the countryside, its headquarters the priory of St Lazare in Paris. Then, assisted by a pious widow, Louise de Marillac, he established the Company of the Maidens of Charity (1633), of which there were some forty houses by 1656, to work among the poor. To try to ensure a better quality of priest, Vincent de Paul introduced the idea of spiritual retreats for parish priests. Captured in his youth by Barbary pirates and compelled to work as a slave in Tunis, he later turned his attention to ameliorating the lot of the unfortunate galley slaves.

Vincent de Paul's spiritual director was Pierre de Bérulle who himself played a prominent part in reviving the spiritual life of the French Church, for, inspired by the example of Philip Neri who had set up the Oratory in Italy, he created the French Oratory. In particular it was designed to help train priests, and it was largely through the work of the Oratorians that so many French seminaries took shape in seventeenth-century France, at Paris, Langres, Mâcon, Laon and elsewhere. The seminary of St Sulpice at Paris, founded by the local curé, J.J. Olier, became a nursery for the French episcopate.

The most spectacular feature of the new monasticism was its practical nature. The monks did not live enclosed behind high walls, but as active soldiers of Christ. They taught the catechism in schools and visited the homes of the sick and poor, attended to the wants of prisoners and orphans, and conducted missions in towns and villages.

The religious house could be a well of holiness from which spiritual waters flowed, channelled into some remarkable writing of which Loyola's *Spiritual Exercises* formed a prototype. They were intended as a guide to pious meditation and an avenue for the man or woman who sought an ecstatic union with God. The soul, emptied of self, passed through the annihilation of darkness, to experience the 'naked love of God'. 'Prayer', as Luis of Granada put it, 'is rising above oneself and all created things, uniting oneself with God and submerging oneself in this sea of infinite sweetness and love.' It was a message implicit in the *Interior Castle* of Teresa of Avila, and the poetic mysticism of John of the Cross, who wrote in 1578:

> This life I live in vital strength
> Is loss of life unless I win You:
> And thus to die I shall continue
> Until in You I live at length. . . .
> This life I do not want, for I
> am dying that I do not die.

Ignatius of Loyola, Teresa and John of the Cross were rare practitioners of piety, but they had humbler followers whose faith was shored up by mystical experience, such as Margaret Mary Alacoque who at Paray-le-Monial in 1673–7 visualized Jesus 'heart aflame with holy fire'. Influenced much by the devotional writings of John Eudes and Cardinal Bérulle, she felt Christ taking his heart from his breast and putting in hers, setting her heart on fire with his love. Some of these holy men and women may have allowed their imagination too much licence, so that the imagery of love such as the sacred heart seemed almost a form of sexual compensation. A flood of pious devotional manuals found a ready market among the laity as well as among the clergy.

REFORM OF THE EPISCOPATE AND PAROCHIAL CLERGY

In the late sixteenth and early seventeenth centuries, at the top of the Church the personnel of the episcopate experienced a partial facelift as the number of worldly and political prelates grew less. The majority of bishops made some attempt to hold diocesan synods and to conduct the visitations which the Council of Trent required. Bishops tried to ensure that the priests in their dioceses abandoned vicious living and conformed to their vocation. The ideal bishop of the Catholic Reformation was Charles Borromeo, the archbishop of Milan. Born of a noble family, as a papal nephew he had a gilded start to his clerical career, for his uncle, Pius IV, appointed him at an early age a papal secretary of state but the sudden death of his brother led to a change of direction, partly promoted by his reading of Loyola's *Spiritual Exercises*. He adopted an ascetic life-style and became a leading reformer, as archbishop holding regular provincial and diocesan synods, whose decrees, published in 1582, were widely circulated.

The most permanent achievement of the Catholic Reformation was to be found at the parish level, as the Church acquired a better-instructed and more conscientious priesthood. The bishops were vigilant in dealing with clergy accused of womanizing or drunkenness, imposing penalties on priests who habitually frequented inns and wine shops, as on those who went hunting or engaged in other worldly pursuits unsuitable to their vocation. Constant attempts were made to ensure that the clergy were properly garbed in a black soutane or cassock, 'to be always dressed', as the bishop of Paris said in 1620, 'in a long, neat and decent soutane' and 'to have a tidy beard and hair style with a neat tonsure'. The bishops tried, apparently with some measure of success, to diminish the amount of absenteeism and to insist that the clergy resided in their parishes. By 1672–3 of the curés of 138 parishes in Paris, there were apparently only six who were non-resident.

While the story of the Church in the large archdiocese of Lyons may not have been wholly representative of the western Church as a whole, its history does embody some of the more salient features which brought about the steady infiltration of the Tridentine decrees into the French Church. In the mid-sixteenth century the city of Lyons, a rich, bustling commercial metropolis, seemed to be moving towards a religious crisis. Relations between the cathedral chapter, the members of which, entitled to be called counts, were wealthy and aristocratic, and the municipal government had reached so low an ebb that the council showed some favour to the Huguenots who were actually able to acquire control of the city in 1562–3. There was, however, a reaction against the Huguenots which opened the way for a reconciliation between the cathedral and the city which the dissemination of the Tridentine ideals strengthened.

From the 1550s onwards increasing attempts were made, as the diocesan statutes of 1566 and 1577 showed, to discipline errant priests. Friars and Jesuits were invited to preach evangelical sermons in different churches; such preachers had the advantage of being acquainted with recent work in theology and of current devotion, such as the cult of the Virgin and the rosary. An alliance was reforged between the élite of the laity and the Church, the laity becoming more active in the Church's life, participating in pious confraternities, and following rules of life which upheld moral austerity. The decline in testamentary benefactions, a feature of the mid-sixteenth century, was stemmed resulting in a marked increase in bequests to the Church.

The Catholic Reformation in Lyons mainly affected the ranks of the affluent bourgeoisie, for the poorer classes and the country people were distanced from the urban élite as they were also from many of the clergy. In the countryside the Catholic Reformation was to make perceptibly slower progress. Indeed, the diocesan records reveal massive numbers of complaints of improper clerical behaviour, of failure to wear clerical dress, of widespread ignorance and of drinking and gambling. The archbishop's visitation to the parish of Passin in 1613–14 revealed that the curé, Pierre Morard, was 'clothed in an extremely indecent costume, with a huge moustache like a soldier – which we made him shave off on the spot'.

Nonetheless the impact which these changes slow but sure had on the priest and his flock was fundamental. The new priest had been instilled with a concept of his vocation which stressed his spiritual calling and separateness from the world, marked by his distinctive costume, for 'those who appear in long curly hair or gaudy clothing . . . are not part of the ecclesiastical estate'. Visitation records in the diocese of Lyons showed that there was a gradual but conspicuous improvement in the standard of clerical behaviour and the performance of clerical function. Non-residence and pluralism declined. The curés were better educated and better paid, for there was some increase in the amount of tithe as well as a re-assessment of Mass stipends and other fees. The new type of priest was both keener and often more authoritarian, intolerant, for instance, of religious or semi-religious activities, such as those undertaken by the different confraternities which were not run directly under his supervision. He was to the fore in the conduct of the local hospitals, charities and schools where he taught the catechism; but as a member of a rural élite he conceivably became less closely identified with his flock than he had once been.

The spiritual ideals of the Catholic Reformation were in many respects a purged version of medieval spirituality, draining off the popular elements which had in medieval culture led to some blending of the sacred and profane. Whereas in the past the laity had not communicated frequently, they were now encouraged to take communion more regularly. The role of the priest as confessor was strongly stressed; and the confessional box took its place as a new architectural device in the parish church. The Eucharist became even more than it had been in the past a centre of veneration, leading to portrayals in art which glorified the consecration of the elements rather than fastening attention on the Last Supper. Pius V required the simple cabinets or ciboria in which the consecrated Host was kept to be replaced by tabernacles.

Side by side with this emphasis on spirituality there went an austere puritanism which was determined to root out anything that by reason of its indecency and worldliness was detrimental to true religion. The festal side of religion was particularly suspect. Marriage, for instance, was to be celebrated 'without tumult, mockery, taunts, scuffles, jokes, foul and immoderate speech which is customary'. The popular rituals which accompanied deaths and funerals were forbidden. All secular activities were banned from the church. Sunday markets were prohibited. The Church was concerned to uphold a rigid moral standard, especially in matters which might be conducive to sexual misconduct. 'Public baths', it was asserted, 'give rise to scandal because of the mingling of the sexes. One sees in summer naked boys of fifteen and twenty and even full grown, on boats and ships, where everyone can see them, all of which constitutes a sordid spectacle for the Christian and a great danger for the purity of the young persons.'

All practices, though long rooted in past custom, which savoured of pagan superstition were suppressed. Catholic and Puritan alike condemned the May Day festivals in the course of which, as a Church council at Milan in 1579 described it, men and women 'cut down trees, branches and all, parading them in the streets and squares of the towns and villages, and then planting them with wild and ridiculous ceremonies'. The bishops sought to eliminate masquerades and festivities, among them those connected with the celebration of St John's Day, as 'shameful relics of paganism'. At Annecy in 1683 the bishop ordered the 'people under pain of excommunication, to suppress and abolish entirely the torches and fires customarily lit on the first Sunday of Lent'.

The priests' attempts to abolish these age-old customs created some degree of tension between themselves and their flocks, perhaps more especially with the young men who resented the priests' attempt to exert social and moral control over their private lives. In a subtle way the priest became increasingly disassociated from the community though it was he who had brought the Catholic Reformation to the people.

The parish priest did not go entirely unassisted, for, apart from faithful laity, there were in most Catholic countries regular missions conducted by Jesuits, Oratorians and other religious which were directed specifically at the conversion of the countryside. The French Oratory began its preaching mission in the villages of the diocese of Paris at the chief church festivals. The missioners who attracted public attention by making bonfires of undesirable books and items of luxury, what John Eudes called 'joy-fires', planted wooden crosses, and got their congregations to sing vernacular hymns to popular tunes. Normally they came in small groups of four to six and stayed until all the parishioners had confessed and taken the sacrament of penance. 'Our missions', as John Eudes described them, 'in the smaller parishes never last less than six weeks. Otherwise you conceal the wickedness, but do not cure it.'

As a result of all this devoted effort Catholic Europe emerged in some respects more Christian than it had been in the closing years of the Middle Ages, if by that is meant that there was a more dedicated priesthood and a laity more committed to the teaching of Christ. Yet it was surely true that the majority of people conformed to what was expected of them rather than that they were very deeply committed.

MISSIONARY ACTIVITY

By the end of the fifteenth century Europe had ceased to be the world. With the progressive exploration of distant continents a new world was opening to which the Church felt obliged to preach the gospel. In the wake of the explorer, soldier, trader and colonist there came the missionary. By the bull *Romanus Pontifex* Pope Nicholas V confirmed the Portuguese occupation of lands discovered in west Africa. In 1493 Pope Alexander VI adjudicated that all lands west of the Azores were allotted to the Spaniards, and lands to the east to the Portuguese. The crown controlled the missionary Church in Spain's rapidly expanding dominions overseas, establishing some forty-three bishoprics and seven archbishoprics in South and Central America between 1500 and 1800 and acquiring from the Pope the right to nominate to the bishoprics.

No one doubted that the Church had an obligation to convert the non-Christian inhabitants of these newly discovered lands to the Christian faith so saving them from the pains of hell for which they were otherwise inevitably destined. The Spanish king, the Pope reminded him, was obliged to 'bring to the Christian faith the peoples who inhabit these islands and the mainland . . . and to send to the said islands and to the mainland, wise, upright, God-fearing and virtuous men who will be capable of instructing the native peoples in good morals and in the Catholic faith'. The Spaniards who had only recently triumphed over Islam by the conquest of the Moors of Granada, brought with them a touch of their conquistadoring spirit to the New World. Their leaders, often a ruthless and cruel bunch of roughnecks, were superstitiously devout, believing that their almost miraculous victories were God-given. Geronimo de Medieta infelicitously described Cortés as a new Moses. They owed it to God to liberate the native people from their thraldom to the worship of images and savage pagan superstition. The Elizabethan Catholic Thomas Stapleton, who believed that the world was moving apocalyptically towards a truly reformed Church, averred, 'God hath of his wonderful mercy and goodness . . . opened and revealed unto us as it were a new world, of which neither by writing or otherwise we have heard anything before. . . . He hath by his Providence ordained that the . . . countries of Asia and Africa have become of plain and open idolaters, of Moors and Saracens, very good Christians.' The Spanish crown itself gave priority to the conversion of the native peoples, stating that this should be accomplished peaceably and without oppression.

The intentions were doubtless excellent, but inevitably coercion too was to play its part in the work of conversion. The conquest of the New World had been by the cross and the sword, and in its conversion both were to have a part. As the first Jesuit provincial of Brazil, Father Abchieta, bluntly put it, 'there is no better way of preaching than with the sword and the rod of iron'. Moreover, whatever the zeal of the missionaries, mainly friars, the work of conversion could only be superficial, involving what was often a purely symbolic renunciation of the old gods, the acceptance of baptism, and conformity to the demands of the teaching of the Church. It was hardly surprising that for many Christianity became sometimes an amalgam of ancestral worship with western European religion, retaining many of the older non-Christian elements.

The Church, in general, adopted a humane attitude towards the early converts. 'We declare', Pope Paul III stated in his bull Sublimis Deus in 1537, 'the Indians, like all other peoples . . . may not be deprived in any way of their freedom or property (even though they do not belong to the religion of Jesus Christ), and can and must enjoy them in freedom and legitimately.' But time and time again its principles were circumvented by the greed of the colonists. As early as 1511 a Dominican, Antonio de Montesinos preaching in Santo Domingo on Christmas Day, criticized the settlers. 'Tell me, by what right or injustice do you keep these Indians in such cruel and horrible servitude? Why do you keep them so oppressed and weary, not giving them enough to eat nor taking care of them in their illnesses? For with the excessive work you demand of them, they fall ill and die, or rather you kill them with your desire to exact and acquire gold every day. . . . Are these not men? Have they not rational souls?' The natives had a champion in another Dominican, Bartolemeo de las Casas. 'It would', he said 'profit the king more to lose all his temporal possessions in the Indies . . . than to let all these Spaniards persevere in evil . . . casting ignominy on God and his Christian religion.' The ruler of Spain, the emperor Charles V, listened to las Casas and in the so-called New Laws of 1542 sought to protect the American Indians' rights, abolishing the *encomienda* system which had allowed the settlers to exact tribute and labour from the natives in return for protection and instruction in the Christian faith. The theologian and lawyer Francisco de Vitoria, teaching at Salamanca, also reaffirmed that it was not only wrong to suppose that the natives were naturally inferior to the Spaniards but necessary to accept that they possessed rights which were valid whether they were Christian or not.

This was splendid stuff but for the colonist on the spot it had an air of make-believe. Although the American Indian peasants were technically free, the settlers, wanting wealth and labour, exploited and virtually enslaved them; the indigenous peoples were heavily depopulated in the closing years of the sixteenth century by plague and oppression. While there were many heroic figures among the missionary priests, there were also deep shadows in the missionary situation. The actual number of those working in the missions proportionate to the number of priests was small. Indeed, the seventeenth-century secretary of the Congregation de Propaganda Fide, Mgr Ingoli, stated that the religious orders often sent their more troublesome and ineffective members abroad from where they returned as quickly as they could. The orders were riven by intense and sometimes bitter rivalry. The evangelization of Mexico had been undertaken by the Franciscans (1523), the Dominicans (1526) and the Augustinians (1533); and they resented the Jesuits who were comparatively late arrivals on the scene (1572). By 1580 the Jesuits had 107 houses in Mexico and by 1603 some 345.

The work of conversion was made less effective by enforced mass baptisms. The first bishop of Mexico Juan de Zumarraga mentioned in 1551 that more than a million had been baptized in New Spain since 1524. If the round figure was questionable, it suggests that the understanding which the converts acquired of their new faith was limited. Many colourful practices, part of the pre-Christian heritage, were incorporated into the Christian faith, so that the externals of Catholic worship screened a pattern of ancient beliefs. One of the most popular of these chapels was that of the Virgin of Guadeloupe, who had appeared miraculously to a converted Indian labourer, Juan Diego, in 1531. The chapel was built on the site of a shrine to the Aztec earth-goddess, Tonantzie at Tepeyac Hill, north of Mexico City. In recognition of the importance the chapel continued to have in Mexican religious life Pope John Paul II was to visit it in 1979.* Latin American

---

* In 1996 the chapel was the centre of a bitter wrangle as its aged abbot Guillermo Schulenberg questioned the historic existence of Juan Diego. Some believers were horrified by the suggestion and claimed that the abbot was the victim of a power struggle between high church dignitaries over the large annual income netted by the basilica.

Catholicism was threaded by a strong devotion to the Virgin Mary, the intercessor often depicted as the suffering mother of an androgynous Christ, providing compensation for a frequently exploited peasantry, their attention diverted from present misery by a rich ritual whose effect if not purpose was to promise compensation in the next world.

While the Church was ready to employ Indians as catechists, it was reluctant to sponsor training for a native clergy. Bishop Zummaraga of Mexico had certainly founded a college with this in mind but by 1540 he was having second thoughts 'since the best students among the Indians are more inclined to marriage than to continence'. In 1555 the first Church council of Mexico forbade the ordination of anyone of 'moorish race', which was held to include Indians, those of mixed race, the *mestizos* and mulattos or pure Negroes. In 1576 Pope Gregory XIII, referring in his bull *Nuper ad nos* to the missionary priests' regrettable ignorance of native languages allowed half-castes to be ordained; but this provoked such criticism in America that a royal order forbade the practice. Church councils explained that the *mestizos* and Native Indians were unable to meet the stiff demands which the Council of Trent had laid down for candidates for the priesthood. Nor was the ban removed until the third Church council of Lima in 1772. The first three Indian priests were actually ordained in 1794. It had taken roughly three hundred years to reach this step. Indians, Negroes and peoples of a mixed race were thus treated in religious as well as in other matters as second-class citizens.

The separateness of the Indians from their White co-religionists was further promoted by the clergy's unwillingness to offer the sacraments to converts because, as a Church council had declared at Lima in 1552, they were not well enough instructed in the faith to understand the sacraments' meaning. The Church inevitably gave the impression of being, and indeed in most respects was, a western European institution. Most missionaries had only a sparse knowledge of native languages and had to rely on native catechists and interpreters whose own understanding of Spanish and Portuguese was limited. The teaching cannot have been for the majority very much more than a set of formulas learnt parrot-fashion, creating what has sometimes been called a 'catechumen-Catholicism', an odd mix of formal ceremonies intermingled with ancient native beliefs and customs.

The missionaries seemed agents of the civil power without whose co-operation they would have found it difficult to do their work. They depended on the local governor for grants of land and forced native labour. Their work among the Indians was undertaken in the so-called '*reductiones*', reservations of natives sometimes removed forcibly from a nomadic life and obliged to live in a segregated community governed by priests and soldiers.

Of these the most interesting was the Jesuit settlement of land in the vicinity of the Parana river granted to the society by Philip III of Spain in 1609 and inhabited by the Guarani Indians. After the Jesuits had successfully warded off attacks by hostile Portuguese and Spanish colonists,

Philip IV virtually agreed to recognize this vast territory, consisting of about thirty *Reduction[e]s* and inhabited by some hundred thousand Indians, as autonomous, though it had to pay tribute to Spain. The Jesuits governed their republic on rigidly paternalistic lines. Each settlement was self-sufficient, with its own buildings, schools and churches, sheltered from the corruptions of White colonists who were banned from entry. The land was held in common but no money was allowed. Although the Jesuits, running their own marketing in a distinctly capitalistic way, were not aiming at creating an ideal or socialist society, they had, however, shown a genuine spirit of communal care in their treatment of the Indians, so that it was a social and personal tragedy for their order when for political reasons Spain and Portugal were obliged to bring the experiment to an end in 1750.

Outside the missionary areas, the Spanish American Church was structured along traditional lines, monolithic in character, privileged and powerful, controlled by the crown and untainted by heresy. In Mexico an archbishopric and nine bishoprics had been instituted by 1605. Splendid churches were built, richly decorated in the exuberant Baroque style. In the vice-royalty of Peru where the Jesuits had arrived in 1568 a university had been established at Lima in 1557. It was in the towns that most priests preferred to work. Tempted by the ownership of property, the religious orders accumulated large estates, sometimes worked by what was virtually unfree labour. The bishops, appointed by the crown, enjoyed rich stipends. The European heartland was preserved in the urban areas where the Church maintained the social, religious and racial values of a superior race. Yet while few colonists were to query the teachings of the Church, which they believed to be necessary for the preservation of social order until the ideas of the Philosophes began to infiltrate into intellectual circles towards the end of the eighteenth century, there was a residual anti-clericalism.

Similar conditions prevailed in the Portuguese colony of Brazil where the Jesuits had arrived as early as 1549. It is hardly surprising that, some centuries later, what has been called liberation theology should be the indigenous product of Latin America.

In the Americas the Spaniards and Portuguese had created an empire in which they had planted their Church. The government paid the missionaries' stipends and gave them military protection. In other non-European lands, the European explorers and settlers had less of a stranglehold, sometimes only attaining a kind of working relationship with the native inhabitants which was based on mutual trading interests and negotiated with the local native potentate; infrequently they created settled colonies of which Portuguese Goa, first occupied in 1510 and made an archbishopric in 1558, was for long the most important. In Asia the Christian settlers formed a religious enclave in a dark sea of encompassing unbelief. There were, moreover, major differences between the situation in South America and Asia, not merely a very different set of religious beliefs, represented by the age-old sophistication of Hinduism and Buddhism but an entirely distinct set of cultural values.

As a result the Church was never to achieve in Asia the paternalistic superiority that it enjoyed in the Americas. Only in the Philippines which became Spanish in 1564–5, did the Catholic Church, carried by the missionary efforts of the Augustinians, the Dominicans who had been sent from Mexico and the Jesuits, attain dominance which it has since retained, though even in the Philippines enclaves of paganism long continued to survive. Elsewhere it did little more than dent the age-old religious pattern of belief in Asia.

This was not for want of trying. Indeed, what was attempted and achieved bore witness to the dynamic nature of the Catholic Reformation. The pioneer was Francis Xavier whom Loyola had appointed Jesuit provincial in India. Like Loyola a Basque by race, Xavier was aggressive in manner and passionate in disposition – fear of the French pox, so it was said, kept him from a colourful love life – but he was a man of overwhelming energy. On his arrival at Goa he worked on the Coromandel coast among the Paravas, a poor fisher people who had been baptized more or less forcibly by the Goan clergy. Later from Malacca he sailed for Japan where he laid the foundations of a Christian community there and died in his forty-sixth year in December 1552 on the isolated island of Sancian in the Canton river as he sought to penetrate China.

His actual achievements were less than his reputation, for he was an inadequate linguist who never acquired more than a rudimentary knowledge of Tamil and was fundamentally incurious about the new world which he had entered; and even by the standards of his own age his attempts at instruction seem naive. He forbade the fishers to go out to sea on Sunday, and commanded them to give a part of the Friday's catch to the Church. However, Xavier's letters home helped to inspire the missionary vocation of others. He became the centre of a cult both in the Far East and at Rome where he was canonized in 1622.

Xavier served as a forerunner to the efforts which the Church made to penetrate both China and Japan. In India its success, outside the Portuguese colony of Goa, was very limited. It sought to Latinize the surviving Christian community, the Syrian Church, allegedly founded by the apostle St Thomas, and by dubious means brought it under the control of the archbishop of Goa, at the rigged synod of Diamper in 1599. The only effective and original missionary effort in India was the work of an Italian Jesuit, Robert de Nobili who perceived that if he was to win sympathizers he must to some extent identify with the people to whom he was preaching. He learned classical Tamil and Sanskrit and dressed as an Indian holy man in robes of ochre, refusing to wear shoes of leather or to cut his hair. He showed respect for his Brahmin friends by accepting the caste system, imposing ashes from sacred cows and omitting some details from the rite of baptism (e.g. insufflation and the application of saliva) which might be thought to be offensive by the

Indians. Although he was denounced for tolerating Hindu superstitions, he had the support of the Pope, Gregory XV.

De Nobili's efforts in India may to some extent explain the relative success which the missionary Church had in China and Japan where the Jesuits saw the need to accommodate the Church's teaching to the religious and philosophical convictions of the people they were seeking to convert. In 1583 a Jesuit, Matteo Ricci, was given permission to settle in the provincial capital of Kwantung on condition that he agreed to dress as a bonze and did not try to leave the town. He made very slow progress learning Mandarin and converted only a few Chinese most of whom lapsed after a change in the governorship led to his removal to Shao-Chou in 1589. The more Ricci mastered the language the more he became aware of the real difficulty of translating Christian theology into Chinese, but discovered through his reading of the Chinese classics that there seemed to be some concepts which could be regarded as precursors to the revealed teaching of the Church, words such as 'Heaven' and 'the Sovereign on High'. His Confucian-like meditations were temporarily interrupted by political events, more especially by the Japanese invasion of China and Korea under Hideyoshi, between 1597 and 1600, which had the approval of the Jesuit visitor to Asia, Valignano. But Ricci managed to make his way to the imperial capital Peking where his skill with clocks won the favour of the emperor. Ricci showed greater understanding of the people among whom he was working than most missionaries. If his seventeen years' sojourn had produced no more than a handful of converts, his readiness to adopt Chinese garb and to accommodate his teaching to Chinese ideas and even to Confucius's ancestor worship laid the foundations for a degree of success for the priests who followed him. When he died in 1610 the emperor himself provided a burial place.

It was the Jesuits' skill in mathematics and astronomy as much as their sense of mission which won imperial favour for other missionaries, such as the German Johann Adam Schell von Bell who was made a mandarin of the first class for advising the Chinese on the reform of the calendar, made necessary by the advent of a new imperial dynasty; and his successor Ferdinand Verbiest who not only succeeded him as president of the board of astronomy but tried to translate Aquinas into Chinese. In 1615 Pope Paul V allowed Chinese priests to say Mass in their own language, and a former Chinese peasant, Lo Wen-Tsao was in 1674 made vicar-apostolic for northern China. Although there were some dangerous crises, such as the attempt in 1664 to expel the European missionaries, aroused by fear that the European powers might intervene in China, the Catholic Church there grew. By the early eighteenth century, the Chinese Church had three dioceses, Macao, Nanking and Peking, as well as 117 missionaries and 244 churches and chapels, a mere rivulet in the densely populated country, but even so an impressive tribute to the missionary enthusiasm stimulated by the Catholic Reformation.

The Japanese mission had had a more troubled history and a disastrous conclusion. Xavier had arrived in Japan dressed as a bonze, representing himself as an envoy of the Portuguese king. At first, Japan's political situation favoured the Christian missionaries, for Japan was not then a unitary state, power resting with some two hundred and fifty *daimyos* or local feudal chiefs while Buddhism was momentarily in decline. While Xavier stayed for no more than twenty-seven months in Japan, he was much impressed by the Japanese whom he described as the 'best [people] who have as yet been discovered, and it seems to me that we shall never find among heathens another race to equal the Japanese'. The Jesuits who followed him won the support of some of the local *daimyos*, so much so that on the initiative of the Jesuit Alessandro Valignano a seminary was established which trained native catechists. After some set-backs two Japanese were ordained as priests in 1601, one of whom, Sebastian Chimwas, died a martyr in 1622.

Such success was, however, shallow. There were bitter clashes between the missionaries themselves, especially after the arrival of the friars. By the early years of the seventeenth century under the lead of the powerful Hideyoshi the country was regaining its political unity. The shogun was suspicious that the Christians, whom he regarded as a subversive force in league with treasonable local chiefs, were engaged in plotting with the Spaniards in the Philippines to invade Japan. Ancestral Shintoism and native Buddhism both seemed threatened by advancing Christianity. A series of persecutions was launched culminating in the outlawry of Christianity by the shogun Iyezaza in 1614. In the Great Persecution of 1637 it was estimated that some thirty thousand Christians in Kyushu were massacred. Many more apostatized. To all intents and purposes the Church had been eliminated in Japan; though pockets of Christian believers seem to have survived until the nineteenth century.

Apart from the Philippines the Catholic Church had its greatest success in Cochin China and Tonking where the Jesuit Alexandre de Rhodes won the confidence of the governing classes. Like Ricci and de Nobili he learned the native language, managing to reduce Vietnamese, a tonal language, to the Latin alphabet. He created a company of native catechists to help in the work. Although there was some intermittent persecution, a strong native Church came into existence in Indo-China which was to outlast its fellow Churches both in Japan and China.

The Jesuit missionary policy was strongly criticized, especially by the friars who accused them of compromising the Christian faith because of their willingness to seek to understand and even to sympathize with the religion of the people among whom they worked. The Jesuits argued that what they were doing was in accordance with papal teaching. The secretary of the Congregation De Propaganda Fide, Francesco Ingoli, had declared in 1659,

Do not regard it as your task and do not bring any pressure to bear on the peoples, to change their manners, customs and uses, unless they are evidently contrary to religion and sound morals. What could be more absurd than to transport France, Spain, Italy or some other European country to China? Do not introduce all that to them, but only the faith which does not despise or destroy the manners and customs of any people. . . . Do not draw invidious contrasts between the customs of the peoples and those of Europe; do your utmost to adapt yourselves to them.

This was surely what the Jesuits could claim to be doing. Their adversaries argued that they were tolerating customs and superstitions which ought to be eliminated; there could not be any compromise with local culture in China any more than there could be in Europe. At first the Inquisition seemed willing to accept the Jesuit policy, but a Dominican Father Navarrete wrote a lengthy book, published in 1676–9, denouncing the Jesuits, which caught the attention of the vicar-apostolic at Fu-Kien, Father Pallu, whom he had earlier met in Madagascar. Pallu, acting in collaboration with his friend Charles Maigrot, renounced all compromise with Confucianism and Chinese rites. Although the Jesuits had won the support of the Chinese emperor K'ang Hsi, the Sorbonne condemned the Jesuit attempt at accommodation which led Cardinal de Noailles to urge the Pope Clement XI to follow suit. He sent an envoy, Charles de Tournon, ill and unsympathetic, who reported adversely on both the Malabar rite, practised by de Nobili's followers, and the Chinese rites. The Chinese emperor was furious and decided to expel all missionary priests who did not accept the Chinese rites. The Catholic community in China became divided, and failing to get Rome to change its mind, it withered away to a fragmented minority. In 1742–4 Benedict XIV in the bulls *Ex quo singulari* (1742) and *Omnium Sollicitudinem* reaffirmed the papal condemnation of the Chinese rites, a decision which was not overturned until 1939. The rigorism of the Catholic Reformation had destroyed the Church in China.

The missionary enthusiasm had other outlets. The French had settled in Canada, in Nova Scotia and New Brunswick (Acadia) in 1603; Quebec had been founded by Champlain in 1605. In the wake of the settlers the religious orders followed, seeking to evangelize the native Indians. The Recollects arrived in 1615 and were joined by the Jesuits and the Sulpicians as well as by the Ursuline nuns brought by Marie de l'Incarnation to provide schools and hospitals. But success among the Indians was limited, and the missionaries were caught in the crossfire of the conflict between the Hurons, supported by the French, and Iroquois, which led to the martyrdom of the two Jesuits, Jean de Brébeuf and Gabriel Lallemant in 1649. Canada formed the jumping-off ground for a number of other missionary expeditions further south, to Lake Superior, the upper Missouri and the Mississippi.

Whatever reservations there may be as to the density and depth of the conversion of these non-Europeans, the propagation of the Christian faith was historically a matter of the greatest moment. It was not something which the Council of Trent had itself ever foreseen. Its sights had been still set on the threat from Islam and the reconquest of Protestant lands, but the Church's attempt to attract followers in Muslim lands, as ever, failed. The Jesuits and Capuchins had set up houses in Ottoman territory, at Istanbul, Aleppo, Damascus, Sidon, Tripoli and Cairo; but they made little headway. Islam, carried by Arab traders, managed to stem the shallow evangelization of the Congo which had been attempted by the Portuguese after its discovery, and where the son of the native African king became the first Black bishop, as they did also in Christian missions in Angola and Monomatapa. By the late seventeenth century Turkish power was in decline, especially after the Turks were obliged in 1683 to raise the siege of Vienna which devout Catholics attributed to the intervention of the Blessed Virgin. It was only in the twentieth century that Islam appeared once more on the offensive. In the closing years of the Middle Ages the Church had been troubled and European civilization was contracting. By the end of the seventeenth century the cross had been planted in every continent, and with the cross had gone the sword which brought many dominions under European rule.

The Catholic Reformation had revitalized the Roman Church and deepened its spirituality. It had widened its membership, nominally by millions, so compensating for any loss it might have sustained by the inroads of Islam or defections to Protestantism. Its musical, artistic and architectural heritage formed a rich testimony to the triumph of the cross. Yet its success was not in all respects unqualified. It had injected a powerful Puritan strain into the practice of religion. The Council of Trent forbade the painting or sculpture of nudes in religious art. Popes Paul IV and Clement VIII tried to eliminate the nudes on Michaelangelo's ceiling in the Sistine Chapel. The Council of Trent tried to purge Church music of its earthiness, and a similar rigour threaded the Church's pronouncements on theatrical performances, dancing, drinking, fashionable dress and popular festivals. The sexual code which it upheld was equally rigorous.

It continued to be a 'persecuting' Church, intolerant of all who deviated from its teaching on doctrine or morals, and ready to use the sword and the stake to bring them into subjection. The Inquisition was still an acceptable instrument of the faith.

Although both Protestants and Catholics were equally responsible for the savage persecution of witches which occurred between 1550 and 1650, bishops who were proponents of Counter-Reformation piety and under the influence of the Jesuits, especially in southern Germany, were to the fore in this sinister work. So Johann von Dornheim, bishop of Bamberg between 1623 and 1633, who had a special witch house constructed in which there was a torture chamber embellished with appropriate texts from Scripture, burned some 600 witches. His colleague, Phillip Adam von Ehrenburg of Würzburg in eight years burned some 500 which included nineteen Catholic priests, young children of seven or eight who were charged with having sexual intercourse with demons, as well as his own nephew and sundry old women. The more seemingly devout the bishop, the more likely he was to sponsor the brutal intimidation of all who offended by their religious or social nonconformity.

All in all the Roman Church continued to be a hieratic institution which found it difficult to accommodate itself effectively to new developments in science and knowledge, condemning Galileo, and in other ways standing on the traditions of the past.

In all this the Catholic Reformation bears comparison with its Protestant counterpart. Catholics and Protestants were now separated from each other by a doctrinal abyss, but the two movements of reform were not antithetical. They seemed two sides of a single coin, aiming at a similar objective, the resuscitation of the Church and the salvation of the individual. Both Catholic and Protestant stood for a coercive moral and doctrinal discipline which they were ready to maintain by the sword. Both were intrinsically puritan, averse to worldly amusements and popular culture. Both had an exalted conception of the role which the priest or clergyman played in society in seeking to revive what both saw as a purer strain of Christianity. The Protestant and Catholic Reformations gave a spiritual blood tranfusion to the body of the Church, but they could not entirely eradicate some continuing symptoms of decay.

CHAPTER EIGHT

Strife, Enlightenment and Renewal, c. 1600–1815

'I read Prayers and administered the H. Sacrament this morning at Weston Church being Christmas Day,' James Woodforde wrote in 1790. 'Gave for an Offering 2s. 6d. Mr and Mrs Custance [the local squire and his wife] at Church and the Sacrament. . . . My old clerk, Js. Smith, old Tom Cory, old Nat. Heavers, old John Peachman and old Christ. Dunnell dined at my House on roast beef and Plumb Pudding. I gave also each to carry home to their wives 1s 0d, 0. 5s. 0d. Sent Old Tom Carr not being able to come being ill, his Dinner and with it, 1s 0d. I lighted my large Wax-Candle being Xmas Day during Tea-Time this afternoon for abt an Hour.'

The author, James Woodforde, was from 1776 to 1803 rector of Weston Longueville in Norfolk, a living in the gift of New College, Oxford, of which he had once been a fellow. He was to be a faithful if conventional parish priest, dispensing hospitality, visiting the sick and the poor, and suspicious of dissent and the onset of Methodism. Loyal to the established order in Church and State, contemporary France in his later life filled him with horror. 'The king of France Louis 16', he wrote in his diary for 26 January 1793, 'inhumanly and unjustly beheaded on Monday last by his cruel, blood-thirsty subjects. Dreadful times I am afraid are approaching to all Europe. France, the foundation of all of it.'

His contemporary John Wesley was another clergyman who had been a fellow of an Oxford college, Lincoln, but he was a very different sort of person. No man of his age was to make such an impact on the religious life of the world. In a preaching career of nearly fifty years he was to travel some quarter of a million miles, to preach 40,000 sermons and to bring the gospel to an innumerable multitude of people. Wesley's preaching, unlike Woodforde's, was not to be confined to a small corner of England. Although, apart from an early visit to Georgia, he did not travel much outside the British Isles, he conceived the world to be, as he expressed it, his parish. Like Woodforde he too kept a journal, but it was very different in character. Where Woodforde recalled what he ate, sometimes in gargantuan detail, Wesley remembered the meetings he had attended, the sermons he preached and his evangelistic experiences.

One of the most memorable of these occurred early in 1739. Invited by his fellow evangelist George Whitefield to preach at Bristol, Wesley broke reluctantly with tradition by speaking in the open air rather than in a church. 'At four in the afternoon,' he wrote in his *Journal* for 2 April 1739, 'I submitted to be more vile and proclaimed in the highways the glad tidings of salvation, speaking from a little eminence, in a ground adjoining to the city, to about three-thousand people.'

Wesley's preaching sometimes affected his congregations in a traumatic fashion. 'I went', he wrote a fortnight later, 'to Baldwin Street [in Bristol] and expounded the fourth chapter of the Acts. We then called upon God to confirm His word. Immediately one that stood by (to our no small surprise) cried out aloud, with the utmost vehemence, even as in the agonies of death. . . . Soon after the other persons were seized with strong pain, and constrained to "roar for the disquietness of their heart".' In later life Wesley's preaching had a less dramatic effect, but the impact which he, his brother Charles, and his preachers had upon their hearers the length and breadth of England was ultimately to revolutionize the religious life of the Protestant Church, not merely in Britain but throughout the world.

Two years after Wesley's death a very different event, anti-religious in character, took place on 10 November 1793 in the cathedral of Notre Dame at Paris, which, semi-secularized by the revolutionary government, had been decorated to celebrate the Revolution's triumph of reason over religion. A pyramid, adorned with busts of Voltaire, Rousseau and Benjamin Franklin, had been erected in honour of Philosophy. At the climax of the festival a young woman, actually an actress from the Paris Opera, '*image fidèle de la beauté*, costumed in a long white robe with a blue mantel and a red bonnet on her head and carrying a pike emerged from the Temple of Philosophy and was enthroned as the Goddess of Reason. It was decided that the cathedral should henceforth be called the Temple of Reason. In republican eyes the hydra of religious superstition had been effectually overthrown and the Christian faith put to flight.

These three themes represent some of the features which conditioned the story of the Christian Church in the eighteenth century. Woodforde, a clergyman traditional in type, stood for that element of continuity which linked the present with past tradition. Contrariwise John Wesley, though a friend to tradition, represented the reaction to the formalism which had come, so he and his fellows had been persuaded, to dilute the original enthusiasm of the early Church.

By contrast with two types of churchmanship the ceremony which took place in Notre Dame, an ephemeral piece of shambolic pageantry as it may have been, pointed to the flotation of radical notions, secular in tone and anti-religious in character, which were to pose a growing challenge to the privileges and faith of the Christian Church, even to the extent of questioning its very existence. 'Here', as a visitor to Paris observed in the summer of 1793, 'there are people of repulsive appearance saying that the existence of God was a hoary superstition, that Hell was a myth, and man a being without a soul, who ought to indulge all the pleasures to which his nature prompted him, without concern either for religion or moral principle.'

In the two centuries which preceded the French Revolution and the ending of the Napoleonic Wars there was to be a slow yet irreversible change in the cultural background which was ultimately to have a profound effect on the future history of Christianity. Medieval culture had been essentially Christian, for though Christianity as a syncretistic faith had absorbed significant elements from the classical and hellenic past with later a tincture of Germanic and Celtic paganism, its thought patterns and life styles took shape within the penumbra of the Christian revelation and the testimony of Scripture. The Protestant and Catholic Reformations had been the outcome of the culture shock which had affected the Church in the closing years of the fifteenth and early years of the sixteenth centuries.

In the two centuries that followed, both the Protestant and Catholic Reformations were being slowly if nearly imperceptibly dismantled as waves of change washed at the high cliffs of traditional Christianity. Outwardly, as the lives of Woodforde and Wesley alone demonstrated, Europe remained Christian in habit and practice; children, receiving social and religious indoctrination at the hands of parents and schoolteachers, became for the most part at least nominal God-fearing members of their respective churches, whether Protestant or Catholic. The churches continued to play an influential, even at times a crucial, part in public life.

Yet the signs of Christianity's diminishing strength were there. It was not merely that even in Catholic countries the political influence of the Pope was steadily evaporating but that new thought-patterns, as yet perhaps in the main the academic play-things of a minority, were beginning to emerge: in the slow development of a more precisely scientific view of the universe, as instanced by the discoveries of Galileo, Newton and Laplace; in the abandonment, again by a minority, of revealed faith in favour of a mechanical deistic interpretation of human destiny; and even in some circles in a naive atheism, of which d'Holbach was a proponent. The stark cataclysm of the French Revolution was a testimony to what lay below the surface where indeed it was by and large long to remain.

The churches still sought to retain the sanctions which curbed criticism of their beliefs or activities, in the shape of excommunication, censorship and invocation of the penal law; but the sanctions were becoming less effective, if on occasions sometimes severe, than they had been in the past, as religious intolerance and persecution became socially unacceptable.

Significant too was the impact of the world outside Europe which Europeans were beginning to exploit and colonize, which revealed the existence of religious systems and sophisticated civilizations even older than Christianity. As the cultural background began slowly to change, so the way was prepared for the ending of the monopoly over faith and life which the churches had enjoyed for so many centuries.

ROMAN CATHOLICISM AFTER THE COUNCIL OF TRENT

That such notions would have been openly publicized could have been predicted at no time in the previous two centuries. The Roman Catholic Church, its structure strengthened, its teaching more precisely defined, its spirituality stimulated by the Catholic Reformation, testified to the continuity of religious tradition. Superficially it would have seemed to be as strongly entrenched in the eighteenth century as it has been a century earlier; but it was operating within the ethos of a changing society in which the religious passions of the past were beginning to wane. The Thirty Years War in which the leading combatants had been initially the Protestant German princes and the Protestant king of Sweden, and the Catholic rulers of Austria and Spain was to be the last major war in which religion was still a basic ingredient. The religious terms of the Peace of Westphalia were condemned by Pope Innocent X in the bull *Zelo Domini Deus* as 'damnable, reprobate . . . empty of meaning and effect for all time', because they recognized the concept of religious toleration; but the aftermath showed that the Pope's influence over the course of political events was increasingly marginal.

Yet *prima facie*, even in the so-called 'age of the enlightenment', the Roman Church remained a deeply entrenched institution, faithful to traditional custom. Although the Catholic Reformation had sought to discourage superstitious manifestations of popular piety, in the remote countryside but also in many town churches the veneration of saints and belief in the miraculous were as strongly rooted as ever. Had not the Blessed Virgin intervened personally to prevent a disastrous repetition of the Lisbon earthquake of 1755? Pilgrims flocked to Rome, especially in jubilee years. Curial administration functioned efficiently. The bishops performed their duties conscientiously. Even the French bishops, who were predominantly chosen by the French king from men of aristocratic birth – only one commoner became a bishop between 1715 and 1789 – did not neglect their duties.

In Catholic countries the priesthood remained a privileged caste, normally exempt from taxation and military service. Some endeavour was made to ensure that they upheld the standards of pastoral care laid down by the Council of Trent and that those who were ordained were men of good character, properly trained and examined by what was known as the *Concursus*, a form of training and a method of appointment to ecclesiastical office which compared favourably with clerical education and the system of patronage in the Protestant Church of England.

Catholic Europe still had a very high population of monks and nuns. As three of the eighteenth-century Popes had themselves been members of religious orders it was hardly surprising that the majority of those whom they canonized were religious. While some, influenced by contemporary philosophy, were beginning to question the justification for purely contemplative orders which lacked 'social utility', the religious orders engaged in practical social or teaching work continued to grow in membership.

In Protestant countries Catholics lived to a greater or lesser degree under the shadow of harsh penal legislation. While the penal laws in England were only sporadically invoked, they formed a constant reminder of their underprivileged status. Nearly eighty-thousand strong in the eighteenth century the Catholics were still debarred from membership of the English parliament, charged a double-rate on the annual land tax, excluded from practising at the bar, and banned from keeping a school. Such laws were not systematically enforced but even as late as 1767–71 there was a spate of prosecutions. In England Catholic chapels were not allowed to have a bell or a spire nor were the religious allowed to wear their habits in public. In 1778 a bill was passed for the relief of the Roman Catholics but it caused a backlash among the Protestant community, leading to rioting in Scotland and then in London where, egged on by the neurotic Lord George Gordon with his cry of 'No Popery', the mob sacked and burned Roman Catholic chapels. The outbreak was less a manifestation of any deep attachment to the Protestant faith than a fear of the foreign influence which the Pope still represented.

English Roman Catholicism was an inoffensive society, passive rather than enthusiastic in its nature and headed by the old gentrified families, though in the closing decades of the eighteenth century there were signs of a perceptible growth in Catholic numbers among the urban and professional classes. Some of the Roman priests who had been educated on the Continent were themselves men of liberal temper, notably Joseph Berington who had been dismissed from his professorship at Douai for his criticism of scholasticism and who became in the 1780s a leading light in the liberal 'Cisalpine' group. A further Relief Bill was passed in 1791 but Roman Catholics in England were still underprivileged citizens. Their history had testified nonetheless to the continued buoyancy of the Catholic faith.

RELIGION IN ENGLAND

Protestantism was threaded by similar elements of continuity which took it back to the Reformation of the sixteenth century. Developments in the history of the Church of England in the seventeenth and eighteenth century were, however, peculiar to England, in part because of the crucial ties which existed then between the English Church and the monarch who, under Jesus Christ, was recognized as the Church's supreme governor. Attempts to damage or destroy this link, whether they came from Roman Catholics or Puritans, were felt to be religiously as well as politically subversive. If it was fundamentally a matter of political convenience for the Church to have the support of the crown and the crown to have the prayers of the Church, there was in the so-called divine right of kings a significant religious element. 'The state of Monarchy', King James I told parliament on 21 March 1610, 'is the supremest thing upon earth; for kings are not only God's lieutenants upon earth and sit upon God's throne, but even by God himself they are called Gods.' Not surprisingly the prayer book, amended in 1662 at the restoration of the monarchy, included prayers of thanksgiving for the foiling of the Catholic plot to blow up the Houses of Parliament on 5 November 1605, and to commemorate the execution of the Church's royal martyr, Charles I, on 30 January.

The execution of Charles I was to be a hiatus in the history of the Church of England, demonstrating that whatever its claims the national Church, which had been brought into being with such difficulty in the closing years of Elizabeth's reign, was never again to be the Church of the whole nation. By the early seventeenth century the Church of England had indeed acquired a fuller authenticity than it had had during the long and arduous process of its gestation. Its apologists, most notably Richard Hooker, described it as both Catholic and Reformed, as a *via media* between the two extremes of Catholicism and Puritanism. Its services were embodied in the prayer book of 1559 the beauty of whose language has rarely been surpassed. Its doctrine was crisply outlined in the Thirty-nine Articles. It was to acquire a code of discipline in the Canons of 1604; and in the translation of the Bible known as the Authorised Version, completed in 1611, it had another superb vehicle of numinous religious prose.

The Church was enriched in the seventeenth century by men distinguished for both ability and sanctity, none more so than Bishop Lancelot Andrewes, renowned in his own day for his sermons, somewhat pedantic and turgid to modern ears but whose *Precatae Privatae*, written in Latin and Greek testified to his search for holiness. George Herbert, who died at forty after a short ministry of three years in the quiet Wiltshire village of Bemerton, wrote gracious poems on the Church in the *Temple* and described the parson's life in *A Priest to the Temple*. Jeremy Taylor, who served as chaplain to Charles I, wrote classic treatises entitled *Holy Living* and *Holy Dying*. Nicholas Ferrar, a London merchant in the service of the Virginia Company, retired together with his family to Little Gidding where they formed a religious community given up to prayer, schooling the children and caring for the sick and the poor, what the hostile Puritans, scenting a whiff of Catholicism, described as 'The Arminian Nunnery'. Ferrar died in 1637 and Little Gidding was sacked by the Parliamentarians nine years later. The record of the Caroline Church was positive in terms of spirituality, pastoral performance and learning, but it had utilized the law and made use of its privileged position to discipline its critics.

There were, however, storms brewing which were to threaten its integrity and even its existence. The Roman Catholics had been largely contained; for though Rome had strong supporters among the old Catholic families and even made occasional converts, the failure of the Gunpowder Plot had alerted the Protestants to the Catholic threat, which they largely identified with the menace of Spain, and the Puritans in particular were over-industrious in finding in the remotely Catholic practices and teaching of some English churchmen suspicious signs of Roman inclinations.

What made the religious situation increasingly tense was the degree of polarization within the ill-defined boundaries of the national Church between those who were High Churchmen or in contemporary terms Arminians (so called after the Dutch theologian Harmensz or Arminius who had criticized Calvinism) and the Puritans, a broad band of Protestants, sometimes aggressive and self-righteous. To a greater or lesser degree the Protestants demanded the further rigorous extension of Protestant doctrine into the practice of the English Church, including the abolition of episcopacy, and the elimination of various minor rituals such as the sign of the cross in baptism, and the wearing of the surplice. They were above all Bible-men, soaked in the language and teaching of the scriptures in the context of which they sought to place their contemporary world. They were strongly moralistic, opposed to theatre-going and the playing of games, more especially on the Sabbath the strict observance of which they determined to maintain. Contrariwise the Arminians wished to restore Catholic practices which accorded with the traditions of the early Church, bringing back the altar to its eastward position, treating the Eucharist with due reverence and ensuring that the churches themselves were restored to the 'beauty of holiness'.

The High Church party had the backing of the crown. James I had been mortified by his experience of the Presbyterians in Scotland, where in 1596 Andrew Melville had addressed the king as 'God's sillie vassall', and declared that 'there are two kings and two kingdoms in Scotland. There is Christ Jesus the King and His Kingdom the Kirk, whose subject King James the Sixth is.' When at his accession to the English throne the Puritans presented him with the Millennary Petition, expressing their desire for a further reformation of the Church, James I, presiding at the subsequent Hampton Court Conference, showed his open dislike for the Puritan party. His son, Charles I, was even more opposed to such Puritan notions, his opinions reinforced by the alignment between Puritans and Parliament-arians in opposition to the crown.

Charles's ecclesiastical adviser was William Laud, archbishop of Canterbury from 1633, a genuine scholar, a former president of St John's College, Oxford. He had a high sense of duty and religious principle and a stern policy on matters relating to Church order and discipline, especially when dealing with those who opposed the reinstatement of ritual which made his critics suspect him, if incorrectly, of looking Romewards, drawing upon himself increasingly bitter obloquy. He used legal instruments, more especially the Court of High Commission which dealt with all ecclesiastical offences, to impose uniformity and to browbeat, punish and even mutilate offenders. A difficult situation was worsened by events in Scotland where in

1637 the crown sought to reinforce unpopular episcopal rule and to impose a new prayer book based upon the English Book of Common Prayer, all of which was deeply resisted by the Scotch Presbyterians who drew up the Covenant to defend the Protestant Church while the Scotch General Assembly abolished both episcopacy and the prayer book.

In the subsequent Civil War between the crown and parliament religion was a major ingredient both in its causation and continuance, though historians remain divided as to the emphasis which should be placed on the war's religious aspect. The opposition to Charles I, who was himself sincerely dedicated to the Church of England, was in large measure Puritan inspired. The Root and Branch Petition to Parliament of 1641, signed by some fifteen thousand Londoners, called for the abolition of all government by an ecclesiastical hierarchy. The Grand Remonstrance demanded a reduction in episcopal power and the abolition of 'idolatrous and Popist ceremonies introduced into the Church by the command of the bishops'. Archbishop Laud had long been the target of Puritan criticism. Deeply unpopular because of his rigorous Church policy, 'the sty of all Pestilential faith . . . the great and Common Enemy of all Goodness and Good men' as Harbottle Grimston ungallantly described him, Laud was impeached and kept in prison for three years and then in 1644 condemned to death by a bill of attainder. Laud's judicial murder, for it was no less, showed the direction in which events were moving. To win Scottish support the Westminster Assembly of Divines accepted the principal notions of the Covenant which the Scotch Presbyterians had drawn up in 1638. The Solemn League and Covenant which parliament accepted in 1644 implied the virtual extinction of the Church of England, for episcopacy and all its trappings was abolished and the Book of Common Prayer was replaced by the Puritan Directory of Public Worship. Some two to three thousand out of ten thousand clergy were deprived of their livings. Officially the Church of England had been dissolved and replaced by a Presbyterian system of Church government, but the structure of the Church of England remained in skeletal form. There remained a group of devout Laudians, some now in exile on the Continent, who waited for the dust to settle, concerned only to keep alive its ceremony, liturgy and episcopal order. Emasculated the Church of England might be but its potential remained, for the Presbyterians had no monopoly of religious power and by their inbuilt austerity, forbidding the celebration of Christmas Day, vandalizing the churches, destroying idolatrous ornaments and stained glass, alienated many.

The Commonwealth was to be a period of religious experimentation. Oliver Cromwell, highly emotional and deeply religious, was a man of 'free spirit' and like many of his army officers really belonged to the Independents or Congregationalists, who regarded the congregation as the proper nucleus of Church government and did not accept the belief for uniformity in religious matters on which both the Church of England and the Presbyterians insisted. The Instrument of Government, issued in 1653, promised an unusual degree of toleration, for while it excluded episcopalians and papists from its provisions, it declared that 'such as profess faith in God by Jesus Christ, though differing in judgment from the doctrine, worship or discipline publicly held forth, shall not be restrained from, but shall be protected in, the profession of the faith and exercise of their religion'.

A welter of religious groups, some with very radical political aspirations and others with bizarre religious ideas, came into existence: Levellers, Diggers, Ranters, Fifth-Monarchy Men who looked to the second advent of Christ, Adamites who worshipped in the nude, Muggletonians and many others, strongly scriptural, with their sights fixed on the New Jerusalem, seeking to build a new heaven as well as a new earth.

Of these the more important, apart from the Independents, were the Baptists and the Quakers. The Baptists had seceded originally from the extreme Puritan group known as the Brownists when John Smyth, the Brownist leader, left for Holland to form the first Baptist Church. The first Baptists were known as the General Baptists to differentiate them from the more Calvinistic Particular Baptists. Their best known member was the author of *Pilgrim's Progress*, John Bunyan, who spent twelve years for his faith in Bedford gaol for refusing to recant his faith.

A significant group of dissenters who came into existence during the Commonwealth were the Quakers or the Society of Friends. Their founder, George Fox, a weaver's son, left his family home at Fenny Drayton in Leicestershire to seek enlightenment. After much mental and spiritual torment he experienced the Inner Light of the Living Christ in 1646. He stopped going to church and became a preacher, voicing the message that he believed God had entrusted to him. Frequently imprisoned, he persevered, travelling through England and visiting Ireland, the West Indies and North America before his death in 1691. The Quakers relied on the guidance of the 'Inner Light' representing a sense of God and his operation in the soul, constituting an authority superior to the teaching of the scriptures and any established Church, enabling a man to be freed from sin and so wedded to Christ that he would perform good works. The Quakers tended to keep apart from their fellows, wearing special clothes and adopting particular verbal observances. They foreswore music and art, but were industrious and philanthropic. For conscientious reasons they refused to pay tithes or to bear arms. Never very numerous, the Society of Friends, with their devotion to philanthropic and educational pursuits, were to contribute much to English social life.

Once the Church of England was restored in 1660 it had to try to create a uniform religious society which should be sufficiently comprehensive to incorporate some of its critics, more notably the Presbyterians, into a united religious edifice. But too much had occurred since the death of Charles I to allow this to happen. Those who refused to accept the Church settlement made in 1662 were ejected from their livings to form the growing body of dissenters. Religion in England had in fact become permanently fragmented, for while the Church of England, established in law, remained the national Church, there were cracks in its facade which betokened a steady weakening of its hold over the nation. It had surrendered its right to tax itself and in 1717 it lost its own parliament, Convocation, which was not to be reinstated until 1852.

Yet although the Church's unity had been irretrievably sundered and its privileged position marginally weakened, its links with the crown had been restored. The order that the royal arms should be placed in all churches underlined the close association between the crown and the Church. The alliance was, however, in many respects an uneasy one, for Charles II turned out to be a covert Roman Catholic, his brother and successor, James II, an overt one. Both may have genuinely believed in religious toleration which was anathema to High Churchmen. James II tried to return the Church to Catholic practice and doctrine but his plans were brought to nought by a combination of Church, gentry and aristocracy against him. Yet some of the clergy, headed by Archbishop Sancroft of Canterbury, would not recognize the legitimacy of his successor William III, a Dutch Calvinist, and subsequently formed a small separatist group of High Churchmen known as the Non-jurors. William III's successor, Queen Anne, was a loyal churchwoman, remembered by Queen Anne's Bounty which released Church properties formerly in the possession of the crown to strengthen the Church's finances; but the accession of George I, a German Lutheran in 1714, was unwelcome to many clergy, even if they could not support the Stuart pretender since he was an avowed Roman Catholic.

Nonetheless the alliance between the Church and the crown or, rather, the established order, was to continue throughout the eighteenth century. The bishops appointed by the government in power gave it their ready support. Many of the parochial clergy were disaffected with the Whig government which remained in office until after the accession of George III, but they were strong supporters of law and order, believing that radical ideas, whether in politics or theology could lead to the subversion of Church and State. 'In reference to the poor', the bishop of Bristol said in a sermon, 'I would conclude that they are under strong obligations to submit to their present condition without murmur or complaint.' An increasing number of the clergy were appointed magistrates; in 1761, 1,038 clergymen were nominated justices of the peace, in 1836 there were 3,266. The Church of England still appeared as the guardian of established society, though not necessarily to the disadvantage of its pastoral function.

The bishops nominated by the Whig governments in the first half of the eighteenth century were expected to support the policies of the government which had appointed them, but they were neither mediocrities nor political yes-men. Drawn from a wider social range than the aristocratic Catholic bishops of France they were for the most part well-read men, who performed their duties conscientiously, riding round their extensive dioceses to perform the rite of confirmation, and giving their warm support to the many philanthropic societies which came into existence. Yet their heavily bewigged features – the Roman Catholic Church deplored the wearing of wigs by the clergy on the grounds that the priest had to celebrate the Mass bare-headed – and the comfortable state in which they lived underlined their alignment with the country's governing classes.

The parish clergy were so varied in character that generalizations are impossible. That they were in general separated from the higher clergy by a social as well as a financial gap can hardly be doubted. While the bishops were Whig in sympathy, the clergy tended to be Tories. The country curate continued to live on a pittance, often having to eke out his meagre stipend by taking outside employment, but there was to be a gradual and marked improvement in the material position of the parochial clergy, their incomes augmented especially in the later part of the century by the rising value of tithes, improvements in agriculture and latterly by the boom created by the Napoleonic Wars. There was also an improvement in their social standing.

The ways in which they fulfilled their pastoral function were for the most part formal and traditional: prayer book services in the parish church, marked by lengthy sermons and without much choral singing, except in great churches and where there was a small group of amateur instrumentalists who accompanied the psalms. The interest and enthusiasm which greeted the Methodist revival with its hymn singing, extempore prayers and stirring sermons, often taking place outside the church, was understandable.

If the apparent conservatism of eighteenth-century churchmanship may help to explain the growing support for the Methodist revival the Church of England still played a significant, possibly an undervalued, part in the nation's life. It continued by and large to be a 'broad Church', more united than divided (though party fractures were beginning to appear), located midway between 'lukewarmness' and 'enthusiasm'. Its abuses, most notably pluralism and consequent neglect of duty, were widely canvassed, especially by later historians; but the standard of performance by the clergy, higher and lower, was more impressive than detractors then and later made out, and a gradualistic basis for the broader administrative reforms of the next century was being laid, as for instance may be demonstrated by the renewed activities of the rural dean and the work of educational and missionary societies, such as the Society for Promoting Christian Knowledge and the Church Missionary Society. Far from being the idle and uncaring product of an increasingly secularized society many parish priests responded to the religious needs of the age and were conscientious in the performance of their religious obligations, engaged in the work of catechizing, in the promotion of charity schools and stimulating devotion through the religious societies, founded in many towns in the late seventeenth and early eighteenth centuries, and at a later date in the societies for the reformation of manners. If newly built areas in recently industrialized parts of the country remained largely unchurched, many new churches were constructed; ecclesiastical art and church music were encouraged, nor was the cause of Church reform ever entirely lost sight of. The Church of the Elizabethan settlement was still operative, if undergoing contraction as a voluntarist religious society came into being. To some it may well have appeared that in the eighteenth century the English Church was marking time rather than making progress, and that this was equally true of the contemporary dissenting Churches.

REPRESSION AND TOLERATION

Both the Catholic and Protestant Churches were not merely privileged but active and influential, concerned to maintain their status by invoking the power of the secular arm to protect their privileged position. In the Roman Church scientific theories thought to be prejudicial to the Christian view of the universe remained banned. Copernicus's works had been placed on the Index; Galileo, threatened with prison for stating that the earth moved round the sun, had been obliged to recant in 1633. Their works were made available in 1757, but it was not until 1822 that they could be freely read, nor until 1992 that Galileo was finally rehabilitated. After an investigation into Galileo's condemnation by the Holy Office which lasted eleven years, its head, Cardinal Poupard, pronounced in 1992 that 'all the participants in the trial, without exception, have the right to be seen as acting in good faith'. With greater generosity Pope John Paul II commented on the 'tragic mutual incomprehension' which had occurred, adding 'It cannot be excluded that we may find ourselves facing a similar situation. Theologians must keep themselves constantly informed on scientific developments to see whether they need to incorporate them, or revise their ideas.'

Rulers still resorted to the threat of expulsion to deal with religious dissenters. In 1685 Louis XIV had revoked the Edict of Nantes which some ninety years earlier had granted coexistence to the French Huguenots. The expulsion was both cruel and ill-advised, for the Huguenots were among the most thrifty and industrious of his subjects who were to enrich the countries, Great Britain, Holland and Brandenburg, where they took refuge. But the intolerance of dissent was never far below the surface as Voltaire's publicizing of the Calas case was to show. The unfortunate Jean Calas was a Huguenot shopkeeper of Toulouse who was accused in 1762 of murdering his son (who almost certainly committed suicide) because the son wanted to become a Catholic, and was thus condemned by the Catholic magistrates to be broken on the wheel. His execution, the injustice of which was soon everywhere admitted, represented the survival of deep religious prejudice.

In 1731 Archbishop Firmian of Salzburg issued a savage decree expelling the Protestants from his diocese, some twenty to thirty thousand in number, of whom several went as refugees to people Pennsylvania. The later Austrian emperor, Joseph II, was a champion of toleration, but the edict which he put into force in 1781 offered only limited freedom to Lutherans, Calvinists and the Greek Orthodox. It excluded atheists and deists and pronounced that a Roman Catholic who was contemplating conversion to Protestantism must spend six weeks being instructed in the Roman faith.

The Spanish Inquisition, which had always been more an instrument of the Spanish crown than of the Church, was a declining force, louder in its bark than cutting in its bite, but its grim panoply of power could still be used to curb and even to burn relapsed heretics, sceptics, bigamists and sorcerers.

The Protestant countries were less harsh in their treatment of those who dissented from the established faith but they were reluctant to relax the penal laws, fearful that too much freedom might encourage subversion and prove morally dangerous since churchmen continued to believe that scepticism and infidelity were a pathway to immorality. 'We need', as Dean Swift put it, 'religion as we need our dinner, wickedness makes Christianity indispensable and there's an end to it.' The English Act of Toleration of 1689, designed to unite all Protestants and which excluded Roman Catholics, Unitarians and unbelievers, granted limited toleration to all dissenters, though they were to continue to be barred from public office until 1828.

In Catholic countries the Jews were still victims of religious and racial intolerance. They were forbidden to live in Spain and Portugal, victimized in Poland and the Ukraine, and in Rome they were obliged to live in a ghetto by the Tiber behind high walls. They had to rent their houses from Christians and to wear a distinguishing badge. It was hardly surprising that they were to be among the first to offer a warm welcome to the French soldiers when they occupied Rome and set up a Roman republic during the Napoleonic Wars.

Yet the values of the religious establishment in respect of toleration were neither static nor unchallenged. There was a growing belief in its virtue, even among religious people. While men did not cease to believe in witchcraft, they were gradually ceasing to burn witches, not because they thought that sorcery did not happen but because of a growing conviction that the nature of the evidence, which had often been extracted by torture, was unreliable. The last condemned English witch, Jane Wenham, died in 1712, that in Scotland in 1721, in Germany in 1775, in Spain under the auspices of the Inquisition in 1781, in Switzerland (at Glarus under a Protestant judge) in 1782 and in Poland in 1793.

To an increasing number of people toleration seemed politically and economically advantageous as well as spiritually acceptable. The Calvinist elector of Brandenburg readily cooperated with his Lutheran subjects and welcomed religious refugees. The Low Countries were probably the most tolerant European country, but nowhere was toleration so specifically laid down as in the American state of Pennsylvania the charter of which declared that no one was 'at any time to be compelled to frequent or maintain any religious worship, place or ministry whatever, contrary to his or her mind'. If toleration seemed for the most part a child of economic interest combined with political prudence, there was a growing conviction among Christians that the Church ought to be a society of voluntary believers who were as individuals entitled to find their own way to God rather than a closed corporation legally binding on its members and exclusive in its privileged position.

The growth in the practice of toleration and the acceptance of it as a concept was itself an indication that the mould into which the Protestant and Catholic Reformations had cast the Churches was being slowly modified, if not fractured. Both Reformations had stood for a defined, definite and prescriptive doctrine, a precise discipline and moral austerity, all of which were backed by law and even by force of arms. While from time to time the Popes were to reaffirm the teachings of the Council of Trent, and the Protestant Churches stood by the authority of scripture and the doctrine of justification by faith, the fortifications were being slowly dismantled. Even within the Church of Rome there was some questioning of papal authority, criticism of monastic orders, a demand for a vernacular liturgy and doubts about clerical celibacy. Such murmurings were to be easily silenced, but that they existed at all suggested some subtle change was taking place in the religious climate. There were modifications in the Reformation setting of Protestantism. The German pietists were criticized for modifying Luther's teaching. Calvinism, though not dormant, was no longer dominant. English eighteenth-century theology lacked the religious urgency of the sixteenth-century reformers. Before the century ended critical analysis was beginning to erode the authority of scripture. While it is always difficult to make judgements about a fall in moral standards, there is some evidence to suggest that the more austere moral principles, especially those relating to sexual behaviour, were being adhered to less and less. The establishment of foundling hospitals and the increase in illegitimacy rates in some west European countries might suggest a slow elision of moral standards.

JANSENISM

Theologically the rise of Jansenism which was to divide the French Church in the seventeenth century was in many respects an indication of some erosion of Counter-Reformation churchmanship, even though *prima facie* its objectives were not dissimilar. Neither a homogeneous nor a monolithic movement, it affected many aspects of French religious and political life and spread outside France. It had originated in a theological dispute brought about by the failure of the Council of Trent to tie together in an acceptable fashion the difficult doctrines of free will and grace, so long a matter of theological dispute. How far, theologians asked, was it possible to believe that men and women could be fully free to attain their moral objectives without devaluing grace?

Jansenism took its name from a book *Augustinus* by Cornelius Jansen, the bishop of Ypres, who had spent ten years of his life writing a large volume of 1,300 double pages which was published two years after his death in 1640. Jansen stressed, as the Protestant reformers also taught, that good works without faith must be unavailing, and that efficacious grace freely given by God from his gracious mercy is the only key to salvation. The Sorbonne declared the work to be heretical and subsequently it was condemned in 1653 at Rome by the bull *Cum Occasione*. Such views were suspect as a compromise with Protestant thinking.

What might have seemed essentially a recondite theological problem was to spread to the wider world, in part through Jansen's disciples, the chief of whom was his friend and collaborator Du Vergier, Abbot of St Cyran. Du Vergier, who was viewed with such suspicion by Cardinal Richelieu that he spent five years in the prison of Vincennes, regarded the resurgence of Augustinianism as a means of meeting the Protestants on their own ground and as a basis for improving the moral standards of clerical life. His friend, Antoine Arnauld, managed to win the support of some of the French bishops, and acquired strong backing from the Cistercian nuns of the two convents of Port-Royal in Paris. His sister, Angélique who was the abbess, persuaded by a visiting Capuchin father, imposed a stern spiritual discipline on her nuns.

Jansenism, suspected by its critics of being proto-Protestant, was an unconscious expression of a reaction against much that had been achieved theologically and politically by the Counter-Reformation. It called for a different theological approach and a more rigoristic spiritual discipline, exemplified by Antoine Arnauld's book *De la frequente Communion* in which, among much else, he argued that long days of penance were a requisite before communion.

The Jansenists did not confine their attention to spiritual and theological matters. They were instinctively distrustful of the Jesuits, Bishop Jansen himself having queried the canonization of Ignatius Loyola and Francis Xavier. They wished to promote the authority and independence of the bishops against the Pope, whose authoritarianism they questioned, and the French king. Looking back to what they held to be the conditions of the primitive Church, they put forward an exalted view of the role of the parish priests as the true successors, as Edmund Richer put it, of the seventy disciples of Jesus. While the Roman Church, as the papal bull *Unigenitus* stated in 1713, condemned the proposition that the 'reading of the Holy Scripture is for all', the Great Bible in French which had appeared in 1696 had been largely the work of the Jansenist Sacy. In carrying their assault from the realm of theology to that of authority, the Jansenists provoked disapproval and condemnation at Rome and eventually aroused the wrath of the French king, Louis XIV, himself.

The Jansenists fell foul of authority in the State as well as in the Church. The nunneries of Port-Royal became the target of the Jansenists' foes. Two hundred bowmen enforced the dispersal of the disaffected nuns from one Paris convent, but the other, Port-Royal des Champs, which Mme de Sévigné described after a visit there in 1674 as 'a paradise: a desert to which the devout of Christendom have retired: a holiness effused over the surrounding countryside', continued to be the movement's headquarters until it was destroyed by royal order between 1710 and 1713.

Royal action against the Jansenists had been delayed by a quarrel that had developed between Louis XIV and the Pope, which underlined the extent to which politically the king was the master of the French Church. The king, who was by law allowed to administer the revenues of a bishopric when it was vacant (what was called the *règale temporelle*) decided to extend his powers in this respect; but the two bishops involved appealed to the Pope. The king angrily made a show of force by requiring the French clergy to reaffirm the king's powers in the so-called Gallican Articles of 1682, of which the most important stated that the king was virtually independent in temporal matters which concerned the Church, and that in any case a general council was of superior authority to a Pope. As a result Pope Innocent XI refused to invest the new bishops whom the king had nominated, so that by 1689 there were some thirty-five French dioceses without bishops.

This tiff, which underlined the increasing limitations of papal power and the growing oversight over the Church exercised even by Catholic princes, was brought to an end by the king's own unprepossessing religious devotion which led him to revoke the Edict of Nantes and expel his Huguenot subjects. He had become convinced that Jansenism was itself a potentially subversive force. In 1713, two years before Louis died, Pope Clement XI issued the bull *Unigenitus* (it was given the force of law in France in 1730), condemning some 101 propositions supposedly made in his study of the New Testament, *Moral Reflexions* by the Jansenist Quesnel, incorporating, so it was alleged, the Augustinian doctrine of grace.

Although Jansenism had been severely mauled, it left trailers behind it. Less concerned with the niceties of theology, its sympathizers, strong in the French Parlements, saw in it a tool to criticize the absolute rule of both Pope and king. Nor was its influence confined to France. The reforming synod of the Church which was called by the Grand Duke of Tuscany in 1786 at Pistoia was powerfully imbued with Jansenist ideas. Jansenist influence in the Low Countries had an even more disturbing effect. In 1700 the canonist Bernard van Espen had published a book *Jus Ecclesiasticum universum* in which he had queried papal absolutism, giving the Pope purely a primacy of honour. In 1723 the Dutch Jansenists, who had refused to accept the bull *Unigenitus* separated from Rome, electing an archbishop of

Utrecht, who was consecrated by a missionary bishop who had left France because of his Jansenist sympathies, so creating a small schismatic Church, the so-called Old Catholic Church.

THE DISSOLUTION OF THE JESUITS

Jansenism eroded rather than directly attacked the spirit of the Catholic Reformation. A much more direct assault resulted in the dissolution of the Society of Jesus which had provided the Catholic Reformation with its storm troopers. The attack on the Jesuits reflected the comparative weakness of the eighteenth-century papacy. For the most part with the exception of Benedict XIV, the eighteenth-century Popes were amiable nonentities. Benedict XIII, a pious and ascetic Dominican, seemed a throwback to an earlier age who would have readily imposed the more austere measures of the Council of Trent. Benedict XIV, a learned canonist, was readier to accommodate Tridentine policy to contemporary conditions, for he made concessions to national states, acknowledging the growth of secular influence in Church matters; and his successors were in many respects even more subservient to the self-interested, secular policies of Catholic princes. The Catholic powers, Austria, Spain, France, Portugal, Bavaria and Poland, exerted considerable, even decisive, influence at papal elections.

There was some criticism of papal absolutism. In 1763 Nikolaus von Hontheim (writing under the pseudonym Febronius) published a book *De Statu Ecclesiae* (*On the State of the Church*) which was critical of papal authority. Von Hontheim, who had been a pupil of the Jansenist Van Espen, became professor of Roman law at the university of Trier and in 1748 suffragan bishop. His object in writing the book was to help in the process of the reunification of Christendom by removing some of the obstacles which had caused division. He argued that many of the claims which Popes had made in the past were not supported by history and that the Pope enjoyed only a primacy among bishops; in practice his authority was actually less than that of a general council of the Church. The Vatican reacted unfavourably to this resurfacing of conciliarism, placing the book on the Index and obliging von Hontheim, who at first denied that he was really the author, to recant. 'I have recanted like Fénelon', he said in 1780, 'to avoid quarrelling and unpleasantness. But my recantation hurts neither the world nor the Christian religion, and will never profit the Curia of Rome. The world had read, examined, accepted my book. My recantation will move intelligent men as little as the various refutations by monks or papal flatterers.' Von Hontheim was right in thinking that his book was widely read. Of twenty-six German bishops, sixteen refused to publish the edict of condemnation.

The demand for the dissolution of the Jesuits underlined the dilemma

lbi Cathedral, begun 1282, a symbolic fortress of the faith against the Albigensian (Cathar)
retics. (Mansell Collection)

Heaven and Hell, depicted in a thirteenth-century mosaic on the ceiling of the Baptistry at Florence. (Alinari/Mansell Collection)

Erasmus, c. 1466–1536, Dutch scholar, theologian and man of letters. After a painting by Holbein (Earl of Radnor Collection). (Hulton Getty)

Martin Luther, 1483–1546, German reformer. Luther's actions during the sixteenth century heralded the beginning of the Protestant Reformation. Portrait by Lucas Cranach the elder, 1520. (Hulton Getty)

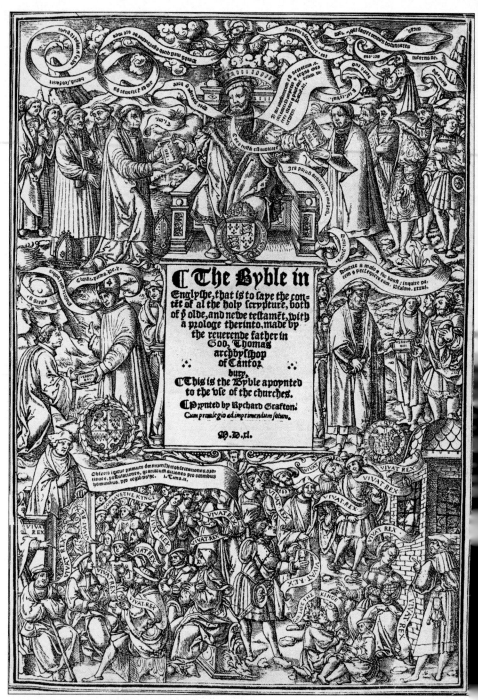

Holbein's title-page from the Great Bible (1539), showing Henry VIII giving the first English Bible to Archbishop Cranmer and Thomas Cromwell, dispensing it to the clergy (on the right) and the laity (on the left). The nobility respond with the words 'Vivat Rex' and the common people with 'God save the King'. (Mansell Collection)

The burning of Bishops Latimer and Ridley outside Balliol College, Oxford, 1555. From John Foxe's Book of Martyrs, published in 1563. (Bodleian Library: SA Oxon. a. 73, p. 1, No. 1)

The Canadian Martyrs, Fathers de Brébeuf and Lallemant, c. 1649. Pioneer Jesuit missionaries working in the French province of Quebec, de Brébeuf and Lallemant were captured and killed by the Iroquois Indians. From a painting by Huret. (National Archives of Canada/C-001470)

P. MATTHÆVS RICCIVS MACERAT. of the Society of Iesus, the first propagator of the Christian Religion in the Kingdo of China.

LY PAVLVS GREAT COLAVS OF the Chinese propagator of y Christian Law.

Jesuit Matteo Ricci and Ly Paulus in local Chinese costume. Ricci worked in China for seventeen years during the late sixteenth and early seventeenth centuries. He was permitted to stay in Kwantung on condition that he wore traditional costume and did not try to leave the town. (Mansell Collection)

Hogarth's caricature (1762) entitled 'Credulity, Superstition and Fanaticism' points to the cruelties and abuses which have gained credence as religion. (Trustees of the British Museum: Brit. Mus. 1868 8.22.1624)

John Wesley, 1703–91. Wesley's preaching career spanned fifty years, his words reaching thousands of people. Portrait by Nathaniel Hone, 1766. (National Portrait Gallery)

which confronted the Pope. The Jesuits' missionary enthusiasm, their skill as educators, as confessors and conductors of parish missions, and their unqualified loyalty to the Pope had made them the recognized spearhead of the Catholic revival. From the start they had their critics and enemies, most notably among other religious orders, the Franciscans and Dominicans, who attacked them for propagating moral casuistry. By the eighteenth century there were other charges for it was said, not wholly unjustly, that they had lost their distinction as educators, for their curriculum was thought to have become too classical and old-fashioned. Papal decrees, in part the result of their being traduced by their enemies, had damaged irretrievably their mission in China.

Their fall was, however, brought about as much by political as by religious factors. In Paraguay they had created a republic in the reservations or *Reductiones* where the Guarani Indians lived in safety from the settlers and in apparent harmony among themselves, but the settlers resented the comparative independence which the *Reductiones* enjoyed, and the local bishops criticized the Jesuits' immunity from episcopal control. Rumour suggested that the Jesuits had both amassed treasure and were sponsoring a semi-communalistic society. In 1750 Spain and Portugal negotiated a treaty which involved changes in the frontier affecting Paraguay, as a result of which seven of the thirty *Reductiones* would pass to Portugal. The Indians would be obliged to migrate. Their general ordered the Jesuits to comply, but the missionary priests, by 68 votes to 2, stood firm, with the sequel that when the Indians refused to budge, bloodshed ensued, for which Spain and Portugal held the Jesuits to be responsible.

By taking up the sword they had in fact played into the hands of their enemies, for Portugal was governed by a dictator, Pombal, a strong anti-clerical who had already advocated the destruction of the order 'either by rigorous reform or abolition'. Accused of fomenting revolution and illicit trading, the Jesuits were expelled from Portugal and their property was confiscated. Since they were charged with crimes against the State rather than offences against religion the Pope appeared impotent to save them.

These events coincided with a scandal detrimental to their reputation in France. A Jesuit father, Lavalette, had reorganized Jesuit property in the West Indies, in Martinique and Dominica, engaging in trade and borrowing more and more money to tide over a growing debt. It was therefore a cruel trick of fate that the two ships which he had despatched home laden with sugar and coffee should have been intercepted and seized by the British, leaving Father Lavalette with a debt of more than 3 million livres. While the French Jesuits argued that the responsibility for repayment of the debts rested with the West Indian mission, the Parlement of Paris, more sympathetic to Jansenism than to Jesuitry, declared that the French society was itself responsible for the debt, now amounting to 5 million livres, and in 1762 ordered the sequestration of all Jesuit property in France. Members of the order were to be expelled unless they took an oath of loyalty to the French king and agreed to abide by the anti-papal Gallican Articles of 1682.

Spain, Naples and Sicily followed the examples of the governments of France and Portugal. In 1767 the Jesuits were expelled and their passports were confiscated. The refugees, both from metropolitan Spain and its American colonies, suffered great hardship, more especially as for some time the Pope refused to give them sanctuary in the Papal States.

These events placed the Pope in a terrible dilemma. The elderly Clement XIII depended upon his secretary of state, Cardinal Torrigiani, who was a warm supporter of the Jesuits, and in the belief that the Church was under threat issued the bull *Apostolicae Pascendi* (1765) in support of the Jesuits. Similarly he responded to other anti-clerical legislation in the Italian state of Parma by declaring the laws null and void in the brief *Monitorium*. The Catholic princes, scenting a reappearance of political papalism, reacted vigorously. French troops occupied Avignon and Venaissin, Naples, the papal enclaves of Benevento and Pontecorvo. 'The Grand Lama of the Vatican', Frederick the Great of Prussia commented, 'is like a tight-rope walker who has grown old and in the sickness of old age wants to repeat the triumphs of his youth, and so falls and breaks his neck!'

When in fact the 'Grand Lama' did die, on 2 February 1769, the cardinals elected a Franciscan friar, Ganganelli, as his successor. Clement XIV, by nature an indecisive and tired man, tried delaying tactics, but the pressure from the Catholic powers became too great for him to resist. They threatened to close down monasteries, to abolish papal nuncios, to strip Rome of its privileges and even to invade by force the States of the Church. 'Toothache', as the Spanish ambassador reminded him, 'can only be cured by extraction.' With a sad heart the Pope issued the bull *Dominus ac Redemptor*, suppressing the order, on 21 July 1773.

The Jesuits were dispersed but continued for a time to survive as an entity in Prussia and Russia and elsewhere. For a time they actually continued to do the same jobs they had been doing previously, even, as in Catholic Switzerland, living in community, subject now to the authority of the local Catholic bishop. Others became secular priests. Their comparatively few remaining members, for recruitment was a real problem, lived on in a twilight existence until the Pope reconstituted them as a religious order in 1814.

CHURCH AND STATE

The decline and fall of the Jesuits reflected the growing secularity of the age. Secular power had always been a determinant in Church affairs, and theoretically as the Gelasian letter of 496 had intimated there was a real dichotomy between the authority exercised by the lay and clerical estates.

Since the Reformation the English king or queen had been supreme sovereign of the Church. By the *cujos regio ejus religio* clause of the treaty of Augsburg in 1555, the religion of the German princes in principle determined the faith of the state. In Catholic Spain, France and Portugal the crown exerted extensive control over episcopal appointments. In the Russian Orthodox Church the fiat of the tsar was a decisive factor in the Church. The interference of the secular power in Church affairs was justified on the grounds that the lay power as much as the ecclesiastical held its authority from God and was acting in accordance with God's will, and ideally there should be no conflict.

In the eighteenth century a new ingredient, the ancestry of which could be traced to an earlier debate, was inserted into the situation, the influence which was exercised on members of the ruling establishment by the intellectuals, the Philosophes, an influence by and large hostile to clerical authority. Catholic sovereigns, as their treatment of the Jesuits was to demonstrate, were ready to ride rough shod over the rights of the Church and even to reorganize it without previous consultation with its head or members. What happened in Austria showed how a Catholic country presided over by a Catholic monarch could act independently in ecclesiastical matters.

The Austrian empress Maria Theresa, who was a devout Catholic, had been much influenced by her doctor Gerard von Swieten and her confessor, both of whom favoured Jansenist ideas. Pious as she was, she agreed to limit the privileges which the Catholic clergy enjoyed in her dominions, ending the clergy's exemption from taxation, abolishing the right of sanctuary, doing away with some saints' days and introducing monastic reforms. These changes were taken much further by her son, the emperor Joseph II, who restructured the Church, forming new dioceses and reorganizing the parochial system and financing these changes by the confiscation of monastic property, all without seeking prior permission from the Pope. Monasteries which were purely contemplative were abolished. Some four hundred houses were closed and the monastic population was reduced from 65,000 to 27,000. Apart from using the proceeds to help the parishes, the emperor also founded four hospitals and a school of surgery in Vienna.

The influence of the 'enlightenment' over the emperor showed itself most obviously in his desire to diminish the superstitious elements in religious observance. He forbade his subjects to kiss relics or kneel in the streets when the Host passed by. Friars were forbidden to take novices or to beg; hermits were banned. Some of these changes were so unpopular with the people, devoted as they were to past custom, that they remained null and void.

'Josephism' caused consternation in Rome, which had come to expect sympathetic support at least in religious matters at the court of the Hapsburg emperor. Eventually the Pope, Pius VI, decided to take the bull by the horns and to the embarrassment of the emperor announced that he would visit Vienna in 1782. He was the first Pope to leave the Papal States for three centuries, but his journey did not cause the emperor to abandon his policy.

The emperor's example was followed to a greater or lesser extent by the rulers of Naples, Parma (whose duke had in 1768 aroused papal wrath by issuing edicts significantly limiting papal power in his state), Piedmont and Tuscany where Joseph's younger brother and eventual successor as emperor, Leopold, was grand duke. The grand duke introduced a series of reforms aimed to reduce the power of the religious orders, to reform parish life, to eliminate superstitious practices and to encourage congregational participation in the liturgy, so reflecting the strong influence at his court of Jansenist ideas and of Bishop Ricci of Pistoia in particular. A majority of the bishop's diocesan clergy, meeting at Pistoia in September 1786, accepted these reforms, but they proved so unpopular with the people, who reacted violently to the disappearance of cherished traditions, that the grand duke had reluctantly to modify his religious programme.

THE ORTHODOX CHURCH IN RUSSIA

What was happening in the Russian Orthodox Church was not wholly out of line with the developments which had taken place in the west. In matters of religious practice the Orthodox Church had led an insulated existence. After Constantinople fell to the Turks in 1453 the Orthodox leadership had passed from Constantinople to Moscow, for the tsar, as the monk Philotheus of Pskov told Tsar Vasili III in 1510, 'is on earth the sole Emperor of the Christians, the leader of the Apostolic Church which stands no longer in Rome or in Constantinople, but in the blessed city of Moscow. Two Romes have fallen, but the third stands and a fourth there will not be.' The Turks as Muslims tolerated the Greek Christians in their territory but placed them, including the patriarch of Constantinople, under severe restrictions, obliging them to pay burdensome taxes and banning all religious processions. Cut off from a self-generating theological and spiritual resources, the Greek Orthodox Church, though it survived, stagnated. It was to Moscow rather than Constantinople, which became a patriarchate in 1589, that the Orthodox Church had to look for leadership. Such leadership was to be intermittent, frustrated both by the Church's unyielding loyalty to traditional thought and liturgy, and by the extent to which the Church, following Byzantine custom, became not merely co-equal but subordinate to the lay power, redeemed only by a deep continuing reservoir of spirituality and mystical theology.

In the first half of the seventeenth century the Russian Church had even experienced a measure of spiritual revival, leading to an improvement in the quality of the parochial clergy, insisting on the observance of fasts, regular preaching and abstention from drunkenness, so placing an emphasis on the life of self-discipline. Such rigorous devotion was well demonstrated in the autobiography of the archpriest Avvakum whose day ended with a recital of 600 prayers to Jesus and 100 to the Blessed Virgin, accompanied by 300 prostrations.

This resurgence of religious practice, which had the support of the Romanov tsars, was jeopardized by the injudicious and arbitrary policy of Nikon, appointed patriarch in 1652–3. The new patriarch provoked strong opposition by insisting that Russian religion ought to conform to the standards of the four ancient patriarchates (Constantinople, Alexandria, Jerusalem and Antioch), and with that in mind ordered that the Russian service book should be amended to conform to the standard of the Greek Church. Such changes were outwardly trivial, replacing, for instance, the sign of the cross by two fingers as had hitherto been traditional in Russia by three fingers as with the Greeks; but Nikon struck deep at the heart of Russian tradition. His critics argued that the changes he was trying to make were indefensible since the custom and practice of the Russian Church as an autocephalous patriarchate (though fifth in rank after the other four patriarchates) should be the norm rather than that of Constantinople. Fundamentally the dispute was a clash between the intrinsic conservative forces in the Russian Church and the innovatory policy of patriarch Nikon, a quarrel in part obscured by the patriarch's own intransigent nature. In the subsequent schism, a separate sect came into existence known as the Old Believers (perhaps more accurately the Old Ritualists), the *Raskolniki*; their leaders were imprisoned, tortured and executed – Avvakum spent ten years in exile, twenty-two years in detention and was eventually in 1682 burned at the stake. In spite of persecution the Old Believers survived, though they were to fragment into two groups of dissenters.

Not content with reforming the liturgy, Nikon cherished political ambitions. He aimed to be a Pope. Moscow had, however, inherited the Byzantine tradition by which tsar and patriarch, *imperium* and *sacerdotium*, were co-equal. Nikon challenged this assumption, not merely claiming supreme power in religious matters but the right to participate in affairs of state. The result was in a sense a foregone conclusion. Nikon went into voluntary retirement and was eventually deposed and exiled. A Church council which met at Moscow in 1666–7 accepted his reforms, but disavowed the patriarch.

This internal conflict which split the Russian Church paved the way half a century later for the more complete subordination of the Church to the State. When the patriarch Adrian died in 1700, Tsar Peter the Great left the position vacant; and in 1721 by the *Spiritual Regulation* he abolished the patriarchate, replacing it by the Spiritual College or Holy Synod. The synod, consisting of three bishops and nine other clergy, was not even based on the canon law of the Orthodox Church but on Protestant Church constitutions in Germany. The tsar, as 'Supreme Judge of the Spiritual College', in general represented by a layman as Chief Procurator, was henceforth dominant in the Church which had become virtually a department of the state. Peter and his successors were concerned to diminish the influence previously exerted by monasteries in the state, new monasteries could only be set up by special permission. The tsarina Elizabeth confiscated monastic property; her successor Catherine II, a patron of the Philosophes and a friend to the Jesuits, dissolved many monastic houses and limited the number of monks in the remainder.

In spite of its drastic subordination to the state, which did much to condition its history for the next two centuries, the Russian Church found its essential genius in the cultivation of spirituality through personal holiness, such as was, for instance, to permeate the life of Tikhon of Zadovesk (1724–83), Bishop of Voronezh, whose deep mystical experience blossomed in works of charity.

THE PHILOSOPHES

In the long term the pervasive influence of secular thought was to provide a greater challenge to the Christian Church than the advancing impact of secular power. Philosophical scepticism can be traced back to the Renaissance but in the seventeenth century it was in part a reaction to the harsh Calvinist theology. Its exponents were not necessarily unbelievers, though criticism could elide into atheism, but they were powerful critics both of revelation and of the Church.

In England in the mid-seventeenth century a group known as the Cambridge Platonists stressed that there was in fact no incompatibility as between reason and revelation, but that reason was, as Benjamin Whichcote put it, 'the divine governor of man's life'. A similar point was hammered home by another group, the Latitudinarians. Slowly the movement of thought became more inimical to revelation. 'Revelation', as John Locke asserted, 'cannot be admitted against the clear evidence of reason.' Locke, like the Cambridge Platonists and the Latitudinarians, did not doubt the existence of God, but he was holding a door open for those who denied the truths of revealed religion. 'Reason', he wrote in his *Essay Concerning Human Understanding*, 'is natural *revelation*, whereby the eternal Father of Light, and fountain of all knowledge, communicates to mankind that portion of truth which he has laid within the reach of their natural faculties. *Revelation* is natural *reason* enlarged by a new set of discoveries communicated by God immediately, which reason resides the truth of, by the testimony and proofs it gives that they come from God.' Cautiously the way had been opened for the possibility of questioning those areas of Christian doctrine which seemed to be irrational.

There was thus posited the concept of a natural as opposed to a revealed religion. Natural religion accepted the existence of God and retained what in Christianity seemed to be natural rather than irrational. A small group of English writers, John Toland in *Christianity Not Mysterious*, Matthew Tindal in *Christianity as Old as Creation* and Anthony Collins in his *Discourse of Freethinking*, known collectively as the Deists, argued that the Church had invented many of its doctrines to protect the vested interests of the priesthood. 'It is come, I know not how,' stated Bishop Butler, the author of the *Analogy of Religion* and one of the most distinguished apologists for Christianity, 'to be taken for granted by many persons, that Christianity is now at length discovered to be fictitious.' The Deists questioned many of the Church's basic beliefs, suggesting that they were accretions welded on to the truths of natural religion. They denounced the miraculous properties of Christianity, including the belief in the Incarnation, as superstitious inventions, ridiculed the notion of hell and held that the light of nature and human reason were a sufficient guide to human happiness. For the contemplative monastic existence and the life of abnegation they had only contempt.

While the Deists exerted only a minor influence in English intellectual life, there was a continental movement of similar views and greater influence. While for the most part its advocates retained a belief in God and immortality – though some were atheistic – they queried acceptance of the supernatural and miraculous. They argued that Christian dogma and the teaching of the Christian Church were basically obscurantist, tending to deprive men of their rational faculties which, if properly used, could lead to human happiness and even to the perfectibility of human society. Rejecting the doctrine of original sin, they had a basically optimistic view of human nature.

Such thinkers, constituting collectively what is often called the Enlightenment or *Aüfklarung*, were influential in German intellectual and literary circles. Hermann Reimarus, who was professor of Hebrew and Oriental Studies at Hamburg from 1727 to 1768, repudiated the miracles and accused the Biblical writers of frauds, contradictions and fanaticism. Reimarus influenced the playwright and critic Gottfried Lessing who rejected Christianity as a historical religion, interested himself in New Testament criticism and in the *Wolfenbuttel Fragments*, published in 1774–8, gave publicity to Reimarus's attack on historic Christianity.

The French Philosophes were less directly concerned with textual criticism and historic Christianity than with the propagation of a rational humanitarianism, attacking what seemed to them to be the dark recesses of clerical domination. Montesquieu used his satiric powers to good effect, but the leading exponent of radical philosophy who was a strong critic of orthodoxy and the Catholic Church against which he directed his slogan 'Écrasez l'infame' ('crush what is infamous') was Voltaire. He believed, however, like other Deists, in the immortality of the soul, and held that some form of religion was a necessary means of social and political control.

Such views were represented in the anti-Catholic *Encyclopédie*, published in thirty-five volumes between 1751 and 1780. In 1759 the *Encyclopédie*, of which Denis Diderot was editor, was suppressed because of the Church's disapproval but it continued to circulate clandestinely. Jean Jacques Rousseau who was one of the contributors to the *Encyclopédie*, was in religious matters a pilgrim who came ultimately to belief in a simple natural religion, in the existence of God, the immortality of the soul and the pursuit of human happiness through the guidance of conscience. His 'civil religion' which he outlined in the *Social Contract* outlawed all dogmatic intolerance. A man of emotion rather than the intellect, his suppositions were governed by sentiment rather than reason; but his influence in France and abroad was substantial as one of the founding fathers of liberal humanism.

Although the Philosophes' influence did not penetrate deeply below the fashionable and affluent classes, they enjoyed a popular status. Voltaire's body was, for instance, brought back to Paris and interred with pageantry in the Pantheon. Their ideas certainly won the favour of the major rulers of Europe, among them Frederick the Great of Prussia at whose court Voltaire was a guest between 1750 and 1752, and Catherine II of Russia whom Diderot visited in 1773–4. Their ideas were taken up by many in fashionable and aristocratic circles. 'I do not believe', the Princess Palatine commented in 1772, 'that there are a hundred persons in Paris, whether among the churchmen or among people in the world, who have real faith or even who believe in our Lord.'

THE SPRINGS OF RELIGIOUS REVIVAL

Although the majority of people conformed, Christianity was under threat from prevailing intellectual trends. What was needed was a revival of true Christian faith which would inject adrenalin into popular religion and help to counter the growth of secular indifference and infidelity. In Catholic countries this took the traditional form of teaching missions, directed at stirring the listeners' emotions. Leonard of Port Maurice, a Franciscan missioner, for instance, regularly wore a heavy chain round his neck and a crown of thorns on his head as he addressed the people. Leonard, who was to be canonized in 1867 and nominated the patron of popular missions in 1923, was one of the first to make regular use of the Stations of the Cross, the fourteen stations which represent the road to Calvary, as a means of popular devotion. In 1742 Alfonso Liguori, who was preaching missions in the environs of Naples, drawing great congregations to hear him, founded a religious order, the Redemptorists, to undertake such missions in the countryside. The reaction to such missions was often deeply emotional. Women fell to the floor and cried for mercy; men and women scourged themselves for their sins. When the Capuchin Father Diego was holding a mission, people began to queue to get places in the public square at dawn, even though his preaching did not actually start until six in the evening. By comparison the scenes at John Wesley's early meetings seem small beer. The Catholic missions were traditional in their approach and teaching, intended to stir the listener to a renewed faith in the Church.

Protestant evangelistic efforts were concerned to return to pure and apostolic Christianity. Among Protestant Churches the German Lutheran Church had lapsed into a life of religious formalism and seemingly spiritual stagnation. P.J. Spener, influenced by Jean de Labadie, a former Jesuit who had become an evangelical pastor, became convinced of the need to revivify the Lutheran Church and make it an instrument of the Holy Spirit. At Frankfurt where he was minister he arranged devotional meetings, *collegia pietatis*, twice a week in his church, in 1675 publishing the influential *Pia Desideria* in which he put forward recommendations for deepening and renewing the spiritual life of the Church, by more intense reading of the scriptures, by greater participation of the laity in the Church, by emphasizing the practical and charitable exercise of religion, and by a needful reformation of theological studies at the universities. The book closed with the over-optimistic hope that the Jews would be converted to Christianity and that papal Rome would fall. Spener's ideas had an enthusiastic response, spread by the hymns of Paul Gerhardt, among them 'O Sacred Head, sore wounded', but were bitterly attacked by some orthodox Lutherans. They charged him with modifying Luther's doctrine of justification by the stress which he placed on the indwelling Christ who would lead the true believer to the life of holiness. They disapproved also of the way in which Spener's friend, A.H. Francke, whose writings were to be much esteemed by John Wesley, tried to reform the faculty of theology at the university of Leipzig by making the lectures more devotional in character and content. Pietism, however, found a platform at the newly founded university of Halle, and though it was to become somewhat diffuse and mystical in its teaching, the movement did much to breathe new life into the faltering Lutheran Church.

Spener's godson, Count Nikolaus von Zinzendorf, was himself to be the leader of an evangelistic group which had wide influence in central Europe, England and America. Brought up under the influence of A.H. Francke, von Zinzendorf founded a spiritual colony at Heernhut on one of his estates to which had migrated descendants of the Protestant Bohemian Brethren. Zinzendorf, like Spener, criticized contemporary Protestantism as too formal and sought to give it new life by implanting 'the religion of the heart', founded on a close relationship with Christ as the saviour of the world. 'As soon as a truth becomes a system, one does not possess it. Religion is a religion of the heart; I was ready to use erotic symbolism to express the divine love.' Religion had to be felt experience. It was this which was the true answer to scepticism and unbelief.

Hence the characteristic features of the life and religious observances of the Heernhut community which was to be followed by his disciples in England and America. Zinzendorf was criticized by the orthodox Lutherans and was obliged to leave Saxony in 1736. Although he had had no specific intention of founding a distinctive religious society, rather intending to infuse new life into Lutheranism, he had in effect brought a new evangelistic group, the Moravian Church, into existence. In 1737 he received Moravian episcopal orders from the Berlin court preacher, D.E. Jablonski; and his church in Britain, then described as the Unitas Fratrum, was to be recognized by an Act of Parliament in 1749.

Zinzendorf and his followers insisted that their primary aim was not to proselytize their fellow Christians but rather to share their good news with them and to strenghen them in their membership of their own churches. Even when the Moravians settled in Georgia, their objectives were not at first missionary, though they later sought to instruct the negroes there. By the standards of the time their intentions were astonishingly oecumenical.

Although the Moravians did not, as a Moravian conference in 1742 put it, try 'to draw any People to us', their piety and communal life-style attracted attention and support, more particularly from John Wesley who had been much impressed with their behaviour during his voyage out to Georgia and during his stay there. The Moravians' tenets, constant intercession, use of the 'lot' in decision making and their belief in the virtue of stillness, 'the waiting upon God' for grace rather than actually struggling to achieve it, brought a growing following, especially among women; though Wesley was to break with them over their fundamental quietism.

Their communal fellowships were based on the German models of the settlements at Heernhut and Heernhaag, one of which was set up at Fulneck in Yorkshire, with separate houses and uniforms for the 'brothers' and 'sisters', with the choral singing and love feasts fitted into the growing impulses of the evangelical revival. Their worship was threaded by deep emotion; they sought a 'deep response from the blood of the lamb', 'bathing in his wounds', describing Christ as the bridegroom, and Communion as a 'conjugal penetration of our bloody husband', imagery that verged on the erotic, as the splendid paintings by G.V. Heidt in the hall at Heernhaag demonstrate.

The Moravians won the sympathetic regard of Archbishop Potter and the saintly Bishop Wilson of Sodor and Man, both of whom accepted membership of Zinzendorf's Order of the Mustard Seed. With the support of the colonial proprietors in particular, who were eager to attract hard-working settlers to their estates, Parliament in 1749 recognized the Moravians as 'an antient episcopal church'. However, this was still less than what Zinzendorf wanted, since although the Moravian Church was legitimized, it was still a foreign church with a status similar to that which it enjoyed in Saxony, Wurttemberg and Prussia and from 1764 in Russia. Zinzendorf's desire was for his United Church to be accepted as an integral part of the Church of England.

The act was the high water-mark of Moravian influence in England, for subsequently it was to be subject not merely to a series of financial problems but also to bitter criticism both from orthodox churchmen and some Methodists, as indicated in Henry Rimius's *Candid Narrative of the Rise and Progress of the Heernhuters* (1753). It continued, however, to be a minor force in the evangelical revival, to which it had contributed significantly through the Fetter Lane Society with which Wesley had been closely associated. By 1760 it numbered twelve congregations; in 1994 there were thirty-two, located in very similar areas of the country.

While the Moravians did not set out to convert other Christians, they accepted the call to baptize the heathen. In 1732 they settled on St Thomas's island in the West Indies, intending to convert the blacks, the following year despatching a mission to Greenland and shortly afterwards making their historic first settlement in South Africa. They could well have claimed to be the first international Protestant Church.

Both the German Pietists and the Moravian Brethren tended to relegate the intellectual and rational aspects of religious belief to a minor place, putting their trust in faith and experience which were to be the chief features of the major evangelical revival which transformed the religious life of eighteenth-century England and America. Their primary objective was a return to the supposed condition of 'Primitive Christianity', a nickname which some of his youthful friends actually bestowed on John Wesley, hoping to cut through the doctrinal accretions which had served to obscure the revealed faith of the Bible, by reasserting the moral standards of Christian teaching and by breaking through the structural formalism of the Churches. The appeal was primarily to the heart and soul rather than to the mind. Above all it was a rejection of the 'Almost Christian' attitudes which seemed aptly enough to describe the average Christian conformist, and a call for the renewal of spiritual experience, bringing the believer by prayer, worship and fellowship into a closer relationship with God through the saving action of Christ.

The first streams of revival can be traced in Britain to the early decades of the eighteenth century. Here and there men and women gathered together to form religious societies which were designed through prayer and Bible reading to promote holiness of heart and life. Evangelical preachers made their appearance, more especially in the green Welsh valleys, like Griffith Jones of Llandover who held forth in fields and churchyards, bringing the Church into closer contact with the people. Another such Welsh evangelist was Howell Harris who wrote of his conversion on Whit Sunday 1735: 'I felt suddenly my heart melting within me, like wax before fire, with love to God my Saviour and also felt not only love and peace but a longing to be dissolved and to be with Christ.' Such preachers were reacting against the seeming formality of contemporary Anglicanism and its apparent failure to preach a personal religion rooted in faith in the atoning work of Christ.

The evangelical revival in Britain represented the confluence of many streams, but unquestionably the dominant figure was John Wesley. Son of a Lincolnshire parson, instilled with the high churchmanship embraced by both his parents, Samuel and Susanna, but infused with the heritage of a Puritan ancestry which gave a moral rigour to his boyhood at Epworth rectory, as a fellow of Lincoln College, Oxford, he became aware of the spiritual impoverishment of a formal churchmanship. So he sought to revive what he believed to be the traditions of the early Church, keeping its fast days on Wednesdays and Fridays, taking Holy Communion as regularly as possible, and seeking to fertilize personal devotional life by a regime of prayer, the regular reading of the Bible and other devotional books, a process for which he believed early rising, at five or even four in the morning, was a necessary preliminary. His younger brother, Charles, then a student at Christ Church, Oxford (where John had also originally studied), who had been imbued with similar ideas, brought together a small group of like-minded young men, some four or five in number, to foster such pious habits. The group was regarded with some degree of mockery by their fellow students who bestowed on them the pejorative nickname of Methodists or Bible Moths.

John Wesley who had been given leave of absence to help his father at Epworth returned to Oxford to act as college tutor in 1729. His return gave the Holy Club, for such was the name by which these small groups were known, a dynamic boost, for his enthusiasm and charm had a compulsive influence. Groups of the Holy Club began to appear in many colleges led by the Wesleys' friends, usually young graduates. They did not confine themselves to pious exercises but tried to give a practical expression to their beliefs by visiting the Oxford prisons, not merely taking religious services there but helping the prisoners by giving them some of the necessities of life and securing for them legal advice; they set up a school, and extended their charitable activities to the workhouses. Some of the dons regarded such a display of religious enthusiasm with apprehension, more particularly when one of the founder-members of the Holy Club, William Morgan, died after suffering a nervous breakdown which Wesley's critics believed might well have been brought on by his religious austerity.

Although the Holy Club appeared to prosper, beginning to attract a small following among the townspeople of Oxford, in practice it had really made a very small impact on the religious life of the university. John Wesley himself was disappointed and depressed, feeling the effects of a failure of a romantic attachment and disquieted by finding that in spite of his zeal he seemed to lack deep spiritual serenity. After refusing to consider the possibility of succeeding his father, who was near his death bed, as rector of Epworth, he decided that he should go to preach the gospel in the newly founded British colony of Georgia in the belief that there, more especially by working with the native Red Indians (the Creeks, Choctaws and

Chackasaws), he would find a more satisfying opportunity to practise true Christianity and win salvation.

The Georgian venture was a failure. The colonists, rough and unsophisticated, had little time for what seemed to them the finicking posturing and High Church discipline of the Wesley brothers. They failed too to make any real contacts with the Indians about whom they became in any case quickly disillusioned. John again fell in love but, as happened regularly through his life – and his eventual marriage to Mary Vazeille in 1751 was to be an unremitting disaster – it led only to unhappiness, trouble and recrimination. Brought before the local magistrate, the young woman's uncle, he fled from Savannah through marsh and forest to take ship at Charleston for England.

If the Georgian experience had not brought him the serenity of spirit he was seeking, it was in one respect central to his future and that of the Church. For it was on the ship out from England that he had first made contact with the Moravian Brethren and he was much affected when one of them, Spangenberg, told Wesley that for all his belief he did not have the witness or assurance of the Spirit. 'I went', he wrote during his voyage back to England, 'to convert the Indians, but, oh, who shall convert me?' On his return he was in constant contact with the Moravian Peter Böhler who had himself experienced 'instantaneous conversion' and repeatedly hammered home to Wesley that he must 'know the Saviour'. It was in a distressed state of mind, 'sorrowful and very heavy, being neither able to read, nor sing nor pray' that he went, reluctantly on 24 May 1738, to a society in Aldersgate Street, 'where one was reading Luther's preface to the Epistle to the Romans'. About a quarter before nine, while he was describing the change which God works in the heart through faith in Christ, 'I felt my heart strangely warmed. I felt I did trust in Christ, Christ alone for salvation; and an assurance was given me that he had taken away my sins, even mine, and saved me from the law of sin and death.'

Whatever spiritual or psychological interpretation we give this event, it was a watershed in Wesley's life, not because he emerged from it a different man but because he was assured in a way that he had not been previously of the basis of his faith. It set the course which he was to follow for the long years of his life, representing in Ronald Knox's words 'the conquest of sin to be an assured fact, instead of being a daily and almost hopeless struggle'. He was not to resign his Oxford fellowship the stipend of which he continued to draw until his unfortunate marriage in 1751. But Oxford had ceased to be the centre of his thought or activities.

He was beginning, albeit cautiously, what was by some to be called rather grandiosely the 'apostolate of England' by preaching the gospel of salvation, at first in churches and then as more and more churchmen began to be worried by the circumscribed tone of his message in churchyards and market places. It was at the invitation of another Oxford graduate and former member of the Holy Club, George Whitefield, who had been preaching in the open air to the largely unchurched miners of Kingswood near Bristol that Wesley himself began to preach in the open air. It was a revolutionary innovation which captured the imagination of an increasing number of people.

So began that life-long extended commitment, an immense missionary enterprise as Wesley moved, first simply on horseback, later by chaise, throughout the length and breadth of the British Isles, travelling, so it is estimated, some 250,000 miles and preaching some forty thousand sermons, sedulously noting down the main events of each day in his Journal, always neat and meticulous in his appearance, genteel and never impassioned but so charismatic as to seem engaged in a love affair with his congregation. 'I everywhere see God's people perishing for lack of knowledge,' he told his former Oxford pupil James Hervey on 20 October 1739, 'I have power (thro God) to save their souls from death. Shall I use it, or shall I let them perish because they are not of my parish?' There were occasions when members of his congregation, especially women, were so affected by his preaching that they became hysterical, cried out and fainted. While he found such a response disconcerting, he eventually accepted such events as a sign of God's work.

Wesley was not everywhere greeted warmly, as not unnaturally some of the clergy were angered by the intrusion of an unlicensed preacher (though Wesley maintained that he had a licence to preach from the university) on their pitch, refused him permission to preach in their church and some even spurred on the local thugs to break up his meetings, ringing the bells, driving a baited bull at the table on which he was standing to preach, throwing stones and at least on one occasion, at Wednesbury in 1743, placing his life in danger.

With the passage of time hostility subsided, and a religious society came into being which had more and more the features of a separate Church. Wesley was to insist to the end of his life that he was a loyal minister of the Church of England. But given the established Church's attitude to Wesley and his associates, the coolness of its bishops, the suspicion with which clergy and laity regarded the growth of Methodism, it became increasingly apparent that it could not be for ever contained within the borders of the Church of England, even if the final break was not to occur until after Wesley's death.

There is a danger in supposing that what was accomplished was in large measure Wesley's own achievement. He was certainly the *primus*, though hardly in his own opinion the *primus inter pares*, for in his treatment of others he was a natural autocrat. But he could not have achieved what he did without active helpers. In the first instance his chief supporters had been other Anglican clergy who were sympathetic to his ideals, among them his brother Charles, some of whom were to become the leaders in the incipient evangelical movement within the Church of England. Even more importantly he drew together a body of lay preachers, often men of inferior education and lower social origin, stonemasons, soldiers, teachers, at first until 1752 unpaid but enthusiasts, who were to carry his teaching, often simplified, far and wide and sustained the societies which he had founded. Although some of the local preachers soon gave up their ministry, they gave the local societies the framework of an organization, arranging for the payment of fees or subscriptions, dividing their followers into bands and classes, beginning to devise their own special services and building their own meeting places, in other words laying the foundations of a Church.

There could be no doubt that a massive religious revolution had occurred, creating a spiritual revival which penetrated to the lower classes of society. By 1767, the first year that the Methodist Conference published figures, the membership stood at 25,911; by the end of the eighteenth century it had risen to 109,000. It had spread to Scotland and Ireland, which Wesley visited several times, and had an expanding following in America where its membership reached 12,914 in 1784 and 57,631 by 1790. Methodism in America owed more to George Whitefield than to Wesley; and Wesley himself parted with Whitefield because of his adherence to Calvinistic theology. Wesley disapproved of the colonial insurgents in the War of American Independence, but the American Methodists found a dedicated leader in Francis Asbury.

It was in part to provide a ministry for the American Church, sadly neglected by the bishops of the Church of England, that in 1784 Wesley took upon himself to ordain three men for the ministry in America, setting one among them, Thomas Coke, as superintendent or bishop, and later others to work in Scotland. In taking this action Wesley may have been driven simply by 'ineluctable necessity', the need to ensure that the American Christians had an effective ministry, but from the point of view of the canon law of the Church of England what he had done was inadmissible, and could only mean ultimately the separation of the Methodists from the Church of England.

The Methodists were widely distributed throughout the country, strongest in the towns, London and Bristol and Newcastle in the north, but with a numerous following in some parts of the countryside, more especially in Wales and Cornwall. They lacked aristocratic patronage, apart from that of Selina Hastings, Countess of Huntingdon, whose evangelical enthusiasm and autocratic nature led to the foundations of a Calvinistic–Methodistical sect which became known as Lady Huntingdon's Connexion. Methodism had little appeal to the fashionable who suspected its teachings harbingered subversion and egalitarianism, but it drew the majority of its membership from the lower middle and working classes, which led the French historian Elie Halévy to claim that by concentrating their attention on the heavenly kingdom and on the performance of good works the working classes were deflected from revolutionary activity. The Methodists tended to be industrious and law-abiding, but in spite of Halévy's strong arguments it is doubtful whether they had any significant part in preventing England from experiencing the political and social upheaval which struck France at the end of the eighteenth century.

Nor is it possible to adumbrate the extent to which economic factors had a part to play in Methodism's rapid growth. In the 1730s and 1740s economic depression and unemployment may have contributed to the appeal of the Methodist preachers in Bristol and the south-west; but their primary objective was religious rather than social. Methodism filled a vacuum which the Church of England had itself in part created by its failure to provide churches in the growing industrial areas of the country and by the staid formalism of its theology and liturgy. Methodism offered a theology of rebirth, of justification, sanctification and perfection, a message of hope both in this life and the life to come. Its services could be lively and even charismatic, enriched by extempore prayer and popular hymns, sung in the first instance while the mass of the communicants partook of the Eucharist. 'Gasps', as the hymn puts it, 'my fainting soul for grace as a thirsty land for showers.' John's brother Charles was a poet and hymnist of genius. The warm fellowship of a Methodist meeting had its secular counterpart in the mutual self-help which provided its members with a social bond. 'It is expected', the Rule for the United Societies which Wesley drew up in 1745 stated, 'of all who continue in these societies that they should give evidence of their desire of salvation.' Methodism had a special appeal to women. A Miss Potter had been an early town member of the Holy Club at Oxford. John Wesley fell in love with Grace Murray, prominent in the activities of the Newcastle society and would indeed have married her if his brother Charles had not intervened to prevent it. Wesley himself voiced his disapproval of women preachers, yet women played a prominent role in the work of evangelization. In 1777 the Methodist Sarah Crosby rode some 960 miles to some 220 meetings, at many of which 'hundreds of precious souls were present'.

Methodist society was a society under godly discipline. Wesley obliged his preachers to follow strict moral injunctions, to abstain from strong drink, gambling, theatre-going and balls, and to practise sobriety in dress and manners. Though not immune to female charm and himself unhappily married, perhaps because of his experience, Wesley stressed to his preachers the need for celibacy. However, on this point he had little influence either over the preachers or the laity. Members who contravened the moral rules might be expelled from the society. The Methodists managed to achieve a measure of social solidarity for they were undoubtedly in many places filling a social as well as a spiritual void. They provided a simple but fervent faith, assured by the witness of the Holy Spirit, and created a fellowship which, in spite of pitfalls, seemed to manifest some of the features of the early Christian *koinonia* or community.

Before John Wesley died the Methodist Church had been launched as one of the world's major Christian denominations. In Britain after Wesley's death the principal authority in the Church became the Methodist Conference, but its relative social and theological conservatism caused splinter groups to come into existence which had a more pronounced working-class appeal; Alexander Kilham, an advocate of complete separation from the Church of England, founded the Methodist New Connexion in 1797; the Independent Methodists started up in the north of England in 1808; in 1810–11 the Primitive Methodists were inaugurated, the fruit of an evangelistic movement led by Hugh Bourne and the American Malcolm Dow who introduced the camp meeting at Mow Cop in Staffordshire; and in 1815 the Bible Christians, originating with a local preacher, William O'Bryan, in north Devon, were founded. In spite of this fragmentation, Methodism was to increase its membership both in Britain and the United States.

Methodism had been only one of the outcomes of the evangelical revival which had also stimulated the Evangelicals within the Church of England. With their special stress on conversion and salvation by faith and a deep moral earnestness they were on the eve of becoming a major influence in the Church of England, more especially in the sponsoring of missionary work and social reform.

RELIGION IN NORTH AMERICA

Religious revival was simultaneously at work in North America. Religion in North America had reflected the pattern of colonial settlement; predominantly Puritan in New England and Anglican in the South; but it became more and more diversified with the arrival of non-British settlers, the Dutch Reformed in New York, the German-speaking Mennonites in Pennsylvania and the Swedish Lutherans in Delaware, each Church carrying with it its characteristic form of ecclesiastical organization.

The Puritan settlement in New Plymouth had been founded by English men and women who had migrated from Scrooby in Nottinghamshire to Holland in search of religious freedom before they embarked in 1620 on the *Mayflower*. Ten years later another Puritan group, the Congregationalists, who had a controlling interest in the New England Company under the lead of their first governor John Winthrop began the colonization of Massachusetts.

The American Puritans, like their forebears in Europe, wanted a purified gospel, a further reformation of the Church and a godly social order. They based their beliefs on the New Testament covenant which God offered to all those who had faith in Christ. The inhabitants of New England had to give a written acceptance, or 'owning' as it was called, of that covenant. English and continental forms of piety were transmuted into something more distinctively American by the changed environmental conditions. The early settlers spoke of New England as like the Israel of old. 'This is the place', as Edward Johnson of Woburn, Massachusetts, wrote in 1654, 'where the Lord will create a new Heaven, and a new Earth in, new Churches and a new Commonwealth together.' 'The Worde of God', as it was said of the colony of New Haven, was 'the onely rule to be attended unto in ordering the affayres of government'. 'We shall', John Winthrop said, 'find the God of Israel is among us . . . that man shall say of succeeding plantations; the Lord make it like that of New England.'

Serious-minded, earnest, imbued with a manifest destiny, the Protestant colonists sought to ensure that the social order was moulded according to the Christian teaching that the churches monopolized. The Puritans were not imposing a theocracy but they were determined to uphold a godly discipline. Even in Anglican Virginia laws were passed against immorality and luxury, and making attendance at Sunday service obligatory. The churches of Massachusetts were unready to tolerate Baptists or Quakers. They had, by and large, a narrow view of their obligations to the native Red Indians, the 'veriest *Ruines of Mankind*' as Cotton Mather described them, 'brutish in all their inclinations' as the Franciscan Louis Hennepin called them. Only occasionally did signs of a visionary mission appear, as in the work of John Eliot of Massachusetts who translated the Bible for the Algonquin Indians. More representative was the comment of Thomas Shepherd who wrote of the defeat of the Pequot Indians in 1637 as 'divine slaughter by the hand of the English'.

The pattern of settlement became increasingly religiously diversified. Roger Williams, expelled from Massachusetts for spreading 'diverse new and dangerous opinions', made Rhode Island an unusual centre of religious toleration. Lord Baltimore's colony of Maryland was Catholic. The most astonishing development was the foundation by the Quaker, William Penn, of the colony of Pennyslvania which he had acquired from Charles II in 1681 in settlement of a large debt owed to his father. Under Penn's beneficent and liberal guidance the colony housed the most tolerant religious regime in the world, for it allowed freedom of religion to all who believed in God and was fair and just in its treatment of the Red Indians.

By the closing years of the seventeenth century there were complaints that with the second and third generations of settlers religion was losing something of its early lustre. A synod in 1679 complained of 'much sabbath-breaking', of 'sinful heats and hatreds' and of 'a great and visible decay of the power of Godliness among many Professors in the churches'.

The unbalanced intensity of the Puritan ethic seemed to manifest itself in the wave of religious hysteria which swept the Massachusetts village of Salem (now Danvers) in 1692 when a group of adolescent girls from the parish church, who had been experimenting with divination, claimed to be bewitched by a Barbadian slave girl, Tituba, employed by the local minister, and two old women. Tituba confirmed that she was a witch who had made a covenant with Satan. There followed a spate of hysterical confessions, resulting in the hanging of nineteen persons and the impressment to death of one who had refused to testify. Although some of the clergy had been cautious, they had been unable to deny the reality of witchcraft. Whether or not the Puritan establishment was to blame for what had occurred, the Salem witch trials probably threw less light on Puritan religion than on the contemporary psychology which Puritanism had helped to create.

What occasioned the Great Awakening of the 1740s may still defy explanation. Some have found social as well as religious factors at work: economic depression, a virulent epidemic of diphtheria, increased urbanization and the greater intrusion of material values. The greater diversity of religious sects – in 1742 New York City had nine churches to meet the needs of eight denominations – lessening the influence of Puritans and Anglicans may have contributed to some degree of religious unsettlement.

The revival made its first major appearance among the Dutch-speaking inhabitants of New Jersey, who responded warmly to the preaching of Theodore Jacob Freylinghausen, who condemned the formality of religion and called for conversion and commitment. He was followed by Gilbert Tennent and his brothers, John and William, who revived religion among the Presbyterians, and by Jonathan Edwards, the most interesting of the evangelists who superimposed Calvinist ideas on pietism which had been so far the revival's chief feature.

Edwards, who was minister at Northampton, Massachusetts, attacked the 'licentiousness' of the young people of the town, and the extent to which men and women had become self-reliant, failing to recognize their dependence upon God. His preaching, solid rather than charismatic, electrified his congregations, having in some instances a disturbing personal effect on his listeners. In 1742 he drew up a covenant for his congregation to sign, binding them to live their faith visibly. He called a roll of the town's sins 'which shut men out from God's mercy and kindled the divine wrath to their destruction'. Edwards was strongly Calvinistic in his approach. Salvation depended on a radical conversion of the heart which God alone can give.

This too was the message of the English evangelist George Whitefield who in 1740 addressed packed congregations in New England, New York, Philadelphia, Charleston and Savannah. He preached, as a local farmer explained, 'like one of the old apostles, and many thousands flocking after him to hear ye gospel and great numbers were converted to Christ'.

The revival was comparatively short lived, but its effects were permanent. It spread beyond the borders of New England to the middle colonies and to the South; the Presbyterian Samuel Davies preached to back-country Whites, the Red Indians and Blacks. Yet the Great Awakening also assisted in the further fragmentation of the Church. The Church in New England was split into four groups, the Moderates and Radical New Lights, the Old Lights led by Charles

Chauncey of Boston, averse to over-enthusiasm, and the Old Calvinists. The resurgence of Calvinist thinking reinforced the innate Puritanism of American religion but in reaction religious liberalism was to veer towards Unitarianism. The principal beneficiaries of the Great Awakening were probably the Baptist churches, which increased in number from 96 in 1740 to 457 in 1780, so exceeding the total number of Anglican churches.

The fragmentation of Puritanism in the North and the growth of Dissent in the South provided further opportunities for the intrusion and growth of other Christian groups, so producing the religious fluidity henceforth so much a feature of the American religious scene. Independence from British rule, achieved in 1783, was a further incentive to the development of religious pluralism. The American revolution had brought together religious groups in pursuit of political aims. The American Constitution (of 1787) provided for full religious liberty, forbidding the imposition of any religious test as a qualification for office, and declaring that no law should be made 'respecting an establishment of religion or prohibiting the free exercise thereof'. It had provided a soil in which both plants and weeds could grow, and it did not challenge the belief, sustained by further waves of emigration and the arrival of new cults, that in some particular fashion America was God's own country.

THE FRENCH REVOLUTION

The evangelical revival was not spent before the French Revolution erupted, offering what at one stage seemed a serious threat not merely to orthodoxy but to the Christian religion itself. On the eve of the Revolution the French Church appeared in a relatively healthy state, for while there were indeed some scandalous figures in the noble-born episcopate the worst abuse was possibly the custom which allowed the crown to nominate to the titular headships of rich monasteries. These sinecure offices were conferred on princes of the blood and noble families who had no qualifications for presiding even in titular fashion over any religious society, let alone ones vowed to poverty, chastity and obedience, vows peculiarly inapplicable to the holders of 'commendatory' abbeys. Yet in the main the French higher clergy seemed conscientious in the performance of their duties.

The parochial clergy appeared well respected and were held in affection by many of their parishioners. The mass of the laity conformed, at least nominally fulfilling their obligations. Even before the outbreak of the Revolution there were, however, some ominous signs that support for the Church was flagging. Statistics in the dioceses of Rouen, Rheims and Mainz, showed that there had been a drop in religious vocations. While the majority of Frenchmen made their Easter communion, there were some signs of abstentions, as, for instance, in the diocese of Chalons. Church attendance in Paris appears also to have been in decline.

These were no more than straws in the wind, but the wind was eventually to become a howling gale. The sceptical, anti-clerical ideas of the Philosophes had a following among the fashionable classes and the intellectuals. There was as always a residual anti-clericalism, rooted in the envy of the wealth and privileges of the higher clergy, clerical exemption from taxation, the imposition of censorship and lack of toleration (while Parisian yobs were apt to jeer at the religious in their habits). But on the eve of the Revolution all this amounted to little more than a gentle breeze, far away from the hurricane which was to ensue and sweep the whole edifice away.

When the States-General met at the palace of Versailles on 4 May 1789 the clergy, some 46 bishops and 208 curés, formed the First Estate but on 19 June some two-thirds of the lower clergy and one-fifth of the bishops voted to join the Third Estate to form the National Assembly. The National Assembly set in train a series of Church reforms which were designed to remove the abuses which hindered the Church in its task: a reduction in the wealth and privileges of the higher clergy and a corresponding improvement in the stipends of the lower clergy, a reform of monasticism. Surplus church income and property could be used to contribute to help pay off the national debt largely caused by the French participation in the War of American Independence, and so stave off the national bankruptcy which had initially caused the crisis which brought the National Assembly into being.

The National Assembly, which had some strong support among the curés, especially those of a Jansenist turn of mind, pushed ahead with radical proposals. It granted toleration to Jews and actors, allowed Protestants to hold public office and abolished censorship in matters of religion and morality. Tithes were abolished with feudal dues. Most significant of all by some 510 votes to 346 it agreed that all Church property should be confiscated and sold, from the sales of which the clergy would be fairly paid. The purchase of Church lands would help to ensure that the new proprietors of the lands, mainly drawn from the bourgeoisie and the richer peasantry, would never willingly allow a clerical reaction to occur. The Revolution had now a stake in the land, and in further reform of the Church.

The monasteries were next on the list. The Assembly passed a decree in February 1790 suppressing contemplative and mendicant orders; those religious who left their monasteries were to be offered reasonable pensions. For the moment on grounds of social utility educational and charitable orders were allowed to continue, but for the future the taking of monastic vows was forbidden. These reforms culminated on 12 July 1790 in the Civil Constitution of the Clergy which restructured the French Church by reorganizing the dioceses, reducing them in number and aligning them with the civil departments. The financial injustices of the past were to be rectified by the new salary system. Both bishops and curés would henceforth be chosen by electoral bodies. Although the constitution had defects, a majority of the clergy, even of the bishops, gave it their approval.

In promulgating the Civil Constitution of the Clergy the National Assembly had been making use of the powers utilized by the French crown, as they had for instance been laid down in the Gallican Articles of 1682, for determining the nature of the French Church, but there had been no consultation with the Church or the Pope, who failed to give his approval. In response the people of Avignon overthrew their papal overlord and asked to be incorporated in the French state. If this action was intended to blackmail the Pope into compliance it failed, for he declared the Civil Constitution to be a schismatic document. The worried king havered, and the clergy tried to find a compromise but neither side was likely to give way. On 27 November 1790 the National Assembly passed a decree requiring all clergy in office to take an oath to observe the Civil Constitution.

Schism divided the French Church, between those loyal to the Pope and those who accepted the Constitution which included most of the clerical members of the National Assembly, and Bishops Talleyrand and Gobel. As bishoprics fell vacant, so the new procedure of election was followed, but the Pope would refuse to accept the new nominees. Of the 160 bishops then in office only four took the oath, and three of these were men of dubious moral character and doubtful religious convictions. While some prepared to leave the country and seek refuge abroad, those who remained were comparatively impotent. The parish priests were divided, but many still believed with the prospect of better salaries in front of them that the Revolution was servicing the Church. Everywhere there were signs of chaos and confusion.

Unfortunately, acceptance of the Civil Constitution of the Clergy was becoming a necessary guarantee of patriotism. Those who did not subscribe were potentially guilty of treason. The mob threw a mock-guy of Pope Pius VI into a bonfire with a placard around his neck bearing the inscription 'fanaticism, civil war'. Non-juring priests were identified with the national enemy, the Austrians, to the protection of whose armed forces the king and the royal family had unsuccessfully tried to flee.

The National Assembly's successor, the Legislative Assembly, decreed that every refractory priest who was denounced by twenty 'active' citizens (soon reduced to six in number) was liable to be deported. The king, a conscientious Catholic, tried to veto the laws but on 10 August 1792 the monarchy fell. A new oath of loyalty to the constitution was imposed on all clergy: 'I swear to be faithful to the Nation, to maintain with all my power Liberty, Equality, the security of persons and property, and to die, if need be, for the execution of the law.' In the ensuing violence of the massacres in September three bishops and some two hundred and twenty priests died.

With the Catholic Church virtually outlawed, it was doubtful whether the Constitutional Church could hold the floodgates against further religious change. Its control over education wavered. The Catholic faithful avoided its services, preferring to register their marriages (as Protestants had been allowed to do since 1787) rather than to submit to marriage by constitutional clergy. There were new signs of erosion of the faith as former monks and nuns were banned from teaching and divorce was legalized. The 'red' curé of Saint-Laurent at Paris, De Moy, demanded the banning of all clerical dress and a civil burial service the theme of which would be 'sleep without hope of awakening'. Patriotic symbolism, represented by Voltaire's burial in the Pantheon on 11 July 1791 and the festival of the Federation on the Champ de Mars the previous year, became a substitute for religious ritual.

In effect what looked very like a new religion was in the process of manufacture, its theme universal brotherhood, its basis the 'culte de la raison et de la loi'. There were few who questioned that religion was a social necessity but the age-old sanctions were disappearing. Louis XVI, having made his confession to a non-juring priest, was executed on 21 January 1793. In the south-west, a bloody rising in the Vendée, caused by social unrest, poverty and attachment to the old faith, reinforced the revolutionaries' belief that the former Catholic Church was actively in league with the enemies of France.

As the influence of the Constitutional Church itself began to wane, so the attack on the Catholic Church escalated. The Paris Commune banned the midnight Mass at Christmas and approved a new calendar which omitted Sundays and saints' days. Approximately thirty to forty thousand priests, most of them seculars, managed to migrate to England, Spain and the Papal States. Some thousands were put to death, often brutally, so that judicial murder was for a time the order of the day. Priests were encouraged to abjure their vocation, such abjuration like clerical marriage being a guarantee of good citizenship. Under pressure forty-seven of the eighty-five constitutional bishops gave up their orders and perhaps as many as twenty thousand clergy followed suit. Bishop Grègoire remained faithfully at his post but the short-lived Constitutional Church appeared to be already in a state of disintegration.

The movement for de-Christianization, sponsored though not specifically led by the National Convention, was most marked in Paris, but it had its promoters, some fanatics, some crooks, some idealists, many renegade priests and monks among them, in many a provincial town. At Nevers Fouché, himself a former member of the Oratory, inaugurated a Feast of Brutus at the church of Saint-Cyr, condemned clerical celibacy and declared that the only religion was that of morality. The flask containing the holy oil for the anointing of French kings was taken from Rheims Cathedral and smashed. Churches were vandalized and looted, and sometimes became the scene of drunken revels. Aristocratic and royal tombs were violated and demolished as reminders of feudal tyranny. Confessional boxes were burned. Church bells, iron grilles and railings were melted down to be converted into arms.

The Christian Church in France was then placed under greater strain than it had been at any time since its foundation. Yet the new religion, if it can be so called, was itself a curious hotch-potch which lacked an enthusiastic following. The new calendar, starting with the birth of the Republic rather than with the birth of Christ, was based on the seasons of the year but omitted all Church festivals and replaced Sunday with what was termed the *dècadi*. Its apparent climacteric was the Festival of Reason on 10 November 1793 [20 Brumaire] which was presided over by a local actress robed as the goddess of liberty in Notre Dame Cathedral at Paris, an example followed by other towns. The cult of the Supreme Being was ordered to be observed throughout France. Frenchmen, as the atheist philosopher Salaville sarcastically phrased it, were 'trying to be republicans in time but royalists in eternity'. The movement for de-Christianization was deistic rather than atheistic. Without belief in a supreme being, the immortality of the soul, some system of reward and punishment, there could be, its advocates believed, no fundamental incentives to virtues. The new cult which had the largest following was called Theophilanthropism and flourished particularly in those places where the assault on Christianity had been most effective such as Paris where in 1798 the sect had sixteen established places of worship. But the republican cults, for all their attempts at pageantry, were too rational and cold to win popular support. Their faith and their festivals lacked the essential ingredient of mystery implicit in religious ritual. Civil marriages and burials were void of the consolation that the old religion brought to the newly married and to the bereaved. The hopes which idealists had raised in the early days of the Revolution disappeared in a widespread fog of disillusion.

The ending of the Terror, which followed the execution of Robespierre in July 1794, had been followed by a steady evaporation of anti-Christian legislation and by a slow but very patchy recovery of the faith. The Convention still forbade the ringing of church bells and the wearing of clerical dress, but it had at least in February 1795 guaranteed the free exercise of religion. The Constitutional Church, whose clergy were no longer being paid by the state, showed a momentary flicker of revival under the able leadership of Henri Grègoire, the bishop of Blois. Meanwhile the Catholic Church, though with a strong reservoir of underground support, lacked leadership, for its exiled prelates, totally intransigent in attitude, showed little understanding of the problems of their former flock. But slowly the prison doors were opening, the churches began to be repaired and the Mass said. Groups of nuns came together surreptitiously in communities, sometimes giving a safe refuge to non-juring priests who, wearing lay costume, held Mass in private houses.

This process of religious renewal was uneven and was at least temporarily delayed by the anti-religious policy which the government of the Directory followed. In the autumn of 1797 the government, frightened by the possibility of a political reaction promoted by a religious revival, ordered all to take oaths of submission to the laws of the Republic. The Directory's anti-clerical policy was exported to other countries by the victorious French armies in Belgium, the Rhineland, Switzerland and Italy. The Pope, powerless to do anything else, was obliged to make the concessions which the conquerors demanded of him. A ballet in La Scala, Milan, showed the Pope surrendering to the French army and dancing a fandango as he donned the cap of liberty.

The concessions demanded by the French and to which the Pope reluctantly agreed were greatly to diminish the power and privileges of the Church. The Pope agreed to give up papal overlordship of Avignon and Bologna, to pay 30 million livres tournois and to allow the French to export some one hundred art treasures. The Cisalpine Republic in northern Italy ordered that all Church property should be confiscated and that monasteries should be dissolved in the hope that this might solve its financial difficulties. Further south the Roman Republic was as rigorous, arresting or expelling the cardinals, dissolving the Roman congregations, banning monasteries, expelling the foreign clergy and abolishing the legal obligation to be present at Mass and the wearing of clerical dress, forbidding religious processions in the streets and looting churches of their art treasures.

In practice the French occupation of Rome had virtually brought the central administration of the Church to a halt. The Pope who was himself now a prisoner and a puppet of the French died at Valence on 29 August 1799, described by the local registrar as 'Jean Ange Braschi, exercising the profession of a pontiff'. The Catholic Church was confronting a crisis of the first magnitude which might still threaten its very survival.

Yet there was an underground swell which showed that popular Catholicism remained a strong force. There were outbreaks of violence in favour of the old religious order, peasant risings in Belgium, the Catholic cantons of Switzerland and southern Italy. 'Our religious revolution is a failure,' General Clarke told Bonaparte, 'people have become Roman Catholic again; maybe we are at the point when we need the Pope to bring to the Revolution the support of the priests, and by consequence of the countryside.'

This was a point of view to which Napoleon Bonaparte, recently elevated to the office of First Consul by a *coup d'état* which overthrew the Directory, was gradually moving. Bonaparte was fundamentally not a religious man, sympathetic to Rousseau's criticisms of 'pure Christianity' as politically and socially subversive. But as a shrewd political pragmatist he believed that religion was natural to man as a bonding factor in society. He would allow the Church to function on sufferance, so long as it was under his masterful control. The Church had to be harnessed to his imperial ambitions.

There was another changing aspect of the situation. Since the Catholic Church was no longer in a position to maintain an intransigent attitude, it had to accommodate itself to the practical situation in which it found itself. Its leaders, more as a matter of pragmatism than principle, agreed that the Church ought not to be bound to any particular form of government but that it should accept a *de facto* regime and operate within its framework. It was to be a policy which the Church was going to have to follow for the next two hundred years.

After three months of deadlock, the papal Conclave, meeting in San Giorgio, Venice, had elected Cardinal Chiaramonti as Pope Pius VII. The new Pope was not a man of great ability or intelligence, but in his secretary of state Cardinal Consalvi he had an industrious and skilled diplomat. A Concordat, concluded on 15 July 1801, at least temporarily brought a pacification of the French Church. It admitted that Roman Catholicism was the religion of the majority of the French nation, but the Pope approved the newly organized dioceses and accepted that the state should appoint the bishops. All religions were granted freedom to worship, obliging the Catholic Church reluctantly to acquiesce in a policy of toleration. In practice the Pope recognized that the Church was controlled by the state, but at least the Concordat had disinterred Catholicism from what had seemed a little earlier to be its likely grave. Napoleon's triumph reached its peak when the Pope was personally present as Napoleon crowned himself French emperor at Notre Dame on 2 December 1804.

Within a decade the Napoleonic empire was to be in its death throes, but before that occurred the Catholic Church was subjected to a series of further damaging shocks. For after the Concordat and the imperial coronation Napoleon's relations with the Pope deteriorated sharply. Accommodating as Pius VII was, he became the victim of Napoleon's flatulent megalomania. Angered by the Pope's refusal to annul the marriage of his brother Jerome (who wanted to marry an American Protestant) and his readiness to give refuge to his alienated brother Lucien, and, what was worse, by the Pope's unwillingness to align himself with his war-aims, he ordered the French army to occupy Rome. The Pope became a prisoner in the Quirinal. 'My predecessor', Pius is rumoured to have said, 'lived like a lion when in prosperity but died like a lamb. I have lived like a lamb, but know how to defend myself, and die like a lion.' Napoleon annexed the Papal States, declaring that Rome was an 'imperial free city'. 'If the Pope preaches rebellion', he told his general Murat, 'against the spirit of the Gospel, arrest him.'

In response Pius issued a papal bull *Quam memorandum*, comparing the emperor's seizure of the Papal States, though not by name, to King Ahab's seizure of Naboth's vineyard, excommunicating all who were involved in the occupation of papal territory. Once more the Pope crossed the Alps, travelling first to Valence and thence to Savona where he lived for three years under house arrest. He lived there very quietly and simply, even doing his own laundry, his sole luxury indulgence being the taking of snuff. Napoleon's return in the Hundred Days led the Pope to take refuge at Genoa, but with the solitary figure exiled to St Helena the Pope was free to preside for the last eight years of his life over the rehabilitation of the Catholic Church.

A decade of republican and imperial rule had brought chaos and confusion to the Catholic Church. In Rome the cardinals had been expelled, the Inquisition was abolished and the clergy who refused the oath of loyalty were expelled or sent to camps in Corsica. More positively the French introduced much needed improvement in the city's government and promulgated toleration, liberating the Jews from the ghetto. Elsewhere there was some breakdown in Church government as bishoprics were left vacant. Napoleon's brother Joseph, as king of Spain, sought to impose controls over the Spanish Church along lines similar to those which Napoleon had followed in France, but his success was very limited, for the Spaniards identified natural resistance to the French with loyalty to the Church.

In Germany the situation had been made the more complicated by the Austrian emperor's reluctant agreement to surrender the title of Holy Roman Emperor, which was decreed in 1806. It was the end of a millennium during which Pope and emperor had been once in practice and still were in theory the twin pillars of the western Christian world. Some thought that Napoleon himself aimed to be crowned 'emperor of the west' – he had actually been crowned king of Italy at Milan – and that his infant son, Napoleon, was entitled king of Rome gives some credence to the idea. The disintegration of an institution, the Holy Roman Empire, which seemed to many already politically moribund might well seem a 'non-event', but it served as a preface to further measures of secularization, for not merely did the three ecclesiastical electors, the archbishops of Mainz, Cologne and Trier, lose their territorial power but German princes, albeit Catholic by religion, such as the newly entitled kings of Bavaria and Wurtemburg used the opportunity to strengthen their control over the Church in their lands and to introduce ecclesiastical reforms which involved the dissolution of many monasteries and the confiscation of Church property.

Napoleon's final defeat at the battle of Waterloo at the hands of an Irish Protestant, the duke of Wellington, and the subsequent congress of the victorious powers at Vienna was not only a milestone in world politics but a watershed in the history of the Church. In the course of the eighteenth century the shackles of the Protestant and Catholic Reformations, though not cast off, had been in many respects weakened. Secular thought, leading in the direction of scepticism and to radical enquiry into the texts of the scriptures, had grown apace. Both these trends were to appear in more marked fashion in the nineteenth century.

The experience of the French Revolution and its aftermath was the third factor which was to condition much of what was to happen in the Church in the next century. For both Catholic and Protestant churchmen excesses of the French Revolution showed plainly where the propagation of infidelity and scepticism could lead. If political and social subversion were to be avoided, with its corollary the possibility of gross immorality, then the Church had to be regenerated and restored.

The French Revolution had strengthened the Church's in-built reactionary nature and its suspicion of change. Yet simultaneously it had led to a growing realization of the need to renew its spiritual life and its evangelistic impulse. There was, however, also a growing minority of Christians who thought that this could only happen if the Church was more closely identified with the social and political aspirations of the people, and that the time had come for the Church to liberate itself from the umbrella of the establishment which gave it sanctuary. The nineteenth century would show the extent to which religious conservatism and radicalism were to jostle each other within the context of an increasingly secular society.

But if by the early nineteenth century the Church was in crisis, the merits of the eighteenth-century Church may have been too easily dismissed. It was indeed guilty of discrimination, censorship and intolerance, and was wedded to an established system of society whose conventions it readily accepted. But it had, however, done much to promote humane values, for the eighteenth century was an age of philanthropic enterprise, concerned with the welfare of orphans and debtors, prisoners and prostitutes, the sick and the poor. The bases of religious revival had been laid as John Wesley and his associates rode the length and breadth of Britain, and Catholic friars tramped the countryside to seek religious renewal through parochial missions.

The very architecture of eighteenth-century churches, square chambers marvellously decorated with stucco angels and cherubs like unworldly drawing rooms, showed how the Church and the world had come together. The Church moved away from the stark realism of the Reformation and kept the ugliness and sadness of religion at bay. Buildings full of light and colour, their domes brilliant with frescoes suggesting the divine illumination of heaven, their sanctuaries creating a union between celebrant and congregation and forming a splendid theatrical setting for the drama of the Mass or the resonance of the choir.

The Counter-Reformation had tried to impose musical austerity and simplicity, expressed at its best in the plainsong of Palestrina. Although this remained the basis of Catholic worship, in spite of attempts to discourage the growing popularity of oratorios, Church music underwent something of a metamorphosis, as in Protestant lands it responded to the genius of Bach and Handel and in Catholic countries to that of Haydn, Mozart (who was personally drawn to freemasonry which the Church condemned) and Beethoven, music that was brilliantly original and stimulating, allowing the profane to intermingle with the sacred, and so ultimately serving to humanize the Church.

Eighteenth-century religion, if at times – as it must have seemed to many a congregation – dull and prosaic, remained a positive feature in a world that was actually beginning to undermine its foundations. Life was still in many respects barbaric and cruel, but the eighteenth century was an age of improvement in which religion continued to be a major ingredient.

CHAPTER NINE

An Age of Ecclesiastical Imperialism, c. 1815–80

On Saturday 28 June 1860 some seven hundred people crowded into the lecture hall of the new University Museum at Oxford to hear a debate arranged by the British Association for the Advancement of Science on the theory of natural selection, enunciated by Charles Darwin in the *Origin of the Species* published the previous year. Darwin was not himself present, for, as he explained, his 'stomach had utterly failed', but he had a champion in Thomas Huxley, reluctant as he had at first been to engage in open debate with Darwin's critics. Among these was Samuel Wilberforce the bishop of Oxford, whose rhetoric was soon to show that though he had taken a first in mathematics, his grasp of science was less than adequate. As he moved towards the peak of his peroration, the bishop said, 'I should like to ask Professor Huxley, who is sitting by me and is about to tear me to pieces when I have sat down, as to his belief in being descended from an ape. Is it on his grandfather's or his grandmother's side that an ape ancestry comes in?' Huxley whispered to his neighbour Sir Benjamin Brodie 'the Lord hath delivered him into mine hands'. 'If then, said I, the question is put to me would I rather have a miserable ape for a grandfather or a man highly endowed by nature and possessed of great means and influence and yet who employs those faculties and that influence for the mere purpose of introducing ridicule into a grave scientific discussion I unhesitatingly affirm my preference for the ape.' There was a storm of applause. In an attempt to defend the bishop, Fitzroy, the head of the government's meteorological department 'lifting an immense Bible first with both hands and afterwards with one hand over his head, solemnly implored the audience to believe God rather than Man'. But Huxley evidently had the benefit of the debate.

Ten years later, 18 July 1870, a wet and stormy summer's day, witnessed the last gathering of the Vatican Council at which the decree on papal infallibility was to be approved. Thomas Mozley, the acting correspondent of *The Times* described the scene:

The storm, which had been threatening all the morning, burst now with the utmost violence. . . . And so the 'placets' of the Fathers struggled through the storm, while the thunder pealed above and the lightning flashed in at every window and down through the dome. 'Placet', shouted his Eminence or his Grace, and [a] loud clap of thunder followed in response. The storm was at its height when the result of the voting was taken up to the Pope, and the darkness was so thick that a huge taper was necessarily brought and placed by his side as he read the words 'Nosque, sacro approbante Concilio, illa, ut lecta sunt, definimus et apostolica auctoritate confirmamus'. And again the lightning flickered around the hall, and the thunder pealed. The 'Te Deum' and the Benediction followed: the entire crowd fell on their knees, and the Pope blessed them in those clear sweet tones distinguishable among a thousand.

Manning commented crisply that 'critics saw in the thunderstorm an articulate voice of divine indignation against the definition. They forgot Sinai and the Ten Commandments!'

The shores of Lake Tanganyike in Africa in January 1873 formed a very different setting for the ending of the epic career of the explorer and missionary David Livingstone. After his earlier triumphs which had made him into a national hero, he had to some extent faded from the public consciousness, but the description he had written of a massacre of slaves by Arab raiders at Nyangwe on 15 July 1871 brought him again before the public eye. The *New York Herald* sent its roving correspondent H.M. Stanley to find Livingstone and eventually at Ujiji by the shores of Lake Tanganyike in November 1871 they had the historic meeting which captured the imagination of the world. Livingstone was obsessed with finding the real source of the River Nile and forced himself, suffering though he was from dysentery and anal bleeding, carried by his devoted Africans, on through the drenching tropical rain until he reached the village of Chilombo, a local chief, where he died. He was given a hero's burial in Westminster Abbey and a packed commemorative meeting was held in the New York Academy of Music where the Governor's Island Band played the *Miserere* from *Il Trovatore* and Rossini's *Crucifixus*.

These episodes, distant from each other as they are in time and space, exemplify some facets of the Church's history in the nineteenth century. If only a few thinking men as yet believed that scientific investigation represented the search for truth and moral rectitude in opposition to ecclesiastical obscurantism, the Oxford debate, if in the long run ultimately inconclusive, itself pointed to the growing conflict between the progressive scientific and traditionalist religious views of the universe. On the other hand the decisions of the Vatican Council underlined the Church's firm attachment to tradition, and its conviction of its divine mission. Contrariwise David Livingstone, who never made more than a few converts, stood as an envoy for an advancing Church which became in spite of itself an expression of White imperialism, which would girdle the world in America, Africa and Asia.

In the eighteenth century, in spite of the potentially rich evangelistic revival, the influence of the Church had in many respects contracted.

Principles adumbrated in the Catholic and Protestant Reformations had been modified. The papacy had been placed on the defensive. The close relationship which had subsisted between the Churches and the State became upset as the State became ever more and more the senior partner. The spread of sceptical philosophy which rejected the Christian revelation was to constitute an intellectual challenge to faith while the development of textual criticism as applied to scripture, a study especially fertile in Germany, put at risk the fundamentalist or literal interpretation of the Bible which had so far held the ground. The century had closed in the hectic violence of the French Revolution and a European war, with a repudiation of the Church and its teaching in France and a partial collapse of the administrative structure of the Roman Church.

These developments conditioned the direction that the Churches were to take in the nineteenth century. After the allied victory over Napoleon, the Churches, deeply disturbed by the possible disintegration of social order and the damage to their own authority which the Revolution had wrought, were determined that nothing like this must be allowed to occur again. Radical forces which threatened Christian belief and ecclesiastical authority had to be countered, restrained and eliminated. Theologically and politically, the established Churches took deeply conservative attitudes and gave their blessing to legitimist governments.

There was a positive and progressive side to this story. Conscientious churchmen were convinced by their experience of revolution that only a strong Church, which was itself spiritually alive, could successfully combat indifference and infidelity. They held that if there was to be a truly just society which would take to heart the Church's teaching the abuses which had blunted the Church's effectiveness had to be eliminated. By and large in their attempts to refurbish their image the Churches were, however, limited by the nature of their structure, by the age-old diocesan and parochial organization and by the vested interests of the clerical order. As a consequence there was to be a renewed emphasis on the authority of the priesthood and sacred ministry; priests were to be better trained as new seminaries and theological colleges were founded. But the training was primarily theological and did not necessarily conduce to the priest's ability to cope with the contemporary problems of the laity from whom in some respects the priest or minister was to become increasingly separate.

The Churches had soon to cope with other new developments, the problems created by the enormous growth in population – the population of the United Kingdom was to double in the first half of the nineteenth century – as well as by increasing social mobility, promoted by improved communications, the building of better roads and of railways. The Churches found they had to provide priests and ministers, churches and schools, in urban industrial agglomerations where the working class had already become increasingly alienated from the Churches' influence.

The cultural changes which were to occur in the nineteenth and twentieth centuries did not augur wholly well for the future of the Christian churches. They had to survive in a world which was becoming industrialized on a massive scale, giving rise to developments in science and technology which did not merely put an increasing strain on traditional religious belief but which also created social problems with which the churches were not well-equipped to cope. By the closing years of the twentieth century mass education was producing generations of children who were less frequently indoctrinated by their parents or schools in the simple tenets of religion. For them Bible stories, once the staple diet of the Sunday school, were often little more than tedious fairy tales. Philosophy and political thought were implicitly less and less concerned with religion, and even in tone anti-religious. Art has been largely secularized since the Renaissance; and such brief forays as artists made from time to time into religious subject matter, as did the pre-Raphaelites, seemed in essence little more than nostalgic romanticism. It is perhaps in music, more especially choral music, that the Christian faith continued to find a rich expression.

Nonetheless there was to be at first an immensely creative burst of energy on the Churches' part, paid for to some extent by the profits of the world's burgeoning industry, which led to the expansion of the Churches overseas. But this era of expansion was to be followed by a period of religious deflation, more or less coinciding with the sequel to two world wars, followed by an eventual re-evaluation of Christian ideology as the Churches began to come to terms with the aftermath of two centuries of cultural change.

For in spite of its apparent massive conservatism, the Church was not as monolithic as it might appear. Even within the Roman Church, notably in France, there were minority groups who held that the Church ought to accommodate itself to the needs of secular society, and to accept such principles as freedom of conscience and toleration, which it had previously rejected. Although the liberals were few in number, they were intellectually influential and though often condemned officially, they held the key to the future. In the Protestant Churches, there were some groups of dissenters who were politically as well as socially, if not theologically, liberal in attitude. All in all, the concept of a 'free Church' in a 'free state' was to become an increasingly practical proposition, as the American experience of a plurality of Churches existing in a religiously neutral state was to demonstrate.

Whatever the underlying weakness of the Church, it was to experience a measure of rejuvenation in the nineteenth century. There was to be a real resurgence of religious fervour, a deepening of devotion and of spiritual insight, which was expressed in a worldwide wave of missionary endeavour which swept over every continent. The nineteenth century was to testify to a boom time in religion, and for the first time the Church could claim to be truly universal. It was to be an age of ecclesiastical imperialism.

THE RESTORATION OF PAPAL AUTHORITY

Little of this could have been foreseen in 1815. More immediately the Roman Church was faced with rebuilding its shattered administration and reimposing its authority. It had emerged from the cauldron of war and revolution convinced that liberal ideas were an embodiment of satanic forces which had to be exorcized and destroyed. The Church supported the restoration of legitimism in France, Spain and Portugal and negotiated concordats with Catholic princes which would confirm the Church's privileged position in society. But it could not wholly ignore the changing world. While Pius VII concentrated on the life of devotion, his able secretary of state, Cardinal Consalvi, was ready to talk with English Protestants in the hope of furthering the movement for Roman Catholic emancipation, and with Russia where the presence of a million Catholics in that part of Poland incorporated within Russia created a major problem. Pius VII's successor, Leo XII, was a devout rigorist, unpopular with the Romans for his censorious attitude to carnival time, who adhered to an obsolete paternalism. Nor was his successor, a Camaldolese monk, Bartolomeo Cappellari, Gregory XVI, any more flexible; politically naive, unversed in politics, an obstinate and authoritarian doctrinaire, he was an exponent of scholastic theology but so determined to repress liberalism that he even refused to countenance the Catholic movement in Poland because it might appear politically subversive. When he died in 1846, the conclave elected the bishop of Imola, Giovanni Mastai-Feretti, of whom as Pius IX liberals had at first high hopes. Only time was to tell how misplaced such hopes were.

The popes had so far deplored any attempt at modernization. Papal government of the city of Rome remained unjust and inefficient. The Jews were confined to their ghetto. Church courts were restored, the laicization of the administration was delayed. Gregory XVI refused to consider the possibility of building a railway. Yet Rome had regained its position as the centre of the Roman Church; in some sense the city had recovered its charisma. Enriched by the sculptures of Canova and Thorwaldsen, it attracted visitors from all over the world, especially in 1825 which Leo XII proclaimed as a jubilee year.

The popes effectively recovered their sacral authority as the cornerstone of the Church's unity. Whatever attempts had been made in the eighteenth century to dilute papal power, the Pope reappeared with his spiritual and jurisdictional primacy intact together with temporal sovereignty over the Papal States. The Petrine position was exalted by influential intellectuals such as Joseph Görres in Germany, by Joseph de Maistre in *Du Pape* (1819) and Chateaubriand in France. The stage was being set already for the declaration of papal infallibility in 1870.

The reassertion of papal authority was a positive ingredient in the recovery of the Church, in respect of its privileged position and even more significantly its spirituality. Appreciative of the support given to their legitimist claims, Catholic monarchs gave the Church their patronage. In France although the Concordat of 1801 had not been formally revoked, the Church recovered much of its power: divorce was outlawed, blasphemy severely punished. The last Bourbon king of France, Charles X, so it was said, 'atoned for the thoughtless sins of his youth through equally thoughtless exercises of devotion in his old age.' In the Iberian Peninsula, where the Church was manifestly in need of reform, it recovered its privileged position. In Spain where there was an anti-clerical reaction in 1820, resulting in the closure of monasteries and the expulsion of the religious orders, the downfall of the liberals in 1823 meant the restoration of the old order of the Church. In Germany where the ending of the Holy Roman Empire brought the disappearance of the ecclesiastical principalities, Rome negotiated concordats with the Catholic rulers preserving Rome's jurisdictional primacy but allowing a reservoir of power in terms of appointments to individual princes. While Austria did not entirely repudiate Josephism, the Pope could count on Metternich's support.

In Europe the papacy's greatest success was possibly in Protestant Britain. In the eighteenth century Catholicism there had had a small but faithful following, headed by gentry who had remained loyal to the faith and serviced by a priesthood, some four hundred in number. Roman Catholics were still subject to penal legislation, restrictions that were in practice inconvenient rather than burdensome. With the incorporation of Ireland in the United Kingdom in 1800, it could only be a question of time before the penal laws were abolished. Although George III and many English churchmen still held that Roman Catholic emancipation represented a threat to throne and altar, in 1829 the Roman Catholic Emancipation Act opened all offices under the crown except for four (the posts of Lord Chancellor, the Keeper of the Great Seal, the Lord Lieutenant of Ireland and the High Commissioner of the Church of Scotland) to Roman Catholics. 'The year 1829', the future Cardinal Wiseman commented, 'was to us what the egress of the catacombs was to the early Christians.'

The number of Roman Catholics in Britain grew massively, especially with the migration of Irish labour; but the faith also attracted an increasing number of converts from the upper and middle classes. In the process the Catholic Church in England underwent something of a metamorphosis. Previously it had been largely dominated by the Catholic laity, for because the Church could not own property, lay Catholics acted as trustees for the chapels and often appointed the chaplain. The influence of the old Catholic laity was now on the decline as the Church became steadily more ultramontane in its administration, teaching and devotional practice.

It had a flamboyant leader in Nicholas Wiseman, a 'ruddy strapping divine', a controversialist of charm but by temperament an autocrat. He negotiated the restoration of the Catholic hierarchy in England, of which as the first archbishop of Westminster he was ultimately the main legatee. When the Pope eventually gave his assent to the re-establishment of the hierarchy in 1850, Wiseman attracted attention by a triumphalistic pronouncement in which he asserted that 'Catholic England has been restored to its orbit in the ecclesiastical firmament, from which its light had long vanished.' English Protestants were naturally alarmed at what they conceived to be the threat of a Roman takeover but it did not halt the growth and consolidation of the Catholic community. In the eighteenth century there may have been eighty thousand Roman Catholics in England; the religious census of 1851 put their numbers as three-quarters of a million or 31–2% of the population.

The vehicles which were used to propagate the faith, the religious orders of men and women, the parish missions, the religious schools, the introduction of devotional practices more particularly associated with the Blessed Virgin Mary, were very similar to the means by which in other more predominantly Catholic countries the laity were stimulated in spirituality. But the English Roman Church had become more specifically Rome oriented. It was hardly surprising that Cardinal Manning, a convert from Anglicanism, who succeeded Wiseman as archbishop in 1865, should have become one of the most fervent promoters of the doctrine of papal infallibility at the Vatican Council.

In other non-Catholic countries the Roman Church was less successful. The revival of Slavophil feeling in Russia, strongly championed by the Orthodox Church, had unfortunate repercussions for the Catholic subjects of the tsar, more especially in Poland. The Jesuits, whose order had been reconstituted by the Pope in 1814, were expelled from Russia where they had once been acceptable refugees in 1820. Tsar Nicholas I ordered the dissolution of approximately five hundred monasteries and nunneries. The union of Belgium and Holland into a united state in 1815 meant the incorporation of a predominantly Catholic Belgium into a Protestant Dutch kingdom. When the Belgians acquired independence in 1830, the new constitution, representing more liberal Catholic tendencies, guaranteed the right to free association and the freedom of education; not tenets of which more conservative Romans would have approved.

For the conservative Roman curia all that smacked of liberalism constituted a danger to faith and social order. Spiritual rebirth and the restoration of traditional values were the just answer to the tribulations of society. Many Roman Catholic writers looked backward to a romantic rediscovery of medieval religion, but there was a small minority of thinking Catholics who believed that the Church's future depended ultimately on its capacity to accommodate itself to modern thought and social progress. The turbulent Breton priest, Robert de Lammenais, once a conservative himself, steadily relinquished his previous belief in the partnership of legitimist monarchy with the Church, substituting the will of the people for monarchical government. The Church, he now argued, should be separated from the State which should grant freedom to the press and of education. Supported by able allies such as the aristocratic Charles de Montalembert and the priest Henri Lacordaire, he set up a religious congregation, the Congregation de St Pierre, and a paper *L'Avenir* to circulate his views which caused consternation not merely to the ultramontanes and the royalists but among conservative statesmen, including the Austrian chancellor Metternich.

Lammenais characteristically convinced himself that the Pope would lead the people to freedom from unjust temporal government and in an impetuous gesture decided to go in person to Rome to seek the Pope's approval. At Rome he was cold-shouldered and kept waiting. Worse was to come, for a papal encyclical *Mirari vos* of 10 August 1832 condemned his views, culled, so it was alleged, from 'a certain religious indifferentism, which faith must reject', 'this false and absurd maxim, or better this madness, that everyone should have and practice freedom of conscience'. Bitterly disappointed by his reception Lammenais at first stood firm but then decided to recant. But when he heard that the Pope had condemned the Polish uprising, Catholic in impulse, against arbitrary Russian rule, he wrote *Paroles d'un croyant* in which he spoke challengingly of a new age in which religion would rescue the people from despotic tyranny. The book, apocalyptic in tone, was condemned in the encyclical *Singulari nos*; and Lammenais sadly left the Church, never to return.

If Lammenais was the quondam high priest of liberal Catholicism, he had followers who urged that the Church ought to accept the basic principles of 1789, including freedom of the press, freedom of religion, the separation of Church and state, views that were anathema to the established authorities as pointing in the direction of a religious indifferentism which would concede that one religion was as valid as another. It seemed too to suggest that the temporal sovereignty of the Pope was by no means good for the Church. In 1831 Mazzini had founded Young Italy with the motto 'God and People', aiming at liberation from dogma and the creation of a new religion of humanity while a Piedmontese priest Vincenzo Gioberti put forward ideas for the unification of Italy in a federation headed by the Pope.

THE ROMAN CHURCH IN NORTH AMERICA

If the revival of religion in Europe was hampered by the heavy-handed traditionalism of the Church's leaders, the scene on the other side of the world appeared very much brighter for the future of Catholicism, at least in North America. At the start of the nineteenth century the United States was a predominantly Protestant country, but the impact of immigration, mainly from Ireland and Germany, began to change the religious balance. Under the able guidance of John Carroll, the bishop of Baltimore, the small Catholic community burgeoned; a seminary was founded and four dioceses, Boston, Philadelphia, New York and Bardston (renamed Louisville in 1841) were established. When Carroll died in 1815, there were probably around a hundred and fifty thousand Catholics; but by 1860 the numbers amounted to some 3.5 million, making the Roman Catholics the largest single denomination in the country. About twenty dioceses had been founded between 1820 and 1837.

That the Church so depended on Irish and other immigrants – in 1852 the hierarchy consisted of thirty-two bishops of whom twenty-three were foreign-born – created a religious and cultural problem. There was at first an angry reaction among the Protestants to the expansion of the Catholic community. A Catholic convent at Charleston, Massachusetts, was burned down in 1834; two churches were destroyed in Philadelphia in 1844 while a political party the 'Know-Nothings' was formed to defend America from foreigners and Catholics, despatching seventy-five members to Congress in 1854. But the process of acculturation was assisted by the very plurality of religion which would hardly have been acceptable in Catholic Europe. As in England before Emancipation, the Church was not itself allowed to own property which was administered by trustees, mainly laypeople who exerted a measure of control over their priests. While the system was resented by the bishops and clergy, who fought what was ultimately a winning battle, lay participation in Church affairs helped at first to moderate foreign and ultramontane influence.

In Canada the Catholic community also grew rapidly under the lead of John Plessis, the bishop of Quebec. The treaty of Paris in 1763, which had been confirmed by the Quebec Act of 1774, had guaranteed the 'free exercise of faith of the Church of Rome', and though anti-Catholic sentiment persisted, fostered by the first Anglican bishop of Quebec, George Mountain, the Catholic Church consolidated its control, more especially in the French-speaking province of Quebec.

THE ROMAN CHURCH IN LATIN AMERICA

In Latin America where the Roman Church had so long held a dominant and privileged position it was to be long dogged by its colonial inheritance. The leaders in the movement for independence from Spain had been educated in the anti-clericalism of the European Philosophes and distrusted the Church as an outworn vehicle of the *ancien régime*. In general most of the newly independent republics were ready to accept the Church's legal establishment, but Bolivar excluded religion from the constitutions which he drew up for Colombia in 1819 and Bolivia in 1826. Yet whatever their distrust of the Church, the politicians valued it both for its role as a powerful force for social cohesion and as a means of social control, and in a sense as a part of the natural inheritance from the discredited yet inalienable colonial past.

There was, then, fertile ground for discord between the Church and the state. The bishops, mainly Spanish born, were hostile to the new governments and many retired home. There was disagreement over the appointment of new bishops, for while the republics claimed to inherit the right of appointment, the *patronato real*, which the Spanish kings had enjoyed, Rome, while recognizing if with some reluctance the new states, reserved the rights of appointment to itself. There was a spate of prolonged vacancies, with consequential effects on Church discipline and a decline in the number of ordinands. Contrariwise the republics claimed wide powers over the churches. In 1851 in Colombia the president sought to appoint parochial clergy while President Rodriguez of Paraguay even assumed the headship of the Church.

Nor was the Latin American Church united. The parochial clergy, native-born, readily accepted the jurisdiction of the state. A group of churchmen led by a Peruvian cleric, Francisco de Paula González-Vigil, whose book was described at Rome as 'diabolical', denounced the autocratic paternalism of Rome. Civil governments attacked the religious orders, criticized the control which the Church exerted over education and the excessive numbers of festivals and holy days which, so the anti-clericals argued, acted as a disincentive to economic enterprise. In a continent where the indigenous population lived on the borderline of poverty the Church was not unjustifiably criticized for its wealth and privilege. While liberals attacked the Church as a barrier to progress, the Church tended to support more conservative regimes such as those of the Argentinian dictator Juan Manuel de Rosas between 1838 and 1852 and Garcia Moreno in Ecuador who was to dedicate his nation to the Sacred Heart in 1873.

The Church's real influence was being steadily eroded by growing secular interference. The South American republics gradually introduced the civil administration of births, deaths and marriages; civil marriage became the norm in every state in the course of the century. Tithes, which Pope Alexander VI had granted to the Spanish crown in 1501 which had with independence reverted to the Church, at first continued to be paid but were eventually liquidated (by Argentina in 1822, Chile in 1825, Mexico in 1833 and Venezuela in 1834). The states engaged in the confiscation and redistribution of Church property; Church tribunals became subject to civil courts and the states gradually extended their control over education, limiting religious instruction. To encourage immigration the republics also promoted religious toleration. In some republics the Church was separated by law from the State; in Colombia in 1853, in Mexico under Juárez in 1859 and in Guatemala under Barrios in 1879.

This enforced diminution of the jurisdiction and powers of their Catholic hierarchies did not mean that the states did not continue to exercise some degree of surveillance over the Church. The Church in Mexico became more especially the victim of despoliation. President Juárez even suggested in 1868 that the American Episcopal Church should consecrate a bishop to head a Mexican national Church. The regime of President Guzman Blanco in Venezuela in the 1870s instituted a virulent persecution of the Church, leading to the closing of monastic houses, though after his downfall in 1888 the policy was to be reversed. It was perhaps symptomatic of the widespread suspicion of the Church that when the Panama Canal began to be built in 1903 the government removed all holy water stoups on the ground that they were likely receptacles for mosquitoes. The influence of freemasonry, with which many of the South American politicians were connected, was itself a potent force in the spread of anti-clerical feeling. Yet the Church did not merely survive but buttressed by popular religiosity, by a rich ceremonial which had absorbed earlier folk myths and by devotion to female saints like Saint Rose of Lima, whose cult formed a healthy contrast to the male machismo, in some respects it flourished, even became strengthened by the persecution to which it was then occasionally forced to submit.

MISSIONARY ACTIVITY IN THE ROMAN CHURCH

The Church's greatest strength lay in its missionary zeal which was especially dear to contemporary Popes. Some forty-four new missionary bishoprics were set up by Gregory XVI who had been himself a former prefect in charge of the Congregation for the Propagation of the Faith. The first Indian bishopric, causing some conflict with the Portuguese see of Goa, had been founded in 1819 and Polynesia became a vicariate apostolic in 1833. The Jesuits sought to revive the mission in China and after a slow start and a period of persecution managed to re-establish their foothold there. The Sino-French treaty of Whampoa in 1844 guaranteed a limited amount of religious freedom which enabled the China mission to steadily expand its work. The most spectacular growth was to occur in Indo-China where after a violent persecution initiated by the emperor Ming Mang the Church prospered. The missionaries of the Society of the Holy Ghost directed their efforts at converting the Blacks of Mauritius and Réunion. Seven priests and three friars arrived at Senegal in West Africa in 1843, but soon succumbed to the climate. Réunion, Senegal and Sierra Leone were the stomping ground – if that is the right expression – for the Sisters of St Joseph of Cluny founded by the devout Anna Maria Javouhey in 1807. In South Africa the vicariate of Cape Town was set up in 1837 and the French occupation of North Africa led to the establishment of a bishopric at Algiers in 1838 and a vicariate apostolic at Tunis in 1843. If the great age of ecclesiastical imperialism occurred in the last half of the nineteenth century there were few parts of the world which were not by 1850 untouched by Roman Catholic missionary activity.

THE CHURCH OF ENGLAND IN THE EARLY NINETEENTH CENTURY

The Protestant Churches lacked the monolithic structure and the well-established discipline of Rome. They had no centre of unity and were often at odds with each other. They enjoyed a freedom of expression which could be, as it was in Germany, ventilated in radical textual criticism which would never have been tolerated by Rome. Yet diverse and amorphous as were the Protestant Churches, they were to be as much affected by current trends as the Roman Church, by the erosion of their influence through the process of secularization and by the need to accommodate their teaching and life to the modern age. Like the Roman Church they were to experience both a measure of growth and spiritual regeneration simultaneously with approaching contraction.

The Church of England was a state Church. The experience of the French Revolution, reinforced by the witness of the flood of French emigré priests who took refuge in England, confirmed English churchmen in their belief that the British constitution was sacrosanct. They suspected anything that was flavoured with radicalism. The majority of the English bishops opposed the first parliamentary reform bill in 1832. For the most part British politicians saw the established Church as a means of social control and of preserving the social and political order. But there were already clear signs that the partnership was beginning to wear thin, more especially as it could no longer be said that in practical terms parliament consisted of a majority of committed Christians, let alone Anglicans. Yet parliament was the medium through which ecclesiastical legislation must pass. In this process the State was steadily to take over or to modify the Church's role in English society, through the compulsory registration of births, deaths and marriages in 1836 and the introduction of a civil marriage law and fifty or so years later the secularization of cemeteries, whose growth showed the extent to which death as well as life was creeping outside the Church's sphere of influence. The gradual abolition of Church tithes began in 1836; the compulsory payment of Church rates was ended in 1868. The property of the Irish Church was redistributed in 1836 and 1869. In his short second term of office Sir Robert Peel, with the cooperation of the much-criticized Bishop Blomfield of London, set up the Ecclesiastical Commission which was in subsequent years to redraw diocesan boundaries, redistribute cathedral revenues and establish new dioceses. Such reforms were designed to make the Church of England more efficient, but in their long-term effect they were denuding the Church of its authority and reducing its function in society. A series of bills from the Test and Corporation Acts in 1828 to the Religious Disabilities Removal Act of 1891 had gradually eliminated some of the special privileges the established Church had enjoyed. In this and other ways the Church was thus excluded from its involvement in many areas of social concern and activity, the responsibility for which passed to the State and to secular organizations. It was a pointer to the Church's contracting influence.

The French Revolution and its aftermath had left Anglicans as it had the Roman Catholics with the conviction that true and pure religion was the best buttress against the breakdown of morality and social order. Well-meaning bishops and clergy, supported by pious noblemen and merchants, promoted societies for the suppression of vice and the enhancement of morality. The besetting abuses of the Georgian Church, pluralities, nepotism and absenteeism, were gradually eliminated. Yet to many thinking churchmen these reforms seemed cosmetic rather than radical. The government might subsidize the building of new churches but there was no guarantee that congregations would fill them. In the early nineteenth century the Evangelicals probably provided the most influential spiritual force, but their conception of the Church was limited; their principal concern was with the salvation of the individual rather than his incorporation in the divine body of the Church.

It was in these circumstances that the Oxford Movement came into being, forming the most effective agency of spiritual revival within the Anglican Church. The ideas which it was to propagate were not new and had been circulating for some time within High Church circles, but they were to find a focal point in the university of Oxford in the mid-1830s. The Whig government had introduced an act to 'rationalize' the Protestant Church of Ireland, top-heavy with bishops and occupying a privileged position in a predominantly Roman Catholic country, by reducing the number of Irish dioceses and redistributing its revenues. High Churchmen were deeply offended by the way in which a secular government was seeking to determine the life of a society which by its nature lay outside its jurisdiction. Such action, justified or not, was implicitly sacrilegious. It was what John Keble in his Assize sermon delivered at Oxford on 14 July 1833 called 'National Apostasy', for the Church, as Keble and his Oxford friends, E.B. Pusey, the learned professor of Hebrew, Hurrell Froude and J.H. Newman), was fundamentally a divine society, instituted by Christ, which was governed by bishops and priests who drew their authority directly from Christ. The Church was in danger and must be saved through a renewal of its sacramental life.

For the twelve years during which the agitation was at its height the Oxford Movement stirred what seemed to some, if unjustifiably, the dying embers of the Church of England. Its leaders sought to inject into an institution which appeared to them to be spiritually flabby a meed of spiritual adrenalin, urging Christians to lives of holiness and devotion encouraged by regular attendance at the Eucharist and by decent and ceremonial performance of the liturgy, so transforming the Church into a sacramental community. Yet there was a paradox at the heart of their message. While they denied that parliament had the authority to interfere with the divine life of the Church, they did not challenge the Church's establishment. They looked backward to stress the government's responsibility for forwarding Christian values. It was this paradox which was eventually to lead Newman to leave the Church of England for the Church of Rome which occurred when he was received by the Passionist Father Dominic on 9 October 1845.

What the Oxford Movement, or Tractarianism, as it is sometimes called, achieved for the Church of England remains a matter of debate. Of its leaders John Keble, a rather mediocre poet with an enthusiastic readership, opted for a quiet and holy life as a parish priest and spiritual guide at Hursley in Hampshire, Hurrell Froude was a wilder, less well-balanced spirit, given to occasional self-mortification, Pusey, prodigiously learned was no leader (albeit those who held to his notions were called Puseyites) and after his wife's death in 1837 became an austere dévot, rarely lifting his face from the ground and repressing every smile. Newman, gifted beyond measure as a writer, subtle, supple and superb, yet to some devious in debate, found his true role as a prophet in the Roman Church, less recognized in his own age than in later times. When he was vicar of St Mary's Oxford, undergraduates thronged to his sermons and copied his mannerisms. The tracts in which the leaders circulated their views were widely read in many town and country rectories. The Oxford Movement was to penetrate eventually to the grass roots of the Anglican Church, enriching its sacramental life and providing for a genuinely caring ministry. It spread swiftly. When, for instance, in 1851 the Revd Francis Witts attended a clerical meeting, he carefully abstained from wearing a surplice because it was 'viewed as a symbol of ultra High Church or Puseyism', but, he noted, some eighty out of the hundred clergy attending were doing so, reflecting in his opinion 'the preponderance of the High Church'.

Yet too much must not be claimed for it. The Oxford don Mark Pattison, disillusioned with the movement of which he had once been a vigorous supporter, described its terminal days at the university as the end of a nightmare. It was intrinsically a backward-looking movement, entranced by the romance of Gothic revivalism, teaching the present through the revitalization of the past, which only offered a partial solution to the problems which were affecting the Church of England in the 1840s. There was some truth in the historian F.W. Maitland's comment that the Tractarians seemed anxious to prove that the Church of England was 'Protestant before the Reformation and Catholic afterwards'. Yet it cannot be denied that it added a dimension of warmth and vitality to English Church life, in part expressed through the revival of the religious life for men and women.

In the mid-nineteenth century Tractarianism, so called from the tracts by which its message was to be circulated, had only a minority following. The Evangelicals probably had a wider popular appeal. 'St Mary's Church Cheltenham' (a well-known centre of evangelicalism), it was reported in 1842, 'was as usual very crowded. Mr Close [Francis Close, a well-known evangelical preacher] preached extempore with much of his known fluency, self-possession, impressiveness and ability. The body of his sermon was argumentative, against the Millennarians. Great numbers of communicants of every class, old and young, male and female, rich and poor, servants and artisans attended, and although the words of administration were not pronounced individually the service was of very long continuance: begun at 11 am it was not concluded till a quarter to 3 pm.' Above all the Evangelicals provided a spiritual and comfortable harbour for the affluent middle classes who championed their cause. They were essentially respectable. By helping to eliminate the coarseness and vulgarity characteristic of high society in the late eighteenth century they fostered a moral revolution. They asserted the supremacy of scripture, made the pulpit rather than the altar the centre of their devotion. They rejected the doctrines of baptismal regeneration and the Eucharistic sacrifice. They were very much to the fore in missionary work and philanthropic enterprise, taking the lead in bringing an end to the slave trade and in improving working conditions in factories. But by and large they held the social order to be sacrosanct and believed that social reformation should be the work of redeemed individuals. By the mid-century there were signs that their influence was waning, though their message tended to become more strident. It is probable that the real strength of the Church of England lay neither with the Tractarians nor with the Evangelicals but in the dominance of broad churchmanship, and that the growth of partisanship was to constitute a continuing major weakness which in part accounted for the decline of Anglicanism as a religious force in the late twentieth century.

In practice there were signs that the Church of England was already losing ground. The religious census of 1851 gave the Church of England a membership of 5,292,551 but allotted 4,536,204 to the dissenting churches and 383,630 to the Roman Catholics. After John Wesley's death in 1791 Methodism's fissiparous tendencies fractured the unity of the movement, leading to the foundations of other Churches, the New Connexion, the Primitive Methodists and Bible Christians, more radical in their organization and proletarian in composition. Yet in 1859 the number of Methodists was estimated to be 1,385,382 by comparison with 793,142 for the Independent Churches (Presbyterians and Congregationalists) and 589,978 for the Baptists. The Dissenters represented a strong moral force, puritanical, likely to be supporters of the Temperance movement, and critical of the privileged position of the Church of England. They had too support among the working classes which the established Church lacked. They were possessed by a strong missionary fervour, desirous of bringing the good news of Christ's saving power to the heathen. Their continued expansion was itself a testimony to the spiritual growth still characteristic of the nineteenth-century Church of England.

RELIGIOUS EXPERIENCE IN NORTH AMERICA

The American religious experience was very different, conditioned less by what was happening in the European Churches than by historic, indigenous factors. The new republic deliberately occupied a neutral stance in religion, so allowing for religious plurality. The first three presidents, Washington, Adams and Jefferson were all rationalists. Thomas Paine as a severe critic of orthodox Christianity was widely read. Yet Americans were a religious people, convinced that God had chosen America for a particular purpose, with a mission in their own country and in the world. In spite of its great diversity American religion helped to give unity to the State and to endow it with a sense of moral purpose.

The turmoil of war had left many congregations without their ministers. The Anglican Episcopal Church suffered badly, partly as a result of an exodus of clergy who remained loyal. Although the first American bishop, Samuel Seabury, was himself a loyalist, his fellow bishops, William White of Philadelphia and Samuel Provost of New York tried to structure a Church more democratic in character than its English counterpart, giving laymen a voice in the choice of bishops. The Episcopal Church had a thin following but because its adherents were affluent it exercised much influence. Dissenting congregations were more numerous: Presbyterians, Congregationalists, Baptists divided between those of the North, theologically moderate, and those of the South, scripturally conservative. Their membership soon outstripped the Episcopalians. The end of the war had left American Methodism cut off from the Church of its origins, but under the lead of Francis Asbury it grew with astonishing speed in part because of the Church's democratic nature and its simplistic theology. Another Church, the Disciples of Christ, founded by Scottish immigrants, Thomas Campbell and his son Alexander, attracted working-class people by its evangelical fervour and strict attention to the Bible. The flood of immigrants soon paved the way to an astonishing religious patchwork. The Roman Catholics became a formidable force in spite of bitter attacks, verbal and violent, from their Protestant critics to whom the fast breeding population, largely Irish, appeared to threaten the cultural and religious homogeneity of America. The German Lutherans infiltrated the Mid-West. Indeed, every European Church was to find a niche on American soil.

American religion was instinctively fissiparous and experimental, promoted by political and social upheaval and by the opening up of the frontier. Revivalism, a feature of American religion in the eighteenth century, became the 'grand absorbing theme and aim of the American religious world', often millennial in its teaching, and charismatic in its worship and behaviour: Shakers, Universalists, Freewill Baptists. Barton W. Stone, rejecting the 'labyrinth of Calvinism' for the 'rich pastures of gospel liberty' with James McGready drew thousands to camp meetings which they arranged at Gasper River and Cane Ridge in Kentucky. The crowds, exhausted and expectant, experienced swoonings, ecstasy and uncontrollable shaking as the Holy Spirit supposedly manifested itself. Such camp meetings became a familiar feature of American evangelistic experience, spreading throughout the South and across the Mid-West.

Among such converts was the Methodist Peter Cartwright who for sixty-five years was at the forefront of evangelizing activity from the Appalachians to the Mississippi, presiding over the frontier circuits and by his muscular Christianity winning adherents. 'God in a remarkable manner', Bennet Tyler said, 'was pouring out his Spirit on the Churches of New England.'

It was through New England that the New Light movement swept like a prairie fire in response to the evangelistic preaching of Charles Grandison Finney. His innovative ideas included protracted nightly meetings, exhortations by women, praying for people by name and a familiar invocation of God. His theology was a modified form of Calvinism, but he insisted that repentance would lead to an immediate assurance of salvation. Finney met with spectacular success in Rome, Utica, Troy and Rochester where he claimed to have made 100,000 converts and what he termed the 'Burned-Over' district in Upper New York State between the Catskills and the Adirondacks. Although he was criticized by old-style preachers, he was a pioneer of American urban evangelism.

The Mormons were an astonishing manifestation of a heterodox Christian faith which became a major Church in spite of what might seem on the surface a fantastic foundation. For the founder, Joseph Smith, came after a series of visionary experiences in the 1820s to the conclusion that all existing religions were at fault. He produced a 'translation . . . by the gift and power of God' of inscriptions on golden plates that he claimed to have found buried in a large hill near his home. The Book of Mormon told of two peoples of Hebrew extraction who had supposedly migrated to America. Smith also asserted that Christ had visited America after his death and resurrection. The Mormon faith grafted on to Christian revelation was to have an immense appeal to people who were trying to find historical roots and to establish their identity.

Persecution led to the movement of the community to Utah, Smith having been murdered at Carthage, Illinois, in 1844 in part because of his autocratic government. Brigham Young emerged as a leader of a self-sufficient theocracy in the valley of the Great Salt Lake in 1847. By Young's death in 1877 he had directed the establishment of some three hundred and fifty settlements, comprising a population of 100,000. Federal pressure induced the Mormons to give up polygamy which Smith had introduced, but in general the Mormons formed an industrious and socially responsible community whose tenets spread, for each Mormon was a missionary for his or her faith, throughout the world. In 1996 the Mormons number some 9.4 million, of whom half live in the United States.

World-wide too was to be the appeal of the Seventh-Day Adventists. A Baptist farmer, William Miller, as a result of studying the Old Testament, concluded that Christ would return to earth in 1843–4. His followers, said to number 50,000, sold their property and went to the tops of hills to await Christ's coming. When the year passed without Christ's appearance, some nevertheless persisted in their beliefs, holding either that Miller had just made the wrong calculation or that Christ had come spiritually and not been recognized. From these groups sprang the Seventh-Day Adventists under the lead of Mrs Rachel D. Preston who observed the Old Testament Sabbath as the weekly day of rest instead of Sunday. They believed in the inerrancy of scripture and the imminence of the second coming, and upheld a strict moral code which included abstinence from alcohol, tobacco, tea and coffee.

American religion fostered social and religious experimentation, involving some repudiation of the sexual and moral norm. The Shakers who bore some resemblance to the Seventh-Day Adventists seem to have originated in a Quaker group in England in the mid-eighteenth century, their leader Ann Lee or Mother Ann being known as the 'female principle in Christ'. She led a band of six men and two women to America in 1774, settling in the woods of Watervliet near Albany in New York. Nicknamed Shakers from the shaking by which they were possessed under the stress of spiritual exaltation, they held property in common, abstained from alcohol, professed celibacy and separation from the world.

The Oneida community was more bizarre. It was the brain child of a Presbyterian minister, John Himfrey Noyes who was convinced from chapter 24 of St Matthew's Gospel that Christ's second advent had actually materialized and that the Christian Church had been spiritualized. From Romans chapter 7 he deduced that at conversion all sin is cleansed, and the individual is henceforth in a state of perfection. For this he was expelled from Calvinistic Yale and his preaching licence was removed. He took refuge at the family farm at Putney, Vermont, forming a Christian community where property was shared and free love was practised, for Noyes argued that the exclusive attraction of a man and woman in marriage was incompatible with absolute Christian fellowship. He was arrested for adultery and in 1846 with thirty-one adults and fourteen children moved his community to a farm in Oneida community. Here he taught biblical communism, divine healing, male continence (for which he was not a good advertisement), eugenic experiment and theocratic democracy. There were religious services and Bible readings every day. The commune proved so popular that Noyes had to restrict its numbers to 300. The economy, based on the manufacture of animal traps and travel bags and silver work, was well managed but the community was dissolved in 1881, five years before Noyes's death.

A much earlier communal experiment, not wholly dissimilar in its nature, had been set up by a former German Lutheran Johann Rapp at New Harmony on the Wabash river in south-west Indiana. Rapp and his followers awaited Christ's return at New Harmony where he sought to recreate the first-century Church. The estate at New Harmony was eventually sold to the British radical Robert Owen who attempted to create a Utopian secular society, but the inhabitants of New Harmony migrated to Economy, north of Pittsburgh where the curious community, pietistic, millennial, perfectionist, endured until 1916.

The White churches seem, by and large, to have been unconcerned with the Red Indians or the Blacks. Some abortive attempts were made to convert the Cherokee Indians. Blacks shared some of the White churches, Baptists, Methodists, Presbyterians, usually sitting apart, either at the back or in the balcony; but Afro-American Christianity was already in the making as Blacks turned from White paternalistic Christianity to their own churches, made warm by colourful ceremonial and singing.

In this respect the American Civil War was something of a watershed. The Churches were divided on the issue of slavery. In the North religion was invoked by the anti-slave propagandists, Theodore Dwight Weld and Harriet Becher Stowe whose *Uncle Tom's Cabin* was published in 1852. But the Southerners were equally convinced of the holiness of their cause. Leonidas Polk, the bishop of Louisiana, became a major-general in the Confederate Army. The scars of the conflict remained, dividing religious communities. While the northern Methodists held that slavery was 'contrary to the laws of God, man and nature', some twenty-five thousand Methodist lay people and 1,200 clergy in the South had been slave owners. The divisions facilitated the foundation of a Methodist Episcopal Church, South, in 1844, and the creation of a Southern Baptist Convention.

In many respects American religion was idiosyncratic and even crude. It was symptomatic that the Churches produced no distinguished theologian, but yet the religious impulse throbbed with life. It was soon to find expression in missionary work overseas. In the ultimate reckoning American religious development in the nineteenth century was one of the more positive aspects of Christian history, and another if different expression of ecclesiastical imperialism.

THE ORTHODOX CHURCH

The Orthodox Church which counted millions of adherents in eastern Europe and Asia, in some respects seemed to be marking time, insulated from western Christianity, still subordinate to secular governments and identified with ethnic and national causes. While the largest of these Churches was the Russian Orthodox, autocephalous Churches came into existence as the Balkan states threw off Turkish rule. The Turks still kept the ancient patriarchates of Constantinople, Antioch, Jerusalem and Alexandria in subservience; but elsewhere the Orthodox Church played a prominent part in encouraging the Christian peoples to throw off Turkish rule. Grudgingly the patriarch of Constantinople granted independence to the newly established national Churches, to Greece where it became the state Church, its religious monopoly preserved, as it still is, by law against propaganda of outside Churches, in 1833; to Romania, which threw off the patriarch's authority in 1864, in 1885; to Bulgaria which copied Romania's example in 1870 but which did not have its autocephalous status accepted until 1945; and to Serbia in 1879. The Serbs had actually obtained the right to build churches and schools in the 1830s, but the newly independent Church had a chequered career. Lacking a well-educated clergy, it easily fell victim to intrigue and instability. Although the Church was strongly identified with the Serbian people, it formed a comparatively uninfluential enclave in the state unlike the small principality of Montenegro where, until the marriage of the reigning prince Danilo, prince and bishop were identical. The Greek Church was afflicted constantly by tales of scandal and corruption; in 1875 three bishops were charged with simony by bribing politicians to gain high office. In response the synod charged the bishops' accusers of heresy. The bishops were often appointed by political influence; the parochial clergy were poor and ill-educated. National independence had given a fillip to monasticism, and bishops were appointed from among the monks. The most famous of the Orthodox monasteries, that of Mount Athos, was international in its composition, including Russian, Serbian and Bulgarian houses in addition to seventeen Greek ones.

Throughout the nineteenth century the Russian Orthodox Church was still the handmaid of the State, the principal official the procurator of the Holy Synod, who in the person of General Protasov (1836–55) and later of Konstantyn Pobedonostev kept the Church fully subordinate to the State, so that for the most part bishops rarely espoused liberal or critical tendencies, either in theology or politics; the westernizing cultural influences which had crept into the seminaries in the eighteenth century were eliminated in the nineteenth. Tsar Alexander I, a mystic with oecumenical leanings, had encouraged the foundation of a Bible Society along the British model, but his successor the autocratic Nicholas I forbade the circulation of the Bible in Russian because it was likely to encourage subversion. Nor was it until 1863 that the New Testament in Russian was again published, the Russian Old Testament following in 1875.

The Church was closely associated with the slavophil reaction which resulted in the oppressive treatment of religious minorities, and in particular of Roman Catholics in the Ukraine and Poland. The Slavophils, though criticized by westernized Russian liberals, and indeed in some respects suspect to the authorities, found in the Orthodox Church the reservoir of genuine Russian culture, and the preserve of the true Christian faith protected from Romanism and Protestantism. Supine in its subordination to an autocratic government as the Russian Church might appear to have been, inadequate as seems to have been the training of bishops and clergy, it played a creative part in Russian society, not merely as a custodian of tradition but as a social force. Its roots were in the countryside where the parish priest drawn from the same social milieu as his flock identified himself with his people. It was the churches, Solzhenitsyn wrote much later, that 'trip up the slopes, ascend the high hills, come down to the broad rivers, like princesses in white and red, they lift their bell rows – graceful, shapely, variegated – high over mundane timber and thatch, they nod to each other from afar, from villages that are cut off and invisible to each other they soar to the same heaven'.

Moreover, as if to compensate for the hiatus in its political and social teaching and for its traditional theology the Church preserved and promoted a rich spirituality, reflected, for instance, in the life of St Serafim of Sarov, an ascetic who abstained as far as possible from food and sleep, and spent his days in solitary contemplation, only after seventeen years of seclusion emerging in 1825 to give counsel to the stream of devotees who came to consult him. The monasteries increased greatly in number, from 452 in 1810 to 1,025 by 1914.

The core of Russian spirituality lay in a pattern of mystical devotion expressed in repetitive prayer which seems to have originated with the eighteenth-century Russian priest Paissy Velichovsky who became a monk at Athos and was eventually from 1763 abbot of the Romanian monastery of Niameto. From 1829 until its dissolution in 1923 the monastery of Optima Pustin near Tula became the headquarters of what is sometimes described as this neo-Hesychast tradition, drawing innumerable students and worshippers. In the mid-1860s its leading starets or elder, Father Ambrose, attracted scores of visitors, was consulted by the unorthodox Tolstoy and held in great admiration by Dostoevsky who embodied some of his teaching in *The Brothers Karamazov*.

The Church provided spiritual theologians of some distinction, among them Alexei Khumyakov who developed the concept of '*sobornost*' or catholicity as an essential ingredient in the Orthodox faith, an idea which was to be taken much further by Vladimir Soloviev who elaborated a quasi-mythological cosmology centred upon the divine wisdom, Sophia. In the Church where the divine wisdom is channelled through the Incarnation the believer is thus brought in touch with the cosmic whole.

Russian spirituality found expression in the writings of some of the great novelists, notably Dostoevsky who had embraced Christianity after the experience of a Siberian prison. He discovered basic evil in a totalitarian concept of authority: in his story of the Grand Inquisitor he described how Christ was himself confronted by totalitarianism. 'The preachers of materialism and atheism', he wrote prophetically, 'who proclaim man's self-sufficiency are preparing indescribable darkness and horror for mankind under the guise of renovation and resurrection.'

It was hardly surprising that, in reaction to a state-dominated Church and as an expression of unregulated mysticism, there should be an outcrop of bizarre sects. Such were the Khlisti who believed that they were inspired by the Holy Spirit and consequently were free to indulge their carnal desires. Contrariwise the Skoptsi, founded by Kondraty Selivanov, recommended castration as the avenue to salvation. The Dukhobers, located mainly in the mountain villages of the Caucasus, a small prophetic movement which taught that property and warfare were sinful, were persecuted for their refusal to do military service. Tolstoy intervened on their behalf, and they were eventually allowed to migrate to Canada where subsequently they were to scandalize the authorities by indulgence in arson and nudism.

The Church's spiritual vitality found a more normal expression in a surge of missionary activity which led in 1840 to the setting up of a bishopric for Alaska where the first bishop, John Veniaminov, Father Innokenty as he was known best, laboured in the inhospitable wastes of the Aleutian archipelago, if only with variable success. The Russian monk Makary Glukharev who in the 1830s worked in the wild Altai Mountains of central Asia actually made only 675 converts in fourteen years, but under his successors some twenty-five thousand or half the population accepted the Orthodox faith. It was perhaps paradoxical that the Russian Church should have had its greatest success in Japan under the lead of Ivan Kasatkin, the Church's adherents numbering some thirty thousand in 1912 and served by forty priests and deacons.

Reforms, Revolutions and Reaction under Pius IX

What was happening in the Russian Christian community may seem a far cry from the critical issues, seemingly as much political as religious, which were to confront the Roman Church from the middle of the century. The accession of a new Pope, Pius IX, gave a glimmer of hope to liberal Catholics. Initially he gave promise of a policy of reform, issuing an amnesty for political prisoners, setting up a commission to build railways in the Papal States, introducing street lighting by gas. He made gestures in the direction of a free press, and of lay participation in the running of the Papal States. The liberals nicknamed him the 'Papa Angelica' while Mazzini renewed his call to the Pope to 'unify Italy'. Yet in practice he had raised hopes which he would be unable to fulfil. 'Each day', Metternich told the Austrian ambassador in Paris, 'the Pope shows himself more lacking in any practical sense. Born and brought up in a liberal family, he has been formed in a bad school: a good priest, he has never turned his mind towards matters of government. Warm of heart and weak of intellect, he has allowed himself to be taken in and ensnared, since assuming the tiara, in a net from which he no longer knows how to disentangle himself, and if matters follow their natural course he will be driven out of Rome.'

In the year of revolutions, 1848, which saw Metternich himself driven from power, Metternich's words were prophetic. Pius's position was extremely difficult. He had no desire to take on the mantle of a leader in the movement for Italian unification, nor did he wish to break with Austria, a Catholic power which had long protected the Holy See. Least of all did he wish to concede his temporal sovereignty which he believed to be providentially essential for his independence as head of the Roman Church.

At first he seemed at the mercy of events. The Piedmontese who had declared war on Austria clamoured for papal support, but the Pope with some justification felt unable to give his blessing to a war fought against another Catholic power. As a consequence he broke away from the Risorgimento movement which had looked to him to give a lead in the unification of Italy. To conciliate the rising tide of opinion in Rome he had granted a constitution and appointed as his chief minister Count Pellegrino Rossi, reputed to be a free-thinker with a Protestant wife, but Rossi was murdered by democratic extremists. Vilified by Mazzini and the Republicans Pius left Rome for the Neapolitan city of Gaeta, carrying the Blessed Sacrament with him in the same ciborium that his predecessor Pius VI had used when a captive of Napoleon. In Rome a so-called constituent assembly under the guidance of Mazzini and Garibaldi voted to end the temporal power of the Pope and proclaimed a Roman republic. The French invited Pius to take up residence at Avignon; the British offered him sanctuary at Malta. But the Pope remained at Gaeta until French intervention made possible his triumphant return. 'The re-establishment of the Papal authority', General Oudinot told the crowd in St Peter's Square, 'is manifestly a work of Providence, and I am not a little proud that France should have been its instrument.'

These events made an indelible impression on the Pope's mind. Henceforth he would never be able to disengage himself from the belief that the maintenance of his temporal power was a necessity for his divinely ordained governance of the universal Church. As a consequence he was to be diverted into political entanglements which did little for his spiritual prestige. Although he regarded the Piedmontese king with some affection, it was the Piedmontese, aiming at the unification of Italy, whom he regarded as the Church's enemies. Nor did the Piedmontese help to destroy this impression by passing a series of anti-clerical laws, reorganizing the Church and dissolving some 334 religious congregations involving a personnel of some 5,500 people. The Pope was forced into dependence on the French emperor, Napoleon III, who saw that to placate the French Church would strengthen his own position, though he was averse to the extreme ultramontanism injudiciously propagated by the papal nuncio Saccini. In September 1864 the French emperor concluded an agreement with the Piedmontese promising to withdraw from Rome within two years on condition that Piedmont promised not to attack the Papal States. The temporal sovereignty of the Pope was based on political sufferance.

It was in such a situation that the Pope issued the *Syllabus of Errors*, a widespread condemnation of the ills which seemed to threaten the integrity of the Church. Elicited more particularly by the anti-clerical legislation of the Piedmontese government, the list represented the Pope's deep conviction that the spread of liberalism and nationalism brought the 'corruption of manners and minds', subversion and infidelity. The most telling of the eighty errors condemned was that 'the Roman pontiff can and should reconcile and harmonize himself with progress, with liberalism and with recent [viz. modern] civilization'. Liberal Catholics, Montalembert in France, Acton in England, Döllinger in Germany, recoiled with alarm at this public embrace of political and social reaction, underlining the charge that Rome was a bastion of insulated conservatism.

Pius IX would not so have interpreted it. Of limited intellect, surrounded by men, some of them, like the papal secretary of state Antonelli, much more worldly than himself, he saw his task in increasingly apocalyptic terms. 'You tell me to have confidence in the Emperor [Napoleon III],' he told Antonelli, 'but I repeat to you that I trust only God and that He is my own support.' He was calling the heavenly battalions to his aid. In 1854 he had proclaimed the Immaculate Conception of the Blessed Virgin to be a dogma. Although there was no scriptural support for the belief that Mary was miraculously exempt from the taint of sin, since the Middle Ages it had long been an article of devotion. But it was symptomatic of his intransigence that Pius should have proclaimed the belief upon his own authority without consultation with the bishops.

His high conception of his office reached its summation in the proclamation of papal infallibility, enunciated in the bull *Pastor Aeternus* which declared that the Pope was infallible when he spoke *ex cathedra*, that is when, exercising the office of pastor and teacher of all Christians, he defines with his supreme apostolic authority a doctrine concerning faith or morals to be held by the universal Church. This doctrine was not new; it had been taught by Cardinal Bellarmine in the early seventeenth century, but as its critics were later to make plain it was not well based on historical grounds.

Even before the *Syllabus of Errors* had been published, Pius IX began to consider the advisability of calling a general council, the first since Trent, by which the doctrine of papal infallibility could be promulgated as the voice of the Church. The summons to the council made on 29 June 1867, when the bishops were meeting at Rome to celebrate the supposed eighteenth centenary of the martyrdom of the apostles Peter and Paul, defined its object as 'to bring necessary and salutary remedies to the many evils whereby the Church is oppressed'. Its original terms of reference were wide: 'the integrity of the faith, the gravity of divine worship, the eternal salvation of men, the discipline of the secular and regular clergy, and its wholesome and solid culture, the observance of ecclesiastical laws, the amendment of manners and the instruction of Christian youth'. Eventually the discussion was short-circuited, partly because of the deteriorating political situation which threatened war between France and Germany, and partly because of the Pope's eagerness to ensure the proclamation of papal infallibility.

While the council was not actually rigged, it was manipulated so that in spite of a strong minority opposition, which included some of the more learned among the bishops such as the Church historian Hefele of Rothenburg, the result was a foregone conclusion. While few denounced the doctrine as unacceptable, many thought that it was inexpedient, among them the French bishop, Dupanloup of Orlèans, who held that it was already so widely believed that it was unnecessary to promulgate it, particularly since doing so would have the effect of antagonizing contemporary governments and making relations with the Orthodox and the Protestants more difficult. Moriarty, the bishop of Kerry, admitted to Newman that as a professor of theology he had taught that papal infallibility was a true theological opinion, but he was opposed to its declaration as an article of faith. On 3 February 1870 Moriarty informed Newman that:

> We have at the utmost 200 [bishops] on our side; but we represent the Church *militant*, in Hungary, Germany, half of France, England (except Westminster [Manning] and Beverley, perhaps another), all North America. From Ireland I am only sure of one with me. The majority represent the Curia Romana, Italy, Spain, Belgium, Ireland, South America. It is composed of men who have not come into conflict with the unbelieving mind, or into contact with the intellectual mind of the time. When I read the school of theology in which they were trained I am not surprised that they treat every doubter as a heretic.

The Pope's supporters were intransigent in attitude. Their opponents complained that their speeches were deliberately curtailed. But the real pressures used to ensure the acceptance of the decree were psychological. Opposition smelt of heresy and treason. The Pope who should surely have taken a neutral stance, became identified with his own cause. Always excitable, possibly a legacy of early epilepsy, he showed plainly enough where his preferences lay. To the Dominican cardinal Guidi who suggested that the Pope should consult the bishops as witnesses to the Church's tradition, the Pope responded 'Witnesses of tradition; there's only one; that's me.' 'The Pope', the English bishop Ullathorne of Birmingham, wrote, 'takes every opportunity of expressing his views on the infallibility, both in audience and in letters that at once get into the papers.'

The fathers of the council pressed on in the debate in the darkening European scene as the clash between France and Prussia presaged war. Most of the opponents of the measure did not wait for the vote but with some relief packed their bags and made for home; 'we return, therefore, without delay to our flocks, to whom, after so long an absence, the apprehensions of war and their most urgent spiritual wants render us so necessary'. When the vote was taken as thunder growled and lightning flashed 533 bishops voted placet and only two, the American Fitzgerald of Little Rock and the Neapolitan Riccio of Cajazzo registered a negative. The following day war broke out between France and Prussia.

What followed immediately was something of an anti-climax. All the critics among the bishops eventually submitted, though the last to do so, the Bosnian Strossmayer, waited until 1872. There was indeed a minor schism, led by the German Church historian Ignaz Döllinger who had voiced his views strongly in the *Letters of Janus* and the *Letters of Quirinus*. Excommunicated for refusing to submit, he joined the Old Catholics, a group of German, Austrian and Swiss Catholics who had seceded from the

Church rather than accept infallibility, and was consecrated as bishop by the Church of Utrecht which had separated from Rome in 1724. In practice most Catholics took the doctrine in their stride, uncertain as to its meaning, for in some sense the dogma remained a dead letter.

The great powers fearing a dangerous attempt to bolster papal authority, were uneasy at what was happening. Prince Hohenlohe, the foreign minister of Bavaria, had written on 9 April 1869 that 'it is evident that this pretension [i.e. infallibility] raised to a dogma would pass beyond the purely spiritual domain, and would become a question eminently political, raising the power of the Pope, even on the temporal side above all princes and peoples of Christendom'. The Prussian Bismarck and the Austrian von Beust, both Protestants, expressed their concern. The English prime minister, W.E. Gladstone, issued a portentous broadside: 'Rome had refurbished and paraded every rusty tool she was fondly thought to have disused.' The Vatican tried to allay such fears which were in practice groundless, for while the Pope intended a confirmation of his spiritual authority, he had not foreseen any extension of his temporal jurisdiction.

It was indeed plain that the Pope's temporal power was contracting to vanishing point as the Piedmontese occupied Rome, a sequel to the withdrawal of the French garrison only a fortnight after papal infallibility was promulgated as an article of faith. The papal army, numbering some eighteen thousand, had made a token resistance, in part to underline that the Pope had been obliged to surrender to brute force. The empress Eugénie had despatched a French warship to evacuate the Pope, if he wished, to France, but Pius preferred to remain as a voluntary captive in the Vatican which together with St John Lateran and Castel Gandolfo were all that were left to him. Since he refused to negotiate with the new Italian government, the government imposed a unilateral settlement. The Law of Guarantees treated the Pope as a full sovereign, allowed him his own postal and telegraph service and allocated him an annual sum of 3 million lire which he refused. Although Italian anti-clericals criticized the settlement as too generous, it was to govern relations between Italy and the papacy until the Lateran Treaty of 1929.

THE *KULTURKAMPF*

Although the treatment meted out to the aged Pope captured the sympathies of Catholics and Protestants alike, secular governments were encouraged to take advantage of the Church's weakness to bring it more fully within the compass of the state. Bismarck, intent on limiting the influence of the Catholic Church which in areas like Bavaria and the newly acquired Alsace-Lorraine could work to Prussia's disadvantage, took strong measures to curb the Church's privileges. His struggle on behalf of the Prussian State to contain the powers of the Roman Catholic Church came to be known as the *Kulturkampf*, literally the battle for secular culture. In 1871 he suppressed the Catholic department of the Prussian ministry of Public Worship. Next year he appointed Paul Falk as Minister of Public Worship and Education. Falk introduced the May Laws which instituted a Supreme Ecclesiastical Court under the control of the State, ordered all candidates for the priesthood to pass through a state gymnasium, brought all Church seminaries under State control and made civil marriage obligatory in Prussia. The Pope responded with a strong condemnation in the encyclical *Quod Nunquam* (1875). Bismarck broke off diplomatic relations with the Vatican and urged the Italian government to strengthen the Law of Guarantees; the Church was deprived of its financial support from the State and the religious were ordered to leave the country. The Church had strongly resisted the government's policy. Some five out of the eleven Prussian bishops spent several months in prison in 1874–5; more than a thousand parishes were left without their pastors.

But Bismarck's eagerness for conflict began to wane, in part because the issues were bound up with internal problems. Bismarck's broadside against the Church was not merely provoked by the doctrine of infallibility but by the rise of a Centre or Catholic Party led by Ludwig Windthorst which championed the independence of the papacy and opposed Bismarck's party, the National Liberals. The German chancellor was above all a political pragmatist. He had underestimated the degree of Catholic opposition, and now wished to win Catholic support to quash a more dangerous enemy, the Social Democrats. The reconciliation between Church and State, and the abandonment of anti-Catholic laws, apart from the expulsion of the Jesuits, was not to be complete until Leo XIII succeeded Pius IX; nor indeed was the damage to the Church ever fully repaired.

The *Kulturkampf* gave a stimulus to anti-Catholic legislation in other countries, in Switzerland, Austria, Belgium and Italy. In Italy the fall of the right-wing government of Visconti Venosta and Minghetti and its replacement by the more radical administration of Agostino Depretis, who sympathized with Bismarck's anti-Catholic policy, led to a new crop of anti-clerical legislation. The Clerical Abuses Bill of 1876 imposed penalties on the clergy for criticism of the state; outdoor religious processions were banned. Pius, who never made any attempt to win over moderate opinion, responded with a stinging encyclical in which he urged Catholics to restore his rights and denounced the actions of the Italian government as a threat to the freedom of the Church.

THE ROMAN CATHOLIC CHURCH IN FRANCE AFTER 1870

The French situation was more complicated. In the aftermath of defeat in war Paris had been taken over by the radical Commune which initiated a brutal persecution of religion. Churches were looted and secularized; nuns were accused of monstrous crimes. Among the dead were the archbishop of Paris and some fifty priests. But after the ending of the Commune there was a conservative reaction in favour of the Church. The National Assembly would have liked to restore the monarchy in the person of the Bourbon pretender, the Comte de Chambord, but de Chambord refused to allow the substitution of the fleur-de-lys by the republican tricolour. 'Henry IV said Paris was worth a mass'; said the Pope, who had himself encouraged de Chambord to accept, commented sadly, 'but Henry V finds France not worth a napkin.' The Church, by its support for the legitimist claims and the French bishops' support of the Pope's claims to temporal power, had made a disastrous alignment with conservatism. Its political stance in the decade which followed confirmed the republicans in their belief that the Church was a dyed-in-the-wool reactionary institution. Because the Church had nailed its flag to the monarchist mast, the Abbe Frémont wrote, 'the clergy of France has finally convinced everyone who believes in things popular and democratic that between the Church on the one hand and progress, the Republic and the future on the other, there is no relationship possible but the most deadly hatred'.

The relations between the French Church and State were governed by the Concordat of 1801 which had declared Catholicism to be the religion of 'the great majority of French citizens'. The State provided funds, the *budget des cultes*, for the payment of the clergy, but was granted the right of appointment to the bishoprics. Appended to the Concordat were the Organic Articles recalling the Gallican Articles of 1682 which could be used to delimit clerical power; but were in fact rarely put into operation. Until the end of the Second Empire official relations between Church and State had remained amicable since it was to the advantage of both to work in cooperation.

The Church's influence in France was, however, plainly on the wane as anti-clericalism and unbelief made inroads. Catholicism remained strongly entrenched in Brittany, Normandy, Maine, Anjou, the Vendée, the Massif Central, Alsace-Lorraine (which in 1871 had become German territory) and the Franche Comté, but elsewhere support for the Church had dwindled. Paris in particular had seen a marked decline in Church attendance; in 1841, 47 per cent of those eligible to take their Easter communion had done so; half a century later the percentage had fallen to 16 per cent. What happened in Paris was repeated in the growing industrial towns. There was a mass of nominal Catholics who may have made their Easter communion but in many parishes there was an almost total loss of male support and the congregations had dwindled to a few elderly women. 'The spirit of the masses', so it was reported by the *Procureur-général* in 1860, 'can be summarised in two words, indifference or hostility to the clergy.' The Church's main support came from the better-educated, more affluent classes, local nobility, magistrates, landed proprietors; but among intellectuals, doctors and lawyers anti-clericalism was rife. The anti-clericals depicted the clergy as schoolmasters intent on condemning the moral failings of their parishioners and often themselves falling into scandal. They described the obligation of celibacy as unnatural. Loyalty to the Pope was unpatriotic.

The Church had steadily lost ground. Its bishops, no longer drawn from the aristocracy, were generally well educated but were separated from the parochial clergy over whom they exercised an arbitrary authority. The priests, drawn mainly from the peasant and working classes, were educated in seminaries where the curriculum was outmoded and old-fashioned. Yet the Church still possessed substantial influence. The Loi Falloux of 1850 had permitted the formation of Church schools, which by 1870 were instructing some 40 per cent of the nation's children. In 1875 the Church was allowed to set up its own universities. There were some 51,000 parish priests, 116 congregations of men (which had increased from 59 in 1856) and by 1875 some 127,000 nuns. The Church had a strong ultramontanist journal in *L'Univers* edited by the uncompromising Louis Veuillot. Another gesture which inspired the faithful had been the erection of a great church on the hill of Montmartre dedicated to the Sacred Heart, to the building of which the Pope had contributed. But all this afforded no compensation for the Church's apparent failure to win over the working labourers and peasants or to overcome the challenge of anti-clericalism and unbelief. Its association with right-wing politics laid up massive trouble for the future. The resignation of Marshal MacMahon in January 1879 was to unleash an anti-Catholic campaign which would continue unabated for decades.

When Pius IX died on 7 February 1878 it was the end of an era. For all the dark shadows which embraced the Church during his pontificate, and for which his intransigent conservatism and political ineptitude must bear some responsibility, he had won the regard and affection of countless Catholics. He was in some ways the Queen Victoria of the papacy, a rather ordinary, courteous, good-humoured man, notorious as a begetter of puns both good (as when, during the Vatican Council, referring to the extent to which he was subsidizing the expenses of some of the bishops, he said wryly 'Non so se il Papa uscirà di questo Concilio fallible od infallible, ma questo è certo che sarà fallito' ['I do not know if the Pope will go out of this Council fallible or infallible, but this is certain that he will be bankrupt'] and bad (as when after hearing of Napoleon's surrender at Sedan he said 'La France a perdu ses dents'). Pope for thirty-two years, an even longer reign than that of his medieval predecessor Alexander III, he had tried to fulfil his task to the best of his ability. But he seemed steadily to have lost his grip on reality, and his tenure was a political disaster for the Church. His outlook was myopic. He failed to come to terms with the real social and intellectual needs of the Church and laid up for it problems in the future.

Yet his pontificate had had another side. He had reasserted the spiritual authority of his office. A man of prayer, he had stimulated devotion among the faithful for whom he seemed a true father in God. Pilgrimages gave an opportunity for the promotion of homely piety: in France, for instance, to the cult of the Sacred Heart at Paray-le-Monial; to La Salette, an Alpine village near Grenoble where on 19 September 1846 the Blessed Virgin had appeared to a peasant boy and girl; and to Lourdes, where in 1858 another peasant girl, Bernadette Soubirous, had a vision in a grotto where a miraculous healing spring appeared. For the ordinary Catholic, far removed from the world of high politics, Pius IX appeared simply as a good priest. The Catholic hierarchy had been restored in England, Scotland and Holland. The College of Cardinals, less dominated by Italians, had become more widely representative. In 1846 there had been eight foreign and fifty-four Italian cardinals; in 1878 there were twenty-five foreign and thirty-nine Italian cardinals. Even more important if Europe remained the centre of Church government, the Catholic Church had spread into every continent. It was outside Europe that Christianity grew, creating a worldwide Church.

THE MISSIONARY CHURCHES

The missionary endeavour of the Church in the eighteenth century had been unimpressive. The Roman Church's missions to the Far East had more or less deliquesced as a result of discord between the Vatican and the Jesuits over the appropriate strategy for conversion. The charter of the British Society for the Propagation of the Gospel, founded in 1701, laid down that its object was to provide for the spiritual needs of British people overseas, and to evangelize the non-Christian races of the world, but the actual scope of what was achieved was slight. The Moravian Brethren, imbued with a genuine missionary spirit, sponsored small missions in 1732 to the Negroes of St Thomas in the West Indies, then to Greenland and later to South Africa. The Danish Lutherans had a mission station at Tranquebar in India.

It was, however, not until the closing years of the eighteenth century that missionary societies really took off, simultaneously with the French Revolution and the Napoleonic Wars. The foundation of these societies may be seen specifically as an aspect of the Evangelical revival in England, for they had strong supporters among its leaders, notably William Wilberforce and other members of the Clapham Group. Zachary Macaulay, who had also been to the fore in the campaign against slavery, became in 1795 the governor of Sierra Leone, a colony founded for freed slaves. Missionary enthusiasm embodied in such organizations as the societies for the reformation of manners and for founding church schools was itself an expression of the deep conviction that real religion was the best antidote to the tide of subversion and infidelity which had engulfed the world in its present troubles. An evangelical John Venn presided over the Church Missionary Society set up in 1799. The London Missionary Society was founded by a group of Anglicans and Dissenters. The Baptist Missionary Society had been started at Kettering in 1792 by ministers from the

Northamptonshire Association of Particular Baptist Churches, in part stimulated by the revival of religion known as the Great Awakening which had been taking place in America. The British and Foreign Bible Society was founded in 1804 to distribute the Bible at home and abroad. Similar organizations sprang up in Germany, France, Scandinavia, Holland and the USA. The Roman Church under the umbrella of the Congregation for the Propagation of the Faith was equally active. The New World was about to be called in to redress the balance of the old. Missionary societies attracted the warm support of church-goers in all denominations. The annual income of the Church Missionary Society which had rarely exceeded £3,000 before 1813 amounted to £14,000 in 1814, reached £34,000 by 1823–4 and by 1843 topped £115,000. The missionary box was to be found on many a sideboard or table in working-class as well as middle-class homes.

It can hardly be doubted that the motivating force in missionary work was basically religious, to preach the gospel and to convert the heathen to the true religion. The salvation of souls was its primary objective. The Baptist missionary William Carey, who declared 'Expect great things from God and attempt great things for God', had sailed for Bengal in 1793 and became an indefatigable evangelist, translating the Bible into Bengali as well as parts of it into some twenty-four other languages. In the pursuit of their ideal missionaries were to suffer substantial hardship and often displayed great courage with few rewards. Constantly they and their wives fell victim at a youthful age to the unhealthy tropical climate. Sixteen out of twenty-seven missionaries working in Sierra Leone died before 1817. Moreover, they had often to face the hostility of those among whom they were working, even to the point of death. In Madagascar, for instance, Queen Ranavalona ordered her officials to 'seize every Christian . . . and without trial bind them hand and foot; dig a pit on the spot and then pour boiling water on them and bury them'. As they lived in an alien society the missionaries often failed to make many converts. In eighteen years Alexander Duff of the Church of Scotland made only thirty-three converts, while when the American Congregationalists left Thailand in 1849 they could register only a single baptism. Ten years later, after having been in Thailand since 1840, the Presbyterians baptized their first convert, Nai Chine. The Utrecht Missionary Society which entered New Guinea in 1861 made twenty converts in twenty-five years. If to later historians the expansion of the missionary Churches was one of the great success stories of modern times it cannot have appeared so to many a missionary. Yet, carried by the missionaries, Christianity invaded the non-Christian world of Africa and Asia like a new-found virus.

Inevitably most missionaries had a limited insight into what they were trying to accomplish. Most of them were probably less well educated than their contemporaries at home. While some spent a great deal of time translating the Bible into native languages, they were not otherwise fluent in communicating their ideas which were difficult to translate into a native tongue. They tended too to be ignorant of the culture and religions of the people among whom they worked. Fundamentalist in their interpretation of scripture, they regarded all native religions as a form of idolatry. Themselves the product of a White civilization, which they esteemed to be Christian, they took from it its conventional features, building churches and meeting houses in the European style and obliging their converts to don trousers and skirts. The forms of religious service, though translated into a native language, were reproductions of the familiar liturgy of their home church, replete with hymns. They sought to exercise a strong superintendence over the moral lives of their converts, banning polygamy (which was, for instance, a natural ingredient in some African societies, the number of wives denoting a man's importance) and upholding Sunday observance. They were, if unconsciously, imposing the habits and ethos of the White European Churches which they took as their model on native cultures and religions which they only partially understood and for which they had only little sympathy. The setting up of separate Christian mission stations sometimes as a refuge for freed slaves, with their own stores, schools, hospitals and churches, led to the segregation of converts from their own tribal societies. It was inevitable that Christian missions should be equated in the minds of the natives with political domination by the European colonialists.

Many missionaries believed the native people to be naturally inferior to the Whites. 'The negro brain', a contemporary anthropologist wrote, 'bears a great resemblance to a European female or child's brain, and this approaches the ape far more than the European while the negroes approach the ape still further.' At best the missionary's attitude tended to be paternalistic, treating the natives as children. It was a long time before the Churches were ready to entrust the natives with any responsibility or to consider their ordination. The first Black African bishop, Samuel Crowther, a freed slave who had studied at the Church Missionary Society College at Islington before ordination by the bishop of London in 1843, was made a bishop in 1865; but Crowther's church in the Niger broke up after being rent by internal friction and charges of corruption, so confirming the conviction of many missionaries that natives were not well suited to leadership. In his latter years Crowther was treated unjustly by his White colleagues. It was to be long before the European-based missionary societies relinquished their responsibility for native Churches.

While it would not be wholly correct to state that the Christian religion simply marched in the van of expanding colonialism – first the gun, then the cross, there is no doubt that the occupation and colonization of native territory did operate to the advantage of the missionary Churches. Colonial overlordship replaced what might well have been a hostile, pagan, as well as sometimes a cruel and oppressive, regime by a form of government which, paternalistic as it might be, stood for elementary justice and order, even if there were some notable exceptions like Leopold II's exploitation of the Congo. The missionaries, some of whom were strongly critical of colonial regimes, came to accept that a takeover by the mother country might be a necessary preliminary to the Christianizing process which they believed to be essential to the welfare of the native.

Nor can there be any doubt that colonization itself helped to promote the acceptance of the Christian faith, since for many native peoples Christianity seemed another expression of White power of which they stood in awe. It is not, indeed, easy to explain satisfactorily why the Christian Church proved as successful as it was to be in attracting converts. As in much earlier history the acceptance of the faith by the great men of the tribe, as in Anglo-Saxon England, could be a determinant. Attracted by the glamour of the Church and by a belief in the superior power of the Christian God, and the rewards that he could bestow on his followers in after life, native chieftains were persuaded to accept the Christian faith, so opening the way for the conversion of their people. The conversion of Tonga's King George, as of Tahiti's King Pomare in 1819, brought in train the conversion of their people, in Tonga's case to Methodism. In Fiji the conversion of the chief Thakombau, previously an enemy to the missionaries, led in 1854 to the success of the Christian mission. In the early history of missionary enterprise in New Zealand the support which the Maori chieftain Hongi gave to the mission provided a vital factor. But when Hongi was brought to England, where he was received by George IV, he took the opportunity to buy guns with which on his return he defeated, enslaved and ate – for the Maoris were then cannibals – his enemies.

The missionaries brought 'goodies': education, medical help, hospitals, material support, the prospect of a job, all of which were an inducement to a poor people to accept instruction in the faith. Statistics showed that those who lived in the Moravian mission stations in South Africa had a much higher life expectancy as well as a better quality of life. It would, however, be too cynical to suppose that many did not in fact find in the Christian faith a resolvent of long-standing fears, and a spiritual satisfaction and happiness which they had not before experienced. Doubtless some were impressed by the unselfish, caring lives of many of the missionaries. They were brought to share in the love and lustre of Christian living, and to a sense of divine purpose.

The tangled interstices of missionary history may be seen at work in the complex story of the conversion to the Christian faith of the Pacific island of Tahiti to which some thirty missionaries, most of them strict Evangelicals, sailed in 1796 under the auspices of the London Missionary Society. At first they had little success, for the virtues they sought to communicate had little attraction for the pleasure-loving natives. By 1799 many missionaries had died and others had 'gone native' while the natives held the missionaries responsible for the spread of disease. But the native chief Pomare I, who aspired to control the whole island, realized that the missionaries could help him achieve this objective. In the civil war which followed the missionaries helped to supply the king with ammunition and gave their support to his successor, Pomare II, whom Herman Melville described as a 'sad debauchee and a drunkard, and even charged with unnatural crimes'. After three years the young prince was driven into exile, but returned by force of arms and was baptized. His subjects for the most part followed suit, for the recalcitrant were promptly executed. The New Testament was translated into Tahitian, schools were introduced, observance of the Sabbath was made obligatory, dancing and strong drink banned, sexual irregularities punished and Church attendance made compulsory. But the missionaries could not control the anchorage at Papeete where men from the whalers took advantage of the favours of the native girls, making it, as one missionary critic put it, a 'vortex of iniquity, the Sodom of the Pacific'.

After the death of Pomare II there was a renewal of political instability during which a variant Christian sect, the Mamaia, came into existence, challenging the established mission, retaining the sacraments but allowing erotic dancing, drink and polygamy. Then in 1836 French Roman Catholic missionaries arrived on the island to the anger of the Protestants who managed to get Roman Catholic teaching made illegal and the Roman fathers expelled, an arbitrary action which even aroused the wrath of the British foreign secretary Lord Palmerston. The missionaries sent by the British, the French priest declared, 'appear to have undertaken, of late, to invade all the islands of the Pacific Ocean. The English government favours them for ends purely political.' Yet in practice as the British government had insufficient interest in the island to colonize it, it was the French who took over in 1842. The English Protestant missionaries found their activities restricted and eventually withdrew, leaving the field to the French Roman Catholics.

The divisions between the different forms of the Christian faith must have often confused the would-be convert. In India Roman Catholics were charged with being more concerned to convert the Protestants than the heathen, partly on the grounds that the Protestants as heretics condemned to hell were in much greater need of salvation than the heathen who would rest in limbo. In Indo-China where a strong Roman Catholic community had been created the French positively discouraged Protestant missions just as the Dutch in Indonesia were to do to the Roman Catholics.

Africa was to be the most fertile field for the propagation of Christianity in the nineteenth century. Christianity was not, of course, new to Africa. In the north-east corner the ancient Coptic Churches of Egypt and Ethiopia had survived, largely isolated from the outside world. The first Ethiopian bishop, Frumentius of Axum, had been consecrated by Athanasius, the patriarch of Alexandria in the fourth century, and for long the Ethiopian Church was subordinate to the patriarch who appointed the abuna or head of the Ethiopian Church, which only achieved its full independence in 1959. The Coptic churches, which had once strongly championed the orthodox Nicene creed, leaning backwards in their orthodoxy had strayed in the fifth century into the heresy of Monophysitism of which they were henceforth to be the surviving adherents. So the Ethiopian Church followed the Coptic liturgy, developed its own customs (which, for instance, included the sacrifice of a live animal at the dedication of a church) and absorbed others, some seemingly pagan, like the barbaric dances and the beating of drums, and others judaic, for the Church observed both the Sabbath and the Sunday and distinguished between meats which were clean and unclean.

In the seventeenth century the Jesuits made some headway in Ethiopia, for years isolated from the Christianity community in the west yet rumoured to be the land of a great Christian prince, Prester John. In 1622 the Ethiopian king Sisinnius accepted the Roman faith, but the reconciliation with Rome was short-lived, since the Ethiopians were deeply affronted by the injudicious and radical reforms which the Jesuit patriarch Mendez tried to impose on the Church. The Jesuits suffered expulsion and execution, and the Church relapsed into its traditional form, remaining strongly nationalistic and theologically divisive, traits further exemplified in the eighteenth century when another new heresy arose, that of the Three Births (the eternal generation by the Father, the birth from the Virgin Mary, and the Unction of the Holy Spirit), which caused protracted controversy. The Church suffered again in the twentieth century: from 1936 under the Italian occupation (during which the spectre of reunion with Rome was again raised), and then after the overthrow of the restored Emperor Haile Selassie in 1974 under the strongly anti-clerical Marxist government, but it was to re-emerge still a fundamental if suffering part of Ethiopian society. The Coptic Church in Egypt had an attenuated existence for while in much earlier years its theological affinities with the faith of Islam had won it tolerance from the Muslim rulers, in the late twentieth century it has become on occasions the target of violent Islamic fundamentalism.

In East and West Africa mission stations had been established under the aegis of Portugal, the Capuchins in Angola where they were said to have baptized 600,000 people between 1645 and 1700, and the Jesuits in Mozambique which was constituted a papal vicariate in 1612; but for these native Africans the Church became identified with Portuguese domination.

The French Lazarists worked, though with very variable success in the island of Madagascar where the London Missionary Society was to penetrate in 1818, winning the favour of the king Radama; but in 1835 his successor Queen Ranavalona reversed his policy and initiated a long and cruel persecution which lasted until her death in 1861.

Christian missions had secured a foothold in the early nineteenth century on the West African coast. Sierra Leone had been purchased by the British government from the native chieftain Naimbarna in 1787 to provide a settlement for Blacks who had served with the British in the American War of Independence; their numbers were augmented by freed slaves, some rescued by British ships from foreign slavers. The Sierra Leone Company had been formed in 1791 through the efforts of William Wilberforce and his fellow Evangelicals to promote the 'civilization of Africa and the abolition of the slave trade', but at first it was a rumbustious settlement, totally unintegrated since the slaves represented a multitude of races. It was transformed into an effective colony through the evangelical enthusiasm of its governor Zachary Macaulay, while Walter John, who came as a missionary in 1817, tried hard to encourage the evangelical virtues: industry, paternalism and piety. Gradually, after 1860, the churches were to be handed over to native pastors, and thereafter, in part because of the inroads made by Islam, the influence of the Churches was to decline.

In 1828 the Basel mission, supported by Danish traders, started work in Ghana, then the Gold Coast, but with little success until the missionaries developed the future colony's economy through the cultivation of cocoa. Christianity in Nigeria was an export from Sierra Leone. Both Anglicans and Methodists, the latter led by Thomas Freeman, the son of an African father and an English mother, worked steadily in the Niger area while the United Presbyterian Church set up a mission in Calabar in 1851. While the Churches made some progress in the work of conversion in west Africa, the process was a slow one, and the future came to depend upon the annexation of these territories by colonial powers. Islam remained a strong, proselytizing force, but there were in Africa until the middle of the nineteenth century, and even later, vast areas, as yet unexplored, out of reach of the Christian Churches.

THE CHURCHES IN SOUTH AFRICA

South Africa was to be the launching pad for missionary exploration into the interior. The Christian Church had been established there with the arrival of the Dutch in 1652, their religious needs supplied by the pastors of the Dutch Reformed Church appointed by the Dutch East India Company and subject until 1795 to the *classis* or presbytery of Amsterdam. There were, however, neither the men nor the money to undertake mission work among the native people, who were mainly Hottentots, for there were only seven congregations in 1800; nor indeed did the Dutch Calvinists believe in the baptism of the heathen, holding that the practice should be reserved for the children of Christian parents. Although the French Huguenots were required to conform to the Reformed Church, German Lutherans were allowed to practise their faith, nor was the Reformed Church as yet segregationalist for mixed marriages were not banned until the synod of 1857. But from the first arrival of non-Dutch missionaries there was growing hostility between the different faiths, and the collision was to produce ultimately the concept of apartheid; it was also to push the missionary Church into expanding its activities beyond the dominant White periphery into tribal lands to the north and east.

In 1737 the Moravian Georg Schmidt had arrived at Cape Town, settling at Genadendal where, though he was ignorant of their language, he worked among the Hottentots, but in 1744 he returned to Europe. Late in 1792 three other Moravian pastors, Hendrick Masveld, Daniel Schwinn and Johann Kuhhel, restored the mission at Genadendal which they made a self-supporting community, with such success that it soon had seven mission stations and 7,100 members, some 28 missionaries and 13 native settlements. The Moravians were supported by the British, who at the invitation of the exiled prince of Orange, had occupied the colony between 1795 and 1803. Between 1804 and 1806 the Cape returned to the Batavian government whose governor, J.A. de Mist, issued an edict of religious toleration, allowing, however, the Dutch Reformed Church to exercise control, and restricting the British missionaries to native areas. The British gradually modified this policy after South Africa became a British colony.

Although there was a steady influx of British settlers, some five thousand arriving in 1820, the Dutch formed the majority of the population, most of them farmers who employed cheap native labour chiefly Hottentots, in conditions not very far removed from slavery (the employment of slave labour was itself illegal). They extended their farms towards the frontier area where they came into conflict with native tribes, more especially the Bantus who were less assimilable than the Hottentots. Without prejudice the colonial government continued to subsidize all Churches. In 1830 the Dutch Reformed Church, with some eighteen congregations and nineteen clergy received £4,000 (by 1860 it was £9,000); the Church of England with six clergy and six congregations, £2,000; the Roman Catholics and the Scottish Presbyterians £200 a piece. In 1843 the Dutch Reformed Church was virtually made separate from the state, though it was not until 1875 that the state ceased to subsidize the Churches. The foundations were then laid for what was religiously to be a pluralistic society.

The first missionaries, mainly from the London Missionary Society, soon appeared, enthusiastic, pietistic, in some sense spiritually arrogant, but with a strong sense of justice for the deprived. Johannes Theodorus Vanderkemp, a Presbyterian minister and a reformed rake who had been a Dutch cavalry officer for sixteen years, arrived in 1799 and set up a settlement of Hottentots at Bethelsdorp where he gave the landless Blacks a place of refuge. Unkempt in appearance, independent in mind, deeply committed to his evangelical principles, he was shocked by the Boers' treatment of the natives, in his turn arousing their hostility. He had tried first to establish contact with the Kaffirs, the cattle-raising Bantus, and though the Kaffirs' king's sister tried to seduce him, the Kaffirs did not respond to his message. He had greater success among the Hottentots whom he taught to read and write. Going native and marrying at the age of fifty-six a seventeen-year-old Malagasy slave girl did not, however, add to his reputation. The Boer farmers managed to interpret the labour laws in their own favour, and a much harassed Vanderkemp died of apoplexy in 1812.

In 1820 John Philip arrived at the Cape as Superintendent of the London Missionary Society, making his settlement a refuge for the Hottentots, leading the Boer farmers to complain that he was causing a labour shortage. He championed native rights, managing with the influence of his evangelical friends who included the colonial secretary Lord Glenelg to get some alleviation of the law. 'In the course of about a century and a half,'

Philip wrote, 'the Hottentots had been despoiled of their lands, robbed or cajoled out of their flocks and herds, and with a few exceptions, reduced to personal servitude.' For the natives, degraded by circumstances, self-help and religion were in Philip's view the main panacea for their ills.

The missionaries were to take the gospel further afield to areas which were rapidly becoming a no man's land between regions settled by African tribes, notably the war-like Zulus and Matabeles, and territory under colonial control. In 1825 Robert Moffatt, a Methodist, formidable and dour, established a mission station at Kuruman in Bechuanaland which he was to convert from a wilderness and to make a flourishing centre of Church activity. Moffatt built a church and translated the Bible into Sichuana and though the Africans were at first slow to respond they were pressurized by Moffatt's indomitable energy into a flourishing community.

It was to Moffatt's mission station that David Livingstone (who was to marry his daughter Mary) came in 1840. As a boy Livingstone had worked as a piecer in a textile mill at Blantyre but by going to night school he had educated himself and attended medical classes at Glasgow in the hope of working as a medical missionary in China. Foiled by the outbreak of the Opium Wars he was sent by the London Missionary Society to Africa where his restless curiosity and desire to push further afield led him to move from Kuruman, first at Mobätsa in 1843 and then to Kolobeng. In 1852 his mission station there was destroyed by the Boers who had accused him of being a gun runner. Although Livingstone was no such thing, he had supplied some arms to the Bechuana chief Sechele both to defend himself against the Boers and to help in the hunt for food.

The tensions between the Boers and the missionaries had become a continuous part of everyday life. Boer resentment against colonial rule led in 1836 to the Great Trek and the subsequent foundation of the independent Boer republics of the Transvaal and the Orange Free State. While many of the pastors of the Dutch Reformed Church disapproved of the trek, the trekkers themselves endowed their exodus with a semi-religious significance, a replica of the Israelites' flight into the Promised Land, for many of them were pious Bible-reading men and women, members of an evangelical sect, the Doppers, so rigidly puritanical that they even objected to the singing of hymns. What at first developed was primarily a lay religion, patriarchal in character, biblical, austere in behaviour. But the Boers had a deep sense that they were a 'gathered people', fulfilling a destiny in accordance with a divine purpose, upheld, as the Puritans had been, by a belief in a special covenant with God. 'Like Moses,' said Gerhardus Maritz in 1838, 'I have seen the promised land but am not destined to live in it.' The constitution of Wynburg in 1837 made the Dutch Reformed Church the national Church of the first voortrekker state; it also explicitly condemned the work of the British missionary societies. In the Transvaal the Dutch Reformed Church was split into two halves, the Hervormde Kerk, and the Gereformeerde Kerk which remained loyal to the Dutch Reformed Church in its wider form. But it was the Hervormde Kerk which became the established Church in the Boer republics, its clergy paid by the State and its teachings based on the Synod of Dort, virtually refusing toleration to Roman Catholic or Protestant bodies. In 1858 the Hervormde Kerk had declared that 'this nation will not have any equality of blacks with whites not in Church not in state'. While the Boers could not deny the premise that God had created all men equal, they argued that the process of history had brought about a cultural diversity between Blacks and Whites which could not be effectively bridged and which was better preserved for the happiness of both communities. From 1881 the Blacks were to have their own separate places of worship. In practice apartheid was given a religious as well as a racial basis.

Since the Great Trek of 1836 the map of southern Africa had changed rapidly. In addition to the Cape Colony, the frontiers of which had expanded since 1815, White settlement had grown not merely through the setting up of the Boer republics but as a result of the establishment of the British colonies of Natal and British Kaffraria. As a consequence African-governed land had shrunk, though there were still relatively powerful native states in Zululand and Basutoland. Neither the Bantus nor the Zulus responded with any degree of enthusiasm to the Christian message or showed any willingness to adopt Christian values. As a result an increasing number of missionaries as well as colonial statesmen began to abandon the notion of carrying on evangelistic work within the confines of an indigenous native culture, coming to the conclusion that before Christianization could be effective, native culture must be replaced by what was to all intents and purposes the values and customs of European civilization. They argued that the quality of African tribal life, violent, oppressive and polygamous, needed to be refined if the native peoples were to enjoy the benefits of Christian rule. The absorption of natives into a pattern of colonial government seemed not merely commercially profitable but likely to enhance the quality of native life and make for a more just society.

The newly appointed governor of the Cape in 1854, Sir George Grey, envisaging a federation of White states, British and Boer, had come from trying to pacify and win the confidence of the Maoris in New Zealand. He tried now to 'pacify' the eastern frontier of the Cape by establishing White settlements in tribal areas, utilizing the services of the missionaries to promote not merely religion but education and health. In Natal Sir Theophilus Shepstone, son of a Methodist missionary, had the idea of setting up native reservations that would preserve native culture which through Christian missions, preferably undenominational, would itself be refined by Christian teaching.

Such ideas were not foreign to David Livingstone who in some respects argued along similar lines, but Livingstone had a passion which his contemporaries lacked and in some sense not merely opened up areas of Africa hitherto closed to the Christian Churches, but broke the mould of missionary enterprise. He was a determined, excessively energetic man, complex, enigmatic, convinced that he was right, 'a more dangerous enemy than a useful friend', as his devoted John Kirk observed. He subjected his wife Mary, though they were separated from each other for three years, to steamy heat, continuous discomfort as well as to constant illness and the pains of child-bearing. But Livingstone was truly a man with a mission. 'In the glow of love which Christianity inspires I swore', he wrote as a young man, 'to devote my life to the alleviation of human suffering.' Ill at ease with some of his fellow Whites, he showed greater insight than they into the native mind and won the affectionate loyalty of his native carriers. 'Anyone who lives among them forgets they are black, and feels they are just fellow men.' Yet he appears to have made hardly any converts to the Christian faith.

Although Livingstone was a man of firm, even simple faith, he was not primarily an evangelist. Gripped by a wanderlust to investigate lands unknown, he was to penetrate to the interior of Africa. A new world opened up before him; new names appeared on the map of Africa, the Victoria Falls which he discovered when following the course of the Zambezi in 1855, the lakes of Nyasa, Shirwa and Bangweulu. When he returned to Britain in 1856 he was fêted by the public, awarded the gold medal of the Royal Geographical Society, honorary degrees at Oxford and Glasgow, and the fellowship of the Royal Society.

He returned to Africa to explore further to find the river, the basin of the Upper Nile, which 'seems', he wrote, 'to open a highway for the progress of the Gospel in the interior of Africa'. He had resigned from the London Missionary Society which had insufficient resources to fund his exploration; 'the proposition to leave the untried, remote and difficult fields of labor as they have been ever since our Saviour died for man, involves my certain separation from the LMS.' He was subsequently appointed British consul at Quliemane in East Africa, ever thereafter wearing the peaked cap with the yellow band that was the badge of his office.

Livingstone saw no conflict between his missionary vocation and his life as an explorer.

Nowhere have I ever appeared as anything else but a servant of God, who had simply followed the leadings of his Hand. . . . My views of what is missionary duty are not so contracted as those whose ideal is a dumpy sort of man with a Bible under his arm. I have laboured in bricks and mortar, at the forge and carpenter's bench, as well as in preaching and medical practice. I feel that I am 'not my own'. I am serving Christ when shooting a buffalo for my men, or taking an astronomical observation, or writing to one of His children who forget, during the little moment of penning a note, that charity which is eulogised as 'thinking no evil'.

In opening up Africa he was, he hoped, paving the way for its Christianization, for its freedom from the scourge of the slave trade and from its interminable internecine tribal wars. The gospel would surely be served by commerce which would enable the African to become self-sufficient and even rich. 'I hope', he wrote in 1858 of a proposed expedition up the River Zambezi, 'it may result in an English colony in the healthy, high lands of central Africa.' The African would be brought to a higher standard of living 'by a long continued discipline and contact with superior races by commerce'.

'I beg', he said at a crowded meeting in the Senate House at Cambridge in 1857, 'to direct your attention to Africa. I know that in a few years I shall be cut off in that country, which is now open; do not let it shut again! I go back to Africa to make an open path for commerce and Christianity.' In response to the meeting the Universities Mission to Central Africa came into existence, its first head Charles Frederick Mackenzie, 'quite a brick of a bishop', as Livingstone called him, a muscular but attractive personality who with a 'jolly rollicking set of fellows', High Anglicans for the most part, worked among the Zulus of Natal. Equipped with a crozier in one hand (with which he jabbed his carriers who believed it to be a new kind of musket) and a gun in the other he conducted his mission, so fervent an enemy of the slave raiders that he helped arm the Manganja against the slave raiding Ajawa, an action which was injudicious and provoked criticism at home. After Mackenzie's early death from malaria in 1861 the mission moved in 1864 to the island of Zanzibar, long a centre of the slave trade where in 1873, partly as a result of the mission's propaganda, the sultan was persuaded by Sir Bartle Frere to close the slave market on the site of which the Anglican cathedral was subsequently to be built.

The missionary attitude to Africa was almost inevitably paternalistic, but there were those like Vanderkemp and John Philip who were concerned to protect the native peoples from the more corrupt features of white civilization. The Africans had another champion in John William Colenso who became bishop of Natal in 1853 and was subsequently to be deprived of his office for his theological liberalism. Colenso held that there were good elements in native African culture which should be preserved. He allowed polygamists to be baptized and insisted that it was immoral to force them to put away their wives.

THE CHURCHES IN ASIA

The background to the story of Christian missions in Asia was very different, in part because they already had a long pedigree. In the sixteenth century the Mogul emperor Akbar had expressed an interest in the Christian faith. The Portuguese enclave of Goa, long the seat of an archbishopric, was strongly Catholic. Protestant activity had been somewhat more restricted since while the East India Company appointed chaplains, it did not encourage outside missions, nor was it until 1813 that it changed its charter to allow missionaries freer entry into its territories.

Yet it was India that attracted a veritable flood of fervent missionaries in the early nineteenth century, for whereas Africa for long remained a dark and unknown terrain, India was a well-mapped land. The American Congregationalist John Scudder arrived in Bombay as early as 1813. Thomas Middleton became first bishop of Calcutta where he founded the Bishop's College in 1814. The American Presbyterians were at work in the Punjab in 1833. The Basel Mission, Lutheran and Reformed in impulse, was working among the destitute classes on the west coast from 1834. The Leipzig Lutherans reached South India by 1840. And in the twentieth century a college was set up in the Danish colony of Serampore in 1919 'for the instruction of Asiatic, Christian and other youth, in Eastern Literature and European Science.'

But the work of evangelizing India's millions was neither easy nor particularly successful. The Churches, Protestant and Catholic, were dogged by the problems of caste. In the seventeenth century the Jesuits, aware that high-caste Brahmins were likely to be rich and influential, tried to placate all sides, even going as far as to build different entrances to their churches and dividing the castes from each other by low walls. The native Christian priests were drawn mainly from the high castes, but the steady improvement in the economic position of the lower castes led to a demand for admission to seminaries, their advocates recalling that St Peter had himself been a fisherman, an argument which the Vatican felt in 1836 obliged to accept. Yet caste division continued to cause bitter controversy. Two prelates who favoured the lower castes were recalled to Rome on the grounds of sexual scandal but it was widely thought that they were the victims of high-caste enmity. It was only slowly that the Jesuits began to admit that the majority of converts to Catholicism came from all castes. Christianity made only a slight indentation in India's millions. Hinduism by its own religious pre-conceptions found Christianity relatively unattractive while for the most part Islam in India as elsewhere was impermeable. Out of a population of some 150 million in 1851, it was reckoned that only 91,093 were esteemed to be Christian and of that number only some 14,661 were communicants. Yet there were at this time some 339 missionaries working in India for some nineteen different missionary societies, often at odds with each other. While there is little to suggest that the mutineers in 1857 were especially hostile to Christians, the change in the political situation making British India a reality may have given a fillip to the slow growth of the Christian Church in India.

Burma, like Sri Lanka, strongly Buddhist, remained long immune to missionary activity. The pioneer missionary was an American Baptist, Adoniram Judson who set up the first mission society in America, the American Board of Commissioners for Foreign Missions in 1810 and sailed for India in 1812. He was to spend thirty-three years in Burma, married four wives, all supposedly models of religious virtue, but it was ten years before he made a convert; his first convert was baptized in 1819 and by 1824 he had twenty-four. Judson was uncompromising in preaching the gospel of sin and repentance, of which he argued that Buddhism was void; the atonement of Christ was designed to correct 'the radical moral evil' of the Burmese people. When he was working among the Karens he observed a woman wearing twelve or fifteen necklaces. Judson was affronted. 'I saw that I was brought into a situation that precluded all retreat . . . I asked myself "Can I baptize a Karen woman in her present attire? No."' Suspected of being a spy in the pay of the British, he was put in prison. Reluctantly he moved his mission under the protection of the British (who had led a successful expeditionary force against the Burmese king in 1824–5) to Moulmein whence he carried out a rather more successful mission among the primitive Karens who lived in the jungle between Burma and Thailand. The Karens cherished a notion that they had once had a knowledge of the true God but subsequently lost it but that foreigners would help them to recover it. Austere with a touch of mysticism – his favourite authors Fénelon and à Kempis – Judson eventually became something of a national hero. Whether Judson liked it or not missionary activity in Burma became identified with British imperialism.

In China and Japan where the Roman Catholics had once acquired a strong footing the work had more or less to be done all over again, and in both countries the way was opened by external pressure from foreign powers. The Presbyterian Robert Morrison had originally gone to Canton in 1807 as a translator to the East India Company under the auspices of the London Missionary Society; subsequently he translated the Bible into Chinese, published in twenty-one volumes in 1823, and compiled a Chinese dictionary. But missionary work had to be secretive, for the officials were hostile and he made very few converts. Then there occurred the Opium Wars and by the subsequent treaty of Nanking in 1842 the way was opened for missionaries to enter China. In the wake of the gunboats came the preachers representing many different societies, some of whom became injudiciously involved in the T'ai Ping rebellion against the Manchu government, for the rebellion had religious elements, including demands for the extirpation of opium and the destruction of idols, which appealed to some of the missionaries. Its leader, Hong Xiuquan, who held a huge area of Eastern China which he named the Heavenly Kingdom for eleven years, called himself the younger brother of Jesus Christ. The rebellion brought about great bloodshed before it was crushed in 1864 by an army led by General Gordon. Further conflict between China and Britain, ending in 1858, had already led to a treaty which explicitly allowed for the protection of the Christian religion in China.

The opportunity for evangelistic work was seized eagerly by British and American missionaries,so that by the end of the nineteenth century there were some 641 at work in China. One of the leading figures was James Hudson Taylor who founded the China Inland Mission in 1865. Theologically conservative, regarded with some suspicion by some of his colleagues, Hudson Taylor, who adopted Chinese costume, sought to identify with the Chinese. Yet it is doubtful how deeply Christianity had penetrated, though it had certainly won converts.

Commodore Perry opened up Japan to the outside world in 1853, and subsequently in 1858 the Japanese allowed the Americans freedom of worship, though for the Japanese Christianity remained a banned religion and as late as 1867 there was some renewal of persecution. Christianity was legalized in 1873 and full freedom of religious belief was granted in 1889. Yet the Roman Catholics discovered that there were small communities which had continued to hold to the tenets of the faith since the persecution of 1640. A Roman Catholic vicariate apostolic was founded in 1866, and by 1891 there was an archbishopric and three suffragan sees. In 1887 the American Episcopal Church with its counterpart in Canada united with the Church of England to form the Nippon Sei Ko Kwai, the Holy Catholic Church of Japan. In 1882 there were about 145 missionaries at work and some five thousand Japanese Christians; and the speed of the conversion may be estimated by the fact that six years later, in 1888, there were some 451 missionaries and 25,514 Christians.

THE EVANGELIZATION OF THE PACIFIC

The Pacific too offered a fair field for missionary activity, if it became not infrequently entangled with more mundane issues. The native peoples were still primitive and poor, battered by tribal strife, and an easy prey to the wiles of the White man, be he missionary or trader. Many of the traders were cruel and grasping, engaged in 'blackbirding' – kidnapping natives for sale as indentured labour. The murder in 1871 of the devoted first bishop of Melanesia, John Coleridge Patteson, was in revenge for the kidnapping of natives to supply labour in Fiji and Queensland. Whites readily purchased vast tracts of land from the natives for absurdly small sums. The natives relished the goods that the missionaries brought as well as the schools and hospitals they set up, but the Whites brought also damaged goods in the shape of venereal disease and measles which had a high mortality rate.

In Australia, settled as a convict colony in 1788, the Churches slowly took shape, the first Anglican bishop W.G. Broughton being appointed in 1836. Anglican chaplains ministered to the convicts who were long obliged to attend the services of the Church of England, an abuse to which the future Roman Catholic bishop Ullathorne, who was in Australia from 1833 to 1844, helped to draw attention. The Benedictine J.B. Polding was appointed Catholic bishop for Australia in 1834. Samuel Marsden, an evangelical protégé of Wilberforce, had been made second chaplain 'for the service of the Church in the settlement of Botany Bay' in 1793. Marsden, a pioneer in land settlement who was responsible for shipping out the merino sheep in 1809, was, apart from being also a stern disciplinarian, a fervent supporter of missionary endeavour.

It was through Marsden's efforts that the Christian Church was first established in New Zealand, to which he paid some seven visits between 1814 and 1831. But the French Marist Jean Pompallier had also made claims for the Roman Church. When by the treaty of Waitangi, signed with the Maori chiefs in 1840, the British took over New Zealand, a bishop was appointed, 31-year-old George Augustus Selwyn, a handsome athlete and a man of great moral earnestness and immense industry. It was he who built up the Church of England on the island, drew up its constitution, called its first ecclesiastical synod and guided it in its first faltering steps after it was separated from the State in 1844. It was more significant that Selwyn supported the Maoris whose language he had mastered on the voyage out from England. The tragedy was that he could not help being involved in a brutal and protracted war with the Maoris for which the British bore much responsibility. 'The only wonder is', Selwyn commented sadly, recalling that the Roman Church had been more sympathetic than the Anglicans to the Maoris' grievances, 'that the whole people did not become Romanists.' As it was, a group of Maoris, at least half of whom had accepted Christianity, apostatized and conjured up a faith compounded of Christianity and native superstition – Pai Marire. Its supporters claimed that at the death in battle of a certain Captain Lloyd, as his victors drank his blood from his penis, the angel Gabriel appeared, promising to drive the English from the land. The captain's head was to be pickled and carried about to make possible communication with Jehovah. 'The Hau-Hau' (so-called from its followers' war cry), Selwyn commented, 'is simply an expression of an utter loss of faith in everything that is English, clergy and all alike.' It would take long for the Church to recover the lost ground.

By 1878 there were few places, however remote, to which the Church had not penetrated. There had been a chaplain at the small remote island settlement of St Helena, in the south-east Atlantic, first appointed by the East India Company, since 1671, even if the appointments seem to have been somewhat unsatisfactory. Of eighteen chaplains appointed between 1671 and 1830 it was recorded that at least eleven were drunk or quarrelsome. 'Mr White our chaplain and his wife', it was said in 1732, 'have for a long time led very scandalous and immoral lives.' Piers Claughton was appointed St Helena's first bishop in 1859. The rocky island of Ascension, 700 miles to the north-west, had been first settled by the Royal Marines to prevent its use in any attempt to rescue Napoleon from St Helena, but was serviced from 1844 by a royal navy chaplain. The volcanic island of Tristan de Cunha, 1,300 miles south-west of St Helena, had a chaplain from 1851 appointed (until 1980) by the Society for the Propagation of the Gospel (SPG). The Falkland Islands had had a resident chaplain since 1859. Allen Gardiner, the courageous founder of the Patagonian Missionary Society which sought to evangelize the inhospitable Tierra del Fuego in 1850–1, had intended to establish a mission station on Keppel Island.

The development of Christian missions throughout the world was perhaps the most distinctive feature in the history of the Christian Church in the nineteenth century. They introduced a set of new ideas about the universe and a different attitude to living which at its best expressed a respect for life often lacking in non-Christian societies. They were, for instance, in part responsible for the abolition of the Hindu custom of suttee, or burning widows on funeral pyres, and the exposure of young children. They upheld the causes of the neglected and deprived members of society, lepers, widows, outcasts, the disabled. If some went native or in other ways fell by the wayside, many missionaries, both men and women, gave an example of Christian living rooted in the gospel. In their wake there came colleges and schools and hospitals.

Yet they often challenged native culture and broke up tribal society without effectively putting anything better in their place.* Nor could the propagation of Christianity be separated from the technological, commercial and military superiority of the great powers. The missionaries themselves stressed the virtues of White civilization. Robert Moffatt spoke of the 'vacant mind of the savage'. 'They have', commented the Roman Catholic Vicar Apostolic Bishop James Richards of natives in his charge, 'no visible symbols, no idea of the existence and attributes of a Supreme Being, nor of a future state, or rewards and punishments arising out of the moral qualities of our actions in life.' The missionaries' obvious objective was to replace existing religions by the Christian religion, but it was only slowly that the Churches sought to shed their externality, and to understand and absorb the culture of the peoples whom they came to convert.

ALTERNATIVE FAITHS

Whatever qualifications may be made as to the nature of the Church's expansion throughout the world, there could be no doubt that its achievement was massive. Yet traditionalists were confronted by a growing intellectual challenge. In the early eighteenth century the Church's teaching had been criticized by the Deists but they had never been more than a minority movement. A more serious challenge had come from the Philosophes who had influenced the course of the French Revolution.

The nineteenth century was to witness the proliferation of alternative panaceas for the evils of the world, even though for the most part they had only minimal support. Some looked back beyond the institutional Churches which to them seemed to represent the relics of reaction and the vested interests of

---

* In his travel book *The Missionaries* (London, 1988) Norman Lewis drew attention to the insidious effects of the policy followed by the North American fundamentalist sect, The New Tribe Mission, threatening the ethnic identity and even the existence of some Indian tribes in Paraguay and Venezuela. The Chamula Indians of Mexico suffered a similar brutal experience as a result of the preaching of American Evangelical missionaries.

the priesthood to a religion of humanity of which Christ of the gospels was an exemplar. The anti-clericals were already claiming that their quarrel was not with Christianity but with the Church. The well-worn argument that Christianity is a progressive force if it embodies the teaching of Christ rather than the ecclesiastical tyranny of the Church, an argument in part engineered by St Paul, was being put forward by Jeremy Bentham as early as 1825.

The socialist tradition which embodied similar views can be traced back to the early decades of the nineteenth century, reflected in the writings of Saint-Simon who argued that the basic principle of real Christianity was that men must behave as brothers to each other, and that it was the working classes who alone could foster such brotherhood. 'Religion', he urged, 'should direct society towards the great aim of the most rapid amelioration of the poorest class.' The priesthood had failed in its vocation for priests no longer 'laboured in a direction useful to the progress of science'. His ideas were taken up by a group of followers, Rodrigues, Enfantin and Bazard, who formed a Saint-Simonian Church. 'Moses has promised to man universal brotherhood, Jesus Christ had prepared for it, Saint-Simon has realized it.' Members of his churches – there were six in France – dressed in different shades of blue to indicate their place in the hierarchy. They supported the emancipation of women, curiously expecting a female Messiah to manifest herself on the banks of the River Nile.

The Saint-Simonians made comparatively little impact but other groups followed, intent on repudiating orthodox and institutional Christianity and providing what was usually a bizarre alternative. The Utopian socialist Charles Fourier found in the goodness of God the key to man's aspirations, and its social expression a cooperative of workers. P.J. Proudhon, proto-anarchist and syndicalist, declared that the Church denied justice and obstructed the advance of science and progress and in its theology taught a false view of human nature – 'la condemnation du moi humain, le mèpris de la personne, le viol de la conscience' ('the condemnation of the human self, contempt for the personality, the rape of conscience').

If for such thinkers as these 'l'homme est destiné à vivre sans religion', there were others who believed that although Christianity did not provide the answer some form of religion was a human necessity. In his *Cours de la Philosophie*, published between 1830 and 1842, Auguste Comte, who had been a disciple of Saint-Simon, asserted that there were three phases in human development, theological, metaphysical and 'positive', all to be deduced from observable experience. For the foundation of truth, so Comte believed, was experimental science which showed that Christianity was aberrant. He constructed a new religion, borrowing from the Roman Catholics a religious apparatus with priests and sacraments and a calendar in which scholars and scientists were commemorated instead of the saints. He provided a moral pattern, in many ways demanding and puritanical, divorced from discredited Christianity. In 1848 he set up the Positive Society which was designed to reconstruct society according to his ethical principles. Positivism, like Unitarianism which in some ways it much resembled, appealed to a limited number of high-minded people – in England the novelist George Eliot, Frederic Harrison, Herbert Spencer and the politician Lord Morley were sympathizers – but in its stress on morality without traditional religion it was reflecting the way in which an increasing number of people, moral but agnostic, were trying to live.

The Unitarians were as high-minded as the Positivists with whose ideals they had some sympathy, but they came within the umbrella of Christianity. With a long lineage which could be traced back to sixteenth-century thinkers like Socinius they blossomed more especially in nineteenth-century America, where they had a scholarly exponent in Charles W. Eliot of Harvard University. In Britain, where they were an offshoot of the Presbyterians, and flourished in Liverpool and Manchester like the Positivists, they had an able leader in James Martineau. They appealed to the intellectual middle class by reason of their rationality, for they had no formal creed, rejecting the doctrines of the Trinity and Divinity of Christ, insisting on the impersonality of God, though they based their teachings on the Scriptures. Their following was limited and by the end of the twentieth century they seemed, at least in Britain, to be in decline.

If Unitarianism had a religious foundation, Marxism was intrinsically anti-religious. The rise of Marxism was in the long term to provide a more sinister threat to Christianity, but it had not by the eighth decade of the nineteenth century made more than a limited impact on social thinkers. Karl Marx, grandson of a rabbi but baptized as a Christian, had had socialist forebears in Baur and Feuerbach, both reared in Hegel's philosophy, and through them had by 1841 become convinced of atheism. He came slowly to believe that religion should be rejected not merely because it was an illusion created by man but because it was socially reprehensible, providing a false panacea for the ills of society. 'Religion', he wrote in 1843, 'is the sigh of the oppressed creature, the heart of a heartless world, the soul of a soulless environment. It is the opium of the people.' With the transformation of society, religion would wither away. Marx's influence, though it could be seen at work in the Paris Commune of 1871, was as yet limited. But in the future, though as a semi-religion it was ultimately to be the faith that failed, it was, supported by totalitarian regimes, to be the most potent adversary that Christianity had to face.

DEVELOPMENTS IN THEOLOGY

The intellectual history of the nineteenth-century Church, like its political and social history, reflected the tension between traditional theology and its remoulding by new forces, secular in origin. The thinkers of the Enlightenment had been basically anti-Christian but by their scepticism they had pierced the barrier of traditional religious thought. Ideologically the philosopher Immanuel Kant was for long a dominant influence. In his *Critique of Pure Reason* he had put forward a theory of knowledge which cut at the roots of traditional metaphysics, dismissing revelation and asserting that Natural Theology was an illusion. He found the base of truth in the voice of conscience which validates a belief in freedom, in immortality and the existence of a just Supreme Being. Kantian idealism was to be a pervasive force in nineteenth-century theology as writers tried to reconcile the teachings of scripture with the rationale of the modern world increasingly transformed by advances in science and mathematics.

Two other philosophers, critical of Kant's ethical interpretation, were equally influential in shaping religious thought. Friedrich Schleiermacher asserted that religion was neither to be understood as a code of ethics, as Kant had implied, nor as a scheme of belief but as self-consciousness or awareness as a consequence of which the individual comes to realize his own absolute dependence upon God. His contemporary, Hegel, believing that Schleiermacher's conception of God was inadequate, brought God back into the process of history as a rational and dynamic creator, supremely revealed in the Holy Trinity. God unfolds his purpose through the dialectic of history.

As a result of the circulation of such ideas scholars began to venture on a comprehensive reinterpretation of theology in the light of modern knowledge, sometimes with destructive results. F.C. Baur who had been both a disciple of Schleiermacher and Hegel applied Hegelian dialectic to his interpretation of the origins of the early Church, expressing its history as a conflict between divergent views, represented by St Peter and St Paul, which was resolved by a synthesis which resulted in the setting up of the Catholic Church. The application of Hegelian dialectic to doctrine, the Atonement, the Trinity and the Incarnation had less happy results while his treatment of St Paul and the dismissal of the authenticity of most of the Pauline epistles created controversies. Baur's contemporary, Ludwig Feuerbach applied Hegelian dialectic to Christianity to reach the conclusion that Christianity was an illusion, what he described as the 'dominance of subjectivity'. He was to influence greatly Marx and his fellow Communists.

Side by side with the attempt to align modern philosophy with Christian theology, only fluctuatingly successful, there went the increasingly historical approach to the text and contents of scripture, involving an investigation of the books of the Old and New Testaments as ancient historical documents, not necessarily dictated by verbal inspiration but to be interpreted in the light of the social context in which the books had been written.

Since a canon of scripture had been drawn up in the fourth century and approved by a Church council held at Rome in 382, it had been broadly agreed that the collection of books constituted writing inspired by God, even if there were to be differences of opinion as to the inspired authority of individual books. Few would probably have argued that the biblical writers wrote at the direct dictation of God, but most commentators would have agreed that, apart from small contradictions due to the errors of copyists, the books were preserved by God from propagating major error. As the nineteenth-century bishop Van Mildert of Durham put it, the writers 'constantly received from the Holy Spirit such a degree of assistance as might suffice to give every part of Scripture its sanction and authority, as the Word of God'.

The interpretation of the text was, however, another matter. In the Middle Ages there had been a wide variety of approaches which gave some opportunity for reading into the text more than its literal meaning. The English reformer John Wycliffe had argued for a literal interpretation; and the bias of Protestantism (as of reformed Catholicism) had been towards a literal, neo-fundamentalist approach to what theologians still conceived as the revealed Word of God. This meant that they were more likely than not to accept the Mosaic authorship of the Pentateuch, the historicity of Genesis, and of Noah's Ark and the Flood, and the story of Jonah.

What was not yet effectually questioned was the authenticity of the text itself. When in 1678 the French scholar Richard Simon alleged that Moses could not have been the author of the Pentateuch, basing his views on the existence of duplicate accounts of the incident and varieties of style, he was expelled from the French Oratory. It was in eighteenth-century Germany as a consequence of the Enlightenment that scholars began to treat the Bible in the same critical way as they did other literature. Lessing, who had won a reputation as a writer and playwright before he turned to the study of theology, put forward heterodox views on the nature of Christianity, believing religion to be humanitarian morality without the benefit of revelation. The gospels, he concluded, were a set of records which had been compiled from the oral narratives of the apostles and other witnesses and so were a proper subject for historical enquiry. Johann Eichhorn, who made a study of the biblical books and parallel Semitic writings, held that the Old Testament documents such as Genesis had been continuously re-edited and were of a composite character. In his *Biblical Theology*, published in 1835, Vatke applied a theory of development to the story of Israelite religion, casting doubts upon the trustworthiness of some of the Biblical accounts. What was at issue was not simply the structure of the text but its historic reliability.

No wonder that conservative theologians such as the Oxford Tractarian Dr Pusey were deeply suspicious of German scholarship. They were disagreeably surprised by the attempts to compile a biography of Jesus in human terms. The first was written by D.F. Strauss, published originally in 1835 (of which the novelist George Eliot was to make an English translation in 1846), and the second was *La Vie de Jesus* by the French scholar J.E. Renan, published in 1863. Both books were to be best sellers. Strauss repudiated the supernatural elements in the gospels which he attributed to the growth of an unintentionally creative legend, the 'myths' which came into existence after the death of Christ and before the writing of the gospels.

Renan's life, beautifully written, also refuted the supernatural element and depicted Christ as an attractive human religious leader, a man of charm and integrity about whom legend had wreathed a catena of miraculous stories. Strauss was deprived of his professorship at Tübingen, Renan of the chair of Hebrew he held at the Collège de France, but both books caused a profound sensation and in some sense brought biblical criticism before a wider reading public.

The heterodox character of religious philosophy and biblical criticism, especially in Germany, alarmed the orthodox. In 1860 seven scholars, six from Oxford, one from Cambridge, with one exception all clergy of the Church of England, published a selection of essays *Essays and Reviews* in which they argued for the necessity of free enquiry in religious matters. Theology, the editor H.B. Wilson argued, is itself subject to the laws of development and dogma, itself may have to be adapted to changing conditions of thought. 'The object', another of the authors, Benjamin Jowett wrote, 'is to say what we think freely within the limits of the Church in England. . . . We do not wish to do anything rash or irritating to the public or the university, but we are determined not to submit to this abominable system of terrorism, which prevents the statement of the plainest facts and makes a true theology or theological education impossible.' For *Essays and Reviews* had produced a storm of protest from the bishops and clergy. Two of the authors were sentenced to the deprivation of their livings for a year. The Convocation of Canterbury censored the book. Of the clergy, 10,906 or nearly half of the English clergy, confirmed their belief in the divine inspiration of the scriptures and the eternity of punishment.

The furore occurred more or less simultaneously with the deprivation on grounds of heresy of J.W. Colenso, Bishop of Natal of his bishopric by the bishop of Cape Town, Robert Gray. In his book on the Old Testament *The Pentateuch and the Book of Joshua Critically Examined*, the first part of which was published in 1862, Colenso criticized its content, judging it to be no more inspired than 'Cicero, Lactantius and the Sikh Gooros'. A mathematician by training, to show the absurdity of some of the statements in scripture, he estimated that six men were said to have had 2,748 sons and that each priest was obliged to consume a daily diet of 88 pigeons. For preaching heretical sermons on the Eucharist and eternal punishment, the bishop of Cape Town excommunicated Colenso and deprived him of his diocese, but Colenso appealed to the Privy Council which found in his favour. In 1865 he returned to his diocese, leading to a split in the Church of Natal which lasted until 1911.

Colenso was in some respects a maverick, not particularly well equipped as a scholar to explore the difficult field of biblical criticism, but to many he seemed to confirm the belief that the Church was intellectually obscurantist. The scientists Lyell and Darwin were to contribute to his legal expenses. Slowly the Protestant Church began to realize that if theology was not be become fossilized, it had to respond not merely to textual discoveries but to new philosophical and scientific ideas.

Protestant theology, to the alarm of more conservative scholars, was escaping from the closet of the past, more especially in Germany. The influence of what came to be called the Tübingen School affected all theological scholarship, even though it was not until the 1870s that British theologians showed much awareness of its existence. One of its most influential figures was Albrecht Ritschl, a pupil of F.C. Baur and from 1864 until his death in 1889 professor at Göttingen. Ritschl moved away from the Tübingen School, looking back to Schleiermacher. He distrusted dogma and metaphysics nor, though he stressed the historicity of Christ through whom God was revealed to man, was he much concerned with Christianity as a historical faith. It was his particular forte to marry religion with experience. Religious consciousness lay at the root of religious belief rather than dogmatic statements. What Ritschl emphasized were 'value-judgements' which, as with Kantian moral judgements, affirm 'not what *is* but what *ought*'. Ritschlians stressed the Kingdom of God, rejecting its interpretation in a mystical sense, but comprehending it as an objective ideal to be realized 'in and through the events of everyday experience'.

The Ritschlians were defective in their lack of appreciation of dogma and history, but in seeking to discover a modus vivendi between traditional orthodoxy and a purely humanitarian conception of Christ they were to exert much influence. Between the ending of the Napoleonic Wars in 1815 and the death of Pius IX in 1878 a new world had come into being as Africa was opened up to commerce and Christianity, as the frontiers in North America were pushed further and further west, as Asia was brought more fully within the orbit of European politics. The speed of communications was improved by the spread of railways and the invention of steamships. The population grew at a great rate. The Churches, Roman Catholic and Protestant, took advantage of this fast-changing world, even though intellectually they found it difficult to come to terms with it. They consolidated their position at home, regaining some of the ground they had appeared to be in danger of losing in the late eighteenth century and stemming the threat of infidelity and subversion which the French Revolution had highlighted. They expanded slowly but effectively into the non-European lands, so that by the end of the nineteenth century the Christian Churches had the allegiance of many millions and Christianity had become a great world religion.

Yet with hindsight it appears that the foundations of this spectacular ecclesiastical imperialism were already being undermined: by the growing secularization of life, by the extent to which the Churches were already becoming socially marginalized, by hints in the Old World of a slow seepage in membership, by the threats to traditional teaching exerted by advances in science and technology and by the study of the scriptural texts. Would the Church in the twentieth century be able to absorb and overcome these threats to its life and influence as it entered into a world the balance of which was to be wildly upset by war and social upheaval?

CHAPTER TEN

The Church in War and Peace, c. 1880–1945

It was Edinburgh in the early summer of 1910, the setting the Council Hall on the ridge of the Mound, where 1,200 delegates representing some 160 societies were gathering for the World Missionary Conference. The delegates, from every Church except the Roman, were for the most part staid-suited men, middle-aged and elderly, but here and there there was a touch of colour, a Chinaman in a jacket of rich peacock blue, an Indian Brahmin with a white beard and a Negro from Liberia.

Under the inspired leadership of Dr John R. Mott, the American Methodist who was chairman of the conference, much preparatory work had been done before the conference met, and its mood was buoyant and optimistic. The delegates believed, as the archbishop of Canterbury (who had been at first reluctant to attend, fearful that he might be committing the Church of England to a project too interdenominational in character) reminded them, that it was a conference 'without parallel in this or other lands'. 'The place of missions in the life of the Church', he went on, 'must be the central place and none other . . . it may well be that some standing here to-night shall not taste of death till they see the Kingdom of God come with power.' The conference was indeed itself powered by a driving sense of urgency. 'God', said young William Temple, 'has been building up a Christian fellowship which now extends into almost every nation, and binds citizens of them all together in true unity and mutual love . . . the result of the great missionary enterprise of the last hundred and fifty years. . . . Here is the one great ground of hope for the coming days – this world-wide Christian fellowship.' 'The evangelization of the world in this our generation' became the conference's watchword.

The delegates departed with high expectations, unaware that within four years their hopes were to be dashed as the nations divided in a bitter war in which the Churches were as split as the nations. Thirteen volumes were needed to print the papers and speeches given at the conference and the one that had preceded it, the Pan Anglican Conference held at London in 1908; but no single speech alluded to the possibility of the coming catastrophe. The churchmen had talked as if they were living in a secure world which was capable of being turned to Christ if only men and women had more faith and knowledge. They took the continuance of human progress and freedom for granted, so that although they had indeed laid the foundations for future understanding between the Churches the visions which had filtered through the Scottish air in June 1910 were to prove insubstantial dreams, and the oratory re-echoed from empty walls.

'On the morning of that day [9 April 1945],' the doctor of the concentration camp at Flossenburg wrote some thirty-five years later, 'between five and six o'clock the prisoners were taken from their cells, and the verdicts of the court martial read to them. Through the half-open door in the room of the huts I saw Pastor Bonhoeffer, before taking off his prison garb, kneeling on the floor praying fervently to his God. At the place of execution, he again said a short prayer and then climbed 120 steps to the gallows, brave and composed.'

Dietrich Bonhoeffer was only one of the innumerable men and women who fell victim to the totalitarian tyranny of the Nazi regime. He was thirty-nine years old, had been ordained in 1931, and then became closely associated with the oecumenical movement. From the late 1930s his criticism of Nazi policy towards the Church made him suspect to the authorities as, with Martin Niemoller, he opposed the regime's Aryan legislation. He was one of a minority of Germans who not merely felt deeply about the treatment of Jewish Christians (that is, those born Jewish but subsequently baptized), but was desperately concerned with the fate of the Jewish people. He was forbidden to speak in public, prevented from printing or publishing and ordered to report regularly to the police. After the abortive attempts on Hitler's life, his association with the conspirators – for his brother-in-law Hans von Dohnyani was one of the plotters – meant that his long travail could have only one conclusion.

Bonhoeffer's vision of the Church was the result of long meditation in the darkness of Nazi Germany. The Church, he argued, was a historical fellowship and a God-established reality, 'Christ existing in community', the actualization of Christ in the realities of existence, which required that the Church should be freed from the trammels of tradition and given a 'non-religious interpretation', in the phrase that Bonhoeffer coined 'religionless Christianity'.

The contrast between the corporate civility and the unhurrrying debates of Edinburgh in 1910 and the German concentration camps must be a symbolic prelude to what was to happen to the Christian Churches between the ending of the pontificate of Pius IX in 1878 and the conclusion of the Second World War in 1945. It was to be a time of metamorphosis, political, social and technological which was bound to make an impact on religion all over the world. The Catholic Hapsburg Empire had disintegrated. Tsarist Russia had collapsed, destabilizing the Orthodox Church. The Churches were to be encompassed by storms which at times seemed to verge on hurricanes threatening their very survival.

If the Churches were to survive, and in some measure to flourish, they had historically to come to terms with the course of events, and restate their position, politically, socially and even theologically. In the Roman Church the underlying conflict between the Church's basic authoritarianism and traditionalism, which Pius IX had largely epitomized, and more liberal forces was only slowly to give ground to more progressive ideas. In this process the Church was to find itself often at odds with secular governments, most notably in France, nor was the expedient peace which it was to negotiate with Mussolini in 1929 a happy augury for its future political relations. If overseas the number of Catholics continued to grow, the Church in general was to experience to an ever greater extent an internal crisis, shown already in a shortfall of candidates for the priesthood and in some countries by falling attendance at the Mass, all of which was only to come more completely into the open in the closing years of the twentieth century. Protestantism, if less monolithic, was to be confronted by not dissimilar problems: questions over the nature of authority, controversy over the interpretation of scripture and after the turn of the century by signs of diminishing congregations; but it was also concerned in a way that the Roman Church was not with the movement for better understanding between the Churches, with the ultimate object of reunion.

The story of all the Churches has to be interpreted against a backcloth of steadily increasing secularization. Scientific and technological advance were outstripping theological cosmology, obliging the Christian to rely more and more on a purely fideistic view of the universe. More serious than the inroads made on faith by intellectual scepticism was the growing indifference to religious values which became more pronounced after the First World War. The First World War, in itself a negation of Christian values, even though the clergy of the national Churches had given it their blessing, had set in train a social and moral revolution which was to strain the Church's traditional teaching.

And in the political upheaval which followed in its wake, the Churches were to be confronted with a more brutal persecution than they had ever before experienced, even under the pagan Roman emperors, as the ruthless leaders of Bolshevik Russia tried to stampede the Orthodox Church out of its very existence, and Nazi dictatorship sought to make the Church subservient to its own semi-pagan philosophy. No century witnessed as many Christian martyrs as the twentieth. Paradoxically nothing was to afford more positive proof of the Churches' underlying vitality, Roman, Protestant, Orthodox, than their ultimate survival. The eighty years which were to elapse after the death of Pius IX were to be for the Churches in many respects a time of trial, which, if by no means void of positive achievement, was going to help fashion their history in the closing decades of the century.

THE PAPACY AFTER PIUS IX

For the Roman Church the death of Pius IX in 1878 marked the end of an era, and it now remained to be seen how far the policies which he had embodied would be endorsed by his successor.

In one of the shortest papal elections in modern times, at the third ballot, the cardinals elected the 68-year-old bishop of Perugia, Giocchino Pecci, as Leo XIII. Since he had known to be physically frail, some expected that this was merely a stop-gap election, but they were mistaken; for twenty years the Pope was to guide the destinies of the Roman Church with masterly skill. He had as high a view of his function as his predecessor and as profound a conception of the Church. It was symbolic that he should in 1892 have brought back to the Lateran Basilica (where he was himself to be buried) the remains of the most magisterial of his predecessors, Innocent III, hitherto interred at Perugia. But Leo XIII was also a political realist. He realized that his predecessor's intransigence had done a disservice to the Church and that the Church had, without surrendering its basic principles, to put in hand what he termed somewhat paradoxically the 'Christianization of modern life and the modernisation of Christian life'. Pius's former secretary of state suspected him of harbouring liberal notions: 'non è Pio, non è Clemente, Leone sensa dente' ('He is not Pius, he is not Clement but Leo without teeth'). But this was not so. While he was to make moves to promote a *rapprochement* between traditional Catholicism and contemporary culture, he was no liberal. He did not reverse his predecessor's policy but rather changed its course. Gambetta may have been correct in describing him as an 'opportuniste sacré'.

There seemed, however, to be every likelihood of some shift of policy. He was helped in Germany by Bismarck's own growing realization that the *Kulturkampf* had been a mistake. Bismarck introduced a cautious policy of reconciliation with the Catholic Church to win its support against the Social Democrats. Falk was replaced as minister by the more conservative von Puttkamer and laws were introduced which modified but did not entirely abandon the anti-clerical legislation, for Bismarck had no wish to sound a retreat which would give comfort to the Romans. The Pope, for his part much concerned by the current anti-clerical policy of the Italian government and so wanting friends in Europe, was at least prepared to go some of the way with the Church's former enemy. Bismarck withdrew most of the discriminatory measures, and as a sop to papal pride cunningly invoked the Pope's mediation in a dispute between Germany and Spain over the Caroline Islands. The Pope as diplomatically conferred on Bismarck the Order of Christ. It was perhaps a stalemate rather than a victory, for the German government's supervision over the Church had not been very significantly reduced.

But in Italy the situation was humiliating. The Italian state passed a series of anti-clerical laws, suppressing religious orders and confiscating their property, secularizing Church welfare organizations and banning religious instruction in schools. The Italian government proved so intransigent that Leo (on 15 June 1887) demanded the restoration of the Pope's temporal power and the return of Rome to papal rule, demands angrily rejected.

Still the 'prisoner in the Vatican', the Pope sought compensation by rallying his friends outside Italy. Twice the Austrian government offered him asylum; but even with Austria, relations were marred by the treatment of the Catholic Church in Hungary, for the Pope disapproved of the grant of religious toleration there in 1894–5 nor were the Austrians best pleased by the support which he gave to the Catholic Croatians whose vigorous leader, Bishop Strossmayer of Diakovár from 1849 to 1905, was a determined nationalist. The Austrians looked askance at the attempts to bring about a reconciliation between the Church and State in France.

By the close of Pius IX's pontificate the French government had passed securely into the hands of the Republicans who were determined to exploit their victory by a renewed onslaught on the privileges of the Catholic Church in the hope that this might eventually bring the Concordat, which governed relations between Church and State, to an end. Since they had no wish to alienate the believers among their supporters, they fell short of launching a frontal attack, seeking to delimit the Church's influence by imposing a series of restrictions on its activities. Hence Republican measures were now allowing work on Sundays, permitting municipal authorities to impose controls on religious processions, abolishing army chaplaincies, restoring divorce to the civil code, encouraging the laicization of burial ceremonies and removing prayers from the opening of parliament. The Republicans' main target was education which, they argued, gave the Church a whip hand over the impressionable minds of the young. In 1879 the minister of public instruction, Jules Ferry, introduced a bill banning non-authorized religious from teaching, aimed more specifically at the Jesuits. In the event some 900 to 1,000 religious were expelled from some 261 houses. It seemed to many as if the government was hell-bent on separating the Church from the State. 'Separation', as Bishop Deputy Freppel told the French parliament, 'that is your goal. Yesterday it was the separation of parish and congregation, to-morrow and the day after to-morrow it will be the separation of Church and State.'

Leo XIII, conservative as was his outlook, saw the expediency of making an accord with the French government. In this he had the support of many of the bishops, worried by falling congregations and the continuance of de-Christianization, and believing that it was their prior duty to foster the faith among individuals rather than to promote a programme designed to Christianize society. Moderate conservatives, concerned by the support which the Church had been giving to right-wing monarchists, joined with moderate Republicans, averse to radical socialism, to improve the relationship between Church and State.

The key figure in the process was to be the tough-minded Cardinal Lavigerie, Archbishop of Algiers. Originally a monarchist, he had become convinced that a *rapprochement* with the Republic would preserve the Church from marauding raids by left-wing radicals. On 12 November 1890, at a dinner given in honour of the officers of the Mediterranean fleet, Lavigerie commended 'unqualified adherence' to the government as 'in itself in no way contrary to the principles which are necessary to the life of civilized and Christian nations'. While his speech angered monarchists and right-wing Catholics who scented betrayal, it won wide support from moderate opinion. The 'toast of Algiers' was to inaugurate the '*ralliement*' which was to create, if but temporarily, a better understanding between the Catholic Church and the French State.

In effect it brought into being a breathing-space in which both sides saw the wisdom of coexistence. The Pope gave the '*ralliement*' his blessing in the encyclical *Au milieu des sollicitudes* of 17 February 1892. It was, however, soon to prove something of a Pyrrhic victory. Many French Catholics put their hopes in the formation of a Catholic conservative party which would displace the Republicans, but such hopes soon proved to be vain. What really doomed the '*ralliement*' was the external crisis created by the arrest of the French army officer, the Jew Alfred Dreyfus, on a trumped-up charge of betraying military secrets to the Germans. Dreyfus was sentenced to life-imprisonment on Devil's Island. Gradually doubts were expressed as to whether there had been a serious miscarriage of justice, a fear expressed powerfully in Emile Zola's open letter *J'accuse*, for which the author was convicted of libel. Subsequently, in 1898, Commmandant Henry of the French military intelligence admitted that he had forged one of the documents central to Dreyfus's guilt. Even so the French government acted tardily, even after Henry committed suicide, and some years elapsed before Dreyfus was granted a free pardon.

The Dreyfus case involved the Catholic Church, if to some extent unjustly, for Dreyfus appeared the victim of anti-Semitism which had been promoted in some quarters of the French Church, represented, for instance in Drumont's *La France Juive*, published in 1886, which went into 127 editions in two years. The journal *La Croix* of the newly formed religious order the Assumptionists was outspokenly anti-Semitic and anti-Dreyfusard. The Church was also known to be sympathetic towards army officers as a conservative force unpolluted by freemasonry and radicalism. In the backlash to the Dreyfus case the French Catholics became the unfortunate if not wholly undeserved scapegoat.

If it was not the Dreyfus case alone which destroyed the high hopes of the '*ralliement*', it was a nail in its coffin. The Republicans, buffeted by tales of scandal and corruption, needed to find a cause which drew away attention from their own ills. They were to find it in a further burst of anti-clerical legislation. In 1901 the French parliament ordered all religious orders to seek authorization on penalty of the confiscation of their properties and the dispersal of their members. It was yet another blow aimed at the Church in the hope of bringing the concordat between Church and State to an end, but the aged Pope was to die before the final denouement occurred.

Leo XIII died in 1903 at the age of ninety-three. At the close of his lengthy pontificate the decline in the Church's political influence had not been effectually stemmed. A new crisis for the Church had broken out in

France. Relations with the Russian government, with which an agreement had been reached in 1882, were strained. The papal secretary of state, Cardinal Rampolla, was so unpopular with the Austrians that they imposed a veto on his candidature. Catholicism seemed at its strongest in backward countries like Ireland and Spain where in spite of lip service paid to the freedom of religion public ceremonies of other faiths were largely inadmissible.

Nonetheless the Catholic Church had not stood still in the closing decade of the nineteenth century. The Church began to face squarely up to the social problems generated by an increasingly industrialized and urban society, and to seek a *rapprochement* with the working classes from which in some countries it had become alienated. In France Albert de Mun's Cercles and its sequel the Association Catholique de la Jeunesse Française envisaged the development of a Christian democracy; Catholiques d'Ouvriers had a membership of 40,000 in 1880. In Belgium J. Cardejn laid the foundations of the Jeunesse Ouvrière Chretienne. Catholic unions, however, were in a minority and how far they stemmed the process of de-Christianization among the working class may well be doubted.

The Pope had himself addressed the problem in the bull *Rerum Novarum* of 1891. Rejecting both economic liberalism and socialism, the bull recommended the creation of Catholic associations 'composed of workers alone or mixed [i.e. with owners or employers]', a phrase which Leo had personally inserted into the document. The bull reminded secular governments of their responsibility for ensuring distributive justice, including the payment of a just wage and the provision of good working conditions. Although *Rerum Novarum* in its concern with economic issues was a landmark and a positive encouragement to those who were seeking to set up working-class unions, it marked no great advance in Catholic thinking on the nature of society. Yet as an expression of the Pope's desire to establish the Church's hegemony in these spheres, it implied rather than stated explicitly that the Church was beginning to see its role less as the established religion, even in Catholic states and rather as an autonomous group existing in a secular state. While it could not accept the validity of religious toleration since this implied that all faiths were of equal value, it seemed to recognize that in a pluralistic society it was realistic to pursue a *modus vivendi.*

The Church continued, however, to maintain a rigid discipline within its own confines. Leo had shown some awareness of the Church's need to take advances in modern scholarship into account, for he encouraged scientific study and in 1883 he opened the Vatican archives to all comers, irrespective of creed. But his approach was cautious and ultimately conservative. He put his trust in the revival of Thomist scholasticism, and remained deeply suspicious of what savoured of modernist theology. He endeavoured to draw up guide lines for biblical study through the establishment in 1902 of a permanent biblical commission. The encyclical *Prudentissimo* (1893) declared that the Bible was 'written under the inspiration of the Holy Ghost. The divine inspiration, far from admitting the existence of error, by itself excludes all error.' Offenders found themselves firmly rapped on the knuckles. Lenormant, who described Genesis as a sacred legend, had his book placed on the Index of proscribed texts. Alfred Loisy in France and George Tyrrell in England were themselves expounding a modernist theology which was to bring upon them the wrath of Leo's successor. Although the Pope spoke of the reunion of 'separated brothers', he had pronounced Anglican orders as invalid in the encyclical *Apostolicae Curae* issued in 1896. Yet his achievement cannot be underestimated. He had broken through the ring of isolation with which Pius IX had fenced in the Vatican from the outside world, and in so doing had strengthened the moral prestige and standing of the Roman Church.

Whether this policy would be followed by his successor was questionable, for conservative elements in the Church were uneasy at the modest compromises that he had made. The favourite at the ensuing conclave, the papal secretary of state, Cardinal Rampolla was thought to be too close to the late Pope and possibly responsible for the failure of the *'ralliement'*; the Austrians imposed a veto on his election. The conclave, consisting of thirty-eight Italian and twenty-four foreign cardinals, among them for the first time an American, elected the patriarch of Venice, Cardinal Sarto.

The village postman's son, remembering the traditionalism of Pius IX and the piety of Pius V 'who in past centuries had courageously fought against sects and rampant errors' took the name Pius X. It was an ominous choice. No one doubted the devotion of this 68-year-old priest, which was to form the main ingredient in his canonization in 1954. He saw his task above all in spiritual terms, his motto *'instaurare in Christo'*. He encouraged the faithful to take communion which Jesus had intended 'to be the daily remedy and the daily food for our daily shortcomings', tried to purify church music, eliminating its orchestral and operatic qualities and promoting the Gregorian chant recently retrieved by the monks of Solesmes. He reformed the missal, improved instruction in the seminaries and began the revision of canon law under the lead of Monsignor Gasparri, an immense task completed by 1916. He warmly supported international Eucharistic congresses. The administrative structure of the Church, in many respects chaotic and out of date, was rationalized. Pius X surrounded himself by a coterie of like-minded advisers, rigorous, able, but narrow, the Spanish Capuchin Vives y Tuto, Gaetano De Lai and the aristocratic but intransigent secretary of state Merry del Val. Careful as he was to care for the spiritual good of the Church, he was unlikely to wish to come to terms with the changing world.

Like Pius IX he had a high view not merely of the Church as a divine society but also of his own office, commissioned by God and not amenable to the wills and whims of men. The world outside the Church was a sea of darkness, the Church itself a fortress besieged by the minions of Satan, free thinkers, freemasons, socialists and secularists. He would have no truck with Protestants, was unwilling to receive President Theodore Roosevelt in audience in 1910 unless the president cancelled a proposed visit to the Methodist church in Rome; the president very properly refused. He held that governments had an intrinsic obligation to respect the rights of the Church as a divine institution. He threatened to break off relations with Austria when the government refused to suspend a professor of canon law at Innsbruck university suspected of modernism. In Portugal where the end of the monarchy and the proclamation of the republic had been followed by anti-clerical legislation, limiting religious freedom and suspending religious instruction in schools, the papal nuncio was expelled in 1913. But it was to be in France that papal intransigence was to prove most disastrous.

Here the anti-clerical legislation which had been promised shortly before Leo XIII's death came to a head with a law of separation in 1905. The new prime minister, Emile Combes, who had once been a failed ordinand and had written a thesis on Aquinas but had later become a freemason and a freethinker, was determined to break the power of the Church. Further religious congregations were dispersed. Nuns were expelled from hospitals, crucifixes were torn down from the walls of the law courts, Church schools were closed; and to add insult to injury a new battleship was named the *Ernest Renan*, so named after the radical author of the unorthodox *Life of Jesus*. Pius X had already a dim view of the French Church, believing the episcopate to be insufficiently tough; and he was made very angry by learning that the French president Loubet was to pay a state visit to the king of Italy. Merry del Val's injudicious letter of protest on this occasion which was circulated to other governments led France to recall its ambassador from the Vatican. A fresh cause of friction occurred when the Pope ordered two French bishops to resign, Géay of Laval who had apparently entered into a romantic correspondence with a mother superior and Le Nordez of Dijon who had been foolish enough to don a masonic apron, but though Combes suspended the payments of the bishops' stipends, he would not let them resign.

Everything was now in train to bring the Concordat which for a century had governed the relations between the Church and the State to a close. By the law of separation, which was passed by 314 votes to 233, the state took over all Church buildings and property, setting up *associations cultuelles* to supervise their future. After an interim period of four years the State would cease to pay clerical stipends. Seminarists would still be excused from military service, and chaplains would continue to be appointed for the services and for hospitals. On the positive side bishops would be henceforth free to communicate with Rome and to rearrange parochial and diocesan boundaries.

In the country at large, more especially in the de-Christianized areas, the measure was popular, for while it took away from the State its right to appoint bishops, it was freed from the financial obligation of paying the clergy. The French Church at first reacted vigorously against the legislation, but second thoughts showed that, with good guidance by the politicians such as the judicious Briand the *associations cultuelles* could work to the benefit of religion, fitting into the existing system of Church government, so that an increasing number of bishops and priests gave the measure a grudging acceptance.

But Pius X had no such inhibitions. In the encyclical *Vehementer*, published on 11 February 1906, he condemned the law of separation, insisting that the State was obliged to give the Church a recognized place in the social order as a divine society, and to pay deference to the claims of God. Nor were the French bishops, trying to get on with their job in difficult circumstances, helped by the Pope's express disapproval of the *associations cultuelles* in a further encyclical *Gravissimo*.

In practice the consequences of this breach between Church and State were less serious than was feared. For while cathedrals and churches had become the property of the State, and were occasionally the target of left-wing vandalism, for the most part diocesan and parochial life went on much as it had done in the past. The clergy were deprived of their presbyteries (though in some instances the communes allowed them to live there rent free), but the Pope could now appoint bishops without depending on the State, and took advantage to instal men of ultramontanist views. The severance of the State from the Church enabled the Church to concentrate on its primary religious and pastoral role, a task all the more important in view of the continuing signs of decline in religion; ordinations, 1,753 in 1901, had slumped to 825 by 1913.

Pius X's disapproval of the French secular state was only one and perhaps a less important ingredient in his onslaught on the modernist tendencies which seemed to him to threaten the integrity of the faith. Modernists did not merely query the Church's attitude to the social order, but in the interests of truth wished to submit the exegesis of the Bible, religious doctrine and philosophy to critical analysis, dismissing their opponents in the words of the German modernist theologian Scheel as 'mental eunuchs'. A leading French modernist Alfred Loisy declared that Christianity must be regarded as an evolving rather than a static faith, arguing, in his *L'Evangile et l Eglise*, published in 1902, like the German Protestant Adolf Harnack, that Christianity and the gospel are not necessarily identical. 'Dogmas are not truths descending from heaven' but changing symbols of an eternal truth. The archbishop of Paris, Cardinal Richard, condemned Loisy's book as likely to 'confuse seriously the faithful's belief in the fundamental dogmas of the Catholic Church'.

The leading English modernist was George Tyrrell, an Anglican who had become a Jesuit. 'I understand a modernist', he wrote, 'to be a Christian of any denomination who is convinced that the essential truths of his religion and the essential truths of modern society can enter into a synthesis.' Dogmas, he explained, seemed merely a human attempt to express the divine force within man in intellectual formulas which lacked the hallmark of divine infallibility. The inspiration of the Bible, the authority of the ecclesiastical hierarchy, the doctrine of the Church were all under fire. Similar criticism came from some intellectual circles in Germany and Italy where Ernesto Bonaiuti tried to make the Church's teaching more palatable.

It is understandable that to the Vatican modernist teaching, which seemed to suggest that ultimately truth was relative rather than absolute, was a dangerous growth, a cancer which must be excised from the Church. On 3 July 1907 Pius X issued a decree *Lamentabili*, listing some sixty-five errors, mainly taken from the works of Loisy, which was directed against 'religious neo-reformism' whose promoters 'profess and disseminate in subtle forms monstrous errors'. A few months later on 8 September 1907 by the bull *Pascendi*, he condemned two errors specifically, agnosticism which was defined as 'the restriction of knowledge to phenomena' and Immanentism or subjectivism.

Anyone who is in any way found to be tainted with Modernism is to be excluded without compunction from those offices, whether of government or of teaching, and those who already occupy them are to be removed. The same policy is to be adopted towards those who openly or secretly lend countenance to modernism, either by extolling the Modernists or excusing their culpable conduct or by carping at scholasticism or the *Magisterium* of the Church, or by refusing obedience to ecclesiastical authority, or any of its depositions; or towards those who show a love of novelty in history, archaeology or biblical exegesis; and finally towards those who neglect the sacred sciences or appear to prefer secular science to them.

So was initiated and sustained an intellectual reaction involving a policy of persecution of nonconformists which seemed reminiscent of a neo-inquisition. 'Councils of vigilance' were set up as watchdogs to hunt out dissentients in every province. A secret network of informers operated under the guidance of the papal secretary of state. Loisy who in his recent book *Autour d'un petit livre* had advocated the liberation of history from outmoded theology was condemned. He agreed to submit to the Holy Office, but in the sequel lost his faith. The English Jesuit George Tyrrell was expelled from his order and excommunicated. Already a victim of Bright's disease which may have made his pen more acidulous, he decided to reject his orders altogether and to adopt a socialistic humanitarianism. When he died the Roman Church refused him Christian burial, and it was left to an Anglican priest to perform the last rites.

Men suspected of modernism were summarily dismissed from office. The historian of the early Church, Duchesne, an impeccable scholar, had his work placed on the Index in 1912 where it was joined by the Abbé

Bremont's life of Sainte-Chantal. The Pope threatened to suspend the theological faculty of Fribourg. Learned journals such as the *Revue Biblique* and the *Annales de philosophie chrètienne* fell under papal displeasure. The distinguished archaeologist Father Lagrange was recalled from Jerusalem.

What may be described anachronistically as papal McCarthyism had no limits. The Pope was as suspicious of socialism as he was of heterodoxy, holding that workers' movements were only legitimate as long as they were under the guidance of the hierarchy. He condemned Marc Sangnier's *Le Sillon* movement in France which was seeking to accommodate Catholicism to left-wing political ideas and suspended the Opera dei Congressis which coordinated associations of Catholic workers in Italy. While there can be little doubt that in his concern for the Church Pius X was a truly pastoral pope his inflexibility did the Church little service and had disastrous effects, acting as a potent constraint on Catholic critical scholarship for a generation or more, keeping its scholars within the narrow confines of neo-Thomism.

On Pius's death on 20 August 1914 the conclave chose Giacomo della Chiesa, the archbishop of Bologna, as Benedict XV. The new Pope had been earlier an associate of Leo XIII's secretary of state Rampolla and for that reason had been regarded with some suspicion by Pius X who though he had made him archbishop of Bologna had not given him a cardinal's hat until May 1914. From the start his pontificate was overshadowed by the outbreak of the Great War which pushed theological controversy into the background. 'When war had broken out', as the Protestant medical missionary Albert Schweitzer observed, 'religion capitulated. It became demobilized. In the war, religion lost its purity, and lost its authority.' The Pope saw it as his task to seek to halt the conflict, declaring his neutrality, condemning the 'useless slaughter' and putting forward a plan in 1917 for a negotiated peace based on natural justice rather than military victory. But no one heeded and many criticized him. The Italians, accusing him of defeatism, nicknamed him Maladetto XV. He was suspected of favouring Catholic Austria against the Orthodox Serbs, and even of wishing for a German victory since the Germans had promised to restore Rome to the Pope after Italy had been defeated. In any case national feeling had led the clergy of every nation to embrace the patriotic cause. The First World War underlined the Vatican's political impotence.

The Pope turned with relief to his main interest, the missionary work of the Church, in the encyclical *Maximum Illud* (30 November 1919) enunciating the principles that should govern future missionary activity, urging that wherever possible local or native clergy should be employed.

Benedict's pontificate which ended in 1922 was a breathing space, almost a hiatus, before the enthronement of a more traditional pontiff, the able and enigmatic Achille Ratti, a mountaineer in his youth and a genuine scholar and palaeographer, who was the compromise choice of a divided conclave. Politically so much more realistic than Pius X – some would say almost disastrously so – he followed in the footsteps of Leo XIII in accepting the credentials of secular states while seeking to safeguard the privileges of the Church as a divine society. He was operating in a totally new situation, a Europe of new states and disturbed vision, which was to become the more unstable as the euphoria of victory faded. As the senior monarch in Europe, he was under some obligation to give a moral lead; he was only partially successful, and in some respects his objectives were themselves flawed.

Benedict XV had managed to reach a measure of entente with the French state in 1915; and his successor sought to continue and implement his policy. In spite of opposition from the Radicals under Clemenceau diplomatic relations with the Holy See were resumed in 1921 and three years later an agreement was reached on the vexed question of Church property. Although anti-clericalism continued to be a feature of French life the experience of the First World War had brought a measure of reconciliation between the Church and the people. The Church had proved strongly patriotic; some twenty-five thousand priests, religious and seminarians had served in the armed forces, of whom 4,608 died. The canonization in 1920 of Jeanne d'Arc, as a national heroine, formed a fitting climax. The Christian cause in France had been further strengthened by the contemporary Christian literary renaissance, expressed in the works of the poet Paul Claudel, the novelist Georges Bernanos, the gifted interpreter of Aquinas, Etienne Gilson, the scholarly biographer of St Augustine, Henri Marrou. The Jesuits at Fourière and the Dominicans at Le Saulchoir encouraged interest in the scriptures and writings of the Church fathers. The Church's concern with social reform received a new stimulus.

Such endeavours provided some evidence as to the rich reservoir of French Catholic spirituality, but how far it stemmed the flight from the Church may be doubted. Father Lhande's book *Le Christ dans le Banlieu*, published in 1927, underlined the numbers untouched by the Church. 'There is', Cardinal Suhard exclaimed when he was bishop of Bayeux, 'a whole region around Caen, containing all great factories where Christ is unknown.' A dozen years later he was to establish the Mission de France which had its headquarters at Lisieux with St Thérèse as its patron designed to prepare young priests to fulfil their vocation in working-class areas.

Pope Pius XI had a measure of success in France, even if the Vatican remained apprehensive at experimental methods of evangelization. In Italy the situation was already extremely serious after the Fascists seized power. Benito Mussolini, originally strongly anti-clerical, saw that it would be politically expedient to come to terms with the Church to counter his critics, more especially the Catholic Democratic Party, the Partito Popolare, led by an able priest Don Luigi Sturzo, the general secretary of Catholic Action. After 1870 the Vatican had discouraged the faithful from any participation in Italian politics, but Benedict XV, moving cautiously towards an entente with the Italian state, had approved the setting up of the Catholic Democratic Party. Pius XI too saw the advantages of reaching an amicable agreement with the Italian state.

In January 1923 the papal secretary of state Cardinal Gasparri had a secret meeting with Mussolini. The Italian leader expressed his willingness to permit religious instruction in schools, the restoration of crucifixes on public buildings, the appointment of military chaplains and an improvement in clerical stipends. The bait worked, for Pius XI, adverse in any case to democratic movements, advised Luigi Sturzo against making a compact with the anti-clerical Socialist Party in opposition to Mussolini. Sturzo was obliged to resign from the secretaryship of Catholic Action and, to Mussolini's relief, went into exile.

Regardless of Mussolini's ruthless suppression of his opponents and the totalitarianism of his government, the Pope agreed in February 1929 to the Lateran Treaty whereby Italy recognized the independence of the Vatican state and the Church gained some concessions with respect to marriage and education. The ending of the fifty-year feud was doubtless a significant diplomatic triumph for the Church, but to some it seemed at the cost of the Church's soul, for it had virtually given its imprimatur to Italian fascism as the Church's conduct during Mussolini's Ethiopian venture in 1935 was to demonstrate. The Italian Church failed to criticize the brutal and ruthless means he took to achieve his end. 'The blessing of God', the bishop of Cremona declared, 'be upon these soldiers who on African soil, will conquer new and fertile lands for the Italian genius, thereby bringing to them Roman and Christian culture.' 'Italy's arms', Cardinal Schuster of Milan allowed, 'brought the triumph of the Cross, opening the gate of Abyssinia to the Catholic faith and civilisation.' In practice this came down to the expulsion of all non-Italian Catholic missionaries, the closing of Protestant missions and the persecution of the native Coptic Church. So much for the triumph of the cross. In Ethiopia it was the sword which had proved victorious.

It was hardly surprising that the Catholic Church should have strongly supported General Franco's campaign against the Spanish republicans, backed by the Communists, which, after three years of appalling bloodshed ended with Franco's capture of Madrid in March 1939. The wealth and power of the Spanish Church had long been criticized by more liberal Spaniards, but in the ensuing conflict neither side showed any quarter. Churches and monasteries were looted and burned; bishops, priests and nuns were massacred. The Church identified Franco's opponents with the Communists, but in pledging its warm support for the Spanish dictator it showed again its basic sympathy with authoritarian regimes. In return it was to receive privileges and favour.

The situation in Germany was more complex since the Roman Church was only one of many Churches, but there too the dread of Communism made it overly sympathetic to the Nazi regime. In the 1920s the Catholic Centre Party through some measure of cooperation with the socialists had helped to provide a political balance, but the Catholic Church failed to give the Centre Party any significant support against the Nazi seizure of power.

Seeming to ignore the ruthless methods by which Hitler had achieved the chancellorship in 1931, the Church in 1933 negotiated a concordat with the new German government. Individual bishops such as Cardinal Faulhaber of Munich or von Preysing of Berlin or von Galen of Munster might protest against Nazi treatment of the Church but neither the Catholics nor the Protestants effectively opposed the crimes perpetrated by the Nazis and the horrors of anti-Semitism and later of the concentration camps. Even Faulhaber stated in 1933 that there were more important matters, such as education, for the Church to consider. In March 1941 Archbishop Grober of Freiburg in a pastoral letter anti-Semitic in tone blamed the Jews for the death of Christ and spoke of the self-imposed curse that they had brought upon themselves. Pope Pius XI was conveniently silent when the Aryan laws were introduced, made no protest at the pogrom of November 1938, but on Palm Sunday 1937 in his encyclical *Mit Brennender Sorge* he had denounced the breaches of the Concordat and the concept of a German National Church as fundamentally anti-Christian, though even there he did not speak specifically of crimes against the Jews. The German playwright Rolf Hochhuth's play *The Representative (Der Stellvertreler)* indicted Pius XI for his failure to do anything to save the Jews; it was an exaggerated assault but there could be no doubt that for diplomatic reasons Pius XI had soft-pedalled.

The Pope's apparent support for anti-democratic regimes was rooted in his dread and detestation of atheistic Communism which he trounced in the encyclical *Divini Redemptoris* (19 March 1937), but also in his traditional view of authority and his conception of the Church. It was his fervent if unrealistic wish for a Christ-centred world, believing that through the suffusion of Christ in the world the world would be saved. In 1925 he had instituted the festival of Christ the King. He sought to give practical expression to his ideal by encouraging the laity through Catholic Action to play their part in the Church's mission. Mindful of the need for the Church to contribute to the amelioration of society, he had issued the bull *Quadragesimo Anno* (15 May 1931), a sort of sequel to Leo XIII's *Rerum Novarum,* and in other encyclicals *Nova impendet* (2 October 1931) and *Caritate Christi* (3 May 1932) he sought to tackle the problems of unemployment; but such documents were theological causeries rather than realistic social programmes.

Like his predecessor he was at his happiest in promoting missions in the overseas Church, supporting the movement to try to create indigenous ministries. He consecrated six Chinese bishops and a Japanese, and the number of native priests in general rose from three thousand to over seven thousand. What was happening in the overseas Church may have contributed to the Pope's confidence in the future, and conceivably to his narrow vision, and his opposition to cooperation with other Churches. For while he encouraged, though with little success, closer relations with the Orthodox Church, he was totally disinclined to take any part in the oecumenical movement or to engage in any dialogue with the Protestants except on the terms of no surrender. In *Mortalium animos* (6 January 1928) he forbade the faithful to confer with non-Romans, denouncing the notion that the Church might conceivably be a federation of different Christian faiths, understandably insisting that the Roman Church was the only true Church.

Pope Pius XI died on 10 February 1939 as the world slumped towards the Second World War. It took the cardinals only a day at the third ballot to elect by a handsome majority the papal secretary of state Eugenio Pacelli as Pius XII. He was an experienced diplomat with a good knowledge of Germany with which he had negotiated the concordat of 1933, but temperamentally he was ill suited to coping with crises. During the Second World War which was to overshadow the early years of his pontificate, like Benedict XV to whom he had been earlier close, he asserted the Vatican's neutrality and made abortive efforts for peace. Through the Pontifical Aid Commission he promoted the relief of war victims and after Hitler's occupation of Rome on 10 September 1943 he offered the Vatican City as a refuge. His critics accused him as they had his predecessor of failing to condemn Nazi atrocities with sufficient vigour. In spite of the dreadful treatment meted out by the Nazis to the Polish Catholics – 3,647 bishops and priests were confined in concentration camps of whom 2,000 died – the Pope seemed to make comparatively little effort to make contact with the Polish Church.

In some sense the Roman Church might well have seemed to be marking time in the past half-century, for the twentieth-century Popes had shown only a limited appreciation of the fundamental problems which affected the Church, relying on traditional solutions. Although they were men of genuine spirituality, they were not inspired leaders. Yet the Catholic Church at least numerically was continuing to advance. In Great Britain, excluding Ireland, in 1912 Catholics numbered 2.33 million out of a total population of 40.8 million and were still growing. In the United States Catholics had increased from 4.5 million (out of a total of 33.5 million) in 1871, to 12 million (out of 78 million) in 1900, and by 1957 were estimated to form 25.7 per cent of the population, constituting the largest single religious group. In Australia where there had been 40,000 Catholics in 1841 by 1885 they numbered 85,000 out of a total population of 3.78 million. In 1971 it was estimated that of about 14 million Christians approximately 8 million were Roman Catholics. This great march forward served sometimes to conceal underlying weaknesses.

THE CHURCHES IN ENGLAND

In the Protestant Churches, so much more diverse in character as in doctrine, somewhat different criteria have to be applied in adjudging their performance, though they were in some ways afflicted by the same problems as the Romans. In Britain before the First World War there was much to

David's painting of Napoleon crowning himself Emperor of France on 2 December 1804 in the presence of Pope Pius VII. (Mansell Collection)

Proclaiming the dogma of papal infallibility at the first Vatican Council, held in the Council Chamber at St Peter's, Rome, 1870. (Mansell Collection)

Pope Pius IX in council, December 1869. (Mansell Collection)

The Oriel Fathers, Manning, Pusey, Newman, Keble and Wilberforce, founders of the Oxford Movement, inaugurated in 1833. (Pusey House Library)

South Sea missionary John Williams, clubbed to death on Erromagna Island, 1839. It was reported that he was later cooked and eaten. (E.T. Archives)

The Shakers, a mid-nineteenth-century American communal movement, so-called because of the shaking by which they were possessed under the stress of spiritual exaltation. Founded by an English woman, Anne Lee, they followed simple styles and austere living, and engaged in ritual dances like the 'square-order' dance shown here. (Shaker Museum and Library, Old Chatham, New York)

Dr Livingstone's last journey before his death at Chitambo village near Lake Bangweolo in 1873. (Mary Evans Picture Library)

Pope Leo XIII, pope from 1878 to 1903. (Mansell Collection)

Billy Graham, American evangelist, at Earl's Court, London. Since his evangelistic work began in 1949, Graham's preaching has led thousands of people to commit themselves to the Christian faith. (Andes Press Agency)

The celebration of the Russian millennium: the service in commemoration of the dead ancestors at St Nicholas' Cathedral in Alma Ata, Kazakhstan, May 1988. (Novosti (London))

e Pope and Archbishop Runcie meeting in Rome in 1989. (John Manning/Times Newspapers
nited)

evd Faith Cully celebrating her first Eucharist at St John's, Fishponds, Bristol, March 1994.
Andes Press Agency)

Desmond Tutu, bishop of Johannesburg and from 1986 archbishop of Cape Town, prominent in the movement against apartheid but also a proponent of reconciliation between the races. (Hulton Getty)

suggest that both the Church of England and the Free Churches flourished. The number of candidates for ordination, now better trained than they had once been through attendance at specialized theological colleges, continued to rise as did the number of baptisms, confirmations and participants at Easter communion. In 1903 some 3,722,317 children were being educated in Church schools. Other statistics were, however, less encouraging. A religious census carried out in London in 1903 showed that Church membership of the Church of England had fallen from 535,715 in 1886 to 396,196 in 1901; Church marriages per thousand also showed signs of decline (1874, 747 per thousand; 1884, 707; 1894, 686; 1904, 642; 1909, 614; 1919, 597). The seepage seemed less to have been a falling off in the working-class membership, which had never been very closely associated with the established Church, than in the steady haemorrhage of its middle-class adherents.

The Church of England in its ministry as in its following continued to be in the main a class-oriented society. Its bishops were usually the products of the English public school (twenty-five Etonians were, for example, bishops between 1860 and 1900) and of Oxford and Cambridge, not infrequently related to the peerage and the landed gentry. Their houses, often still palatial, were staffed by domestics and they found it easy to accommodate themselves to the leather arm chairs of the Athenaeum Club or the benches of the House of Lords. This did not necessarily mean that they could not be good bishops but the episcopal image in some sense remained aristocratic or at least gentrified. The mass of the Anglican clergy came from a similar social background, still occupying a prestigious position after the squire in many a country village. 'The grand atmosphere of many country rectories is one of *paupertas ambitiosa*,' D.N. Bennet wrote in 1914, 'the hat-touchings and curtseyings, the wagonettes driven by the gardeners in livery, the girls to have new frocks for the county ball, the sons to be "educated as gentlemen".' The establishment of new training colleges for the clergy at Kelham and Mirfield opened the way to the admission of ordinands who had not necessarily attended a public school and university and so helped to modify the distinctively middle-class image of the Anglican clergy. While the First World War was to help bring about a social change, vestigially the prevailing ethos in the 1920s and 1930s was still essentially middle class. If the Church of England could never be properly called the Tory Party at prayer, its attitudes were politically and socially profoundly conservative in spite of recognizably socialist groups in the Church.

The strength of its membership probably still came from women (men were more likely to be defectors from membership), though the Church was still male-oriented. In 1897 the Convocation of Canterbury had insisted that all members of parish councils must be men. Whereas the Free Churches began to open their ministry to women, the Church of England remained assertively male. 'The scheme of the ladies who desire ordination has for a long time been familiar to me,' Canon Lacey commented in 1916. 'I have never found occasion to do anything but laugh at it.' When Maude Royden, paradoxically an Anglican who became a minister of the Congregational Temple, tried to attend a meeting of the Life and Liberty movement at Cuddeson Theological College the then principal J.B. Seaton refused to allow her to sleep in the building.

The chief impetus to Anglican vitality in the early decades of the twentieth century were the enthusiasm and activity of the Anglo-Catholics, the legatees of the earlier Tractarians. In the past Anglo-Catholic clergy had been occasionally victims both of prosecution (by the ecclesiastical authorities) and of persecution, as a result of mob prejudice and episcopal action, leading to unsavoury trials of priests who had contravened the canons for ritualism. In spite of continuing disapproval from the more extreme Evangelicals, the Anglo-Catholics had gradually achieved respectability. Anglo-Catholic priests, such as Father Mackonochie at St Andrew's, Holborn and Father Lowder in Portsmouth, working in slum areas, were admired for the austerity of their lives and their unswerving devotion to their people. Moreover Anglo-Catholic theology, originally conservative and even neo-fundamentalist, had come to terms with modern research both in textual criticism and philosophy. There had developed a more positive and richer pastoral life, with growing importance attached to Eucharistic theology and the celebration of the communion. The incidentals of Eucharistic worship – the importance of confession, the eastward position of the celebrant, the candles on the altar, the use of vestments and incense, the ceremonial mixing of water with wine in the chalice, and the employment of the reserved sacrament as an object of devotion – opened up new vistas in English Church life and were a stimulus to spirituality.

It had taken some time for Anglo-Catholics to make the grade. At first, apart from the high-spirited missionary bishop Frank Weston of Zanzibar, they lacked representatives on the episcopal bench, though they had a friend in Charles Gore, the first principal of Pusey House, the Anglo-Catholic centre in Oxford. Gore subsequently became bishop of Worcester, Birmingham and Oxford; he was a man learned and emotional, autocratic by nature but radical in attitude, as evinced by his presidency of the Christian Social Union and founding of the Community of the Resurrection at Mirfield. Cosmo Gordon Lang, the archbishop of York who was to succeed Randall Davidson at Canterbury in 1928 was a friend and patron of Anglo-Catholics. He was the first archbishop since the Middle Ages to wear a mitre, for copes and mitres had previously been thought to represent a degraded form of Romanism (a photograph taken of Bishop King of Lincoln so garbed, published in a local newspaper caused scandal), but in subsequent years they were to become recognized episcopal costume.

The Church of England had emerged from the First World War with only partial credit. No doubt its chaplains, as those from other denominations, had often performed a courageous and dangerous task in administering the sacraments and bringing comfort to the troops, but many had reasonably enough only a limited capacity for doing their job. While Archbishop

Randall Davidson perspicaciously disapproved of the use of the pulpit as a recruiting agency, many of his fellow bishops and clergy, free churchmen as well as Anglicans, took a bellicose attitude. The bishop of London, Arthur Winnington-Ingram, flamboyant, kindly and silly, wrote in 1915 that 'What the Church is to do, I answer, MOBILISE THE NATION FOR A HOLY WAR', and proceeded to do so to the best of his limited ability. There was only a comparatively small group of conscientious objectors, some sixteen and a half thousand, many of them objecting for religious reasons, Quakers in the main. Fundamentally the First World War was to lead to an erosion of faith.

The Church of England entered into the disturbed decades of the 1920s and 1930s somewhat uncertain of its objectives. Under the lead of William Temple, then bishop of Manchester, the movement known as Life and Liberty sought to give the Church a wider degree of self-government; the Church Enabling Act of 1919 brought into existence the Church Assembly. Its institution highlighted a problem which has not yet been resolved, how to reconcile the Church's cherished freedom and independence, which viewing the Church as a divine society the Anglo-Catholics just as the Tractarians held to be fundamental to its being, with its function as a national Church headed by the monarch and regulated by parliament. This issue became acute with the attempt to revise the 1662 Book of Common Prayer, in part to satisfy the aspirations of Anglo-Catholics who wanted to restore the prayer of consecration to its original place in the liturgy and provide for the reservation of the sacrament, for reservation had been permitted only on a temporary basis in 1911 to facilitate communicating the sick;* as a result of the experience of the First World War, with its heavy casualties, its use had become more regular. The revised prayer book passed easily through the three houses of the Church Assembly but it was defeated twice in parliament, in December 1927 and in June 1928. The defeat had been manipulated by a few Evangelical members of parliament, backed by some right-wing Anglo-Catholics, appealing to a majority of no particular religious persuasion. While the revised prayer book may have been liturgically defective, that the worship of the Church should be determined by a body of men and women in no sense representative of the Christian Church revealed the painful, if not the inadmissible, nature of the establishment. The futility of what had occurred was demonstrated further as clergy continued to use the 1928 prayer book, though it was not authorized, so underlining the indiscipline of the Church and the partisanship which was further promoting its disunity.

---

* The practice of keeping the Bread (and sometimes the Wine) consecrated at the Eucharist in a receptacle or pyx or tabernacle in the Church dated from early times; but while provided for in the Anglican prayer book of 1549 it was disallowed by the prayer books of 1559 and 1662. The attempt to insert a rubric allowing the practice, common in Roman churches, was one of the reasons for the defeat of the 1927/8 prayer book measure. Its intention was primarily to enable Communion to be given to the sick who could not attend the church.

After Randall Davidson's long and diplomatic primacy, Cosmo Gordon Lang came from York to preside over the destiny of the Church of England. He was a Scot with the Celtic gift of second sight and was an excellent operator albeit he lacked the powers of effective and inspired leadership in a Church which his contemporary Bishop Hensley Henson described as 'moving like a rudderless vessel over a rock-haunted ocean'. He had been prominent in promoting the abdication of Edward VIII, but his strong line, seeming to some moralistic and unfeeling, was much criticized. In the life of the Church of England Lang was less significant than his successor, William Temple. An archbishop's son, an Oxford don, a public school headmaster before his preferment to the see of Manchester, Temple, who was blessed with an acute mind and was indeed no mean theologian as well as benefiting from an avuncular disposition, possessed spiritual insight and prophetic vision. Serious-minded, scholarly, deeply religious, yet void of pomposity or prelacy, Temple wished for the freedom and independence of the Church, urged the necessity of social reform and hoped for an essential synthesis of theology and modern culture. There had been within Anglicanism some glimmers of a literary renaissance, as the poems of T.S. Eliot and the novels of C.S. Lewis were to demonstrate. But Temple's archiepiscopate, coinciding with years of war, was tragically short, for he died in 1944. Whether he would have been able to cope with the problems of the postwar Church must remain in doubt, for fundamentally he seemed a man of an earlier epoch, his philosophy in question, his judgement of character sometimes in doubt and his optimism possibly misplaced. The Church Assembly, of which he had hoped so much, was to prove a disappointment. Yet his exemplary wisdom can hardly be doubted.

The Churches reacted to the outbreak of the Second World War with far greater restraint than they had in 1914. In the immediate pre-war years there had been a substantial growth in Christian pacifism, with some distinguished leaders, such as the Cambridge professor Charles Raven, and the charismatic if emotionally confused H.R.L. Sheppard, the founder of the Peace Pledge Union and dean of Canterbury. But in the changing international situation pacifism shrunk to a small rump, and the majority of British Christians saw participation in the war as a moral obligation to fight against the powers of evil which Hitler and the Nazis seemed to symbolize. The Churches were, however, far less blatantly nationalistic than they had been in 1914, and tried, if with very limited success, to restrain the nation's leaders, more especially the incomparable but fiercely belligerent Winston Churchill, from sacrificing in the effort to achieve victory the moral principles for which the nation was supposedly fighting. The major politicians, among them Churchill and Eden, were not for the most part committed Christians, but they readily presented the war as a Christian crusade against the forces of evil. Some Church leaders, including Temple himself but most notably George Bell, the bishop of Chichester, a fervent spokesman for humanity, criticized the demand for unconditional surrender as the price of victory, and condemned the saturation bombing of German cities, a line which may well have robbed Bell of his opportunity to succeed Temple. But at least it served to demonstrate that there were British churchmen who were concerned in so far as it was possible to give a Christian content to the waging of war and the making of peace.

The fortunes of the Free Churches in these years were not so very different from those of the established Church. Before the outbreak of the First World War they were prospering, constituting some 15 per cent of the population by comparison with the 60 per cent attributed to the Anglicans. It was at this time that the Baptists, the Methodists and the Congregationalists reached their maximum membership. Moreover the Free Churches possessed certain advantages which the Anglicans lacked. They had greater appeal to the working class, more especially in the north of England, and their members displayed a more marked interest in social reform and political liberalism, and were ready to consider favourably the demands for a female ministry. Contrariwise the puritanical morality which they espoused including abstinence from alcohol, lacked appeal to the young.

A new religious force had appeared with the foundation of the Salvation Army, so called from 1878, which owed its initiation to General Booth, a former Methodist preacher. Working in the poorer areas of industrialized cities, its simplistic evangelical faith, propagated at open-air meetings supported by brass bands and public testimonies met a religious need that the more conventional Churches were unable to supply. The army's social activities, its care for the sorely deprived, gave it a moral authority. Although its headquarters were in London, it was rapidly to spread throughout the world.

Much later in date and very different in its aims and organization but international in its scope was what came to be known in England at first as the Oxford Group (though it had no connection with the university or city) and later, from 1938, as Moral Rearmament. Founded by an American Frank Buchman, formerly a Lutheran minister, the group sponsored what Buchman envisaged as an authentic form of Christian life, propagated by 'sharings' and 'guidance' of interested participants at organized house parties and conferences. It had its principal headquarters at the former Palace Hotel, Caux, above the lake of Geneva. While the movement was regarded with some suspicion by the conventional churches, it made some appeal to the non-committed, more especially professional men and women. Although it claimed to reconcile workers in industrial disputes and found some support among trade unionists, it was politically non-aligned and its religious and social impact was amorphous.

GERMAN PROTESTANTISM

German Protestantism differed from its British counterpart because of the political circumstances which affected its life. After the ending of the First

World War the Lutherans were largely unsympathetic to the ideals of the
Weimar Republic and, swayed by their fear of Communism and influenced
by the Church's Erastian tradition, at first greeted the rise of National
Socialism. The Nazis pressurized the evangelical Churches into forming a
united German Christian Church under the Reichsbishof Ludwig Müller
who aimed to bring about a synthesis of Nazism and Christianity, which
involved, for instance, incorporating the Evangelical Youth into the Hitler
Youth. In 1939 the Conference of Lutheran Church leaders declared that it
had 'learnt from Martin Luther to distinguish clearly between the spheres of
Reason and of Faith, of Politics and Religion and of the State and the
Church. The Evangelical Church holds the State in reverence as an Order
set up by God, and requires from its members loyal service within that Order,
and instructs them to apply themselves with full devotion to the furthering of
what volkishly and politically is the constructive work of the Führer.'

In April 1933 legislation had been promulgated purging the Civil Service
of all those of non-Aryan descent. This impelled a number of German
Evangelical pastors led by Martin Niemöller, Walter Kunneth and Hans Lilje
not merely to declare stoutly that the Evangelical Church must enjoy
'complete freedom from all political influence', but that the exclusion of
non-Aryans from the Church would be incompatible with the belief in the
Holy Spirit. Bonhoeffer urged that while the Church had no right to dictate
to the State, it was the Church's duty to question its legality if there were a
breach of natural law, such as would be constituted by a denial of the rights
of non-Aryans as fellow Christians.

Contrariwise the German Christians supported the non-Aryan legislation,
insisting that those of Jewish descent should, as the synod of the Old
Prussian Church laid down, no longer be allowed to preach or hold Church
office. The more extreme members of the Church aimed to eliminate what
was specifically Jewish, as for instance, the teaching of St Paul from
Christian teaching. After the failure of von Stauffenberg's plot against
Hitler in July 1944 a church newspaper commented: 'While our brave
armies, courageous unto death, are struggling manfully to protect their
country . . . a handful of infamous officers made an attempt to murder the
Führer. The Führer was saved. . . . For this we give thanks to God with all
our hearts and pray, with all our church congregations, for God's assistance
and help in the grave tasks that the Führer has to perform.'

A small part of the Evangelical Church, the Confessing or Confessional
Church, so called because it was intended to indicate that its members were
less motivated by confessional allegiance than by adherence to the true
Christian faith as expressed in the formularies of the Lutheran Church,
more especially that of Augsburg, continued to make protests at the Nazi
treatment of the Church, if with some hesitation and reservation. For it was
concerned less with Nazi treatment of the Jews than with the treatment of
non-Aryan Christians which it saw as an invasion of the Church's liberties.
Its leader Pastor Martin Niemöller, who had first welcomed the Nazis, was

eventually arrested in 1937 and sent to a concentration camp. Henceforth the Church, whose objections to the German Christians had been more religious than political, was driven underground.

The German Protestants, like the Catholics, never protested effectually against the devastating evils of anti-Semitism, such as the events of the infamous Kristallnacht of 9 November 1938 when 119 synagogues were burned to the ground. 'If', the clear-sighted Dietrich Bonhoeffer wrote, 'the synagogues burn today, the churches will be on fire to-morrow.' But Bonhoeffer was to pay for his outspokenness with death. The majority of German theologians acquiesced in the regime or found exile abroad. Among the latter the most distinguished was Karl Barth, a Swiss who held chairs at Göttingen, Munster and Bonn until he was obliged to leave Germany for refusing to take an oath of unconditional allegiance to the Führer. Perhaps the failure of the German Churches lay not in the seeming inability of bishops and pastors to protest against what was taking place but in the absence of any spontaneous reaction by the ordinary Church people to the monstrous things that were being perpetrated in their name.

THE REPRESSION OF THE ORTHODOX CHURCH

Yet the agony of the German Churches at the hands of the Nazis pales by comparison with the fate of the Orthodox Church in Soviet Russia. The Orthodox Church's identification with the tsarist state meant that it would be at risk once the tsardom had been abolished. The Church might have hoped that freed from its dependence upon the State it would now be at liberty to determine its own life. But this was to misunderstand the nature of the new State and the extent to which the Bolshevik regime inherited the authoritarianism of tsarist Russia. At first the signs were not wholly unfavourable, for the provisional government allowed the establishment of an all Russian Church Council consisting of laity as well as clergy which instituted a series of reforms including the abolition of the Holy Synod and the restoration of the patriarchate which Peter the Great had suspended in 1711. On 4 November 1917 Tikhon, the Metropolitan of Moscow, was elected patriarch.

This, however, proved to be a false dawn, even before the council dispersed in the summer of 1918. With the victory of Lenin and the Bolsheviks the Church might still have hoped, as had happened in Western countries where anti-clericalism was a strong force, as in France, that the Church would be simply made separate from the State. A decree of separation was indeed promulgated on 5 February 1918 depriving the Church of all its property and also, in effect, of its freedom, for while local communities might allow a congregation to use a church for religious purposes, the Church in practice had henceforth no legal rights.

The new Russian state was to follow a policy of militant atheism the ultimate object of which was the elimination of Christianity, as an expression of the old reactionary order, both by propaganda and violence. 'The party', Stalin, himself a former seminarist observed, 'cannot be neutral towards religion. It conducts an anti-religious struggle against all and any religious prejudices.' While the original constitution of 1918 had specifically allowed 'freedom of religious and anti-religious propaganda', amendments reduced this to a series of meaningless guarantees. The Church was banned from teaching, publishing and from circulating the Bible or any religious tracts, from holding catechism classes or Sunday schools or from organizing any social or charitable activity. Contrariwise the state sponsored the indoctrination of its citizens with anti-religious propaganda, supplemented by the desecration, closure and destruction of churches, by the imprisonment and execution of bishops, clergy and Christian laity.

After the initial shock of apparently regaining its freedom and then losing it so swiftly, the Church's leaders, so long used to subservience to the State, attempted to come to terms with the Communist regime. From their point of view the Communists also favoured a *rapprochement* which, they believed, would strengthen their authority over the masses, and help ultimately to reduce the Church to such a state of submission that its natural extinction would follow. On 1 February 1918 the patriarch Tikhon had excommunicated the 'godless rulers of the darkness' and condemned the murder of Tsar Nicholas II; but subsequently he was sent into confinement. While he was in prison a group of Christians who called themselves the 'Living Church' with the connivance of the Communists sought to take control over the Church, instituting a series of further reforms. Before Tikhon died, having been released from prison, in somewhat mysterious circumstances, probably browbeaten by his captors, he seemed to take a more conciliatory line towards the Communists.

Tikhon was succeeded by a locum tenens, Peter the Metropolitan of Krutitsy, who was exiled to Siberia where he died in 1936, Sergius the Metropolitan of Nizhni-Novgorod, acting in his stead. At first, like Tikhon, Sergius argued for a genuine separation of the Church from the State, but after a period in prison he took a more compliant line towards the regime. In return the government agreed to recognize the patriarchal synod and allowed Sergius to reside in Moscow. In July 1927 he pledged his loyalty to the Soviet government and ordered the clergy to follow his example. 'We wish to be Orthodox and at the same time to recognize the Soviet Union as our civil fatherland. Every blow directed against the Union . . . we regard as a blow directed against us.' Sergius's action was strongly criticized, more especially by the Russian Orthodox abroad, but those who opposed in Russia suffered imprisonment and death. Yet under the lead of Maximus, Bishop of Serpukhov, a friend of Tikhon and a former physician who was himself to be executed in 1930, an underground or catacombs Church came into existence, disowning Sergius's policy and proclaiming itself to be the true Orthodox Church.

In practice Sergius had formulated what was going to be the Church's official policy towards the State until the dissolution of the Communist regime: complete loyalty to the State involving a readiness to turn a seemingly blind eye to the State's policy of persecution which was to be particularly virulent in 1929–30 and 1937–8. To the Russian clerics, who were perhaps doing no more than following the Church's traditional policy towards the state, this may have been the price of survival. They could argue that they were at least tolerated and that although severely restricted religious worship continued. But it was folly to seek to persuade the West that religion was free. Under Stalin's legislation of 1929, all religious associations with a membership of twenty or over were obliged to register with the state before they were allowed to meet. They had to provide a list of their members' names, which was itself a disincentive since a committed member might well find it difficult to obtain employment. The instruction of the young was totally forbidden. The majority of churches were closed and often secularized, only an estimated 4,255 out of the 57,105 active in 1914, surviving in 1941. Where there had been 57,105 priests in 1914, only 5,665, many of them aged, were active in 1941. Only some 30 of nearly 1,500 monasteries and convents remained open. The theological seminaries had been closed. In the churches that were open the congregations consisted mainly of elderly women. Even without the anti-religious propaganda and the brutal persecution, countless imprisonments and executions, the Orthodox Church might well have seemed to be dying of inanition.

That it survived was in part due to its deep sources of spirituality, its closeness as it were to the soil of Mother Russia. But it was also a result of historical forces. The German invasion of Russia was to provide an opportunity for a measure of *rapprochement,* for Stalin wished to avail himself of every possible resource to defeat the enemy. He realized that the Church had always identified itself with the nation, and so in return for the Church's support he was ready to grant it some concessions. How far the Church's patriotic attitude was the key to the opening of a period of genuine spiritual rejuvenation may be doubted, but by the end of the Second World War the Russian Church seemed at least to be emerging from the bottom of the pit, though it had to endure a long Calvary before the ungodly were in seeming retreat.

What theological development there was in the Orthodox Church was naturally to occur in the Russian Church in exile, or in the Greek Church. Sergei Bulgakov, originally a Marxist, had been ordained a priest in 1917 and left Russia, settling in Paris as dean of the newly established seminary for emigrés, the Institut-Saint-Serge. Bulgakov urged that only the Church, through which the Divine Wisdom or Sophia is channelled, can adequately overcome human self-love and disintegration and so restore wholeness to humanity. He was condemned by the Moscow patriarchate as a heretic. His younger contemporary Vladimir Lossky, who set up the Brotherhood of St Photius in Paris and who was loyal to Moscow and so critical of Bulgakov, was strongly committed to an authentic Orthodox faith based on the patristic writings. There was simultaneously some hints of a revival of theological scholarship in the Greek Church, in the writings of John Romanides and Christus Yanneras, in Romania in the work of the dogmatic and ascetic theologian, Dumitru Staniloue. While the Orthodox Church had deep resources of spirituality, there was a danger that it might die of intellectual paralysis.

RELIGION IN NORTH AMERICA

The American religious experience was in many ways very different from that of the European Churches, though a vigorous Orthodox Church took root in the New World to meet the religious needs of the many Greeks and other eastern Europeans who migrated to the United States. But much of the stress that was battering at the frontiers of faith in the Old World in the closing decades of the nineteenth and early years of the twentieth century was absent from North America. In an age of fast-growing economic enterprise the Churches were to participate in the nation's growing affluence. Free of any state control religion still seemed an essential ingredient in America's providential destiny.

The older Protestant Churches, Episcopal, Congregational and Presbyterian, if with a smaller following than the Baptists and Methodists, formed the social spearhead of American religious life, catering for the spiritual needs of an affluent middle class and patronized by millionaire families such as the Rockefellers and the Vanderbilts who generously gave their wealth to fund the building of new churches, colleges and seminaries. It was hardly surprising that the Churches' ethical teaching should suggest that worldly success could itself be an indication of God's blessing, as some Protestants had taught in the late seventeenth century, and that the rich man's duty lay in the practice of individual acts of charity rather than in seeking to bring about a socialistic restructuring of society.

The Roman Catholics had become the largest Christian denominational group numbering some 10,658,000 by 1906. Their support came above all from a large working class, constantly reinforced by immigration. In 1908 the hierarchy was freed from its even nominal subordination to the Congregation of the Faith in Rome. It had a firm and diplomatic leader in Cardinal Gibbons, the archbishop of Baltimore, who won the respect and confidence of the political establishment, for he had even felt able to justify the morally dubious Spanish-American War of 1898.

In general Roman Catholics, for so long regarded with suspicion by their Protestant neighbours, had acquired respectability, though perhaps not enough as yet to allow the election of a Roman Catholic as president, as the candidature of A.E. Smith in 1928 was later to show. The Irish, Polish and Central European immigrants found, like the Irish labourers in England, that their local Catholic church was a familiar religious sanctuary as well as a comforting social centre. While the first generation of immigrant Catholics often had linguistic difficulties and retained their ethnic identity, the future generations were absorbed more easily into American society, the Church acting as the catalyst in this process.

The Black churches, Methodist, Episcopal and Baptist, remained, like their communities, largely segregated from their White Protestant counterparts, but as the Blacks moved north in search of employment, so Black colleges and universities were founded, and the Blacks began to form a new middle class. In this process a Black theology, expressed originally in the Negro spirituals, began to be articulated.

In the late nineteenth century Protestant theologians had been disposed to regard American prosperity as a sign of God's approval; but in the early years of the twentieth century there were indications of a more positive response to the findings of biblical criticism and to the necessity of formulating a social gospel. Writers such as the Baptist Walter Rausenbusch discovered in Jesus's teaching a deep concern for human welfare in the community and a responsibility on the Church for trying to resolve the problems of poverty and deprivation.

It was, however, the Conservative Protestants who became the more influential force in American religious life in the early twentieth century. They were worried by the seeming erosion of their faith by modernism and were drawn more and more to a fundamentalist interpretation of scripture. Revivalists such as Billy Sunday and Dwight L. Moody taught that the Bible was free from error since it was God's Word and God cannot err. They were strongly patriotic. Except for the Quakers, the Mennonites and Jehovah's Witnesses the American Churches had greeted America's entry into the war in 1917. 'Christianity and Patriotism are synonymous terms,' Billy Sunday exclaimed, 'and hell and traitors are synonymous.' They were likewise strong supporters of the Constitutional Amendment in 1919 which forbade the sale of alcohol and were to oppose its repeal in 1933.

In 1919 a World Christian Fundamentalist Association had been founded to fight against modernist tendencies in doctrine and morality. The religious back-lash against postwar secularization, especially in matters relating to sex and entertainment, had a particularly strong following among the Northern and Southern Baptists and had the blessing of the Democratic politician William Jennings Bryan. The religious conservatives attempted to cleanse colleges and seminaries of those who were circulating subversive liberal views, so helping to preserve America from the threatening onset of 'infidelity'. They were particularly concerned to prevent the public teaching of the Darwinian theory of natural selection as atheistic in direction and likely to corrupt American youth. In 1925 John Thomas Scopes, a high-school teacher from Dayton, Tennessee, was brought before a court of law for teaching evolution in defiance of state law. William Jennings Bryan took the lead in prosecuting Scopes on behalf of the World

Christian Fundamentalist Association. Scopes, who was defended by Clarence Darrow, was fined $100 but in public opinion Bryan's arguments had done much to discredit his cause; he died five days after the trial's conclusion of a diabetic disorder induced by exhaustion. For some decades fundamentalism retreated into the background, though it was only hibernating.

A much more sinister expression of right-wing thinking with some religious implications was the revival of the Ku Klux Klan which was reorganized in 1915. Although the Churches disclaimed any connection with the Klan, its objectives, principally anti-Black but also anti-Semitic and anti-Catholic, made some appeal to more conservative Protestants. In its ceremonial the Klan made use of Christian symbols, more especially in its flaming cross. By 1923 it had an estimated membership of 3 million.

By the 1930s both fundamentalism and liberalism seemed to be waning. Influential teachers in the Protestant colleges were more likely to be of the school of Karl Barth and Emil Brunner. The two most influential publicists of popular theology in the 1930s and 1940s were the brothers Reinhold and Richard Niebuhr. While Reinhold accepted mankind's basic imperfection, he urged that the Church should involve itself in movements for social change. While the clash of disparate and selfish interests could not be ignored, the hope of greater justice in the future must not be abandoned. His brother Richard stressed even more than Reinhold the prevalence of sin as part of the human condition but equally the Christian's responsibility for promoting social justice in accordance with God's purpose for mankind. Man's salvation was made possible by his acceptance as a genuine penitent through the grace of God perfectly displayed in the love of Jesus Christ. Their critics charged the Niebuhrs with going too far to compromise with existing social systems.

All told there could be little doubt that whatever its flavour, religion remained a very vital factor in American life. While there had been a wave of pacifist propaganda in the 1930s, after Pearl Harbour only one member of Congress, Jeanette Rankin, voted against the declaration of war, which the Churches accepted as an unfortunate necessity in the fight against evil.

THE CHURCH IN LATIN AMERICA

In Latin America the Church was still the legatee of the struggles which had steadily reduced its power and influence in society. The connection between Church and State weakened as republics legalized separation, in Brazil after the ending of the empire in 1890, in Uruguay in 1919 and in Chile in 1925. Although the Church in Mexico had been separated from the State it did not enjoy any freedom but was rather for long to be subject to persecution. The Mexican revolution of 1910 had taken on some aspects of a religious crusade against the Church, its leaders stressing the suffering and exploitation of the natives victimized by Hispanic and clerical elements in society. The revolution's apostle, Emiliano Zapata, who was assassinated in 1919, was depicted wearing a wide white hat which had some of the symbolic attributes of the halo. Anti-clerical legislation was embodied in the constitution in the Articles of Queretaro in 1917. The religious persecution continued until the third decade of the twentieth century during the presidency of Callao. Bishops were imprisoned or banished. Convents and schools were closed. All religious services were suspended. Between 1926 and 1929 some seventy-eight priests, religious and lay Catholics were killed.

There were all the elements of a religious civil war as armed Catholic bands, known as the Cristeros from the crosses which they wore around their necks and their war-cry 'Viva Cristo Rey', carried on the battle. President Callao had even sponsored in 1925 the setting up of a rival church, the Mexican Catholic Apostolic Church. In 1932 Pope Pius XI condemned the Mexican government's action; and the government responded by expelling the apostolic delegate for the third time. President Cardenas ordered the confiscation of Church property and decreed that socialism, Marxism, atheism and sex education should be taught in all schools. Yet resistance to the government's anti-religious policy remained strong, and under Cardenas's successor, General Camacho, there was some relaxation of policy and a cautious move towards reconciliation. It was his experience of the plight of the Mexican Church which led the British novelist Graham Greene to write *The Power and the Glory*. The Mexican experience was not typical of South America as a whole, though in Peru under Victor Raul Haya in the 1930s there was a populist anti-Catholic movement, but it pointed to underlying tensions in Latin-American society which were to condition the history of Christianity there in the second half of the twentieth century.

THE MISSIONARY CHURCHES

It was in the Churches outside Europe that a seeming boom in religion was continuing to take place. In old Europe, as in Latin America, the Churches were still the legatees of their past history, but outside Europe, where the Churches were in some sense both the originators and the beneficiaries of what was happening, Church membership was increasing. The Roman Church, as the largest denomination, was also the largest beneficiary. Each successive Pope was a strong supporter of missionary activity. Leo XIII's pontificate had seen the foundation of 248 new sees, 48 vicariates and 2 patriarchates, and the establishment of hierarchies in North Africa (1884), India (1886) and Japan (1891). Protestantism grew proportionately. Between 1851 and 1901 the Protestant community in India increased tenfold.

Political as well as religious circumstances favoured the expansion of the Churches. Between 1880 and 1914 Africa was almost totally taken over by the colonial powers, whose influence penetrated more and more deeply, carried by trade and force of arms, to every continent. Colonization by its very nature made the work of the Churches easier, and even conceivably helped to make the message of Christianity more attractive to the native who did not always distinguish between White religion and White rule. The missionaries were not indeed the purposive agents of colonialism, the morals of which they sometimes severely criticized, as they did in respect of Leopold II's treatment of the Congo, but they were colonialism's legatees. Some of them could not help recognizing that colonization might provide a providential dispensation for the preaching of the gospel. It maintained law and order, which enabled the Churches to carry out their work. 'I should consider myself worse than despicable,' a Methodist missionary on the Gold Coast, Dennis Kemp commented, 'if I failed to declare my firm conviction that the British Army and Navy are today used by God for the accomplishment of His purpose.' The Church approved Cecil Rhodes's seizure of the territory of the Matabele king Lobengula. The order of the White Friars, which Cardinal Lavigerie had founded, who wore native costume, appeared to some to be a religious branch of the French Foreign Legion.

The missionaries could not avoid being in competition with each other, as different faiths converged on the same territory, sometimes with tragic results. No episode provided a better illustration of what was at stake than the 'Christianization' of Uganda where religious idealism, denominational rivalry, political chicanery and colonial imperialism were all at work.

The Bugandan king – the Buganda were the most important tribe – the 'large-lustrous eyed' Kabaka, Mtesa, a cruel autocrat who had 'a larger collection of wives than any human being of whom we have record', had told H.M. Stanley in 1875 that he would welcome Christian missionaries, in the belief that he could play them off against Islam, a powerful influence in Uganda. Deeply affected by Stanley's appeal, an eccentric recluse, the millionaire Sir Robert Arthington donated money to the Church Missionary Society to finance a mission on Lake Victoria. The mission was headed by a shrewd if dour Scots engineer, Alexander Mackay, who had few illusions about the warlike peoples among whom he was to live for fourteen years. He created workshops, made a loom, a spinning jenny and a printing press and learned the native language, winning Mtesa's support by translating the gospels into Swahili. 'I hope', he had said, 'to connect Christianity with modern civilization.'

But the Protestants were not the only missionaries among the Buganda. While Dr Cust of the Church Missionary Society had tried to persuade Cardinal Lavigerie that it would be impolitic to introduce religious competition into the as yet unconverted land, two White Fathers arrived in 1879 and won Mtesa's favour, in part by giving him some flamboyant French dress uniforms. In return the Bugandan king gave them a banana plantation and thirty head of cattle. Mackay tried to warn the king by telling him that the Catholics worshipped a woman called Mary.

The religious rivalry became more acute with Mtesa's death and the accession in 1884 of the eighteen year old Mwanga, a young man who had been instructed in the faith by both Catholics and Protestants but was drawn towards Islam, in part because it was more tolerant of his pleasure in sodomy. One of his page boys, who was under tuition from a Protestant catechist, refused the king's sexual overtures and in a rage Mwanga turned on all the Christian boys, picking them off at first in ones and twos, and then resorting to an act of mass carnage; of the twenty-six Christians who suffered, some burned to death in a slow fire, thirteen were Catholic and thirteen were Protestant. The new bishop of Eastern Equatorial Africa, James Hannington, was speared to death on his arrival. The White Fathers temporarily withdrew. There was talk of abandoning the Protestant mission altogether, but Mackay was allowed to stay until 1887, possibly because of his invaluable skills as an engineer.

The Bugandan state, in which both Britain and Germany were interested as a fertile land with a potential for development, was deeply disturbed politically. In 1888 Mwanga decided to resolve the problem of the contending religious groups by putting both Whites and Arabs on an island in Lake Victoria where hopefully they could be left to starve. When the plot was discovered Mwanga's younger brother, Kiwewa was enthroned in his stead. Kiwewa selected a prime minister who was a Roman Catholic but came to rely on a Muslim, Ali Bey, who persuaded the young king that the Christians intended to force him off his throne. Since Kiwewa, however, refused to be circumcised as the Muslims insisted, he was replaced by yet another brother, Kalema, who put Kiwewa and thirty members of the royal family to death.

The native Christians rose against the Muslims and after a year of strife defeated the Muslim army at Bulwanyi, in 1890 restoring the dethroned Mwanga who had presented himself as a supplicant at the Roman Catholic mission. Meanwhile the great powers, meeting at Berlin in July 1890, were seeking to determine the extent of their own influence in Africa. So welcome were the offers made by the German Dr Carl Peters that he won over the Catholics in Uganda while the Protestants backed Britain. Mwanga, now restored to the throne and addicted to the drug bhang, was bewildered by the competing religious forces challenging the centuries old paganism by which his kingship was sustained but, believing the Protestants might be seeking to avenge the murder of Bishop Hannington, gave his favour to the Catholics, intolerant as they were of sodomy.

The country had been brought to the brink of civil war. At this stage there entered on the scene Frederick Lugard, the representative of the recently constituted Imperial British East Africa Company, determined to frustrate the possibility of a German annexation. He came with a small army, mainly Sudanese and a Maxim gun. While he dealt forcefully with the Muslims, he could not prevent in January 1892 the outbreak of war between the religious factions. 'Uganda', the Anglican bishop Tucker observed in

December 1890, 'was like a volcano on the verge of an eruption.' The Protestants fired the Catholic cathedral (for which after claims for damages from the French government, the British made an ex gratia payment of £10,000), but at Mengo Hill the Maxim gun determined that the Protestants would win the day. Mwanga with six Catholic fathers and the bishop Monsignor Hirth fled, the bishop moving to the province of Budu which remained strongly Catholic whence he wrote that the 'whole of Budu has become a Catholic province. The Protestants, though ten times more numerous, have been driven out.' It was left to Lugard, himself a free thinker, to determine Uganda's political and religious future. Six provinces were allocated to the Protestants, six to the Catholics, three to the Muslims (who lost two of them when they rebelled). Whatever the validity of the methods by which Lugard had imposed his solution, the Church Missionary Society concluded that the interests of the Church would be best served by the incorporation of Uganda and Kenya in the British Empire which occurred in June 1895.

The situation in Uganda remained explosive, but its Christianization went on apace, carried on with evangelical enthusiasm under the leadership of a CMS missionary G.K. Baskerville. Within twelve months he had sold 1,100 copies of his translation of the Bible, some 4,000 copies of the New Testament, 13,500 copies of the gospels and 40,000 copies of Bible stories. In 1911 it was estimated that out of a population of 660,000, no less than 282,000 had become Christians. In 1964 the Pope canonized the Ugandan martyrs who had suffered in the dark years of internecine religious and tribal conflict.

The violent aspects of the missionary operation did not go uncriticized at home. After Bishop Mackenzie had become involved in armed action against the slave traders, Dr Pusey observed that 'it seems to me a frightful thing that the messengers of the Gospel of peace should in any way be connected, even by their presence, with the shedding of human blood'. Events in Uganda, though public opinion was horrified by the martyrdoms, added to the disillusionment. The only person, Sir Charles Dilke affirmed, who benefited from the British presence in East Africa was Mr Hiram Maxim. The radical M.P. Labouchere added sourly that he did not believe that 'it is the mission of the State to prevent these Protestant missionaries from cutting the throat of Roman Catholic missionaries, nor is it their business to prevent the Catholic missionaries cutting the throat of the Protestant missionaries'. A few questioned the ultimate validity of what the missionaries were trying to do, 'regarding', as Mary Kingsley put it, 'the native minds as so many jugs only requiring to be emptied of the stuff which is in them and refilled with the particular form of dogma he is engaged in teaching, in order to make them the equals of the white races'.

But such criticism was minimal. With the support of the Churches and governments at home the missionary societies were advancing fast to bring the gospel to the unenlightened. By 1901 the British had some 2,750 male missionaries and 1,700 women at work in the field and the annual income of the societies, of which the CMS was the most important, amounted to £1,500,000. North America had sent 1,630 men and 1,200 women, Germany 880 men and women.

In spite of setbacks the Church had boundless confidence in its future. Nor was there any shortage of candidates for missionary work. St Augustine's College, Canterbury, which had been founded in 1848 to train priests for the overseas Church was flourishing. Unmarried women in particular found a vocation in mission work and a degree of responsibility which they might have found it difficult to acquire at home. Between 1887 and 1897 some 214 Christian women joined the Church Missionary Society. 'Three ladies for East Africa', the journal of the CMS advertised in 1887, 'must be wholehearted missionaries, physically strong and thoroughly understanding the principle "In honour preferring one another".'

In the missionary Churches as at home the First World War constituted a watershed, inevitably distracting evangelical activity, as missionaries, if of combatant age, offered themselves for military service or in the case of the French were conscripted for the army. Financial support for the missionary societies temporarily declined. Many natives were perplexed and bewildered by the bitter conflict between Whites which seemed to contradict the basic teaching of Christ which they had been seeking to instill.

As the war reached Africa, and in East Africa the Germans long managed to keep the Allied forces at bay, so involuntarily the Africans were brought into the conflict in part as military porters and carriers if not as combatants. The missionaries from whatever side they came had no doubt of the righteousness of the cause for which they were fighting. Bishop Weston of Zanzibar raised a contingent of 2,000 native carriers. 'The Archbishop of Canterbury', General Smuts wrote to him, 'was much interested in my picture of you marching with an enormous crucifix at the head of your black columns.' As Germans were interned, or left for home, so other missions under the control of Allied governments took over, in the Cameroons the Paris Missionary Society replaced the Basel Mission and in Togoland Frenchmen of the Society of Africa Missions took over from the German Fathers of the Divine Word.

Once hostilities had ended the missionary societies showed renewed vigour as another era of Christian expansion opened, though the shadows of the immediate past were not easily cast aside. Slowly and patchily they began to refashion and recast their earlier assumptions about the character of the missionary Church. While in attitude they remained basically paternalistic, they began to realize, as pronouncements by Popes Benedict XV and Pius XI had shown, that for the good health of a native Church it was essential to develop an indigenous ministry. By 1914 the White Fathers had ordained the first two Black Catholic priests for East Africa; though it was not until 1939 that the Pope appointed a Black Catholic bishop Joseph

Kiwanaka. In this respect the Protestants were more forward, in part because the training to which they submitted future ordinands was less intense than that of the Roman Church. The Church Missionary Society had some fifty-four African clergy at work by 1914, though it was not until 1947 that the Anglicans made Aberi Balya a bishop in Uganda.

Missionary activity was henceforth to become more diversified, somewhat less concentrated on evangelism (though this varied much from society to society) and more devoted to the building and maintenance of schools, to the staffing of hospitals and to social work. In this field Albert Schweitzer was a unique phenomenon, enjoying ultimately a reputation in the world not unlike that of Mother Teresa in more recent times. A fine student and interpreter of the organ music of J.S. Bach, a theologian and founder of a medical mission at Lambaréné in the Congo, Schweitzer made a singular impact on the contemporary Church. A pastor's son, Alsatian by birth which accounted for his being unsympathetically twice interned by the French in the First World War, he had early reacted against current theological scholarship. As the title of his famous book *The Quest of the Historical Jesus*, published in 1906, suggested, he sought to get at the root of Jesus's real teaching which he found in Jesus's belief in the imminent end of the world, a view which was much criticized by both conservative and liberal theologians. A critic described his heterodox views as a 'peculiar mixture of agnosticism and animistic pantheism'.

Schweitzer said of his decision to become a medical student, 'This new form of activity I could not represent to myself as talking about the religion of love, but only as an actual putting it into practice.' In 1913 he had given up his academic career to devote himself to the care of sick natives at Lambaréné in the primeval forest of the Congo, serving at his own expense. The Paris Missionary Society, suspicious of his heterodox theology at first objected to his acceptance as a missionary doctor who had only Christian love to offer but insufficient Christian belief, and he was initially inhibited from preaching. After his internment he lived at Strasbourg but returned to Lambaréné in 1924 to restore the hospital which had fallen into a state of complete dilapidation.

For Schweitzer religion consisted only in doing good, 'as being good, to preserve life and as being evil, to destroy life, to injure life, to repress life', a path of good which enabled man to 'step for a moment out of the incomprehensible horror of existence', a philosophy summed up in the phrase 'reverence for life'. 'We are Dives. . . . Out there in the colonies, however, sits wretched Lazarus, the coloured folk.' 'Who', he wrote at the end of his book *On the Edge of the Primeval Forest*, 'can describe the injustice and cruelties that in the course of centuries they have suffered at the hands of Europeans. . . . Anything we give them is not benevolence but atonement.' Schweitzer was unique, fitting into no category.

In South Africa while the tensions which had led to the outbreak of the Boer War had been primarily political, they had religious ingredients which were to persist after the Union of South Africa had been formed, in the exclusivity of the Dutch Reformed Church and its distant, if not positively hostile, relations with other Protestant and Roman Churches. The balance of the Dutch Reformed Church had been itself upset as a result of the discovery of diamonds and gold at Kimberley and Witwatersrand, resulting in the immigration of 'poor Whites' and later cheap Black labour, so changing a predominantly rural society into an urbanized industrial agglomeration. But the religious values of the Dutch Reformed Church were rooted in a pastoral economy. It seemed unable to adapt itself to a changing situation, though in 1870 in the Transvaal the performance of the Roman Mass had ceased to be an offence, and it strove therefore to preserve its traditions against the impurities, religious and social, of English and Black settlers. The Dutch Reformed Church maintained its control over education which by the Education Bill of 1882 and under the guidance of S.J. du Toit became a means of preserving Afrikaner values.

THE BLACK CHURCHES OF AFRICA

In Africa there were comparatively early signs of a religious reaction against the paternalism of the White Churches, leading to the formation of Black Churches. As in America these started with small groups, revivalist in character, favourable to apocalyptic teaching, and with a powerful injection of native superstition. In part they were a product of the expanding frontier served only sparsely by White missionaries; but in the main they were an assertion of religious independence against White-dominated Churches. They brought into worship colour and ceremonial, dancing and music, which the White Churches, often dull and staid, lacked. Some had a short life but others had an enduring following, often with a substantial membership.

The Black Churches grew only slowly, numbering possibly as many as thirty by 1913, a hundred and thirty by 1925. The first of such Churches seems to have been the Tembu National Church, founded in 1884 by a Black Methodist minister, Nehemiah Tile. A similar movement had occurred in the Transvaal in Sekukuniland initiated by a White missionary who was soon dismissed from office by the Africans whose cause he had espoused. In 1892 another Methodist minister Mangena Mokoni established the so-called Ethiopian Church (it bore no relation to the Church in Ethiopia but referred to a verse from the Psalms (Ps. 68:31) in the Transvaal, winning followers by declaring that his was a Church for the Africans. He managed to interest the American African Methodist Episcopal Church which appointed James Dwane as his collaborator, but Dwane, apparently doubting the validity of his own orders, became an Anglican, seeking, however, to preserve his Church's identity.

In 1888 a Native Baptist Church, led by Mojola Agbebi, broke away from an American Southern Baptist mission in Nigeria. 'Our Christianity ceases to be London-ward and New York-ward but heaven-ward.' This Church, which by 1914 had twice as many members as the Southern Baptist Mission in Nigeria, used native nomenclature, native dress and native languages for its worship. These early sects, usually described as Ethiopian in type, were normally secessions from Protestant Churches or missions and retained orthodox doctrines and ceremonial, if modified by native custom.

Side by side with such Churches were more radical groups, the so-called Zionists, generally the creation of a single individual who was convinced that he had a special call, often enshrined in a vision directly from God. They incorporated Christian elements in a Black culture, with an emphasis on penance, faith-healing and often messianic and millennial expectations. Their appeal was in the main to lower social groups, more particularly to women who might act as prophetesses or diviners. The appearance of Halley's Comet in 1910 acted as a spur to Enoch Mgijima's Israelite Church which he founded as a result of visions which he had received after seeing the comet. Timothy Cekwane, who claimed he had experienced the stigmata, was also inspired by the comet to set up the Church of Light on the holy mountain of Ekukhanyeni. The prototype for many of these Churches was the Christian Apostolic Church in Zion founded by John Alexander Dowie in Chicago in 1896, which stressed faith healing, expected the imminent second advent of Christ and forbade alcohol, tobacco and pork. William Wade Harris who had been a teacher in an American Episcopalian school in Liberia established a Church led by twelve apostles which was to stretch through British territory to the Ivory Coast with a following not far short of a hundred thousand.

After the First World War the Black Churches were to proliferate at an amazing speed. In 1946 it was estimated that there were 1,300 such Churches. George Khambule who founded a Church in 1919 after a mystical experience set up a heavenly telephone in his vestry so that he could receive direct instructions from God. In the Congo Simon Kimbangu, after a visionary experience, began to heal the sick, attracting a following which continued to grow even after his arrest in 1921 and sentence to thirty years' imprisonment. His prison cell at Elizabethville became a shrine, and his Church of Christ on Earth, estimated to have 3 million adherents, was later to be affiliated to the World Council of Churches.

In Nigeria the Aladura or praying movement, the Church of the Lord, originated as a result of the rumour that the Churches had not done enough to help the victims of the influenza epidemic which occurred after the First World War. Its first evangelists, rejecting the use of medicine, advocated the curative properties of pure rain water. Originally associated with the Faith Tabernacle of Philadelphia, under Josiah Olunowu Oshitelu, a former Anglican catechist who had received a vision in 1925, it became the Church of the Lord (Aladura) which by 1947 had adherents throughout Africa, attracted by its charismatic ceremonial. In 1929 an African Greek Orthodox

Church was founded by Reuben Spartas (originally called Mukasa) 'for all right-thinking Africans, men who wish to be free in their own house'.

These Churches represented a search for a Black religious identity. They were not, however, particularly politically conscious, though John Chilembwe of the Ajawu Providence Industrial Mission in Nyasaland was shot in 1915 charged with inciting a rising against the British. But, like the Afro-American Black Churches, they did represent an attempt to escape from the prosaic conventions of the mainline Churches, and conceivably to find a setting in which they did not merely provide a sense of community but a means of preserving tribal custom and native culture.

THE CHURCHES IN ASIA

In India the Churches were by the early twentieth century showing a greater understanding of and sympathy for native culture. Some missionaries, including the officers of the Salvation Army who arrived in the 1880s, adopted local costume to seek a cultural identity with the natives. Hinduism's attitude to Christianity was ambivalent for there were many Hindus like Swami Daya and Saras Vati who feared that the advance of Christianity represented a threat to the integrity of ancient culture and championed the maintenance and purification of Hinduism. But there were other Hindus, attracted by Christian ethics – though in general the Hindu argued that Hindu spirituality was of a higher quality than Christian spirituality – who believed in the coexistence of the faiths. Some Christians, such as the Anglican missionary J.N. Farquhar and an Indian Christian minister, Krishna Mohan Banerjea, argued that Christianity was the natural fulfilment of what was implicit in the Hindu sacred writings, and even suggested that Vedic or Hindu texts might replace the Old Testament in the Christian liturgy. The Roman Catholic Brahmabandhab Upadhyay, a Hindu holy man in appearance, taught that it was possible to synthesize Hinduism and Christianity. But such views as these had only a small minority following.

More significant were practical religious experiments which were influenced by Hindu custom by which Christian teachers sought to make a synthesis with Hindu spirituality. Christian teachers founded *ashrams* or semi-monastic communities, based on Hindu practice, such as that set up by the religious poet Narayan Vaman Tilak in 1917, and the Christa Seva Sangh, founded by an Anglican clergyman Jack Winslow.

Although it was not until 1912 that the Anglican Church made an Indian, V.S. Azariah, a bishop, the Christian Churches, in spite of their minority following, wielded an influence in India out of proportion to their numbers, for Indian Christians, educated in Christian colleges, found places in Indian education and the civil administration. By and large the Churches continued to draw their membership from the higher castes, but later a movement for mass conversion brought many converts from the lower castes, a development which high-caste leaders as well as Mahatma Gandhi strongly condemned. Although the membership of the Christian Churches was limited, Christian influence permeated Indian life, and would survive independence.

CHINA

China, it was observed at the Edinburgh Conference of 1910, was the 'chief storm centre of opportunity in the whole world'. 'Not since the days of the Reformation, not indeed since Pentecost', Bishop Bashford of North China declared rhetorically, 'has so great an opportunity confronted the Christian Church. The Far East as a whole stands at the parting of the ways. No such opportunity is likely to confront the Christian Church again till the day of Judgement.' If this was so, it was an opportunity either missed or mismanaged. The aftermath to the suppression of the Boxer rebellion, anti-Western in origin as a result of which the Christian Churches and missionaries had suffered in lives and property, and the subsequent fall of the Manchu Empire had in fact provided an opportunity for the expansion of Christian work in Chinese colleges and schools. The new republic's leader, Sun Yat-sen was a baptized Christian who had been educated by missionaries; his successor Chiang Kai-shek was to be baptized in 1930.

The Churches took advantage of the favourable climate for evangelization, seeking to establish roots in Chinese culture, so that Chinese Christian sects like the Family of Jesus and the Little Flock attracted a substantial following. The Roman Church which had set up an apostolic delegation in 1922 itself encouraged the transfer of responsibility to a native-born clergy. But the war with Japan (1937–41) which had damaging effects on all Churches, led to the deaths of a bishop, a prefect apostolic, some fifty-five priests and seventeen brothers and sisters. After the war ended the Churches sought to repair the damage they had suffered. It was estimated in 1941 that there were still some 3,128,157 Chinese Catholics. But the signs for the future became increasingly ominous. The outbreak of the Japanese-American war in 1941 led to the internment of foreign missionaries (who still made up three-fifths of the working clergy), casting responsibility on the native clergy, numbering 2,008 out of 5,005 in 1946. Pope Pius XII gave every encouragement to the Chinese Catholic Church, creating Tien Ken-Sin, later archbishop of Peking, the first Chinese cardinal, making a number of new dioceses and beatifying as martyrs those who had suffered in the Boxer rebellion. But the civil war resulting in a Communist victory was to spell disaster for all the Christian Churches in China. Christianity did survive but it was to emerge much emaciated.

JAPAN

Once the Japanese government had relaxed its policy of persecution in 1873, all Churches made full use of the opportunity to evangelize, setting up schools and colleges, and winning adherents in the urban, industrialized areas, but making little or no impact on the countryside. The policy of placing control of the Church in the hands of native Japanese was followed by both Protestants and Catholics. The first Japanese bishop, Januarius Hayusake of Nagasaki was consecrated by Pius XI in 1927. The Church sought to act as the champion of the oppressed, more especially women and workers, but there was an increasingly uneasy relationship with the growing forces of patriotic nationalism, euphoric after victory in the Russo-Japanese War and operative in the invasions of Korea and China. The Japanese criticized the Church for its foreign bishops. A law on religious corporations in 1939 which sought to reduce foreign influence led to the replacement of foreign prelates by Japanese, a move much disliked by Rome. Japanese Christians seemed eager to assert the national identity of their religion. Kanzo Uchimera, who founded the Non-Church movement, rejected conventional Church structures as a Western invention, using study groups for the propagation of scripture. The outbreak of the American-Japanese war in 1941 was to be an obvious setback for the Christian Church in Japan.

PHILIPPINES

There was one other distinctively Christian country in Asia, the Philippines which, from the time of the Spanish conquest in the sixteenth century, had been essentially a colony of the Spanish Church which provided the hierarchy and the majority of the religious. In the revolution against Spanish rule in 1896, some of the native Filipino clergy supported the insurrection which was condemned by the hierarchy. After the American victory in 1898 the Filipino Church accommodated itself to the new order. But the ending of Spanish rule resulted in free access to Protestant missionaries who were to concentrate on the conversion of the Catholics. Religious freedom provided also an opportunity for the foundation of fringe Churches such as the Iglesia ni Cristo set up in 1914 by Felix Manalo who asserted that he was the angel 'having the seal of the living God' mentioned in Revelation 7:2. More serious from the point of view of the Roman Church was the nationalist Iglesia Filipina Independiente, founded in 1899 by a Filipino priest. Its liturgy was Catholic but theologically it was to drift towards Unitarianism and after a long struggle it was to fall victim to an increasingly resurgent Roman Catholic Church.

THE OECUMENICAL MOVEMENT

The proliferation of missionary societies, the competition between the faiths more and more highlighted the scandal of division. In the expanding Church of the late nineteenth and early twentieth century divisions within the Churches, causing controversy, bitterness and even bloodshed (as in Uganda and Madagascar) made serious churchmen increasingly concerned to promote understanding between the Churches. More and more cooperation between competing Christians appeared an essential ingredient, as was made clear at Edinburgh in 1910, in the conversion of the world to the truths of the Christian gospel. But there were also other reasons for encouraging reunion and oecumenical understanding. The signs of contraction in the membership of the older Churches were continuing to demonstrate the wisdom of trying to form a common front against the forces of secularization and unbelief. Furthermore the Churches were confronted with the missionary expansion of Islam which constituted almost as great a threat to the integrity of Christendom as it had done five centuries earlier. The Church's renewal seemed then to many Christians to depend on the restoration of its unity, though by unity its advocates meant less absorbtion into a single Church than the creation of an organic union which allowed for legitimate differences while providing an abiding solidarity, a concept unacceptable either to the Roman or Orthodox Churches.

Some preliminary moves in this direction were made in the late nineteenth century. Some 1,500 representatives of 140 missionary societies foregathered in London in 1888, and at a later conference held in New York in 1900 about 1,700 representatives from 115 missionary societies and some 48 countries came together. But the real historical landmark was the World Missionary Conference held at Edinburgh in the summer of 1910. 'I think bold to say', John R. Mott told his audience, 'that the Church has not yet seriously attempted to bring the living Christ to all living men.' To achieve this the scandal of division must be healed and the Church unified in its message.

It was much easier to propagate this vision than to fulfil it. The outbreak of the First World War not merely isolated the Churches but promoted a belligerent nationalism within their ranks. But the call to oecumenical understanding was to be renewed under the lead of the Swedish archbishop of Upsala, Nathan Soderblom, at the first of the postwar oecumenical conferences held in 1925 at Stockholm. Subsequent international conferences such as the Oxford Conference on Life and Work in 1937 testified to the strong belief among Protestants in the desirability of the ultimate unity of the Church, and an understanding of the inter-dependence of its component parts in a world embattled by evil forces. One product of all this was the World Council of Churches formed at Utrecht in 1938.

Efforts were made to coordinate the activities of the numerous Protestant missions and to foster contacts with the Orthodox; but the Orthodox found the pan-Protestant movement confusing as well as theologically dubious. From such activities the Roman Catholics, strong in their belief that they were the only true Church, stood studiously aloof. Although Benedict XV had received a delegation of bishops from the American Episcopal Church in a friendly fashion in 1919, Pius XI had condemned the oecumenical movement in his encyclical *Mortalium animos* in 1928. Indeed, when as late as 1940 Archbishop Hinsley of Westminster, who had inaugurated a social movement, the Sword of the Spirit, designed to foster democratic spiritual thinking at a meeting of the society at the Stoll Theatre, Kingsway, attended by non-Catholics as well as by Catholics, joined with non-Catholics in the Lord's Prayer, he provoked the strong disapproval of his fellow bishops, and full membership became confined to Roman Catholics.

The key words of the Edinburgh Conference had been the 'evangelization of the world in this generation', but such high-sounding aspirations had no hope of being implemented and remained a pipe-dream. Yet the growing desire for unity and the threat presented by falling congregations did in practice precipitate within some Protestant Churches a movement towards reunion. The secretary of the Baptist Union J.H. Shakespeare suggested tentatively, though hardly realistically, that there should be re-union between the Church of England and the Free Churches. The British Methodist Churches agreed to reunite in 1928, a decision implemented in 1932, so bringing the declining if competing congregations of the Methodist Churches under Wesleyan control. Some Methodists interpreted this move as a positive Protestant response to the threat seemingly posed by Anglo-Catholicism and Romanism. In 1929 the United Free Church and the Church of Scotland ended the lengthy Presbyterian schism. In France where as a result of the separation of Church and State three distinct Protestant Reform Unions had come into being, union between two of them was achieved in 1938, though a minority of the French Reformed Evangelical Churches, fearful of contamination by liberal theology, preferred to go its own way. The National Synod of the French Reformed Church, meeting in the Church of the Holy Spirit at Paris in December 1938, elected Marc Boegner, who had been a leading light in the oecumenical movement, as president of the National Council.

Although the oecumenical movement fostered some degree of friendliness between Churches, in effect it stopped short of inter-communion, nor was there in practice much crossing of boundaries between different congregations. If there were, for instance, occasional joint services between Anglicans and Free Churchmen, the positive results of the oecumenical movement had so far been limited; nor had it apparently done much to halt the decline in attendance or belief, or even to act as yet as a very significant catalyst for a forward movement in the Christian Churches.

DEVELOPMENTS IN THEOLOGY

The theological climate changed slowly as the cliffs of tradition were eroded by the historical criticism of the texts of scripture. The Roman Catholic Church remained theologically hidebound, its theologians confined to a neo-scholastic waste land, nor was it until after the mid-twentieth century that it became open to the findings of modern scholarship.

Outside the Roman Church what might be described as liberal theology was long to dominate the scene, its major figure the Prussian scholar Adolf Harnack who was professor at Berlin from 1889 to 1921, dying in 1930. His interests were primarily historical, his major opus the *History of Dogma* which traced the development of Christian doctrine down to the Reformation, revealing his deep mastery of patristic sources. Like Ritschl, to whom he owed much, he was suspicious of metaphysics and stressed Christianity's ethical genius, more especially its contributions to human brotherhood, to the exclusion of what was doctrinal. Distinguished as a textual critic, reaching indeed conservative conclusions on the authorship of the synoptic gospels, as a patristic scholar and Church historian, he was for long the doyen of the theological scene.

Harnack praised *The Apostolic Fathers*, a patristic study by J.B. Lightfoot, professor at Cambridge from 1861 to 1879 and then bishop of Durham, one of the most skilled interpreters of the New Testament in his day, neither speculative nor philosophical, but a historian of the early Church of depth and clarity. It was the Cambridge school which dominated English theology in the late nineteenth century: Lightfoot's pupil, B.F. Westcott, less distinguished as a scholar, and F.J.A. Hort, a 'sacerdotalist' but more speculative.

British theology was not in the main stream, by and large lacking a philosophical bent. The exception to this was a series of essays, *Lux Mundi*, published in 1889 and edited by Charles Gore, Tractarian in inspiration, which was intended to show that new knowledge could be confined within the essentials of traditional Christianity. The attempt to reconcile the claims of reason and revelation helped to give a boost to the intellectual respectability of the Tractarians but the book was regarded as insufficiently radical by the more liberal and condemned by the conservatives as being in Liddon's view 'the inspiration of inveracity', seeming to replace the authority of the Church by private judgement.

It was the continental theologians whose analytical approach, dominated by the 'higher criticism', the application to the texts and meanings of scripture of the standards applied in literature, designed to establish the historicity of the story and the authority of its teaching. It was applied, for instance, by Hermann Gunkel, professor at Giessen and Halle between 1907 and 1932, to the interpretation of the Old Testament. But it was the synoptic gospels, the dating of which was a matter of continuous debate, which were the focus of investigation, leading sometimes to radical conclusions. Wrede, for instance, concluded that the messianic consciousness of Jesus was the product of early Christian teachers who corrected or changed the historical record to suit their own presuppositions. G. Bertram deduced that the narrative of Christ's Passion reflected the liturgical needs and practices of the early Church.

Dismissive of what they construed to be the non-historical events, the infancy narratives and the Resurrection appearances, the textual critics questioned the historicity and authenticity of the gospel writers. Kirsopp Lake, an English theologian who migrated to the United States, challenged the sufficiency of the evidence for the Empty Tomb, and in general suggested that the story of the early Christian Church bore the imprint of the mystery religions. In his book *The Quest of the Historical Jesus* Albert Schweitzer concluded that Jesus's teaching reflected his belief in the imminent inauguration of the kingdom of God and the consequent millennium, and that when this did not happen he as the Messiah came to the belief that the kingdom of God could only be brought about by his own self-chosen suffering and death. Schweitzer's book was much criticized, but it demonstrated the theologians' current concern to reach a historical understanding of scripture and of the New Testament in particular, by a meticulous investigation of the text.

Such notions lay behind the extremely influential work of the German scholar Rudolf Bultmann who was professor at Marburg from 1921 to 1951 and the originator of the so-called 'form-criticism'. Bultmann argued that the gospels needed to be 'demythologized' so as to discern their inner meaning. As they stood they represented a view of the universe which was unacceptable; but if the myths which they described, such as the story of the Virgin Birth, were explained then the underlying significance of the text would appear. The Word of God was not necessarily to be identified with the words of scripture. Form-criticism deepened theological understanding and so enabled the reader to glimpse below the surface, making it possible to discern, for instance, the pre-Christian gnostic ideas embedded in St John's Gospel. Demythologization, its advocates claimed, would help to establish the essential meaning of the gospel and so promote the 'unfolding of faith itself growing out of that understanding of God, the world and man which is conferred in and by faith'.

Bultmann had many followers. The Oxford theologian R.H. Lightfoot, for instance, was to express some doubts as to the historicity of the narratives in the synoptic gospels. His tentative doubts were taken further by Dennis Nineham who argued that the exact truth of the New Testament stories was irretrievably lost and that they constituted a mixture of fact and fiction not easily disentangled.

It was inevitable that there should be a reaction to the reductionism of the liberal theologians which seemed not merely to query the historical reliability of the gospels but to challenge their doctrinal content, so reducing credal statements to purely subjective observations based on faith. The prophet of the reaction was Karl Barth, a young Swiss pastor from the small Swiss town of Saferwil who in 1911 concluded that liberal theology was gravely deficient, as he was to make plain in his epochal *Commentary on the Epistle to the Romans* (1919) in which he spoke of God's judgement and grace through the medium of St Paul. The basic sin, he concluded, was human autonomy and the claim to self-sufficiency; the basic answer, admission of dependence upon God. He substituted the man–God relationship by the God–man relationship, assured that we ought not to seek to estimate God's place in human history but our place in God's. God, he argued, is a perfectly pure event, *actus purissimus*, who has given of himself through Christ to humanity, bridging over 'the distance between God and man – in that he tears it open'. Barth held that the Church had to be detached from politics (he had himself refused to take the oath of loyalty to Hitler) and in 1934 was partly responsible for drawing up the Barmen Declaration by which the Confessing Church asserted its primary task – to preach the gospel of the free grace of God. He was deprived of his chair at Bonn and returned to Basle where he died in 1968, the grand old man of theology.

His influence was pervasive, his disciples innumerable. In England Sir Edwyn Hoskyns, the Cambridge theologian who translated his commentary on Romans, promoted his views. In Germany Dietrich Bonhoeffer, who had visited Barth at Bonn in 1931, was much affected by his teaching but went beyond it by stressing the social relevance of the gospel in which Barth had seemed only peripherally interested, and by his insistence that Christ exists in community.

In practice it seemed as if Barth had decapitated liberal theology, but there was a growing feeling that Barth's approach had the effect of isolating Christian thought from the currents of contemporary life. Barthianism represented a retreat into the high mountains of theological exposition, recalling the great reformers of the sixteenth century, rather than a journey down the mainstream of existence. It still left theologians with an unresolved problem: how to make theology relevant to modern life without surrendering its fundamentals.

CHAPTER ELEVEN

The Crisis of the Modern Church

Less than a century after the First Vatican Council the fathers of the Church gathered at Rome for a further general council. The day, 11 October, 1962, dawned fine after days of rain as the 3,281 prelates left the papal palace and walked in ranks of six, their golden mitres and copes glittering in the sun, across St Peter's Square into the splendour of the basilica. At the close of the procession Pope John XXIII was carried in the *sedia gestatoria* by Roman aristocrats in red breeches and capes, escorted by the Swiss Guards in their blue and orange uniforms and iron breast plates, a fitting reminder of the ceremonial of the past. To the irritation of the master of ceremonies, the Pope alighted at the door of the church and walked up the aisle, seating himself on a simple brocade chair rather than on a high pontifical throne. On the Pope's instruction the gospel was sung in Arabic and Old Slavonic as well as in Latin and Greek. The Mass ended, the cardinals and patriarchs made an act of obeisance, kissing the Pope's ring, and, to represent the rest of the clergy, two archbishops, two bishops and two representatives of the Dominicans and Franciscans followed suit, the bishops kissing the Pope's knee, the religious his red slipper.

In the discourse with which he opened the council the Pope spoke optimistically about the Church's future:

In the daily exercise of our pastoral office we sometimes have to listen, much to our regret, to voices of persons, who, though burning with zeal, are not endowed with much sense of discretion or measure. They say that our era, in comparison with past eras, is getting worse. . . . We feel that we must disagree with these prophets of gloom, who are always forecasting disaster as though the end of the world were at hand. . . . In the present order of things Divine Providence is leading us to a new order of human relations, which by men's own efforts, even beyond their very expectations, are directed towards the fulfilment of God's superior and inscrutable designs. Everything, even human differences, leads to the greater good of the Church.

He continued,

The Church should never depart from the sacred patrimony of truth received from the Fathers, but at the same time, she must ever look to the present, to new conditions and new forms of life introduced with the modern world, which have opened avenues to the Catholic apostolic. Our duty is not only to guard this precious treasure (as if we were concerned only with antiquity), but to dedicate ourselves with an earnest will and without fear to that work which our era demands of us.

The salient point of this Council is not, therefore, a discussion of one article or another of the fundamental doctrine of the Church. . . . But, the Christian, Catholic and Apostolic spirit of the whole world expects a step forward towards a deeper penetration and a developing realization of the faith in perfect conformity to the authentic doctrine which should be studied and expounded through modern research and modern scholarly discipline.

He added boldly, 'the substance of the ancient doctrine of the deposit of faith is one thing. The way in which it is presented is another.' He rejected the doctrinaire condemnation of error which the Church had made in the past. 'Nowadays . . . the spouse of Christ prefers to make use of the medicine of mercy.' He looked forward to Christian unity, that 'great mystery Jesus Christ petitioned with fervent prayer from his heavenly father on the eve of his sacrifice'. The council was to be for the Church the great leap forward, *un balzo in avanti*.

Twenty-six years later, the menace of Communist totalitarianism seemingly lifted, churchmen came together in Moscow to celebrate the millennium of the Russian Orthodox Church. For a week in early June 1988 the Russian Orthodox Church with the approval and the participation of the State celebrated the millennium of Prince Vladimir's conversion to the Christian faith. The proceedings started with the liturgy on Sunday 5 June, a swelteringly hot day, in the blue and gold cathedral of the Epiphany which had replaced the patriarchal cathedral after its destruction in 1934. While leading foreign churchmen attended, among them Archbishop Runcie and Cardinal Jan Willebrands, representing the Vatican, as well as representatives of the Jamaican Methodists, the Japanese Catholics, American Presbyterians and the radical Brazilian theologian Father Leonardo Buff, local worshippers were kept away behind special crowd control barriers.

In the course of the following week a council or *sobor* of the Church met in the monastery of the Holy Trinity and St Sergius at Zagorsk to legislate for the future, passing statutes which provided for the Church's capacity to order its own life and lifting some of the restrictions which the State had hitherto imposed on its activities. The climax came with a grand meeting at the Bolshoi Theatre on Friday 10 June attended by representatives of the State including President Gromyko and Mrs Gorbachev, and of world Churches. In his address, only one of several speeches which lasted some hours, Metropolitan Yuvenali of Krutitsy and Kolomena, the archdiocese of Moscow, alluded to the period of repression which had followed the Revolution of 1917 'so difficult for the people' but welcomed the omens for a bright future.

Next Sunday dawned chill, overcast and windy, but a vast crowd assembled in the grounds of the Danilov monastery to attend the liturgy concelebrated by seven prelates representing as many nationalities. The chief Roman Catholic guest, the Polish primate Cardinal Glemp, reminded his hosts that the millennium afforded incontrovertible proof that God was reviving the faith of his people. It did indeed seem as if a new era in the history of the Church had opened, so much so that after the sufferings of the past seventy years the event seemed little short of miraculous.

The scene next shifts from Moscow to London where four years later on 11 November 1992 the General Synod of the Church of England meets to debate and reach a decision on the vexed question of the ordination of women to the priesthood. The debate, as Anglican debates tended to be, was cool and civilized. The bishop of Birmingham Mark Santer asked 'What kind of good news is it that only men may represent Christ in the priesthood of the church?' 'For too long,' David McClean the chairman of the House of Laity pronounced, 'the special gifts of women have been unused and undervalued. May we now take the marvellous opportunity to unlock those gifts to enrich the Church and strengthen it in the service of God?' The bishop of Durham asked 'Is it not disgraceful that we have so little faith in the catholicity of Christ's incarnation for all, and in the catholicity of the sacrament of his body and blood, that we confine that sacrament to men's hands? Surely women's hands are as human and as able to be hallowed by God's grace and calling.' The bishop of Ely thought the issue was not a mere matter of fashion or civil rights, but of the doctrine of the Trinity and Incarnation.

But there were others who felt as strongly that the Church of England was about to refute its heritage as well as its catholicity, betraying the faith, making difficult relations with the Roman and Orthodox Churches, and so in danger of precipitating a schism within its own ranks and sinking to the status of a sect. 'The invariable practice of 2000 years is terminated in a single clause.' 'We are asked', Peter Geldard said, 'to push down one of the walls that holds the very house together.'

The motion required a two-thirds majority which was obtained by only a narrow margin – 67.3 per cent of the three houses: those of the bishops, 39 for and 13 against; of the clergy, 76 for and 74 against; of the laity, 169 for and 82 against. The archbishop of Canterbury George Carey, who had no doubt of the rightness of the decision, believed that it was a very happy augury for the future of the Church of England. 'The step I hope we shall take today is a development in the Church's tradition. The ordination of women to the priesthood alters not a word in the creeds, the scriptures, or the faith of our Church.'

All these meetings, Roman, Orthodox, Anglican, were permeated with a strong element of optimism and hope for the future, even if that at London left in some respects a sour taste behind it, but sufficient time has not yet elapsed to make a final judgement as to whether such optimism was justified.

The ending of the Second World War had left western Europe and America full of hope for the future. The only major menace remained Stalinist Russia and its satellites, but even here there was some expectation of a period of peaceful coexistence. The creation of the United Nations gave hope of preserving the world from major wars, a hope that in spite of occasional crises was to be justified; though interracial and internecine violence continued to be rampant.

The Churches shared in such hopes. Even President Truman decreed that 13 May 1945 should be designated a national day of prayer. General Chiang Kai-shek affirmed that Chinese Christianity might provide an answer for an unbelieving world, while General MacArthur saw in Japan's defeat a providential dispensation which was to be marked by Christian services. Some nations asserted that by their constitutions they were Christian: Spain, Portugal, Italy and Ireland, Roman Catholic; Greece, Orthodox; Iceland, Protestant. In England and Scandinavia the Churches were established by law (though Church and State were to be separated in Sweden in 1994).

It was symptomatic of the times that major Western countries should be governed by Christian democratic governments, Catholic in origin but supported by conservative Protestants: Konrad Adenauer in Germany, and Alcide Gasparri in Italy. General Franco remained in power in Spain, a close ally of the Catholic Church. But, in general, the drift was politically towards a more liberal Catholicism. In France the postwar government appointed the left-wing Jacques Maritain as its ambassador to the Vatican. When the Mouvement Republicain Populaire gave way to the Gaullists the reconciliation between the Church and state was reaffirmed.

In other ways there was at first much to suggest that the Church's optimism about the future of Christianity was justified. The Second Vatican Council was to inaugurate what seemed to be a time of renewal in the Roman Catholic Church. There was strong support in Protestant churches for the oecumenical movement and the World Council of Churches. Churches took measures to remodel their liturgies in the hope of attracting congregations, eliminating what seemed obscure and obscurantist. In Germany the Lutherans redrafted their service books between 1955 and 1964; the Church of England between 1960 and 1980, culminating in the publication of the Alternative Service Book. Rome introduced the vernacular into the Mass. There were numerous new translations of the Bible: the Jerusalem Bible in 1966, the New English Bible in 1970 and the Good News Bible in 1976. If to conservative worshippers in all churches the language seemed often banal and lacking much sense of the numinous, the attempts at least showed the Churches' concern to demonstrate their relevance to the modern world. By and large immediately after the war Church membership went up in most countries. Oxford and Cambridge college chapels, often empty before the Second World War, burgeoned. The young were drawn even more to less conventional or semi-religious movements. Moral Rearmament, for instance, anti-Communist in direction, which urged spiritual renewal and social reconciliation, attracted a numerous following. At the start of the second half of the twentieth century religion might have seemed to be taking flight again after the doldrums of the inter-war years.

Time has shown that such hopes were largely illusory, and that many features, social and intellectual as well as religious, were in some respects placing Christianity on trial. It was not merely that the Churches were long to be menaced by the threat of atheistic Communism, but that the ethos of the late twentieth century was to be penetrated more and more by religious indifferentism and moral relativity.

ROME AND THE SECOND VATICAN COUNCIL

The Roman Church was faced by the need to adapt itself to a fast-changing environment. For some time there had been a growing groundswell of discontent with its centralized bureaucratic government, for while the college of cardinals had increased in number, control appeared to rest in the hands of the Pope and a small number of curial advisers. It was government by old men, both with the wisdom which experience brings but with the prejudice of old age. The Church's finances were wrapped in impenetrable mystery. The laity had only minimal participation in the Church's government. To many Catholics the Church's theology and moral teaching seemed too inflexible; and its leading theologians, Karl Rahner, de Lubac, Congar, Daniélou, Küng, were regarded with suspicion by the curia. Yet this authoritarian bureaucracy did not lack the capacity for change. It possessed a deep reservoir of spirituality, and more especially in the new Churches outside Europe an enthusiastic body of the faithful. The last half of the twentieth century was to reveal both the continued conservatism and yet fresh resilience of the Roman Church.

Pope Pius XII who as Eugenio Pacelli had been secretary of state to Pius XI, authoritarian by nature and conservative by instinct, edged cautiously into the postwar world. Although in *Humani generis*, issued in 1950, he was to warn the faithful against the application of modern criticism to the study of theology he had some years earlier, in *Divino afflante Spiritu* (1943) allowed the exegetes of scripture to use modern historical methodology. He had encouraged the laity to take part in the Mass (*Mediator Dei*, 1947) and approved the relaxation of fasting before the Eucharist and the celebration of evening Masses which the conditions of war had promoted. He certainly showed greater awareness of other Churches than his predecessors, and in 1949 so far approved the oecumenical movement as to allow Catholics to enter into dialogue with non-Romans on matters of faith. But Pius's intellectual timidity and basic conservatism of attitude made him afraid of changes which seemed to threaten the Church's traditional role.

As a result of his earlier experience as a diplomat, he was a very cautious politician, fearful of Communism the teachings of which he strongly condemned. On 30 June 1949 he signed a decree, appropriately enough published on 14 July, the anniversary of the storming of the Bastille, in which he threatened to excommunicate all who 'knowingly and with full consent defend the materialistic doctrines of Communism or any who assisted in bringing about a Communist regime', a matter of some relevance in Italy where the Communist Party under Togliatti was to become strong. He made advantageous concordats with the fascist regimes of Dr Salazar in Portugal (1950) and General Franco in Spain (1953). Although General Franco, like the Spanish kings, continued to appoint bishops, a right which King Juan Carlos was to surrender in 1976, the Spanish state helped the Church to pay for stipends, buildings and colleges. Non-Catholic buildings were not permitted to put up public signs. Freemasonry and Communism were banned. Pius was suspicious of liberal tendencies in the French Church, more especially of the literary renaissance with which it was associated. He was suspicious too of worker priests whom he believed to be potential agents of Communism.

He was equally opposed to attempts to bring theology into line with intellectual enquiry. As a sequel to the publication of *Humani generis*, the liberal Jesuits, de Lubac, Roudet and Bouillard were banned from teaching. De Lubac, held to be the *enfant terrible* of *la theologie nouvelle* was even forbidden to reside in a house where there were students. The work of the Dominican scholar M.D. Chenu, who taught that it was necessary to place Thomas Aquinas in the context of his times to understand his theology, was placed on the Index. More understandably the Vatican condemned the ideas of the former Jesuit Teilhard de Chardin who had fallen into what *Humani generis* described as the heresy of immanentism.

If Pius was concerned to come to terms with the modern world what he tried to do was always qualified by his basic belief in his Petrine authority. The model which sustained him was a rigid conception of Catholicity, which found expression in his anti-modernism. His theology and devotional life were rooted in traditional spirituality, focused on the Blessed Virgin Mary, whose bodily Assumption he declared in *Munificentissimus Deus* (1 November 1950) to be an article of faith, and for whom he devised a special feast by the encyclical *Ad coeli reginam* to be celebrated on 31 May. He was the first Pope to approve the devotion to Our Lady at the small Portuguese town of Fatima which had become a popular resort for pilgrims after she supposedly appeared there in May 1917 to three illiterate children.

The Pope's latter years were clouded by increasing ill-health, and he agreed to be treated by the Swiss gerontologist Dr Paul Niehaus who applied the 'living cell therapy', involving the injection into his patient of the ground up tissues of newly slaughtered lambs. More and more he had placed reliance on a small coterie of advisers who pursued their own interests to the detriment of the Church. His funeral was grisly, for as a result of faulty embalming the coffin exploded.

Pius XII had died on 9 October 1958. On 28 October Angelo Giuseppe

Roncalli, the patriarch of Venice was elected at the twelfth ballot. The new Pope, who took the name John XXIII, was in his seventy-seventh year, though twenty-four of the fifty-one cardinals at the conclave were themselves older. Although he was the candidate of the more conservative cardinals, he was plainly regarded as a stop-gap who would not sponsor radical innovations, in practice he was to be the most significant and positive head of the Roman Church in the twentieth century.

If not a man of outstanding intellect, he was a worthy Church historian who had written a series of volumes on his hero the Counter-Reformation reformer St Carlo Borromeo, on whose festival he chose to be crowned. His earlier career had been spent in the Vatican's diplomatic service, as apostolic delegate to Bulgaria, Turkey and Greece and latterly as nuncio to France where he had lubricated relations with de Gaulle, more especially over his demand for the deprivation of French bishops who had collaborated with Marshal Pétain.

Fundamentally a traditionalist, Pope John yet had an instinctive insight into the crisis of his times. He never lost his peasant shrewdness and sense of humour, and after the elegant Pius XII he brought a much-needed breath of fresh air into the Vatican, reviving, for instance, the custom which had fallen into disuse after 1870 of visiting personally the Regina Coeli prison and one of the Roman hospitals at Christmastide.

For the Church he was the herald of the wind of change, even if in the years to come the wind subsided into a gentle breeze. What he sought was the renewal of the Church, *aggiornamento*, which would bring the Church into touch with the needs of contemporary society. He can have had little idea of the floodgate he was opening, which his eventual successors were to seek to confine and even to close. He formulated his plans on 25 January 1959. 'Trembling with emotion,' he told his congregation at the church of St Paul Without the Walls, 'and yet with humble resolution, we put before you the proposal of a double celebration: a diocesan synod for Rome and an oecumenical council for the whole Church.' The synod, the first in Rome's long history, intended as a prelude to the council, met in St John Lateran from 24 to 31 January 1960. It was traditional in its findings, reminding Roman priests that they must always wear either the cassock or the soutane, avoid attendance at operas and race meetings, nor be alone with a woman and only use cars in case of urgent need. It gave little inkling of what was to follow.

Behind the scenes as preparatory committees and secretariats were set up, the conservative curialists were agitated, the cardinals especially the aged Pizzardo (at eighty-six) and the influential Ottaviano (at seventy-three) apprehensive, and even obstructive. Where the Pope saw the council as a God-sent opportunity for restoration and renewal within the Church, the conservatives wished that it would confine its attention to reaffirming the truth of traditional teaching and the condemnation of contemporary errors. The conservatives were to fight a rearguard action with a measure of success.

But the number of liberal and radically minded Catholics had grown in Western countries and looked at the council as a new omen. The brilliant young professor from the university of Tübingen, Hans Küng, praised the council as an advance on the Council of Trent which had reinvigorated the Church four hundred years earlier. He advised a reform of the Roman curia, the abolition of the Index, a reassessment of the Reformation and the institution of the Mass in the vernacular. The forward-looking archbishop of Paderborn, Lorenz Jaeger, asserting that the earlier Vatican council had been an expression of ecclesiastical authoritarianism, urged that the new council should reflect the collegiality of the Church. Prominent was the Jesuit Father Augustin Bea, former rector of the Pontifical Biblical Institute, who, in spite of age and frailty, underlined the notion that the council would be, in the Pope's own words, 'not a speculative assembly, but a living and vibrant organism which would embrace everyone in the light and love of Christ'. In 1960 the Pope put Bea in charge of a new curial office, a Secretariat of Unity, with Monsignor Willebrands as its secretary. It was to prove the most radical department of the curia.

In practice the council could not be as oecumenical as some would have wished, though some eighteen non-Roman Churches sent observers. The Orthodox Churches, as usual, were split, for the patriarch of Constantinople, Athenagoras, much resented that an invitation had been sent to Alexis, the patriarch of Moscow. Of the 2,449 prelates who attended, there were some 800 from missionary dioceses, including 296 from Africa, some 93 from the Philippines and Japan and Indonesia, and 84 from India. There were 217 bishops from the USA, 531 from Latin America, 400 from Italy, 159 from France, 95 from Spain, 68 from Germany, 42 from the United Kingdom, 33 from Ireland and 27 from Portugal. There were some 135 from the Low Countries, the majority of whom (111) were from overseas dioceses. There was an exiguous contingent from eastern Europe, 13 Poles led by Cardinal Wyszynski, 3 Hungarians, 2 Yugoslavs, 3 Czechs and the apostolic administrator of Tebiai in Lithuania, small in number but symbolically significant, given the continued domination of Communism in these lands. The Maronites of the Lebanon were led by Meouchi, the patriarch of Antioch, the Melkites by their 84-year-old patriarch, Maximos IV. There were also representatives of the Malankars, the Copts, the Chaldeans and the Armenians, all Uniat Churches. There were bishops of every shape and size, of every colour, some so poor that they had difficulties eking out a living, and others, like the Americans, enjoying the facilities of Rome's luxury hotels.

The Council opened on 11 October 1962. Pope John did not personally attend the proceedings but he kept a fatherly eye on what was happening, intervening only to resolve a dispute over a schema on revelation. Nor was the convening of the council the sole achievement of his short pontificate. He had initiated an ongoing dialogue with non-Romans and non-Christians, setting up the Secretariat for Christian Unity under the presidency of

Cardinal Bea in June 1960. In his encyclical *Ad Cathedram Petri* of 29 June 1959 he spoke of non-Catholics as 'separated brethren and sons'. On 20 December 1960 he received Archbishop Fisher of Canterbury, the first archbishop to visit Rome since the Reformation, and he approved the despatch of five Roman Catholic observers to a meeting of the World Council of Churches held at New Delhi in November 1961. He sent personal envoys to greet the oecumenical patriarch, Athenagoras, at Istanbul. He showed his sympathy for the Jews by deleting words thought to be offensive from the liturgy for Good Friday.

Nor did Pope John confine his pastoral role to purely religious matters. In the Cuban missile crisis of 1962 he urged both the Americans and Russians to use caution to avoid the possibility of nuclear conflict, and was deservedly awarded the Peace Prize of the International Balzan Foundation. His encyclical *Mater et magistra* of 15 May 1961 carried forward the social teaching of Leo XIII and Pius XI; and in *Pacem in terris* of 11 April 1963 he stressed how important it was to secure the recognition of human rights, distinguishing between Marxist ideology and actual policies followed by Communist states, arguing for coexistence. Even the Soviet states were impressed by the Pope, resulting in a surprising visit to the Vatican by Nikita Khrushchev's son-in-law early in 1963. But the Pope's health was failing fast and he died, a victim of stomach cancer, on 3 June 1963. The churchman who had been dismissed by his critics as a silly and ineffectual old man had turned out to be the most dynamic and constructive of twentieth-century popes.

It remained to be seen whether the council would continue to fulfil his high hopes, and his successor to implement them. The conclave of some eighty cardinals, the highest number yet so to function, at the fifth ballot elected Giovanni Montini, the archbishop of Milan, as Paul VI. Montini, who earlier in his career had worked in the papal secretariat, had been archbishop of Milan since 1954, proving an active pastor, seeking, if with only limited success, to bring the city's industrial working class into contact with the Church. Suspected of harbouring liberal aspirations, he had lacked the favour of Pius XII, and had only in 1958 been named a cardinal by his successor, John XXIII. He took as seriously as his predecessor the work of the Second Vatican Council which concluded with a fourth session on 8 December 1965.

During Paul's early pontificate some important procedural changes had been introduced, including the admission of laymen and women as auditors. New decrees were promulgated, recognizing the collegiality of the bishops, who, it was laid down, when acting together with but not independently of the Pope constituted the highest authority in the Church. It was a claim which had been canvassed during the Conciliar movement in the later Middle Ages, but it had been rejected at the Council of Trent. The notion had been revived by some eighteenth-century thinkers of whom Febronius had been the most important. Conservative churchmen still opposed it, believing that it did not sufficiently safeguard the primacy of the Pope.

In conformity with this decree Paul VI promised to set up a synod of bishops to discuss and debate as well as to proffer advice, and in 1971, 1974 and 1977 he called international episcopal synods to deliberate on the priesthood, on evangelization and the catechism. Commissions were set up to consider how the breviary should be revised as well as the lectionary, the order of the Mass, sacred music and canon law. Most importantly, in spite of strong protests from the more conservative faithful, he permitted the use of the vernacular in the liturgy.

The Second Vatican Council had in many ways restructured the practice of the Catholic Church, completing the cycle of liturgical change inaugurated under Pius XII, using as the criterion for change the congregation's capacity to understand what was going on and to take part. In addition to permitting the saying of the canon of the Mass in the vernacular, in certain circumstances communion in both kinds was permitted. Another development was the use made of concelebration by which priests celebrated Mass together rather than as private individuals. After five hundred years the Latin Tridentine Mass practically disappeared and was replaced by a service the language of which was, as was the case with most new service books, somewhat pedestrian in character.

Doctrinally the new constitution on the Church had radical possibilities, for while the Petrine headship was unchallenged, the concept of a papal monarchy was put on one side in favour of collegiality with the bishops together with the Pope holding a collective responsibility as the heirs of Christ's apostles. There was besides a somewhat different vision of the Church itself, defined as God's people, not fundamentally restricted to members of the Roman communion but consisting of all baptized Christians. The council had furthermore recognized the validity of religious toleration. To traditionalists the barricades so carefully and painfully built up over the centuries to preserve the purity of the faith and the integrity of the Church were about to be dismantled. In practice the curialists were going to be able to slacken the pace of change, but the Second Vatican Council was nonetheless a landmark in the history of the Christian Church if for its aspirations rather than its actual achievements. In some sense the Catholic Church might almost have seemed to have been Protestantized. In any case the Church could never be quite the same again.

Pope Paul VI, like John XXIII, was ready to enter into dialogue and friendship with non-Catholic Churches. He and the patriarch of Constantinople, Athenagoras, agreed to end the schism which had split the two Churches since 1054, withdrawing on 7 December 1965 the anathemas which their respective predecessors had launched against each other. On 20 March 1966 Pope Paul received Fisher's successor, Michael Ramsey, Archbishop of Canterbury, in audience. He broke with past papal tradition by travelling far afield, to Bombay to the International Eucharistic Congress, to New York to address the United Nations, to Jerusalem and to Istanbul, to Geneva to give an address to the International Labour Organization and the

World Council of Churches, to Uganda in 1969 to celebrate those who had been martyred there for the faith, to Sardinia to honour Our Lady of Bonavia in April 1970, to the shrine of Our Lady at Fatima in May 1967 to pray for peace, for like his predecessors he was devoted to the Blessed Virgin Mary whom he had made, in spite of some opposition, 'Mother of the Church'. To emphasize the international character of the Church he had greatly increased the numbers of the college of cardinals, from 80 to 138, reducing the number of Italians and adding many representatives from the Third World.

The pontificate of Paul VI might seem to be a momentous achievement, but it was not an achievement without some grave qualifications. The Pope was a cautious rather than a radical progressive, a natural worrier with a strong strain of indecision in his character. There seemed to be a growing uncertainty in his mind as to where he was leading the Church. Desirous as he undoubtedly was of implementing the decisions of the council, he was concerned that the Church should not drift too far outside its traditional frontiers. He was disconcerted by the fierce opposition to the liturgical changes led by Monsignor Marcel Lefebvre, and by rising demands for more radical reforms including an end to the obligatory celibacy of the clergy by the more liberal faithful. He reacted strongly by reasserting the fundamental requirement of clerical celibacy in the encyclical *In Sacerdotalis caelibatus* of 24 June 1967. He followed this up by *Humanae vitae* on 25 July 1968 which condemned artificial methods of birth control. It was much criticized by many of the faithful as well as by non-Roman Churches, being specifically rejected by the Lambeth Conference of Anglican bishops. The Pope was much put out by the hostile criticism and was never to issue another encyclical. 'A little like Hamlet', *Amletico*, as his predecessor had described him, Pope Paul VI found it increasingly difficult to reconcile the vision of the Church as the Vatican council had conceived it with inner doubts as to whether the changes which were taking place might jeopardize the Church's mission to the world.

When the conclave met in August 1978, the cardinals elected Albino Luciani, the patriarch of Venice, who in tribute to his two eminent predecessors took the name of John Paul I. His was a strange appointment, probably representing the cardinals' wish to choose a candidate who lacked the sophistication, even the capacity, of his immediate predecessors and who had little experience of curial committees. In some respects he almost appeared a modern-day Celestine V. Of working-class origins, a devoted pastor, not intellectually distinguished, essentially simple in his tastes, he was critical of the wealth and ceremonial of the Church, dispensing with the pomp of coronation. It is impossible to say what sort of Pope John Paul I would have made, for within three weeks 'God's candidate' was dead of a heart attack. Because Vatican officialdom made a hash of revealing the circumstances of the Pope's death, in default of a medical autopsy, rumour spread suggesting that the Pope had been poisoned because he intended to clean up the Vatican Bank which was controlled by the dubious Archbishop Marcinkus, or even to revise the encyclical *Humanae vitae*, but this scenario was implausible. Nonetheless the surmise that the cardinals had made an election which the Church might regret and that had he lived Pope John Paul I might well not have been up to the job seemed to have something to be said for it.

The conclave which met in October 1978 at the eighth ballot, by a majority of 103 votes out of 109, elected the Polish cardinal, Karol Wojtyla, Archbishop of Cracow, as the new Pope; out of respect for his predecessor he took the name John Paul II. Unlike the previous Pope he was already a widely known and respected figure on the world stage. Of modest background, an athlete and later a skier, a dramatist and actor, a poet of some distinction and a philosopher, he was a man of parts, indeed a Renaissance figure. The first Slav to become Pope, the first non-Italian since the early sixteenth century, he had obtained his doctorate at Rome for a thesis on St John of the Cross, and he had been to the fore at the Second Vatican Council whose decisions he sought to implement in Poland. His Polish background provided the key to the understanding of the Pope's character, for he saw himself, as the Poles have throughout their history seen themselves, as a defender of Christian civilization against the forces of barbarism and unbelief.

He promised to promote 'with prudent but encouraging action' the fulfilment of the Vatican council. To some it seemed as if prudence rather than encouragement had the upper hand. Yet he was to win golden opinions by his warm, charismatic personality and his espousal of humane causes. He laid down firmly in *Redemptor hominis* in 1979 the principles on which society should be based, asserting that the roots of true freedom and human dignity were to be found in the Church. In *Dives in misericordia* issued in December 1980 he urged men to behave towards each other with charity, mercy and love. In *Laborem exercens* of September 1981 he declared the need for a new economic order, founded on the rights of workers and the dignity of labour, which should be neither capitalist nor Marxist. How far such encyclicals had a practical effect may be doubted, but they brought home the Pope's pastoral concern for all the peoples of the world. He was untiring in insisting on the rights of the poor and in his concern for the peace of the world, but he was incorrigibly reactionary in his interpretation of his office, in effect consciously or unconsciously repudiating the vision of the Church that many Catholics had gleaned from the proceedings of the Second Vatican Council.

He was nonetheless an energetic and charismatic spokesman for the Church. His role was underlined by what became the most characteristic feature of his pontificate, his spectacular personal journeys to every country in the world where he was in general met with great enthusiasm, though in Holland and in some places in North America progressive Catholics resented what they felt to be his reactionary policy. In 1982 he visited

Britain, the first time a pope had ever made such a visit, and joined the archbishop of Canterbury in prayer in Canterbury Cathedral. A year earlier on 13 May 1981 he had been shot in St Peter's Square by a Turk, Mehmet Ali Agca, for reasons which are obscure, though some believed that the assassin had been acting on Communist orders. He had been obliged to undergo major surgery, but the attempted assassination only added to his popularity.

There were, however, an increasing number of Catholics who were made anxious by the personality cult which he seemed to have created for himself. They were worried by the great expense of the journeys which many of the faithful who contributed funds could ill afford. They questioned whether the Pope's absence from Rome had a deleterious effect on the Vatican which had been rocked by rumours of financial scandal and corruption. It was the more disconcerting that whatever lip service the Pope may have paid to the concept of collegiality, in practice his rule was authoritarian. He would not give up an iota of his claims to universal jurisdiction, and indeed sought to reimpose discipline on erring members, chastising liberals and others who dissented from his policy. In reaction to the more liberal line followed by John XXIII and Paul VI he maintained strongly the Church's traditional teaching, not merely on doctrinal but on moral matters. Ruthlessly conservative he condemned contraception, reaffirming Paul VI's encyclical *Humanae vitae*, abortion and homosexuality, and upheld the celibacy of the clergy. He resolutely opposed 'liberation theology' which called on the Church to support the workers and the oppressed in the class struggle, condemning its begetters such as the Brazilian theologian Leonardo Buff. The Dutch scholar Edward Schillebeeckx was criticized for putting forward heterodox views on Christology and the German bishops, with the Pope's approval, withdrew Hans Küng's licence to teach theology. In 1987 the American moral theologian Charles Curran was similarly suspended from teaching at the Catholic University of America. John Paul's appointments to bishoprics further manifested his conservative slant. The influence of Opus Dei, the worldwide Catholic society suspected by some of favouring political and possibly religious reaction, was much esteemed by him. Its founder was canonized during his pontificate. The Pope's conservative policy was reaffirmed in the encyclical *Veritatis splendor* (1993) which was the Vatican's answer to contemporary dissent in the Church: 'A new situation has come about within the Christian community itself, which has experienced the spread of numerous doubts and objections. . . . It is no longer a matter of limited and occasional dissent, but of an overall and systematic calling into question of traditional moral doctrine, on the basis of anthropological and ethical presuppositions.' The encyclical countered the 'illusory freedom' to which such 'relativism and scepticism' gave rise, even among some seminarians and faculties of theology, by reaffirming the Church's traditional teaching, based on permanently valid moral norms and natural law, the interpretation of which seemed the prerogative of the Pope and the hierarchy, restating the ban on artificial birth control and opposition to homosexuality, pre-marital sex and abortion. 'If acts are intrinsically evil, a good intention or particular circumstances can diminish the evil, but they cannot remove it.'

The Pope had had high expectations for the regeneration of Catholicism in Eastern Europe after the disintegration of Communism, which he appeared to attribute to his dedication of the whole world to the Immaculate Heart of Mary on 25 March 1984, hoping that religion in tune with nationalism would help to create social justice, but his idealism was to be painfully fractured as Christians warred with each other in Croatia, Serbia and Bosnia-Herzegovina. By 1996 there were some signs that the Pope's great stamina was being sapped by ill-health, though he was still travelling abroad to encourage the faithful. In some sense his pontificate has been epochal in the life of the Church, but on his death or even conceivably on his resignation there seems every likelihood of a struggle between the liberals and conservatives as to his successor. The election of a new Pope after John Paul II will be momentous for the future of the Roman Church, still poised on dilemmas about fundamental doctrinal and moral issues. For there is no doubt, in spite of John Paul II's strong guidance, that the Church remains in some respects in a state of ferment. In 1971 the Swiss theologian Hans Urs von Balthasar observed that the clergy formed 'the clear trouble spot of the Church'. In Western Europe as in North and South America, though not in Poland or in the eastern Churches, the authority of the Church was questioned and some expressed doubts as to what constituted the essential function of the priesthood. What was, some of the faithful asked, to differentiate the priest from the layman? If ordination conferred on the priest the right to administer the sacraments, this function seemed to be in itself insufficient to legitimize a vocation to the priesthood. If the priest was to fulfil his basic function he had too to become involved with the world. While in earlier ages of the Church it was thought proper that the priest should separate himself off from the world, many now believed that the priest should identify with the world so as to save the world for Christ. He had to abandon his prim uniform, the cassock and the clerical collar, and become at least outwardly as other men.

He must, also, so some liberal theologians added, share the same labour as other men. In the Second World War when French seminarians and members of Catholic Action had been obliged to work in German factories, the French bishops told them to try to combine their manual labour with a pastoral role towards their fellow workers. After the war ended, priests who were members of the Mission de France tried to live as workers. While some French bishops applauded the experiment, others thought that it tarnished the priest's image, more especially leading him to be influenced unduly by political and social radicalism. In 1953–4 the Pope intervened to bring the experiment to an end, but the desire for some expression of solidarity with the working class persisted among many young priests. When in 1969 another group, largely French in composition, met in conference at Chur, its aims so aroused the hostility of the Vatican that it was subsequently disbanded. In Latin America the priests' wish for identification with the working class led to the growth of liberation theology which, though viewed with displeasure by the Vatican, continued to have a steady following on the Continent and in Latin America.

A different but thorny problem was raised by the obligation of celibacy, as the flight of priests from the Church in order to marry became the more marked. While the Church was bound to recognize that celibacy had not been a feature of the early Christian priesthood, it was reluctant to admit that a married priest was a viable option. In 1965 Pope Paul VI had specifically requested that celibacy should not be discussed at the Vatican Council for though celibacy was 'not demanded by the very essence of the priesthood, as the practice of the Ancient Church and the tradition of the Eastern Churches show. . . . Celibacy is in many respects proper to the priesthood', a ruling which he confirmed in the encyclical *Sacerdotalis caelibatus* in 1967. Defectors from the celibate state were labelled 'pitiable deserters'. But the demand for the abandonment of celibacy as an obligation and for the possibility of a married priesthood remained strong. The announcement by the distinguished British theologian Charles Davis that he intended to marry was a reflection of what was to be a growing trend. The affair of Eamon Casey, the bishop of Galway, a prelate distinguished for his pastoral sense, who was disclosed to have had a long-standing relationship with a woman by whom fifteen years earlier he had a son, leading to his resignation, raised questions which seemed to some to lead ultimately in the direction of a married clergy.

The Dutch Catholic Church, liberal in attitude, was in this respect a thorn in the side of the papacy. The Dutch Church was suffering particularly from an acute shortage of priests, for whereas 325 men had been ordained in 1950, only 48 came forward in 1970. Some Catholics argued that the requirement of clerical celibacy was a disincentive to ordination. There were the makings of a schism which were only averted by the timely diplomacy of the Dutch cardinal, Alfrink. At the Roman synod of 1971, Alfrink, supported by the Canadian bishops, argued for the removal of the obligation to celibacy, but was strongly opposed by the Italians, the Sri Lankans and the bishops from the United States. While the synod did not accept Alfrink's arguments, it agreed to recommend that in exceptional circumstances the Pope should allow the ordination of a married priest (i.e. married before ordination). There was henceforth to be a slow trickle of married men into the priesthood.

Rome was apprehensive at the spread of what seemed to the curia to be subversive propaganda. The Pope did what he could to chasten Dutch liberals by appointing known conservatives to vacant Dutch sees, such as Simonis to Rotterdam in 1971 and Gijsen to Roermond in 1973. But the problem would not go away, and though the historian lacks the crystal ball, it seems not improbable that the rule of clerical celibacy may well be relaxed in the not too distant future.

Whether Rome is ever likely to accept women priests seems much more doubtful, for while the ordination of women became a commonplace in the Protestant Churches in the 1970s and 1980s, and was even accepted by a majority vote in the Church of England in 1992, there are few hints of flexibility in the Roman position. The Pope's pastoral letter of 1965 had indeed emphatically rejected all discrimination against women on the grounds of their sex. In 1970 Paul VI made St Teresa of Avila and St Catherine of Siena doctors of the Church, a rank hitherto reserved to men. In parishes in San Salvador women acted as pastors, administering the sacrament; but the Roman Church continued to be strongly opposed to the ordination of women, as the Pope again made plain in an apostolic letter in May 1994 in which he declared that the Church has no authority to confer priestly ordination on women. In the Eastern Orthodox Church the paradoxical situation existed whereby a priest had to be married before his ordination but could not marry after it while the episcopate was confined to celibate monks. In Greece some 264 Orthodox priests and monks had petitioned the synod to be allowed to marry after ordination, but in vain. At the Rome synod of 1971 Cardinal Flahiff of Winnipeg stated that there was no fundamental doctrinal argument against the ordination of women, a view upheld by the radical Jesuit theologian Karl Rahner. But not surprisingly the Congregation of the Faith by the decree *Inter Insigniores* in 1977 confirmed that the ordination of women to the priesthood was totally inadmissible.

Beyond these questions of Church order there were perhaps even more searching issues, of which the democratization of the Church and greater participation of the laity in its affairs was only one. The Roman Church was still strong in membership and in the loyalty of the faithful. Numbering some 944 million worshippers out of a world population of 5.4 billion, it constituted the largest single religious denomination in the world. Its membership continued to rise as world population itself grew. Yet it will enter the twenty-first century with many unresolved problems, theological as well as moral, which could bring about major changes in its constitution and teaching.

THE CHURCH IN THE UNITED KINGDOM

Other Christian Churches, notably the Protestant Churches in the United Kingdom, were confronted by problems not wholly dissimilar to those faced by the Roman Church. In the immediate postwar years there had been some renewed signs of vitality in the British Churches. The Church of England took steps to modernize its structure and reform its liturgy. The Pastoral Reorganization Measure of 1949 in an effort to remedy some of the problems of a defective and outmoded parochial framework decided to get rid of over-large rectories and to improve the parson's stipend by merging together livings which were then to be run by a team ministry. The Parish and People movement which was started in 1949 aimed to enrich worship by making it more sacramental and participatory, and as a consequence the principal Sunday service became in many churches the Sung Eucharist. Allied to this renewed emphasis on communion were the house churches, modelled on the practices of the French worker-priest movement where the Eucharist was celebrated on weekday evenings in private homes, first introduced in England at Halton, Leeds, by the vicar E.W. Southcott in 1956.

Side by side with these experimental changes moves were made to create a specialized ministry, involving the appointment, for instance, of industrial chaplains who would seek to represent the Church on the shop floor. The intellectual respectability of Anglicanism found a continuing expression through the substantial sales of works by popular Anglican writers, most notably T.S. Eliot, C.S. Lewis, Dorothy Sayers (whose radio play *Man Born to be King* had a very wide audience) and John Betjeman.

Such changes were probably cosmetic rather than radical and had their own built-in defects. The amalgamation of livings led to the loss in many villages of a resident parson, and ultimately to a marked reduction in the parson's influence in society as a whole. The amalgamation of livings in a group ministry may have been inevitable, but its pastoral effects were deplored while the new services acted as a deterrent to those who still relished the familiar liturgy. The replacement of Matins as the main Sunday service by the Eucharist discouraged some non-communicants from attending Church, and so narrowed the congregations. All in all what was happening mainly affected the middle-class worshipper and made little impact upon the working class.

Immediately after the ending of the Second World War there had been some promising signs of outward Christian activity expressed in the various ways by which Christian individuals and groups tried to ameliorate or resolve contemporary social and racial problems. Christian Action, which had been founded after a meeting at Oxford Town Hall on 5 December 1945, under the leadership of John Collins, former chaplain of Oriel and later canon of St Paul's, became a politically radical if theologically conservative broad Church society, later focusing its attention on the problem of seeking to eliminate apartheid in South Africa. Collins's efforts were later diversified into the Campaign for Nuclear Disarmament which had been provoked by renewed anxieties raised by the possibility of a nuclear war between the great powers. Very different in their objectives were the Samaritans formed by an Anglican vicar Chad Varah in 1953 to help those contemplating suicide, branches of which soon spread throughout the country. The Samaritans like other groups closely associated with the Churches such as Oxfam and Christian Aid were not specifically Christian in membership but they were authentically Christian in their activity.

Within Anglicanism the balance of power was shifting from the Anglo-Catholics to the Evangelicals. The Anglo-Catholics had become inward looking and insufficiently innovative, fascinated by ritualistic practices which the Roman Catholics were beginning to relegate to the cellar, too focused on an esoteric subculture, what one critic described as ecclesiastical Trotskyism. But the Evangelicals made increasing headway, the Inter-Collegiate Christian Union (ICCU) replacing the once predominant Student Christian Movement as the most influential Christian group at British universities. The ICCU missions conducted by John Stott at Oxford and Cambridge were authentically both Protestant and Anglican. Evangelical teaching was propagated by the American evangelist Billy Graham whose crusade at Harringay in 1954 attracted crowds of 1,300,000 in three months; the Lord Mayor of London and the Archbishop of Canterbury were beside him at the last meeting. 'I am convinced', Graham said, 'there is going to be a spiritual awakening such as you have not seen since the days of Wesley.' There remained, however, in Evangelicalism a tang of biblical fundamentalism and antiseptic moralism which seemed later to be a feature of Archbishop Carey's sometimes ingenuous pronouncements.

Even so in the process of regaining influence the Evangelicals did in fact discard some of their rigidity, as the proceedings at the National Evangelical Congress held at Keele in 1967 showed; they adopted a more distinctively oecumenical attitude, abandoning their narrow partisanship and accepting a sacramental order with greater enthusiasm. Their influence was such that some prominent bishops, such as David Sheppard of Liverpool and two archbishops of Canterbury, Donald Coggan and George Carey, were drawn from their number.

Canterbury had five archbishops after Temple's death to the close of the twentieth century: Geoffrey Fisher, Michael Ramsey, Donald Coggan, Robert Runcie and George Carey. While the archbishop's power was limited, for each Anglican province was autonomous and his role was predominantly 'patriarchal' in character, as a coordinator, his influence as head of the Anglican Communion remained substantial, for the Anglican Communion of which he was nominally the head was worldwide, probably numbering some 70 million adherents in parts of the former British Empire and in the American Episcopal Church in the United States. Since 1867 the bishops of the Anglican Communion had met together in the decennial Lambeth Conference to discuss problems of mutual importance; there convened 242 bishops in 1908, 252 in 1920, 462 in 1968; but the growing size of the conference diminished its usefulness.

The archbishops have had an uneasy task in seeking to guide the Church of England in a volatile period, during which at times it has seemed in danger of losing both its identity and its influence. Fisher had many of the traits of the successful headmaster (which indeed he had been for eighteen years), and was an excellent administrator, authoritarian by nature, not deeply theological but pastorally concerned as evidenced by his visit to

Pope John XXIII at Rome in the interests of trying to further a better understanding between the Churches.

Michael Ramsey, whom Fisher had personally thought unsuited to be archbishop, was a silent man of genuine humility, deep scholarship and profound holiness. While he had little interest in administration, some forward steps were made in this direction under his guidance. The Church Assembly, which could be described as the Church's legislative assembly, never very satisfactory as a representative body, was replaced in 1970 by the General Synod in which the three houses of bishops, clergy and laity had wider powers than they had exercised in the assembly, so helping to give the Church a greater degree of independence from the State. The assembly set about revising the prayer book under the Worship and Doctrine measure of 1974, resulting in the Alternative Service Book, magisterial in size if flawed in its language, which was designed to meet the needs of the different groups in the Anglican Church. A commission was set up under Owen Chadwick to investigate the way in which the Crown made appointments to high office, issuing in a recommendation that such appointments should in future be made by a semi-representative commission, which would present two names to the prime minister. The change became law in Donald Coggan's archiepisocopate in 1977. The form of subscription to the Thirty-nine Articles was changed and replaced by a simpler affirmation of the faith 'which is revealed in Holy Scripture and set forth in the Catholic creeds and to which the historic formularies of the Church of England bear witness'.

Ramsey, oecumenical and Catholic-minded, following Fisher's example, visited Pope Paul VI. Whereas Fisher had been coolly received by the curial officials who had pointedly described him as Dr Fisher rather than as archbishop, Paul VI and Michael Ramsey worshipped together in the church of St Paul's Without the Walls where the Pope placed his own episcopal ring on Ramsey's finger (the latter's widow subsequently gave the ring to Archbishop Runcie). Although the plans for a reunion between the Anglicans and the Methodists which Ramsey had cherished were defeated in the General Synod, by his serene wisdom Ramsey had kept together the increasingly fragmented Church of England.

After the short but inconspicuous tenure of the see by the evangelical Donald Coggan, Robert Runcie became in 1980 the 102nd archbishop. Civilized and humane as a person and pastor, Runcie's prudent policy papered over the cracks which were threatening the Anglican Communion, his delicate and acute political antennae serving the nation well. Indefatigable in seeking to preserve the 'interdependence' of its constituent parts he travelled widely throughout the world, visiting Africa on some eight occasions. Sedulous in his pursuit of understanding and Christian unity he greeted Pope John Paul II warmly in Canterbury Cathedral in May 1982, the most impressive of five meetings which they had had with each other, at Accra, Canterbury, Bombay, Assisi and Rome. Runcie had a deep concern for social justice which raised the hackles of some political traditionalists.

'The Church', he stated in 1982, 'has a special concern to speak for the vulnerable, the inarticulate, those who are weak in bargaining power – those who are in our country at the bottom of the heap.' The practical expression of this statement was the publication of the report *Faith in the City*, perhaps the greatest achievement of Runcie's archiepiscopate, which was aimed to redress the social imbalance in deprived urban areas, and which led to the establishment of the Church Urban Fund. In pursuit of deepening the relationship between Canterbury and Rome Runcie encouraged the work of the newly founded Anglican–Roman Catholic International Commission. With non-Anglican Protestant Churches, such as the Evangelical churches of Germany and the Lutheran churches of Sweden and Finland he enjoyed a warm accord.

It is, however, fair to say that for all the archbishop's good sense and wise guidance, the cracks in the fabric of the Church of England became more explicit. This was displayed in the irresponsible preface to *Crockford's Clerical Directory* for 1987–8, which deplored the way in which bishops were being appointed and directly criticized the archbishop for favouring candidates of a liberal theological stance and unduly neglecting Evangelicals and Anglo-Catholics. It led sadly to the suicide of the author, a prominent Oxford historian, Gary Bennett, a personal friend of Runcie who had somewhat deviously at first sought to deny his authorship. Another personal tragedy occurred in 1987 in the kidnapping and harsh imprisonment of Terry Waite in the Lebanon where he had gone in an attempt to rescue hostages there. Runcie had appointed Waite his Assistant for Anglican Communion Affairs with a roving commission to keep him in touch with what was happening in the Anglican Communion. But the principal contention dividing the Church which overshadowed the close of Runcie's archbishopric was the debate over the ordination of women.

THE ORDINATION OF WOMEN AND DISESTABLISHMENT

Apart from a few odd historical sects, for the greater part of their history the Christian Churches had only ordained men; but the growth of feminism, a greater awareness of women's rights and a changing social culture precipitated a demand that in all matters women should be treated the same as men. The advocates of the movement quoted St Paul's words: 'Neither Jew nor Greek, neither slave nor free, neither male nor female, you are all one in Jesus Christ.' There were practical reasons for women's ordination, since women priests would fill the gaps left by the fall in the number of male candidates to the ministry. The critics of women's ordination pointed out with some justification that the ordination of women would constitute a breach of two thousand years of tradition, and be a contravention of the Catholic order of the Church. The male priesthood, it was said, represented both the order of creation and of redemption and was rooted in scripture. The fatherhood of God and the maleness of Christ required that men should preside over the Eucharist. The ordination of women seemed to the more Catholic-minded theologically and historically inappropriate. Whether the movement for the ordination of women represented simply an admission by the Church that it had so far failed to recognize the proper role of women in its ministry or whether, more probably, it was an expression of social expediency rather than a matter of religious principle, must remain uncertain, but it seemed very likely that it was another outcrop of contemporary militant feminism. The Free Churches, without a definite sacramental Catholic view of the priesthood, had already appointed women as ministers. In 1946 the Danish Lutherans elected a woman as a pastor but encountered some difficulty in procuring a bishop to ordain her. Two years later the Danish government intervened to permit the choice of a woman as pastor providing a bishop was ready to ordain, a step which some Danish churchmen criticized as constituting interference by the state in Church affairs. Likewise the Swedish government, in spite of criticism from the Church Assembly, in 1967 passed legislation allowing women to become priests. Norway followed the Danish and Swedish examples.

An Anglican group to promote the ordination of women had been set up in the 1930s but it was only in the 1960s that the question really surfaced. In the Second World War as a matter of pastoral urgency Bishop Hall of Hong Kong had ordained Florence Li Tim Oi as a priest in 1944. Bishop Hall's action was repudiated by the Chinese House of Bishops of 1946. She reverted to lay status and her priestly role was not regularized until 1970 (she died in 1992). Archbishop Temple had disapproved of the bishop's action but he had commented that the theological arguments against the non-ordination of women 'seem to me quite desperately futile'.

The Lambeth Conference of Bishops, meeting in 1968, was mildly encouraging and three years later the Anglican Consultative Council, meeting at Limuru in Kenya, though without any explicit authority and acting against the advice of Archbishop Ramsey, recommended by 24 votes to 22 that if a province of the Anglican Church wished to ordain women it should feel free to do so. In 1972 two women priests were ordained in the diocese of Hong Kong. The American bishops of the Episcopal Church, by 74 to 61 votes, agreed that women could be ordained but laid down that the bishops should not act independently. In spite of this qualification in July 1974 three retired American bishops and one from Costa Rica ordained eleven women in Philadelphia, one being herself the daughter of a bishop. In 1972 women were ordained canonically in Canada and in 1977 in New Zealand.

It was soon plain that what was at issue was not simply the ordination of women to the priesthood but the possibility of their being consecrated as bishops. In 1990 Penelope Jamieson was appointed bishop of Dunedin in New Zealand. The critics of women's ordination were outraged by the election in 1989 of a Black divorcée, Barbara Harris as a suffragan bishop of Massachusetts, which a protester at her consecration described as a 'sacrilegious imposture'. But the preacher at the service, which was attended by some fifty-six bishops and had to be held because of the huge congregation of some eight thousand in the Hynes Convention Center, compared Bishop Harris's consecration to the Annunciation of the Blessed Virgin Mary. 'He has', he said, 'chosen this thing to confound the wise . . . I would say that this day has gotten through the eye of the needle.' Jane Holmes Dixon had been appointed bishop suffragan in Washington. In 1993 it was proposed to elect Mary Macleod (a divorcée with sparse academic credentials who with her husband was co-rector of St John's Charleston, West Virginia) as bishop of Vermont. There seemed no historical reason why there should not be ultimately a predominantly female episcopate and even, supposing the Roman Catholic Church accepted women priests, a female pope, so in fact making the medieval legend of Pope Joan a practicable possibility in the twenty-first century.

The Church of England, bitterly divided on the issue, havered. Archbishop Ramsey was at first hostile but came eventually to the conclusion that the scriptural arguments against the ordination of women were weak. Archbishop Coggan was favourable; and in 1975 the General Synod agreed that there were 'no fundamental objections to women's ordination'. Archbishop Runcie, striving to keep the Church together, was unenthusiastic. 'In regard to the ordination of women,' he told the General Synod in 1984, 'I have consistently driven down the middle of the road, and I am surprised to find that I have survived this dangerous ordeal.' But although he believed that it was inopportune to introduce the measure he eventually committed himself to it, having come to believe as he confessed in 1988 that 'the ordination of women to the priesthood would actually be an enlargement of the Catholic priesthood rather than its overturning'.

The opponents of the measure who belonged mainly to the Anglo-Catholic wing, supported by some extreme Evangelicals, held that the archbishop was subordinating a moral issue to ecclesiastical expediency. In 1987 the Church of England agreed to ordain women to the diaconate. The number of women deacons rose by 13 per cent from 596 to 674 by 1991, so in part helping to fill the gaps created by the slow but steady decline in the male ministry. Once the decision had been made to ordain women as deacons, it was obviously going to be difficult to prevent their ordination to the priesthood. Even by 1978 there were over 150 women priests at work in other churches of the Anglican Communion. On 11 November 1992 the General Synod by a hardly-won majority agreed to the ordination of women to the priesthood.

The consequences of this move were not immediately plain. The measure was endorsed without difficulty by Parliament, and in 1994 a number of women were ordained for the first time to the priesthood in the Church of England. The Church of Ireland had already taken the step, as subsequently, and by a narrow majority, were to do the Church in Australia and in 1994 the Episcopal Church in Scotland. However, by a narrow majority in 1994 the Church in Wales rejected the measure. Its more immediate effect was to cool what had been the increasingly friendly relations with the Roman and Orthodox Churches. It was a decision, the Vatican announced 'which the Church does not see itself entitled to authorize and which constitutes a great obstacle to the whole process of Anglican Catholic reconciliation'. In the encyclical *Mulieris Dignitatem* Pope John Paul II rejected the possibility of women's ordination.

Although the decision appeared to be greeted by a majority of the Anglican laity, the Church remained deeply divided, high Anglicans arguing that by taking an action which only represented a part of the mind of the Church, the Church was in danger of narrowing itself to a sect. The principal opponents of the measure, led by the former bishop of London, Graham Leonard, who, though married, was soon to be received into and ordained a priest in the Church of Rome, toyed with the notion of a uniat Church, a 'personal prelature' of semi-autonomous groups which would retain Anglican features but accept the magisterium of Rome, as had happened in a number of parishes in the American Episcopal Church in 1980. Some 200 or so clergy, sometimes with their congregations, moved to Rome. Those clergy who found the priesthood of women unacceptable but who wished to remain loyal to the Church in which they had been ordained, holding with some apparent justification that the traditional and orthodox teaching of the Church had been overturned by a partially representative General Synod whose function was not to create new doctrine, found themselves in danger of being treated as second-class citizens, their hope of preferment for the most part blocked. The solution offered to them of committing them to the care of so-called Provincial Episcopal Visitors or 'Flying Bishops' seemed bizarre if not schizophrenic. The ordination of women may have been socially inevitable, and conceivably theologically justified, but the procedure by which it was brought about in the Church of England seemed in many respects flawed. Whether, as its advocates claimed, it will serve to strengthen the Church of England history alone will show.

Over the Church of England there continues to be, albeit long-term, the increasing possibility of its disestablishment. It could not be claimed that a church, attended by some 1.2 million people every Sunday, is fully representative of the nation nor even of a majority of Christian believers. The right of some twenty-four of its bishops with the archbishops to sit in the House of Lords, to the exclusion of the leaders of other Churches, seems to many an anachronism. The matter is further complicated in that since the sixteenth century the sovereign is, under Jesus Christ, head of the established Church. At his or her coronation the monarch swears to 'maintain and preserve inviolately the Church of England, and the Doctrine, Worship, Discipline and Government thereof as by law established'. While it is plain that many past sovereigns have been only nominally committed members of the

Church of England, the matrimonial problems of the Prince of Wales, and his subsequent divorce in 1996, must raise some difficulties for the ecclesiastical establishment. The divorce would not necessarily affect his coronation should he become king, though, given the pluralistic society that Britain has become, it seems very likely that the rite would have to be modified to allow the participation in the ceremony of representatives of other Churches and other faiths, a development that in itself must weaken the concept of the establishment. But given that the Church of England has so far steadfastly refused to marry divorcees, his remarriage, should it occur, must pose problems for the Church.

Those who defend the establishment agree that at worst it is no more than a harmless anachronism, even positively that its royal connection makes it a focal point of unity by underlining the vestigial Christian presence in the nation. If the Church were to be disestablished, the duty now placed on every incumbent to baptize, marry and bury all his parishioners, a duty by no means any longer invariably carried out, would lapse. Supporters of the establishment argue that such likely developments would constitute a further victory for secularism. Contrariwise supporters of disestablishment argued that it would liberate the Church from its dependence on the State. Under Archbishop Ramsey the Church had secured a degree of institutional freedom from the State which served to foreshadow a movement towards disestablishment: the setting-up of the General Synod in 1970, the right to determine its own liturgy through the Worship and Doctrine Measure of 1974 and the appointment of a Crown Appointments Commission. But the Church of England still remains dependent on the will of a parliament which is clearly not necessarily a Christian assembly. If it has largely won its right to recommend the choice of candidates for bishops, it is still possible for a prime minister to disregard the first choice, as Margaret Thatcher did when she nominated Mark Santer, the second choice, to the see of Birmingham instead of Jim Thompson who was thought to be politically unsound [he was later appointed to the see of Bath and Wells]. To many people, including churchmen, the retention of the establishment seems pastorally and politically indefensible, and the likelihood of its abolition in the twenty-first century not improbable.

In the 1990s the Church of England was severely damaged by a financial crisis resulting from the mismanagement of its funds by the Church Commissioners who to ensure that they had the resources for increased clergy pay and pensions had speculated unwisely, so decreasing the Church's assets by some £800 million. Although the Commissioners managed to replenish the coffers of the Church by the sale of its assets, it looked likely that in the future the laity would have to pay for their clergy, as the Roman Catholics had long been doing; and there were other implications: further reductions in the number of full-time clergy and changes in the parochial structure, the greater employment of non-stipendiary ministers, the closure of churches and neglect of their fabric. The faithful could no longer effectively sustain the full cost of the maintenance of cathedrals and ancient parish churches, a rich part of the national heritage which sooner or later seemed likely to become a charge on the wider community.

Yet buffeted as the Church of England was by so many problems – its financial crisis, the aftermath to the admission of women and consequent flight of some clergy to the Church of Rome, doubts about the establishment, lack of appeal to the young – its capacity for resilience should not be overlooked. There were signs that the seepage in membership was being stemmed. Attendance at Sunday services had remained more or less stationary since 1988, standing at 1.2 million and there was evidence of a slight increase in confirmations. There were some flourishing churches, more often evangelical and charismatic, whose neo-fundamentalist approach was in some respects disconcerting and intellectually damaging to the rationale of the faith. But the real strength of Anglicanism remained in the quiet ordinariness of communal parochial life, not in missionary movements, or radical social programmes but in the peace engendered by the beauty of simple worship. For while conceivably the Church of England in the future might either dwindle to the status of a sect, like the Dissenting Churches, or simply remain a fine facade represented by the rich choral and ceremonial order of its cathedral worship which casts a veneer over its inner weaknesses, it seems more likely that the dedicated labours of its parochial clergy and the often unacknowledged devotion of the ordinary men and women in the pew will enable the Church still to contribute in a positive fashion to the spiritual and social wellbeing of the nation.

ROMAN CATHOLICS IN BRITAIN

By contrast with the established Church, the history of the Roman Catholic Church in England in the latter years of the twentieth century seemed less fraught. The immediate postwar archbishops of Westminster had not been outstanding, but Heenan was to be an attractive and enthusiastic pastor, intent on regaining the lapsed and in spreading the faith. 'Bring back', he said, 'the Mass to every village in this isle.' His successor Cardinal Hume was a civilized, very highly regarded head, more liberal in attitude than Heenan. It was a sign of the changed relationship between the British government and the papacy that an apostolic delegation had been established in 1938 and an apostolic pro-nuncio appointed in 1982.

In the postwar years there had been a substantial growth in the number of converts from the middle class, more especially among intellectuals, the faith articulated, if somewhat idiosyncratically, in the works of two leading novelists, both converts, Graham Greene and Evelyn Waugh whose *Brideshead Revisited* was a fascinating study in divine grace. Although they had originally resisted the Education Act of 1944, the Roman Catholics, unlike the Anglicans, were to be its beneficiaries. With increases in the number of converts, priests, convents and schools and the continued proliferation of religious orders the Catholics could look ahead with some confidence, for at least 10 per cent of the population were practising members of its churches, and in the north of England the percentage was even higher – in Liverpool where Irish influence was dominant as much as 80 per cent.

But in the closing decades of the twentieth century the rate of increase slowed down and eventually ground to a halt, for as in North America, strong as the Catholic position remained, there were some signs of disenchantment. Some Catholics were increasingly worried by the Vatican's ruling on birth control. If in earlier times converts had been attracted by the notion of obedience to a divinely constituted authority, by the 1970s and 1980s authority of this sort was not what the young wanted; nor did the conservatism of Pope John Paul II who made a visit to Britain in 1982 at some expense to the faithful win the support of the more liberal minded.

In practice in England Catholicism as much as Protestantism was confronting a crisis which gave rise to some questioning of traditional belief and brought an erosion in its numbers. While the Roman Church had performed 137,000 baptisms in 1964, these were reduced to 70,000 by 1976. The number of converts which between 1959 and 1972 had averaged 12,490 a year shrank between 1969 and 1972 to 4,436. There were some signs of falling attendance at Mass, in the number of candidates for the priesthood and in religious vocations. Between 1975 and 1990 adult membership of the Roman Church fell by 23 per cent by comparison with 19 per cent in the Church of England.

Even in Ireland, still a stronghold of the Catholic faith, where 80 per cent of the population normally attended Mass, there were signs of contraction, especially among Irish youth. It was reckoned in 1993 that only 56 per cent of those between the ages of eighteen and twenty-five went to Mass each week. The religious orders lacked novices. The number of the religious dropped from 25,172 in 1970 to 15,634 in 1986. In Irish schools there was a significant increase in the number of lay teachers, rising from 4,923 in 1971 to 10,375 in 1991 while the number of teachers in religious orders correspondingly dropped.

This was no more than what the Church of England and in some sense less than what other Churches, except for the Pentecostal, Afro-Caribbean and Orthodox Churches, were experiencing. In the Anglican Church statistics showed a steady fall in the number of candidates offering themselves for ordination, in the number of baptisms and marriages, and in Easter communicants. British Churches, it was estimated in 1994, were losing members at the rate of 1,500 a week, with the Anglican Church the worst affected, with half a million fewer people on the rolls in 1994 than there had been in 1975, a drop of 21 per cent. The Methodist and Presbyterian Churches lost 23 and 24 per cent of their membership respectively in fifteen years; and attendance at Roman Catholic Churches has fallen by 19 per cent since 1975. Anglican ordinations which had numbered 636 in 1963 were down to 437 in 1970 and 273 in 1976. Baptisms fell from 40 per cent to 28 per cent of live births between 1980 and 1990; in 1988 some 189,200 baptisms were registered or 29 per cent of live births. On a normal Sunday some 1,154,000 Anglicans went to Church in 1991–2, though many more would have described themselves as nominal Church of England. The Roman Catholics numbered some 5,500,000 or one in ten of the population; the Church of Scotland, 785,000; the Methodists, 430,000; the Baptists, 160,000; the United Reformed, 121,000; and the Quakers 18,000.

In practice the Church of England had been largely squeezed out of the educational field for the ethos of many so-called church schools was often not detectably different from non-church schools. The maintenance of such control as it was able to exercise over education cost the Church a great deal of money without any obvious dividend in religious terms. In any case religious education was often ineffective; Sunday schools were in decline, some Anglican and Free Church theological colleges were closed, nor were state schools, often multi-racial, effectively able and willing to conduct the morning religious assemblies which the law required. Between 1969 and 1984, 1,086 Anglican churches were declared redundant, some of them handed over, if reluctantly, to other faiths. The dissenting Churches were similarly affected. The Methodist Kingsway Hall was sold in 1970. Nor were schemes designed to regenerate church life more than modestly successful; the ongoing Decade of Evangelism launched in 1990 seemed to go off rather like a damp squib.

REUNION AND OECUMENICISM

It was the steady contraction of Church life which gave added force to schemes for reunion, and for the furtherance of the oecumenical movement among the Churches. Among the schemes for the reunion of Churches, the most effective stimulated by the confused message of the missions, was the creation of the Church of South India in 1947, followed by similar schemes for North India and Pakistan. Even so the establishment of the Church of South India did not go unopposed, nor did Anglicans participate in the setting up of the United Church of Zambia or the United Church of Canada. The most ambitious of the schemes affecting the British Churches was adumbrated at the Nottingham Faith and Order Conference in 1964 which voted to request the British Council of Churches 'to covenant to work and pray for the inauguration of union [of the Church of England with the Methodists] by a date which we dare to hope should not be later than Easter Day 1980'. Such hopes were from the start unrealistic. Backed by Archbishop Ramsey the project was approved by the Methodist Church, by the Moravians and the Churches of Christ; but in spite of enthusiastic championing by David Brown, the bishop of Guildford (who was unfortunately to die of a heart attack immediately after the vote was taken), it was rejected in General Synod, mainly by the votes in the House of Clergy. 'The way marked out by a whole generation of ecumenical leaders', Kenneth Greet said sadly, 'has proved to be a cul de sac!' or, in the words of another commentator, it had served to reduce 'the Church of England from comprehension to irrelevance'.

There were, however, successful mergers to create the United Church in Canada, the Uniting Church in Australia and the United Reformed Church in England. Nine American denominations planned to unite as the Church of Christ. Such schemes were, however, a mere drop in the pan and showed that the deep theological divisions between the Churches, rooted in their past history could not be easily repaired.

Nonetheless, whatever the motive forces which brought it about there was a greater degree of tolerance and understanding between Christians where in the past acrimony and even bloodshed had marred relationships between the Churches. Oecumenicism had become a positive force led in the immediate postwar years by the prestigious figure of Visser 'T Hooft. An Oecumenical Institute had been set up at Bossy near Geneva, and a world conference, meeting at Amsterdam in 1948 was attended by representatives from the Old Catholic and Orthodox Churches as well as from the Anglican and Protestant Churches, leading to the formation of the World Council of Churches, first instituted ten years earlier, as a permanent institution. Its second assembly met at Evanston on the outskirts of Chicago in August 1954, but Archbishop Ramsey's experience there only served to confirm his suspicions that such jamborees were largely futile excuses for churchmen to give boring and platitudinous speeches with little effect.

Such high-profile meetings were accordingly far less important than the local oecumenical projects which brought together Christians in a common objective, leading to an exchange of pulpits, common services and cooperative social services, if usually falling short of inter-communion. The building of a new church dedicated to Christ the Cornerstone at Milton Keynes in Buckinghamshire opened in 1992, was intended for common and equal use by all denominations. By and large such gestures encouraged the congregations making them aware of their common Christian faith rather than converting the doubters. Oecumenicism did not halt the decline in Church membership or impress secular society which in so far as it was aware of the oecumenical movement at all saw it rather as an index to the weakening of the Church's authority than as a surer proclamation of the Church's gospel.

With Rome the ice only slowly thawed, for the Vatican did not find it easy to reconcile itself to what seemed the pernicious concept of religious pluralism. 'To look for "reunion" in religion', the Catholic bishop Beck commented, 'except on the conditions explained by Pope Pius XI in the encyclical *Mortalium Animos* is to look for a will o' the wisp.' The Roman Church would admit only to reunion on its own terms. But at least the way was open for friendly dialogue, manifest in the setting up of a permanent Anglo-Roman Joint Preparatory Commission in 1967 which though it looked forward to a realization of union between the Churches never amounted to much more than a humane exchange of views. Visits of archbishops to Rome and of Pope John Paul II to Canterbury in 1982 showed that some at least of the ice which had separated the two communions had melted. Five cardinals had taken some part in Runcie's own enthronement at Canterbury. Runcie who had a good rapport with Bishop Christopher Butler, the former abbot of Downside, and Cardinal Hume, indicated personally that he would have been ready to recognize the primacy of the Pope in a federal union of Churches but this would not have been acceptable to Rome which had never rescinded its 1896 declaration against the validity of Anglican orders. Hence there seemed no real likelihood of a visible and sacramental unity of the Churches in the immediate or even in the remote future.

Nonetheless in spite of obstacles to reunion, to which the decision to ordain women to the priesthood added, there was a degree of common bonding which was a remarkable testimony to the realization so contrary to the experience of earlier centuries, that Protestants and Catholics were actually 'brothers and sisters in Christ'. In 1980 an Anglican and Catholic bishop took part in a common confirmation service in the shared church of All Saints at Telford New Town in Shropshire. St Andrews at Much Hadham and the newly built church at Milton Keynes were also shared churches. At Liverpool the Roman archbishop Warlock and his Anglican colleague David Sheppard worked together in striking amity. In November 1992 both the Catholic archbishop of Armagh and the Church of Ireland primate attended a service at St Margaret's Westminster to celebrate the quatercentenary of Trinity College, Dublin. In the 1990s by the so-called 'Porvoo declaration' – Porvoo is a Finnish cathedral – the Church of England formed an alliance, entailing full communion with the Nordic and Baltic Lutheran churches, so creating what might be the genesis of an international North European Protestant Church. Five of the churches, the Danish Lutheran church was the exception, had preserved the apostolic succession. Whether such common action was a product of the Church's growing weakness or of its tardy realization of its common brotherhood in Christ it represented a substantive Christian achievement.

ROMAN CATHOLICS IN FRANCE

The experience of the continental Churches, rooted in a very different past, was necessarily distinct from that of the British Churches even if some features of their recent history were not dissimilar. The Roman Catholic Church in France had emerged from the Second World War with a somewhat tarnished reputation, in part because many of its bishops and priests had collaborated with the regime of Marshal Pétain, himself a devout Catholic, and had played a very small part in the French Resistance. On his accession to power General de Gaulle was only dissuaded from a wholesale deprivation of French bishops of their office by the tactful diplomacy of the future John XXIII, then papal nuncio to France. In the 1950s and '60s the liberal element in the Church came to the fore again, working through the Catholic unions the Jeunesse Ouvrière Chrètienne and the Jeunesse Agricule Chrètienne to seek to bring the faith to the non-Christianized. This too was the objective of the Mission de France, in part stimulated by the publication in 1943 of the Abbé Godin's *France pays de Mission* which underlined the secular and pagan character of contemporary French society. Priests went to work in factories, seeking to share the lives of the workers and so bridge the gap between the Church and the alienated working class.

Conservative Catholics regarded this development with suspicion, believing that priests were more likely to be imbued with radical socialist ideas than the workers with Catholic values. The Vatican, equally fearful that the Church would be tainted with Marxism, brought the experiment to an end in 1953–4, henceforth only permitting priests to work in a factory for three hours a day. In spite of the Vatican's condemnation, some seventy-three out of ninety priests refused to submit, believing that to do so would be a betrayal of the interests of the working class. Some years later after the issue of the decree *Presbyterorum ministro* in 1965, which permitted a priest to do manual labour, there was still a number of priests in France, Holland and Italy engaged in part-time industrial work.

Catholic militants were at the core of the many contemporary movements for social reform, advocating some accommodation with socialist and even Marxist teaching. Often influenced by the optimistic assumptions of the outlawed Jesuit theologian Teilhard de Chardin, and by the ideas of the radical reformist Emmanuel Mounier, the founder of the influential review *L'Esprit* which promoted movements for social reform, partly through the medium of *Action Catholique*, the Church brought some influence to bear on secular society. There were priests who were ready to collaborate with the Marxists to build a better world. The Dominicans especially embraced this ideal, aiming as Jean Cardonnel put it 'to deconfessionalize and declimatize the faith' in the interests of 'liberating Christianity from the Church'. The Dominican theologian M.D. Chenu praised the worker priests as valiantly attempting to take the Church into an unbelieving world; he was also to give his support to the students' revolutionary programme in 1968. In the late 1960s small groups of priests, described as '*les prêtres contestaires*', discarding their clerical garb sought to endow the priesthood with a new role, that of forging a more genuine sense of identity between the Church and the world.

It was hardly surprising that such developments caused concern both in Rome and among French conservatives who believed that the Church might be in danger of abandoning its traditional and sacramental role in pursuit of ephemeral social amelioration. The Catholic paper *Le Monde et la Vie* advocated right-wing views. The reform of the liturgy brought in 1974 a positive conservative reaction from Marcel Lefebvre, the former archbishop of Dakar, who argued that the new reforms of the Vatican council put the Church in danger. He set up a seminary at Ecône in Switzerland to train clergy according to his own viewpoint, ordaining some thirteen priests and thirteen deacons in the presence of a congregation of 1,800 people in 1976. Hurt and angry Paul VI deprived the elderly prelate of his right to celebrate the sacraments, but Lefebvre was indomitable, setting up another seminary in France and in 1984 ordaining fourteen more priests. He established a priory in the diocese of Bordeaux, a chapel in Glasgow and a Carmelite house in Belgium. His followers seized the Paris church of St Nicholas-du-Chardonnet in 1977, making it the headquarters of the movement. In 1988 to ensure its future he consecrated a bishop to succeed him.

Lefebvre's movement represented only a comparatively small segment of the Church and after his death in 1991 it was likely to evaporate; but the episode underlined the significant divide between the 'integrists' and the reformers which sometimes even penetrated into parish life itself. While districts such as Lorraine and Brittany remained traditionally conservative, there were priests in other areas who continued to advocate a socialist political programme, and in the interest of unity even joined with the minority Protestant Church in sponsoring youth movements. Estimates made in the late 1970s showed that 80 per cent of French priests no longer habitually wore the cassock and were against compulsory celibacy. It seemed improbable that these outward looking attitudes attracted doubters to a Church which still remained, at least in the towns, predominantly bourgeois in composition. The episcopate, encouraged by the Vatican, continued to take a strong line against contraception, which remained illegal until 1967, abortion, legalized in France in 1974, and pre-marital sex. Meeting at Lourdes in 1969 the bishops by 107 votes to 6 pronounced in favour of clerical celibacy. But the bishops were in no position effectively to reassert their authority.

The French Church was experiencing a progressive decline in its following as religion became more and more marginalized. Attendance at Mass varied much from region to region, reaching in the 1980s as much as 80 per cent in Brittany and strongly Catholic parts of France, but probably amounted to no more than 10 per cent in Paris and 4 to 5 per cent in industrial towns. There had been some thirty-six thousand priests in 1980 but they were ageing and recruitment was low, and the number was expected to fall to twenty thousand by 1995.

In France as elsewhere there was no lack of experimental movements on the religious fringe, such as, for instance, the Boquen community in

Brittany led by a homosexual priest the Abbé Bernard Besret (who eventually emigrated to the USA) which championed social and sexual as well as religious liberation, renouncing all dogma and authority. Mostly such communities had a short life, but even if they were flashes in the pan they showed that there was at least a continued concern to find a religious basis for existence.

THE CHURCHES IN POSTWAR GERMANY

For nearly half a century the story of the Churches in Germany was overshadowed by the divided nature of the country. The Churches had emerged from the Second World War with a tarnished reputation, the Confessing Church alone having stood for Christian principles in the face of totalitarian dictatorship. Conscious of their responsibility for acquiescing in, if not positively aiding, the tyranny of the immediate past, some Protestant clergy under the lead of Martin Niemöller published the Stuttgart Declaration on 19 October 1945 admitting their collective guilt and the need for penitence; the Roman Catholic bishops, meeting at Fulda, made a similar declaration. But many Germans resented such self-abasement.

The Churches were geared to a fresh start, repudiating those who had collaborated with the Nazi regime such as Bishop Marahrens of Hanover. But the leaders were figures from the past, notably Martin Niemöller who became foreign secretary of the Federated German Church, and Otto Dibelius, who was restored to the see of Berlin–Brandenburg from which the Nazis had expelled him in 1933. Such men were courageous but essentially conservative in attitude and so lacking the flexibility which the new situation required. The German chancellor from 1949 to 1963, Konrad Adenauer, was himself a devout Catholic who had spent some of the war years in a monastery. In western Germany where there were more Catholics than Protestants, the Catholics were strong supporters of Adenauer's party, the Christian Democratic Union, and at least until 1965 the bishops actively worked against the rival Social Democratic Party. The religious as well as the political ethos of western Germany was therefore strongly anti-Communist and rightest in attitude.

Martin Niemöller had declared that Christianity was to be a crucial ingredient in Germany's future, but the division between East and West operated to the Churches' disadvantage. In July 1949 the Evangelical Church had adopted a joint constitution and for a time representatives of both East and West met together in the *Kirchentag*, but the strident anti-Communism of the Evangelical Church in the West made it increasingly suspect to the East German government which in 1957 insisted that the Evangelical Church in East Germany should disassociate itself from its partner in the West.

The East German government's Office for Contact with the Churches was transformed into a State Secretariat for Church Questions, designed to keep the Church subservient to the State. The government sponsored a campaign for the recruitment of Free German Youth which included an initiation ceremony (*Jugendweihe*) which required the young to profess atheistic principles of Marxism and Leninism. The Churches held that membership of such an organization was incompatible with Church membership. The strained relations between Church and State in eastern Germany were exacerbated further by a letter which Bishop Dibelius wrote to Bishop Hans Lilje of Hanover in which he asserted that the authority exercised by the East German government over the Church was illegitimate, so inferring that its citizens were thereby released from any moral obligation to obey its laws. The bishop was subsequently prevented from travelling to that part of his diocese which lay within East German control, for the Berlin Wall was constructed in 1961. In 1968 the East German government took away the special protection from the Church which it still enjoyed (such as laws against blasphemy) and drew up a new constitution for the Evangelical Church, safeguarding freedom of religion and conscience, but declaring that the Churches must regulate their affairs and activities 'in a manner consistent with the constitution and law of the GDR' (i.e. the East German government).

In practice, though the Protestant and Roman Catholic Churches contrived to live under repressive restrictions, there was some sort of modus vivendi, as the Churches realized, as had been their experience in most Communist countries, that if they were to operate they had to some extent to collaborate. Karl Scharf who succeeded Otto Dibelius as bishop of Berlin when he eventually retired (in his eighty-seventh year) managed to negotiate an agreement which led in 1973 to the creation of separate bishoprics for east and west Berlin, which enabled the Churches to work together without dissolving their union. The East German government very reluctantly permitted the celebration of the 450th anniversary of the publication of Martin Luther's theses in 1967, and somewhat less grudgingly the fifth centenary of his birth in 1983. But by the time of reunification the Churches in East Germany had been emasculated, the number of children baptized declining and the congregations growing elderly.

In West Germany the situation was different, even if in the last decades of the twentieth century there were indications of religious decline. After the war the Churches had recovered rapidly. The Catholic Church benefited from the concordat which the Church had negotiated with Hitler in 1933, the clauses of which, though not observed by Hitler, favoured the Church, so much so that some criticized the Church's seemingly privileged position. The West Germans who were members of a church paid a tax, in the region of 9 per cent of their personal taxation, out of which they could contract if they wished, but the numbers who did so, some 15 per cent, were relatively small. There were, however, signs that an increasing number were contracting out – some 60,000 in 1967; 202,000 in 1970; in 1991 some 35,000 in Berlin alone – and there was a small but growing demand for the tax's abolition. Although it has been estimated that 56 million out of 78 million were Church members, there were signs of declining attendance; it was reckoned in 1980 that only 2 per cent of the nominal members of the Evangelical Church actually attended Sunday services. Elsewhere the figure averaged some 20 to 30 per cent, and was higher than in Britain or France. The reunification of the two Germanys obviously presented the Churches with new problems as well as fresh opportunities.

CHRISTIANITY IN RUSSIA AND EASTERN EUROPE

Christians in Eastern Europe, apart from those in Greece and Turkey, lived for the greater part of the last half of the twentieth century in the darkening twilight of totalitarian tyrannies which aimed to eliminate religion. In Soviet Russia, Poland, eastern Germany, Czechoslovakia after the invasion of 1968, Hungary especially after the abortive rising of 1956, Yugoslavia, Bulgaria, Romania and Albania, all Churches suffered to a lesser or greater degree from repression and persecution. After the ending of the Second World War the incorporation of new territories in the Soviet sphere of influence had brought some millions of Catholic and Orthodox within the scope of anti-religious policies. The Marxist states took a severe, even a brutal line towards the Churches which, by the criteria of Marxist ideology, were propagating a false faith and encouraging political reactions leading to the subversion of the state.

While some of the churches were, under certain conditions, allowed to remain open, the State made every attempt to indoctrinate its people with Marxist tenets. Teachers at schools and universities were obliged to instruct their pupils in scientific materialism and Marxist philosophy, and so to promote atheism while the Churches and Christian parents were forbidden to engage in any form of religious education. Atheist clubs, social in character, were set up. More positively, aware of the psychological attractiveness of church ritual, Communist states set out their own alternative rituals, among them special ceremonies to celebrate marriage and the coming of age or naming days. In 1955 a Palace of Weddings was opened at Leningrad. Spring and New Year festivals provided alternatives to Easter and Christmas. In the Soviet Union anti-religious museums had been long established, as in the former cathedral of the Virgin of Kazan at Leningrad, to depict the corruption, folly and irrationality of Christianity. Communist regimes hoped that as a result of such indoctrination, supported by unstinting pressure, congregations, consisting in the main of ageing people, mainly women, would ultimately become extinct.

The pressures which the State exerted were more sinister than the policy it articulated, for it was employed to deter and savage those associated with the Churches: practising Christians faced imprisonment, labour camps, torture and even death. Trials were rigged to discredit Christians by accusing them of collaborating with the Nazis or of engaging in illegal currency transactions. At the very least commitment to Christian belief might make it difficult to enter higher education or to get a job.

The apparent reconciliation which had occurred at the height of the Nazi invasion of Russia in 1943 between the Soviet state and the Orthodox Church heralded a false dawn. The patriarch had indeed been restored, the theological academy at Zagorsk reopened, as were some churches, but the new patriarch, Alexei was circumspect. Whatever progress had been made in the restructuring of the Church was largely brought to nought by the renewal of a policy of repression by Nikita Khrushchev. Churches were again closed and at least two thousand monasteries shut their doors between 1960 and 1961. The number of theological seminaries was reduced from eight to three. 'Does an honest man go to a theological school, in our century of science and technology?' a Soviet critic commented, 'The Rector and inspector select any sort of rabble . . . lovers of an easy, dishonest life . . . criminals who should be remoulded by work.'

A campaign of vilification of clergy and believers was waged, accusing them of drunkenness, sexual perversion and corruption. Religious activists were despatched to harsh labour camps after rigged trials; such were the fates of the Russian priest Gleb Yakunin who in 1976 had established the Christian Committee for Believers' Rights and was sentenced in 1979 to ten years, five in a labour camp and five in exile, and the Baptist pastor Georgi Vins. There were only a few signs of a genuine thaw under Brezhnev. Churches still found obstacles placed in their way when, as the law required, they tried to register. Where there had been 51,005 clergy in 1914, there were only 6,674 in 1988. The number of churches had declined steeply more especially as a result of Khrushchev's policy of repression: 54,174 in 1914; 18,000 in 1945; and 6,893 in 1988. The story was similar with respect to monasteries and convents: 1,025 in 1914; 21 in 1988; and the number of religious had slumped from 94,629 in 1914 to 1,190 in 1988. To dissuade young men from becoming monks the patriarch had decreed that no one should receive the tonsure before he reached the age of thirty.

In their attitude to the state the Church authorities appeared sycophantic, ever ready to justify the regime to the outside world, presumably because they believed that it was only by compliance that the Church could be saved from an even worse fate. Church affairs were placed under the surveillance of a Council for Religious Affairs which was instrumental in ensuring that the Church toed the line required by the state. The patriarch Pimen, who held office from 1971 until his death in 1990, was a passive figure, neither a theologian nor a statesman, rumoured to be much under the thumb of his formidable female secretary Nadezvida Nikolaevna Dychenzo whom he nicknamed Nadezhdez of Moscow and All Russia. Relations between the Church authorities and some of the younger priests, who resented their elders' seemingly supine policy, were as a consequence often strained.

Other religious denominations suffered equally from Russia's atheistic government. The largest Protestant group, the Baptists, probably numbering some three hundred thousand, were themselves splintered in 1960 by differences over the policy they should adopt towards the government. The larger group, the Baptist Union, had complied with the law requiring the registration of all churches, but a smaller group which included two heroic protesters, Georgi Vins and Gennadi Kryuchkov, who paid for their intransigence by long terms of imprisonment, remained unregistered, continuing to exist as an underground movement.

The worst legatees of this repressive policy were probably the Uniat churches, which had so much earlier accepted the supremacy of Rome but had been allowed to keep their own traditions including the Eastern rite and a married clergy. They were the target both of the Soviet state and the Orthodox Church. Stalin feared that the Ukrainian Catholics, allied to Uniat churches in Central Europe, in Transylvania and Ruthenia, living in what had once been the Austro-Hungarian Empire, might well become a focal point for anti-Russian and pro-Ukrainian agitation. He obliged the Moscow patriarchate to bring pressure to bear on the Catholics to force them to return to the Orthodox allegiance. Two Uniat priests were made Orthodox bishops and a conference or *sobor* of renegade clergy held at Lvov in 1946 confirmed the Uniat Church's reunion with Orthodoxy. In 1963, after serving seventeen years in prison, ostensibly for collaborating with the Nazis, the Uniat metropolitan Slipyj was released and allowed to go into exile at Rome where he was later to denounce the Vatican for its failure to protest at the unjust treatment which the Uniats had endured both at the hands of the Soviet authorities and the Orthodox Church.

As late as 1984 the Soviets were still shutting Uniat churches, and it was only after 1987 that the Uniat Church began slowly to emerge, surviving but damaged. A synod of exiled Ukrainian bishops meeting in Rome confirmed the headship in their Church of Bishop Stenink, an octogenarian, who had been secretly consecrated a bishop eleven years earlier but had never submitted. The Orthodox, led by Metropolitan Filaret of Kiev, continued to inveigh against the Uniats, asserting that the Uniats were now legally united to the Orthodox Church. Filaret claimed that their followers, 'gangs of violent people', were seizing Orthodox churches, causing the Orthodox Holy Synod to protest against the cruel and illegal actions of the Ukrainian Catholics. The Vatican, presumably fearful of damaging its relations with the Orthodox Church, remained for the most part passive.

The Uniat Churches in other Communist states endured a similar fate. A rigged synod held at Presov in 1950 declared an end to the Uniat union with Rome and the absorption of the Czech Uniat Churches in Orthodoxy. When Dubcek came to power he restored the Uniats but on his fall the new government, while not banning the Uniats altogether, gave over much of the Church's property to the Orthodox Church. In Romania the Uniat Church was as ruthlessly destroyed.

The experience of Churches in other Communist countries was not dissimilar to what had happened in Soviet Russia, if somewhat less severe. The Baltic republics which had been incorporated into the Soviet Union in 1940 were to be subjected to a repressive religious policy, made the more so because religion had become tied up with national identity; in Lithuania the Roman Catholics suffered, in Estonia and Latvia the Lutherans. The Lutheran St Stanislas Cathedral in Vilnius became a warehouse and then an art gallery; St Casimir's was turned into an atheist museum. There was only one seminary in operation, and a shortage of young priests. Where there had been twelve bishops in 1940, as a result of exile, imprisonment and death there was soon only one, Bishop Paltarokas of Panvezys. On his death in 1958 the Lithuanian Church was placed under the control of apostolic administrators, whose appointment had to be vetted by the Soviet authorities.

Poland was a strongly Catholic state where there was no real possibility of the Church being dislodged from its central position in the country's life, though the Communists at first employed their familiar tactics of putting priests in prison, confiscating the property of the religious orders and seeking to indoctrinate the young with Marxist–Leninist philosophy, though it allowed the Catholic University of Lublin to function. That religious life continued to play such a part in Polish life owed much to the leadership of Archbishop Stefan Wyszynski who managed to reach an agreement of sorts with the state, though subsequently he was to be confined to a monastery for three years. Later he was to secure the strong support of the trade union movement, led by the future leader of Solidarity, Lech Walesa. The Poles' passionate devotion to the faith was shown by the great numbers who still went as pilgrims to the national shrine of our Lady at Czestochowa, some 1¼ million in 1975. Even in 1976 there were 19,046 priests, 30 seminaries and an attendance rate of 55 per cent at Mass.

Hungary was another predominantly Catholic country, but there the Church's experience was very different from that in Poland. The primate of Hungary, Joseph Mindszenty, archbishop of Estergom, who had protested strongly at government policy, was arrested in 1948, charged with espionage and breach of currency regulations. He was sentenced to life imprisonment, but in 1956 took advantage of the abortive rising against the Russians to seek sanctuary in the American Embassy at Budapest where he was to remain for the next fifteen years. In 1971 he was allowed to go to Rome and subsequently to live in a Hungarian seminary near Vienna where he wrote his memoirs. By this time he had become a thorn in the side of the papacy which wanted to improve its relations with the Hungarian state and so soften the State's policy towards the Catholic Church. When the Pope told Mindszenty to resign, the obstinate old man refused and was subsequently deprived of his office. The Pope, as an Italian newspaper observed, had offered Mindszenty's head on a plate to King Herod. The Hungarian government had dissolved all religious orders – in 1950 there had been 11,538 monks and nuns but thirty years later there were only some 500 – though curiously in the mid-1980s the State had allowed the foundation of a new order of nuns, the Community of the Protectresses of Hungary.

The Communist government of Czechoslovakia was equally intolerant of both Catholics and Protestants. While some eight thousand nuns continued to work in hospices and hospitals, the male orders disappeared. Relations between the Vatican and the State were subject to strain, for a number of Czech clergy who favoured the government formed an association *Pacem in Terris* from whose membership the government in 1973 insisted that all bishops should be chosen. The Vatican thereupon forbade such appointments to be made, leading to vacancies in the dioceses which were then run by clerical administrators appointed by the government.

Yugoslavia was not merely an artificial combination of disparate states but their strong national feeling was rooted in religious loyalty. Apart from the Muslims in Bosnia, Croatia and Slovenia were predominantly Catholic, Serbia, Orthodox. Croatia had been a Nazi puppet state in the Second World War; the Catholic Church there was accused of approving the massacre of some 300,000 Serbs, among them 3 bishops and 128 priests, and the destruction of some 300 Orthodox churches. When the war ended and the various states were united under Marshal Tito, the Serbs, mainly Orthodox, wrought vengeance, murdering many Catholics, among them some twenty-eight Franciscan friars thrown to their deaths from a bridge.

The head of the Croatian Church, Archbishop Stepinac of Zagreb, who had welcomed the Germans and the creation of a separate Croatian state, though he had also protested against the deportation of Jews and the mass execution of Serbs, fell out with the Communist regime which had made civil marriage compulsory, shut down all Catholic newspapers and confiscated Church property. Tito, angered by Stepinac's stand, had him brought to trial in 1946. He was condemned to sixteen years forced labour, dying in 1960 still under house arrest. The Pope had somewhat provocatively made him a cardinal in 1952 and his tomb was to become a focal point for Croatian national feeling.

After Stepinac's death relations between Church and State in Yugoslavia were less fraught than in other Communist satellite states, in part because Serb national feeling identified with the Church, though the Serbian Church itself suffered from a shortage of clergy and a comparatively poor active membership. Patriarch Germain of Belgrade championed the Serbs in Kossovo against the Albanians (who were Muslim), and in 1959 opposed the setting up of an autonomous Church of Macedonia; in the subsequent civil strife in the 1990s the Serbian clergy strongly supported their compatriots in the fight against the Bosnian Muslims and the Catholic Croats.

The most extraordinary religious phenomenon was, however, the development of a Catholic shrine to our Lady at Medjugorge which was to attract pilgrims from all over the world until the outbreak of civil war in Yugoslavia deterred travellers. In 1981 the Virgin was reported to have appeared to six children aged eleven to eighteen. A commission which had been set up by the bishop of Mostar to investigate the incident, consisting of nine theologians and two psychiatrists, by a handsome majority reported that the appearances were unlikely to be genuine. In spite of the bishop's efforts to play down what was claimed to have happened, the shrine, strongly supported by its Franciscan guardians, became an international centre of pilgrimage, attracting between 8 and 10 million people in 1987, encouraged by the Communist authorities who relished the profits of the tourist trade. In the Bosnian civil war the monastery served as a base for the Spanish troops of the United Nations.

In Romania the Orthodox Church escaped the worst excesses of Communist repression, for the patriarch Justinian, an able man, Western-educated, managed to collaborate with the government. In 1973 there were apparently 780 students at the seminary at Sebiu, 8,627 priests, 540 monks and 1,443 nuns active in Romania. The patriarch congratulated Ceauşescu on his opposition to the Russian invasion of Czechoslovakia in 1968, but with the growth of Ceauşescu's megalomania, so his attitude to the Church hardened, and monasteries and seminaries were suppressed, monks and clergy imprisoned. On Justinian's death in 1975 his successor, Justin of Jussy, took a sycophantic attitude to the increasingly tyrannical and incompetent regime.

Of all the Communist states Albania was the most repressive in its treatment of Christianity, indeed of all religions. While the majority of the population, 72.8 per cent were Muslim, some 17.1 per cent belonged to the Orthodox Church (the Albanian Church was recognized as an autocephalus Church in 1967) and 10 per cent were Catholics. Under Albania's dictator Enver Hoxha the most extreme anti-religious legislation was passed, even religion in private being banned. Bishops were imprisoned and shot, the clergy sent to manual labour. The festival of Christmas was abolished and even Christian names were forbidden. Religion was forced underground but it survived.

The survival of religion in Communist Europe was an astonishing, even a miraculous, phenomenon. It was hardly surprising that it should have done so in Poland where Catholicism was so deeply rooted, nor perhaps in Czechoslovakia or in Hungary; but in Russia it had been virtually living in the catacombs for nearly seventy years. No state except Albania was, however, sufficiently committed to the destruction of religion to pursue a policy of complete elimination nor indeed sufficiently competent to bring this about. So the Church lived on, managing to maintain a few seminaries and attracting some men and women to the religious life. The roots of Orthodoxy were popular, its basic attraction mystical and spiritual rather than intellectual, focused on an age-old and unchanging liturgy rich in colour and music. Orthodox theology had become crystallized, the energy of the Church sapped, its vision harassed but whether in practice it was weaker than some Churches in Western countries may be doubted. The Churches were to emerge like dinosaurs from a primeval swamp.

And emerge they did, in the backwash of the failure of Communism to the destruction of which they appear only very partially to have contributed. President Mikhail Gorbachev's liberalizing policy of *perestroika* at once transformed their situation. When he met Patriarch Pimen and five other metropolitans on 29 April 1988 Gorbachev promised that there would be a new law of freedom of conscience 'to reflect the interests of religious organizations'. A more liberal commissioner for religious affairs, Konstantin Kharchev, was appointed and though his liberalism soon led to his removal, a new era for the Churches had dawned. Churches long converted to secular use were gradually returned, sometimes, however, causing bitter disputes as to their ownership. Monasteries were restored; by 1989 the twenty-one surviving monasteries had become thirty-five. Seminaries and schools were set up. Priests appeared on television and took part in political debates. The American evangelist Billy Graham was invited to preach in St Vladimir's Cathedral, Kiev. In 1988 the millennium of the foundation of the Russian Church was celebrated at the Bolshoi Theatre and broadcast on Russian television. On 1 December 1989 Gorbachev was received in audience by Pope John Paul II. The frontiers opened to the importation of Bibles and religious books as well as, it must be added, to pornographic literature.

How far these extraordinary events were in some respects window dressing it is difficult to estimate. The millennium of Russia's conversion, celebrated as it was with pomp and ceremony, was mainly an advertisement to the outside world and the cost of organizing the pageantry, from which for the most part the Russian faithful had been excluded, constituted a heavy burden on a Church no longer rich. It was politically significant that it was Moscow rather than Kiev, the capital of the Ukraine where Prince Vladimir had been baptized in 988, which was the chosen location for the celebration. Church leadership remained inevitably a legacy from the Soviet era, its leaders themselves victims of decades of fear and compromise, passive and indecisive. The Moscow patriarchate gave only a limited guidance and seemed unable to exploit the potential explosion of religious enthusiasm among the faithful. Many of the bishops were still elderly time-servers, ready to greet the more liberal regime but ill equipped to lead a regenerated Church. The hierarchy, isolated from reforming principles, seemed more concerned with administrative and financial matters than spiritual renewal. 'Church life', as a critic put it, 'is not responding today to the principle of democratisation and *glasnost*.' The Church, like the tsardom, was in many respects a nostalgic relic of the past. Its leaders were still divided from the activists and it had few skills for attracting young people or reviving parish life; theologically it had hardly entered the twentieth century. Cradled in the past, it was as yet only partially committed to religious revival. In 1996, recalling past controversies, an acrimonious debate broke out between Alexei II, the patriarch of Moscow, and

Bartholomew I, patriarch of Constantinople, who claimed the spiritual headship of orthodoxy, over the jurisdiction of the Orthodox Church in Estonia. Time would alone tell how far it was going to be able to take its natural place in Russian life again.

In the Baltic States where resistance to Soviet rule had often had a religious component, religious freedom came like a breath of fresh air. In Lithuania there were signs of a Catholic revival as Vilnius cathedral was restored to public worship. In 1989 the Pope appointed three new bishops and made Bishop Sladkevicius, long banned from office by the Soviets, a cardinal. In Estonia the leading Lutheran Harri Motsink had been imprisoned and exiled, but with the coming of *perestroika*, the Soviets gave concessions to the churches, including the abolition of the punitive taxes levied on the clergy. But the Estonian Lutheran Church, unlike the Roman Church in Lithuania and the Lutheran Church in Latvia, remained long politically circumspect. 'Our senior people', it was admitted, 'have not trained themselves to take the initiative; rather they keep out of the limelight, away from the gaze of the authorities', but Church membership slowly began to rise. In Latvia signs of religious renewal in 1988–9 were more marked, and feeling against those who had compromised was so strong that the recently elected archbishop Erik Mesters was voted out of office.

In the other Communist satellite states religious freedom was restored. In Poland the Catholics, made euphoric earlier by the election of their countryman as Pope, again became predominant, so much so that there was a reaction against the powerful influence which the Church exerted, for the Church had been instrumental in passing tough anti-abortion laws (abortion was made illegal unless the mother's life was endangered or in cases of rape or incest) and in making religious education compulsory. Protestants, Orthodox and non-Christian alike, were fearful that the revived triumphalism of the Roman Catholic Church led by a conservative curia and a politically reactionary Pope augered badly for oecumenical understanding. The Romanian patriarch was obliged to resign but managed to worm his way back to office. The death of the Albanian leader Hoxha in 1985 began a slow thaw, making it possible in 1991 for the Catholics there to greet the most distinguished living Albanian, Mother Teresa, and two years later in April 1993 Pope John Paul II visited Albania to consecrate four new bishops. The most tragic outcome of the collapse of Communism was the disintegration of the former Yugoslavia into its component parts which as its corollary renewed the bitter religious differences of the past between Muslim, Catholic and Orthodox.

RELIGION IN NORTH AMERICA

In the last half of the twentieth century the United States seems at least superficially the most religious nation in the world, numbered in church attendance and religious belief. A poll taken in 1991–2 estimated that 40 per cent of the population were believers (by comparison with 20 per cent in Britain and 58 per cent in southern Ireland) and that the Churches had the confidence of 40 per cent of the population (by comparison with 18 per cent in Britain). The number of children attending Sunday schools which came to 24.6 million in 1945 had reached 38.6 million by 1956. All politicians willingly paid tribute to America's providential destiny. 'Our government', President Eisenhower declared, 'makes no sense unless it is founded on a deeply religious faith.'

While the main-line Churches continued to flourish, there were, however, to be signs of growing religious instability and even some degree of disillusion. The ending of the Second World War had resulted in a resurgence of evangelical feeling, so that some 14 millions out of 42 millions who belonged to the National Council of Churches could be described as evangelicals. No less than 80,000 students came to Dallas in 1972 for the Congress of Churches for Christ Expo. Liberal and intellectual Christians were increasingly disconcerted by the re-emergence of a strong neo-fundamentalist theology in alliance with political and moral rightism. Its exponents set out to counteract the secular humanism which, as it seemed to them, had even penetrated the higher echelons of American theology, as expressed in the much publicized 'Death of God' school of thought launched in 1966–8 by disenchanted Barthians such as Thomas Altizer, Gabriel Vahanin and Paul van Buren.

The growth of the religious right was attributed to a moral malaise which, it was feared by its supporters, might ultimately pave the way for a Communist takeover. It found symptoms of the malaise in unlimited sexual freedom, the growth of the pornography industry, the widespread use of drugs, in the high divorce rate, in the feminist movement, in sex education, abortion on demand, the movement for gay rights and after 1981 the spread of AIDS. More positively the religious right stood for strong military defence. The anti-Communist crusade, led by Senator McCarthy, was in line with the evangelical revival. They supported the state of Israel, called for the reimposition of prayer in public schools (which had been prescribed by decisions of the Supreme Court in 1962 and 1963) and the outlawry of abortion which was equally abhorrent to Evangelicals and Roman Catholics alike as a contravention of divine law. In 1973 the Supreme Court had legalized abortion, allowing abortion to be carried out in the final three months of pregnancy in cases of extreme foetal abnormality or a threat to the mother's life.

The militant group Operation Rescue even set out to blockade abortion clinics, quoting the phrase from the book of Proverbs 'Rescue those who are being taken away to death; hold back those who are stumbling to the slaughter'. In March 1993 a protesting member of a pro-life organization, Rescue America, shot dead Dr David Gunn when he arrived at his abortion clinic at Pensacola, Florida. The killer asked that he might use the Bible as a legal document in his defence.

Numbering perhaps as many as 50 millions, backed by conservative Catholics as well as Mormons and Jews, the 'moral majority' brought pressure to bear on public elections, ensuring, for instance, a majority of delegates to the National Convention which voted for Reagan in Alaska, Alabama and Iowa. Jimmy Carter, a 'new-born' Christian himself, owed his success to the support of 51 per cent of Protestants and 18 per cent of Catholics who also claimed to have experienced rebirth. Both Presidents Reagan and Bush owed much to the support of the 'moral majority' but President Clinton's election in 1992 hinted at their declining influence, though the president's own private life served to give their views some credence. By the mid-1990s Clinton's social liberalism actually seemed to strengthen the political influence of the Christian right within the Republican Party.

One of the more influential leaders of the 'moral majority' was Jerry Falwell who had founded the Thomas Road Baptist Church at Lynchburg, Virginia, which he built up into a flourishing congregation with an average Sunday attendance of some four thousand and a string of religious and social activities. In 1964 he had erected a thousand-seat auditorium for his church services, setting up the Lynchburg Christian Academy three years later. The Liberty Baptist College, founded in 1971 with some seven thousand on its rolls in 1985, was designed to send students trained in Falwell's neo-fundamentalism to act as pastors. But his principal mode of propagating the faith was through *The Old-Time Gospel Hour* which attracted a very large audience, and raised substantial funds, $35 million from 2½ million people on its mailing list in 1979, and some $115 million in all between 1977 and 1980. Falwell like others of his ilk was not above using a form of spiritual blackmail to attain his ends, threatening, for instance, to close down his programme unless his listeners contributed more funds.

Falwell epitomized a significant and in some respects an unhealthy aspect of American religious life in the late twentieth century: the extent to which a religious group, often narrow in outlook, intensely enthusiastic and tightly organized could exploit, if with the best of intentions, an audience drawn from the lower middle and working classes in the supposed interests of the gospel.

The media, radio and television, were in North America to be potent weapons in the hands of the churches. The most influential figures even in the pre-war years had been the radio parsons, the Detroit Catholic priest Charles Coughlin who had an estimated audience of 10 million, Monsignor Fulton Sheen, and Norman Vincent Peale, the minister of New York's City Marble Collegiate Church.

Old-fashioned revivalism had in fact been grafted on to a new stock, proliferating its fruit, good and bad, at an amazing rate and without any equivalent as yet in the Old World. Its major prophet was Billy Graham the confidant of presidents, who was to carry his missionary message to every corner of the world, drawing immense audiences to hear his simplistic, evangelistic call to religious commitment. In fact Billy Graham represented a moderate fundamentalism, more tolerant and less inflexible than that of its more extreme exponents, Carl McIntire, John R. Rice and the rigid teachers trained by Bob Jones University at Greenville, South Carolina. In such circumstances religion became big industry. In the mid-1970s and 1980s spending on religious programmes on television increased from some $150 million to $600 million. The leading preachers, Pat Robertson, Oral Roberts, Jim Bakker, Jerry Falwell, James Robertson Swaggart became as well known as pop and film stars.

Commercial television was in the process of commercializing religion, its advocates selling their own particular brand of faith with the same half-truths and innuendos as their secular counterparts sold soap, jeans or perfume, promising to the purchasers God's blessing and healing powers. Their teaching was fundamentalist, scriptural and usually put forward with deep emotion in a highly charged, indeed psychologically disturbing atmosphere. Its appeal to impressionable people was undeniable. The scenario varied from a stately building to a circus tent. The immensely architecturally impressive Crystal Cathedral in Orange County, California attracted huge congregations to hear its Presbyterian revivalist preacher Robert Schuyler, one of the more restrained exponents of the gospel. The tele-evangelists promised salvation through new birth, the forgiveness of sins and in some instances powers of miraculous healing. Oral Roberts exercised his supposed gift of healing on television as well as at revivalist meetings, for those who could not watch television were invited to send money for a handkerchief which, it was claimed, had healing power. Many of the revivalists preached the imminent second coming of Christ after a period of tribulation. Jerry Falwell held that he was preaching to the 'terminal generations before Jesus comes'. The evangelists' message was basically socially conservative. They had no wish to change the structure of society but to convert the individual; in Falwell's words 'the Gospel does not clean up the outside but regenerates the inside'.The faithful contributed offerings which made evangelism into an expanding commercial enterprise. Religion was run like any other secular business. Immense profits were made for its ministrants which the more grasping seem to have converted into luxurious life-styles. The balance sheets, often unconvincing, showed that a disproportionate amount was spent on administration which usually included the support of the evangelist and his wife in a significant degree of comfort and luxury; and the residue spent on purely religious and charitable purposes was proportionately marginal.

While the majority of the evangelists were probably respectable God-fearing men, sincere in their objectives, there were undoubtedly some bogus practitioners, and from time to time the taint of financial and sexual scandal led to a measure of disillusion, bringing about the removal of some well-known figures, notably Swaggart, involved in seamy sex, and Jim Bakker, sentenced originally for forty-five years for defrauding his followers of some $158 million (£100 million), at least temporarily from the revivalist scene. In 1992, 44-year-old Edward Gallimore who held his congregation spellbound at the evangelistic tabernacle in Martinswell, southern Virginia, was charged with bigamy with a sixteen-year-old high school girl. Gallimore justified polygamy from the Old Testament but was a stern critic of drink, drugs, cosmetics and long hair. Revivalism seemed to be often threaded by double standards. Yet rent as it could be by scandal and the whiff of hypocrisy it did not appear significantly dented, and there was a real possibility that the American form might be carried from the New World to the Old where some of its leading preachers had already had varying degrees of success.

In some respects revivalism might appear to overlap with the charismatic movement which in 1980 had an estimated following of some 29 million; but it affected all Churches. It seems to have originated in 1960 at St Mark's Episcopal Church at Van Nuys, California, when the rector Dennis Bennett and his congregation experienced a baptism of the Holy Spirit accompanied by glossolalia or speaking with tongues. The authorities in both the Protestant and Catholic Churches reacted with disapproval. The bishop of Los Angeles banned speaking with tongues. Bennett resigned and moved to Seattle where he turned his church, St Luke's, into a thriving congregation. The movement spread to other churches and to Europe, invading, in spite of some episcopal disapproval, the Catholic community as well; the first Catholic charismatic conference took place at the Catholic University of Notre Dame. The search for an ecstatic religious experience may help to explain the rapid growth of the Holiness and Pentecostalist churches.

Such activities illustrated North America's continued appetite for religion. 'The typical American', so wrote the sociologist Will Herberg, 'has developed a remarkable capacity for being serious about religion without taking religion seriously.' Be that as it may, there was an infinity of religious groups, at the very least more than eight hundred, by no means only Christian but Buddhist and Hindu in origin which formed communes to engage in transcendental meditation and to seek the way of perfection through love, sometimes interpreted in a very liberated fashion. Their adherents seemed often to be brain-washed as well as scatter-brained. The fastest growing of all were the Pentecostalist churches, originally attracting poor Blacks and Whites in the southern states, but spreading throughout the country as well as abroad with increasing middle-class support. Other so-called churches had a Christian gloss but little else that was distinctively Christian, such as Ron Hubbard's Church of Scientology and the Unification Church of Sun Myang Moon which had a magnetic hold over its numerous members.

Not dissimilar religious developments took place in the Black community. Still segregated largely from the Whites, Black religion, flourishing particularly among the Black Southern Baptists and in the Black Methodist

Episcopal Church, became more and more significantly a medium for emphasizing Black identity and synthesizing Black hopes. In 1931 George McQuire, a Black Episcopal priest, received Old Catholic orders and set up the African Orthodox Church as a specific Black church. A Black Jewish group, the Church of God and the Saints of Christ, attracted a following, as had earlier Father Divine (George Baker), the flamboyant and self-indulgent founder of the popular Peace Mission. But the major prophet of the Black churches was Martin Luther King, the pastor of the Dexter Avenue Baptist Church in Montgomery, Alabama, who first caught public attention as a leader in the bus boycott aimed to break White racism. He became the first president of the Southern Christian Leadership Conference in 1951 and subsequently the charismatic leader of the Civil Rights Movement where he tried to urge on his followers a peaceful resolution to the racial conflict. His murder in 1968 was a watershed, polarizing the debate between those who believed in an uncompromising stand and those who argued in favour of peaceful coexistence.

The former looked to a 'Black theology' as a justification for a more radical and revolutionary programme, arguing in favour of separation and isolation from the White community and its churches rather than integration. While the roots of 'Black theology' lay buried deep in the bitter experience of Negro slavery, its first manifestation the Negro spirituals, it was a distinctively new concept stimulated by the Civil Rights Movement and probably originating in a statement by the National Committee of Negro Churchmen in 1966. Among the first of its proponents was James Cone who published *Black Theology and Black Power* (1969) and *God of the Oppressed* (1975). The Bible was interpreted as a handbook for liberation which would help to bring an end to oppression and discrimination and to further political justice and freedom. The most spectacular growth in membership occurred among the African-American Churches. The Church of God in Christ averaged gains of nearly 200,000 members and 600 congregations a year since 1982, making it the fifth largest denomination in the country.

The White churches remained divided from each other, and schemes for their reunion met with relatively little success. Although the Lutheran churches managed to discard their ethnic differences between 1960 and 1962 to form a large unified denomination, a scheme for bringing together the Presbyterians and the Episcopalians failed. The Episcopalians, solid and affluent, were themselves unhappily split by a majority decision to ordain women to the priesthood; by 1992 there were two women bishops. Like other Protestant churches, they suffered very heavy losses in membership.

A new religious phenomenon was provided by the great increase in the Hispanic population. While the majority were nominally Roman Catholic, their participation in American Catholic life was below average. A sizeable majority, some 10 to 20 per cent, attended the Protestant churches, Baptists and Methodists, while they were also drawn to the Pentecostalists and other more fringe cults.

By 1960 North American Roman Catholics, from 40 to 50 million in number, constituted the most diligent Catholic Church in the world, but even the Catholics could not escape the impact of social change, the rising tide of feminism, the call for the recognition of gay rights, the issue of contraception and the demand for the abolition of clerical celibacy, all issues which were of some concern to the Catholic laity. They too were confronted by a crisis of authority as it became clear than many of the decisions made at the Second Vatican Council were not being effectively implemented. In particular the publication of the encyclical *Humanae Vitae* in 1968 had adverse effects on attendance at Mass and on monthly confession. Statistics showed that there was a growing decline in the Church's revenue, in enrolment in parochial schools and in the number of seminarists, and religious. Visits by Pope John Paul II left many American Catholics with mixed feelings. It was doubtful whether – for a statistical survey showed that only 32 per cent of American Catholics believed in papal infallibility – he had done much to reassure the faint-hearted or to stem the continuing ferment in the Church.

Outwardly religious as America continued to appear, it could not escape the impact of secularization. Indeed, paradoxically many of the churches by copying the methods of big business had themselves become secularized. Yet there were some signs that American religion might be beginning to relax its hold on society. In *Rome* v. *Wade* in 1973 the Supreme Court had legalized abortion, overruling many state laws. The struggle over religious education continued as fundamentalists sought to retain the theory of biblical creationism, even setting up special schools which would save their children from the deleterious effects of secular humanism, but it seemed a lost cause. The election of President Clinton introduced a programme of which many in the moral majority were likely to disapprove. Anti-religious radicalism, attracting some intellectuals, was on the look-out to invoke the law to preserve the State's neutrality on religious issues. The champion of atheism, Madalyn Murray O'Hair tried to get the inscription 'In God We Trust' removed from the coinage and 'Under God' out of the pledges. More significantly there were signs of a changing pattern of behaviour – high divorce rates, the greater openness of homosexuality, the great increase in abortions – which could lead to a steady evaporation of the moral consensus.

FERMENT IN LATIN AMERICA

In Latin America the Roman Church had struggled for some time with limited success to free itself from the strait-jacket of its colonial past. While a third of the population was nominally Roman Catholic, the Church's effective influence was not proportionate to its numerical strength. In most South American countries only 10 to 15 per cent of the population attended Mass. A census in Brazil in 1962 showed that some 70 per cent did not do so, and that there was a serious lack of vocations, so that many parishes were understaffed or served by foreign priests. In Bolivia it was estimated that there was only one Catholic priest for 17,000 people. The religious vacuum was to some extent filled by the Protestant churches and more especially by the exceptionally fast-growing Pentecostalist churches. Afro-Brazilian cults spread among the indigenous population.

In Brazil where there was so wide a gap between rich and poor, radical or basic communities came into existence where peasants and workers tried to apply scriptural teaching to the solution of contemporary social problems, such as land reform. As a result of the severe shortage of priests lay people sometimes took on the responsibility for baptisms and weddings, only occasionally visited by a priest to say Mass. By and large such communities maintained contact with the bishops, but Rome was worried by the decline in sacerdotal authority and suspicious of the liturgical experiments, often lively and popular, to which this seemed to give rise.

The Roman Church's continuing problems, apart from its association in the popular mind with past power, privilege and wealth, were accentuated by the fact that the Church was mainly supported in financial terms by a conservative upper and middle class who were averse to the growing radicalism which some in the Church now appeared to sponsor. Paradoxically the Church's roots really remained in the countryside rather than in urban areas, but the rural environment was itself changing fast as a result of economic exploitation, secular education and the impact of radio and television.

The bishops like their middle-class congregations were apprehensive of a prospective Church riddled by Marxist ideology and wedded to the class war. While the Vatican was ready to acknowledge that the Church's 'institutionalized power' had in the past led to abuses, it urged strongly that the cure for such abuses lay in improved pastoral care and some structural reform rather than in revolution.

But to the many left-wing priests drawn to so-called liberation theology such reforms were no more than inadequate palliatives. They argued that it should be the Church's priority to champion the poor and oppressed, even if this did lead to violence and revolution. God, they averred, acts in history to set his people free, and it is consequently incumbent on the Church to look for signs of liberating theology by fighting against injustice and oppression, and by promoting human brotherhood. The leaders of the Christians for Socialism which had a strong following of priests in Chile argued that Latin America's evils originated with capitalism and exploitative colonialism which Christians fighting side by side with Marxists should join together to overthrow.

The bishops, paternalistic in attitude but not as reactionary as their critics made them out to be, were naturally unable to condone such extremism. Radical change, as Dr Norman suggests, would result in 'the politicization of parts of the Church's leadership, not the Christianizing of secular political society'. Meeting at Punta de Tralca in 1974 the bishops forbade priests to join the movement. Desirable as was social reform, the bishop of

Osorno was to tell the synod of bishops at Rome in 1974, liberation theology *per se* could only promote further secularization.

At the same time the bishops tried to dissociate themselves from notoriously illiberal regimes, such as that of General Stroesner in Paraguay where priests had been imprisoned without trial and the Jesuit Francisco de Paula Oliva of the university of Asuncion had been expelled in 1969. In Peru where Marxism continued to have a strong following among intellectuals and became militant in the rural areas the bishops supported measures for social reform and surrendered some of the Church's privileges. In Brazil Halder Camara, from 1964 archbishop of Olinda and Recife, was a tireless worker for social reform, but characteristically Rome appointed as his successor a conservative canon lawyer.

Some of these problems were highlighted by what had happened in Argentina. When in 1943 General Peron, backed by the workers, attained power on a programme of *justicialismo*, he was at first supported by the Church but as a result of his increasing authoritarianism relations with the Church deteriorated. While his wife Evita seemed deliberately to cultivate a holy image as a secular Virgin Mary, her husband sponsored an anti-clerical programme, ordering crucifixes to be removed from public buildings, forbidding religious instruction in schools and introducing divorce. Priests who protested were arrested, mobs burned church buildings and even the episcopal palace at Buenos Aires.

Although the anti-clerical legislation was not repealed, Church and State were reconciled after Peron's fall in 1955. The bishops who met at Medellin in 1969 declared that the Church as the sacrament of Christ belonged to the poor, that it was incumbent on the clergy not merely to preach that this was the gospel but that they themselves should live in conditions of exemplary poverty. Lest this should be taken for too radical a political statement, the following year they stressed again that the Church's task was fundamentally spiritual and religious and not political or social, and that priests had no right to support revolutionary or terrorist movements in order to gain their objectives.

But such a policy of political involvement appeared to be justified to those involved in the battle. For radical priests Fidel Castro appeared as a model in spite of his anti-clericalism. He had accused the Falangist clergy of Cuba of supporting the Bay of Pigs invasion, and he ordered the expulsion of Spanish and foreign priests and the confiscation of their property. Of 130 priests at work in Cuba only 80 were left to care for a population of 6.5 million, nominally Catholic. Although a pro-Castro group of clergy came into existence under the lead of Father German Lence, the Church remained on probation; but Cuba remained a model for those engaged in fighting in their own countries against capitalist exploitation, which was often backed by American money.

As a consequence the Church was caught between two fires and suffered accordingly. In Mexico where the Church had so long endured persecution, a slow reconciliation began in the Presidency of General Camacho and culminated in an agreement between the Vatican and president Salinas in 1992. In Nicaragua the Church by and large supported the left-wing insurgents and in spite of Vatican disapproval priests held portfolios in the left-wing government. Archbishop Romero who was murdered became a martyr. The army slew six Jesuits. In San Salvador some members of religious orders were victims of the death squad. In Guatemala three priests and a sister were expelled for helping the guerrillas. Plainly, neither the Vatican nor the bishops had resolved what was to be the relationship between the Church and society in Latin America.

CHRISTIANITY IN AFRICA

After the Second World War the missionary Churches entered a new era as the countries in which they operated threw off colonial rule and acquired or were granted their independence. As a consequence the Churches were themselves freed in part from their dependence on the home country, and though they did not lose their connection with the missionary societies either for the supply of ministers and teachers or for funds, the native Churches came more and more to be run by indigenous clergy and adapted themselves with greater understanding to native custom. As a result in some places the membership of the Church grew rapidly but in others the Churches were to experience great difficulties because of internal strife and government policy and in some countries, China, Iran, Burma, the Churches were for a time to be virtually suppressed.

Africa which paradoxically was where the Church continued to grow in membership has been a disturbed continent during the last half of the twentieth century, defaced by devastating famine and rent by strife, exemplified by the massacres in Rwanda in 1994 in which the clergy as well as civilians were both participants and victims, but it had become increasingly free from colonial domination. The Churches seemed more and more willing to absorb native ceremonies which were pagan in origin into their own liturgies so long as they were religiously indifferent. Although this policy sometimes created problems, such as when Rome recalled Emmanuel Milengo, the archbishop of Lusaka, known as the 'Zambian Witch Doctor' for exorcizing those possessed by devils, it made the Churches more attractive to their native worshippers. A policy of Africanization of the clergy gathered speed. In 1939 Pope Pius XII had consecrated the first two African bishops. By 1960 there were 22 Catholic African bishops; in 1978, 237 out of 335 were African. John XXIII created the first African cardinal, Laurean Rugambwa, bishop of Rutopo; a decade later twelve Africans had red hats. The Protestant Churches followed a similar policy. Among the representatives, 175 African bishops were to attend the Anglican Lambeth Conference of 1988. The speed of

Africanization was not rapid enough for some Africans but the net result was impressive.

The Churches in general had supported the movements for independence. Many of the pioneer politicians who played a major part in attaining independence had themselves been educated by missionaries, and in some cases remained committed Christians: Hastings Banda of Malawi, Kenneth Kaunda of Northern Rhodesia whose father had been a Protestant missionary, Jomo Kenyatta of Kenya, Julius Nyerere of Tanzania who had taught in a Catholic school, Moise Tschombe in the Congo and Kwame Nkrumah in the Gold Coast.

Although the Churches benefited by being freed from the stigma of colonialism, they were to be harassed by the rise of harsh dictatorships, the prevalence of corruption in high places, by prolonged and bloody civil war, and the continued advance of militant Islam. In Ethiopia the deposition of the emperor Haile Selassie and the subsequent lengthy Marxist dictatorship subjected the ancient Coptic Church to a period of repression from which it was at length to emerge as a traditional centre of national piety. Liberia, though still under the influence of American Protestant churches, relapsed into calamitous conflict which crippled the work of the churches; in October 1992 five nuns were gunned down by trigger-happy rebels.

In the Sudan the heavy-handed Islamic regime subjected the Christians of the south to a policy of persecution. In 1964 all European missionaries, some 278 Catholics and 28 Protestants were expelled, leaving the care of some 40,000 Catholics, whom Pope John Paul II was to visit in 1992, to 32 native priests. In Somalia, where it was forbidden from 1963 to propagate the Christian religion, the country was abandoned to civil war and famine. Missionaries were expelled from Burundi where in 1977 the Verona Fathers were told to leave because they had tried to protect the Hatha tribe decimated by civil strife, seemingly endemic in the region. In Uganda while the bloody and insensate dictatorship of Idi Amin persisted the Church was to experience sporadic persecution; the Anglican archbishop Luwum and others were cruelly murdered. In Zaire there were for a time laws curtailing religious freedom, banning the use of Christian baptismal names and religious instruction in schools. In the former Spanish colony of Equatorial Africa religious worship was at length forbidden and all foreign missionaries expelled in 1978, leaving only some twenty native priests. In 1967 Guinea expelled all foreign priests and three years later the archbishop of Conakry was arrested and sentenced to hard labour for life because of his alleged complicity in a plot against the government. In Chad the government in the name of promoting 'African authenticity' followed an anti-Christian line. In the former Portuguese colonies of Angola where the majority of the population was Catholic and of Mozambique where some 20 per cent were Catholic the Church had suffered from its long and close identification with colonial rule. Even before the outbreak of civil war ecclesiastical institutions had been nationalized, foreign priests told to leave and the Churches Africanized.

Yet the extraordinary fact is that in spite of the difficulties which confronted the Churches costing priests and laity blood, sweat and toil, Christianity still grew with greater speed in Africa than anywhere else in the world. It was almost as if the challenges to which the Churches had to submit injected them with new life. In 1922 the Roman Church in Africa had been organized into 50 vicariates apostolic and 28 prefectures; some fifty years later there were 49 metropolitan sees, 269 dioceses, 13 vicariates apostolic and 14 prefectures. On the island of Madagascar where there had been some 120,000 Catholics at the start of the century, the Church numbered 1.5 million out of a total population of 7.9 million at its close. The number of Anglican bishoprics and provinces likewise increased. The province of East Africa was divided into Kenya and Tanzania in 1970, Nigeria was separated off from West Africa in 1979. Burundi, Rwanda and Zaire were made separate from Uganda in 1980. Even in that stricken state, 2 dioceses became 10 before 1968, 22 by 1978 and 30 ten years later.

In South Africa the principal issue affecting the Christian churches was internal, the problems caused by the government's policy of apartheid, upheld by the Dutch Reformed Church, but increasingly criticized by the other Churches. The advocates of apartheid argued that while God had created Blacks and Whites as equals, yet because they were apparently of a different blood and culture it was in the interest of each race to preserve and enhance what was best in the culture of each community. 'In order to remain faithful to his divine calling,' so C.B. Brink, the Moderator of the Hervomde Kerk stated at Pretoria in 1953, 'the Afrikaner has to retain his identity, he has to love himself, that which he had become through the grace of God, in order to be able to love his neighbour he had to separate himself in order to be a blessing to the millions of non-Whites. Thence he derived his *apartheid idea*.'

Apartheid, the Hervomde Kerk declared in 1960, provided 'the only just solution of our racial problems'. The Reformed Church seemed still to feel that the Afrikaners were a people called by God to a special destiny. 'The history of the Afrikaner', Dr Malan commented, 'reveals a determination and definition of purpose which makes one feel that Afrikanerdom is not the work of man but the creation of God.' 'We are standing like Luther at the time of the Reformation; with the back against the wall,' Verwoerd declared.

The racial legislation of the South African government further divided the Churches. In 1927 sexual relationships between Blacks and Whites had been banned even though it was not until 1948 that apartheid became public policy. The Native Laws Amendment Bill of 1957 tried to restrict the attendance of Blacks at public worship. In practice the South African state objectives were primarily political and social rather than religious, and the government was largely at first indifferent to the pressures that the Churches were seeking to apply.

But if the Dutch Reformed Church stood by exclusivity, other Christian Churches played an active part in seeking to dismantle apartheid. Trevor Huddleston, a Mirfield father who went as parish priest to Sophiastown, a

Johannesburg slum and was subsequently banned from South Africa brought home the evils of the policy in his best-selling book *Naught for Your Comfort* (1956). Ambrose Reeves, the bishop of Johannesburg until he was forced to leave for Swaziland in 1960, urged the Church to ally with radical politicians to defeat government policy. 'We believe', Geoffrey Clayton, the archbishop of Cape Town, declared, 'that obedience to secular authority, even in matters about which we differ in opinion, is a command laid upon us by God. But we are commanded to render unto Caesar the things which be Caesar's and to God the things that are God's. . . . We feel bound to state that if the Bill [the Native Laws Amendment Bill of 1957] were to become law in its present form we should ourselves be unable to obey it or to counsel our clergy and people to do so.' The most sterling critic of apartheid was the Black churchman Desmond Tutu, Bishop of Johannesburg from 1986 and later archbishop of Capetown, a courageous and humane man. Once apartheid collapsed and a Black government under Mandela was set up in 1994 the Churches would undoubtedly play a significant part in the work of reconciliation.

Meanwhile the Black churches continued to grow throughout the continent, probably numbering as many as three thousand by 1970. There were more than nine hundred such churches in Soweto alone. These churches tried to incorporate native customs, in some cases recognizing polygamy, into a Christian framework, their services often vibrant with dancing, singing and Christian testimony. By and large their theology was scriptural but simplistic and fundamentalist. There were educated Blacks, as in America, who sought to adumbrate a specifically Black theology which, as Dr Boesak, actually a Coloured minister of the Dutch Reformed Church, asserted, 'must mean a search for a totally new social order' and a rejection of White domination 'based on exploitative values'.

THE POSITION OF THE CHURCHES IN ASIA

The success in 1947 of the Indian movement for independence meant that the Christian Churches would have to shed further their alien features; but the foundations of Christian *ashrams* on Hindu lines and the restructuring of the liturgy to absorb Indian ingredients had only minimal success. For most Indians still thought of Christianity as an alien culture and a by-product of British imperialism and American capitalism. In an attempt to iron out their own difficulties the Protestant Churches moved towards unification. The South India United Church, an organic union of Presbyterians, Congregationalists and the Dutch Reformed had been formed in 1906 and further strengthened in 1908 by the addition of the Malabar district of the Basel Mission. The union negotiated at Tranquebar in 1919 preserved some episcopal elements but was regarded with suspicion by Catholic-minded Christians. The Church of South India, consisting of Anglicans and Methodists, was formed in 1947, and proved sufficiently effective for a Church of North India to be set up in 1970. Although there were some forty thousand Anglicans in the Nandyal district who refused to join, the Church of England admitted the Church of South India into a state of 'limited Communion'.

After independence, Rome, freed from the bitter disputes over jurisdiction with the Portuguese patriarch of Goa, synchronized diocesan boundaries with the political borders of India and Pakistan. Pope Paul VI attended the 38th Eucharistic Congress in Bombay in 1964.

In Sri Lanka, a strong bastion of Buddhism, independence in 1948 brought some delimitation of the Church's influence, for the government nationalized private schools, removed the Catholic nursing sisters from the state hospitals and in 1966 replaced the Christian Sunday by the Buddhist Poya Day, computed according to the phases of the moon.

In other parts of Asia the Church was in thrall. Although the Burmese constitution guaranteed religious liberty, the Christian missionaries worked under a cloud, only winning converts among the animistic mountain tribes of the north; between 1966 and 1970 some 262 Catholic missionaries were obliged to leave the country, and the Churches more or less went underground.

In Vietnam under French patronage the Roman Catholic Church was dominant, though a curious syncretistic faith, Catholic, Buddhist and Taoist, known as Caodaism, had won a following in the 1920s. The Church suffered serious injury in the civil war. After the partition of the country in 1954 North Vietnam as a Communist state expelled all foreign missionaries. South Vietnam also obliged them to leave, but a strong Catholic community continued to exist, numbering some 2.8 million out of a total population of 47 million. In Laos which fell into Communist hands in 1975 the work of the Church was much impeded, and even more so in Cambodia where many Catholics were massacred as representatives of a foreign faith. In Sabah or North Borneo the Christian community suffered persecution at the hands of the Muslims who expelled the Roman Catholic bishop and twenty-six priests; but by the early 1970s the situation had improved sufficiently to allow Archbishop Ramsey to visit the state.

In China the Churches were to experience a period of severe persecution. After their victory the Communists had at first encouraged the formation of a National Chinese Church. Between 1957 and 1962 some forty-five Chinese bishops were appointed by the state, only to be disowned by Rome. In 1951 the Three Self-Help Patriotic Movement (self-support, self-government, self-propagation) was founded, with the object of winning Protestant cooperation in the fulfilment of its aims. The slide towards a deliberate anti-religious policy culminated in 1966 with the Cultural Revolution. Churches were closed and desecrated. Priests and pastors and committed lay Christians were imprisoned and ill-treated. 'They found out', said one of the latter 'that I was a Christian. . . . They wanted me to "confess" at a public meeting. I refused. So they smashed everything in the house, burnt my Bible, my hymn-book – and then made me eat the ashes. They cut my hair, slung placards over my front and back and made me collect the night-soil.' Isolated and brutally persecuted the Christian Churches might well have seemed to be on the verge of extinction; but in spite of a systematic policy of ruthless extermination, Christian groups continued to function underground.

The ending of the Cultural Revolution and the death of Mao Tse-tung saw a surprisingly rapid re-emergence of the Churches, in some respects seemingly strengthened by their ordeal. Churches were reopened and rebuilt, though because of the shortage of priests and trained teachers their resources were limited and they came to depend upon the fervour of the faithful laity, small in number. The Protestant Churches, except for a few conservative evangelical groups, worked together in a common understanding. Stripped of their former foreign associations the Churches became more essentially indigenous Chinese institutions, and seemingly spiritually the stronger for the process. Chinese Roman Catholics were less advantageously placed since the quasi-independence from the jurisdiction of the Vatican which they had developed aroused Rome's suspicions while the Chinese authorities resented Rome's recognition of Taiwan where the Church flourished.

In Taiwan where the Catholic Church had concentrated its missionary energy the membership grew at speed, from 12,326 to some 290,000 in a decade. The other area of rapid Christian growth was in South Korea, by contrast with Communist North Korea where the 57,000 Catholics remained more or less isolated. In South Korea in the early 1970s there were over a million Catholics out of a total population of some 40 million. But the greatest area of growth was in the conservative evangelical Full Gospel Church which had half a million members, 1,000 full-time staff and 50,000 house groups. The Yoido Full Gospel Church boasted a seating capacity of five thousand, a fifty-piece orchestra and a choir of two hundred. It had also a built-in radio and television, and an estimated growth rate of 10,000 new members a month. Although the Church supported a major welfare programme, it did not press for social change or industrial action and accommodated itself to the comparatively illiberal regime which reacted fiercely to hostile opinion. The Roman Catholic bishop of Wonju, for instance, was sent to prison for criticizing President Park.

There was, however, in reaction to religious and political conservatism, a feeling of the need in the Church for social awareness. Korean theologians developed the concept of '*minjung*' theology which, as one of its main exponents Hyan Younghak, professor of religion and culture at the Ewha Women's University, Seoul, from 1946 to 1986, explained, was a concern for the Church as a 'community of sinners' rather than a ruling and saved élite. 'We have', he commented, 'lost sight of our people as they exist in the concrete world. . . . The minjung are the ones who are carrying on their shoulders the sins of the world. They are the scapegoats, the lamb of God and the suffering servant.'

After the ending of the Second World War the Churches in Japan had slowly revitalized. The government had been obliged to grant freedom of religion and even to decree the abolition of Shintoism as a state religion; but militant nationalism identified with the traditional faith was never far below the surface. The Japanese churches came to the fore in the peace movement and even sponsored some of the more conventional customs of Western Christian culture such as white weddings and the celebration of Christmas. The rate of growth of Japanese Christianity was relatively modest, and in some respects it still remained an alien faith. There were some Japanese who sought to graft Christianity on to Japanese culture; the Japanese theologian Kosuke Koyama suggested that the Buddhist life-style of concern was relevant to the Christian message. 'The relationship between Buddhism and Christianity', he wrote, 'is not that between "true religion" and "false religion". It is to do with two different yet intertwined understandings of the history of human greed.'

The Japanese occupation of the Philippines in the Second World War had damaged the churches there but once peace came they resumed their vital part in national life. Although the Vatican advocated caution the Roman Catholic Church under the lead of Cardinal Sin criticized the unjust regime of President Marcos and played some part in bringing about his downfall. The Protestant churches, if, as in Japan, infiltrated by fundamentalist teachers, appeared to win adherents, the Iglesia Filipina Independiente, having thrust off its Unitarian bias, came to a close understanding with the Episcopal Church.

AGENCIES OF RELIGIOUS RENEWAL

The nature of political and social change had led to a modification of missionary methods of evangelization with more emphasis placed on teaching and social work and, except in the extreme fundamentalist Churches, less stress on individual conversion and salvation. Yet by and large the Churches employed the same methods for promoting spiritual renewal as they had in the past. The religious orders had once been the spearhead of mission work in the parochial field, but after 1960 the influence and impact of the older monastic orders was on the wane. The Capuchins who numbered 15,710 in 1965 were down to 11,497 by 1984. The Jesuits were shrinking and out of favour with the Pope: 16,894 in 1914; 36,038 in 1965; and 29,426 in 1974. On the other hand, the Swiss Benedictine abbey of Einsiedeln, which had an uninterrupted history of vocational activity since its foundation in 934, its noble baroque buildings designed by Caspar Moosbrugger, a lay brother, and completed between 1704 and 1770, still housed some 153 monks, serving 16 Swiss parishes and visited by 100,000 pilgrims a year; but Einsiedeln was essentially a teaching community, located in a stable society untouched by war and political instability. There were of course, some notable exceptions, among them certain American communities, but in general the picture was one of shortage of vocations and general decline, which affected the Anglican as well as the Roman orders.

Women's orders showed less of a pronounced reduction, in part because they were intimately associated with looking after the sick and disabled. Although the idea of celibacy was foreign to African society, congregations of native sisters were still growing there, increasing from nine in number in 1920 to seventy-nine in 1960. To the distress of some conservative Catholics the Vatican had relaxed some of the harsher rules governing the convent life, more especially modifying the requirement to wear purposely a decorative but austerely uncomfortable habit.

The Greek monastic republic of Athos had never been a centre of spiritual renewal, priding itself on its isolation from the outside world and more especially from any hint of feminism, but it had once been an esteemed centre of spiritual austerity. It too was in a state of what seemed likely to be terminal decline, with less than 1,500 monks in residence and some houses virtually desolate.

The Christian communities which attracted most attention and a genuine following were on the fringe of traditional monasticism and characterized by a touch of individualistic religiosity. After a raffish career in the French army Charles de Foucauld had explored in North Africa to return home in 1890 to the Catholic faith and membership of a Trappist house at Notre-Dame-des-Neiges. Longing still for a more austere regime he became a servant of the Poor Clares in the Holy Land. Ordained a priest in 1901, he then lived the life of a hermit at the Algerian oasis of Benis Abbes, moving four years later to the wild Hoggar mountains where he dwelt among the Tuaregs. He deliberately did not seek converts but his ascetic and caring existence made him admired both by French soldiers and local Arabs. In 1915 he was murdered by local people, seemingly because he perhaps unwittingly became involved in the Holy War of the Senussi.

In 1933 René Voillaume, following the example of de Foucauld who had been beatified in 1927, re-established a small religious community of the Little Brothers of Jesus on the edge of the Sahara, not aiming directly at the conversion of the local people but attesting the love of God through the manner of their lives. In 1936 a community of the Little Sisters of Jesus was set up in the Sahara at Touggourt. The Pope gave his approval to the Little Brothers of Jesus in 1968.

Another community which appeared a beacon of Christianity, especially to the young was founded in 1940 by Roger Schutz, the son of a Swiss reformed pastor, as a centre for refugees and was located in farm buildings at Taizé near Cluny in Burgundy. During the German occupation Schutz returned to Switzerland, but after the liberation of France he came back with seven brothers, four Swiss and three French, all of whom took monastic vows. Taizé became a world-renowned centre for Christian unity and prayer, visited by people from all denominations, especially the young.

There were other communities which sought by embracing a disciplined life to be centres of spiritual renewal. Iona off the western coast of Scotland, long ago the centre of St Columba's mission, housed a community set up by George Macleod to express the theology of the Incarnation in social life. Officially recognized by the Church of Scotland in 1951, its members were ministers and laymen of the Church of Scotland who lived there in preparation for the work which they were pledged to undertake in the mission fields or in industrial towns. Other religious communities were founded at Grandchamp in Switzerland and an oecumenical sisterhood of Mary was established at Darmstadt in Germany. The concept of living in the world rather than away from it and of demonstrating the reality of Christ through life rather than by indoctrination, suggested by such experiments in Christian living, made an appeal to many Christians and even non-Christians. In this respect Mother Teresa's life formed an exemplar, winning her a world-wide reputation which to some seemed a little exaggerated. After training with the Sisters of Loreto in Italy, Mother Teresa, born an Albanian, worked among the poor in Dublin and Bengal where she was eventually to devote her long life to caring for the waifs, the sick and the dying of Calcutta. Her nunnery was approved as the Missioners of Charity in 1950. It numbered some 1,700 sisters and 300 brothers working in 250 homes, pledging their lives to look after the poorest of the poor.

In a further effort to promote religious renewal the Vatican approved the setting up of secular institutes or pious unions to stimulate a religious life by imposing a religious discipline within the framework of secular life. The most influential of these was Opus Dei, founded in Spain in 1928 by J.M. Escriva de Balaguer, then twenty-six years old. While it included priests as well as laymen in its membership it was designed primarily to promote a lay spirituality through which the members would devote themselves to God without abandoning their lay profession, blending practical work, evangelistic zeal and political and theological conservatism. It had its detractors who accused it of secretiveness and élitism, but it spread through the world, was raised by the Pope to the standing of a 'personal prelature', and exercised great influence at the Vatican. Its founder was canonized by Pope John Paul II in 1993. More positively it enhanced devotion and promoted social work for the deprived in Europe, America and the Third World, but its intrinsic conservatism, political as well as moral, made the organization an object of suspicion and dislike to many liberal Catholics.

Pilgrimages to holy places which had always managed to combine religion and tourism continued as a means of bringing people together in community in pursuit of a common religious aim. In spite of their often seemingly dubious historical antecedents, pilgrimage shrines fostered a sense of piety, the ceremonial creating a religious ethos which stimulated belief. Some 6 million pilgrims went to Lourdes at the centenary of the shrine in 1958. Others were drawn to our Lady of Fatima in Portugal, to our Lady at Knock in Ireland, visited by Pope John Paul in 1979, to Kerizinen in Brittany in spite of the disapproval of the bishop of Quimper and to

Medugorje in Yugoslavia in spite of the disapproval of the bishop of Mostar. The pilgrimage continued to be an expression of popular religion.

The revivalistic mission, originating in America but exported all over the world, became a familiar feature of late twentieth century religious life, often with powerful financial supporters. Billy Graham's mission at Earl's Court in 1966 lasted a month and cost £3.5 million. Such missions often had the support of the local clergy, more especially if they were strong Evangelicals. The preacher's message tended to be simplistic and scriptural in content, and his approach was sometimes sensational and even crude, directed at the emotions rather than the intellect, designed to catch the naive and the impressionable. In spite of huge audiences their long-term impact was probably very limited.

In some respects the charismatic movement was associated with revivalism in that it was an appeal to personal experience, seeking the gift of the Holy Spirit, its manifestations affording a pleasant contrast to the barren and boring ritual of a conventional church service. In the 1960s and 1970s it spread fast, even penetrating to the Catholic Church, for in 1965 Cardinal Suenens of Malines led a charismatic pilgrimage to Rome. While it made a particular appeal to the young, fitting in with their desire for spontaneity and freedom, it obscured the discipline of the liturgy and promoted what might seem to some to be a dangerous individuality.

The British 'House Church' movement, which had a small but growing membership, was an apparent by-product of the charismatic movement, drawing its supporters from Christians frustrated by the formalism and inflexibility of the main-line churches. The groups, evangelical in teaching and only loosely bound together, were 'Restorationist' in outlook, wishing to recover the New Testament pattern of life and worship. Worship which took place in private homes was informal, often accompanied by hand-clapping and dancing. It was aligned to the Evangelical Alliance and the festival called Spring Harvest.

THE 'FRINGE' CHURCHES

THE PENTECOSTAL MOVEMENT

It was plain that while membership of the main-line Churches was tending to contract, in the search for religious renewal the 'fringe' Churches were still growing. In Britain between 1975 and 1990 the membership of all recognized Churches fell, but there was an estimated 40 per cent increase in the numbers of the Independent Church, 8 per cent in the Pentecostalists and 4 per cent in the Afro-Caribbean churches. It would take too long to mention the many brands of fringe religion; but there was no doubt that the world-wide Pentecostalist movement, itself an expression of charismatic Christianity, was amazingly successful in its recruitment.

Its origins can be traced to meetings held at Los Angeles in 1906 where the congregation was said to have experienced the gift of the Holy Spirit, including speaking with tongues. It seems to have been imported into Britain by F.B. Barrett, a Methodist minister at Oslo, who had been influenced by the Pentecostalists in New York; he was later invited to conduct revivalist meetings at All Saints' Church, Sunderland. In the United Kingdom its principal agency of propagation was at first the Foursquare Gospel Alliance which between 1925 and 1935 under the lead of the Welsh evangelist George Jeffrey conducted many revivalist services. In 1924 the Assemblies of God in Great Britain and Ireland had been constituted to bring together some seventy similar Pentecostal societies. After the ending of the Second World War the movement won a very substantial following in North America, Scandinavia and Central and Southern America, especially Brazil, but it penetrated also to Eastern Europe and spread to every part of the world.

That the Pentecostalists and other charismatic groups lacked intellectual credibility was no disadvantage to their power to attract or to their growth. Their uncritical appeal to the authority of the Word of God was beguiling because of its very simplicity and the authority they claimed for it. At their services, often enlivened by charismatic gestures, the worshippers aroused by the insistent rhythm of song and dance, believing that they were governed and seized by the Holy Spirit, experienced a feeling of liberation from sin and joy in their salvation. In California for some time they attracted recruits from the former drop-out generation, the Jesus freaks, but Pentecostalism was a world-wide phenomenon, appealing in general to the poor and unlettered who found in the warm fellowship its followers generated a compensation for the difficulties of everyday existence. The message their preachers offered was medieval in the simplicity of the options it provided and the fears on which it was based; for those who do not turn to Jesus only the eternal fires of hell await. The Pentecostalist movement, though seemingly often misguided and naive, raised questions which the older Churches had to answer, most especially as to whether they had unduly neglected the doctrine of the Holy Spirit.

JEHOVAH'S WITNESSES

Another religious society which attracted a world-wide following was the Jehovah's Witnesses. The movement's founder, Charles Taze Russell, a rich haberdasher of Alleghany, Pittsburgh, who had set up Zion's Watch Tower Society in 1884, was a conceited and egotistical but charismatic figure. After his death in 1916 his work was continued by one of his followers, 'Judge' Rutherford, who presided over the society for thirty years until his death in 1946.

The Witnesses are run with great efficiency like a business house, each member being responsible for distributing the Society's official publications and acting for his or her faith as a religious commercial traveller. The Witnesses have a confused and inconsistent theology, with an Arian view of Christ whom they hold to have been incarnate in the Archangel Michael before his own incarnation. The culmination of their gospel is the Second Advent of Christ, variously calculated but once dated for 1984. After the final battle of Armageddon, 144,000 of the saved Jehovah's Witnesses will be taken up to rule with Christ over the new heaven. They claim that the Christian Church is under 'the supervision and control of the Devil' and should therefore be condemned as the dominion of Anti-Christ.

In pursuit of their teaching, regarded by several governments as subversive, they experienced some persecution. They were outlawed in New Zealand and Australia in 1940–1, and deemed by the Supreme Court of Canada in 1947 not to be a 'religious body'. In Greece some two thousand Witnesses have been arrested since 1984 for proselytization, 48 of whom have been imprisoned, while a further 415 were jailed for their conscientious objection to military service. There can, however, be no question that their religious marketing proved to be remarkably successful. The Witnesses' congregations grew steadily, increasing from 182 in 1914 to 356 in 1928 and 727 in 1955. When in 1955 they held a convention on the rugby ground at Twickenham, it was attended by a crowd of 42,000 people, some 182 of whom were to be baptized in the local swimming pool. Growth was also, by and large, the experience of many other fringe Christian groups, for while the main-line Churches were contracting, their 'illegitimate' offspring were expanding.

RELIGIOUS EXTREMES

Charismatic movements were as prismatic as the proverbial rainbow and in practice as in belief often sinisterly eccentric. On the one hand they might seem comparatively harmless, as the capers of the so-called 'Toronto Blessing', which had originated in the Vineyard Church at Toronto airport in 1994, and involved barking, laughing, embracing and collapsing in convulsions as a manifestation of the Holy Spirit. On the other hand there were the numerically small but disturbing millennial movements such as that which culminated in the mass suicide of some 900 members of the Temple of the People at Jonestown, Guyana, in 1978, a fate not wholly dissimilar to that which in 1993 overwhelmed the Branch Davidians.

A breakaway sect of the Seventh-Day Adventists, who had formed a community called Mount Carmel at Waco in Texas, they were led by David Koresh, a self-proclaimed messiah. Not averse to indulging in worldly delights which included the seduction of the wives and daughters of his followers, Koresh preached the imminent end of the world and the Last Judgement. This came for him in a way that he can hardly have expected, in part as a result of the blunders of US officialdom, leaving some fifty-three adults and twenty-one children dead. Even after this catastrophe, the few surviving members remained faithful to the precepts of their deranged messiah. Minimal in their religious importance, such socially and spiritually aberrant movements demonstrate how religion, like other extreme forms of fanatical belief, can be as addictive and dangerous as any drug.

CHURCHES AND CHANGES IN MORAL VALUES

In the closing decades of the twentieth century the Churches have been faced by a revolution in morals and manners which to many seems to threaten traditional ethical values. Christian morality was largely the fruit of Judaic tradition as expressed in the Old Testament, sustained and modified in the New Testament by the sayings of Jesus and St Paul and in time incorporating some elements of non-Christian cultures.

Fundamentally Christian teaching as articulated by St Paul and promoted by some patristic writers, most notably St Augustine, appeared suspicious of human sexuality. It did not easily abandon a potent Manichaean ingredient with its implicit distrust of the body at war with the spirit. It was based implicitly on male superiority, even though it recognized the rights of women idealized in the cult of the Blessed Virgin Mary and innumerable female saints. If the Church reckoned virginity and celibacy as a status superior to the married state, it came comparatively early to recognize that marriage was natural for most men and women. As early as the end of the second century Clement of Alexandria, albeit the author also of a tract on ascetic theology, stated that marriage had both physical and spiritual constituents and represented a united dedication to God who has endowed both partners with the capacity to love physically as well as spiritually. So the nuclear family became the essential unit in Christian society, its original image a romanticized and indeed imaginary picture of the Holy Family. Sex could only be rightly practised by two people of different gender contracted to each other by marriage. Its bonds were indissoluble, its object the procreation of children, for pleasure could not in itself be regarded as a valid objective for sexual activity.

Conversely it condemned all sexual activity outside the marriage bed, whether fornication or adultery and condemned homosexuality as unnatural. Neither divorce nor remarriage were permissable. The Church had thus developed a strait-jacket which in theory demanded unwavering conformity to the moral law which it had articulated. Christians were to keep themselves unspotted from the world. Historically such precepts had been regularly ignored by priests as well as by lay people; but at least ideally the Church's teaching had not until recent times been significantly breached.

In the twentieth century social mores, at least in Europe and North America, have changed at a fast rate and are eroding the traditional teachings of the Church. It is not merely that the Sabbatarianism which the Church had for so long sought to enforce was disappearing, except in remote regions of the Scottish Highlands, but also that sexual habits are undergoing mutation in response to a shifting culture and in part to advances in medicine. Cohabitation without marriage or before marriage has become a relatively normal practice. Artificial birth control has become widespread in more developed countries. Abortion is becoming more and more a familiar product of sexual relationships. In England where abortion was legalized in 1968 there are annually some 140,000 or more registered abortions, a figure which is, however, far less proportionate to the population than in the United States, where the increase in abortions and the use of contraception generally in the White population actually appears to threaten, eventually, to upset the balance of the population in favour of the Blacks and Hispanics. Laws legalizing abortion have been passed in France, West Germany and Italy (in 1977). Although Swedish churchmen have protested, the Swedish government in 1977 gave women the right to decide for themselves.

Divorce too has become increasingly prevalent, especially in North America. In England and Wales the number of divorces went up from 23,000 in 1963 to 150,000 in 1980 and has since continued to rise. In 1989 12.7 divorces were granted for every 1,000 married couples. When in 1974 the Italian State introduced a divorce law, protests by the Pope persuaded the government to introduce a referendum which went in favour of divorce, suggesting that even in a highly Catholic country the laity accept divorce as a norm. In Spain, in spite of opposition from the Church, divorce became legal in 1981. In England, where there has been a staggering increase in the number of one-parent families, of all pregnancies 28 per cent or more are outside marriage and the number is growing steadily.

Slowly homosexuality has become more and more accepted, in spite of some continuing homophobia, as a natural condition and a proper basis for an accepted partnership. In most countries, at least in America and Europe, laws against homosexual practice have been relaxed. Exceptions remain, however, such as Ireland and Cyprus. The death penalty for sodomy was abolished in 1861 in England and Ireland and in 1889 in Scotland, but the Criminal Law Amendment Act of 1885 actually extended the penal law to include all homosexual activity whether in public or in private. This was changed by the law of 1967, which as a result of the Wolfenden Report legalized all private relationships between adult males over the age of twenty-one. There can be little doubt that, though the process has been a slow one, homosexuality has come out of the closet and will stay out. There has been among homosexual groups a demand for the Churches to accept homosexuals for ordination and to bless gay partnerships.

The Churches' reaction to this loosening of moral bonds has been somewhat predictable. The Roman Catholic Church has taken an unyielding line, for it vehemently opposes divorce, birth control and abortion, which Pope John Paul II describes as the murder of an innocent individual, and equates with the genocide of the Jews. When in 1990 the Belgian government passed legislation relating to abortion, the Belgian Catholic bishops protested so strongly that the Catholic King Baudouin resigned rather than sign the bill. However, as he returned to the throne a mere two days later it was not very much more than a gesture. Anti-abortion groups in the United States, often Protestant and fundamentalist, have sometimes attacked abortion clinics with violence. In 1996 a conservative Catholic bishop, Fabian Braskowitz of Nebraska, threatened to excommunicate all church members who supported birth control or advocated women's rights.

The Roman Church in Ireland was still strong enough to ban abortion until recently when a movement to allow it was passed by a wafer-thin majority in a referendum instituted by the Irish parliament. It continues to oppose contraception and birth control, but even in a country where vending machines selling condoms were illegal, it was not uncommon in the summer of 1992 to see young people in Dublin wearing tee-shirts with the inscription 'Wear a Condom. Just in Casey', a reference to Eamonn Casey, the disgraced bishop of Galway, who fathered a son. The Church agreed that 'being homosexual is not sinful or a sin' but remained condemnatory of homosexual genital acts. Being a homosexual, as Cardinal Ratzinger worded it in 1986, implied 'a strong tendency towards an intrinsic moral evil'. When the French Roman Catholic Father Marc Oraison wrote a book pleading for greater understanding of homosexuals, the book in spite of having an imprimatur was placed on the Index.

The Church of England has been inclined to take a similar line. 'Let it be understood', Archbishop Fisher said categorically in 1953, 'that homosexual indulgence is a shameful vice and grievous sin from which deliverance is to be sought by every means.' In 1957 Ramsey, then Archbishop of York, had greeted warmly the findings of the Wolfenden Report, but it was only approved by a small majority in the Church Assembly (by 155 votes to 138) and the Church of Scotland rejected it altogether. In 1992 Archbishop Carey's intervention prevented the publication of an innocuous 'gay' prayer book by the SPCK. However, a gay prayer book, We Were Baptized, compiled by two American Methodists and with a foreword by Archbishop Tutu, was published in 1996.

There are, however, indications that the Churches might have to review their moral teaching just as they are beginning to overhaul or at least to reinterpret their doctrinal theology in the light of changing circumstances. The new Roman Catholic catechism tries to take into account the changing nature of society, widening the range of offences to include, for instance, that of drug-taking, but has been criticized for its continued male chauvinism. Although it continues to condemn birth control, it has virtually turned a blind eye to the fact that so many of the faithful disregard its ruling; indeed the highest sale of condoms proportionate to the population is reported to take place in a predominantly Catholic country, Colombia. It makes no concessions in respect of abortion or homosexuality. Abortion represents the meeting of two worlds, the religious and the secular, for while the religious regard the destruction of the foetus as murder, the pro-abortionists argue that what is at issue are women's rights and the health of the mother. Increasingly publicized, if unduly exploited and magnified by the media,* are the number of priests, more especially in the United States and Canada, but also in Ireland, charged with sexual deviation. Cardinal Hans Groer, the archbishop of Vienna, was retired for fear of sexual scandal. In 1995 the Pope removed, from the see of Evreux, Jacques Gaillot, notorious for his support of radical causes, including birth control and the marriage of priests, and who had admitted his homosexuality. In 1993 the bishop of Gloucester, a monk highly reputed for his holiness, felt obliged to resign on a charge of indecency with a young novice. The radical American Episcopalian, Bishop Spong of Newark, ordained a practising homosexual, but the experiment turned sour when the man turned out to be a proselytiser. In 1992 the bishop of Washington was said to have ordained to the priesthood a woman who was self-admittedly living in a lesbian relationship, but in 1996 the retired bishop of Iowa, Walter Righter, was charged with violating the doctrine of the American Episcopal Church by ordaining a homosexual in 1990; his later acquittal at least made possible the ordination of gay men in the American Episcopal Church. Ten traditionalist bishops, however, led by Bishop Stanton of Dallas, sought to frustrate such a move. Similarly Bishop Finlay of Toronto invoked the law to deprive a young parish priest who was openly homosexual of his charge of the parish of Unionville. There are very few outward signs of any softening in the judgement of the main-line Churches on moral issues. Since the Church of England still refuses to marry divorced persons, Princess Anne, the daughter of Queen Elizabeth II, Supreme Governor of the Church of England, had to remarry in the Church of Scotland, which is less rigid in its rules on this matter.

Whatever the future has in store for the Churches with respect to changes in moral criteria, it seems evident that if they are not to be isolated from the society they seek to serve, they may in some respect have to re-state their moral theology. It seems obvious to many that homosexuality, for instance, should not be a barrier to ordination, nor, in spite of the scandals to which allusion has been made, is there anything to suggest that a homosexual would be any less able to fulfil his pastoral vocation than his heterosexual counterpart. Past history has shown that the interpretation of Christian theology and worship have evolved rather than remained static, and that in fact the Churches' future depends on this happening.

THEOLOGY IN THE LATE TWENTIETH CENTURY

The need to reassess the Church's teaching in doctrine as well as morals might well seem to call for theologians of the stature of St Thomas Aquinas

---

* See Philip Jenkins, *Paedophiles and Priests, Anatomy of a contemporary Crisis*, Oxford, 1996.

who in the thirteenth century managed to reconcile so remarkably Christian teaching with Aristotelian philosophy. At a university sermon in the 1930s Dean Inge, peering from the pulpit of St Mary's, Cambridge at the professors of divinity sitting in the pews below him, commented that 'the trouble with this age is that there are no major prophets and too many minor ones'. The late twentieth century has been modestly replete with prophets who have sought with greater or lesser success to relate the study of theology to the needs of the fast-changing world.

From this process the fundamentalist theologians have to be excepted. Given their premise that the Word of God is inerrant and inspired, they have been able to create a logical structure of faith which has undoubtedly attracted many people, perhaps simply because of the authority seemingly enshrined in *sola scriptura*. But to those outside this enclosed world, fundamentalists appear to lack an open mind, disdaining biblical criticism unless it falls into line with their essentials, engaging in polemics rather than dialogue.

Fundamentalism, intrinsically anti-historical as well as anti-intellectual, has, however, to be differentiated from conservative evangelical theology which, if rigid in its teaching and uncompromising in its attitude, has been much more intellectually credible. It has had distinguished exponents in the Protestant Reformed Churches, especially in North America, such as the Baptists Carl F. Henry and Harold J. Okenga, the pastor of Park Street Church, Boston and the first president of the National Association of Evangelicals. Conservative evangelicals have not ignored scientific and cultural developments but reaffirmed the basic assumptions which they drew from the gospel as they had been originally adumbrated by the sixteenth-century reformers, that scripture constitutes the key to divine revelation and is the sole means of saving grace. It alone can provide the criterion by which human history has to be judged, enunciating, as Carl Henry put it, 'the religious realities that human unregeneracy desperately needs and cannot otherwise provide'. With these fundamental doctrines in mind, they were unequivocal in their condemnation of what seemed to them ethical relativism, demanding a return to the moral absolutes which they deduced from scripture. The German Lutheran scholar Helmut Thielicke, who strongly attacked the Nazis' attempt to promote a German Christian theology, was equally critical of scholars who seemed to him to subject the Word of God to human agency, strongly stressing, as did other conservative evangelicals, the Reformation teaching on *sola scriptura* and *sola gratia*.

This strong and stern promulgation of faith through redemption by Jesus Christ, revealed in the gospels and experienced by the individual through the power of the Holy Spirit in the Church was in some sense a legacy of the continued influence exerted by the Barthians in the Church. Although Karl Barth did not die until 1968 and his teaching was to be modified by his disciples, his influence long remained pervasive in schools of Protestant theology.

Barth had been mainly concerned to safeguard the absolute primacy of God to which human history was subject, declaring that rather than seeking to place God within the context of human society, human society had itself to be judged by the truth of God's absolute revelation in scripture. By such a criterion the fresh understanding of the universe offered by scientific advance and even steps towards the amelioration of society appeared largely irrelevant. To an increasing number of theologians the traditionalism of the conservative evangelicals and the neo-conservatism of Karl Barth and his disciples seemed an inadequate way of demonstrating the relevance of the Christian gospel to the modern world.

But Barthian ideas had not been confined to the Protestant Churches. The Swiss Jesuit, Hans Urs von Balthasar, who had been a student chaplain at Basle where he had been much influenced by Barth, was a scholar in the Barthian tradition, if in the main concerned with a renewed emphasis on spirituality. In 1950 he had left the Jesuits to promote with Adrienne von Speyr the Secular Institute at Basle to stimulate religious life within the laity. Von Balthasar was above all a contemplative and spiritual theologian who sought to encourage spiritual renewal as a means of regenerating the Church and the world, fastening on the theme of beauty as the positive core of revelation and calling on the faithful to indulge in what he called a 'kneeling theology', studying the lives of the saints to rediscover the glory of the Christian vision of God. In earlier life at Lyons as a student of the *nouvelle thèologie* he had been a friend of the Catholic poet Paul Claudel, and for a time was coolly regarded at the Vatican. In later life he became a severe critic of his more radical colleagues whom he charged with fostering what he called an 'anonymous Christianity' by seeking to 'baptise secular and religious movements outside the Church'.

Indeed, the most remarkable feature of late twentieth-century theology is its radical renaissance in the Roman Church, more especially the rediscovery of the Bible which the Romans had so long kept under wraps. Until the 1950s Roman Catholic scholars had still to accept the single authorship of the book of Isaiah, the priority of St Matthew's Gospel and the Pauline authorship of Hebrews and the Pastoral Epistles. The Second Vatican Council had, however, given a more flexible ruling on the nature of exegesis: 'the exegete', it said, 'must look for the meaning which the sacred writer, in a determined situation and given the circumstances of his time and culture, intended to express, and did in fact express, through the medium of a contemporary literary form'. 'It is', as the Sulpician Raymond Brown of the Union Theological Seminary, New York, put it, 'crucial that we be aware that the Church interpretation of a passage and the literal (i.e. the original) sense may be different.' 'The literal sense of scripture uncovered through historical-critical research', he went on, 'may challenge the Church; and it is incumbent on scholars not to present that challenge hostilely but by way of invitation. Scripture would not be the Word of God if it always confirmed Christians or the Church.' Such ideas opened new windows letting in a gust of fresh air which was bound from time to time to cause discomfort in conservative curial circles.

In the first instance there was a burgeoning of fresh insights into patristic and scholastic theology with some attempt to re-align them with developments in modern science and philosophy. The Canadian Jesuit Bernard Lonergan, originally a student of the Counter-Reformation scholar Francisco Suarez, made a valiant effort to reconcile the scholastic method with the findings of modern science and philosophy, as he demonstrated in his two important books *A Study of Human Understanding* (1957) and *Method in Theology* (1973). The renaissance of Thomist studies was a powerful force in regenerating Catholic theology and bringing it into touch with the modern world.

Karl Rahner was another Jesuit, his inner life shaped by Loyola's *Spiritual Exercises*, from 1937 a professor at the university of Innsbruck, near in spirit to Lonergan, who endeavoured to reconcile the scholastic philosophy of Aquinas and Bonaventure with German idealistic philosophy; hence the phrase 'Transcendental Thomists' sometimes used to describe scholars of his ilk. He had indeed some success in accommodating scholasticism to the needs of modern theology.

More influential and controversial than Lonergan or Rahner, and in some respects less of a pure theologian, was the French Dominican Yves Congar who had studied under M.D. Chenu at Le Saulchoir, then located because of the anti-clerical legislation of the French State at Kain-la-Tombe in Belgium. Mobilized as a war chaplain he became a prisoner of war at Colditz, an experience which helped to shape his future development. He became concerned to preserve what seemed of enduring value in Catholic modernism and as a result was soon on a collision course with the Vatican. Rome had condemned his mentor Chenu's essay on 'A School of Theology, le Saulchoir', which in the opinion of the Dominican 'master of the sacred palace' Mariano Cordoviario promoted a school of cultural anthropology rather than an academy for the propagation of revealed truth.

Congar now became the target of Rome's displeasure for the support which he gave to oecumenicism, 'a false eirenicism' as his critics called it, and for his defence of the French worker priests. For this he was exiled in 1947 to the École Biblique, only to return to favour under Pope John XXIII, who appointed him a consultor to the Second Vatican Council. Congar, who stood for what he would have described as the 'humanization of God' in the Church, wished to re-adapt the Church to the world by a reform of its structures and by giving greater participation to the laity. He defined tradition succinctly but with insight as 'the permanence of a past in a present in whose heart the future is being prepared'. A polymathic scholar rather than a systematic theologian, Congar was perhaps more than any other Roman Catholic responsible for the 'shift in sensibility' which was to breathe fresh life into the Church's thinking, however much it was resented by more conservative churchmen.

A fellow Dominican who studied under Congar and Chenu at Le Saulchoir was Edward Schillebeeckx, from 1957 until his retirement in 1983 professor of dogma and the history of theology at the university of Nijmegen. It was his primary object to seek to relate the Church to the needs of the modern world by urging the Church to promote the belief that it is through God that society can be made more humane and just – a goal which should itself be the Church's objective. To that end he steadily abandoned the scholastic method and the mechanical approach which it seemed to generate, reaching conclusions which tested and angered the curial theologians, bringing him on a number of occasions, as in 1968, 1976 and 1981, into conflict with the Vatican. The authorities were alarmed by his critical attitude to the priesthood, his apparent subordination of dogma to experience (as instanced in his interpretation of the post-Resurrection appearances of Jesus) and his conviction that the needs of the community should be put before the exigencies of Church order. His personalist and existentialist ideas, expressed in his study *The Church with a Human Face* (1985) made him a forward and constructive figure in theology.

In his radical approach he was by-passed by Hans Küng, a Swiss who at the early age of thirty-two became professor of fundamental theology in the Roman Catholic faculty of theology at the university of Tübingen. For many years he was the Church's *enfant terrible*. His theology was strongly scriptural and Christological, 'interested' as he put it, 'in the Jesus who meets us today, within the horizons of the world, humankind and God, as the challenge to the faith which he personally embodies'. 'Christianity exists only where the meaning of Jesus Christ is activated in theory and practice.'

But his understanding of scripture made him, like Schillebeeckx, critical of the Church's existing structure, which he condemned as too often promoting 'spiritual absolutism, a formal and often inhuman jurisdiction and a traditionalism fatal to genuine revival'. He was interested in dialogue with other faiths and in the oecumenical movement, and increasingly hostile to papal authoritarianism. In particular he was strongly critical of the papal encyclical *Humanae vitae* and challenged papal infallibility. He argued that in the interest of Christian unity all Churches might have to change and that religion should never be static. For the Church was only viable if it was a genuine expression of the kingdom of God.

Eventually Pope John Paul II withdrew the teaching permission, the *missio canonica*, which Küng required in order to offer instruction in a Roman Catholic theological faculty, and he was transferred to a chair at the independent Institute for Ecumenical Research. Few modern theologians have had such influence over the Protestant as well as the Roman Catholic Church as Küng, who was instrumental in reminding Christians that their Churches had to be justified by the criterion of the gospel freshly interpreted.

Protestant theologians enjoyed a degree of freedom from the supervision of the 'magisterium' that the Roman Catholics lacked but whether they were more constructive may be doubted. The Protestant Churches certainly produced a catena of scholars who, indebted as they were likely to be in their several ways to Barth and Bultmann, were concerned to reconcile theology and modernity. The Scottish theologian Thomas F. Torrance tried, if with limited success, to bring together the methodology of theology and science, finding profound similarities in their basic approach.

One of the most influential of modern Protestant theologians was Paul Tillich who after being suspended by the Nazis in 1933 found refuge in the United States, first at New York and then at Harvard. He had a wide readership, attracting attention by the thesis he put forward that God had to be regarded as the ground of all being, instantiated in Christ in logos, the antithesis of which was destructive non-being represented by sin, suffering and death; these destructive elements can be overcome only by the 'power of New Being' in Christ which brings reconciliation and so heals the estrangement which pervades all life and society. Tillich's ideas were popularized (and to some degree misrepresented) in Bishop John Robinson's *Honest to God*, published in 1963, which sold more than a million copies in four years. Its supposed radicalism was, rather like that of David Jenkins, the bishop of Durham some years later, somewhat overstated; but Robinson and Jenkins represented an honest effort to take theology out of the slough of the antiquarian past. What Tillich tried to do, as Robinson also attempted to do, was to escape from the specialized language of theology which needed a glossary for the non-instructed reader into modern idioms which could be understood by the educated layman.

The writings of another distinguished Protestant, Wolfhart Pannenberg, professor respectively at Mainz, München and Mainz, were less accessible intellectually to the general public but were arguably of greater significance, for Pannenberg set out to respond to the atheist critique of religion by endeavouring to find a common ground for believer and non-believer in a theory of knowledge the validity of which did not itself require religious faith. Aware of human and natural science and taking into account both Christian tradition and the findings of the latest biblical exegesis Pannenberg advanced a concept of reality which could be described as both genuinely Christian and yet intellectually acceptable to non-Christians as well as to Christians.

Jürgen Moltmann, who held a chair at Tübingen, was a post-Barthian whose experience as a prisoner of war and of the dialogue in which he later engaged with Jewish and Marxist writers, led him to the conviction that the essential and converting feature of the Christian faith was its concern and hope for the future. The resurrection of Christ was the definitive and culminating gesture of God's promise for the world, which looked ahead to the future, for just as Christ was transformed from death to new life, so God, working through the Church, the 'messianic fellowship of believers', can transmute the community. Influenced no doubt by Bonhoeffer's belief that the Church had to be deeply involved in society if it would be true to its vocation, Moltmann taught that theology made it obligatory on the Christian to sponsor social, even revolutionary change, since Christianity involves the acceptance of a distinctive life-style, which requires an acceptance of human rights and solidarity with the poor, all of which were rooted in the eschatological destiny of a humanity made in the image of God. Moltmann was a prophet of his times in seeking to relate biblical faith to the mind and ethos of modern society.

It was hardly surprising that Moltmann should have had some influence over the development of liberation theology in the Church in Latin America. Liberation theology, as we have noted earlier, originated in the social conditions of a continent where two-thirds of the population lived in grinding poverty. Its advocates were above all concerned to find a theological solution to contemporary problems of race and gender, seeing Christianity as a 'praxis of love and solidarity with the oppressed'. 'The Church must have', as Gustavo Gutierrez phrased it, 'a preferential option for the poor.' If, as Juan Luis Sobrino urged, men would follow Jesus, then they must follow him by struggling for justice against injustice and oppression.

Not dissimilar ideas lay behind the development of an intrinsic Black theology in North America and Africa, though there were to be differences of attitude between their proponents on the two continents. But the Bible, and in particular the plight of the Children of Israel, was invariably invoked to underline the call of a God who was above all a champion of the oppressed; only by liberation can the 'beloved community' of God be created.

Even more specialized was so-called 'feminist' theology, a product of North America and a relative newcomer, though it had been in 1895 that Elizabeth Cady Stanton produced *The Women's Bible* to illustrate the extent to which the Church had long presented a portrait of women that seemed to demonstrate their basic inferiority to men. In her *Church and the Second Sex* (1968) Mary Daly stressed the Church's patriarchal attitudes, becoming herself ultimately so convinced that she was fighting a losing cause in trying to 'feminize' Christianity that she lost her faith. Feminist theology partook of the language of protest and was perhaps more socially than theologically significant. It did, however, constitute a relevant reminder of the extent to which Christian theology had been in the past interpreted in essentially masculine terms.

At the other end of the spectrum from the conservative theologians were the radicals who so humanized the gospel that it was difficult to see that their views fitted into a supernatural context at all. Such were the group of American scholars who in the late 1960s, reacting against the Barthians, formed the so-called 'Death of God' School, Thomas Altizer, Gabriel Vahanin and Paul van Buren. They voiced a disenchantment with the supernatural and a wish to interpret theology in purely naturalistic terms, for which in England the Cambridge intellectual Don Cupitt was the spokesman. Cupitt was particularly critical of Christianity's anthropomorphic features, its unhealthy attitude to sex and asceticism, and its authoritarian imagery. God, Cupitt advised, had to be 'interiorized' through a life-style, which resembled the Buddhist 'way' embodied in the teaching of Jesus. In Cupitt's conception God ceased to be an objective presence, and religious conviction was subjective and autonomous.

The plethora of theologians demonstrates that if there has not been a presiding genius in the late twentieth century, yet at least many minds have been at work in seeking to address the relevance of the Church's teaching to the modern world. It would be fanciful to say that although scholars such as Tillich and Küng have had a wide reading public, the impact made by theology even on the Church, let alone the outside world, has been more than limited. In some sense academic theology has become increasingly marginalized. Theologians, like scholars in other disciplines, have evolved a language in which to present their ideas that requires a glossary before it can be understood by the non-specialist. The theologians of the early Church had also used a specialized language but they were writing for an audience still basically familiar with the images and language of religion. In the late twentieth century this is no longer the case. In such circumstances it can be understood why the simplistic, even crude imagery and the emotive terms used by revivalists, the pentecostalists and other sectaries gather a wide following.

Epilogue

Where is the Christian Church likely to stand at the start of the twenty-first century? Its history shows that from the days of its foundation the Christian Church has been a power structure sustaining its way of life by authoritarian sanctions, whether spiritual or secular in character. The spiritual sanctions, enshrined in New Testament teaching, were rooted in Judaism; 'if you do not behave or believe in such and such a way God will withhold from you blessings in this life and assuredly deprive of you of eternal life in the world to come.' In time the Church developed a whole series of effective penalties to support its claims and maintain the privileges of its priesthood: excommunication and the withdrawal of spiritual privileges, a penitential system that was a curious combination of the promise of forgiveness and the threat of punishment, and ultimately the reward of heaven or more likely the pains of hell, constituting a system of physical as well as psychological intimidation and terror. Such sanctions had for long enjoyed secular backing, involving trials, torture, imprisonment and death. The Church's ultimate appeal was to the sword, evoking wars which were religious or semi-religious in character, with the carnage and cruelty, slaughter and rapine which form the accompaniment to all wars, past and present.

These proscriptions, still characteristic of fundamentalist Islam (which may in some respects be described as a debased form of Christianity) have virtually disappeared. The Christian Churches have indeed become involved in national wars, as in 1914–18 and 1939–45, invoking the Thomist principle of the just war to bless the armies; and they have been still involved in the deplorable explosions of national ethnicity as in northern Ireland and the former Yugoslavia. In the genocidal strife between the Hutus and Tutsis in 1994 in Rwanda, where 70 per cent of the population belong nominally to the Roman Catholic Church, many Christians, and even priests and nuns, at least acquiesced and even participated in the massacre of their fellow Christians, for tribal feeling took precedence over religious commitment. It is, however, unlikely that a war will in future ever be fought primarily for religious reasons; the last such war curiously enough occurred in 1846–7 in the strife between the Catholic and Protestant cantons in Switzerland.

The power of the sword with which secular governments at the behest of the Churches browbeat, tortured and executed their critics and those who dissented from their teaching has happily vanished. The Inquisition has long disappeared. Ecclesiastical courts, if still occasionally invoked to deal with erring clergymen, rarely attempt to utilize their jurisdictions; though the Holy Office of the Roman Church keeps a beady eye on potential critics of Church doctrine. Excommunication is a device now rarely employed. Censorship in the name of religion and morality is on the wane. Where laws against blasphemy still exist, the growing demand for their abolition in so-called Christian countries (though not in Islamic lands) is likely to prove successful. The Christian Churches can no longer to any credible extent rely on the power of the sword or the rigour of the law to help them maintain their privileged position, control their members or support their position in society. Even in rigidly Catholic countries, such as Ireland, as the debates over abortion and homosexuality exemplify, such sanctions have increasingly limited force.

Where religious sanctions survive they cannot be wholly ignored but they carry comparatively decreasing weight. It is only among the more extreme evangelicals and some dissenting sects that Christians are likely to be told that if they do not accept Jesus Christ as their saviour and lord they may be in danger of being damned to everlasting fire in hell. The proliferating sects of America and Africa, lacking political sanctions, have been freer in their use of spiritual sanctions to discipline their flocks. But even for the committed traditional Christian the concepts of heaven and hell, which once so overshadowed daily life, seem to be of little pertinence or relevance. The Christian appears indeed reluctant to give up his belief in eternal life, subjecting the dead to a charade of social and religious imagery, a tribute of affection or respect for the deceased but only a vestigial expression of religious belief. Except for the spiritualist – and spiritualism is at best a dubious phenomenon – belief in an afterlife has been greatly eroded. The hope of heaven and the fear of hell have only a peripheral hold over even the committed believer.

The decline in the efficacy of religious sanctions has been promoted further by recent scientific and intellectual developments which seem to tilt at what some might consider the threadbare windmills of Christian theology. A rationalized world-view at odds with a supernatural understanding of the universe, the creation of which may seem a purposeless and aberrant accident of science, or at best a complex chemical equation, attracts a greater following, at least among intellectuals. The tremendous advances in science and technology which enabled man to land on the moon and which promise breath-taking and alarming developments in genetic engineering raise questions which stir further the stirrup-cup of belief, even if they do not necessarily conflict with a view of the universe as divinely inspired.

Contained within such a secular ethos, even if the main tenets of the Christian faith, the Atonement, the Resurrection, remain in some sense no less credible, they seem more irrelevant to daily life. Their sources are under daily inquisition. The textual authority of the Bible has been increasingly challenged, its historicity appearing more and more implausible, its divine origins questionable. Many of the principal characters of the Old Testament may appear on closer examination to be fictional beings, created hundreds of years after they had supposedly lived, nor is the authority of the New Testament as historically acceptable even for professing Christians as it has been in past centuries. For the most part Church members do indeed turn a blind eye to these and similar developments, condemning without much thought new interpretations when they have been put forward as, for instance, by Dr David Jenkins, the former bishop of Durham, preferring by and large to find consolation in the more nostalgic yet historically dubious poetry of the Christmas story. Most Christians are people with faith but little or no theology; though this is not necessarily an obstacle, as doubtless the disciples of Jesus had themselves earlier discovered, to the excitement of Christian living. However, few modern historians would feel as did the Venerable Bede and many after him, that they could certainly discern in the course of history proof of the providence of God.

That the Christian Churches appear in the closing years of the twentieth century to be confronted with a dangerous continuing crisis which affects their future can hardly be doubted. On the one hand, there seems a possibility that the Churches might become closed sects, clusters of believers in an unbelieving world from which they have become isolated, relying on the authority of scripture fundamentally interpreted, morally enclosed, a prospect which would seem more likely to make itself felt in the many Protestant Churches than in the world-wide membership of the Roman Church. On the other hand, the Churches may, in as yet unforeseen ways, conceivably through trial and tribulation, adapt further to meet the needs of an ever-changing society, becoming increasingly immersed in secular culture, both in terms of doctrine and morals, shedding to a greater or lesser extent their supernatural framework. 'No form of Christianity in the nineties', Anthony Freeman a radical Anglican vicar wrote in 1993, 'can be the same as the Christianity of 1662, or 1066, or of any past time, because to say the same thing in new circumstances is to say something different.' As the Irish Augustinian Father Byrne expressed it in 1993, the Church which stands still will stagnate and perish while that which adapts will flourish. In some fashion like the Roman God Janus, Christianity has to look two ways, both to the traditions of the past and to the challenge of the future.

Whatever its future, Christianity is unlikely to disappear, if only for purely anthropological and historical reasons. In practice the survival of religious systems has very little to do with the rational principal or intellectual perception. Indeed, in certain respects, religious faith is not unlike sex and may have a similar capacity to endure and to survive. The analogy between sex and religion appears forcibly in John Donne's *Holy Sonnet XIV* with its innate sexual conceit:

> Batter my heart, three person'd God; for you
> As yet but knocke, breathe, shine, and seeke to mend;
> That I may rise, and stand, o'erthrow mee, and bend
> Your force, to breake, blowe, burn and make me new . . .

> Take mee to you, imprison mee, for I
> Except you enthrall mee, never shall be free,
> Nor ever chast, except you ravish mee.

Sex is a basic natural attribute, the instinctive root of all being, in whatever
ways it may express itself. It may be irrational in the demands which it makes
upon men and women which they cannot escape and to which in some
manner they feel bound to submit. It is capable of raising men and women to
the height of ecstasy, but it can equally lead to degradation and humiliation.
To prevent moral anarchy and exploitation, sex has itself to submit to some
measure of self-discipline, whether individual or communal, subordinating its
innate predatory power to humane values and rational judgement. Religion
seems to share in many of these features. It is capable of promoting
exploitation but also of generating the greatest joy and happiness, and is less
a product of the intellect than an expression of something deep within the
human psyche. Like sex, religion seems to meet a primal urge.

However, perhaps we should now draw breath and remind ourselves that
Christianity has survived because first and foremost from the very beginning it
has been a society, a brotherhood, a *koinonia*, sustained by a vision of holiness
and love, and by a deep faith in the purpose and providence of God. It was
less historically important that Christianity should have been a system of
belief than that it was a way of life, embracing certain values enshrined in the
Bible and rooted in the doctrinal statements of the Church. Christianity
represented both a culture and an existence. It has been the inspiration of
some of the greatest art and music, literature and sculpture that the world has
known; its churches, chapels and cathedrals have been an endless testimony
to the faith and skill of those who designed and built them. The churches
have cared for the sick and the homeless, the widow and the orphan. They
have brought consolation to the dying and compassion to the living. They
have founded and sustained schools and universities. They have helped to
create communities which have in practice been threaded, however
imperfectly, by the ethic of Christian love. The Churches, whatever their
shortcomings, have provided examples of self-sacrificing and loving lives of
which Christians believe Jesus Christ to be the exemplar. The Church as a
society still continues to be at the heart of the healing process, so that at times
of great tragedy, such as the massacre of the school children at Dunblane
early in 1996, men and women, not necessarily committed Christians, turn to
it for comfort and fellowship, with hope of redemption through the power of
love. 'Our society still looks to the Church', Archbishop Runcie commented
in 1989, 'as a body able to handle the great questions of life and death when
their enormity becomes too great for easy answers.' Whether Christianity has
its roots in a supernatural world or is simply a manifestation of the highest
form of the human spirit, it is likely to survive until man destroys creation or
the world crumbles into dust.

Select Bibliography

Books for Reference

Barrett, D.B. (ed.), *World Christian Encyclopaedia*, Oxford, 1982
Cross, F.L. and Livingstone, E.A. *The Oxford Dictionary of the Christian Religion*, rev. edn., Oxford, 1983
Farmer, D.H. *The Oxford Dictionary of the Saints*, Oxford, 1978
Kelly, J.N.D. *The Oxford Dictionary of the Popes*, Oxford, 1986

General Histories

Chadwick, Owen. *A History of Christianity*, London, 1995; a distinguished, finely illustrated survey
Gilley, Sheridan and Shiels, W.J. *A History of Religion in Britain*, Oxford and Cambridge, Mass., 1994; a modern treatment by expert historians
Jedin, H. and Dolan. J, (eds), *A History of the Church*, tr. from the French, 10 vols, London, 1965–81, abridged edn, 3 vols, New York, 1992–3
Latourette, K.S. *A History of the Expansion of Christianity*, 7 vols, London, 1947
McManners, J. (ed.), *The Oxford Illustrated History of Christianity*, Oxford, 1990; illuminating chapters by expert historians
Moorman, J.R.H. *A History of the Church in England*, 3rd edn., London, 1973; a reliable guide

Chapters 1 and 2: The Early Church

General

Brox, Norbert. *A History of the Early Church*, tr. J. Bowden, London, 1994; a short but useful survey
Chadwick, H. *The Early Church*, Harmondsworth, 1967; a scholarly introduction
Danielou, J. and Marrou, H.I. *The Christian Centuries*, London, 1964
Duchesne, L. *Early History of the Christian Church*, 3 vols, London, 1929–34; still retains its value
Frend, W.H.C. *The Rise of Christianity*, London, 1984
Harnack, A. *The Missions and Expansion of Christianity*, London, 1908; a classical exposition
Lane-Fox, Robin. *Pagans and Christians*, London, 1960; a stimulating, critical survey
Lietzmann, H. *The Beginnings of the Christian Church*, tr. B. Lee Woolf, London, 1949
——. *The Founding of the Church Universal*, 2nd edn, tr. B. Lee Woolf, London, 1950
——. *From Constantine to Julian*, London, tr. B. Lee Woolf, London, 1951
——. *The Era of the Church Fathers*, tr. B. Lee Woolf, London, 1951

Church and State

Baynes, N.H. *Constantine and the Christian Church*, London, 1972; a classic discussion
Frend, W.H.C. *Martyrdom and Persecution in the Early Church*, Oxford, 1965; an excellent survey
Jones, A.H.M. *Constantine and the Conversion of Europe*, rev. edn, Toronto, 1979
Bernstein, Alan E. *The Formation of Hell: Death and Retribution in the Ancient and Early Christian Worlds*, ULC, 1993

Early Christian Thought and Life

Brown, Peter. *The Body and Society: Men, Women and Sexual Renunciation*, New York, 1988; a stimulating scholarly study
——. *Augustine of Hippo*, London, 1967; an excellent biography

Cadoux, C.J. *The Early Church and the World*, Edinburgh, 1925
Campenhausen, H. von. *The Fathers of the Greek Church*, London, 1963
——. *The Fathers of the Latin Church*, London, 1964; both books suggestive studies of important figures
——. *The Formation of the Christian Bible*, London, 1972
Chadwick, H. *Early Christian Thought and the Classical Tradition*, Oxford, 1960
——. *Augustine*, Oxford, 1986
Cochrane, C.N. *Christianity and Classical Culture*, Oxford, 1944
Geffcken, J. *The Last Days of Greco-Roman Paganism*, English tr., Amsterdam, 1978
Grant, R.M. *Greek Apologists of the Second Century*, London, 1988
Homes Dudden, F.H. *St Ambrose*, 2 vols, Oxford, 1935; valuable if old-fashioned
Kelly, J.N.D. *Early Christian Doctrine*, London, 1958; a good historical survey
——. *St Jerome*, London, 1975; an excellent biography
McLynn, N.B. *Ambrose of Ulian, Church and Court in a Christian Capital*, Berkeley, 1994
MacMullen, R. *Christianity in the Roman Empire*, New Haven, Conn., 1984
Markus, Robert. *The End of Ancient Christianity*, Cambridge, 1990
Marrou, H.I. *Saint Augustine and his Influence through the Ages*, New York, 1957
Momigliano, A. (ed.) *The Conflict between Paganism and Christianity in the Fourth Century*, Oxford, 1963
Norris, R.A. *God and the World in Early Christian Theology*, London, 1966

Heresies

Burkitt, F.C. *Church and Gnosis*, Cambridge, 1932
——. *The Religion of the Manichees*, Cambridge, 1925
Frend, W.H.C. *The Rise of the Monophysite Movement*, Cambridge, 1972
Layton, B. *The Gnostic Scriptures*, London, 1987
Lieu, S. *Manichaeism in the later Roman Empire and Medieval China*, Manchester, 1985
Rudolph, K. *Gnosis*, Edinburgh, 1985
Williams, R. *Arius, Heresy and Tradition*, London, 1985

The Saints

Brown, P. *The Cult of the Saints*, London, 1981; full of fascinating insights
Delahaye, H. *The Legend of the Saints*, London, 1962

Early Monasticism

Butler, C. *Benedictine Monasticism*, London, 1919, 2nd edn, Cambridge, 1961; a classical exposition
Chadwick, Owen. *John Cassian*, 2nd edn, Cambridge, 1968
——. *Western Asceticism*, London, 1958
Chitty, D.J. *The Desert a City*, Oxford, 1966

Roman Britain

Thomas, Charles. *Christianity in Roman Britain to AD 500*, London, 1981

CHAPTER 3: THE CHURCH IN THE DARK AGES

General

Hillgarth, J.N. *The Conversion of Western Europe, 550–750*, 2nd edn, Philadelphia 1986; a useful collection of texts

The Celtic Church

Adamnan's Life of St. Columba, ed. A.O. Anderson and M.O. Anderson, London, 1961
Bieler, L. *The Life and Legend of St. Patrick*, Dublin, 1949
——. *Ireland, Harbinger of the Middle Ages*, Oxford, 1963
Chadwick, N.K. *The Age of the Saints*, Oxford, 1961
Duke, J.A. *The Columban Church*, Oxford, 1932
Hanson, R.P.C. *Saint Patrick His Origins and Career*, Oxford, 1968
Gougaud, L. *Christianity in Celtic Lands*, London, 1932

Hughes, K. *The Church in Early Irish Society*, London, 1966; informative
Mackay, J.P. *An Introduction to Celtic Christianity*, Edinburgh, 1989

The Anglo-Saxons
Barlow, F. *The English Church 1000–1066*, London, 1963; a competent study of the pre-Conquest Church
Bede's Ecclesiastical History of the English People, ed. B. Colgrave and R.A.B. Mynors, Oxford, 1969; an indispensable source
Deanesly, Margaret. *The Pre-Conquest Church in England*, London, 1976
Levison, W. *England and the Continent in the Eighth Century*, Oxford, 1946
Mayr-Harting, H. *The Coming of Christianity to Anglo-Saxon England*, London, 1972; an admirable and readable study
Rollason, D. *Saints and Relics in Anglo-Saxon England*, Oxford 1989
Smyth, Alfred. *Alfred the Great*, Oxford, 1995; a stimulating and critical study
Talbot, C.H. *The Anglo-Saxon Missionaries in Germany*, London, 1972

The Franks
Bulloch, Donald. *The Age of Charlemagne*, London, 1965
Chamberlin, E.R. *Charlemagne*, London, 1986
Gregory of Tours, *History of the Franks*, tr O.M. Dalton, Edinburgh, 1967; an important source for the earlier period
McKitterick, R. *The Frankish Church and the Carolingian Reforms 789–895*, London, 1977
Wallace-Hadrill, J.M. *The Frankish Church*, Oxford, 1983; throws new insight

The Papacy
Homes-Dudden, F. *Gregory the Great*, 2 vols, London, 1905; still useful
Richards, J.M. *Consul of God [Gregory the Great]*, London, 1980
——. *The Popes and the Papacy in the early Middle Ages, 476–732*, London, 1979

The Byzantine and Eastern Church
Atiya, A.S. *A History of Eastern Christianity*, London, 1968
Browning, R. *Justinian and Theodora*, London, 1971; thorough and scholarly
Bryder, A.A.M. and Herrin, J. (eds). *Iconoclasm*, Birmingham, 1977; some suggestive essays
Hussey, J.M. *The Orthodox Church in the Byzantine Empire*, Oxford, 1986; a broad survey
Mango, C. *Byzantium: The Empire of New Rome*, London, 1983; illuminating
Sherrard, P. *Athos: the Holy Mountain*, London, 1982
Ure, P.N. *Justinian and his Age*, Harmondsworth, 1951
Ware, T. *The Orthodox Church in the Byzantine Empire*, Oxford, 1986

CHAPTERS 4 AND 5: THE MEDIEVAL CHURCH

General
Hamilton, B. *Religion in the Medieval World*, London, 1986; reliable
Nineham, Dennis. *Christianity Medieval and Modern*, London, 1993; a stimulating discussion of medieval belief
Oakley, F. *The Western Church in the Later Middle Ages*, London, 1979
Southern, R.W. *Western Society and the Church in the Middle Ages*, Harmondsworth, 1970; a scintillating study

The Papacy
Barraclough, G. *The Medieval Papacy*, London, 1968
Boase, T.S.R. *Boniface VIII*, London, 1933
Cowdrey, H.E.J. *The Age of Abbot Desiderius*, Oxford, 1983; a study of Gregorian reform
Mollat, G. *The Popes in Avignon*, London, 1963
Morris, C. *The Papal Monarchy; the Western Church 1050–1250*, Oxford, 1989; a comprehensive and authoritative survey
Partner, P. *The Lands of St. Peter*, London, 1972; a study of the Papal States
Robinson, L.S. *The Papacy 1073–1198, Continuity and Innovation*, Cambridge, 1990

Sayers, Jane. *Innocent III*, London, 1984
Tillmann, H. *Pope Innocent III*, Amsterdam, 1980
Ullmann, A. *A Short History of the Papacy in the Middle Ages*, London, 1972
——. *The Growth of Papal Government in the Middle Ages*, 3rd edn, London, 1970
Waley, Daniel. *The Papal State in the Thirteenth Century*, London, 1961

The Investiture Contest
Brooke, Z.N. *The English Church and Papacy*, Cambridge, 1931, repr. 1989; still basic
Morrison, K. *Tradition and Authority in the Western Church*, Princeton, 1969
Tellenbach, G. *Church, State and Christian Society* tr. R.F. Bennett, Oxford, 1959, repr. Toronto, 1991

The Conciliar Movement
Crowder, C.M.D. *Unity, Heresy and Reform, 1378–1440, the Conciliar Response to the Great Schism*, London, 1977
Thomson, J.A.F. *Popes and Princes 1417–1517, Politics and Polity in the Medieval Church*, London, 1980
Tierney, B. *The Foundations of the Conciliar Theory*, Cambridge, 1955

The English Church
Barlow, Frank. *The English Church 1066–1152*, London, 1979
——. *Thomas Becket*, London, 1986
Dickinson, J.C. *An Ecclesiastical History of England. The Later Middle Ages*, London, 1979
Gibson, Margaret. *Lanfranc of Bec*, Oxford, 1978
Hamilton-Thompson, A. *The English Clergy and their Organisation in the late Middle Ages*, Oxford, 1947
Harper-Bill, C. *The Pre-Reformation Church in England 1400–1530*, London, 1989
Knowles, David. *Thomas Becket*, London, 1970; a good introduction
Pantin, W.A. *The English Church in the Fourteenth Century*, Cambridge, 1955
Southern, R.W. *St Anselm and his Biographer*, Cambridge, 1990; scholarly and perceptive
——. *Robert Grosseteste*, Oxford, 1986

The Crusades and Relations with Islam
Christiansen, E. *The Northern Crusade*, London, 1980
Daniel, N. *The Arabs and Medieval Europe*, 2nd edn, New York and London, 1979
——. *Islam and the West: the Making of an Image*, Edinburgh, 1960
Erdmann, C. *The Origin of the Idea of the Crusade*, Princeton, N.J., 1977
Godfrey, J. *1204–The Unholy Crusade*, Oxford, 1980
Mayer, H.E. *The Crusades*, tr. J. Gillingham, 2nd edn., Oxford, 1988; a first-class study
Runciman, S. *History of the Crusades*, 3 vols, Cambridge, 1954
Southern, R.W. *Western Views of Islam in the Middle Ages*, Cambridge, Mass., 1962

Monasticism
Brooke, R.B. *The Coming of the Friars*, London, 1975
Hunt, N. *Cluniac Monasticism in the Central Middle Ages*, London, 1971
Knowles, David. *The Monastic Order in England*, 2nd edn, Cambridge, 1963; authoritative
——. *The Religious Orders in England*, 3 vols, Cambridge, 1948–59
Lawrence, C.H. *Medieval Monasticism*, 2nd edn, London, 1989; a good introduction
Lekai, L.J. *The Cistercians. Ideals and Reality*, Kent, OH, 1977
Leyser, H. *Hermits and the New Monasticism*, London, 1984; a fascinating study
Moorman, J.R.H. *A History of the Franciscan Order*, Oxford, 1968

Popular Religion
Brooke, R. and Brooke, C.N.L. *Popular Religion in the Middle Ages*, London, 1984
Cohn, N. *Europe's Inner Demons*, London, 1946; discusses witchcraft
Duffy, Eamon. *The Stripping of the Altars: Traditional Religion in England 1400–1580*, New Haven, Conn. and London, 1992; a stimulating revisionist account of the devotional aspects of the pre-Reformation Church
Finucane, F.C. *Miracles and Pilgrims: Popular Beliefs in Medieval England*, London, 1977
Geary, P.J. *Furta Sacra*, Princeton, N.J., 1978; discusses trade in and theft of relics
Heath, P. *The English Parish Clergy on the Eve of the Reformation*, London, 1969
Kieckhefer, R. *The European Witch Trials. Their Foundation in Popular and Learned Culture*, London, 1976

Moorman, J.R.H. *Church Life in the Thirteenth Century,* Cambridge, 1955
Owst, G.R. *Church and Pulpit in Medieval England,* Oxford, 1961
Rubin, Miri. *Corpus Christi: the Eucharist in Late Medieval Culture,* Cambridge, 1991; a learned and fascinating contribution to liturgical and social history
Sumption, J. *Pilgrimage. An Image of Medieval Religion,* London, 1975; a broad and readable study.
Swanson, R.N. *Church and Society in Late Medieval England,* Oxford, 1989
Ward, Benedicta. *Miracles and the Medieval Mind,* rev. edn, Aldershot, 1987

Spirituality
Knowles, David. *The English Mystical Tradition,* London, 1962
Leclercq, Jean, Vandenbroucke, François and Bouyer, Louis. *The Spirituality of the Middle Ages,* English tr., London, 1968

Heresy and Dissent
Hamilton, B. *The Medieval Inquisition,* London, 1981
Heymann, F.G. *John Zizka and the Hussite Revolution,* Princeton, N.J., 1955
Hudson, Anne. *The Premature Reformation: Wycliffite Tracts and Lollard History,* Oxford, 1988; a valuable contribution to the understanding of Lollardy.
Kaminsky, H. *A History of the Hussite Revolution,* Berkeley, Calif., 1967
Kenny A. (ed), *Wyclif in his Times,* Oxford, 1986
Ladurie, E. Le Roy. *Montaillou, Cathars and Catholics in a French Village 1294–1324* tr. B. Bray, London, 1978; a justly praised account of medieval religious life in a miniature setting
Lambert, M.D. *Medieval Heresy: Popular Movements from the Bogomils to Huss,* London, 1977
Leff, G. *Heresy in the Late Middle Ages,* 2 vols, Manchester, 1967; a judicious account
McFarlane, K.B. *John Wycliffe and the Rise of English Nonconformity,* London, 1952
Moore, R.I. *The Origins of European Dissent,* Harmondsworth, 1977
Obolensky, D. *The Bogomils,* London, 1978
Reeves, Marjorie. *The Influence of Prophecy in the Later Middle Ages,* Oxford, 1969; a skilful examination of an esoteric aspect of medieval religion
——. *Joachim of Fiore and the Prophetic Future,* London. 1976.
Runciman, S. *The Medieval Manichee,* Cambridge, 1947

The Byzantine Church
Brand, C.M. *Byzantium Confronts the West,* Cambridge, Mass., 1968
Hussey, J.M. *The Orthodox Church in the Byzantine Empire,* Oxford, 1986
Lossky, V. *The Mystical Theology of the Eastern Church,* London, 1957
Meyendorff, J. *Byzantium and the Rise of Russia: A Study of Byzantine–Russian Relations in the Fourteenth Century,* Cambridge, 1981
Nicol, D.M. *The Last Centuries of Byzantium 1261–1453,* 2 vols, Cambridge, 1993
Runciman, S. *The Eastern Schism: A Study of the Papacy and the Eastern Church during the XIth and XIIth Centuries,* Oxford, 1955
——. *The Byzantine Theocracy,* Cambridge, 1977

CHAPTER 6: THE REFORMATION

General
Cameron, E. *The European Reformation,* Oxford, 1991; a valuable and magisterial panoramic study
Chadwick, Owen. *The Reformation,* Harmondsworth, 1964; a well-balanced introduction
Leonard, E.G. *A History of Protestantism,* 2 vols, London, 1967
Ozment, S.E. *Protestants: the Birth of a Revolution,* London, 1953
——. *The Age of Reform 1250–1550,* New Haven, Conn. 1988
Prestwich, Menna (ed.) *International Calvinism 1541–1715,* Oxford, 1985
Spitz, L.W. *The Protestant Reformation,* New York, 1986
Thomas, Keith. *Religion and the Decline of Magic. Studies in Popular Belief in Sixteenth and Seventeenth Century England,* London, 1971; an original work full of fascinating insights

Background
Bainton, R. *Erasmus of Christendom,* London, 1969
Hyma, A. *The Christian Renaissance, A History of the Devotio Moderna,* 2nd edn., Hamden, Conn, 1961

Oberman, H.A. *Masters of the Reformation*, Cambridge, 1981
Spitz, L.W. *The Religious Renaissance of the German Humanists*, Cambridge, Mass., 1963

The German Reformation
Bainton, R. *Here I Stand; a Life of Martin Luther*, London, 1955; a justly acclaimed biography
Dickens, A.G. *The German Nation and Martin Luther*, London, 1974
Erikson, Erik H. *Young Man Luther*, London, 1959; a psychological study. Cf. Ian Stiggins, *Luther and his Mother*, Philadelphia, 1981
Fife, R.H. *The Revolt of Martin Luther*, New York, 1957
Oberman, H. *Luther; Man Between God and the Devil*, London, 1985
Scribner, R.W. *The German Reformation*, London, 1986
Strauss, Gerald. *Luther's House of Learning: Indoctrination of the Young in the German Revolution*, New York, 1978; illuminating

The Swiss Reformation and Calvin
Hopfl, H. *The Christian Polity of John Calvin*, Cambridge, 1982; a useful discussion of Calvin's political thought
McGrath, A.E. *John Calvin*, Oxford, 1993
McNeill, J.T. *The History and Character of Calvinism*, rev. edn, New York, 1967
Monter, E.W. *Calvin's Geneva*, New York, 1967
Parker, T.H.L. *Calvin*, London, 1975
Potter, G.R. *Zwingli*, Cambridge, 1976
Wendel, F. *Calvin*, tr. P. Mairet, London, 1963

The Scottish Reformation
Cowen, I.B. *The Scottish Reformation; Church and Society in Sixteenth-Century Scotland*, New York, 1982
Donaldson, G. *The Scottish Reformation*, Cambridge, 1960
Wormald. J. *Court, Kirk and Community Scotland 1470–1625*, London, 1981

The French Reformation
Davis, Natalie Z. *Society and Culture in Early Modern France*, London, 1961
Greengrass, Mark. *The French Reformation*, London, 1987

The Reformation in the Low Countries
Crew, P.M. *Calvinist Preaching and Iconoclasm in the Netherlands, 1544–69*, Cambridge, 1978
Parker, G. *The Dutch Revolt*, London, 1977

The English Reformation
Brigden, Susan. *London and the Reformation*, Oxford, 1989; an admirable discussion of the Reformation at work
Collinson, P. *The Birthpangs of Protestant England*, London, 1988
——. *The Religion of Protestants: the Church in English Society*, Oxford, 1992
——. *The Elizabethan Puritan Movement*, London, 1967; all excellent works
Daniell, David. *William Tyndale*, New Haven, Conn., 1994; an excellent biography
Dickens, A.G. *The English Reformation*, London, 1964; remains the best single account
Haigh, Christopher (ed.). *The English Reformation Revised*, Cambridge, 1987; a series of stimulating revisionist essays
MacCulloch, D. *Thomas Cranmer*, Yale, Newhaven, 1996
Scarisbrick, J.J. *The Reformation and the English People*, Oxford, 1984
Shiels, W.J. *The English Reformation 1530–70*, London, 1985

The Radical Reformation
Clasen, C.P. *Anabaptism: A Social History*, Ithaca, NY and London, 1972
Scott, T. *Thomas Müntzer; Theology and Revolution in the German Revolution*, London, 1989
White, B.R. *The English Separatist Tradition from the Marian Martyrs to the Pilgrim Fathers*, London, 1971
Williams, G.H. *The Radical Reformation*, London, 1962; a wide coverage

CHAPTER 7: THE CATHOLIC REFORMATION

General

Bossy, John. *Christianity in the West 1400–1700*, Oxford, 1985; a stimulating discussion

Delumeau, Jean. *Catholicism between Luther and Voltaire*, London, 1977; original if idiosyncratic in judgement

Dickens, A.G. *The Counter-Reformation*, 2nd edn, London, 1989; a straightforward, reliable introduction

Evennett, H.O. *The Spirit of the Counter-Reformation*, Cambridge, 1968

Kamen, H. *The Spanish Inquisition*, London, 1965

Wright, A.D. *The Counter-Reformation*, London, 1982; provides useful insights into theological developments

The Society of Jesus

Aveling, J.C.H. *The Jesuits*, London, 1981; a good account from the foundation of the Jesuits to the present day

Brodrick, J. *The Origins of the Jesuits*, London, 1940; still retains its value

——. *The Progress of the Jesuits, 1556–79*, London, 1946

O'Malley, J.W. *The First Jesuits*, Cambridge, Mass., 1993; admirably dispassionate

Ravier, A. *Ignatius of Loyola and the Founding of the Society of Jesus*, San Francisco, 1987

The Council of Trent

Evennett, H.O. *The Cardinal of Lorraine and the Council of Trent*, Cambridge, 1930

Jedin, H. *A History of the Council of Trent*, tr. E. Graf, vol. 1, London, 1957

Church Life

Cristiani, L. *St Vincent de Paul, 1581–1660*, Boston, Mass., 1977

Forster, Max. *The Counter-Reformation in the Villages: Religion and Reform in the Bishopric of Speyer, 1560–1620*, Ithaca, NY, 1992

Hoffman, Philip. *Church and Community in the Diocese of Lyon 1500–1789*, New Haven, Conn., 1984

Missionary Activity

Boxer, C.R. *The Christian Century in Japan 1549–1650*, Berkeley, Calif., 1931

Caraman, P. *The Lost Paradise: an Account of the Jesuits in Paraguay*, London, 1975

Mason, J.F. *The Japanese and the Jesuits; Alessandro Valignano in Sixteenth-Century Japan*, London, 1993

Neill, S.C. *A History of Christianity in India*, 2 vols, Cambridge, 1984–5

Parry, J.H. *The Age of Reconnaisance*, London, 1963; covers a wide span

——. *The Spanish Seaborne Empire*, London, 1966

Ricard, R. *The Spanish Conquest of Mexico*, tr. L.B. Simpson, Berkeley, Calif., 1966

Rosse, A.S. *Apostolic Legations in China in the Eighteenth Century*, Pasadena, 1968

Rowbotham, A. *Jesuits at the Court of China*, Berkeley, Calif., 1942

Schurhammer, G. *Francis Xavier*, trs, 4 vols, London, 1973–82

Spirituality

de Boulay, S.A. *Teresa of Avila*, 2nd edn, London, 1993

Peers, E.A. *Studies of the Spanish Mystics*, 3 vols, London, 1947–60

——. *Spirit of Flame [St John of the Cross]*, 2nd edn, London, 1953

CHAPTER 8: THE CHURCHES *c.* 1600–1800

General

Callahan, W.J. and Higgs, D. *Church and society in Catholic Europe of the Eighteenth Century*, Cambridge, 1979

Cragg, G.R. *The Church in the Age of Reason*, Harmondsworth, 1960; a brief but reliable survey

Roman Catholicism

Aveling, J.C.H. *The Handle and the Axe: Catholic Recusants in England from Reformation to Emancipation*, London, 1976

Bossy, John. *The English Catholic Community, 1570–1850*, London, 1975

Chadwick, Owen. *The Popes and the European Revolution*, Oxford, 1981; a comprehensive and authoritative study of European Catholicism

Mathew, D. *Catholicism in England: the Portrait of a Minority, Culture and Tradition*, London, 1948

The English Church in the Seventeenth Century

Fincham, K. (ed.), *The Early Stuart Church, 1603–42*, London, 1993

——. *Prelate as Pastor: the Episcopate of James I*, Oxford, 1990

Hill, Christopher. *The English Bible and the Seventeenth Century Revolution*, London, 1993

Spurr, J. *The Restoration Church of England, 1646–89*, New Haven, Conn., 1991

Trevor-Roper, H.R. *Archbishop Laud*, London, 1940

The English Church in the Eighteenth Century

Mather, R.C. *High Church Prophet, Bishop Samuel Horsley (1773–1806) and the Caroline Tradition in the Late Georgian Church*, Oxford, 1992

Rupp, Gordon. *Religion in England 1688–1791*, Oxford, 1986; especially good on Dissent

Sykes, N. *Church and State in England in the Eighteenth Century*, Cambridge, 1934; still an excellent survey

Virgin, P. *The Church in an Age of Negligence*, Cambridge, 1989

Walsh, J. Haydon, C. and Taylor, Stephen. *The Church of England, c. 1689–c. 1833*, Cambridge, 1993, an important study providing many fresh insights

Ward, W.R. *The Protestant Evangelical Awakening*, Cambridge, 1992; covers the Continent as well as Great Britain

Watts, Michael R. *The Dissenters*, Oxford, 1978; an authoritative investigation

Werner, J.S. *The Primitive Methodist Connexion. Its Background and Early History*, Madison, Wisconsin, 1984

The French Church

Abercrombie, N. *The Origins of Jansenism*, Oxford, 1935

Hufton, Olwen. *Bayeux in the Eighteenth Century*, Oxford 1967

Kley, D. van. *The Jansenists and the Expulsion of the Jesuits from France, 1757–65*, New York, 1975

Kreiser, B.R. *Miracles, Convulsions and Ecclesiastical Politics in Early Eighteenth-Century Paris*, Princeton, N.J., 1978

McManners, J. *French Ecclesiastical Society under the Ancien Regime*, Oxford, 1961

——. *The French Revolution and the Church*, London, 1960; a masterly account

Sedgwick, A. *Jansenism in Seventeenth-Century France, Voices from the Wilderness*, Charlotteville, 1978

Tackett, T. *Priest and Parish in Eighteenth-Century France*, Princeton, N.J., 1977

Developments in Thought

Burke, Peter. *Popular Culture in Early Modern Europe*, London, 1978

Grimsley, R. *Rousseau and the Religious Quest*, Oxford, 1968

Hazard, P. *The European Mind, 1680–1715*, tr. J.L. May, London, 1953

McManners, J. *Death and the Enlightenment*, Oxford, 1981

Sullivan, R.E. *John Toland and the Deist Controversy*, New York, 1982

CHAPTERS 9 TO 11: THE MODERN CHURCH

General

Jedin, H. and Dolan, J. *History of the Church*, London, 1981

    Vol. VII: *The Church between Revolution and Restoration*, London, 1981

    Vol. VIII: *The Church in the Age of Liberalism*, London, 1981

    Vol. IX: *The Church in an Industrial Age*, London, 1981

    Vol. X: *The Church in the Modern Age*, London, 1981

Latourette, K.S. *Christianity in a Revolutionary Age*, 5 vols, London, 1959

The Papacy

Butler, Cuthbert. *The Vatican Council*, 2 vols, London, 1930
Flannery, A. (ed.). *Documents of the Second Vatican Council*, New York, 1975
Hales, E.E.Y. *Pio Nono*, London, 2nd edn, 1956
Hastings, Adrian (ed.). *Modern Catholics, Vatican II and After*, Oxford, 1991
Hebblethwaite, P. *Pope John XXIII: Pope of the Council*, London, 1984
——. *Pope Paul VI, The First Modern Pope*, London, 1993
Rhodes, A. *The Vatican in the Age of Dictators 1922–45*, London, 1973

The Roman Catholic Church in England

Gray, R. *Cardinal Manning*, London, 1985
Ker, Ian. *John Henry Newman*, Oxford, 1990
Newsome, David. *The Convert Cardinals [Manning and Newman]*, London, 1993; very readable
Norman, E.R. *Roman Catholicism in England from the Elizabethan Settlement to the Second Vatican Council*, London, 1985
——. *The English Catholic Church in the Nineteenth Century*, Oxford, 1984; a distinguished comprehensive survey

The Church of England

Bell, G.K.A. *Randall Davidson*, 2 vols, Oxford, 1935
Brose, O.J. *Church and Parliament. The Reshaping of the Church of England, 1828–1860*, Oxford, 1959
Chadwick, Owen. *The Victorian Church*, 2 vols, London, 1961–70; a magnificent study
——. *Michael Ramsey*, Oxford 1990
Chadwick, Owen and Henson, Hensley. *A Study in the Friction between Church and State*, Oxford, 1983
Edwards, D.L. *Christian England*, Vol. 3: *From the Eighteenth Century to the First World War*, London, 1984
——. *Leaders of the Church of England 1828–1944*, London, 1971; a readable study
Hastings, A. *A History of English Christianity 1920–85*, London, 1986; an excellent comprehensive study
Iremonger, F.A. *William Temple*, Oxford, 1948
Kent, John. *William Temple*, Cambridge, 1993
Lockhart, J.G. *Cosmo Gordon Lang*, London, 1949
Machin, G.I.T. *Politics and the Churches in Great Britain, 1832–68*, Oxford, 1977
——. *Politics and the Churches in Great Britain, 1869–1921*, Oxford, 1987
Mews, Stuart (ed.). *Modern Religious Rebels*, London, 1993; includes an essay on Canon John Collins
Norman, E.R. *Church and Society in England 1770–1970*, Oxford, 1976; valuable and often original
Welsby, Paul A. *A History of the Church of England, 1945–80*, London, 1984

Tractarianism

F. Anson, Peter. *The Call of the Cloister: Religious Communities and Kindred Bodies in the Anglican Communion*, London, 1935
Brilioth, Yngve. *The Anglican Revival*, London, 1933; still a good guide
Church, R.W. *The Oxford Movement, 1833–45*, repr. London, 1932; in spite of its age retains its value
Faber, G. *The Oxford Apostles*, Harmondsworth, 1954
Griffin, J.R. *The Oxford Movement 1833–45*, Edinburgh, 1984
Nockles, Peter. *The Oxford Movement in Context, Anglican High Churchmanship, 1760–1850*, Cambridge, 1994
Rowell, Geoffrey. *The Vision Glorious: Themes and Personalities of the Catholic Revival in Anglicanism*, Oxford, 1983

Evangelicalism

Bebbington, D.W. *Evangelicalism in Modern Britain: A History from the 1730s to the 1980*, London, 1989
Bradley, Ian. *The Call to Seriousness: The Evangelical Impact on the Victorians*, London, 1976
Brown, Ford K. *Fathers of the Victorians: The Age of Wilberforce*, Cambridge, 1961

Dissent and Revival

Bolam, C.G., Goring, J., Short, H.L. and Thomas, Roger. *The English Presbyterians from Elizabethan Puritanism to Modern Unitarianism*, London, 1968

Campbell, Ted A. *The Religion of the Heart, A Study of Religious Life in the Seventeenth and Eighteenth Centuries*, Columbia, South Carolina, 1991; a thoughtful survey

Davies, R. and Rupp, Gordon. (eds.) *A History of the Methodist Church in Great Britain*, 4 vols, London, 1965–88; an updated revision of an earlier work

Garnett, Jane and Matthew, Colin. *Revival and Religion since 1700*, London, 1993; useful essays

Green, V.H.H. *The Young Mr Wesley*, London, 1961

——. *John Wesley*, London, 1964

Heitzenreiter, Richard P. *The Elusive Mr Wesley*, Nashville, Tenn., 1984

——. *Memory: Reflections on Early Methodism*, Nashville, Tenn., 1989

Hempton, D. *Methodism and Politics in British Society 1750–1850*, London, 1954

Henry, Stuart C. *George Whitefield*, New York and Nashville, Tenn., 1984 and 1957

Hilton, Boyd. *The Age of Atonement: The Influence of Evangelicalism on Social and Economic Thought 1795–1865*, Oxford, 1988; valuable and original

Howse, E.M. *Saints in Politics: The 'Clapham Sect' and the Growth of Freedom*, Toronto, 1962

Lewis, A.J. *Zinzendorf, The Oecumenical Pioneer*, London, 1962

Miller, P. *Jonathan Edwards*, New York, 1949

Rack, Henry D. *Reasonable Enthusiast: John Wesley and the Rise of Methodism*, London, 1989; an admirable biography

Schmidt, Martin. *John Wesley, A Theological Biography*, tr. N.P. Goldhawk, London, 1962

Smyth, Charles. *Simeon and Church Order*, Cambridge, 1940

Stoeffler, Ernst. *German Pietism in the Eighteenth Century*, London, 1973

——. *The Rise of Evangelical Pietism*, London, 1968

Jones, R. Tudor. *Congregationalism in England 1662–1962*, London, 1962

Underwood, A.C. *A History of the English Baptists*, London, 1947

Walzer, M. *The Revolution of the Saints. A Study in the Origin of Radical Politics*, Harvard, Mass., 1966

The French Church

Dansette, A. *Religious History of Modern France*, tr. J. Dingle, 2 vols, London, 1961–70

McManners, J. *Church and State in France 1870–1914*, London, 1972; first class

Phillips, C.S. *The Church in France, 1815–1907*, London, 1929, 1936; repr. New York, 1967

Vidler, A. *Prophecy and Papacy: A Study of Lammenais, the Church and Revolution*, London, 1954

The German Churches

Anderson, M. *Windthorst*, Oxford, 1981; good on the *Kulturkampf*

Bentley, James. *Martin Niemöller*, Oxford, 1984

Bethge, Eberhard. *Dietrich Bonhoeffer*, London, 1970

Conway, J.S. *The Nazi Persecution of the Churches, 1933–45*, London, 1948

Lewy, G. *The Catholic Church and Nazi Germany*, London, 1984

Wright, J.R. *Above Parties: the Political Attitude of the German Protestant Church Leadership 1918–33*, Oxford, 1974

The Italian Church

Binchy, D.E. *Church and State in Fascist Italy*, Oxford, 1941

Molony, J.N. *The Emergence of Political Catholicism in Italy: Partito Poplare, 1919–1926*, London, 1977

Pollard, J.E. *The Vatican and Italian Fascism, 1929–32*, Cambridge, 1985

The Spanish Church

Peers, E.A. *The Church in Spain 1737–1937*, London, 1938

Lannon, F. *Privilege, Persecution and Prophecy, The Catholic Church in Spain, 1875–1975*, Oxford, 1987; excellent

The Church and Society

Badham, Paul (ed.), *Religion, State and Society in Modern Britain*, Lampeter, 1989

Ceadel, Martin. *Pacifism in Britain, 1914–1945*, Oxford, 1980

Currie, R., Gilbert, A. and Horsley, L. *Churches and Churchgoers: Patterns of Church Growth in the British Isles since 1700*, Oxford, 1977

Gilbert, A.D. *Religion and Society in Industrial England: Church, Chapel and Social Change 1740–1914*, London, 1976
Hoover, A.J. *God, Germany and Britain in the Great War: A Study in Clerical Nationalism*, New York, 1989
Rowell, G. *Hell and the Victorians. A Study of the Nineteenth-century Controversies Concerning Eternal Punishment and the Future Life*, Oxford, 1974
Shiels, W.J. (ed.). *The Church and War*, Oxford, 1983
Wilkinson, A. *Dissent or Conform? War, Peace and the English Churches, 1900–1945*, London, 1986
Wilson, B.R. *Religion in Sociological Perspective*, Oxford, 1982

The Oecumenical Movement
Fey, H.E. *The Oecumenical Advance: A History of the Oecumenical Movement*, London, 1970
Matthews, John. *The Unity Scene*, London, 1986
Rouse, R. and Neill, S.C. *A History of the Ecumenical Movement, 1517–1948*, 2nd edn London, 1967

'Fringe' Movements
Barber, Eileen. *New Religious Movements*, London, 1989
——. *The Making of a Moonie*, Oxford, 1969
Quebedeaux, R. *The New Charismatic Age*, New York, 1976
Wilson, B.R. *Contemporary Transformations of Religion*, Oxford, 1976

Liturgical Change
Spurr, Barry. *The Word in the Desert*, London, 1955; an incisive criticism of modern liturgies

Secularization
Budd, Susan. *Variations of Unbelief: Atheists and Agnostics in English Society, 1850–1960*, London, 1977; a wide-ranging study
Chadwick, Owen. *The Secularization of the European Mind in the Nineteenth Century*, Cambridge, 1975
Charlton, D.G. *Secular Religions in France, 1815–70*, Oxford, 1963
Cox, Jeffrey. *The English Church in a Secular Society*, London, 1976
Gilbert, Alan. *The Making of Post-Christian Britain: a History of the Secularization of Modern Society*, London, 1980
Macleod, H. *Religion and Irreligion in Victorian England*, Bangor, 1993
Martin, D. (ed.), *The Religious and the Secular*, London, 1969
——. *A General Theory of Secularization*, Oxford, 1978
Royle, Edward. *Victorian Infidels: The Origins of the British Secularist Movement, 1791–1866*, Manchester, 1974
——. *Radicals, Secularists and Republicans: Popular Freethought in Britain, 1861–1915*, Manchester, 1980
Wright, T.R. *The Religion of Humanity: The Impact of Comtean Positions on Victorian Britain*, Cambridge, 1986

Russia and the Eastern Churches
Alexander, S. *Church and State in Yugoslavia since 1945*, Cambridge, 1979
Chadwick, Owen. *The Church in the Cold War*, London, 1991
Curtiss, J.S. *Church and State in Russia. The Last Years of the Empire 1900–1917*, New York, 1940
Ellis, Jane. *The Russian Orthodox Church: A Contemporary History, 1964–85*, London, 1986
Frazee, C. *The Orthodox Church and Independent Greece, 1821–1852*, Cambridge, 1969
Pospielovsky, D. *The Russian Church under the Soviet Regime, 1917–1982*, 2 vols, New York, 1984
Zernov, N. *The Russians and their Church*, London, 1945
——. *The Russian Religious Renaissance of the Twentieth Century*, London, 1963

The Churches in Latin America
Bastide, R. *The African Religions of Brazil*, tr. H. Sabba, Baltimore, MD, 1978
Cleary, L. *Crisis and Change. The Churches in Latin America Today*, New York, 1983
Kennedy, J.L. *Catholicism, Nationalism and Democracy in Argentina*, Notre Dame, Ind., 1958
Klaibov, J.L. *Religion and Revolution in Peru 1824–1876*, Notre Dame, Ind., 1977
Lafaye, J. *Quetzalcoatl and Guadalupe. The Fountain of Mexican National Consciousness 1513–1815*, Chicago, 1976

Levine, D.H. *Religion and Politics in Latin America: The Catholic Church in Venezuela and Columbia*, Princeton, N.J., 1981

Mainwaring, S. *The Catholic Church and Politics in Latin America*, 2nd edn, Chapel Hill, N.C., 1966

Mecham, J.L. *Church and State in Latin America*, rev. edn, Chapel Hill, N.C., 1966

Quirk, N.E. *The Mexican Revolution and the Catholic Church, 1910–1929*, Bloomington, Ind., 1975

Schmitt, K.M. (ed.). *The Roman Catholic Church in Modern Latin America*, New York, 1972

Turner, F.C. *Catholicism and Political Developments in Latin America*, Chapel Hill, N.C., 1971

Williams, E. *Followers of the New Faith: Cultural Change and the Rise of Protestantism in Brazil and Chile*, Nashville, Tenn. 1967

North America

Ahlstrom, S.E. *A Religious History of the American People*, New Haven, Conn., 1972

Arrington, L.J. and Bita, D. *The Mormon Experience*, 2 vols, Urbana, Ill., 1992

Dolan, J.P. *The American Catholic Experience*, Garden City, NY, 1985

Findley, J.F. *Dwight L. Moody American Evangelist*, Chicago, 1969

Handy, R.T. *Christianity in the United States and Canada*, New York, 1977

Hennessey, J. *American Catholics. A History of the Roman Catholic Community in the United States*, New York, 1981

Hudson, W.S. *Religion in America*, New York, 1981

McLoughlin, W.G. *Modern Revivalism from Finney to Billy Graham*, 1959

Marsden, G.M. *Fundamentalism in American Culture: The Shaping of Twentieth-century Evangelicalism, 1878–1925*, New York, 1980

Marty, M.E. *Modern American Religion*, Vol. 1: *1893–1919*, Vol. 2: *1919–41*, 2 vols, Chicago, 1986, 1991

Marty, M.E. and Appleby, R.S. (ed.). *Fundamentalism and Society*, Chicago, 1993

——. *Fundamentalism Observed*, Chicago, 1991

Mead, S.E. *The Lively Experiment: The Shaping of Christianity in America*, New York, 1963

Raboteau, Alfred.*Slave Religion: The 'Invisible Institution' in the Antebellum State*, New York, 1978

Walsh, H.H. *The Christian Church in Canada*, Toronto, 1956

Wills, Gary. *Under God: Religion and American Politics*, New York, 1992

Wuthnow, Robert. *The Restructuring of American Religion, Society and Faith since World War II*, Princeton, J.H. 1988

Missionary Activity and the Overseas Church

General

Allen, W.O.B. and McClure, E. *Two Hundred Years. The History of the Society for Promoting Christian Knowledge, 1698–1898*, London, 1898

Canton, W. *A History of the British and Foreign Bible Society*, 5 vols, London, 1904–10

Goodall, N. *A History of the London Missionary Society, 1895–1945*, London, 1954

Hewitt, E. *The Problems of Success. A History of the Church Missionary Society*, 2 vols, London, 1971–6

Latourette, K.S. *A History of the Expansion of Christianity*, 7 vols, London, 1947; very comprehensive from a Protestant point of view

Moorhouse, Geoffrey. *The Missionaries*, London, 1973; very readable

Neill, Stephen. *A History of Christian Missions*, 2nd edn, rev. Owen Chadwick, Harmondsworth, 1986; an excellent survey

Stock, E. *The History of the Church Missionary Society*, 4 vols, London, 1899–1906

Thompson, H.P. *Into All Lands: A History of the Society for the Propagation of the Gospel in Foreign Parts, 1701–1950*, London, 1951

Africa

Gray, R. *Black Christians and White Missionaries*, New Haven, Conn., 1990

Groves, C.P. *The Planting of Christianity in Africa*, 4 vols, London, 1948

Hastings, A. *African Christianity*, London, 1976; highly recommended

North Africa

Crummey, D. *Priests and Politicians: Protestant and Catholic Missions in Orthodox Ethiopia 1830–68*, Oxford 1972

O'Donnell, J.D. *Lavigerie in Tunisia*, Athens, Ga, 1979

Central, East and West Africa

Ajayi, J.F.A. *Christian Missions in Nigeria, 1841–1891. The Making of a New Mission Elite*, London, 1965
Ayandele, E.A. *The Missionary Impact on Modern Nigeria, 1842–1914: A Political and Social Analysis*, London, 1966
Baeta, C.G. (ed.). *Christianity in Tropical Africa*, London, 1968
Chadwick, Owen. *Mackenzie's Grave*, London, 1959
Hangen, H.P. *Mission, Church and State in a Colonial Setting, Uganda 1890–1925*, London, 1984
Jeal, J. *David Livingstone*, London, 1975
Lagergren, D. *Mission and State in the Congo*, Upsala, 1970
McCracken, J. *Politics and Christianity in Malawi, 1875–1945. The Impact of the Livingstone Mission in the Northern Province*, Cambridge, 1977
Northcott, W.C. *David Livingstone in Africa*, London, 1957
Oliver, R. *The Missionary Factor in East Africa*, London, 1952
Pirouet, M.L. *Black Evangelists: The Spread of Christianity in Uganda, 1891–1914*, London, 1978
Ranger, T.O. and Weller, J. (eds.). *Themes in the Christian History of Central Africa*, London, 1975
Pachai, B. (ed.). *Livingstone, Man of Africa*, London, 1973
Rotberg, R. *Christian Missionaries and the Creation of Northern Rhodesia, 1880–1924*, Princeton, N.J., 1965
———. *The Rise of Nationalism in Central Africa: The Making of Malawi and Zambia 1873–1964*, Harvard, 1965
Seaver, George. *Albert Schweitzer*, London, 1947
Taylor, J.V. *The Growth of the Church in Buganda*, London, 1958
Wright, M. *German Missions in Tanganyike 1891–1941*, Oxford, 1971

South Africa

de Gruchy, J.W. *The Church Struggle in South Africa*, Grand Rapids, 1976
Hinchliff, Peter. *J.W. Colenso, Bishop of Natal*, London, 1978
———. *The Church in South Africa*, London, 1968; a brief, reliable history

Black Churches

Barrett, D.B. *Schism and Renewal in Africa, An Analysis of Six Thousand Contemporary Religious Movements*, Nairobi, 1967
———. *African Initiatives in Religion*, Nairobi, 1971
Ossthuizen, G. *The Theology of a South African Messiah [Shabi's Nazareth Movement]*, London, 1967
Peel, J.D.Y. *Aladura, A Religious Movement among the Yoruba*, Oxford, 1968
Shepperson, G. and Price, T. *Independent African: John Cilembwe and the Origin, Setting and Significance of the Nyasaland Native Rising of 1915*, Edinburgh, 1958
Turner, H.W. *African Independent Church* [Aladura], 2 vols, London, 1967
Webster, J.B. *The African Churches among the Yoruba*, Oxford, 1976

India

Boyd, R.H.S. *An Introduction to Indian Christian Theology*, Madras, 1975
Forrester, D.B. *Caste and Christianity: Attitudes and Policies on Caste of Anglo-Saxon Missions in India*, Curzon Press, 1980
Gupta, K.P.S. *Christian Missionaries in Bengal, 1793–1833*, Calcutta, 1971
Hambye, E.R. (ed.). *A Bibliography on Christianity in India*, New Delhi, 1976
Sundklet, B. *The Church of South India: the Movement towards Reunion 1909–1947*, London, 1947

China

Broomhall, A.J. *Hudson Taylor and China's Open Century*, 7 vols, London, 1981–9
Brown, G.T. *Christianity in the People's Republic of China*, Atlanta, Ga, 1983
Cohen, P.A. *China and Christianity: the Missionary Movement and the Growth of Chinese Anti-Foreignism 1860–70*, Cambridge, Mass., 1963
Purcell, V. *The Boxer Uprising*, Cambridge, 1963

Japan

Caldarola, C. *Christianity. The Japanese Way*, Leiden, 1979
Drummond, R.H. *A History of Christianity in Japan*, Grand Rapids, 1971

The Philippines
Anderson, G.H. (ed.), *Studies in Philippine Church History*, Ithaca, NY, 1969
Clymer, K.J. *Protestant Missions in the Philippines*, Urbana, Ill., 1987

Korea
Clark, D.N. *Christianity in Modern Korea*, London, 1986
Palmer, S.J. *Korea and Christianity: the Problem of Identification and Tradition*, Seoul, 1967

Australia
Border, Ross. *Church and State in Australia 1788–1872. A Constitutional Study of the Church of England*, 1962
Sultan, T.L. *Hierarchy and Democracy in Australia: the Formation of Australian Cahtolicism, 1788–1870*, 1965

The Pacific and the Atlantic
Cannan, Edward. *Churches of the South Atlantic Islands, 1502–1991*, Oswestrv, 1992
Davies, J. *The History of the Tahitian Mission, 1799–1830, ed. C.W. Newbury*, Cambridge, 1961; a contemporary account
Gunson, N. *Messengers of Grace: Evangelical Missions in the South Sea 1797–1860*, Oxford, 1978

Theological Developments
Barth, K. *Dogmatics in Outline*, London, 1966
——. *Theologian of Freedom*, ed. Clifford Green, London, 1989
Ellis, Ieuan. *Seven against Christ: A Study of 'Essays and Reviews'*, London, 1980
Ford, David F. (ed.). *The Modern Theologians, An Introduction to Church Theology in the Twentieth Century*, 2 vols, Oxford and Cambridge, Mass., 1989; an excellent introduction
Kent, J. *The End of the Line? The Development of Christian Theology in the Last Two Centuries*, London, 1982
Niebuhr, R. *The Nature and Destiny of Man*, New York, 1941
Rahner, K. *Foundations of Christian Faith*, London, 1978
Ramsay, A.M. *From Gore to Temple*, London, 1960
Reardon, B.M.G. *From Coleridge to Gore; A Century of Religious Thought in Britain*, London, 1971
——. *Liberal Protestantism*, London, 1968
——. *Roman Catholic Modernism*, London, 1970
——. *Liberalism and Tradition: Aspects of Catholic Thought in Nineteenth-Century France*, Cambridge, 1975
Smart, Ninian. (ed.). *Nineteenth-Century Religious Thought in the West*, Cambridge, 1985
Welch, Claude, *God and the Incarnation in Mid-Nineteenth-Century German Theology*, Oxford, 1965
——. *Protestant Thought in the Nineteenth Century, 1791–1914*, 2 vols, New Haven, Conn., 1972, 1985

Index